T0180811

Communications in Computer and Information Science   2114

Editorial Board Members

Joaquim Filipe ⓘ, *Polytechnic Institute of Setúbal, Setúbal, Portugal*
Ashish Ghosh ⓘ, *Indian Statistical Institute, Kolkata, India*
Lizhu Zhou, *Tsinghua University, Beijing, China*

Rationale

The CCIS series is devoted to the publication of proceedings of computer science conferences. Its aim is to efficiently disseminate original research results in informatics in printed and electronic form. While the focus is on publication of peer-reviewed full papers presenting mature work, inclusion of reviewed short papers reporting on work in progress is welcome, too. Besides globally relevant meetings with internationally representative program committees guaranteeing a strict peer-reviewing and paper selection process, conferences run by societies or of high regional or national relevance are also considered for publication.

Topics

The topical scope of CCIS spans the entire spectrum of informatics ranging from foundational topics in the theory of computing to information and communications science and technology and a broad variety of interdisciplinary application fields.

Information for Volume Editors and Authors

Publication in CCIS is free of charge. No royalties are paid, however, we offer registered conference participants temporary free access to the online version of the conference proceedings on SpringerLink (http://link.springer.com) by means of an http referrer from the conference website and/or a number of complimentary printed copies, as specified in the official acceptance email of the event.

CCIS proceedings can be published in time for distribution at conferences or as post-proceedings, and delivered in the form of printed books and/or electronically as USBs and/or e-content licenses for accessing proceedings at SpringerLink. Furthermore, CCIS proceedings are included in the CCIS electronic book series hosted in the SpringerLink digital library at http://link.springer.com/bookseries/7899. Conferences publishing in CCIS are allowed to use Online Conference Service (OCS) for managing the whole proceedings lifecycle (from submission and reviewing to preparing for publication) free of charge.

Publication process

The language of publication is exclusively English. Authors publishing in CCIS have to sign the Springer CCIS copyright transfer form, however, they are free to use their material published in CCIS for substantially changed, more elaborate subsequent publications elsewhere. For the preparation of the camera-ready papers/files, authors have to strictly adhere to the Springer CCIS Authors' Instructions and are strongly encouraged to use the CCIS LaTeX style files or templates.

Abstracting/Indexing

CCIS is abstracted/indexed in DBLP, Google Scholar, EI-Compendex, Mathematical Reviews, SCImago, Scopus. CCIS volumes are also submitted for the inclusion in ISI Proceedings.

How to start

To start the evaluation of your proposal for inclusion in the CCIS series, please send an e-mail to ccis@springer.com.

Constantine Stephanidis · Margherita Antona ·
Stavroula Ntoa · Gavriel Salvendy
Editors

HCI International 2024 Posters

26th International Conference
on Human-Computer Interaction, HCII 2024
Washington, DC, USA, June 29 – July 4, 2024
Proceedings, Part I

Springer

Editors
Constantine Stephanidis
University of Crete and Foundation for
Research and Technology - Hellas (FORTH)
Heraklion, Crete, Greece

Margherita Antona
Foundation for Research and Technology -
Hellas (FORTH)
Heraklion, Crete, Greece

Stavroula Ntoa
Foundation for Research and Technology -
Hellas (FORTH)
Heraklion, Crete, Greece

Gavriel Salvendy
University of Central Florida
Orlando, FL, USA

ISSN 1865-0929   ISSN 1865-0937 (electronic)
Communications in Computer and Information Science
ISBN 978-3-031-61931-1   ISBN 978-3-031-61932-8 (eBook)
https://doi.org/10.1007/978-3-031-61932-8

© The Editor(s) (if applicable) and The Author(s), under exclusive license
to Springer Nature Switzerland AG 2024

This work is subject to copyright. All rights are solely and exclusively licensed by the Publisher, whether the whole or part of the material is concerned, specifically the rights of translation, reprinting, reuse of illustrations, recitation, broadcasting, reproduction on microfilms or in any other physical way, and transmission or information storage and retrieval, electronic adaptation, computer software, or by similar or dissimilar methodology now known or hereafter developed.
The use of general descriptive names, registered names, trademarks, service marks, etc. in this publication does not imply, even in the absence of a specific statement, that such names are exempt from the relevant protective laws and regulations and therefore free for general use.
The publisher, the authors and the editors are safe to assume that the advice and information in this book are believed to be true and accurate at the date of publication. Neither the publisher nor the authors or the editors give a warranty, expressed or implied, with respect to the material contained herein or for any errors or omissions that may have been made. The publisher remains neutral with regard to jurisdictional claims in published maps and institutional affiliations.

This Springer imprint is published by the registered company Springer Nature Switzerland AG
The registered company address is: Gewerbestrasse 11, 6330 Cham, Switzerland

If disposing of this product, please recycle the paper.

Foreword

This year we celebrate 40 years since the establishment of the HCI International (HCII) Conference, which has been a hub for presenting groundbreaking research and novel ideas and collaboration for people from all over the world.

The HCII conference was founded in 1984 by Prof. Gavriel Salvendy (Purdue University, USA, Tsinghua University, P.R. China, and University of Central Florida, USA) and the first event of the series, "1st USA-Japan Conference on Human-Computer Interaction", was held in Honolulu, Hawaii, USA, 18–20 August. Since then, HCI International is held jointly with several Thematic Areas and Affiliated Conferences, with each one under the auspices of a distinguished international Program Board and under one management and one registration. Twenty-six HCI International Conferences have been organized so far (every two years until 2013, and annually thereafter).

Over the years, this conference has served as a platform for scholars, researchers, industry experts and students to exchange ideas, connect, and address challenges in the ever-evolving HCI field. Throughout these 40 years, the conference has evolved itself, adapting to new technologies and emerging trends, while staying committed to its core mission of advancing knowledge and driving change.

As we celebrate this milestone anniversary, we reflect on the contributions of its founding members and appreciate the commitment of its current and past Affiliated Conference Program Board Chairs and members. We are also thankful to all past conference attendees who have shaped this community into what it is today.

The 26th International Conference on Human-Computer Interaction, HCI International 2024 (HCII 2024), was held as a 'hybrid' event at the Washington Hilton Hotel, Washington, DC, USA, during 29 June – 4 July 2024. It incorporated the 21 thematic areas and affiliated conferences listed below.

A total of 5108 individuals from academia, research institutes, industry, and government agencies from 85 countries submitted contributions, and 1271 papers and 309 posters were included in the volumes of the proceedings that were published just before the start of the conference, these are listed below. The contributions thoroughly cover the entire field of human-computer interaction, addressing major advances in knowledge and effective use of computers in a variety of application areas. These papers provide academics, researchers, engineers, scientists, practitioners and students with state-of-the-art information on the most recent advances in HCI.

The HCI International (HCII) conference also offers the option of presenting 'Late Breaking Work', and this applies both for papers and posters, with corresponding volumes of proceedings that will be published after the conference. Full papers will be included in the 'HCII 2024 - Late Breaking Papers' volumes of the proceedings to be published in the Springer LNCS series, while 'Poster Extended Abstracts' will be included as short research papers in the 'HCII 2024 - Late Breaking Posters' volumes to be published in the Springer CCIS series.

I would like to thank the Program Board Chairs and the members of the Program Boards of all thematic areas and affiliated conferences for their contribution towards the high scientific quality and overall success of the HCI International 2024 conference. Their manifold support in terms of paper reviewing (single-blind review process, with a minimum of two reviews per submission), session organization and their willingness to act as goodwill ambassadors for the conference is most highly appreciated.

This conference would not have been possible without the continuous and unwavering support and advice of Gavriel Salvendy, founder, General Chair Emeritus, and Scientific Advisor. For his outstanding efforts, I would like to express my sincere appreciation to Abbas Moallem, Communications Chair and Editor of HCI International News.

July 2024   Constantine Stephanidis

HCI International 2024 Thematic Areas and Affiliated Conferences

- HCI: Human-Computer Interaction Thematic Area
- HIMI: Human Interface and the Management of Information Thematic Area
- EPCE: 21st International Conference on Engineering Psychology and Cognitive Ergonomics
- AC: 18th International Conference on Augmented Cognition
- UAHCI: 18th International Conference on Universal Access in Human-Computer Interaction
- CCD: 16th International Conference on Cross-Cultural Design
- SCSM: 16th International Conference on Social Computing and Social Media
- VAMR: 16th International Conference on Virtual, Augmented and Mixed Reality
- DHM: 15th International Conference on Digital Human Modeling & Applications in Health, Safety, Ergonomics & Risk Management
- DUXU: 13th International Conference on Design, User Experience and Usability
- C&C: 12th International Conference on Culture and Computing
- DAPI: 12th International Conference on Distributed, Ambient and Pervasive Interactions
- HCIBGO: 11th International Conference on HCI in Business, Government and Organizations
- LCT: 11th International Conference on Learning and Collaboration Technologies
- ITAP: 10th International Conference on Human Aspects of IT for the Aged Population
- AIS: 6th International Conference on Adaptive Instructional Systems
- HCI-CPT: 6th International Conference on HCI for Cybersecurity, Privacy and Trust
- HCI-Games: 6th International Conference on HCI in Games
- MobiTAS: 6th International Conference on HCI in Mobility, Transport and Automotive Systems
- AI-HCI: 5th International Conference on Artificial Intelligence in HCI
- MOBILE: 5th International Conference on Human-Centered Design, Operation and Evaluation of Mobile Communications

List of Conference Proceedings Volumes Appearing
Before the Conference

1. LNCS 14684, Human-Computer Interaction: Part I, edited by Masaaki Kurosu and Ayako Hashizume
2. LNCS 14685, Human-Computer Interaction: Part II, edited by Masaaki Kurosu and Ayako Hashizume
3. LNCS 14686, Human-Computer Interaction: Part III, edited by Masaaki Kurosu and Ayako Hashizume
4. LNCS 14687, Human-Computer Interaction: Part IV, edited by Masaaki Kurosu and Ayako Hashizume
5. LNCS 14688, Human-Computer Interaction: Part V, edited by Masaaki Kurosu and Ayako Hashizume
6. LNCS 14689, Human Interface and the Management of Information: Part I, edited by Hirohiko Mori and Yumi Asahi
7. LNCS 14690, Human Interface and the Management of Information: Part II, edited by Hirohiko Mori and Yumi Asahi
8. LNCS 14691, Human Interface and the Management of Information: Part III, edited by Hirohiko Mori and Yumi Asahi
9. LNAI 14692, Engineering Psychology and Cognitive Ergonomics: Part I, edited by Don Harris and Wen-Chin Li
10. LNAI 14693, Engineering Psychology and Cognitive Ergonomics: Part II, edited by Don Harris and Wen-Chin Li
11. LNAI 14694, Augmented Cognition, Part I, edited by Dylan D. Schmorrow and Cali M. Fidopiastis
12. LNAI 14695, Augmented Cognition, Part II, edited by Dylan D. Schmorrow and Cali M. Fidopiastis
13. LNCS 14696, Universal Access in Human-Computer Interaction: Part I, edited by Margherita Antona and Constantine Stephanidis
14. LNCS 14697, Universal Access in Human-Computer Interaction: Part II, edited by Margherita Antona and Constantine Stephanidis
15. LNCS 14698, Universal Access in Human-Computer Interaction: Part III, edited by Margherita Antona and Constantine Stephanidis
16. LNCS 14699, Cross-Cultural Design: Part I, edited by Pei-Luen Patrick Rau
17. LNCS 14700, Cross-Cultural Design: Part II, edited by Pei-Luen Patrick Rau
18. LNCS 14701, Cross-Cultural Design: Part III, edited by Pei-Luen Patrick Rau
19. LNCS 14702, Cross-Cultural Design: Part IV, edited by Pei-Luen Patrick Rau
20. LNCS 14703, Social Computing and Social Media: Part I, edited by Adela Coman and Simona Vasilache
21. LNCS 14704, Social Computing and Social Media: Part II, edited by Adela Coman and Simona Vasilache
22. LNCS 14705, Social Computing and Social Media: Part III, edited by Adela Coman and Simona Vasilache

https://2024.hci.international/proceedings

47. LNCS 14730, HCI in Games, Part II, edited by Xiaowen Fang
48. LNCS 14731, HCI in Games, Part II, edited by Xiaowen Fang
49. LNCS 14732, HCI in Mobility, Transport and Automotive Systems, Part I, edited by Heidi Krömker
50. LNCS 14733, HCI in Mobility, Transport and Automotive Systems, Part II, edited by Heidi Krömker
51. LNAI 14734, Artificial Intelligence in HCI, Part I, edited by Helmut Degen and Stavroula Ntoa
52. LNAI 14735, Artificial Intelligence in HCI, Part II, edited by Helmut Degen and Stavroula Ntoa
53. LNAI 14736, Artificial Intelligence in HCI, Part III, edited by Helmut Degen and Stavroula Ntoa
54. LNCS 14737, Design, Operation and Evaluation of Mobile Communications, Part I, edited by June Wei and George Margetis
55. LNCS 14738, Design, Operation and Evaluation of Mobile Communications, Part II, edited by June Wei and George Margetis
56. CCIS 2114, HCI International 2024 Posters, Part I, edited by Constantine Stephanidis, Margherita Antona, Stavroula Ntoa, and Gavriel Salvendy
57. CCIS 2115, HCI International 2024 Posters, Part II, edited by Constantine Stephanidis, Margherita Antona, Stavroula Ntoa, and Gavriel Salvendy
58. CCIS 2116, HCI International 2024 Posters, Part III, edited by Constantine Stephanidis, Margherita Antona, Stavroula Ntoa, and Gavriel Salvendy
59. CCIS 2117, HCI International 2024 Posters, Part IV, edited by Constantine Stephanidis, Margherita Antona, Stavroula Ntoa, and Gavriel Salvendy
60. CCIS 2118, HCI International 2024 Posters, Part V, edited by Constantine Stephanidis, Margherita Antona, Stavroula Ntoa, and Gavriel Salvendy
61. CCIS 2119, HCI International 2024 Posters, Part VI, edited by Constantine Stephanidis, Margherita Antona, Stavroula Ntoa, and Gavriel Salvendy
62. CCIS 2120, HCI International 2024 Posters, Part VII, edited by Constantine Stephanidis, Margherita Antona, Stavroula Ntoa, and Gavriel Salvendy

https://2024.hci.international/proceedings

Preface

Preliminary scientific results, professional news, or work in progress, described in the form of short research papers (4–11 pages long), constitute a popular submission type among the International Conference on Human-Computer Interaction (HCII) participants. Extended abstracts are particularly suited for reporting ongoing work, which can benefit from a visual presentation, and are presented during the conference in the form of posters. The latter allow a focus on novel ideas and are appropriate for presenting project results in a simple, concise, and visually appealing manner. At the same time, they are also suitable for attracting feedback from an international community of HCI academics, researchers, and practitioners. Poster submissions span the wide range of topics of all HCII thematic areas and affiliated conferences.

Seven volumes of the HCII 2024 proceedings are dedicated to this year's poster extended abstracts, in the form of short research papers, focusing on the following topics:

- Volume I: HCI Design Theories, Methods, Tools and Case Studies; User Experience Evaluation Methods and Case Studies; Emotions in HCI; Human Robot Interaction
- Volume II: Inclusive Designs and Applications; Aging and Technology
- Volume III: eXtended Reality and the Metaverse; Interacting with Cultural Heritage, Art and Creativity
- Volume IV: HCI in Learning and Education; HCI in Games
- Volume V: HCI in Business and Marketing; HCI in Mobility and Automated Driving; HCI in Psychotherapy and Mental Health
- Volume VI: Interacting with the Web, Social Media and Digital Services; Interaction in the Museum; HCI in Healthcare
- Volume VII: AI Algorithms and Tools in HCI; Interacting with Large Language Models and Generative AI; Interacting in Intelligent Environments; HCI in Complex Industrial Environments

Poster extended abstracts were accepted for publication in these volumes following a minimum of two single-blind reviews from the members of the HCII 2024 international Program Boards, i.e., the program committees of the constituent events. We would like to thank all of them for their invaluable contribution, support, and efforts.

July 2024
Constantine Stephanidis
Margherita Antona
Stavroula Ntoa
Gavriel Salvendy

26th International Conference on Human-Computer Interaction (HCII 2024)

The full list with the Program Board Chairs and the members of the Program Boards of all thematic areas and affiliated conferences of HCII 2024 is available online at:

http://www.hci.international/board-members-2024.php

HCI International 2025 Conference

The 27th International Conference on Human-Computer Interaction, HCI International 2025, will be held jointly with the affiliated conferences at the Swedish Exhibition & Congress Centre and Gothia Towers Hotel, Gothenburg, Sweden, June 22–27, 2025. It will cover a broad spectrum of themes related to Human-Computer Interaction, including theoretical issues, methods, tools, processes, and case studies in HCI design, as well as novel interaction techniques, interfaces, and applications. The proceedings will be published by Springer. More information will become available on the conference website: https://2025.hci.international/.

General Chair
Prof. Constantine Stephanidis
University of Crete and ICS-FORTH
Heraklion, Crete, Greece
Email: general_chair@2025.hci.international

https://2025.hci.international/

Contents – Part I

User Experience Evaluation Methods and Case Studies

Human Robot Interaction

HCI Design Theories, Methods, Tools and Case Studies

Research on the Cognitive Mechanisms of Aural Alert Design in Civil Aircraft Cockpit

Lin Du[✉] and Zhi Qiao

Shanghai Aircraft Design and Research Institute, No. 5188 JinKe Road, PuDong New District, Shanghai 201210, China
idu636261@gmail.com

Abstract. Research on the cognitive and behavioral response of flight crews to aural alerts is a challenging and critical area both in the fields of human factors and cognitive psychology. Studying the impact of aural alerts on crew recognition, understanding, task performance, and overall experience provides a theoretical foundation for the design of aural alerts.

This paper summarizes the design of aural alerts in the cockpit of civil aircraft while tracing the evolution of the aural alert system from simple aural alerts to multi-modal alert design leading to the trend of the development of aural alerts towards more user-friendly interaction between humans and computers was concluded. Besides, this section proposes design points for aural alerts, including sound types, cancelable modes and persistence characteristics. It also explores the design features to improve pilots' perception of flight status and their ability to cope with emergencies. Finally, this study analyzes the cognitive mechanism of aural alerts with the methodology of cognitive psychology and human factors engineering. The study evaluates the effects of different designs of aural alert information elements on crew perception, understanding, and task execution. The design of the cockpit aural alert system is crucial for the pilot's understanding of the flight situation and response speed to emergencies, which serves as a vital link between the pilot and the aircraft. Therefore, the design of aural alerts should focus on human-computer interaction and pilots' experience. The cockpit aural alert system must balance flight safety and pilots' experience, improve operational efficiency and enhance overall experience in stressful environments.

Keywords: Aural alerts · Human-computer Interaction · Aircraft Design · Cognitive Mechanisms

1 Overview of Cockpit Aural Alerts Design for Civil Aircraft

The cockpit of an aircraft plays a critical role in civil aviation. It attracts the attention of the flight crew and informs them of abnormal system states that require attention, as well as current fault attributes or corrective action guidance. Aural alerts on civil aircraft consist of two main types, including the tone alerts and the voice alerts.

The design process for aircraft models involves key considerations such as the selection of tone types and the content of the voice alerts. Aural alerts used in civil aircraft

© The Author(s), under exclusive license to Springer Nature Switzerland AG 2024
C. Stephanidis et al. (Eds.): HCII 2024, CCIS 2114, pp. 3–8, 2024.
https://doi.org/10.1007/978-3-031-61932-8_1

contain two main types, namely tones and speech. Table 1 gives the tones commonly used in aural alerts for civil aircraft, and Table 2 gives the voices commonly used in aural alerts for civil aircraft.

Table 1. Tone types of aural alerts commonly used in civil aircraft

Number	Aural Alert Content (Tone)	Comment
1	Trim Clacker	Aircraft trim work instructions
2	Cavalry Charge	The autopilot disengagement
3	Chime	General alerts when alert level alerts occur
4	Triple Chimes	A warning alert occurs
5	C Chord	Alert deviation from the pre-selected height
6	Beeper	APU limit
7	High Low Chime	Cabin emergency calls
8	Siren	Overspeed alerts
9	Fire Bell	For fire alert

Table 2. Voice types of aural alerts commonly used in civil aircraft

Number	Aural Alert Content (Voice)	Comment
1	"STALL"	Stall alert
2	"LEFT Engine Fire"	The left fire alert
3	"Right Engine Fire"	The right fire alert
4	"APU Fire"	The APU fire alert
5	"Smoke"	Used for detect smoke
6	"Configuration"	Used for takeoff and landing configuration alert
7	"Cabin Altitude"	The cabin height is too high
8	"Ice"	Ice alert
9	"Climb, Climb Now, Climb, Climb Now"	For Resolution Advisory

Major civil aircraft manufacturers, such as Boeing and Airbus, incorporate diverse design elements, including form and content. For instance, Boeing's aircraft designs primarily use horn sounds, accompanied by voice prompts featuring phrases like "Terrain Terrain Pull Up." In contrast, the alert tones in the Airbus design mainly consist of C chord tones. For instance, there are notable differences in the aural alert design among models for radio altitude alerts. Specifically, in the Boeing 737NG model, voice alerts are primarily used when the aircraft is at a low altitude, while in the Airbus A330 model, similar alerts are presented as 'C-chord' tones. The design of aural alerts can vary among manufacturers and is influenced by multiple factors.

From a perceptual standpoint, the recognition of aural alerts by crews constitutes a fundamental issue within the realm of aural alert perception, which is generally encompassed by the study of arousal and attention in cognitive science and human factors engineering. Begault et al. [1] from NASA (National Aeronautics and Space Administration) stated that continuous sounds possess greater alerting properties compared to discrete sounds. Kramer et al. [2] discovered a positive correlation between the crew's comprehension of the alert content and the number of repetitions of the main aural alert. Therefore, it is recommended to repeat the alert until it receives acknowledgment from the crew or until the alert state has ceased. Besides, Patterson [3] suggested that aural alerts should be reliable in capturing an individual's attention without being excessively loud, which could elicit a startle response and hinder primary task performance. Xin et al. [4] conducted empirical research on user experience through road VR environment simulation methods, which enhanced driver's experience and comfort, as well as advanced the development of future automated driving technology. Aural alerts should enable flight crews to understand the aircraft system status and situation, guiding them towards implementing optimal countermeasures to ensure the safe completion of the flight mission. As a result, it is important to consider the comprehensibility of alert messages.

2 Key Points in the Design of Civil Aircraft Cockpit Aural Alerts

The research on the cognitive and behavioral response of crew members to aural alerts is a hot spot topic and a challenge in the field of ergonomics and cognitive behavioral research. The study of the impact of the design elements of aural alerts on crew perception, understanding, task execution and experience can provide a theoretical basis for aural alerts information design, which is highly significant for the design of cockpit aural alerts.The design points for aural alerts in human-computer interaction are proposed based on research.

2.1 Types of Aural Alerts

An aural alert can be a separate tone, a voice, or a combination of both when a crew alert uses an aural alert as one of the sensing methods. To help the crew quickly determine the urgency of the alert, different tones are used for different types of alerts. The volume of the alert can be adjusted by the crew in accordance with the ambient noise level. As a result, the alert can be heard in all conditions and the frequency and duration of alerts are appropriate to their urgency and importance.

2.2 Cancellation Method for Aural Alerts

To prevent aural alerts from inadvertently disturbing the cockpit environment, the flight crew can cancel the currently triggered aural alerts by pressing a button. The alert can be manually canceled by the flight crew via the cockpit control panel or other designated equipment. However, when the problem is resolved or the situation is no longer an emergency, the alert should be automatically canceled in the system.

2.3 Persistence Characteristics of Aural Alerts

Aural alerts can be classified into three types: single-trigger, multi-trigger and continuous-trigger. Each type may require different durations to ensure that the flight crew has sufficient time to take necessary action. In terms of important but non-urgent alerts, intermittent reminders can be used to prevent the flight crew from ignoring them. Besides, when it comes to some unsolved issues which caused the alerts, the system should periodically repeat the alert to ensure that the flight crew is aware of it.

3 Cognitive Mechanism of Aural Alert Based on Human Factors Engineering

Factors Engineering Design guidelines and design databases serve as typical design management tools, providing standardized and reusable design solutions to improve the efficiency of design and development efficiency. This paper discusses the core elements of aural alerts, with a primary focus on alert tones and voice alerts. To identify parameters for each aural alert, the study focuses on analyzing design elements such as frequency, volume, intensity, amplitude, spelling, pitch, intonation, speech rate, repetition frequency and interval duration (see Fig. 1).

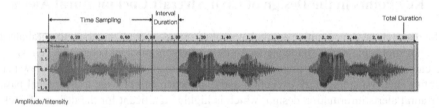

Fig. 1. The design features of aural alerts

The cognitive mechanisms of aural alerts provide the theoretical basis for designing such alerts. Human factors engineering suggests that alert tones should be clear and easy to distinguishable to ensure the flight crews can quickly identify and understand the problem. This paper analyzes the relationship between the design elements of aural alerts and crew cognition, focusing on dimensions such as crew cognition, crew performance and crew comfort. The impact mechanisms of these design elements on crew cognition are explored by analyzing aural parameters and cognitive performance (see Fig. 2). The following conclusions are drawn from the analysis:

- Frequency:
  The tone frequency should be between 200 Hz–4500 Hz which can be distinguished from cockpit noise frequencies, such as those from vibration dampers. The tone should consist of at least two frequencies. Besides, in the case of a single frequency, the tone should be distinguished by other characteristics like intervals between tones).
- Volume:
  The volume of the tone should be sufficient to ensure that it can be easily perceived by the crew in the most severe cockpit noise environments, but not so loud as to interfere

with the crew's ability to take necessary action. If the volume is adjustable, either manually or automatically, the minimum volume should still be perceived by the crew in all cockpit noise environments. Automatic volume adjustment is commonly used to maintain an appropriate signal-to-noise ratio.

- Quantity:
  In civil aircraft, the number of tones should not exceed 10 to reduce crew workload and training requirements, as an excessive number of tones can increase cognitive difficulty for flight crews.

Besides, in emergencies, aural alerts should be designed to prevent confusion and minimize the cognitive burden on the flight crew. Different alert levels should be associated with different sounds or sound patterns to help the crew quickly distinguish the importance of the problems. For instance, high-frequency or high-volume sounds may be used for urgent alerts. The design of aural alerts should take into account

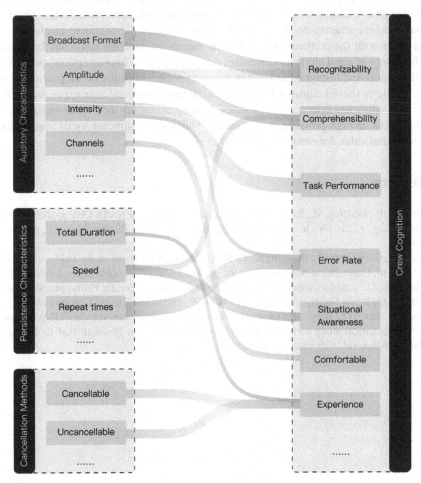

Fig. 2. Mapping of aural alerts characteristics to crew cognition

human physiological characteristics, such as the frequency range and sensitivity of human hearing.

In the aircraft cockpit, a large amount of information is integrated into a limited space, with complex scenarios and high cognitive load. Combining complex task scenarios for user evaluation and validation of the effects on how flight crews perceive, understand, perform and have an overall experience supports the design of aural alerts that more closely match the cognitive characteristics of the flight crew.

4 Conclusion

Cockpit aural alerts are a crucial aspect of communication between pilots and aircraft, directly impacting pilots' understanding of flight situations and their response speed to emergencies. This paper provides an overview of the design of aural alerts in civil aircraft cockpits, revealing trends in the development of aural alerts towards more friendly human-machine interaction. Besides, this paper analyzes the cognitive mechanism of aural alerts with the methodology of human factors engineering, proposes key points for the design of aural alerts and discusses design features to improve pilots' perception of flight status and response capabilities in emergencies. In future developments, cockpit aural alerts should consider human-machine interaction and user experience while balancing safety and operational efficiency, thereby enhancing the overall experience of aircraft crews in high-pressure environments. This holds significant social implications and industrial value for ensuring aviation safety.

References

1. Begault, R., Godfroy, M., Sandor, A.: Auditory alarm design for NASA CEV applications. In: Proceedings of the 13th International Conference on Auditory Display, Montréal, pp. 26–29 (2007)
2. Kramer, G., Walker, B., Bonebright, T.: Sonification report: status of the field and research agenda. In: University of Nebraska-Lincoln, pp. 1–29. University of Nebraska, Lincoln (2010)
3. Patterson, D.: Auditory warning sounds in the work environment. In: Philosophical Transactions of the Royal Society of London, pp. 485–492. The Royal Society, London (1990)
4. Xin, Z., Steve, O., Barret, E.: On-road virtual reality autonomous vehicle (VRAV) simulator: an empirical study on user experience. In: Transportation Research Part C: Emerging Technologies, vol. 126. Elsevier, Amsterdam (2021)

Visualization of Operating System Behavior in a Linux Environment Running in a Browser

Mayo Fukata[✉] and Eiichi Hayakawa

Takushoku University, 815-1Tatemachi, Hachioji-Shi, Tokyo, Japan
`23m307@st.takushoku-u.ac.jp`

Abstract. In recent years, Linux is increasingly used for server operating systems and other applications, and the opportunities to learn the Linux operating system are increasing. In this study, we focus on learning Linux OS. There is a need for a tool that allows beginners to easily try Linux.

Currently, one of the ways to use Linux on Windows or MacOS is to use a Linux environment emulated by a browser. This method is very convenient because the user only needs to access a specified URL with a browser, and JSLINUX [1] is a well-known site. However, the current JSLINUX does not have such features, making it unsuitable for learning.

This system is an implementation of the functionality developed for JSLINUX that is made available on the Web. In addition to the basic functions of JSLINUX, the web application screen displays a CPU state transition diagram, scheduling, and swap information in real time on the side of the console screen. In addition to the basic functions of JSLINUX, the web application screen implements a function to display a diagram that visualizes CPU state transition, scheduling, and swap information in real time on the side of the console screen.

Keywords: Operating system · Student support · Visualization · JSLINUX · Linux running in a browser

1   Introduction

According to a survey by IDC Japan [2], the share of the Linux OS in Japan in 2017 was 24.8%, with a year-on-year growth rate of 13.5%, indicating that the Linux OS is gradually expanding its share. The following resources are available to help beginners learn the Linux OS.

- Preparing a New Computer
- Using WSL
- Create a virtual environment, such as VirtualBox

These are difficult for beginners who want to start learning casually, and they are one of the barriers. In this study, we focused on JSLINUX, a Linux environment that runs on a browser emulated by JavaScript. The browser can be used on any PC connected to the Internet, and can be reloaded to return to its initial state in case of problems. This has

© The Author(s), under exclusive license to Springer Nature Switzerland AG 2024
C. Stephanidis et al. (Eds.): HCII 2024, CCIS 2114, pp. 9–13, 2024.
https://doi.org/10.1007/978-3-031-61932-8_2

the advantage of making it easy to execute dangerous commands that would normally damage the operating system.

In our previous study [3], we added functions to JSLINUX to connect to the Internet through a relay server and to execute commands using GUI operations in conjunction with a Web application. As a result, the system contributed to educational applications by enabling the execution of programs containing APIs. However, since the purpose of this previous study was to expand the range of available applications, it did not specialize in OS learning and did not implement visualization. The purpose of this study is to promote the understanding of the operating principles of the Linux operating system by implementing a function to visualize the movement of processes hidden in the operation of the operating system.

In a previous study [4], we developed software that simulated several CPU scheduling algorithms. The software displayed the computation time for each algorithm so that the advantages and disadvantages of each algorithm could be visually understood. However, since the software in this previous study only displays the CPU wait time and the turnaround time after execution, it does not show the progress of the process, such as the order in which the processes were executed. Therefore, it is not possible to understand how context switching is performed. In this study, the actual LinuxOS processing is displayed in a table for each process, allowing the user to see the process in progress.

In a previous study [5], we developed an OS visualization tool using the kernel tracer LTTNG and asked students in the Department of Computer Engineering to use it as part of their problem-solving assignments. This tool allows you to visualize and experience the scheduler, deadlocks, pipelines, semaphores, queues, and interprocess communication. In the assignment, we asked the participants to run their own programs and observe the behavior of the operating system and the visualized state behind the operating system. This was followed by a questionnaire survey to determine the usefulness of the tool.

However, one problem was that some commented that it was cumbersome to install on their home PC. To solve this problem, an improvement was made that only supported Ubuntu and distributed Ubuntu packages with tools already installed. The tool developed in this research runs in a browser, so it has the advantage of requiring no installation work and can be used immediately as long as you are connected to the Internet.

2 Research Summary

Figure 1 shows a system configuration diagram. The parts to be developed in this study are indicated by blue boxes. In this study, the visualization and replay functions are implemented in the JSLINUX emulator implemented in Javascript. A program that collects resource status is periodically executed on the emulator and the collected information is recorded. In case of real-time display, the recorded information is displayed one by one. In case of slow-motion display, the recorded information is displayed by extending the time axis.

When you run a Python or C program or shell script on JSLINUX, the corresponding process is displayed in the CPU state transition diagram, and the scheduling function displays the process status every unit of time. By observing these, you can visually observe how the operating system is processing.

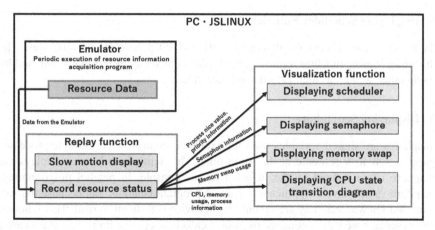

Fig. 1. A system configuration diagram

3 Functions Developed

The following functions have been developed in this study. Figure 2 shows the screen with the added visualization features. The emulator console is on the top left, and the CPU state transition diagram, resource state display, semaphore variable display, and scheduling state display are in order from the top right.

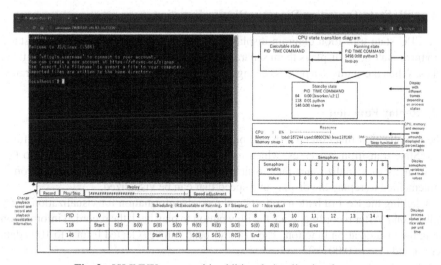

Fig. 2. JSLINUX screen with additional visualization features

3.1 Displaying Scheduler Function

Scheduling is the process of allocating CPU and IO processing to processes. The Scheduling Viewer function retrieves and displays the status of processes assigned by the scheduler, as well as their priority and nice values.

3.2 Displaying Semaphore

Semaphores are shared variables used for exclusion control when multiple processes request access to a resource at the same time. The Semaphore Viewer displays the semaphore range created by the program on the console. In parallel programming, semaphore values have a significant impact on program behavior, but because the values are not known until they are output, the behavior is difficult to read. This function displays semaphore values obtained by system calls in a separate frame to make it easier to understand the exclusive control program.

3.3 Displaying Memory Swap

Memory swap is the process of transferring data that can no longer be stored in RAM to storage. The memory swap display function displays the status of the swap area obtained using a graph. Since swap is turned off by default at startup, a button to turn it on is also provided so that it can be used as needed.

3.4 CPU State Transition Diagram Display Function

The CPU state transition diagram display function divides the detected process states into three states and displays them separately by setting up frames for each of the three states. When the status of a process changes, the process moves to the appropriate frame.

3.5 Replay Function

The visualization function records and plays back the actions of the visualization function. State transition processes, which usually take place in milliseconds, are too fast for humans to visualize and thus difficult to understand. Therefore, this function is implemented to replay the display at a speed that can be visualized.

Clicking the Record button collects and records information for visualization every millisecond. After recording, click the Play button to play back the recorded information using the visualization function. The display speed can be selected from 1 to 1000 data per second ($1\times$ to $0.001\times$).

4 Conclusion

To date, we have completed the study of the scheduling algorithms and processes of the Linux operating system. In addition, development functions, screen structure, UI and data collection methods have been determined.

Recently, the visualization display part was created using HTML, the UI was developed using Javascript, and the data collection program was created using Python.

In the future, a method to place files when loading JSLINUX due to its own creation, a method to execute scripts when loading, and other methods will be investigated and developed.

As a verification experiment, students who are novice OS users will be asked to perform tasks using JSLINUX before and after the added functionality, and their solution times and correct answer rates will be compared.

References

1. JSLINUX. https://bellard.org/jslinux/
2. Oshima, J.: Windows is the majority of server OSs in Japan, with Linux also holding steady bp-A news (2018). https://bp-affairs.com/news/2018/08/20180824-7901.html. Accessed Mar 2024
3. Kasae, Y., Chiba, H., Kurumatani, S., Akama, H.: Wemu: Extension Method of Web Browser's Functions by Virtual Machine on the Web Browser: A Study for Educational Applications. DEIM Forum 2014 F2-3
4. Hasan, T.F.: CPU scheduling visualization. Diyala J. Eng. Sci. 07(01), 16–29 (2014)
5. Dagenais, M.R., de Montreal, E.P., Boucheneb, H., de Montreal, E.P.: Teaching operating systems concepts with execution visualization. In: 121st ASEE Annual Conference and Exposition Indianapolis, 15–18 June 2014

Research on the Application Situation and Trend of Immersive Design

Hongqing Gu[✉]

NetEase Youdao Information Technology (Hangzhou) Co., Ltd., Hangzhou,
People's Republic of China
feeling9063@gmail.com

Abstract. Through a systematic analytical study of 1,219 immersive design documents in the internationally renowned database WOS (Web of Science), we hope to gain a more objective and credible knowledge and understanding of this field. By using bibliometric analysis combined with content analysis, the overall overview, theoretical basis, research hot spots, and dynamic trends of immersive design research are analyzed, interpreted, and discussed. The research results show that immersive design research is developing rapidly, mainly in the fields of computer science, engineering, educational research, imaging science and photography technology, telecommunications, psychology, etc. With the United States as the core of academic research; the theoretical basis of immersive design mainly originates from immersion theory, and hot topics mainly focus on the cognitive elaboration of the ontology of immersive design, the innovative strategies of immersion theory in design, educational applications, product development, and multi-field practice and other topics; immersive design research has significant interdisciplinary and practical characteristics, and cross-level and interdisciplinary cooperation needs to be further strengthened in future research, such as artificial intelligence, machine learning, sensing technology, etc. This cross-level and cross-disciplinary cooperation will break the limitations of traditional design and bring more innovative possibilities to immersive design.

Keywords: Immersive design · Content analysis · Econometric analysis · Vos viewer · Cites pace

1 Introduction

The theory of "immersive" originates from the theory of "flow" proposed by Prof. Mihaly Csikmihalyi in 1975. Also known as the "immersive" Theory, it provides a more systematic introduction to immersive experiences, revealing that the source of people's happiness comes from "flow" [1]. When "flow" arises, a person is able to feel a complete immersion of body and mind. By combining consciousness and action, subjective perception emerges over time, leading to the achievement of an optimal state between consciousness and body [2]. "Immersive design" is a design concept that aims to utilize human sensory and cognitive experiences through design means, creating an

© The Author(s), under exclusive license to Springer Nature Switzerland AG 2024
C. Stephanidis et al. (Eds.): HCII 2024, CCIS 2114, pp. 14–21, 2024.
https://doi.org/10.1007/978-3-031-61932-8_3

atmosphere in which participants can enjoy an optimal state. Its goal is to enable users to smoothly focus their attention, perform desired behaviors, and guide them to specific emotions and experiences [3].

Research on immersive design possesses significant value in the field of design. Firstly, it drives innovation by integrating cutting-edge technology, creating novel design experiences, and interaction methods [4]. Immersive design enhances user experiences by allowing them to be fully immersed in the design process, thus enhancing product satisfaction and usability [5]. Moreover, interdisciplinary collaboration is integral to immersive design research, fostering knowledge exchange, and fostering innovation, and broadening perspectives in design education and practice. Finally, immersive design research has positive societal impacts, enhancing users' interaction with the digital world and advancing the application of digital technology in sectors like education, healthcare, and cultural entertainment. In summary, research on immersive design is of great importance in academic research, contributing to the advancement in the field of design.

In recent years, the application of immersive design in design research has attracted more and more attention. As a result, a large amount of research literature with diverse knowledge structures and a visible interdisciplinary nature has been produced [6]. However, the traditional literature review method alone is insufficient for accurately reflect the practical application of immersive design. Therefore, this paper utilizes relevant literature from the Web of Science database as the data source, visualizes the knowledge structure of the retrieved data, and comprehensively analyzes the research status and development trends of immersive design.

2 Methodology

This paper utilizes bibliometrics and information visualization methods. In order to obtain more rigorous and comprehensive data indicators, two pieces of bibliometric visualization software, VOSviewer and CiteSpace, were used to create a map of scientific knowledge [7]. The map includes networks such as the cooperative countries co-occurrence network, the keywords co-occurrence clustering network, and the reference co-citation clustering network. The networks were empirically analyzed based on the retrieved data [7].

For this study, the Web of Science database was selected to retrieve journal and paper data related to immersive design. To ensure the authority and research value of the literature data, only sources from SCI, SSCI, and A&HCI were included in the search criteria. The search criteria used were (TS = "immersive design" AND TI = "design"), and there was no limitation on the time span. A total of 1219 papers published between 1987 and 2023 were retrieved and exported as TXT files in the format of fully recorded and cited references. The files were then used to generate a visual knowledge map for quantitative analysis.

In the process of analysis, the scientific knowledge mapping method was applied, and software such as VOSviewer and Citespace were also used to visualize and analyse immersion-related literature. The corresponding scientific knowledge maps were created to demonstrate the research progress of immersive design, in order to explore the key paths and evolutionary turning points of this subject area. The specific steps are as follows:

1. In order to present the research status and strength in the field of immersive design, an analysis was conducted using the VOSviewer software. This analysis included examining the distribution of literature, such as publication volume, countries and regions of publication, and affiliations of the authors.
2. By performing co-occurrence analysis of keywords, the hot topics in the field were identified, and clustering analysis was used to highlight the research themes within the entire field of study.
3. By employing burst analysis and knowledge graph analysis, the evolution and future research trends of immersive design are explored.
4. By combining theories and the results of the clustering analysis, the integration of various aspects of immersive design was achieved, including the distribution of output, core topics, knowledge foundation, research hotspots, and future trends.

3   Descriptive Analysis

3.1   Analysis of Publication Volume and Publication Countries

The number of papers published in a certain field reflects the development status and research results of the subject [8]. Figure 1 shows the distribution of the number of publications on immersive design. The analysis shows that the number of papers related to immersive design is generally increasing. Between 1987 and 2000, the overall number of publications was relatively small, proving that the application of immersion theory in immersive design was still in its infancy, and related research had not been taken seriously. The number of articles published showed a gradual upward trend from 2000 to 2016. The number of articles published almost increased every year, and the number

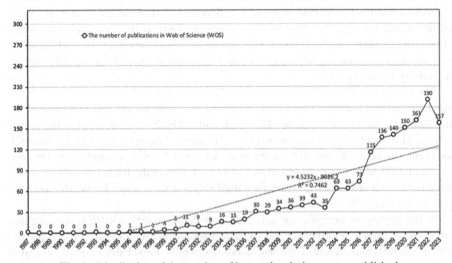

Fig. 1. Distribution of the number of immersive design papers published

of articles published annually did not exceed 100 articles. It was not until 2017 that the annual number of articles published exceeded 100 articles for the first time. Since then, Accelerate the upward trend. The number of published articles declined until 2023, proving that research on immersive design needs to be continuously enriched through interdisciplinary research and more researchers.

The main countries with a high publication output include the United States, China, England, Italy and Australia (Table 1). Among them, the United States has the largest share of research in this field. China shows significant interest in immersive design research, as indicated by its wide range of applications. Furthermore, the main institutions with high research output include Florida State University, CNRS, and the University of Sydney, each specializing in different aspects of immersive design. This centralized pattern of research output can be observed in the United States, while in China, research in this field is distributed across multiple institutions, indicating wide participation without any single institution standing out prominently.

Table 1. The number of published papers and the number of citations in the top 5 countries

Country	Documents	Times Cited
The United States	374	4424
The People's Republic of China	344	4057
England	95	946
Italy	76	653
Australia	75	709

3.2 Analyses of Research Field Hotspots

In today's research fields, immersive design is applied in Computer Science, Engineering, Education Research, Imaging Science and Photography Technology, Telecommunications, Psychology, and some other areas. It focuses on creating immersive experiences and combining with virtual reality (VR), augmented reality (AR), and education. The combination of immersive design with other methods primarily involves sensory experience and cognitive science. It uses virtual reality (VR) and augmented reality (AR) technologies, user interface design, and emotional design, making immersive design an interdisciplinary field (Fig. 2).

It can be seen from the cluster diagram that the research classification of immersive design mainly includes interface design, immersive design and education, immersive technology and immersive experience system. Among them, interface design refers to the scientific design process and interface operation design based on user experience during the immersive design process, so that the performance of immersive design can better meet the needs of users. While immersive design often involves interface design as part of creating the user's interaction with a digital environment, it also encompasses broader considerations such as spatial design, audio design, and user engagement strategies specific to immersive technologies [9]. Interface design within immersive experiences may involve creating intuitive controls, navigation systems, and interactive elements that seamlessly integrate with the immersive environment and enhance the user's sense of presence and agency within that environment.

Immersive design and education refer to the use of immersive technologies and other interactive digital environments to enhance the learning experience for teachers and students [9]. In immersive design, the focus is on creating environments or experiences that deeply engage the user's senses and cognition, often blurring the lines between the physical and virtual worlds. This approach aims to provide learners with more effective and engaging ways to acquire knowledge, skills and understanding.

Immersive design uses cool technology to make digital experiences feel real and exciting. Add digital content to the real world with virtual reality (VR), such as adding interesting characters to a room via your phone. Mixed reality (MR) mixes real and digital content so users can touch and interact with both [10]. Spatial computing helps digital things understand where you are, making it all fit together like magic. Haptic feedback allows users to feel things in the digital world, such as vibrations when touching something. For the first time, immersive design will also use motion tracking technology, 3D audio technology, etc. [11]. All these technologies make digital experiences more interesting and real, and also allow immersive design to be applied to more and richer fields.

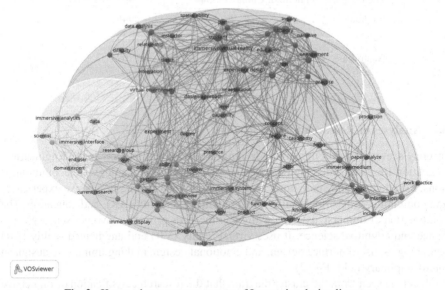

Fig. 2. Keyword co-occurrence map of Immersive design literature

3.3 Highly Cited Literature

The citation frequency of journal articles can objectively reflect the academic value and influence of journal articles in the academic field. Therefore, the citation frequency of journal articles is generally used internationally as a standard to evaluate the level of scientific research. Highly cited papers refer to academic papers that are cited relatively frequently and for a relatively long period of time. If a paper is cited more frequently, it can be considered to have higher academic value to a certain extent. Therefore, research on highly cited papers has also become a hot topic in recent years.

At present, a substantial amount of influential and highly cited literature on immersive design has been published (Table 2). For example, some literature has examined the use of immersive design in higher education. The most cited documents on immersive design appear in journals related to education. This study explores the benefits and applications of VR in different scenarios. It has been confirmed that VR has great potential in educational research and has attracted widespread attention from peers. This educational method can increase students' concentration on teaching content and enhance their interest [12]. Other researcher has explored the importance of considering communication goals, target audience characteristics, content management strategies, triggers, and the socio-physical environment in which consumers live. These findings provide a solid foundation for the subsequent application of immersive design. They constitute classic cases and a knowledge base, providing a research basis for its subsequent application.

Table 2. Highly cited literature

WOS literature	Literature source	Number of citations
Radianti J 2020	COMPUTERS & EDUCATION	554
Moreno P 2008	COMPUTERS IN HUMAN BEHAVIOR	225
Scholz J 2016	BUSINESS HORIZONS	202
Heydarian A 2015	AUTOMATION IN CONSTRUCTION	194
de Freitas S 2010	BRITISH JOURNAL OF EDUCATIONAL TECHNOLOGY	173
Dickey MD 2011	BRITISH JOURNAL OF EDUCATIONAL TECHNOLOGY	127
Chirico A 2018	FRONTIERS IN PSYCHOLOGY	126

4 Conclusion and Discussion

Through immersive design, designers can break the limitations imposed by traditional design and combine technology and creativity to offer users novel ways to interact with products or services. These advancements not only promote the progress of the design industry, but also enrich people's lives with more captivating and fulfilling experiences. This study examines the research on immersive design from the period of 1987 to 2023:

1. The analysis of the output distribution demonstrates a consistent upward trend in the number of papers that focus on immersive design. Despite the late emergence of research in this field, the overall growth trend is clearly evident.

2. The main countries with significant output of relevant research include the United States, China, the United Kingdom, Italy, and Australia. Among them, the United States has the largest share of relevant research volume, as the theory originated there. China has the second largest amount of relevant research, indicating its strong emphasis and extensive application of research in this field.

3. Keywords and cluster analyses show that immersive design has emerged in various research fields such as computer science, engineering, educational research, and psychology. By combining immersive experiences with virtual reality and augmented reality technologies, designers can create more realistic and interactive user experiences. This combination provides designers with more room for creativity and access to technological tools, while also providing users with a more engaging experience. The integration of immersive experiences with virtual reality and augmented reality technologies can promote innovation and development in the design field, build a closer interactive relationship between designers and users, and further enhance the quality and impact of design.

Combined with the above analyses, it can be seen that in the process of continuous development, especially in the last 10 years, immersive design has been used in a large variety of fields [13]. The next research needs to further strengthen the cross-level and interdisciplinary cooperation, such as artificial intelligence, machine learning, sensing technology and so on. This kind of cross-level and interdisciplinary cooperation will break the limitations of traditional design and bring more innovative possibilities for immersive design. At the same time, immersive design will also pay more attention to social responsibility and provide solutions for social progress through immersive design. In addition, there are some limitations in the article, and the results analyzed by the chosen database and search method for the study may deviate from the actual ones, which will be further improved in the subsequent studies.

References

1. Nilsson, N.C., Nordahl, R., Serafin, S.: Immersion revisited: a review of existing definitions of immersion and their relation to different theories of presence. Hum. Technol. **12**(2), 108–134 (2016)
2. Kitson, A., Prpa, M., Riecke, B.E.: Immersive interactive technologies for positive change: a scoping review and design considerations. Front. Psychol. **9**, 1354 (2018)
3. Rieuf, V., Bouchard, C., Meyrueis, V., Omhover, J.-F.: Emotional activity in early immersive design: sketches and moodboards in virtual reality. Des. Stud. **48**, 43–75 (2017)
4. Ruan, Y.: Application of immersive virtual reality interactive technology in art design teaching. Comput. Intell. Neurosci. **2022**, 1–12 (2022)
5. Rebelo, F., Duarte, E., Noriega, P., Soares, M.: 24 Virtual reality in consumer. In: Human Factors and Ergonomics in Consumer Product Design: Methods and Techniques, p. 381 (2011)
6. Chen, Z., et al.: Exploring the design space of immersive urban analytics. Visual Informatics **1**(2), 132–142 (2017)
7. Ding, X., Yang, Z. Knowledge mapping of platform research: a visual analysis using VOSviewer and CiteSpace. Electron. Commerce Res. **22**(3), 787–809 (2020)
8. Liao, H., Tang, M., Luo, L., Li, C., Chiclana, F., Zeng, X.-J.: A bibliometric analysis and visualization of medical big data research. Sustainability **10**(1), 166 (2018)

9. Kharoub, H., Lataifeh, M., Ahmed, N.: 3D user interface design and usability for immersive VR. Appl. Sci. **9**(22), 4861 (2019)
10. Farshid, M., Paschen, J., Eriksson, T., Kietzmann, J.: Go boldly!: Explore augmented reality (AR), virtual reality (VR), and mixed reality (MR) for business. Bus. Horiz. **61**(5), 657–663 (2018)
11. Suh, A., Prophet, J.: The state of immersive technology research: a literature analysis. Comput. Hum. Behav. **86**, 77–90 (2018)
12. Radianti, J., Majchrzak, T.A., Fromm, J., Wohlgenannt, I.: A systematic review of immersive virtual reality applications for higher education: design elements, lessons learned, and research agenda. Comput. Educ. **147**, 103778 (2020)
13. Andreoli, R., et al.: A framework to design, develop, and evaluate immersive and collaborative serious games in cultural heritage. J. Comput. Cult. Herit. **11**(1), 1–22 (2017)

Using Schema Theory to Construct the Designer's Knowledge Framework

Su Guo[✉]

Tongji University, No. 281 Fuxin Road, Shanghai, China
24405922@qq.com

Abstract. Design knowledge is often categorized as tacit knowledge, but it is not randomly scattered within the designer's mind. Schema is used to capture the designer's knowledge, representing the structure of knowledge. This study explores the formation and use of design knowledge among designers through in-depth interviews, analysis of precedent works, and design task testing, outlining the structure of design knowledge frameworks. The research reveals that design knowledge is stored in the form of conceptual schema at different levels. The classification of conceptual schema is closely intertwined with the design process and outcomes. The structural framework of conceptual schema plays a crucial role in the retrieval of design knowledge, with different types of conceptual schemas able to retrieve different knowledge.

Keywords: Schema Theory · Conceptual Schema · Knowledge Framework

1 Introduction

For a considerable period, the process of moving from design problems to solutions has been referred to as a creative leap, where the solution generation process is considered invisible. But it does not exist disorderly in the designer's mind. It has a certain framework that allows knowledge to be systematically accessed during the design process. What is the specific structure of this framework? Can it be explicitly represented? Design knowledge is influenced by the accumulation of experience. There is a significant difference in the knowledge and experience that design experts and novices can access and process [1]. Before growing into experts, designers need to study a large number of design precedents, storing them in the brain through scenarios and experiential memory [2]. The Schema theory originated from Kant's inquiry into "how knowledge is formed and develops," with Bartlett and Piaget analyzing how knowledge is generated and developed through the memory and organization of experiences and cognitive processes, respectively. Minsky systematically explained the structure of knowledge by proposing the theory of the frame, stating that schemata are the structural units representing knowledge [3]. In the field of design research, schema theory has been used to capture designers' knowledge [4], assess the level of design knowledge [5], and represent the internal structure and innovation of design prototypes [6, 7]. However, it has not been systematically used to analyze the inherited framework of design knowledge and how

© The Author(s), under exclusive license to Springer Nature Switzerland AG 2024
C. Stephanidis et al. (Eds.): HCII 2024, CCIS 2114, pp. 22–29, 2024.
https://doi.org/10.1007/978-3-031-61932-8_4

the reasoning rules design thinking. Conceptual schemas serve as indicators to measure a designer's level of knowledge. Designers express complex ideas through simple words (conceptual terms) and phrases, which is precisely the process of conceptual formation or schema development. For example, a designer may use "Belvedere" to express an idea. However, for the designer, the schema of "Belvedere" is not limited to a specific observation deck, but rather a type of architecture, a device of vertical spatial organization aimed at providing dramatic perspectives and assisting users of the building in creating a mental map of their surroundings [8]. As knowledge and experience accumulate, the content and information contained within this concept become richer. During 4–6 years of professional learning, designers acquire knowledge and experience stored in memory, forming a database [9]. When engaged in design practice, the contents of this database are retrieved, converging into a designer's design world. Conceptual schemas, as the basic units of design knowledge, exist in the designer's database and design world. How do they interact? Drawing on schema theory, this study presents three questions regarding the construction of a designer's knowledge framework:

- What is the internal structure of design knowledge?
- What knowledge contents do designers access during the design process?
- How is design knowledge identified, abstracted, and transformed during the design process?

2 Methods

2.1 Study Design

This study aims to understand the process of knowledge and experience accumulation among designers through their professional learning experiences and design practice. The research employed in-depth interviews, precedent analysis method [5], and task testing with 5 designers for data collection. The study consists of three parts: interviews on design knowledge, precedent analysis of works, and design task testing. Each session with the participants was controlled to last for 90 min. The entire interviews were recorded, and all data were analyzed using the qualitative research software NVivo11 for coding. The interview section consisted of 5 questions regarding the understanding of design knowledge, the process of learning design knowledge, participation in design practice projects, experiences with precedent learning, among others. The precedent analysis section displayed a total of 10 visual renderings of design works[1]. Most of the selected examples were from Fortune Magazine's 2019 selection of The 100 Best Designed Products, representing famous examples of designers from the 20th to the 21st century. These examples were chosen to represent different aspects such as form, style, functionality, typology, and usage. The 5 designers were presented with images of design works and asked to verbally describe what they observed in the pictures. The process was recorded and transcribed using speech-to-text tools. For the design task testing, designers are presented with a photo of a bathroom and asked to design a chair for elderly people based on the scene information. The testing time is 40 min, during

---

[1] 1-Aeron chair, 2-iPhone, 3-Porsche 911, 4-OXO Good Grips Peeler, 5-Eames Fiberglass Armchair, 6-Model S Sedan, 7-Nokia 3210, 8-Apple Watch, 9-Poäng, 10-Box Chair.

which designers verbally articulate their thoughts on the design process. Data collection is conducted through protocol analysis.

2.2 Participants

Designers were recruited from design companies and design schools in Shanghai through purposeful sampling. Further selection was carried out using snowball sampling. The recruitment criteria for participants included: undergraduate industrial design major and practical design project experience. Initially, 11 designers were recruited, and then 5 designers were randomly selected from them.

2.3 Tools and Materials

Recording pen, interview script, portfolio of precedent works, task testing questions.

2.4 Analysis

The collected verbal reports are projections of the externalization and internal knowledge structure of designers, reflecting the objective content of design knowledge they possess. Research data were analyzed using the traditional content analysis method to create a main code book: Two doctoral students majoring in design from Tongji University were invited to review the consistency of data collection, which helped in a comprehensive understanding of the viewpoints presented in each interview.

2.5 Ethical Review

The research design, data collection tools, and consent forms were approved by the Research Ethics Committee of Tongji University. Participants were informed about the purpose and nature of the study, and informed consent was obtained before each survey, with participants signing informed consent forms. To ensure confidentiality, numerical codes (D1, D2, D3, D4, D5) were used instead of names for the five participants in the research data, and any data related to personal information was deleted.

3 Results

This study conducted in-depth interviews, precedent work analysis, and design task tests with five designers. The demographic information of the designers is shown in Table 1. The analysis results will be discussed in the following sections.

Table 1. Participant Demographics

Designer	Gender	education	work experience
Designer 1	Female	postgraduate	2years
Designer 2	Male	postgraduate	15years
Designer 3	Female	postgraduate	8years
Designer 4	Male	postgraduate	13years
Designer 5	Male	postgraduate	3years

3.1 Learning and Accumulation of Design Knowledge

Designer Professional Learning Process: Internalization and Integration. Designers study basic general education courses in the first two years of their undergraduate studies, and begin to engage in specialized courses such as comprehensive design exercises in the third year. In the graduate stage, they study subjects like psychology and market analysis, often mentioning design methods. Active learning among designers mostly occurs during the graduate stage, involving areas such as marketing, quantitative analysis, and service design.

Designers study foundational general education courses in the first two years of their undergraduate studies, and start professional courses in the third year, such as comprehensive design exercises. In the graduate stage, they study psychology, market analysis, and frequently discuss design methods. Designers see foundational courses as partial components of design knowledge that become internalized. They generally consider the most important course to be comprehensive design training, typically determined by teachers, with themes such as Bluetooth speakers, MP3 players, aiming to produce works through a complete design process. As the number of comprehensive design projects increases, designers begin to focus on design scenarios and issues. Terms commonly mentioned by designers in in-depth interviews are problem awareness, design process, and user needs. In the graduate stage, designers experience an increase in both the depth and breadth of design knowledge. When addressing challenges or situations lacking smoothness or rationality, designers start focusing on design scenarios and issues. After starting work, designers express that their core skills involve rapidly acquiring information and articulating problems quickly. Design knowledge is integrated into the design process and dispersed throughout every aspect.

Collection and Study of Design Precedents. Designers actively collect design precedents during their undergraduate and graduate studies to enrich their design knowledge. In their undergraduate years, they gather cases related to their personal interests, such as hand-drawn works (D1, D4), automobiles (D1, D4), furniture (D5, D3), and electronic products (D2). During their graduate studies, their focus shifts to cases and materials relevant to the design topics, such as interaction methods (D1), community innovation (D5), healthcare (D1), and elderly-friendly design (D1, D5). Designers collect these cases to understand the latest and best design works, either borrowing from or imitating their appearance and style, or analyzing their creative ideas and concepts. However, as they accumulate work experience, designers begin to reduce their collection of cases and concentrate on exploring cutting-edge technologies, new consumer trends, and social innovations in the design field. They integrate this wealth of design knowledge into their design process to enhance their design proficiency.

3.2 Design Precedent Works Analysis

Analysis Framework for Design Precedent Works. Designers' analysis of the works demonstrates a consistent pattern, as they use professional terminology to categorize the works, and then provide detailed evaluations based on dimensions such as appearance, structure, form, material, function, usage scenarios, ergonomics, experience, and comfort.

Taking the four chair works as an example, designers typically refer to them as "ergonomic chair, recliner, office chair, folding chair," and evaluate them based on dimensions such as form, function, comfort, material, and ergonomics. Their evaluations highlight specific attributes of each design, such as using adjectives like "foldable, portable" for the Box Chair, "ergonomics, functionality, comfort" for the Aeron chair, "fashionable, structured, integral design" for the Eames Fiberglass Armchair, and "comfort, experiential sensation" for the Poäng chair.

This comprehensive analytical approach is particularly evident in evaluating the Box Chair, where designers analyzed it across 9 dimensions: form, function, structure, comfort, material, usage experience, user, manufacturing process, and production transport. Each dimension had further details, such as "hole design" under form, and "foldable > detachable > disassembly process > backrest storage" under function.

3.3 Different Concept Schema Influence Knowledge Retrieval

Designers Use Similar Problem-Solving Steps. The problem-solving steps of designers in the task testing are generally similar and can be summarized as analyzing the question, hypothesizing the problem, defining the problem, seeking solutions, and finalizing the solution and details. After reading the design task's title, designers begin by observing the provided scene images of the bathroom, examining the environment of the entire toilet (D4, D5), and analyzing the behaviors that the elderly might engage in the bathroom (D3, D4). Designers recall experiences to analyze the potential role of the chair in the toilet (D1, D2, D3), the reasons behind using the chair (D3, D4), and analyze possible problematic situations, proposing concepts such as "safety, ease of use, fatigue relief", etc. Subsequently, designers verbally articulate the problems they aim to solve, for example, designer D4 states: "My chair should be usable as a walking aid. First, analyze the problems, one is slipping due to wetness. Second, it can assist in walking. Third, it can be unfolded into a seat or a toilet seat at any time (D4)". Based on the defined problems, they proceed to specific designs, with designers sketching while explaining the structure and usage scenarios of the design proposal, and finally supplementing the details of the design proposal. Designers roughly outline the specific form of the chair, with two designers naming their design results as "Walking Aid D4" and "Bathing Stool D5".

Knowledge Retrieval in Design Tasks. Designers use the same design steps to complete design tasks, which include analyzing the problem, defining the problem, generating concepts, refining concepts, and creating solutions. Semantic analysis reveals that designers draw on different knowledge content in different steps. During the problem analysis phase, designers analyze key words in the task such as "chair", "bathroom", "elderly", and extract contents such as "using the toilet, washing, grandparents, my home, problem-oriented, chair as a result", and so on. Designers observe and analyze the bathroom images, describing not only what they see such as "washing machine, toilet, sink, shower head, steps", but also mentioning "elderly living alone, nursing home, hospital, bending over." By recalling past experiences, designers supplement possible scenarios in the photos such as "my home's bathroom, mobility issues, storage, cleanliness, convenience of use, habits, mobility space, narrow space, alarms, temperature control, faucet", etc., to help enrich the scene for designers.

The most mentioned words during the problem definition and concept generation phase are "slipping, sitting, lightweight, safe and stable, portable, movable, rest, toilet use, fatigue relief, alarm, support, walking aid, walker, toilet seat", etc. In the phase of refining the solution details, words such as "form, shape, assembly, material, disassembly, size, brakes, hooks, cane, armrest, lightweight, carbon fiber, aluminum alloy, chair back curvature, drainage,", etc., are mentioned. For the design outcome "chair", designers also use various expressions during the design process instead of just "chair", referring to it as "stool, bath aid, walking aid, cane, folding chair, massage chair, assistive device", etc.

In the data, terms such as "elderly living alone", "elderly in welfare homes", "normal elderly", "healthy elderly", "elderly with mobility issues", etc., represent different categories within the elderly population. The bathroom, as a setting, activates behaviors and facilities, for example, "washing clothes in the bathroom, well-equipped bathroom, squatting toilets, old-fashioned bathrooms", etc. Designers have accumulated concept schema about different groups of people and situations during their learning and cognitive processes, which are activated by semantic or visual stimuli. The design problems also have schema structures. When the task is focused on "a chair for bathing (D5)", details such as "cannot stand for too long", "temperature adjustment", "adjusting the position of the faucet", "having a showerhead on the chair", etc., are brought up by designers in their descriptions. The design outcomes also help in accessing knowledge. In the specific design task of "chair" in the test, designers accessed information related to chairs such as "seating, stool, folding chair, massage chair", etc., to describe the design scenario or express design intentions. Other items related to bathrooms and elderly use, such as "toilet seats, canes, bath aids, age-friendly equipment", etc., were also accessed during the thought process of the designers.

4 Discussion

4.1 Framework Structure of Design Knowledge Based

Designers' knowledge exists within a hierarchical framework, with conceptual definitions at the top level, specific categories in the middle, different dimensions expressing these concepts at the third level, and specific details at the bottom. This is akin to Minsky's schema structure, where concepts gradually develop into complete schema during the process of knowledge accumulation. The description of the design task "chair" overlaps with the analysis of design precedents because they are both part of the conceptual schema of a chair.

4.2 Experienced Designers Possess More Advanced Conceptual Schema

The learning experiences of designers show a transition from initially borrowing design details to later generalizing design principles and understanding future trends. This signifies the progression of conceptual schema to advanced stages. In the process of analyzing precedents, designers categorize cases by factors such as usage scenarios, structure, function, material, and behavior. Experienced designers have more diverse and innovative dimensions in their schema frameworks, including more detailed end details.

4.3 Influence of Design Learning Process on Conceptual Schema

Researchers have expressed concerns about excessive focus on design outcomes because it can lead to the formation of conceptual schemas based on design results. In this study's design task testing, it was found that designers almost uniformly utilized the same approach to solving design problems, namely the four steps starting from the problem. In these steps, there are repeated elements in the issues considered by designers and the knowledge they draw upon. From the design outcomes, it can be observed how designers utilize past design results and materials to formulate the final solution. This may remind us that design problem schema and design result schema could also be vital components of designers' knowledge content, exerting significant influence on the design process.

4.4 Influence of Design Knowledge Framework on Innovation

Gero proposed the FBS model in design knowledge research, illustrating the relationship between knowledge frameworks and problem solving [6]. Does having a rich conceptual schema for a certain concept mean we can solve all related problems? In this study, we analyzed designers' knowledge retrieval, where different stimuli evoke different knowledge content. Similar conceptual schemas and knowledge frameworks might impact how we retrieve and gather knowledge. Innovations in conceptual schema frameworks could be the core logic behind design innovation.

5 Conclusions

This study explored the structuring of design knowledge, focusing on the core issue of the framework in which design knowledge exists. It analyzed how design knowledge is constructed, its composition, and how it operates in design reasoning. Utilizing schema theory helped capture designers' design knowledge and elucidate its development and transformation during the design process. Due to the limited number of participants, there may be errors in the analysis dimensions of the design knowledge framework, which will be addressed in future research by increasing the sample size to ensure the accuracy of the study.

References

1. Cross, N.: Expertise in design: an overview. Des. Stud. **25**(5), 427–441 (2004)
2. Lawson, B.: Schemata, gambits and precedent: some factors in design expertise. Des. Stud. **25**(5), 443–457 (2004)
3. Minsky, M.: A framework for representing knowledge. In: Frame Conceptions and Text Understanding (1980)
4. Kohls, C., Scheiter, K.: The Relation Between Design Patterns and Schema Theory (2008)
5. Anay, H., Ozten, U.: On the nature of the conceptual schemata development of architecture students. In: ICONARP Int. J. Architect. Plan. **7**(1), 78–98 (2019)
6. Gero, J.S.: Design prototypes: a knowledge representation schema for design. AI Magazine **11**(4) (1990)
7. Dorst, K.: Frame Innovation: Create New Thinking by Design. The MIT Pres (2015)
8. Lawson, B.: How Designers Think, 4th edn. Routledge (2005)
9. Hertzberger, H.: Lessons for Students in Architecture. Rotterdam, Uitgeverij (1991)

Designing Metaphor-Based Character Archetypes for a Story Authoring Tool

Ian Kang and Byung-Chull Bae$^{(\boxtimes)}$

School of Games, Hongik University, Sejong, South Korea
akira319program@gmail.com, byuc@hongik.ac.kr

Abstract. Archetype concepts are widely used in various domains and applications. Building on Schmidt's 32 master character types (16 heroes and 16 villains) derived from Greek and Egyptian myths, this paper introduces 32 master character designs to our authoring tool prototype, aiming to assist users in understanding character archetypes better. We reconstruct the 32 myth-based characters to modernize their unique features in a friendly manner, conveying the hidden meanings of each character through intuitive symbols. Our prototype allows users to select from three archetype categories: protagonists (heroes), antagonists (villains), and helpers. A pilot study with 31 participants shows that some character symbols are relatively easy to recognize due to their well-known metaphors; others are not due to ambiguity or misused metaphors. Based on these findings, we plan to refine our initial designs to facilitate a better understanding and inspire diverse story ideas. Following the revision, we will assess the usability of our prototype tool, mainly focusing on how the character archetype images facilitate story creation.

Keywords: Character Archetypes · Metaphor · Authoring Tool Design

1 Introduction

In Poetics, Aristotle emphasizes the importance of plot and character as two critical elements of tragedy, noting that they are not mutually exclusive. Although many character types can exist, we acknowledge the importance of specific character archetypes as a foundation for developing diverse characters. Particularly, character archetypes can assist authors in creating vivid and coherent characters within the plot. In her book, V. L. Schmidt [7] proposes 32 master character types (16 heroes and 16 villains) rooted in Greek and Egyptian myths. As illustrated in Fig. 1, each archetype encompasses two opposing aspects, akin to yang (hero) and yin (villain).

Archetypes, grounded in Jungian theories, are defined as "ancient or archaic images derived from the collective unconsciousness" and represent "emotionally toned collections of associated images" [5]. The concept of archetypes is extensively employed across various domains and applications, including character

© The Author(s), under exclusive license to Springer Nature Switzerland AG 2024
C. Stephanidis et al. (Eds.): HCII 2024, CCIS 2114, pp. 30–35, 2024.
https://doi.org/10.1007/978-3-031-61932-8_5

design [2,8], robot design [3], dialogue generation for intelligent virtual agents [6], and VR movies [10]. Several methodologies have been adopted for archetype design. Wang et al. [8], for instance, suggest a formalized process to translate verbal descriptions into visual archetypes. Pakrasi et al. [3] apply the Kansei (feeling) engineering design method in their robotic systems. Zhang and Liu [10] explore the relationship between literary elements like Schmidt's character archetypes [7] and plot genres in shaping audience preferences in interactive VR movies.

The burgeoning use of large language models (LLMs) in various fields comes with challenges, particularly in their literary capabilities and creative potential. Coauthoring tools like CoAuthor [1] and Wordcraft [9] have been developed for human-AI collaborative story writing using LLMs to enhance these aspects. Building on this, our previous work [4] has proposed the creation of interactive stories using a large language model. In this paper, we introduce 32 master character designs for our existing authoring tool prototype, aiming to deepen the user's (i.e., the author's) understanding of character archetypes.

No.	Gender	Character Archetype	Characteristics (Heroes)	Characteristics (Villains)
1	Female	Aphrodite	The Seductive Muse	The Femme Fatale
2		Artemis	The Amazon	The Gorgon
3		Athena	The Father's Daughter	The Backstabber
4		Demeter	The Nurturer	The Overcontroling Mother
5		Hera	The Matriarch	The Scorned Woman
6		Hestia	The Mystic	The Betrayer
7		Isis	The Female Messiah	The Destroyer
8		Persephone	The Maiden	The Troubled Teen
9	Male	Apollo	The Businessman	The Traitor
10		Ares	The Protector	The Gladiator
11		Hades	The Recluse	The Warlock
12		Hermes	The Fool	The Derelict
13		Dionysus	The Woman's Man	The Seducer
14		Osiris	The Male Messiah	The Punisher
15		Poseidon	The Artisit	The Abuser
16		Zeus	The King	The Dictator

Fig. 1. 32 Character Archetypes for heroes and villains by V. L. Schmidt [7]

2 Design

We reconstruct the 32 myth-based characters to modernize their unique features. In our design, round lines and expressive facial features for people and objects are fundamental, creating a smooth and engaging mood. We aim to intuitively express each character's hidden meanings using mythological symbols.

For example, Dionysus's heroic aspect, "the Woman's Man," is creatively represented by a man's underwear adorned with hearts. In contrast, his villainous side, "the Seducer," is symbolized by two tilted wine glasses. These symbols metaphorically capture the seductive essence of Dionysus, the renowned god of wine (See Dionysus in Fig. 3).

Transitioning to Artemis, she embodies two distinct yet related archetypes: the Amazon as a hero/heroine and the Gorgon as a villain. Artemis, the warrior, is consistently portrayed with a bow and silver arrows, highlighting her heroic nature. On the other hand, the Gorgon aspect is visually interpreted through snake-like hair, portraying aggression without guilt. However, we have chosen to represent the Gorgon with a more friendly and cute snake design, as shown in Fig. 2. The complete set of 32 master characters, representing the diverse character archetypes, is illustrated in Fig. 3.

Archetype	Hero	Symbol 1	Villain	Symbol 2	Motif
1 Aphrodite	The Seductive Muse		The Femme Fatale		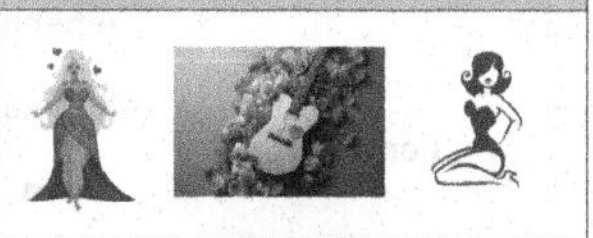
2 Artemis	The Amazon		The Gorgon		

Fig. 2. Character Archetype Design Examples: Aphrodite and Artemis (Images in the Motif are selected from freepik.com and Google Images search)

In our authoring tool prototype [4], the user has the option to select from three categories of character archetypes: protagonists (heroes), antagonists (villains), and helpers. Figure 4 illustrates this selection process. The interface displays 32 master characters, categorized into archetypes. These include 16 heroes and 16 villains, distinguished by color coding - the heroes are highlighted in a green shade, while the villains are marked in a yellow tone. Users can interact with these archetype images by selecting and dragging a symbol image representing their chosen character. Upon clicking on an archetype symbol, the image enlarges and is accompanied by a brief explanatory text. The symbol images for the four helper archetypes - the Magi, the Mentor, the Best Friend, and the Lover - are being developed and will be integrated into the tool.

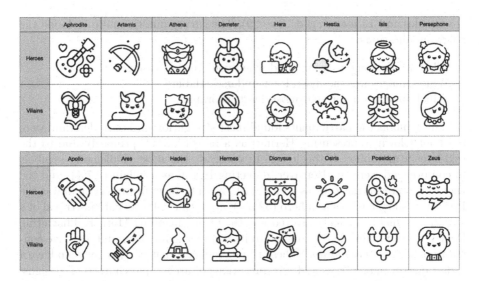

Fig. 3. 32 Master Characters Design (Top: 16 Females; Bottom: 16 Males)

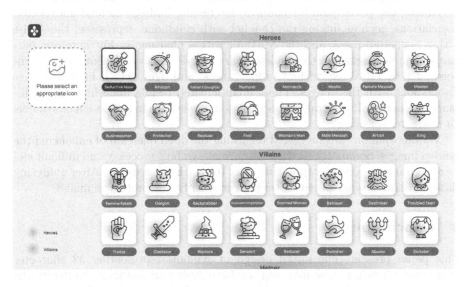

Fig. 4. Selecting Character Archetypes in the Authoring Tool [4] (Color figure online)

3   Pilot Study and Discussion

We conducted a small-scale pilot study to investigate how our symbol design effectively represents each character archetype. We recruited volunteer participants via the university's online community. The study included 31 participants

(18 females and 13 males aged 18 to 29). The survey questionnaire included the following questions:

- What words come to your mind when you see these images?
- Which images are the most/least understandable?
- Which images do you find most/least favorable?

The symbols the participants found most straightforward to understand were the Fool/Clown, representing Hermes as a hero (38.7%), primarily due to the well-known metaphor of the jester. In contrast, the most challenging symbols to comprehend were the Betrayer, depicting Hestia as a villain (9.7%), and the Dictator, representing Zeus as a villain (9.7%). The most favored symbol was the Protector, showing Ares as a hero (32.3%), appreciated for its cute portrayal of a star in the shield; the least favored was the Overcontrolling Mother, illustrating Demeter as a villain (25.8%), owing to its complex symbolism and negative connotation such as '*prohibition*.' These results indicate that participants can have a wide range of perceptions and interpretations of archetypal characters' designs. However, one of our primary goals is to use these images to stimulate diverse ideas and imaginations in the user, thus making such variety more acceptable.

Among the participants' responses, interesting findings include unexpected associations, such as linking the Derelict with childhood depression, the Artist with a pepperoni pizza, and the Nurturer with a pharmacist. Furthermore, participants appear sensitive to supplementary and decorative elements in the symbols, such as facial expressions, appearances, and ages, which influence their associations with the images. These unanticipated results underline the significance of emotional, cultural, and occupational relevance in the design of symbols for character selection.

Various opinions are suggested regarding the open question of enhancing the symbol images. Some suggest that the current symbols mix easy and difficult elements. Others suggest incorporating color to enrich the symbols. After analyzing these constructive perspectives, we plan to modify our prototype images.

4   Conclusion

This paper presents our initial design of symbols representing 32 character archetypes, drawing on well-known mythical gods and goddesses to depict the archetypes of heroes and villains. A pilot study shows that some character symbols are relatively easy to recognize due to their well-known metaphors; others are not due to ambiguity or misused metaphors. Based on the survey results, we will refine our initial images to inspire various story ideas more effectively. Following the revision, we plan to assess the usability of our prototype tool, mainly focusing on how the character archetype images facilitate story creation.

Acknowledgements. This work was supported by the Ministry of Education of the Republic of Korea and the National Research Foundation of Korea (NRF-2022S1A5A2A03052246).

References

1. Lee, M., Liang, P., Yang, Q.: Coauthor: designing a human-AI collaborative writing dataset for exploring language model capabilities. In: Proceedings of the 2022 CHI Conference on Human Factors in Computing Systems, CHI 2022. Association for Computing Machinery, New York (2022). https://doi.org/10.1145/3491102.3502030

2. Mielczarek, N.: A hero, a ruler, and a sidekick walk into a voting booth: visual archetypal characters and their stories in editorial cartoons after the 2020 U.S. presidential election. Vis. Commun. Q. **29**(4), 223–235 (2022). https://doi.org/10.1080/15551393.2022.2129659

3. Pakrasi, I., Chakraborty, N., LaViers, A.: A design methodology for abstracting character archetypes onto robotic systems. In: Proceedings of the 5th International Conference on Movement and Computing, MOCO 2018. Association for Computing Machinery, New York (2018). https://doi.org/10.1145/3212721.3212809

4. Park, J., Shin, J., Kim, G., Bae, B.C.: Designing a language model-based authoring tool prototype for interactive storytelling. In: Holloway-Attaway, L., Murray, J.T. (eds.) ICIDS 2023. LNCS, vol. 14384, pp. 239–245. Springer, Cham (2023). https://doi.org/10.1007/978-3-031-47658-7_22

5. Rizakiah, S., Sili, S., Kuncara, S.: An analysis of main characters in warm bodies film using jung theory of archetypes. Ilmu Budaya Jurnal Bahasa Sastra Seni dan Budaya **2**(4), 412–425 (2018). https://doi.org/10.30872/jbssb.v2i4.1029. https://e-journals.unmul.ac.id/index.php/JBSSB/article/view/1029

6. Rowe, J.P., Ha, E.Y., Lester, J.C.: Archetype-driven character dialogue generation for interactive narrative. In: Prendinger, H., Lester, J., Ishizuka, M. (eds.) IVA 2008. LNCS, vol. 5208, pp. 45–58. Springer, Heidelberg (2008). https://doi.org/10.1007/978-3-540-85483-8_5

7. Schmidt, V.: 45 Master Characters: Mythic Models for Creating Original Characters. Writer's Digest Books (2012)

8. Wang, A., Eason, A.D., Akleman, E.: A formal process to design visual archetypes based on character taxonomies. In: ACM SIGGRAPH 2019 Posters, SIGGRAPH 2019. Association for Computing Machinery, New York (2019). https://doi.org/10.1145/3306214.3338579

9. Yuan, A., Coenen, A., Reif, E., Ippolito, D.: Wordcraft: story writing with large language models. In: 27th International Conference on Intelligent User Interfaces, IUI 2022, pp. 841–852. Association for Computing Machinery, New York (2022). https://doi.org/10.1145/3490099.3511105

10. Zhang, L., Liu, F.: Relative research on psychological character and plot design preference for audiences of VR movies. In: Chen, J.Y.C., Fragomeni, G. (eds.) HCII 2022. LNCS, vol. 13317, pp. 505–518. Springer, Cham (2022). https://doi.org/10.1007/978-3-031-05939-1_35

UI-DETR: GUI Component Detection from the System Screen with Transformers

Sotaro Kato[1] and Yoshihisa Shinozawa[2(✉)]

[1] Graduate School of Science and Technology, Keio University, Yokohama, Japan
[2] Faculty of Science and Technology, Keio University, Yokohama, Japan
shino@ae.keio.ac.jp

Abstract. In the development of system screens, rebuilding consistent graphical user interface (GUI) screens is a costly and time-consuming process. The system screen consists of several parts, which we call GUI components in this study. Especially in the redevelopment of large-scale systems, it requires a great deal of effort to manually identify reusable GUI components from a large number of system screens. Therefore, a method to automatically detect GUI components from the system screen is needed to reduce the workload of operators and to speed up their work. In this study, we propose UI-DETR, an improved model of Detection Transformer (DETR), for automatic detection of GUI components. In particular, in UI-DETR, we improve the object query introduced in Anchor DETR. We attempt to improve the detection accuracy by inputting the positional features of GUI components into the object query. Then, evaluation experiments are conducted on the VINS dataset to validate the effectiveness of UI-DETR.

Keywords: GUI Component · Detection Transformer · Object Query

1 Introduction

In the development of system screens, redeveloping consistent graphical user interface (GUI) screens is a costly and time-consuming process. Currently, when redeveloping GUI screens, in many cases the work of identifying the parts that make up the system from a large number of screens is done manually. Therefore, there is a need to automate the process of discovering the parts that make up the system because it is error-prone and time-consuming.

In this research, the parts that make up the system are called GUI components (Graphical User Interface Component). The research field to detect these GUI components is called GUI Element Detection, and various detection attempts have been made to date. For example, research has been conducted to detect large components such as headers and widgets using only information from images by analyzing and grouping relationships among GUI components from GUI screens [1], and to streamline the process of application redevelopment by generating code directly from the detected GUI components [2]. As these examples show, detection of GUI components is a fundamental task for many software engineers, so the contribution of research is high.

© The Author(s), under exclusive license to Springer Nature Switzerland AG 2024
C. Stephanidis et al. (Eds.): HCII 2024, CCIS 2114, pp. 36–46, 2024.
https://doi.org/10.1007/978-3-031-61932-8_6

In recent years, much research has been conducted on the detection of GUI components using deep learning. In particular, automatic detection of GUI components using Convolutional Neural Networks (CNN) is being performed. However, it is difficult to improve detection accuracy in detecting GUI components with CNN models because it is difficult to extract features between objects in an image. To improve the detection accuracy of GUI components, it is necessary to extract features that take into account the relationships among GUI components. Detection Transformer (DETR) [3] has been proposed as a detection model that takes into account features between objects in an image.

Therefore, in this study, we propose UI-DETR, an improved version of DETR, for automatic detection of GUI components in order to take into account the relationships among GUI components. In particular, UI-DETR improves the object query proposed in Anchor DETR [4]. Attempts to improve detection accuracy by inputting location features of GUI components into the object query. We then conduct evaluation experiments on the VINS dataset [5] to test the effectiveness of UI-DETR compared to CNN models (YOLO [6]) and Transformer models (DETR, Anchor DETR).

2 Related Research

2.1 Object Detection

Object detection is one of the techniques related to digital image processing and computer vision to detect objects of a certain class (categories such as humans, buildings, and cars) in digital images and videos. Object detection has been applied in many fields such as image classification, face recognition, and automatic driving. With the development of deep learning since the 2010s, CNN-based object detection models (called CNN models) have become mainstream in the field of object detection.

Around 2013, the method was split into "Two Stage Detectors," which separates region estimation and class classification, and "One Stage Detectors," which performs region estimation and class classification in a single process. "Transformer-based Detectors" (called Transformer models), object detection models based on Transformer, have been proposed since 2020.

R-CNN [7], SPP-net [8], Fast R-CNN [9], and Faster R-CNN [10] have been proposed for the study of Two Stage Detectors. Two Stage Detectors first estimates candidate regions and performs class classification for each candidate region. On the other hand, AttentionNet [11], YOLO [6], and Single Shot MultiBox Detector (SSD) [12] have been proposed for One Stage Detectors. One Stage Detectors considers object detection as a regression or classification problem and estimates object location and class name.

Furthermore, Detection Transformer (DETR) [3] was proposed in 2020 as an end-to-end learning method. In the Transformer model, models such as Anchor DETR [4], an improved version of DETR's object query, have been proposed. Currently, there is no clear difference in detection accuracy between One Stage Detectors, Two Stage Detectors, and the Transformer model.

2.2 GUI Component Detection

GUI component is a generic term for UI parts that are displayed on the screen. Specifically, there are "Button," "Icon," "Page Indicator," etc. The advantage of using GUI components is that using common GUI components on different platforms creates a sense of unity and allows efficient creation and redevelopment of UI designs.

GUI component detection methods can be divided into the Instrumentation-based method and the Pixel-based method. The Instrumentation-based method requires an accessibility API [13] and runtime infrastructure [14] that exposes information about the GUI components within the GUI screen. On the other hand, the pixel-based method directly analyzes the GUI screens. Therefore, it is a general-purpose method that is not dependent on platforms such as iOS and Android. Since the method we devise in this study is a pixel-based method, we discuss previous studies using the pixel-based method and examples of applications of GUI component detection.

Chen *et al.* [15] performed detection of seven different GUI components on 50,000 GUI screens and evaluated the detection accuracy, effectiveness, and its limitations. The results indicated that it is difficult to obtain high detection accuracy when GUI components are detected by image processing techniques. Therefore, a method combining image processing techniques and deep learning was proposed. In the new method, image processing techniques were used to detect GUI components, and deep learning was used to detect text screens. As a result, the accuracy of detection of GUI components and text screens has been reported to have improved. Xie *et al.* [16] also devised a tool for GUI component detection. Bunian *et al.* [5] then devised a system that takes a UI design as input and outputs visually similar designs. A model based on YOLOv5 [17] has been proposed as a state-of-the-art GUI component detection model. Evaluations on the VINS dataset [5] have reported improved detection accuracy when compared to SSD.

3 Proposed Method

3.1 Overview of the Proposed Method

An overview of the proposed method is described. In recent years, many CNN models have been proposed that are modified versions of the two stage model such as Faster RCNN and one stage models such as YOLO, which are more complex because they consist of multiple convolution layers and residual blocks. Although CNN models are superior in extracting image features, it is difficult to identify the positional relationships among objects. The GUI components targeted in this study are considered relatively easy to detect objects because of their clear contours. However, the similarity of features between classes makes class identification difficult. Therefore, we consider the identification of similarities and relationships among GUI components to be a major issue in this study, and we use the Detection Transformer (DETR), which is capable of learning such relationships. In particular, we attempt to improve the input (object query) to Decoder when using DETR for object detection. Taking advantage of the fact that GUI components are relatively easy to extract contours, we propose UI-DETR that uses positional features of GUI components as object queries. An overview of UI-DETR is shown in Fig. 1.

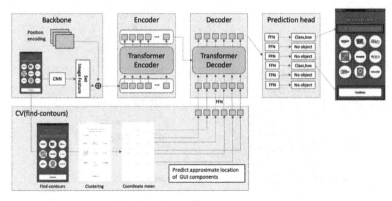

Fig. 1. An overview of UI-DETR.

As shown in Fig. 1, UI-DETR consists of a CNN backbone (Sect. 3.2) to extract image features from input images (GUI screens), Transformer's Encoder and Decoder (Sect. 3.3), and feedforward networks (abbreviated as FFN, Sect. 3.4) to predict GUI components.

3.2 CNN Backbone

The CNN backbone extracts image features from the input image. The size of the input image is an RGB image of width X and height Y. First, the input image is input to the CNN backbone and a feature map of size (H, W, C) is extracted. Next, 1×1 convolution process is used to reduce the number of channels from C to D and convert them to (H $\times$ W, D) in size. This allows the input values to the Transformer's Encoder to be vectors of dimension D and (H $\times$ W) sequence lengths.

In this study, ResNet50 [18] was used as the CNN backbone, based on Detection Transformer [3]. As described above, a feature map of size (7,7,2048) extracted from ResNet50 is converted to a size of (49,256), which is used as the image feature size.

3.3 Transformer

Image features extracted from the CNN backbone are input to the Transformer's Encoder after Positional Encoding is added. Next, object queries are input to Decoder (Sect. 3.5). In addition, the output values from Encoder are input to the Multi-Head Self-Attention layer of Decoder. The output values from Decoder are then used to predict class labels and the coordinates of the bounding boxes with FFN.

Transformer makes it possible to identify each object using the relationships between them. In this study, we use Transformer to address the issue that GUI components have similar image features across classes, because we believe that the accuracy of prediction can be improved by using relationships between objects. The structure of the Transformer is shown in the Fig. 2.

As shown in Fig. 2, Encoder has the same structure as DETR and consists of Positional Encoding, Multi-Head Self-Attention, Layer Normalization, and fully-connected layer (MLP). The "×6" in Fig. 2 means 6-layer stacking.

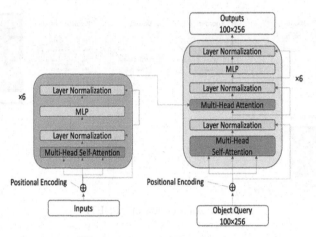

Fig. 2. Structure of Transformer.

Decoder has the same structure as DETR as well as Encoder. Object queries are input to Decoder. The number of object queries is N(100) and the number of dimensions is D(256). Object queries are the target of training. The output values (49, 256) from Encoder are input to Multi-Head Self-Attention as keys and values. Decoder also has a 6-layer stacked structure.

3.4 Feedforward Network

Two types of FFNs are used to predict class labels and the coordinates of the bounding boxes. The structure of FFN is shown in Fig. 3. The output values from Decoder are used as the input values to FFN. The first FFN predicts the class label of the bounding box. The second FFN predicts the normalized center coordinates (c_x, c_y), height h, and width w of the bounding box.

The number of units in the output layer is the number of classes in the first FFN and 4 in the second FFN. The number of units in both input layers is D(256). The number of the bounding boxes to predict is the same as the number of object queries, N(100). However, since N is usually larger than the number of objects in the image, if no objects are detected, the label ϕ is used as a special class. This class is the same as the "background" class in object detection.

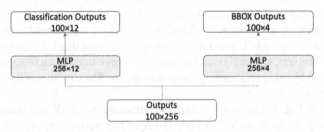

Fig. 3. Structure of Feedforward Networks.

3.5 Object Query Improvements

In the case of DETR, each value of object queries, which are the inputs to Decoder, is learned with a random integer of 0 or 1 as the initial value. However, after training, object queries have no explicit physical meaning and it is unclear how to interpret them. Therefore, Anchor DETR has introduced anchor points and improved object queries to solve this problem.

Object queries in Anchor DETR have an explicit physical meaning by encoding the coordinates of anchor points. This improvement in object queries allowed Anchor DETR to improve accuracy over DETR. However, in the case of GUI component detection, multiple GUI components are often concentrated in an image, and if the initial values of the object queries are not set appropriately, the accuracy will be adversely affected. Therefore, this study aims to further improve object queries by taking into account the characteristics of GUI components. The flow of creating object queries is shown in Fig. 4.

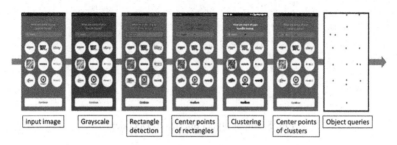

Fig. 4. Creating object queries.

As shown in Fig. 4, the process consists of extracting rectangles, extracting the center points of the clusters by clustering, and creating object queries.

Rectangle Detection. Rectangle detection consists of the process of extracting edge information from the input image, recognizing outlines based on the edge information, and classifying the shape of the figure from the outlines. First, the input image is converted to a grayscale image. Then, a convolution operation is performed using a Gaussian filter to remove noise. Next, after edge extraction, contour lines are extracted using the edge information. The method of the previous study [19] is used for contour extraction. The result of rectangle detection is shown in the third image in Fig. 4.

Extraction of the Center Points of Rectangles. Since the GUI components have clear outlines, Fig. 4 shows that rectangle detection is successfully performed. However, some rectangles overlap and some rectangles are detected consecutively. After extracting rectangles, the number of center points is narrowed down by clustering the set of center points of the rectangles. K-Means method is a typical clustering method. In the case of K-Means method, the number of clusters must be set in advance. Since the number of GUI components in a GUI screen is unknown, DBSCAN is used as a clustering method that does not require pre-determining the number of clusters.

Creating Object Queries. Next, the process of inputting the detected center points as object queries to decoder is described. Figure 5 shows the input method for object queries. The coordinates (x, y) of the center point of each clusters are divided by the width X and height Y of the input image and normalized to a value between 0 and 1. Due to the limitation of N(100) inputs to Decoder, if the number of detected center points is greater than or is less than N, the process is as follows. If the number of detected center points is greater than N, N center points are randomly selected. On the other hand, if the number of center points is less than N, (x, y) coordinates with random values between 0 and 1 as elements are generated for the missing points. The input to Decoder is from the center point (in the order of y-coordinate and x-coordinate) closest to (0, 0). Finally, the coordinates of the center point (x, y) are linearly transformed to D(256) dimensions, which are input to Decoder as object queries. Training of UI-DETR is performed using the same method as for DETR.

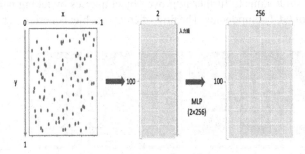

Fig. 5. Input object queries to Decoder.

4 Experiments

4.1 Dataset

In this study, two types of experiments are conducted on the VINS dataset [34]. The VINS dataset consists of screenshot and wireframe images for iPhone and Android applications. The images consist of five types: "Android," "iphone," "Rico," "uplabs," and "Wireframes. In this study, "Android" and "Rico" are considered Android images, "iphone" and "uplabs" are considered iOS images, and "Wireframes" are considered wireframe images. A bounding box with the correct answer and a class label are assigned. The VINS dataset contains 4,807 images.

- Experiment (1): We verify the effectiveness of UI-DETR in detecting GUI components (Sect. 4.2).
- Experiment (2): We verify the effectiveness of improved object queries (Sect. 4.3).

The VINS dataset contains 20 classes of GUI components. The number of GUI components in the VINS dataset is unevenly distributed by class. For example, there are 29,324 Texts, but less than 5 Maps and Check Boxes, and we consider that a reasonable amount of data is needed for training to detect GUI components. Therefore, we select 11 classes with a large number of GUI components to be the target of GUI component detection. The number of classes is 12 including the label φ. Specifically, there are 11 classes: Text, Text Button, Edit Text, Modal, Icon, Switch, Page Indicator, Checked Text View, Image, Upper Task Bar, and Background Image. The same number of images as in the previous study [34] are used to split the data into training, validation, and test data. 4,807 screenshot images are split at 80%, 10%, and 10%, respectively. We use 3,640 images from iOS and Android as training data. We also use 712 images from iOS, Android and Wireframes as test data.

Mean Average Precision (mAP) is used as the evaluation index. AP value is one of the evaluation indices for binary classification tasks and means the area of the lower region of the Precision Recall Curve. The mAP is an index that averages the AP values for all classes.

4.2 Experiment (1)

In the experiment (1), we verify whether UI-DETR is effective in detecting GUI components. Therefore, we compare UI-DETR with CNN models (YOLOv5 [17] and YOLOv7 [20]).

The training parameters for each model are shown in Table 1. YOLOv5 and YOLOv7 use the parameters shown by YOLO in Table 1. In the training of UI-DETR the learning rate of the CNN backbone and the model are set based on previous studies [3]. In UI-DETR, the parameter *eps* of DBSCAN is set to 50. The detection results of UI-DETR and YOLO are shown in Table 2.

Table 1. The training parameters for each model.

	DETR	YOLO
Learning rate (CNN backbone)	10^{-5}	–
Learning rate	10^{-6}	10^{-4}
Epoch count	200	100
Batch size	2	16

Table 2. The detection results of UI-DETR and YOLO.

mAP@0.5	iOS	Android	Wireframes
YOLOv5	76.9	81.3	55.0
YOLOv7	75.0	85.5	56.0
UI-DETR	91.3	87.9	78.2

In Table 2, mAP@0.5 is the result of detecting areas with an IoU (Intersection over Union) greater than 0.5. Table 2 shows that the mAP of YOLOv5 is 76.9% and that of

UI-DETR is 91.3% on iOS, indicating that UI-DETR achieves the highest detection accuracy. On Android, the mAP of YOLOv7 is 85.5% and that of UI-DETR is 87.9%, indicating that UI-DETR achieves the highest detection accuracy. In Wireframes, the mAP of YOLOv7 is 56.2% and that of UI-DETR is 78.2%, indicating that UI-DETR achieves the highest detection accuracy. Transformer model (UI-DETR) is able to improve detection accuracy in detecting GUI components more than CNN model.

4.3   Experiment (2)

In the experiment (2), UI-DETR is compared with the existing methods (DETR and Anchor DETR). The parameters of DETR, Anchor DETR, and UI-DETR are shown in Table 1. Table 3 shows the detection results of DETR, Anchor DETR, and UI-DETR.

Table 3 shows that the mAP of DETR, Anchor DETR, and UI-DETR is 86.2%, 83.2%, and 91.3% on iOS respectively. On Android, the mAP of DETR, Anchor DETR, and UI-DETR is 85.7%, 85.1%, and 87.9% respectively. On Wireframes, the mAP of DETR, Anchor DETR, and UI-DETR is 70.2%, 68.0%, and 78.2% respectively. The highest detection accuracy is achieved by UI-DETR in both iOS, Android and Wireframes.

Table 3. The detection results of DETR, Anchor DETR, and UI-DETR.

mAP@0.5	iOS	Android	Wireframes
DETR	86.2	85.7	70.2
Anchor DETR	83.2	85.1	68.0
UI-DETR	91.3	87.9	78.2

On the other hand, Anchor DETR showed lower detection accuracy than DETR for iOS, Android, and Wireframes. While Anchor DETR is reported to be more accurate than DETR in object detection, the reasons for the lack of accuracy in this study are discussed. Anchor DETR is characterized by the fact that it clearly specifies the detection location for object queries. Therefore, we consider the specification of the detection location to be the cause of the lower detection accuracy. The distance between objects in a GUI screen is shorter than in a typical image. Therefore, Anchor DETR cannot detect two objects at a single anchor point, which we consider to be the reason for the lower detection accuracy.

5   Conclusion

In this study, we proposed UI-DTER to automatically detect GUI components in GUI screens. The results of the comparison with the CNN models, YOLOv5 and YOLOv7 on the VINS dataset show the effectiveness of UI-DETR. Compared to DETR and Anchor DETR, UI-DTER was able to improve detection accuracy, demonstrating the effectiveness of the object query improvement. In conclusion, we have demonstrated the effectiveness of UI-DETR in automatic detection of GUI components from GUI screens.

As future work, in this study, we attempted to automatically detect GUI components from GUI screens for iOS and Android used in smartphones. However, we believe that it is necessary to devise a method to automatically detect GUI components on Web screens as well as such GUI screens. Furthermore, it is necessary to verify the effectiveness of the proposed method in general object detection.

References

1. Wu, J., Zhang, X., Nichols, J., Bigham, J.P.: Screen parsing: towards reverse engineering of UI models from screenshots. In: Proceedings of the 34th Annual ACM Symposium on User Interface Software and Technology (UIST2021), pp.470–483 (2021)
2. Chen, C., Su, T., Meng, G., Xing, Z., Liu, Y.: From UI design image to GUI skeleton: a neural machine translator to bootstrap mobile GUI implementation. In: Proceedings of the 40th International Conference on Software Engineering, pp. 665–676 (2018)
3. Carion, N., Massa, F., Synnaeve, G., Usunier, N., Kirillov, A., Zagoruyko, S.: End-to-end object detection with transformers. In: European Conference on Computer Vision (ECCV2020), pp. 213–229 (2020)
4. Wang, Y., Zhang, X., Yang, T., Sun, J.: Anchor DETR: query design for transformer-based detector. In: Proceedings of the AAAI Conference on Artificial Intelligence, pp. 2567–2575 (2022)
5. Bunian, S., Li, K., Jemmali, C., Harteveld, C., Fu, Y., El-Nasr, M.S.: VINS: visual search for mobile user interface design. In: Proceedings of The 2021 CHI Conference on Human Factors in Computing Systems, pp. 1–14 (2021)
6. Redmon, J, Divvala, S., Girshick, R. and Farhadi, A.: You only look once: unified, real-time object detection. In: Proceedings of 2016 IEEE Conference on Computer Vision and Pattern Recognition (CVPR), pp. 779–788 (2016)
7. Girshick, R., Donahue, J., Darrell, T., Malik, J.: Rich feature hierarchies for accurate object detection and semantic segmentation. In: Proceedings of 2014 IEEE Conference on Computer Vision and Pattern Recognition (CVPR), pp. 580–587 (2014)
8. He, K., Zhang, X., Ren, S., Sun, J.: Spatial pyramid pooling in deep convolutional networks for visual recognition. In: Fleet, D., Pajdla, T., Schiele, B., Tuytelaars, T. (eds.) ECCV 2014. LNCS, vol. 8691, pp. 346–361. Springer, Cham (2014). https://doi.org/10.1007/978-3-319-10578-9_23
9. Girshick, R.: Fast R-CNN. In: Proceedings of the IEEE International Conference on Computer Vision (ICCV), pp. 1440–1448 (2015)
10. Ren, S., He, K., Girshick, G., Sun, J.: Faster R-CNN: towards real-time object detection with region proposal networks. IEEE Trans. Pattern Anal. Mach. Intell. **39**(6), 1137–1149 (2017)
11. Yoo, D., Park, D., Lee, J.Y., Paek, A.S., Kweon, I.S.: AttentionNet: aggregating weak directions for accurate object detection. In: Proceedings of 2015 IEEE International Conference on Computer Vision (ICCV), pp. 2659–2667 (2015)
12. Liu, W., Anguelov, D., Erhan, D., Szegedy, C., Reed, S., Fu, C.Y., Berg, A.C.: SSD: single shot multibox detector. In: European Conference on Computer Vision (ECCV2016), pp. 21–37 (2016)
13. Windows Accessibility API. https://docs.microsoft.com/en-us/windows/win32/winauto/windows-automation-api-portal. Accessed 07 Mar 2024
14. UI Automator. https://developer.android.com/training/testing/ui-automator. Accessed 07 Mar 2024

15. Chen, J., et al.: Object detection for graphical user interface: old fashioned or deep learning or a combination? In: Proceedings of The 28th ACM Joint Meeting on European Software Engineering Conference and Symposium on the Foundations of Software Engineering, pp. 1202–1214 (2020)
16. Xie, M., Feng, S., Xing, Z., Chen, J., Chen, C.: UIED: a hybrid tool for GUI element detection. In: Proceedings of the 28th ACM Joint Meeting on European Software Engineering Conference and Symposium on the Foundations of Software Engineering, pp. 1655–1659 (2020)
17. Altinbas, M.D., Serif, T.: GUI element detection from mobile UI images using YOLOv5. In: Proceeding of the 18th International Conference on Mobile Web and Intelligent Information Systems, pp. 32–45 (2022)
18. He, K., Zhang, Z., Ren, S., Sun, J.: Deep residual learning for image recognition. Proceedings of 2016 IEEE Conference on Computer Vision and Pattern Recognition (CVPR), pp. 770–778 (2016)
19. Suzuki, S., Abe, K.: Topological structural analysis of digitized binary images by border following. Comput. Vis. Graph. Image Process. **30**(1), 32–46 (1985)
20. Wang, C.Y., Bochkovskiy, A., Liao, H.Y.M.: Yolov7: trainable bag-of-freebies sets new state-of-the-art for real-time object detectors. In: Proceedings of 2023 IEEE/CVF Conference on Computer Vision and Pattern Recognition (CVPR), pp. 7464–7475 (2023)

The Current Status of the Application of Virtual Reality Technology in Display Design: A Bibliometric Analysis

Jingyi Liu[✉]

Royal College of Art, Kensington Gore, South Kensington, London, UK
liujingyiad1221@163.com

Abstract. Purpose: To determine the progress and emerging trends in virtual reality technology research in display design over the past two decades.

Methods: Based on 317 relevant literature articles related to virtual reality and display space design collected from the Web of Science (WOS) database, a comprehensive overview was conducted using bibliometric methods, utilizing VOSviewer and CiteSpace to create knowledge maps in terms of keyword co-occurrence, co-citation of references, and research collaboration networks. Conclusion: The current research focus on the application of virtual reality in display space design mainly centers around (1) the study of virtual reality psychotherapy in architectural space design; (2) research on gaze rendering and zoom displays in augmented reality; (3) the application of autonomous virtual environments in spatial contexts; (4) enhancing architectural space perception in immersive virtual reality experiences; and (5) the presence of virtual environment frameworks. Future research will concentrate on topics such as automatic virtual environment recognition and tracking systems, focus display development, augmented reality, product evaluation, and more. Classic literature referenced by multiple articles forms the foundation of current research, providing theoretical guidance and methodological tools. Finally, we discuss several future research directions and challenges in VR-EDR.

Keywords: Exhibition Display Design · Virtual Reality (VR) · Bibliometrics · VOSviewer · Citespace

1 Introduction

Virtual Reality (VR) is commonly described as a medium. Effectively utilizing these technologies in exhibition space design is a crucial future development direction. The technological advancements in the application of Virtual Reality in exhibition and display design research (VR-EDR) allow designers and engineers to explore data and interact with spaces in increasingly natural ways (Berg & Vance, 2017).

© The Author(s), under exclusive license to Springer Nature Switzerland AG 2024
C. Stephanidis et al. (Eds.): HCII 2024, CCIS 2114, pp. 47–55, 2024.
https://doi.org/10.1007/978-3-031-61932-8_7

Over the past two decades, the application of VR in exhibition spaces has seen rapid development, resulting in a wealth of literature. However, there is currently a lack of systematic literature reviews for VR-EDR to assess the current research status, theoretical foundations, and future research directions. Bibliometrics is an effective method for quantitatively visualizing and analyzing existing published literature. It can effectively uncover patterns and underlying information within a large body of literature and has been widely applied in many important scientific research areas (Achuthan et al., 2023). Therefore, this paper will use bibliometrics to address the following three research questions for a comprehensive review of the research and application of virtual reality technology in exhibition design:

1. What are the current research hotspots in VR-EDR?
2. How has the research content of VR-EDR evolved over the past two decades? What are the overall trends?
3. Which scholars and institutions worldwide are the main contributors to VR-EDR research? What are their collaboration relationships?

2 Research Design

2.1 Data Sources

Because high-quality scientific literature undergoes rigorous peer review and strict scrutiny by publishing journals, its research outcomes tend to have higher disciplinary representativeness (Anthony & Chalcraft, 1997). Therefore, this paper selects the commonly used Science Citation Index Expanded (SCI-EXPANDED), Social Sciences Citation Index (SSCI), and Arts & Humanities Citation Index (AHCI) from the Web of Science (WOS) database as the data sources for retrieval. The search terms are set as "virtual reality" AND "exhibition design," with the document type "article" specified. The specific search strategy is TS = ((("VR" OR "virtual reality") AND ("exhibition design" OR "Display design")) (January 1, 2004, to August 14, 2023). The language is restricted to English. A total of 1519 initial documents were retrieved. After screening, irrelevant research content, duplicate data, and other related interfering documents were excluded. Finally, a total of 317 documents were obtained for further quantitative analysis.

2.2 Research Methodology

In order to obtain a more comprehensive and complete data analysis, this paper employs a combination of bibliometrics and data visualization methods. Bibliometrics is a quantitative analysis method that uses mathematical and statistical techniques to describe, evaluate, and predict the current state and development trends of science and technology. To obtain more rigorous and comprehensive data metrics, this paper utilizes software such as CiteSpace and VOSviewer for bibliometric visualization analysis of the relevant literature data.

3   Results and Analysis of Bibliometric Analysis

3.1   Distribution and Trend Analysis of Literature Volume

After screening, a total of 317 relevant articles published from 2004 to 2023 were obtained. (See Fig. 1). Figure 1 reveals that there were no relevant papers published in 2004. From 2004 to 2015, the field was in its initial stages of research, with a relatively low annual publication output. Starting from 2016, the use of virtual reality in display design began to steadily develop, showing a stable upward trend. This trend continued until 2022, reaching a peak period with an average annual publication output of 66 articles. The first half of 2023 already had 40 publications, and it is expected that the total production for 2023 will surpass the annual average publication output of 2022. Overall, there is a stable and rapid upward trend, indicating that the application of virtual reality in display design is increasingly recognized and entering a stable and mature phase of development.

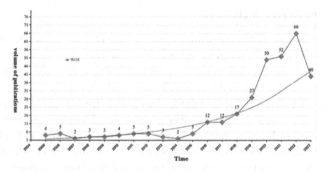

Fig. 1. Annual distribution of outputs of relevant literature

3.2   Analysis of High-impact Journals

After statistical analysis and filtering, a total of 317 valid papers were published in 152 different journals. Table 1 lists the top three high-impact journals in terms of publication volume over the past two decades (2004–2023), along with their respective five-year impact factors (IF). "IEEE Transactions on Visualization and Computer Graphics" is the journal with the highest publication volume in this research field, with a total of 24 papers published. It also has the highest citation count (837) and an impact factor of 5.6, indicating its significant influence in the field of virtual reality display design research. The second-ranked journal is "Virtual Reality," with 17 papers published, 141 citations, and an impact factor of 5.5. The third-ranked journal is "Applied Sciences-Basel," with 9 papers published, 33 citations, and an impact factor of 2.9.

Table 1. Distribution of high-yield journals

Rank	Periodicals	Publishers	Publications	Cited	Average Citation	5-Year Impact Factor
1	Ieee Transactions On Visualization And Computer Graphics	IEEE COMPUTER SOC	24	837	34.875	5.6
2	Virtual Reality	SPRINGER LONDON LTD	17	141	8.2941	5.5
3	Applied Sciences-basel	MDPI	9	33	3.6667	2.9

3.3   Analysis of Research Hotspots

Among the 317 papers within the search scope, a total of 1383 keywords were identified. After using VOSviewer to set the minimum keyword co-occurrence frequency to 2 and merging synonyms, 283 keywords were obtained. These keywords form a keyword co-occurrence clustering map in this research field (as shown in Fig. 2A). These clusters represent the current research focus in the application of virtual reality in display design: Cluster 1 (Red): Research on virtual reality psychological therapy space design. Cluster 2 (Green): Research on interactive design of augmented reality in display spaces. Cluster 3 (Blue): Research on usability testing in dynamic interactive spaces. Cluster 4 (Yellow): Research on enhancing architectural spatial perception in immersive virtual reality experiences. Cluster 5 (Purple): Research on the sense of presence in virtual environments.

Cluster #1 focuses on research related to virtual reality psychological therapy space design, consisting of 121 keywords. This cluster includes keywords such as "anxiety," "emotions," "sense," and "communication," among others. It is widely acknowledged that physical and social environmental factors have a significant impact on human daily behaviors and lifestyles (Birenboim, 2018). Considering the structural characteristics of high-frequency keywords, the research focus of Cluster #1 can be summarized as the application of virtual reality technology in spatial design to reduce negative emotions such as anxiety and depression in humans.

Cluster #2 focuses on research related to the interactive design of augmented reality (AR) in display spaces, consisting of 63 cluster members. This cluster includes keywords such as "augmented reality," "system," "interface," "3D display," and "holographic display," among others. Currently, the challenge of minimizing visual discomfort caused by wearing AR displays remains largely unresolved. Research and development in gaze rendering and zoom displays are important approaches to addressing these issues. Figure 2B shows that the keywords in this cluster are relatively recent, indicating that it represents a recent research hotspot in the field.

Cluster #3, titled "Research on Dynamic Interaction Usability Testing in Space," consists of 42 keywords, including "visualization," "virtual environments," "three-dimensional displays," and "interaction techniques," among others. In recent years, the commercialization of low-cost full-body tracking systems has made natural gesture-based interaction in display spaces increasingly popular, enabling the deployment of natural interfaces beyond the confines of virtual reality labs (Argelaguet & Andujar, 2013). Future research will need to address the broader application of automatic recognition and tracking devices in spatial contexts.

Cluster #4, titled "Enhancing Architectural Space Perception in Immersive Virtual Reality Experiences," consists of 33 keywords, including "distance perception," "haptics," "reality-induced symptoms," and more. This cluster primarily focuses on experimental research regarding the perceptual design of immersive virtual reality in architectural spaces. Researchers in the architectural industry use IVEs for education and training, and measuring human behavior in extreme events (Duarte et al., 2014).

Cluster #5, titled "Research on the Sense of Presence in Virtual Environments," comprises 25 cluster members, including keywords like "framework," "human-computer interaction," "accuracy," "mental rotation," and "spatial navigation." The concept of presence or "being there" provided by virtual environment frameworks is often emphasized in immersive media environments. It is generally believed that a higher level of immersive quality leads to a greater sense of presence, enhancing the effective-ness of mediated experiences (Cummings & Bailenson, 2016). This research direction is expected to be a significant focus in the future of this field.

Fig. 2. A. Literature Keyword Co-occurrence Clustering. B. Literature Keyword Co-occurrence Clustering

3.4 Research Trends Analysis

To further investigate the frontier topics and development trends of VR-EDR, a co-occurrence analysis of the average appearance time of keywords was conducted, resulting in Fig. 3 (Keyword TimeZone). The TimeZone chart visually reflects the frequency and initial appearance time of keywords within the search scope, often used by scholars to identify early trends and future directions of research topics. The TimeZone chart is analytical indicators that combine keywords with the dimension of time, and it can provide more reliable research results (Bitkina et al., 2020).

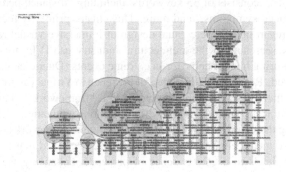

Fig. 3. Keyword Timezone mapTotal Citations to References

3.5 Total Citations to References

In order to further analyze the application of virtual reality in exhibition design, a more in-depth analysis of the content of the retrieved literature was conducted. Due to some references being co-cited, they formed a co-citation network, as shown in Fig. 4. Numerous nodes formed five main clusters, and these clusters were ranked by citation counts. The top one reference in terms of total citations were extracted from each of the five clusters, as shown in Table 2. Cluster #1 (red) - Research on the sense of presence in virtual environments; Cluster #2 (green) - Research on dynamic interaction usability in space; Cluster #3 (blue) - Research on interactive design of augmented reality in exhibition spaces; Cluster #4 (yellow) - Research on enhancing architectural space perception in immersive virtual reality experiences; Cluster #5 (purple) - Research on psychological therapy space design in virtual reality.

In Cluster #1 (Research on the sense of presence in virtual environments), the central position is occupied by the paper 'Measuring Presence in Virtual Environments: A Presence Questionnaire,' published by Bob G. Witmer and others in 1998 in 'Presence: Teleoperators and Virtual Environments.' This paper has a total of 30 co-citations in our co-citation network. This work provides a conceptual measurement basis for research on the sense of presence in virtual environments (Witmer & Singer, 1998).

In Cluster #2 (Research on usability experiments in spatial dynamic interaction), the most popular paper is 'Simulator Sickness Questionnaire: An Enhanced Method for Quantifying Simulator Sickness,' published by Robert S. Kennedy in 1993 in 'The International Journal of Aviation Psychology,' with a total of 22 co-citations in our co-citation network. This paper addresses the issue of Simulator Sickness (SS) in high-fidelity visual simulators (Kennedy et al., 1993). This work provides a conceptual measurement basis for research on the sense of presence in virtual environments (Witmer & Singer, 1998).

In Cluster #3 (Research on interactive design in augmented reality in display spaces), the most influential paper is 'A Survey of Augmented Reality,' which holds a central position in the co-citation network. This paper surveys the field of augmented reality (AR), focusing on real-time integration of 3D virtual objects into 3D real environments (Azuma, 1997). The study demonstrates the significant benefits and potential of using thin films in varifocal displays (Dunn et al., 2017).

In Cluster #4 (Research on enhancing architectural space perception in immersive virtual reality experiences), the most co-cited paper is 'Industry use of virtual reality in product design and manufacturing: a survey,' which discusses the state of development of virtual reality (VR) technology in a groundbreaking survey by Fred Brooks in 1999. The conclusion drawn from the survey was that VR was still in its infancy and 'barely works.' However, in a new industry survey after 2016, it was revealed that virtual reality technology had made significant progress (Berg & Vance, 2017).

In Cluster #5 (Research on the design of virtual reality therapy spaces), the most influential paper is the review article by S.F. Kuliga and colleagues titled 'Virtual reality as an empirical research tool—Exploring user experience in a real building and a corresponding virtual model.' This article highlights the value of virtual reality (VR) in fields like architectural research for studying human-environment interactions, providing detailed observations, precise behavioral measurements, and controlled environmental manipulations (Kuliga et al., 2015).

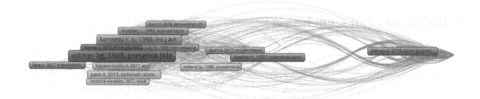

Fig. 4. Reference Co-Citation Clustering Network

Table 2. Classical literature in the top 3 total citations for each cluster

Literature name	Affiliated clusters	Publication time	Total linkage strength	Total citations
Measuring Presence in Virtual Environments: A Presence Questionnaire	# 1	1998	273	30
Simulator Sickness Questionnaire: An Enhanced Method for Quantifying Simulator Sickness	# 2	1993	141	22
A Survey of Augmented Reality	# 3	1997	54	10
Industry use of virtual reality in product design and manufacturing: a survey	# 4	2017	112	10
Virtual reality as an empirical research tool—Exploring user experience in a real building and a corresponding virtual model	# 5	2015	156	13

4   Discussion and Conclusion

1. Relevant literature on the application of Virtual Reality in exhibition spaces has shown a steady upward trend over the past two decades. Professors such as Prof. Manuel Contero, Prof. Francesco Ferrise, and Prof. Monica Bordegoni are considered core authors in the international VR-EDR academic community. Journals like IEEE and Mathematical Problems in Engineering have been core journals for VR-EDR research over the past two decades.
2. By combining Time Zone analysis, burst keywords, and keyword contribution clustering, it has been revealed that the future development directions in VR-EDR will primarily focus on automatic virtual environment recognition and tracking systems, development of focus-display technology, augmented reality, product evaluation, and more.

3. The primary research method employed in this article is bibliometrics. This method provides an intuitive representation of the development trends and evolution of research themes in VR-EDR over specific time periods. By constructing a shared co-citation network from the entire reference collection, five clusters have been identified, aligning with the conclusions drawn from keyword clustering analysis.

References

1. Achuthan, K., Nair, V.K., Kowalski, R., Ramanathan, S., Raman, R.: Cyberbullying research—alignment to sustainable development and impact of COVID-19: bibliometrics and science mapping analysis. Comput. Hum. Behav. **140**, 107566 (2023)
2. Anthony, C.: Encyclopedia of Library and Information Science, 2nd edn. Reference Reviews (1997)
3. Argelaguet, F., Andujar, C.: A survey of 3D object selection techniques for virtual environments. Comput. Graph. **37**(3), 121–136 (2013)
4. Azuma, R.T.: A survey of augmented reality. Presence: Teleoper. Virt. Environ. **6**(4), 355–385 (1997)
5. Berg, L.P., Vance, J.M.: Industry use of virtual reality in product design and manufacturing: a survey. Virtual Reality **21**, 1–17 (2017)
6. Birenboim, A.: The influence of urban environments on our subjective momentary experiences. Environ. Plan. B: Urban Analyt. City Sci. **45**(5), 915–932 (2018)
7. Bitkina, O.V., Kim, H.K., Park, J.: Usability and user experience of medical devices: an overview of the current state, analysis methodologies, and future challenges. Int. J. Ind. Ergon. **76**, 102932 (2020)
8. Cruz-Neira, C., Sandin, D.J., DeFanti, T.A.: Surround-screen projection-based virtual reality: the design and implementation of the CAVE. In: Seminal Graphics Papers: Pushing the Boundaries, vol. 2, pp. 51–58 (2023)
9. Cummings, J.J., Bailenson, J.N.: How immersive is enough? a meta-analysis of the effect of immersive technology on user presence. Media Psychol. **19**(2), 272–309 (2016)
10. Duarte, E., Rebelo, F., Teles, J., Wogalter, M.S.: Behavioral compliance for dynamic versus static signs in an immersive virtual environment. Appl. Ergon. **45**(5), 1367–1375 (2014)
11. Kuliga, S.F., Thrash, T., Dalton, R.C., Hölscher, C.: Virtual reality as an empirical research tool—Exploring user experience in a real building and a corresponding virtual model. Comput. Environ. Urban Syst. **54**, 363–375 (2015)
12. Van Eck, N., Waltman, L.: Software survey: VOSviewer, a computer program for bibliometric mapping. Scientometrics **84**(2), 523–538 (2010)
13. Witmer, B.G., Singer, M.J.: Measuring presence in virtual environments: a presence questionnaire. Presence **7**(3), 225–240 (1998)
14. Kennedy, R.S., Lane, N.E., Berbaum, K.S., Lilienthal, M.G.: Simulator sickness questionnaire: an enhanced method for quantifying simulator sickness. Int. J. Aviat. Psychol. **3**(3), 203–220 (1993)

Universal Hand Gesture Interaction Vocabulary for Cross-Cultural Users: Challenges and Approaches

Elizabete Munzlinger[1,2(✉)] [iD], Fabricio Batista Narcizo[1,2] [iD],
Dan Witzner Hansen[1] [iD], and Ted Vucurevich[2] [iD]

[1] IT University of Copenhagen (ITU), 2300 København S., Denmark
{munzlinger,narcizo,witzner}@itu.dk
[2] GN Audio A/S (Jabra), 2750 Ballerup, Denmark
{enarcizo,fbnarcizo,tvucurevich}@jabra.com

Abstract. This paper highlights the complexity of creating a universal, cross-cultural Hand Gesture Recognition (HGR) vocabulary for global products and systems where worldwide users interact by sharing the same system or space. We revisit the concept of an idealistic universal HGR vocabulary for cross-cultural users and systems that suit all users and present potential development challenges by reviewing the hand gesture taxonomy, lexical, vocabulary, and the current design methods. The analysis emphasizes the importance of creating a cohesive movement towards standardizing HGR vocabulary for innovative products and services that accommodate cultural diversity and converge for a universal agreement at some point.

Keywords: Hand Gesture Interaction · Universal Vocabulary · Lexicon · Taxonomy · Cross-Cultural Users · Human-Computer Interaction · Design Methods · Global Users · Global Products and Systems

1 Introduction

Gestures are nonverbal signals made using the body, such as hand movements, facial expressions, and body posture [9]. Functional gestures are body poses or trajectories that humans intentionally perform using a part of their body to complete tasks that affect the state or behavior of a system or equipment [6]. To be recognized, a functional hand gesture must be part of a vocabulary. Algorithms will recognize, track, and interpret each gesture from the vocabulary [57] in a process called Hand Gesture Recognition (HGR).

HGR is an active and growing research area in computer vision. It has become valuable in Human-Computer Interaction (HCI), expanding the design space and providing a touch-free channel interface for communication, system interaction, and device control [54] and improving user experience by providing a more direct, natural, interesting, and accessible interface [8,32,38].

© The Author(s), under exclusive license to Springer Nature Switzerland AG 2024
C. Stephanidis et al. (Eds.): HCII 2024, CCIS 2114, pp. 56–69, 2024.
https://doi.org/10.1007/978-3-031-61932-8_8

Efforts in solving computational problems for HGR have produced significant advancements that enabled the design of numerous innovative products and services in sectors such as healthcare, gaming, marketing, education, collaboration, mobile, home, robotics, automotive, and cultural and creative industries [7,22,25,36,39,44]. New devices such as wearable sensors like smart rings [10,11,44] and bracelets [50] are populating in addition to the camera-based technology, which is the primary methodology in vision-based hand gesture recognition [24,38,57]. The employment of Machine Learning (ML) approaches in HGR for image segmentation, feature extraction, and classification due to their flexibility and adaptability to handle uncertainty and imprecision in gesture data have led to more robust and accurate systems [8,10,38,55,57,58].

Aside from technical issues related to HGR [9,38,57], a remarkably established challenge is the need for standardized hand gesture vocabularies to be shared between contexts and systems. This missing, is an underlying issue because vocabularies, taxonomy, and lexicons, that are closed related, do not have a shared standard in HGR. The literature on gestural interaction is not homogeneous and is characterized by a lack of shared terminology, leading to fragmented results and making it difficult for research activities to build on top of state-of-the-art results and approaches [6,17,26].

A gestural vocabulary is a set of selected hand gestures that an application recognizes. All the possible gestures that can be part of any vocabulary belong to a lexicon, which is a dictionary containing a full hand gesture description. The gestures have different aspects, such as their relation to the language, communication, world, objects, etc. A taxonomy framework organizes gestures in categories based on its function. This categorization helps to understand each class and type of gesture. The absence of standardization in taxonomy and lexical makes building an adequate vocabulary difficult, resulting in inconsistencies of gestures reflected in studies and commercial products. The variability in gestures found across applications makes it challenging to design a universal HGR that can interpret different gestures accurately if a shared pattern is not stabilised [9].

The common inadequacy are the interchanged commands and vocabulary between domains, conflicts or lack of sense, and vocabulary with divergent meanings between users from different cultures, including some with offensive connotations. Vocabulary coherence is a significant feature even for a very accurate recognition, as divergences from the user perspective of use affect the performance of interactive HGR and limit their global reach to users with different backgrounds, contexts, and origins.

This need of shared vocabulary is particularly pronounced in global contexts, where cultural diversity demands a universal lexicon for hand gestures. The approach to defining a universal hand gesture vocabulary involves a critical analysis of existing vocabularies and need new solutions to identify common hand gestures suitable across cultures. Current design methods also consider cultural patterns, factors, expectations, and preferences. Therefore, they are faced with the challenge of designing products for cross cultural users and need to review those concepts and design methods for a product that caters to a global audience [5].

This paper discusses the foundation and complexities of a universal cross-cultural HGR vocabulary concept for global products and systems and its potential to enhance user experiences and interaction capabilities. We present challenges in identifying or selecting patterns in taxonomy, lexicon, and currently known vocabularies, as well as limitations on current design and evaluation methods. We depict the implications of cultural aspects in designing a culturally aware HGR interaction for global users, products, and systems.

2   Challenges in Hand Gesture Vocabulary Standardization

2.1   Taxonomy, Lexicon and Vocabulary

Although the terms taxonomy, lexicon, and vocabulary are often used interchangeably to refer to gestures or a gesture set in the context of hand gesture systems, they have subtle differences in meaning, and the relationship between these terms can be seen as hierarchical and interdependent.

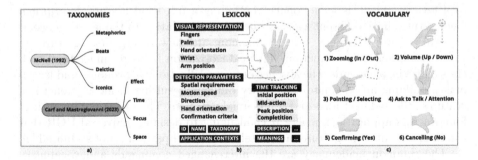

Fig. 1. a) A classic [28] and a recent [6] hand gesture taxonomy; b) Example of possible hand gesture descriptions from a lexicon dictionary; c) A gestural vocabulary composed by a set of selected hand gestures for a given application and associated actions.

Taxonomy is a systematic categorization scheme that organizes hand gestures into categories based on specific criteria, such as their function or form, also relation with communication or language (see Fig. 1a). The most referenced taxonomy categorizes hand gestures as beat, deictic, iconic, and metaphoric [28]. A more recent introduced a new multimodal non-hierarchical taxonomy of gestures from many perspectives such as context communicative or manipulative, level of instruction, body part, and spatial influence [6].

Lexicon refers to a dictionary of all gestures with more structured framework that can includes diverse physical description, technical parameters, semantics, syntax, and usage rules (see Fig. 1b). A well-established lexicon offers a framework for understanding and exploring the gesture in a whole system view.

Vocabulary refers to a subset of gestures from the broader lexicon that a specific system is designed to recognize and interpret (see Fig. 1c). The vocabulary is often tailored to the application's context and can be focused on spatial navigation or object manipulation. Each gesture within the vocabulary is associated with a particular action or command that should be performed by the user to complete a system task.

Diverse other taxonomies for hand gestures observed across fields are explored [4, 6, 17, 20, 26, 43, 47]. For instance, a taxonomy of hand gestures in HCI might categorize gestures only as static or dynamic, each with further subdivisions based on their purpose, varying between the authors. It is common for authors to define their taxonomies based on a range of criteria [26] because available taxonomies do not cover some requirements. Defining a new taxonomy that covers, describes, and justifies a previously defined vocabulary is a easy solution. However, describing categories focused on the needs of a particular system can result in non-reusable taxonomy that reinforces the deficiency of standardization [33, 47] or a widely accepted definition [36].

The lack of pattern or shared lexicon and vocabulary leads to difficulty in products and services reaching the best naturalness of the interaction. Norman [33] highlighted that *"gestures proliferate, with no standards, no easy way of being reminded of them, no easy way to learn"*. This lack is related to several hand gesture application fields [35, 49]. This problem results in diverse systems applying different hand gesture commands for a shared action across systems. This lack of consistency in gesture patterns can lead to user resistance in choosing or continuously using the systems. This resistance can be triggered by increased workload, confusion, and low memorability, making it difficult for users to adapt to new systems.

Although this paper's ultimate concern lies in the outcome of the hand gesture vocabulary, taxonomy, and lexical frameworks constitute a base for designing and systematically exploring potential gesture-based interactions for the interactive system. The various perspectives proposed for categorizing human gestures into different taxonomies play a crucial role in comprehending user input behavior during gesture articulation in computer system interactions [43].

2.2   Design of Hand Gesture Vocabulary

Theoretical models of HCI provide a framework for understanding how users interact with technology and how gestures can facilitate this interaction efficiently. Designing hand gesture vocabularies involves systematically integrating knowledge from HCI, ergonomics, cognitive psychology, ethnography, and computer vision, among other fields. In addition to the known classics HCI desirable usability properties of user-system application HGR needs also some properties related to the nature of the interaction category, that includes expressiveness, articulation efficiency, and articulation flexibility [44].

Human-Based vs Technical-Based. Diverse approaches and methods are available to help creating a HGR vocabulary to achieve those properties. The main approaches to defining the vocabulary are technical-based, which considers specialist knowledge, and human-based, which investigates the people who will use the interface [31].

In the *human-based* approach, user needs and preferences are largely considered. However, these vocabularies are generally only suitable for the intended user group and cannot accommodate an outside user with a different cultural background [2]. The *technical-based* approach poses problems; for example, some gestures may be stressful or impossible to perform, and the mapping of functionalities and gestures is illogical for the users [31]. Additionally, developers or researchers have not devoted enough attention to selecting gestures for command sets and instead often resort to using arbitrary gestures, chosen based solely on available technology [25,36], that are not always reflective of users' preferred choice [4], are not intuitive and needs to be taught and learned [29].

Although the number of gesture-based interfaces has increased, the chosen gestures were usually determined by the researchers conducting the studies, often for convenience or because they aligned with the technology [48]. Even though many designers have relied on technical approaches involving HCI professionals to develop a vocabulary for HGR applications, the user-centered design approach remains the most commonly used method in the literature.

User-Centered Design. The primary methodologies for HGR vocabulary design include *expert-driven, technology-driven, domain-driven, user-centered* designs or *hybrid approaches. User-centered* design methodology places potential users at the heart of the design process. User-defined gestures involve participants naturally generating gestures for predefined commands, allowing for the creation of intuitive and easily remembered gestures [32].

Important issues to consider when choosing the set of gestures for the interface from a user-centered view are ergonomics and intuition [31]. For ergonomic aspects of human-system interaction, the ISO 9241-430 [19] offers recommendations for the design of non-touch gestural input to reduce biomechanical stress.

Users prefer gestures authored by large groups over those that single experts proposed [30], specially when created through user-centered design using end-user gesture elicitation [51,52]. A successful gesture set must be tailored to the application's purpose and user base rather than arbitrarily applied across different applications [31]. Tailoring gestures to the specific user problem, system functions, and application context ensures relevance and usability.

Elicitation Studies. An end-user elicitation study is a user-centered approach design methodology in the practice of participatory design that actively involves users in creating the input action for the system's functions. Although this methodology has become quite popular over the last decade since the publication of a study [51,52], the core method has been around since the early'80s from a particular study to design user-driven key terms for a command line interface [12]. The essence of the methodology is that participants are presented with the effects of action (referent) and asked to perform the signs that could cause those actions. By weighing and calculating agreement scores, the proposed gestures can be mapped to user-friendliness and acceptance.

The elicitation methodology for hand gestures [51,52] propagated as a basis for other researchers to build gesture vocabularies for different domains with a promise to results in a intuitive, memorable, and closely aligned with users' natural interactions gesture set. For HGR, gesture elicitation results in a vocabulary of gestures for a specific purpose likely to be adopted by the users [48]. Through sensible crafting of elicitation tasks, such studies can generate a gesture vocabulary that allows for the reuse of gestures for similar tasks [4].

Even though widely used, according to some designers, elicitation studies face challenges, such as the legacy bias problem [53] in which users tend to transfer gestures they have learned from existing input devices, interfaces, and techniques to new applications. Such biases can be an issue in gesture elicitation, inducing a failure to identify the more appropriate gestures for specified system tasks [53].

Elicitation studies can be considered insufficient for approaching an optimum interaction vocabulary [15], because by simply collecting user suggestions and following the majority principle may not capture the full depth and nuance needed for the most intuitive or effective gesture set. A more nuanced approach that considers the underlying mental models evoked by different gestures – categorized as imitative, instrumented, and intelligent – and restricts commands to those associated with a single mental model could me more efficient [15]. Another relevant issue is that many systems and elicitation studies often use controlled labs that may not reflect the real interactions of typical environments [17], where the result do not reflect the real environment.

Guessability and Agreement. Guessability, from the universal design principles of learnability, refers to the quality of symbols, gestures, keywords, or icons in a user interface that allows users to accurately predict and use them to access desired functions or characters, even without prior knowledge or learning of those symbols. It measures how intuitive and logically connected a symbolic input method is to its actions or outcomes. Wobbrock et al. [51] define guessability in symbolic input as *"that quality of symbols which allows a user to access intended referents via those symbols despite a lack of knowledge of those symbols."* The essence of guessability lies in the immediate, natural alignment between a user's expectations and the system's responses.

The agreement equation formula calculates the agreement among symbols proposed by participants. The agreement evaluation for elicitation studies gained new measurements [45], i.e., *disagreement* and *coagreement* rates, and a statistical significance test *Q-test* for complementing the analysis and, new clarifications and updates [46].

It is essential to mention that, in elicitation studies, the agreement analysis is one step of the study. The main three steps of the overall procedure involved running a gesture elicitation, are: (1) recording gesture, (2) gesture classification, and (3) agreement analysis [41]. Agreement analysis is also calculated by the classic inter-rater reliability methods, largely used for qualitative research [41].

In a meta-analysis, there is little consensus about how to approach reliability in qualitative research in HCI, which leads to authors often struggling to communicate methodological choices with confidence and reviewers may communicate confusing expectations [27]. It is because that fewer research reports describe the method used, and even fewer use the IRR method. This lack of description also discourages the application of those analysts to other researchers [27].

2.3   The Cultural Dimension

The Oxford Dictionary defines *culture* as "*the collective ideas, customs, and social behaviors of a particular people or society.*" The concept of culture in the context of HCI design presents a challenge due to its multifaceted nature and diverse interpretations. Nevertheless, some frameworks describe crucial cultural aspects that are essential for crafting user-centric and culturally aware interfaces.

Culture Frameworks. A theory of cultural dimensions offers a comprehensive framework to understand and analyze the pervasive influence of societal values on individual behaviors and intercultural interactions [16]. The framework outlines six dimensions: (1) power distance; (2) individualism vs. collectivism; (3) masculinity vs. femininity; (4) uncertainty avoidance index; (5) long-term orientation vs. short-term normative orientation; and (6) indulgence vs. restraint.

A second cultural framework for industrial designers to incorporate cultural sensitivity into product development [37] integrates cultural elements with design thinking, categorizing cultural elements into four lenses: (1) population, with lifestyle and demographics elements; (2) environment, with artifacts and setting; (3) consciousness, with influences and trends; and (4) values, with perceptions and traditions elements. This approach enables designers to create culturally relevant and appealing products to a global audience. According to the author, there is no discussion of how many cultural elements designers must screen through to inform and inspire design, as the selection concerns a specific design goal (compatibility, emotionality, functionality and aesthetics) and a clear definition of culture as it relates to product design.

Both frameworks are a reference for HCI studies and products development on cultural aspects. The first theory [16] of cross-cultural hand gestures reveals how cultural dimensions shape gestural communication. For instance, cultures with a high power distance index may prefer hierarchical gestures, while those with long-term orientation may convey commitments or values. This helps create culturally aware hand gesture recognition technologies. The second approach [37] underlines the need of incorporating cultural insights to enhance the usability and acceptance of systems in diverse global contexts. However, for global products that jointly face cross-cultural users, the ideal interface inevitably becomes one-size-fits-all. So, when analyzing the cultural dimension, the objective is to take the opposite path, that is, to neutralize strong cultural aspects to accommodate as many users of cultural diversity as possible.

Communication and Meaning. Verbal and nonverbal forms of communication are essential in human existence, enabling the transmission of information like thoughts, intentions, and emotions to others. Although language is the primary communication means, gestures significantly contribute to human interaction [28]. Gestures naturally complement spoken words, enhancing the clarity of communication. They enable individuals to express a wide range of emotions, feelings, and thoughts, whether verbalized or not [8,21]. This is especially true for emblematic gestures, which allow individuals to convey various thoughts and emotions ranging from approval to hostility [23].

Given the significant role of gestures in conveying a broad spectrum of human emotions and intentions, designing cross-cultural gesture-based communication systems becomes increasingly complex due to the diverse cultural interpretations of these nonverbal signals. Different cultures and individuals might have different understandings and associations with particular gestures [34]. Some gestures might be familiar to the user, but as they already have a meaning for the observers, they could interfere with communication, for example, the emblematic thumb up [36]. Simple gestures such as pointing are self-evident, but usually, each system has its own set of gestures and conventions for the meaning of specific gestures [35]. But, even if a gesture is culturally dependent, other cultures can learn it if presented [31].

Culturally vs. Cross-Cultural Driven Design Approaches. Culturally driven design, also called localized design is defined as a traditional cultural design based on the relationship between people, that combines inherent traditional elements with products applied to form a symbolic product [56]. A gesture vocabulary tailored for the specific application and context of use tends to be ergonomic, intuitive and easy-to-perform [31]. However, they are oriented to local and not global users [29] or translated applications [14]. Application and organization contexts and culture are limiting factors and impact the users' choice in user-defined gestures vocabulary [52].

Driven by the rapid globalization process, the market for design products has also transitioned from a single-oriented to a more diversified market, which has become a significant opportunity for exploring cross-cultural product design and an essential requirement for modern products [56]. Cross-cultural product design requires designers to have an in-depth understanding of the differences between various cultures to transcend boundaries and limitations posed by cultures [56]. This need is an essential barrier to designers of products for cross-cultural users, as getting to know other cultures with relevant depth is challenging.

It is crucial to inquire whether cultural dependence poses a problem since, for general interfaces, it is common to have English as the primary language followed by the option to select national language packages, by applying the same logic of translating hand gesture vocabularies into selectable gesture sets [31]. This setup would work for local systems. However, global products and systems need a more strategic solution to accommodate cross-cultural users sharing a vocabulary simultaneously.

Indicative Pathway Clues to Universality. Even some authors have underlined the nonexistence of a universal gestural vocabulary in several domains [2, 13,17,26,35,40,49], other studies have addressed the needed of designing shared hand gesture vocabularies, supporting the idealistic idea of work towards a universal HGR vocabulary for cross-cultural users and systems, especially for global products. Studies in different application domains have attempted to establish a consensual vocabulary based on various approaches, such as inter-domain and intercultural. Gestures would need standard conventions to ensure the same gestures mean the same things in different systems [34].

If considering domains as context, creating a universal set of gestures would be possible if it focuses on specific domains and context and the commands found can be used as a standard set in any other system that share the specific context [1,25]. A consensus of 22 mid-air gestures evaluated with the agreement rates [51] was already identified between 172 investigated studies, considering their transferability across domains [17]. The effect of cultural background on gesture-based human-robot interaction does not influence the type of gesture used but may affect the preferred gesture when the task has a cultural core [3].

Although the differences in multi-touch gestures are widespread, there is some consensus among designers [18], that agrees the most ubiquitous gestures supported by all multi-touch interfaces are a one-finger touch (which mimics the press of a button, the click of a mouse, or pointing to establish relevance) and a one-finger drag (often used for moving objects or the camera view). A two-finger pinch and spread motion for zooming or scaling objects is also widespread, although not universally used. Developers tend to show less agreement as interactions become more abstract but more consensus with straightforward interaction outcomes, often using one-finger drag and touch [18]. Regarding hand gesture formation, individuals from different cultures use similar hand shapes for the same tasks or operations, with only minor differences observed across participants from multiple countries [42].

It is essential to recognize the influence of culture on systems, for example, when examining collaborative meetings in a global setting. In such situations, users are encouraged to interact in a neutral zone, where many individuals naturally adopt a culture-free approach when communicating with cross-cultural colleagues and stakeholders. This behavior often involves communicating in a second language and putting aside one's cultural background. Cultural understanding is essential for designing a vocabulary, but cross-cultural understanding is also essential for designing a universal hand gesture vocabulary. Therefore, for a globalized market, it is essential to consider that more is needed to design a vocabulary, given that international individuals interact and communicate while sharing the same systems and devices in virtual or hybrid meeting spaces.

3   Conclusion

Designing a universal hand gesture recognition vocabulary poses significant challenges and opportunities within HCI. The vocabulary design demands a complex balance between considering the cultural dimensions to guarantee user acceptability and transcending cultural boundaries to reach the global user.

Although developing universal hand gesture vocabularies for cross-cultural users presents many challenges, some authors have tried to follow this path and presented encouraging results. The evolution of technology and the interaction and integration between people from different cultures in physical or virtual environments have reached a non-return point. The need to offer better interaction experiences in this scenario is becoming increasingly urgent.

Even if a universal HGR vocabulary concept is somewhat idealistic, it should be considered attainable, as it would encourage researchers to continue attempting to decode this problem. The approach to defining such a universal hand gesture vocabulary suitable for cross-cultural users involves analysis of existing vocabularies, lexicons, and taxonomies toward the construction of shared patterns that support the design of vocabularies to promote user engagement and inclusion. The synthesis of a taxonomy, lexicon, and vocabulary specific to HGR systems offers a structured framework for categorizing and understanding gestures, thereby facilitating the design of more effective and user-friendly interfaces.

Furthermore, it is essential to highlight the new implications of cultural aspects in designing HGR systems for cross-cultural users. Recognizing cultural dimensions in the development process adds a layer of analysis since, to create genuinely global products in their scope and applicability, some cultural elements need to be identified and neutralized in the standardization process, which is the opposite of today's design goals. By considering a cross-cultural perspective in a balanced way, designers and researchers can ensure that gesture-based interfaces are more inclusive, improving the user experience for individuals from diverse backgrounds.

In conclusion, the journey towards establishing a universal HGR vocabulary is filled with challenges but worthwhile. By bridging the gap between cultural diversity and technological innovation, we can unlock the full potential of gesture-based communication in global products and systems. This effort advances the HCI field and promotes a more connected and understanding world where technology is a universal language of interaction.

Acknowledgments. Original versions of the hand pose illustrations used in Fig. 1 (b and c) were designed by pch.vector/Freepik from https://www.freepik.com ("Human hand gestures set" pack, https://www.freepik.com/free-vector/human-hand-gestures-set_8609352.htm) released under the Freepik license, free for personal and commercial purpose with attribution.

Disclosure of Interests. The first author is supported by a grant from Innovation Fund Denmark (Award No. 3129-00046B) as part of an industrial Ph.D. research program in collaboration with GN Audio/AS and IT University of Copenhagen.

References

1. Ardito, C., Costabile, M.F., Jetter, H.C.: Gestures that people can understand and use. J. Visual Lang. Comput. **25**(5), 572–576 (2014). https://doi.org/10.1016/j.jvlc.2014.07.002

2. Bailey, S.K.T., Johnson, C.I.: A human-centered approach to designing gestures for natural user interfaces. In: Proceedings of the 22nd International Conference on Human-Computer Interaction, pp. 3–18 (2020). https://doi.org/10.1007/978-3-030-49062-1_1

3. Brito, I.V., Freire, E.O., Carvalho, E.A.N., Molina, L.: Analysis of cross-cultural effect on gesture-based human-robot interaction. Int. J. Mech. Eng. Robot. Res. 8(6), 852–859 (2019). https://doi.org/10.18178/ijmerr.8.6.852-859

4. Brudy, F., et al.: Cross-device taxonomy: survey, opportunities and challenges of interactions spanning across multiple devices. In: Proceedings of the 2019 CHI Conference on Human Factors in Computing Systems, pp. 1–28 (2019). https://doi.org/10.1145/3290605.3300792

5. Cao, X., Hsu, Y., Wu, W.: Cross-cultural design: a set of design heuristics for concept generation of sustainable packagings. In: Proceedings of the 23rd International Conference on Human-Computer Interaction, pp. 197–209 (2021). https://doi.org/10.1007/978-3-030-77074-7_16

6. Carfì, A., Mastrogiovanni, F.: Gesture-based human-machine interaction: taxonomy, problem definition, and analysis. IEEE Trans. Cybern. 53(1), 497–513 (2023). https://doi.org/10.1109/TCYB.2021.3129119

7. Chang, X., et al.: It must be gesturing towards me: gesture-based interaction between autonomous vehicles and pedestrians, pp. 1–25 (2024). https://doi.org/10.48550/arXiv.2402.14455

8. Chaudhary, A., Raheja, J.L., Das, K., Raheja, S.: Intelligent approaches to interact with machines using hand gesture recognition in natural way: a survey. Int. J. Comput. Sci. Eng. Surv. 2(1), 122–133 (2011). https://doi.org/10.5121/ijcses.2011.2109

9. Deshpande, K., Mashalkar, V., Mhaisekar, K., Naikwadi, A., Ghotkar, A.: Study and survey on gesture recognition systems. In: Proceedings of the 2023 7th International Conference On Computing, Communication, Control and Automation, pp. 1–6 (2023). https://doi.org/10.1109/iccubea58933.2023.10392214

10. Gheran, B.F., Vanderdonckt, J., Vatavu, R.D.: Gestures for smart rings: empirical results, insights, and design implications. In: Proceedings of the 2018 Designing Interactive Systems Conference, pp. 623–635 (2018). https://doi.org/10.1145/3196709.3196741

11. Gheran, B.F., Vatavu, R.D., Vanderdonckt, J.: New insights into user-defined smart ring gestures with implications for gesture elicitation studies. In: Proceedings of the 2023 Annual ACM Conference Extended Abstracts on Human Factors in Computing Systems, pp. 1–8 (2023). https://doi.org/10.1145/3544549.3585590

12. Good, M.D., Whiteside, J.A., Wixon, D.R., Jones, S.J.: Building a user-derived interface. Commun. ACM 27(10), 1032–1043 (1984). https://doi.org/10.1145/358274.358284

13. Gope, D.C.: Hand gesture interaction with human-computer. Global J. Comput. Sci. Technol. 11(23), 3–12 (2011). https://computerresearch.org/index.php/computer/article/view/414

14. Hasler, B.S., Salomon, O., Tuchman, P., Lev-Tov, A., Friedman, D.: Real-time gesture translation in intercultural communication. AI Soc. 32(1), 25–35 (2014). https://doi.org/10.1007/s00146-014-0573-4

15. Hitz, M., Königstorfer, E., Peshkova, E.: Exploring cognitive load of single and mixed mental models gesture sets for UAV navigation. In: Proceedings of the 2019 Annual ACM Conference Extended Abstracts on Human Factors in Computing Systems, pp. 1–8 (2019). https://api.semanticscholar.org/CorpusID:198332850

16. Hofstede, G.: The business of international business is culture. Int. Bus. Rev. **3**(1), 1–14 (1994). https://doi.org/10.1016/0969-5931(94)90011-6

17. Hosseini, M., Ihmels, T., Chen, Z., Koelle, M., Müller, H., Boll, S.: Towards a consensus gesture set: a survey of mid-air gestures in HCI for maximized agreement across domains. In: Proceedings of the 2023 CHI Conference on Human Factors in Computing System, pp. 1–24 (2023). https://doi.org/10.1145/3544548.3581420

18. Ingram, A., Wang, X., Ribarsky, W.: Towards the establishment of a framework for intuitive multi-touch interaction design. In: Proceedings of the 2012 International Working Conference on Advanced Visual Interfaces, pp. 66–73 (2012). https://doi.org/10.1145/2254556.2254571

19. International Organization for Standardization: ISO/TS 9241-430:2021 – Ergonomics of Human-System Interaction, Part 430: Recommendations for the Design of Non-Touch Gestural Input for the Reduction of Biomechanical Stress (2021). https://www.iso.org/standard/80270.html

20. Karam, M., Schraefel, M.C.: A Taxonomy of Gestures in Human Computer Interactions. Resreport, University of Southampton (Soton), United Kingdom (2005)

21. Kendon, A.: Gesture: Visible Action as Utterance. Cambridge University Press (2004). https://doi.org/10.1017/CBO9780511807572

22. Koh, J.I., Cherian, J., Taele, P., Hammond, T.: Developing a hand gesture recognition system for mapping symbolic hand gestures to analogous emojis in computer-mediated communication. ACM Trans. Interact. Intell. Syst. **9**(1), 1–35 (2019). https://doi.org/10.1145/3297277

23. Lindenberg, R., Uhlig, M., Scherfeld, D., Schlaug, G., Seitz, R.J.: Communication with emblematic gestures: shared and distinct neural correlates of expression and reception. Hum. Brain Mapp. **33**(4), 812–823 (2011). https://doi.org/10.1002/hbm.21258

24. Lugaresi, C., et al.: MediaPipe: a framework for perceiving and processing reality. In: Proceedings of the 2019 IEEE/CVF Conference on Computer Vision and Pattern Recognition, pp. 1–9 (2019). https://doi.org/10.48550/arXiv.1906.08172

25. Madapana, N., Gonzalez, G., Rodgers, R., Zhang, L., Wachs, J.P.: Gestures for picture archiving and communication systems (PACS) operation in the operating room: is there any standard? PLoS ONE **13**(6), 1–13 (2018). https://doi.org/10.1371/journal.pone.0198092

26. Maricchiolo, F., Gnisci, A., Bonaiuto, M.: Coding hand gestures: a reliable taxonomy and a multi-media support. In: Esposito, A., Esposito, A.M., Vinciarelli, A., Hoffmann, R., Müller, V.C. (eds.) Cognitive Behavioural Systems. LNCS, vol. 7403, pp. 405–416. Springer, Heidelberg (2012). https://doi.org/10.1007/978-3-642-34584-5_36

27. McDonald, N., Schoenebeck, S., Forte, A.: Reliability and inter-rater reliability in qualitative research: norms and guidelines for CSCW and HCI practice. Proc. ACM Hum.-Comput. Interact. **3**(CSCW), 1–23 (2019). https://doi.org/10.1145/3359174

28. McNeill, D.: Hand and Mind: What Gestures Reveal about Thought. University of Chicago Press (1992). https://doi.org/10.2307/1576015

29. Morgado, L.: Cultural awareness and personal customization of gestural commands using a shamanic interface. Procedia Comput. Sci. **27**, 449–459 (2014). https://doi.org/10.1016/j.procs.2014.02.049

30. Morris, M.R., Wobbrock, J.O., Wilson, A.D.: Understanding users' preferences for surface gestures. In: Proceedings of the 2010 Graphics Interface, pp. 261–268 (2010). https://doi.org/10.5555/1839214.1839260

31. Nielsen, M., Störring, M., Moeslund, T.B., Granum, E.: A procedure for developing intuitive and ergonomic gesture interfaces for HCI. In: Camurri, A., Volpe, G. (eds.) GW 2003. LNCS (LNAI), vol. 2915, pp. 409–420. Springer, Heidelberg (2004). https://doi.org/10.1007/978-3-540-24598-8_38
32. Nielsen, S., Nellemann, L.J., Larsen, L.B., Stec, K.: The social acceptability of peripheral interaction with 3D gestures in a simulated setting. In: Proceedings of the 22nd International Conference on Human-Computer Interaction, pp. 77–95 (2020). https://doi.org/10.1007/978-3-030-49062-1_5
33. Norman, D.: Gesture Wars (2011). https://www.core77.com/posts/20272/gesture-wars-20272
34. Norman, D.A.: Natural user interfaces are not natural. Interactions 17(3), 6–10 (2010). https://doi.org/10.1145/1744161.1744163
35. Rakkolainen, I., et al.: State of the art in extended reality – multimodal interaction. Techreport, Tampere University (TAU), Finland (2021)
36. Rico, J., Brewster, S.: Usable gestures for mobile interfaces: evaluating social acceptability. In: Proceedings of the 2010 CHI Conference on Human Factors in Computing Systems, pp. 887–896 (2010). https://doi.org/10.1145/1753326.1753458
37. Rubin, Z.L.: A framework for cross-cultural product design: the designer's guide to cultural research and design. Georgia Institute of Technology (2012)
38. Sarma, D., Bhuyan, M.K.: Methods, databases and recent advancement of vision-based hand gesture recognition for HCI systems: a review. SN Comput. Sci. 2, 436 (2021). https://doi.org/10.1007/s42979-021-00827-x
39. Shamma, D.A., Marlow, J., Denoue, L.: Interacting with smart consumer cameras: exploring gesture, voice, and AI control in video streaming. In: Proceedings of the 2019 ACM International Conference Interaction Experiences TV Online Video, pp. 137–144 (2019). https://doi.org/10.1145/3317697.3323359
40. Taralle, F., Paljic, A., Manitsaris, S., Grenier, J., Guettier, C.: A consensual and non-ambiguous set of gestures to interact with UAV in infantrymen. In: Proceedings of the 2015 Annual ACM Conference Extended Abstracts on Human Factors in Computing Systems, pp. 797–803 (2015). https://doi.org/10.1145/2702613.2702971
41. Tsandilas, T.: Fallacies of agreement: a critical review of consensus assessment methods for gesture elicitation. ACM Trans. Comput.-Hum. Interact. 25(3), 1–49 (2018). https://doi.org/10.1145/3182168
42. Urakami, J.: Developing and testing a human-based gesture vocabulary for tabletop systems. Hum. Factors J. Hum. Factors Ergon. Soc. 54(4), 636–653 (2012). https://doi.org/10.1177/0018720811433052
43. Vatavu, R.D.: Gesture-Based Interaction, pp. 1–47. Springer, Cham (2023). https://doi.org/10.1007/978-3-319-27648-9_20-1
44. Vatavu, R.D.: iFAD gestures: understanding users' gesture input performance with index-finger augmentation devices. In: Proceedings of the 2023 CHI Conference on Human Factors in Computing Systems, pp. 1–17 (2023). https://doi.org/10.1145/3544548.3580928
45. Vatavu, R.D., Wobbrock, J.O.: Formalizing agreement analysis for elicitation studies: new measures, significance test, and toolkit. In: Proceedings of the 2015 CHI Conference on Human Factors in Computing Systems, pp. 1325–1334 (2015). https://doi.org/10.1145/2702123.2702223
46. Vatavu, R.D., Wobbrock, J.O.: Clarifying agreement calculations and analysis for end-user elicitation studies. ACM Trans. Comput.-Hum. Interact. 29(1), 5:1–5:70 (2022). https://doi.org/10.1145/3476101

47. Vuletic, T., Duffy, A., Hay, L., McTeague, C., Campbell, G., Grealy, M.: Systematic literature review of hand gestures used in human computer interaction interfaces. Int. J. Hum.-Comput. Stud. **129**, 74–94 (2019). https://doi.org/10.1016/j.ijhcs.2019.03.011

48. Vuletic, T., et al.: A novel user-based gesture vocabulary for conceptual design. Int. J. Hum.-Comput. Stud. **150**, 1–25 (2021). https://doi.org/10.1016/j.ijhcs.2021.102609

49. Wei, X.L., Xi, R., Hou, W.J.: User-centric AR sceneized gesture interaction design. In: Proceedings of the 22nd International Conference on Human Factors in Computing Systems, pp. 367–378 (2020). https://doi.org/10.1007/978-3-030-49695-1_24

50. Willms, J., Letter, M., Marchandise, E., Wolf, K.: Pull outperforms push as vibro-tactile wristband feedback for mid-air gesture guidance. In: Proceedings of the 2023 Mensch Computer, pp. 138–148 (2023). https://doi.org/10.1145/3603555.3603579

51. Wobbrock, J.O., Aung, H.H., Rothrock, B., Myers, B.A.: Maximizing the guess-ability of symbolic input. In: Proceedings of the 2005 Annual ACM Conference Extended Abstracts on Human Factors in Computing Systems, pp. 1869–1872 (2005). https://doi.org/10.1145/1056808.1057043

52. Wobbrock, J.O., Morris, M.R., Wilson, A.D.: User-defined gestures for surface computing. In: Proceedings of the 2009 CHI Conference on Human Factors in Computing Systems, pp. 1083–1092 (2009). https://doi.org/10.1145/1518701.1518866

53. Wu, H., Fu, S., Yang, L., Zhang, X.L.: Exploring frame-based gesture design for immersive VR shopping environments. Behav. Inf. Technol. **41**(1), 96–117 (2022). https://doi.org/10.1080/0144929x.2020.1795261

54. Yasen, M., Jusoh, S.: A systematic review on hand gesture recognition techniques, challenges and applications. PeerJ Comput. Sci. **5**(e218), 1–30 (2019). https://doi.org/10.7717/peerj-cs.218

55. Yashas, J., Shivakumar, G.: Hand gesture recognition: a survey. In: Proceedings of the 2019 International Conference on Applied Machine Learning, pp. 3–8 (2019). https://doi.org/10.1109/icaml48257.2019.00009

56. Zeng, S., Xu, R., Huang, S.: The application and expression of product modeling design from cross-cultural perspective. In: Proceedings of the 25th International Conference on Human-Computer Interaction, pp. 564–579 (2023). https://doi.org/10.1007/978-3-031-35936-1_42

57. Zheng, Z.: Human gesture recognition in computer vision research. SHS Web Conf. **144**, 1–5 (2022). https://doi.org/10.1051/shsconf/202214403011

58. Zholshiyeva, L., Zhukabayeva, T., Turaev, S., Berdiyeva, M., Jambulova, D.: Hand gesture recognition methods and applications: a literature survey. In: Proceedings of the 7th International Conference on Engineering MIS, pp. 1–8 (2021). https://doi.org/10.1145/3492547.3492578

Applying Co-designing Methods to Information-Seeking Systems with North Carolina Foster Parents

Rachel Rodney[✉] [iD]

University of North Carolina at Chapel Hill, Chapel Hill, NC 27514, USA
rhrodney@ad.unc.edu

Abstract. Considering the significant role information systems play in resource accessibility, my poster will focus on one aspect of my dissertation: establishing connections with vulnerable groups. Presently, one key issue in foster parent retention is the inadequacy of resources and support systems, influencing their decision to cease providing foster care. Child welfare researchers call to include foster parent perspectives in designing interventions, but limited research has applied such data. Therefore, this work emphasizes participatory research methods and prioritizing relationship building with foster parents. I seek to understand the information-seeking behavior of rural North Carolina foster parents and plan to facilitate co-designing workshops with stakeholders. The process of building trust with this community provides insights that will contribute to the participatory development of future inclusive and effective information systems.

Keywords: participatory research · co-design · information-seeking behavior

1 Introduction

Limited research of applying foster parent experiences to designing systematic changes are highlighted by child welfare researchers, indicating the benefit of applying a user experience (UX) approach to navigating the issue of foster parent retention in North Carolina (NC) [7, 24, 25]. In 2023, reports uncovered the crisis of foster parent retention in NC, where there are double the number of foster care youth than there are foster care homes [11, 23, 27]. Looking deeper at factors that influence foster parent retention, there is a strong impact of a foster parent's access to resources and support. An inadequacy of user-friendly resources leaves foster parents feeling unsupported, which is emphasized in rural settings, where there are few resources that are available to foster parents or foster youth [4, 20]. This can influence the decision to cease foster parenting [14, 16, 17, 25]. I propose to map out the information seeking behaviors (ISB) of foster parents in resource limited settings and facilitate participatory design to bridge the gap between available resources and how foster parents are learning about, and accessing, such support.

One of the research questions guiding this study is: How might designers cultivate a co-designing relationship with foster parents to develop accessible resources? Through

© The Author(s), under exclusive license to Springer Nature Switzerland AG 2024
C. Stephanidis et al. (Eds.): HCII 2024, CCIS 2114, pp. 70–78, 2024.
https://doi.org/10.1007/978-3-031-61932-8_9

co-designing, I seek to understand the obstacles in foster parents' information seeking process and how they might envision a more effective process. Preceding participatory studies or co-design, relationships need to be established between the researcher and the community. In this paper, my process of building trust with the foster parent community will provide insights that will contribute to the participatory development of future inclusive and effective information systems.

2 Background

NC is one of nine states in the United States of America that uses a county administered system, where each county develops their own methods of administering foster care [21]. Although the benefits of a county administered system are the localized solutions and resources that can be designed to support the communities within, this system makes way for uneven distribution of resources between counties, supporting foster children disproportionately throughout the state. Currently, 70 NC counties are considered rural, and 30 are considered urban, compounding health disparities available in rural areas and to the foster care system [10, 19]. Having support plays a significant role in the lives of foster children and youth, as well as in the experience of being a foster parent. A couple of factors that influence foster parent retention stem from: (1) not receiving adequate help and support from case workers, and (2) not having enough training on how to work with children who come from unresolved trauma [14, 16, 17, 25]. These factors point to the issue of foster parents not having the knowledge they need about resources. Having ready access to resources can either ensure the success or the failure of child placement [14]. Thus, a deeper look at how the availability of local resources impacts foster parent retention is needed.

Localizing support generally has positive outcomes because it can meet unique needs that vary between the size of the population, average income, etc. However, when applied to providing healthcare and support for communities such as foster parents, living in a resource limited setting might result in difficulties taking foster youth to doctors' appointments, or not having childcare services that accept children who have behavioral problems (which are especially prevalent in foster children). For example, more health practices in urban counties might accept Medicaid, the insurance that foster youth are provided, than health practices in rural counties. A previous foster parent explained that because of the obstacles foster children and youth face when seeking healthcare, they have known foster parents who needed to drive four hours round trip to take their foster child to a mental health appointment. Foster parents are not compensated for gas, and their existing responsibilities are impeded with needing to travel four hours for the nearest mental health doctor that will take a foster child's insurance.

In response to this issue, non-profit organizations and academic institutes create solutions to solve the issues they see in the foster care system. However, the process of foster parents learning about and accessing resources are disrupted by the information seeking system they have been provided. An example overview of an information system for seeking resources is illustrated below (Fig. 1).

The overarching information system visualizes how a foster parent might seek resources from the child welfare service they are working with. The case workers they

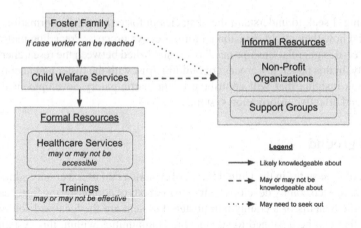

Fig. 1. Example of an overarching information system for foster parents seeking help.

have a connection with are likely to know what formal resources the welfare service has connections with. However, if these resources do not meet the foster parents' needs, it is not guaranteed that the case worker will know what informal resources exist, such as local organizations or support groups. In this case, foster parents need to seek these resources themselves, which may or may not be successful. Thus, I aim to investigate foster parent ISB within resource limited settings using a participatory UX approach.

3 Literature Review

Literature on foster parent retention highlights a gap in interdisciplinary research. Research addressing foster parent retention is largely seen in fields such as Child and Family Studies, Child and Family Behavior Therapy, and Public Health [14, 16, 17, 24, 25]. Several articles call for a specific focus on foster parent perspectives to improve the quality of their experience [7, 24, 25]. Furthermore, leaders call for interdisciplinary fields to tackle problems in the foster care system [6]. Consequently, the potential of ISB and UX studies emerges as a promising avenue for uncovering valuable insights into this aspect of foster parent retention.

ISB and UX provide a closer look at experiences on foster parents seeking information. Foster parent ISB regarding resources has been explored with little direct applications that extend beyond policy suggestions. UX studies have been conducted to improve the experience of digital tools for foster parents, such as a platform for communication between foster parents and case workers, or a system of connecting foster parents with their neighbors [3, 9]. However, these studies focus on the effectiveness of specific tools, as opposed to the behaviors of foster parents which would provide unique insight to the process of how foster parents look for information when they need resources. This work is unique in that I aim to narrow this study to foster parents in rural settings in NC, and that I will employ a qualitative and participatory research approach to do so. Furthermore, any solution that is formed from this research will be developed through co-design.

Overall, my work will be shaped by feminist theory and a social justice framework. The foster care system is not perfect, and social justice issues such as access to healthcare and discrimination persist in various capacities [8]. Thus, my study is informed by feminist standpoint theory, which asserts that knowledge is situated and contextual [5]. Furthermore, situating my work within a social justice framework expands it to encompass the consideration of political and institutional systems that participants navigate in their information seeking processes [1, 29].

4 Methods

Methods my study will utilize are participatory action research (PAR) and co-design. These methods align with my theoretical framework of feminist theory and social justice, as well as motivate two-way collaboration on designing solutions.

4.1 PAR

PAR is research with the intention to enact change [12]. PAR adds value to my work both methodologically and theoretically by recognizing participants' lived experiences and supporting sincere collaboration [13]. The social justice applications of my research addresses improving access to resources. Further, drawing from feminist theory requires that my work reflects the agency of others' experiences [22]. Additionally, supporting sincere collaboration will be an ethical necessity in conducting research, and will be beneficial in supporting long term relationships to implement actionable change.

4.2 Co-design

Co-designing is when the designer/researcher and the community designs solutions together. As a research method, co-designing reveals assumptions that the researcher has about the community, provides an opportunity for users to ideate about a problem they face, and highlights the priority of issues and what form a solution should take. The overall process of building relationships between designers and users as co-designers is the core of user centered design. The ideas that support co-design are found in feminist theory where designers explore the impact of the designed world on a user's identity and agency [5]. Core themes within feminist theory are "agency, fulfillment, identity, equity, empowerment, and social justice," concepts that should be considered to ensure a product is designed inclusively [5].

4.3 Implementation

To implement PAR and co-design, I plan on conducting a qualitative study with foster parents in Western NC to define which resources are most difficult to access and which ones are high priority. An example of this study may be facilitating a conversation with foster parents and conducting a card-sorting activity to see how resources compare to each other. Afterwards, I will synthesize the findings and moderate a co-designing workshop with the interviewed foster parents focusing on prioritized resources.

PAR and co-design will enhance my study's impact with the local community, pairing localized foster parent's experience with the UX design process in a way that shares the power distribution of the study [2].

5   Cultivating Relationships to Enact Change

This work intentionally builds ethical relationships with participants to conduct research for positive social impacts. These relationships will support the effectiveness of participatory methods of the study. Thus, methods for initiating and continuing relationships are crucial in the goal of implementing positive change.

Considering change, Systems Change is a concept "about shifting the conditions that are holding [a] problem in place" [15]. This idea is conceptualized into a model of six conditions, shown below (Fig. 2).

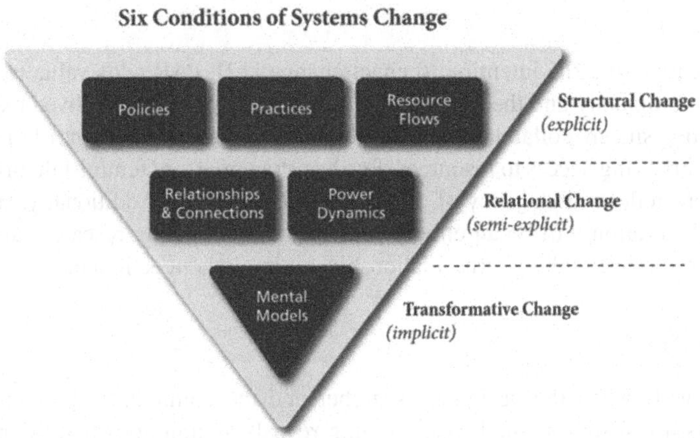

Fig. 2. Six Conditions of Systems Change [15].

As seen in this model, power dynamics and relationships and connections are on the second tier of the model, labeled 'relational change.' The impact of relational change is less tangible than structural change, but more impactful towards transformative change. The connection between relational change and transformative change indicates that relationship building is a crucial part of enacting systematic change. To do so, power dynamics must be evaluated.

Researchers must understand their power dynamics with the community. Looking at the power dynamics of participatory research, Wallerstein et al. (2019) states that "power is operationalized through constructed racialized and gendered hierarchies, institutionalizing the subordination of people of color and other marginalized groups." To consider dynamics within the sphere of social constructs, intentional reflection and communication is required to create and maintain the relationship between stakeholders and researchers [28]. Furthermore, the researcher must identify their personal beliefs about the community and reconcile these ideas through communication with the community

[26, 28]. Considering how to apply the process of building such relationships, Metz et al. (2022) states that:

"growing evidence highlights trusting relationships as a critical element of effective implementation, with important implications for efforts to bring to scale effective policies, practices, and approaches in the context of health services and other related service delivery settings." [18]

The focus on trust-building guides prioritizes the gaining and sharing of trust as a key method in building relationships. Metz et al. (2022) emphasizes trust-building in developing relationships and proposes a theory of change that includes both 'relational strategies' and 'technical strategies.' Relational strategies include communicating authentically and showing an openness to learn from each other. Technical strategies include interacting often, being responsive and having quick turnaround for small milestones [18]. These strategies are implemented in the next section.

6   Methods of Building Trust

For trust and relationship building, I have taken actions to being open and willing to help in any capacity, along with maintaining regular communication with stakeholders. One organization I have begun building relationship with is Seeds of Hope, a non-profit organization in Western NC that supports their local community by providing year-round services to families of children considered at-risk (i.e. a child in the foster care system, adopted, with a disability, or from a low-income family.) Since forming this relationship in 2023, I have expanded my network to include stakeholders who are developing NC resources through the University of North Carolina at Chapel Hill (UNC-CH), or are part of other non-profit organizations supporting foster children and youth in NC.

6.1   Seeds of Hope

The first encounter I had with the director of Seeds of Hope was during their summer day camp. I assisted in guiding kids 5 to 13-years old through various activities, including cheerleading, LEGO building, and gym exercises. Building connections with the children that week left a profound impact on me, prompting me to seek opportunities to return and continue my involvement with the community. Subsequent meetings with the camp director provided insight into challenges faced by the families involved. Since then, I have engaged in online and in-person meetings with the director, and volunteer ed at two holiday events. My primary goal has been to aid and forge connections with families and fellow volunteers within the Seeds of Hope community (Fig. 3).

I found attending these volunteer events to be a natural extension of my initial service-oriented mindset, rather than approaching them solely as a researcher. My involvement with Seeds of Hope, prior to any exploration of issues within the foster care system, has facilitated the development of genuine connections with the camp organizers. As a result, I am excited to dedicate time during June and July 2024 to volunteer at the Seeds of Hope day camp, furthering my commitment to serving and strengthening relationships within the local foster care community. Furthermore, I foresee myself working primarily with

Fig. 3. Holiday volunteer events (Seeds of Hope December Newsletter, 2023). The author helped hand off presents hidden in bags, and passed out breakfast items to families the next morning.

foster parents whose children participate in Seeds of Hope. Foster parents involved with Seeds of Hope will provide a unique perspective, and they present a local community that I can work with closely in the future.

6.2 Family and Children Resource Program (FCRP) at UNC-CH

FCRP, based at UNC-CH, plays a pivotal role in enhancing foster care resources, offering support in areas like training and aiding organizations across NC in addressing challenges. Engaging with FCRP provided valuable insights into the perspectives of case workers and non-profit organizations within the foster care realm. Cultivating this connection has been instrumental in refining my understanding of foster parent information-seeking behavior. In the future, I may continue to collaborate with FCRP staff and researchers. Their expertise on how the foster care system intersects with organizations across NC will help clarify and provide feedback on the study. Additionally, FCRP introduced me to the Foster Family Alliance, expanding my network within the foster care community.

6.3 Foster Family Alliance

Meeting with the director of the Foster Family Alliance unveiled a potential partnership for the study. Over the past year, Foster Family Alliance has undertaken a comprehensive study examining foster parent experiences in NC on a large scale. Leveraging this data will elucidate existing gaps in understanding of foster parent perceptions in NC and enable comparative analysis of experiences across counties.

7 Limitation

Limitations in working with foster parents include being able to recruit them, and schedule time(s) to meet. Foster parents have many responsibilities and may not have time to participate in studies. Some ways to avoid adding to foster parents' workload is to seek secondary data before meeting, to limit how many times we need to meet. Additionally, privacy issues have high stakes in foster care research. Therefore, I need to design the study for anonymity and seek IRB approval before beginning data collection.

8 Next Steps

Forming relationships and learning from community experts has been a critical point in this study. In the future, I expect to continue deepening these relationships and potentially bridging them to improve the process of foster parents seeking resources.

9 Conclusion

This paper emphasized the act of building trust with communities prior to conducting participatory or co-design methods within an ISB and UX context. Specifically, this work considers how researchers and practitioners can work with foster parents, who have unique positions as individuals volunteering their time to care for foster children and youth. Further, although the target population of this study are foster parents, others can leverage this insight in their work. Implications of this work are strategies to translate critical social issues to HCI applications, in addition to building relationships with communities. Furthermore, expected contributions include insights into social justice applications of HCI through qualitative and localized methods, as well as advancing approaches to designing information systems in resource-limited populations.

Acknowledgments. The author thanks organizers in Seeds of Hope, Family and Children Resource Program, and Foster Family Alliance for their time and willingness to collaborate. Additionally, the author thanks her committee members Dr. Maggie Melo *(chair)*, Dr. Brad Hemminger *(co-chair)*, Dr. Willie Payne, Dr. Douglas Walls, and Dr. Paul Lanier for their guidance leading to this work.

Disclosure of Interests. The author has no competing interests to declare that are relevant to the content of this article.

References

1. Acharya, K.: Usability for user empowerment: promoting social justice and human rights through localized UX design. In: Proceedings of the 36th ACM International Conference on the Design of Communication, pp. 1–7 (2018)
2. Agboka, G.: Participatory Localization: A Social Justice Approach to Navigating Unenfranchised/Disenfranchised Cultural Sites. Technical Communication Quarterly (2013)
3. Audige, F: Foster Together—UX Design Case Study. Medium (2022)
4. Baldauf, R.: Kids in foster care often need mental health care. But options are limited in rural NC. NC Health News (2023)
5. Bardzell, S.: Feminist HCI: Taking Stock and Outlining an Agenda for Design (2010)
6. Bjoran, K.: Can UX Help Disrupt a Broken Foster Care System? UX Booth (2017)

7. Brown, J.: Foster parents' perceptions of factors needed for successful foster placements. J. Child Fam. Stud. **17**(4), 538–554 (2008)
8. Chipungu, S., Bent-Goodley, T.: Meeting the challenges of contemporary foster care. Future Child. **14**(1), 74 (2004)
9. Costa, R.: Fjord and UX Research: Prototyping for Child Welfare Services. Justinmind (2019)
10. County Data. NC Rural Center. https://www.ncruralcenter.org/advocacy-and-research/county-data/. Accessed 13 Mar 2024
11. Crouch, M.: With Nowhere Else to Go, Kids Needing Foster Care Sleep on the Floor in County Offices. North Carolina Health News (2023)
12. Foth, M., Axup, J.: Participatory design and action research: identical twins or synergetic pair? In: Wagner, I., Jacucci, G., Kensing, F., Blomberg, J. (eds.) Expanding Boundaries in Design, vol. 2, pp. 93–96 (2006)
13. Gatenby, B., Humphries, M.: Feminist participatory action research: methodological and ethical issues. Women's Stud. Int. Forum **23**(1), 89–105 (2000)
14. Gouveia, L., Magalhães, E., Pinto, V.S.: Foster families: a systematic review of intention and retention factors. J. Child Fam. Stud. **30**(11), 2766–2781 (2021)
15. Kania, J., Kramer, M., Senge, P.: The Water of Systems Change (2018)
16. Larsen, M., Baste, V., Bjørknes, R., Breivik, K., Myrvold, T., Lehmann, S.: Foster parents' experiences of using child mental health and welfare services in Norway: associations with youth, placement, and service characteristics. Child Fam. Soc. Work **25**(4), 884–894 (2020)
17. Mancinelli, E., Dell'Arciprete, G., Salcuni, S.: A systematic review on foster parents' psychological adjustment and parenting style—an evaluation of foster parents and foster children variables. Int. J. Environ. Res. Public Health **18**(20), 10916 (2021)
18. Metz, A., Jensen, T., Farley, A., Boaz, A., Bartley, L., Villodas, M.: Building trusting relationships to support implementation: a proposed theoretical model. Front. Health Serv. **2** (2022)
19. Morales, D., Barksdale, C., Beckel-Mitchener, A.: A call to action to address rural mental health disparities. J. Clin. Transl. Sci. **4**(5), 463–467 (2020)
20. More Foster Parents Needed in Rural Areas. Omni Family of Services (2019). https://www.theomnifamily.com/blog/news/more-foster-parents-needed-in-rural-areas/
21. North Carolina. Child Welfare Information Gateway. https://www.childwelfare.gov/resources/states-territories-tribes/nc/
22. Ogbonnaya-Ogburu, I., Smith, A., To, A., Toyama, K.: Critical race theory for HCI. In: Proceedings of the 2020 CHI Conference on Human Factors in Computing Systems, pp. 1–16 (2020)
23. Pierce, D.: Foster children sleeping in jails, emergency rooms, and DSS offices amid a foster family shortage. Queen City News (2023)
24. Rork, K., McNeil, C.: Evaluation of foster parent training programs: a critical review. Child Fam. Behav. Ther. **33**(2), 139–170 (2011)
25. Saarnik, H.: A systematic review of factors needed for successful foster placements: perspectives from children and foster parents. Child Youth Serv. **42**(4), 374–392 (2021)
26. Sheftel, A., Zembrzycki, S.: Only human: a reflection on the ethical and methodological challenges of working with "difficult" stories. Oral Hist. Rev. **37**(2), 191–214 (2010)
27. Terry, M.: There aren't enough foster parents in North Carolina. Kids are Sleeping in Social Service Offices(WFAE 90.7). Charlotte's NPR News Source (2023)
28. Wallerstein, N., et al.: Power dynamics in community-based participatory research: a multiple–case study analysis of partnering contexts, histories, and practices. Health Educ. Behav. **46**(1_suppl), 19S–32S (2019)
29. Walls, D., Dieterle, B., Miller, J.: Safely social: user-centered design and difference feminism. In: Blair, K., Nickoson, L. (eds.) Composing Feminist Interventions: Activism, Engagement, Praxis, pp. 391–407. The WAC Clearinghouse; University Press of Colorado (2018)

Exploration of Design Intervention in Eliminating Bias: A Persuasive System Design Approach of Introducing Intermediate Scenarios

Xingyu Tu[(✉)] , Hao Chen , Jiatao Wang , and Xiangyang Xin

Shanghai International College of Design and Innovation, Tongji University, Shanghai, China
2333779@tongji.edu.cn

Abstract. While the undeniable health risks of tobacco warrant attention, the substantial existing smoker base and potential challenges associated with mandatory cessation suggest that mitigating its impact is best approached through gradual reductions and awareness campaigns. In the Chinese context, e-cigarettes, as a harm-reduction alternative to traditional smoking, have stirred controversy. This study aims to uncover the reasons behind negative public perceptions of e-cigarettes in China and identify effective strategies for promoting local tobacco harm reduction by facilitating smoker transition. We employed qualitative and quantitative methods to collect and analyze public opinions on e-cigarettes and their users.

The study identified two primary reasons contributing to the negative public perception of e-cigarettes: online information with subjective guidance and the unfavorable impression of the e-cigarette subculture. Utilizing the Behavior Change Techniques (BCTs) and the Persuasive Systems Design (PSDs) framework, we identified design features aimed at shifting the social perception of e-cigarettes from being seen as 'another kind of cigarette' to serving as a medium for promoting healthy behaviors. Subsequently, a product solution was devised based on these findings.

Keywords: e-cigarettes · PSD · BCT · intermediate scenarios

1 Introduction

E-cigarettes, at equivalent nicotine levels, generate fewer cardiovascular and cancer-related toxins compared to traditional combustible tobacco [1]. Furthermore, their nicotine content can be adjusted through oil modulation.

Although theoretically posing considerably less harm than traditional tobacco, e-cigarettes have only achieved a 4.2% penetration rate among the smoking population in China as of 2021. Besides restrictive sales policies, the assertive design and suggestive promotional strategies employed by related companies frequently lead to public discontent. Research also suggests a concern that the entry of tobacco companies into the e-cigarette market may exploit mental illness for increased sales [2].

© The Author(s), under exclusive license to Springer Nature Switzerland AG 2024
C. Stephanidis et al. (Eds.): HCII 2024, CCIS 2114, pp. 79–88, 2024.
https://doi.org/10.1007/978-3-031-61932-8_10

Our survey results among the general public indicate that 69.8% of randomly selected respondents neither use nor recommend e-cigarettes to other smokers, primarily due to their skepticism regarding the harm reduction potential of e-cigarettes. This substantial disparity between subjective bias and actual demand underscores an urgent challenge in advancing the overall population's health.

2 Related Works

The Persuasive Systems Design Model (PSDM) has garnered increasing recognition in both design and business domains, playing a pivotal role in shaping behavioral patterns and lifestyles within numerous public health initiatives.

In theoretical realms, B.J. Fogg introduced the Fogg Behavior Model, which outlines three key elements of human behavior: motivation, ability, and triggers [3]. Cialdini synthesized extensive research into six principles of influence: reciprocity, commitment and consistency, social proof (consensus), liking, authority, and scarcity [4], Kirsi et al. contend that these six elements are not mutually exclusive but rather context-sensitive [5], aligning with the findings of this study. Oinas-Kukkonen consolidated research findings and proposed the Generic Steps in Persuasive System Development along with corresponding principles of persuasion, offering a workflow framework for persuasive system design [6]. Michie reorganized the methodology of behavior change techniques (BCTs) [7], furnishing a toolkit for the subsequent application of behavior change techniques.

In the specific application domain, Rikke et al. highlighted users' value claims as the primary driver of their behavior and needs. Through interviews, they identified the needs and value claims of end users, which served as the foundation for designing the eCHANGE APP. This design process integrated Persuasive System Design Principles and Behavior Change Techniques (BCTs) [8, 9], showcasing a successful case of promoting a healthy lifestyle through thoughtful design.

While persuasive design inherently relies on meeting user value needs, addressing controversial products such as e-cigarettes requires caution. Simply reinforcing the connection between e-cigarettes and health values often results in negative impacts on the Social Acceptance/Rejection element of behavioral motivation [3], Therefore, meticulous decisions regarding design elements are essential.

3 Methods and Process

3.1 Causes of Prejudice

This study employed a qualitative approach by combining online questionnaires and offline interviews to discern the primary causes of prejudice. Initially, we randomly selected 210 participants as Public Group, of which 68 had prior smoking experience, offering a sample reflective of the average public awareness level of e-cigarette products. Subsequently, we recruited 33 traditional cigarette users with previous e-cigarette experience, along with 3 core users who regularly use e-cigarettes, to be our User Group. These participants were all from China.

We initiated the data collection process by distributing a questionnaire to the Public Group. This questionnaire asks participants to share their perceptions regarding the harm reduction potential of e-cigarettes and the reason. Subsequently, we collated and categorized the reasons contributing to negative evaluations, yielding a total of 184 valid questionnaires. The detailed breakdown of reasons for negative evaluations is presented in Table 1.

Table 1. Public group results for Reasons of negative comments: keywords, example post and value.

Reason Label	Keywords	Example Post	Value
User Impression	Smoky, Hooligans, Look, Atmosphere, Face, Tattoo	People who smoke e-cigarettes look like hooligans	43
Actual Experience	Helpless, Addictive, Physical examination, Dizziness, cough, not used to, feeling	I can't get used to it, and sometimes it can cause dizziness	3
Media News	Media, Internet, News, TV, report, paper, magazines	I often hear negative reports	107
Subjective Guess	Guess, Suppose, Never heard of, Unfamiliar	I don't know much about it, but hearing the name is unhealthy	6
Heard from acquaintance	Friend, Relatives, Neighbors, Colleagues	I heard from my colleagues that it has no effect on smoking cessation	21

We then distilled the reasons into a new set of questions and presented them to the User Group, instructing them to rate their level of agreement on a five-point scale (-2 = strongly disagree to 2 = strongly agree).

Interviews conducted by three designers with 36 members from User Group, the average scores for each reason were determined as follows: User Impression = 1.28, Actual Experience = -1.42, Media News = 1.72, Subjective Guess = 1.86, and Heard from acquaintance = 0.67. It was observed that the User Group strongly concurred with the categorization of Media News, User Impression, and Subjective Guess as significant factors contributing to negative ratings.

Combining feedback from both the Public and the User Group, along with additional desktop research, we propose two potential causes of bias:

1. Negative Impression from the E-cigarette Subculture:
2. Subjective information on the Internet.

Young promoters introducing new trends make the e-cigarette subculture appear immature to the public in China. Additionally, one-sided reports on the Internet have increased people's distrust.

3.2 Identification of Intermediate Scenario

After analyzing the system, we believe that we need to find a more motivating sub-theme under the parent theme of health as an intermediate scenario that can improve the negative social image of e-cigarettes and their users and thus reduce public prejudice.

First, we needed to identify the values and needs of individuals interested in vaping. After interviewing 36 User Group, we obtained three major value claims: "health", "differentiation", (result also included the claims of "relaxation" and "inspiring", but they are not typical from traditional cigarettes, so they are not regarded as the value claims of e-cigarettes users). With the sale of multiple flavors of e-cigarettes being restricted, our focus will be on developing persuasive strategies for the values of 'different' and 'healthy,' as illustrated in Fig. 1.

Fig. 1. Values and Needs of People using e-cigarettes instead of traditional cigarettes.

To address the identified needs and values, designers conducted brainstorming sessions and evaluated potential behaviors in four scenarios: technological aesthetics, sports and fitness, fashion trends, and daily wellness. We screened 10 e-cigarette users and 6 designers from User Group and scored them based on their degree of agreement with the four criteria (ranging from 1 to 5). The scenario with the highest average score was then selected as the intermediate scenario, as detailed in Table 2.

The result showed Sports fitness had the highest score. We further subdivided Sports and continued the scoring process with the same criteria, the 16 participants in this phase indicated that daily fitness should be introduced into the system as the mediating element.

To ensure that the scenario derived from this methodology do meet the participation needs of both cigarette and e-cigarette users, the results were validated by questionnaire. we distributed questionnaires to participants with smoking experience among Public Group and all User Group (104 in total), and the results showed that 72.1% of users maintained a frequency of exercise more than 2 times per week, while 81.7% of users expressed their recognition of promoting smoking cessation through exercise, which supported the results in terms of both the user base and user recognition.

Table 2. Results of criteria-based scoring of four scenarios: modes, means and SDs.

Intermediate Scenarios	Criteria Means (SDs)	Final Value
Technology esthetics	$C_1 = 3.19$ (0.66) $C_2 = 3.56$ (0.89) $C_3 = 1.44$ (0.63) $C_4 = 4.06$ (0.57)	3.06
Sports and Fitness	$C_1 = 4.75$ (0.45) $C_2 = 4.00$ (0.73) $C_3 = 4.50$ (0.63) $C_4 = 4.81$ (0.40)	4.52
Fashion	$C_1 = 3.25$ (1.61) $C_2 = 3.31$ (1.66) $C_3 = 1.75$ (0.86) $C_4 = 1.63$ (0.89)	2.48
Diet	$C_1 = 3.06$ (1.29) $C_2 = 3.56$ (1.21) $C_3 = 3.88$ (1.26) $C_4 = 4.69$ (0.48)	3.80

C_1: Audience Size
C_2: Topicality
C_3: Difficulty
C_4: Persistence

3.3 Identification of User Requirements and Design Features

In the process of identifying the intermediate scenario, we gathered user values and needs. These were then linked to the Persuasive Systems Design (PSD) and Behavior Change Techniques (BCT) methodologies. Subsequently, focus group interviews were conducted to translate specific user needs into design elements, as outlined in detail in Table 3.

Table 3. User group results with design elements to support smokers change to use e-cigarettes.

User Values	User Needs	Design element (PSDs and/or BCT)
Health	I. Improve long-term health	1. Feedback and monitoring (BCTs) 2. Goals and Planning (BCTs) 3. Shaping knowledge (BCTs) 4. Suggestion (PSDs)
	II. Reduce impact on others	1. Social support (BCTs) 2. Rewards (PSDs)

(continued)

Table 3. (*continued*)

User Values	User Needs	Design element (PSDs and/or BCT)
	III. Help to quit smoking	1. Repetition and substitution (BCTs) 2. Regulation (BCTs) 3. Suggestion (PSDs)
Distinctive	I. Look cool II. Feel different III. Be a minority IV. Be stylish	1. Identity (BCTs) 2. Personalization (PSDs) 3. Social role (PSDs) 4. Competition (PSDs)

A KANO questionnaire, designed to determine which elements should be included in the design, was assessed by members of the Public Group who smoke and by the entire User Group (104 in total). The results are as follows: Feedback and Monitoring (Must have), Social Support (Must have), Personalization (Must have), Goals and Planning (Nice to have), Rewards (Nice to have), and Rewards (Must have). The detailed results can be found in Fig. 2.

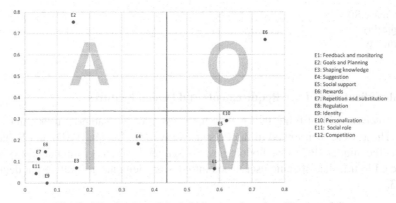

E1: Feedback and monitoring
E2: Goals and Planning
E3: Shaping knowledge
E4: Suggestion
E5: Social support
E6: Rewards
E7: Repetition and substitution
E8: Regulation
E9: Identity
E10: Personalization
E11: Social role
E12: Competition

Fig. 2. Distribution of design elements based on Kano model.

4 Result

The sQuit design solution integrates the five design elements mentioned above, drawing inspiration from sports cars, sports equipment, and other products to shape its styling. This ensures that the product aligns with the conversational needs of users in sports and fitness scenarios.

For the Feedback and Monitoring element, we devised an e-cigarette usage mode that links the allowed usage to the day's exercise. The current remaining amount of usage is then communicated through a light indicator (refer to Fig. 3 for details). This design encourages users to engage in fitness as a substitute for smoking behavior.

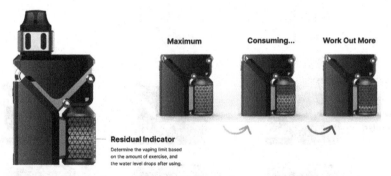

Fig. 3. Light indicator to give feedback on the current remaining capacity.

For the elements of Social Support, Goals and Planning, and Rewards, we integrated them into the product's APP (refer to Fig. 4 for details). The Community module allows users to share their fitness and smoking cessation experiences. The Monitoring Module displays e-cigarette usage, enabling users to set or adjust the capacity. In the Fitness module, users can create fitness plans, and the app provides customized planning suggestions with schedule reminders. The e-pet module gamifies the Rewards element, featuring a customizable pet image and various boosts based on the user's exercise and smoking reduction progress.

Fig. 4. The interface of each functional module of sQuit's mobile APP.

The elements of Personalization, which are reflected in the customization of personal plans and e-pets, the product's V-shaped light is designed to generate light effects with varying colors and intensities based on the user's recent exercise and the type of fitness program. Some examples of which are shown in Fig. 5.

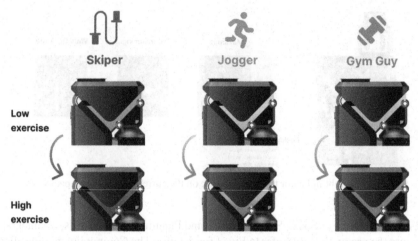

Fig. 5. Produces different lighting effects depending on the fitness of the user.

5   Discussion

This study introduces fitness as an intermediate scenario based on the persuasive design workflow and uses e-cigarettes to promote fitness behavior. We believe that encouraging long-term fitness among e-cigarette users can improve their public image and help reduce negative perceptions. Additionally, exercise can aid e-cigarette smokers in quitting, CLD diagram is shown in Fig. 6. It's crucial to highlight that our focus in selecting intermediate scenario is to promote a healthy lifestyle and sustain motivation. We excluded options with health hazards and prioritized sustainability during the screening process.

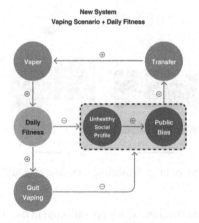

Fig. 6. Analysis of CLD, a new system for introducing fitness as intermediate scenario.

In addition, KANO's findings show that feedback and monitoring, social support, and personalization are essential for users, which may be due to the difficulty of obtaining guidance on smoking cessation in China, or the reluctance of users to seek help due to attitudinal reasons. E-cigarettes, as an emerging product, are more appealing to young people, so the importance of personalization has been increased accordingly.

Considering the widespread and long-term nature of social perception formation, more in-depth and sustained validation is needed to ascertain whether the system is resilient to external risks to demonstrate that the methodological model can have a sustainable impact on public prejudice.

6 Conclusion

In this study, we delved into the obstacles hindering smoker conversion in the Chinese region, particularly in the design and development of controversial products like e-cigarettes. Employing persuasive design and system design methods, we proposed a workflow introducing intermediate scenario to establish a novel smoker conversion system, linking two behaviors: e-cigarette use and daily fitness.

During the design phase, PSD principles and BCT methodology were applied to derive elements transforming e-cigarettes into a medium that stimulates fitness behaviors. The resulting design solution activates the fitness behavior of e-cigarette users through customized lights, electronic pets, and community support. The enhanced user image resulting from fitness engagement aims to diminish public prejudice and counter one-sided reports, thereby overcoming barriers to smoker conversion. Concurrently, it aids light users in achieving smoking cessation.

The introduction of intermediate scenarios offers a fresh perspective on how persuasive design methods can be more effective in contexts marked by subjective bias, improving the existing workflow.

References

1. Jackson, S., Bullen, C.: UK report underscores potential of e-cigarettes to reduce smoking harms. The Lancet **400**(10365), 1747–1750 (2022)
2. Ebrahimi Kalan, M., Brewer, N.T.: Longitudinal transitions in e-cigarette and cigarette use among US adults: prospective cohort study. Lancet Reg. Health - Am. **22**, 100508 (2023)
3. Fogg, B.: A behavior model for persuasive design. In: Proceedings of the 4th International Conference on Persuasive Technology, pp. 1–7. ACM, Claremont (2009)
4. Brown, S.L., Asher, T., Cialdini, R.B.: Evidence of a positive relationship between age and preference for consistency. J. Res. Personal. **39**(5), 517–533 (2005)
5. Halttu, K., Oinas-Kukkonen, H.: Susceptibility to social influence strategies and persuasive system design: exploring the relationship. Behav. Inf. Technol. **41**(12), 2705–2726 (2022)
6. Oinas-Kukkonen, H., Harjumaa, M.: Persuasive systems design: key issues, process model, and system features. Commun. Assoc. Inf. Syst. **24** (2009)
7. Michie, S., et al.: The behavior change technique taxonomy (v1) of 93 hierarchically clustered techniques: building an international consensus for the reporting of behavior change interventions. Ann. Behav. Med. **46**(1), 81–95 (2013)

8. Asbjørnsen, R.A., et al.: Combining persuasive system design principles and behavior change techniques in digital interventions supporting long-term weight loss maintenance: design and development of eCHANGE. JMIR Hum. Factors **9**(2), e37372 (2022)
9. Asbjørnsen, R.A., et al.: Identifying persuasive design principles and behavior change techniques supporting end user values and needs in eHealth interventions for long-term weight loss maintenance: qualitative study. J. Med. Internet Res. **22**(11), e22598 (2020)

A Practical Study of Project-Based Learning in High School General Technology Based on Design Thinking

Chenxi Wang[1]([⊠]), Jiawei Tang[2], and Yuanbo Sun[2]

[1] The High School Affiliated to Beijing Normal University, No.18, Nanxinhua Street, Xicheng District, Beijing, China
Cxw1210652587@163.com

[2] Beijing Institute of Technology, No. 5, Zhongguancun South Street, Haidian District, Beijing, China
yuanbo@bit.edu.cn

Abstract. In the 21st century of rapid technological iteration, technical talents capable of innovative design have become the need of the hour. With the continuous improvement of China's social productivity level, technical education has gradually become an important part of quality education. High school general technology is a basic course for cultivating students' innovative design ability, and for high school education, it is necessary to start from changing students' thinking mode. Design thinking, as a way of thinking and methodology to promote innovative design, is used in the high school general technology classroom, relying on project teaching, which is conducive to the development of problem-based and real-world teaching. Based on Stanford University's "EDIFT" model for instructional design, two rounds of teaching practice were conducted through the action research method to verify the effectiveness of learning. The conclusion of the study hypothesizes that high school general technology project-based learning based on design thinking is conducive to increasing learners' interest in learning, fostering learners' empathy and creativity, cultivating learners' disciplinary core literacy, transforming learners' problem-solving styles, and promoting learners' collaborative learning.

Keywords: Design Thinking · High School General Technology · Project Based Learning

1 Introduction

Design Thinking is originally an innovative way of thinking in the professional field of design, and in the twenty-first century, it has gone beyond the professional field of design and has been widely used in other professional fields, and Design Thinking has been transformed from a professional ability to a basic quality that everyone should have [1]. Technology is the form of accumulation of human material and spiritual wealth, and is an important symbol of the level of social productivity. With the continuous improvement of

© The Author(s), under exclusive license to Springer Nature Switzerland AG 2024
C. Stephanidis et al. (Eds.): HCII 2024, CCIS 2114, pp. 89–94, 2024.
https://doi.org/10.1007/978-3-031-61932-8_11

the level of social productivity in China, technology education has gradually become an important part of quality education. High school general technology is a basic course for cultivating students' innovative design ability, introducing design thinking into the high school general technology course for specific project-based teaching case design, relying on project teaching, is conducive to the development of teaching based on problems and real situations, which not only cultivates the ability of students to apply knowledge to solve practical problems, enhances students' practical ability, innovative thinking, empathy and teamwork ability, but also cultivates the students' disciplinary core literacy.

2   The Relationship Between High School General Technology and Design Thinking Education

The General High School Technology Curriculum Standard (Experimental), which clearly presents technology as one of the eight learning areas [2], puts general technology and information technology alongside subjects such as physics and chemistry, and also serves as a course for the Academic Proficiency Test [3]. From the Ministry of Education's 2017 version of the General Technology Curriculum Standard for General High Schools, it is basically the same as the integrated and project-based teaching concepts, goals and methods of design thinking, which can be used as a reference for innovation in teaching general technology in high schools.

The core literacy of the discipline of general technology is technical awareness, engineering thinking, innovative design, drawing expression and materialization ability. The curriculum standard mentions that "there are two compulsory modules: Technology and Design 1 and Technology and Design 2". The design here mainly refers to the design of technical products, including identifying and clarifying problems, formulating design plans, making models or prototypes, optimizing design plans, writing technical specifications and other design aspects. The basic contents of the two compulsory modules show a progressive relationship......". Although the general technology curriculum standard does not mention design thinking, the curriculum content and requirements of Technology and Design 1 show a basic consistency with design thinking.

The National Technology Education Standards of the United States suggest that design is considered by many to be the solution process at the heart of technology development, and that design is as important to technology as exploration is to science and reading is to language arts. A teaching model centered on design thinking will undoubtedly promote the reform of basic education as well as the advancement of quality education if it can be imported into the teaching of the basic education stage through the present general-purpose technology. Design thinking education with innovative thinking as its basic feature is also in line with the national policy of talent cultivation.

3   Current Problems in the High School Technology Classroom

High school general technology teaching method is single, the traditional teaching mode, students to imitate the production of the main, the lack of design and innovation, practice level is not high, it is difficult to achieve the requirements of in-depth learning.

Many high schools in the process of carrying out general technology, some teachers use old-fashioned teaching content, can not keep pace with the times to innovate teaching activities, many students are passive to accept the teaching. For example, in the process of teaching carpentry, students are repeatedly asked to make Ruban locks, small benches, etc., and the program has not been innovative for many years. In the long run, students lose interest in learning, lose the ability to actively explore and design.

Due to the lack of teachers, insufficient laboratory equipment or class time limitations in high school general technology, most of the courses are carried out by choosing projects that are easier to realize, and even some schools just imitate the real environment of product development, and do not let students really experience the general process of design. Therefore, students' lack of design thinking and design experience limits learners' creativity.

4   A Case Study of Project-Based Teaching of High School General Technology Based on Design Thinking

Design thinking starts with problems and needs, and then uses various means to solve problems and fulfill needs. The five processes of design thinking include empathy, problem definition, conceptualization, prototyping and testing. Through empathy to the user's point of view for demand analysis, through the definition of demand to clarify the problem, through creative conception to find ways to solve the problem, through the production of prototypes to complete the problem-solving model, through the test to optimize the problem, and the above five processes do not exist in isolation, but rather promote each other, iterative process, emphasizing the transferability of the design thinking methodology.

Based on the standard, relying on the textbook, combined with the students' learning situation, we design the project-based teaching cases of the geological version of Technology and Design 1 and Technology and Design 2. The project-based teaching design is based on the five steps of "EDIPT" proposed by Stanford University [4], and takes the smart home as a big project for knowledge teaching and learning.

Empathy - asking questions. The core of design thinking lies in empathy, also known as sympathy or empathy, i.e. starting from the user's needs, putting oneself in the shoes of others, and adhering to a human-centered design starting point. Establishing empathy includes feeling other people's feelings and emotions, experiencing the origin of their words and actions from their attitudes, and recognizing and clarifying their needs and expectations. Specific methods include observing users, interviewing them and experiencing them from their perspective. Students interviewed and observed the target users to find out the specific problems they encountered at home. The case is based on a real-life situation that will stimulate students' interest.

Definition - Clarify the problem. This case clarifies the need to design and create a smart home, but the specific design requirements are not yet clear. We use the method of user journey mapping to analyze the needs of the target user and the problems that need to be solved. The user journey map can observe the user's day-to-day experience at home in an all-round way, and from the user's goals, we can clarify the user's different needs at each stage, so that we can more clearly define the user's experience path and find out where the problem lies. The visualization can be fed back into the design to promote the subsequent design.

Brainstorming - Analyzing Problems.

Brainstorming is a common method of analyzing problems in design thinking. It is based on the principle of unrestricted free association and discussion through the reinforcing effect of stimuli, and is aimed at generating new ideas or stimulating innovative visions. In the stages of clarifying the problem and sketching the appearance of the smart home and the functional design of the smart home, students are able to obtain a large number of ideas by brainstorming and determine the final design solution by comparing the options Table 2x2 Matrix Diagram.

Prototyping - problem solving.

"A million drawings are no match for a prototype". A prototype can be the product itself, or an object made before production that is the same size as the product and uses the same functions. Once the designer enters the prototyping process, many details not considered in the preliminary design will surface one by one, thus prompting the designer in the prototyping process not only to utilize the appropriate medium to express the design concepts in the mind, but also must be done while thinking, to deal with the production of new problems that arise at any time. The form and material of prototyping can be diversified, and the appearance of the smart home can be handmade, cut with a laser cutter, or 3D printed through computer modeling. The functional design of the smart home uses intelligent hardware to complete the hardware construction using graphical programming to realize the functional design.

Testing - Optimizing the Solution.

Testing is a stage that any new product must go through before it is released to the market, because few new products are successful at one time, and most of them are continuously improved during the development of the product in order to achieve final success. Testing is to check whether the product can meet the intended design requirements in terms of structure and technical performance. Smart home testing is based on practicality, safety, innovation, aesthetics, environmental protection, humanization and science. The target users are allowed to evaluate whether the requirements have been met.

In the project-based learning process, breaking the regular schedule arrangement of 45 min in one class and adopting a long class of 135 min in three consecutive sessions, students are encouraged to conduct research and exploration around the smart home project. What students learn from the program is no longer limited to single subject knowledge, but rather the comprehensive ability to collect, process and communicate information when facing real situations and real problems. Students work in mixed groups to complete a complete design project in a collaborative manner. Members of the group take on the roles of project manager, designer and engineer respectively. The project manager is responsible for the coordination and management of the whole project to ensure that the design work is carried out according to the plan, the designer is responsible for the specific design work, including sketch design, program design, effect drawing production, etc., and the engineer is responsible for transforming the design into actual models or prototypes and solving problems in the production. Let students start from the perspective of different functions, so that students become the initiative of learning. Thus better solving the current problems in the technical classroom.

5 Evaluation Methods for Project-Based Instructional Case Design

The research hypotheses (1) high school general technology project-based learning based on design thinking is conducive to increasing learners' interest in learning; (2) high school general technology project-based learning based on design thinking can cultivate learners' empathy and creativity; (3) high school general technology project-based learning based on design thinking can cultivate learners' disciplinary core literacy; (4) high school general technology project-based learning is conducive to transforming learners' problem-solving styles and promoting learners' collaborative learning.

The learning effect of project-based learning is evaluated through two rounds of teaching practice, as shown in Fig. 1. Firstly, the first teaching practice is carried out according to the smart home project-based teaching case, and the second teaching practice is carried out by revising and improving the project-based teaching case according

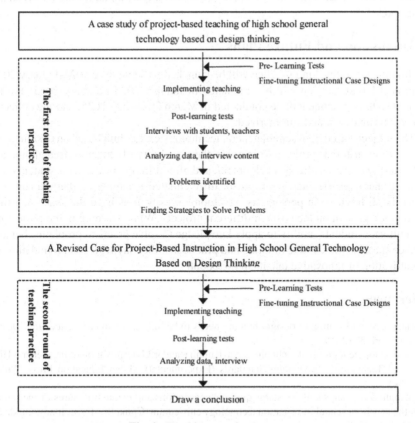

Fig. 1. Teaching practice process

to the first teaching effect. In the process of each practice, we record the students' classroom performance, activity forms, etc., and then analyze and summarize the practice effect by combining with the interviews with some students.

The process of the first round of teaching practice: (1) Pre-learning test for the students of senior X class, detailed understanding of the students' learning situation, and fine-tuning of the teaching design; (2) Implementation of the teaching, in the process of implementation of the teaching, timely record of students' performance, students' difficulties and their solutions to the difficulties that can't be solved; (3)Post-learning test for the students of senior X class, and draw 10 students at different levels for reading visits; (4) Conduct a post-study test questionnaire and interviews with 10 students in senior X class; (5) Analyze the problems in this teaching implementation based on data analysis and own previous records, and put forward solution strategies for the problems.

The process of the second round of teaching practice: (1) Pre-testing the learning of students in senior Y class, detailed to understand the students' learning situation, fine-tuning the teaching design;(2) Implementing the teaching, in the process of implementing the teaching, timely record of the students' performance, the students' difficulties as well as the students' solutions to the difficulties that can't be solved; (3) Post-testing the learning of the students in senior Y class; (4) Post-test questionnaires are analyzed and organized.

6   Discussion and Future Plans

The first theory of teaching practice will be launched in September 2024-January 2025, the project-based revision will be conducted in January 2025-February 2025, and the second teaching practice will be conducted in March 2025-July 2025, and the collected data will be analyzed and summarized.

The project-based high school general technology curriculum based on design thinking can offer different projects to increase the possibility of students' free choice and the flexibility of personalized development, and offer different projects for students with different characteristics and interests for differentiated teaching, so that students can reflect the differences in personality development as well as have the space and time for common growth on the basis of different projects. While learning in the project not only cultivate students' ability to apply knowledge to solve practical problems, but also enhance students' innovative thinking and practical ability, laying a good foundation for the cultivation of innovative talents in the country.

References

1. Yuanbo, S.: Cultivation of design thinking needs to be introduced in basic education. Design **32**(18), 55–57 (2019)
2. The development group of technology curriculum standard:Interpretation of the General High School Technology Curriculum Standards (Experimental). Hubei Education Press, Wuhan (2004)
3. Quanjun, Z.: Analysis of the status quo, misconceptions and countermeasures of the reform of the new high school information technology curriculum. China Sci. Educ. Innov. Guide **36**, 140–272 (2010)
4. Plattner, H.: Bootcamp Bootleg. Institute of Design at Stanford, San Francisco, CA (2010)

On the Influence and Application of Regional Culture in Interaction Design

Yichen Wu[✉] and Ruoyuan Liao[✉]

School of Industrial Design, China Academy of Art, Hangzhou, People's Republic of China
Liaoruoyuan1@outlook.com

Abstract. In the era of smart media, people are deeply immersed in extensive interactions and information exposure daily, and regional differences play a crucial role in shaping aesthetic preferences and interaction tendencies. These regional differences are formed by the influence of mainstream cultures in various areas, giving rise to unique cultural elements for individuals, where regional culture holds a significant position. This article delves into the application of regional culture in interaction design, exploring the collaborative innovation between regional culture and interaction design in the era of smart media.

Keywords: Interaction design · Culture · Sensory

1 Regional Culture and Interaction Design

Regional culture encompasses the historical remnants, cultural forms, customs, and ways of life formed within a specific geographical area. It possesses permeability and inclusiveness, as interactions among people from different regions lead to the mutual permeation and influence of cultural customs. Both material and spiritual aspects of regional elements exhibit characteristics derived from the natural and human environments, including traditional cultural customs and scenic features specific to certain areas, passed down through generations. Regional elements also cover customs, traditions, and beliefs unique to specific regions, showcasing the profound cultural heritage and characteristics of regional cultures.

Cultural experts in anthropology have long recognized the strong correlation between cultural elements and individual behaviors. In the book "Riding the Waves of Culture: Understanding Cultural Diversity in Business" published in 1998, Trompenaars and Hampden-Turner identified cultural differences among managers from various cultures based on seven cultural dimensions.

Hofstede's five cultural dimensions, including power distance, uncertainty avoidance, masculinity-femininity, individualism-collectivism, and time orientation, are widely known in defining cultural differences. These dimensions, derived from Hofstede's global research, directly relate to the behavioral habits of people in different regions.

© The Author(s), under exclusive license to Springer Nature Switzerland AG 2024
C. Stephanidis et al. (Eds.): HCII 2024, CCIS 2114, pp. 95–101, 2024.
https://doi.org/10.1007/978-3-031-61932-8_12

All the mentioned information highlights the strong correlation between culture and behavior. In the realm of interaction design, understanding users' habitual behavior directly influences the design process and outcomes. Integrating regional culture into interaction design helps reduce participation barriers, making it easier for users to resonate and enhancing overall user experience.

Interaction design aims to establish connections between consumers and services by defining communication content and information, facilitating mutual integration to achieve specific goals. This design philosophy particularly emphasizes consumer experience.

Incorporating regional cultural attributes into interaction design not only fosters the formation of online communities but also injects unique cultural identity into brands, adding a human touch. This synergy provides extensive opportunities for innovation in the field of interaction design, enhancing product competitiveness by customizing designs to meet users' cultural needs.

2 Sensory-Driven Regionalized Interaction Design Considerations

As mentioned earlier, due to cultural differences, people in different regions have distinct lifestyles and diverse aesthetic tendencies. This creates regional attributes in users' information and experience needs, as well as the objectives designers aim to achieve. However, there is currently no systematic solution on how to effectively integrate regional culture into interaction design.

Interaction design, originating in the 1970s with the development of computer technology, particularly graphical user interfaces, gained theoretical foundations from Don Norman's work "The Design of Everyday Things". With the rise of the internet and web technologies in the 1990s to the early 2000s, interaction design evolved. The proliferation of mobile devices introduced new directions, and designers began focusing on mobile user experience. Emerging technologies like social media and virtual reality also became part of the design domain.

Analysis of the essence of interaction design reveals its strong connection to human senses, particularly vision, hearing, and touch. These senses are influenced by regional culture, making them vital links between regional culture and interaction design.

Vision: In interaction design, vision is crucial, as the majority of human information is perceived visually. Designers guide users' attention by creating visually appealing interfaces, color combinations, and graphic elements. Cultural influences in vision design affect people's preferences for colors, patterns, and layout, causing users from different cultural backgrounds to perceive and react differently to the same design elements.

Hearing: Auditory elements in interaction design play roles in guidance, prompts, and communication. Sound feedback provides information about the interface's status, such as successful operations or warning signals for errors. Cultural influences on hearing, including music, voice, and sound effects, may vary across regions. Skillful use of auditory elements enhances the richness and vividness of user experiences, and cultural considerations can lead to different selections of music, voice, and sound effects.

Touch: Touch is a direct way for people to interact with products, feeling textures, shapes, and temperatures. In interaction design, tactile experiences aim to establish a more intimate connection between users and products. Preferences for product materials and acceptance of tactile feedback may differ among users from different regions. Considering the influence of regional culture on tactile experiences in design can better cater to user preferences.

Notable successful cases in combining sensory experiences with interaction design, such as TeamLab's multi-sensory immersive art exhibition, emphasize creativity, exploration of life cycles, and the relationship between humans and nature. These cases demonstrate that the integration of senses is not isolated but interwoven, creating a synergistic effect. Understanding regional culture allows for the consideration of "synesthesia", significantly enhancing the acceptance threshold and user satisfaction of interactive behaviors (Fig. 1).

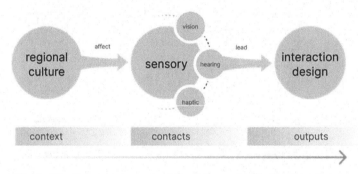

Fig. 1. The flowchart for territorialized interaction design from the senses

Since human behaviors, influenced by regional culture, are strongly associated with the five senses, combining regional culture and interaction design based on sensory behaviors seems to be a viable approach. Through a comprehensive consideration of vision, hearing, and touch, interaction design can be more holistic and aligned with user needs. Cultural sensitivity in the design process is crucial, and successful interaction design should incorporate and respect the unique features of different regional cultures, creating a more attractive and resonant user experience.

3   Possibilities of Regionally Specialized Interaction Design Through Sensory Experiences

Through an in-depth analysis of regional culture and interactive design, we have found that integrating regional characteristics with interaction through sensory connection is feasible. Initially, we need to start from the attributes of regional culture, analyzing different sensory experiences and behavioral characteristics, and then combine corresponding sensory needs for interactive design. To validate the feasibility of this methodological approach, we conducted a specific case experiment.

We opted to design a portable Bluetooth speaker imbued with Jiangsu and Zhejiang cultural attributes as an experiment. Music serves as a form of social behavior, enabling people to exchange emotions and life experiences. The primary purpose of music is to express emotions and provide aesthetic enjoyment, which is also the essence of the existence of audio equipment. After conducting research, we chose the cultural motif of "windows", commonly found in Jiangnan gardens. These latticed windows are mostly set on the interior walls of gardens, often used in corridors and semi-transparent courtyards. Through these windows, the scenery seems to be divided yet also revealed, with dappled light and shadow, visible yet not easily reachable. As visitors move, the scenery changes accordingly, infusing vitality and fluidity into otherwise mundane walls. The patterns of these lattice windows are diverse, each forming a three-dimensional picture, with intricate details offering great beauty and allure (Figs. 2 and 3).

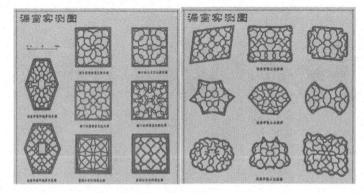

Fig. 2. Measured view of a leaky window in a Suzhou garden, from Suzhou Classical Gardens

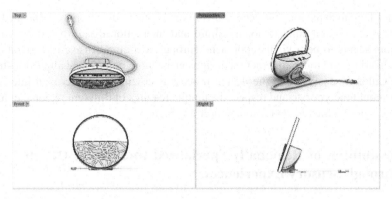

Fig. 3. Jiangnan culture combined with bluetooth speaker

Starting from the characteristics of lattice windows, we discovered that in Jiangsu and Zhejiang culture, windows are not merely architectural elements for ventilation and lighting but are more akin to viewfinders visually. Windows serve as the visual subject, while audio equipment serves as the auditory subject. Within the cultural context, windows carry scenery, corresponding to the "painting" in Eastern culture, while music carries emotions, corresponding to the "poetry" in Eastern culture. Combining the two creates a "scenario". Therefore, in designing this speaker, we integrated the hollow design of classical lattice windows visually. Through the combination of grids and lighting effects, we attempted to recreate abstract "window" scenes in sound. Regarding hearing, the lighting effects change along with the music, symbolizing the end of a piece, thus achieving synesthetic effects. For tactile sensation, we chose a combination of materials resembling ceramic frosted plastic and metal, creating a rustic yet stylish sensation. Starting from the senses, we successfully integrated Jiangsu and Zhejiang culture into the interactive design of the speaker. Through "synesthesia" and the meaning bestowed by culture, users can relive the sentiments of ancient times, simultaneously enjoying the dual beauty of visual and auditory senses (Figs. 4 and 5).

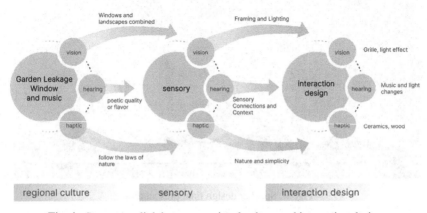

Fig. 4. Senses as a link between regional culture and interaction design

In the experimental design of combining Jiangsu and Zhejiang culture with portable speakers, we attempted to create an interactive experience that aligns with local aesthetics and habits through sensory integration. This experimental design proves the feasibility of regional-specific interactive design through sensory perception. This design approach not only provides users with customized cultural products but also opens up new possibilities for the integration of regional culture and interactive design.

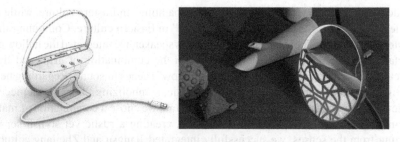

Fig. 5. Speaker design final presentation

4 Conclusion

In the era of smart media, our daily lives are immersed in extensive interactions and information exposure. This digitized social life not only connects us but also highlights the crucial role of regional differences in individual aesthetic preferences and interaction tendencies. These differences stem from the profound influence of mainstream cultures in various regions, forming unique cultural elements where regional culture holds a significant position.

Interaction design, rooted in users' behaviors and focusing on their five senses, is deeply influenced by regional culture, making sensory-driven regionalized interaction design a feasible path. Through an in-depth exploration of the application of regional culture in interaction design, the article uncovers the collaborative innovation potential between regional culture and interaction design in the era of smart media. Regional culture serves not only as a carrier of social heritage but also as a treasury of inspiration and direction for design.

In the current landscape of highly integrated artificial intelligence and traditional media, we believe that the infusion of regional cultural factors will not only enhance the artistic aspect of interaction design but also promote cultural dissemination, foster cultural confidence, and strengthen the cultural and creative industries. The integration of regional cultures provides new avenues for innovation in interaction design, initiating a positive feedback loop. The catalytic effect of culture transitions products from mere functionality to intelligent solutions. The collaborative innovation of sensory-driven regional culture and interaction design in the era of smart media points to a dynamic direction for future design.

References

1. Hofstede, G., Hofstede, G.J., Minkov, M.: Cultures and Organizations: Software of the Mind, 3rd edn. McGraw-Hill, New York (2010)
2. Xiaoying, T., Yihui, C., Yinghe, X., Hanwei, S., Jiaqi, X., Junxian, L.: Research on embodied interaction design of virtual reality landscape spaces for touring spring. Pack. Eng. (24), 297–307+327 (2023). https://doi.org/10.19554/j.cnki.1001-3563.2023.24.032
3. Huan, Q.: Regional expression in the design of tourist cultural and creative products. Pack. Eng. **02**, 306–309 (2022). https://doi.org/10.19554/j.cnki.1001-3563.2022.02.040
4. Jingyan, Q.: Information dimensions and principles of interaction design. Pack. Eng. **16**, 57–68 (2018). https://doi.org/10.19554/j.cnki.1001-3563.2018.16.010
5. Fenko, A., Schifferstein, H.N.J., Hekkert, P.: Shifts in sensory dominance between various stages of user-product interactions. Appl. Ergon. **41**(1), 34–40 (2010). https://doi.org/10.1016/j.apergo.2009.03.007
6. Kewei, L.: Multisensory interaction narrative space design—research and practice of information interaction design courses in art and technology. Pack. Eng. (S1), 625–629+650 (2023). https://doi.org/10.19554/j.cnki.1001-3563. 2023.S1.094
7. Hao, X.: Image History of Jiangsu Gardens (2016)
8. Dunzhen, L.: Classical Gardens of Suzhou (2005)
9. Du, J., Li, Y.: G-Tunes – physical interaction design of playing music. In: Jacko, J.A. (ed.) HCI 2007. LNCS, vol. 4552, pp. 846–851. Springer, Heidelberg (2007). https://doi.org/10.1007/978-3-540-73110-8_93

Supporting Parent-Child Interactions in Child Riding: Exploring Design Opportunities for Digital Interaction Strategies

Qichen Zhan, Ziying Yao(✉), and Lili Guo

College of Mechanical Engineering, Donghua University, Shanghai, China
baroncr7@163.com

Abstract. Digital interaction plays a crucial role in enhancing parent-child interactions. Existing research in Human-Computer Interaction (HCI) has explored how digital interactions enhance parent-child interactions in several settings [1]. However, there is limited understanding of the mechanism and design intervention strategies for enhancing parent-child interactions in child riding setting, especially leveraging digital interaction approaches. Child riding is a significant setting for parent-child interactions [2]. This study aims to explore the following research question: How do digital interaction approaches facilitate parent-child interactions in children's riding process? Methodologically, we conducted semi-structured interviews with the parents with children aged 2–8 years old to identify the interactions during riding process [3]. We analyzed the data using thematic analysis in an iterative, inductive manner. The research findings involve two parts. First, we identified parent-child interaction patterns in child riding and derived a series of insights [4]. Secondly, we explored design opportunities for digitized interaction interventions in child riding, providing a set of design intervention strategies to enhance parent-child interactions in this setting. This study contributes new insights to understanding (1) digitized interaction approaches in child riding settings and (2) digital interaction strategies to enhance parent-child interaction.

Keywords: parent-child interaction · digital interaction · child riding · semi-structured interview · design intervention strategy

1 Introduction

Parent-child interaction refers to the reciprocal communication and social exchange between children and their parents. Parent-child interaction plays a key role in child's emotional development and the cultivation of social skills. Digital interaction plays a key role in promoting virtuous parent-child interactions. Existing research in the field of Human Computer Interactions (HCI) revealed approaches for promoting parent child interactions through digital interactions in a variety of setting [5], including online education, gaming, and place making. However, investigations in child riding settings remains limited [3]. There is limited knowledge about the patterns of parent-child interactions and the design intervention strategies for enhancing it, especially leveraging digital interaction approaches.

© The Author(s), under exclusive license to Springer Nature Switzerland AG 2024
C. Stephanidis et al. (Eds.): HCII 2024, CCIS 2114, pp. 102–111, 2024.
https://doi.org/10.1007/978-3-031-61932-8_13

Child riding is a setting where parent-child interactions frequently occur [6]. Child riding refers to the activity where a child operates and rides a balance bike, a bicycle or similar vehicle, often for recreation, exercise, or transportation. In this setting, parent-child interactions aids in improving a child's learning efficiency and riding safety, creating enriched riding experience. For example, In the early stages of children learning to ride, parents often provide frequent real-time, on-site guidance; the child's feedback in turn helps parents adjust their teaching strategies.

Although parent-child interactions frequently occur in the context of child riding, existing research has not yet sufficiently discussed how to support the positive development of parent-child interaction through digital interaction strategies [7]. This study aims to explore the following research question: How does digital interaction approaches facilitate parent-child interactions in children's riding process?

2 Related Works

2.1 Parent-Child Interactions in Child Riding

With the development of society, there is an increasing emphasis on children's health and social interactions. Simultaneously, as riding environments improved and riding products continue to upgrade, children's riding activities are becoming increasingly popular. This trend has propelled research related to children's riding, spanning across various fields such as safety, education, and cognition [4].

Riding activities not only provide excellent social opportunities but also serve as significant family activities that promote parent-child communication. Studies on parent-child interactions suggest that positive parent-child communication and emotional exchanges are crucial for children's development. Riding activities provide a platform for parents and children to communicate, helping parents understand their children's needs and interests, enhancing mutual understanding and trust between them, and strengthening family cohesion [2]. During riding, parents and children can engage in friendly interactions through teaching skills, planning activities together, sharing experiences, and creating memories, thus indicating promising prospects for further research into parent-child interactions patterns during children's riding experiences.

2.2 Digital Interaction

Digital interaction refers to the process of communication, interaction, and collaboration facilitated by digital technology. Its applications span across various fields including personal life, business, education, healthcare, and more. Digital social platforms and online communication tools have broken the barriers of time, space, and geography, fostering global communication and collaboration. In the realm of social interaction, Fernando Cesar Balbino et al. have redefined digital social networks, making knowledge sharing more natural and convenient within social networks [8]. In the realm of experiential interaction, Virtual Reality (VR) and Augmented Reality (AR) allow users to enter virtual worlds, experiencing immersive digital interactions. Thomas Mejtoft et al. (2023) have improved digital social interaction during fitness activities by studying the application of AR in mobile fitness apps [9].

Existing work reveals the significance of digital interaction in shaping human communication and collaboration. Digital interaction facilitates more convenient, flexible, and enriched forms of communication and collaboration, also bringing new possibilities for parent-child interactions. For instance, Eunkyung Jo et al. have designed the meal-assisting application MAMAS to facilitate mealtime interaction between parents and children, promoting healthy eating habits for children [10]. Mileys, a car game developed by Guy Hoffman et al., integrates location-based information, AR, and virtual characters, enhancing the in-car experience for parents and children, strengthening family bonds and interaction. These efforts suggest that digital interaction can provide more ways and experiences for parent-child interactions during the process of children's growth [11].

Although research has elucidated how digital interaction supports parent-child interactions, fewer scholars have focused on the realm of children's riding. This paper further explores how to leverage digital technology to facilitate parent-child interactions during riding, allowing parents and children to share the joy of riding and strengthen communication, collaboration, and mutual growth.

3   Methods

3.1   Data Collection

This study adopted qualitative research methods [12] and employed semi-structured in-depth interviews to address two research objectives: (i) explore the patterns of parent-child interactions in child riding setting, and (ii) propose design strategies that leveraging digital interaction to facilitate parent-child interactions.

Through exploring the genuine feelings and behaviors of parents and children during the riding process, we aim to understand and identify the patterns of parent-child interactions inherent in the riding setting. Furthermore, we propose design opportunities for digital interaction interventions to enhance parent-child interactions [13].

Our study focuses on families with children aged 2 to 8 years old. These children are all in good health, without any detectable diseases, and have had riding experiences that led to parent-child interactions. These settings help to concentrate our research specifically on children's riding activities. To ensure the diversity and representativeness of our research findings, we recruited ten interviewees from different regions, with varied educational backgrounds, and socio-economic statuses. These participants were labeled P1 to P10, with the numbering ordered according to the date of the interviews. Two of the interviewees are experts engaged in the field of children's transportation, with extensive experience in parent-child riding; the other participants' children have had experiences with balance bikes, bicycles, or both.

The interviews were progressively conducted in February 2024. Due to constraints in time and space, semi-structured interviews were carried out online via Tencent Meeting. Each interview lasted between 30 to 60 min. The online interviews were proceeded with the consent of the interviewees, who agreed to the recording of all dialogues. Participants were fully informed about the research activities. In accordance with the confidentiality agreement, anonymity was maintained for the project and its participants.

The interview content is divided into two parts. The first part aims to elicit the interviewees' views and interpretations of specific events, stories, and emotional experiences in the context of parent-child interactions during children's riding activities. The second part involves digital interaction, intending to understand the pain points in the interaction methods of parents during the riding process, as well as their expectations and visions for the intervention of digital interaction technologies.

3.2 Data Analysis

Data analysis was conducted in two rounds. In the first round of analysis, data were examined and extracted through the theoretical lens of Staged Authenticity, resulting in a wealth of quotes and narratives to express the true interpretation of parent-child interactions during the riding process. During the second round of analysis, the data was coded based on thematic analysis. These data underwent traditional qualitative content analysis [12], a standard and systematic method for interpreting the content and contextual meanings of text data. Our analysis followed the procedures detailed by Hsieh and Shannon [14]; data was selected from the text and clustered into a hierarchical categorization to formulate our findings concerning our research objectives. We now present and discuss these empirical results in two separate sections to achieve our research objectives: (1) digitized interaction approaches in the child-riding setting and (2) digital interaction strategies to enhance parent-child interactions.

4 Finding

The findings of this study involve parent-child interaction patterns during child riding processes (as shown in Fig. 1). We identified two aggregate dimensions: Supportive Interaction and Non-positive Interaction [15]. Through coding, we formed several second-order themes by combining professional terminologies. We found that supportive interaction patterns mainly consist of four patterns: Participatory Support, Emotional Support, Instructional Support, and Material Support [16]. Meanwhile, Non-positive Interaction primarily comprises two themes: Excessive Intervention and Lack of Affection. In this section, we will describe and discuss each of these themes separately.

4.1 Participatory Support

Participatory support is a positive form of communication and interaction, which core lies in cooperation, sharing, and mutual growth. Different from the simple information transmission, participatory support encourages both parties to actively engage in exploring, learning, and discovering new insights, skills, or experiences together [17]. This interaction can establish positive, cooperative, and creative patterns of interaction in interpersonal relationships, promoting the development and progress of individuals and groups.

In parent-child riding interactions, participatory support takes on various forms. Firstly, there is joint riding. As P1 shared, "I prefer riding with my child. During this process, I can tell him how to control the direction of riding, how to observe the riding

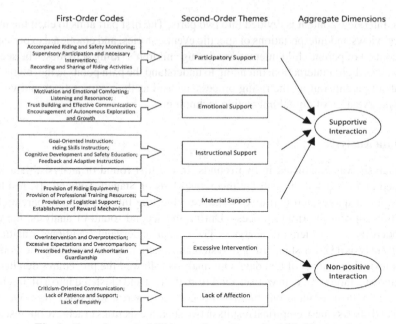

Fig. 1. General parent-child interaction patterns in child riding settings.

environment, and I can share my skills with him in real-time." This joint riding not only allows parents and children to face complex riding environments together but also enables parents to impart riding skills and provide safety education in real-time. Secondly, there is documenting. P5 said, "Since my child was born, I've been using photos and videos to document his growth. These will be the most precious memories." Through documenting, parents can prolong the experiences and emotions shared with their children, free from time constraints to a certain extent. P6 stated, "I prioritize nurturing my child's self-awareness. I want him to think deeply and make decisions independently, so most of the time, I just observe. I only intervene during special occasions." This supervisory participation allows children to have more autonomy and facilitates their rapid growth.

Parents engage in their children's riding activities through various means, fostering positive interactions between both parties and positively impacting the growth of both parents and children. This interaction not only strengthens family relationships but also provides excellent support and guidance for children's development.

4.2 Emotional Support

Emotional support refers to a form of communication in interpersonal interactions that spiritual support and understanding each other, including but not limited to listening, encouraging, affirming, and so on [4]. Through emotional support, individuals can establish relationships of mutual trust, understanding, and support, thereby enhancing psychological well-being and happiness.

In interviews with multiple respondents, some common themes emerged regarding coping with negative emotions during children's riding, fostering safety awareness, and providing encouragement and guidance during the learning process. As P2 stated, "When my child faces negative emotions during riding, such as frustration or disappointment, I choose to communicate with him, hoping that this approach will help him calm down or take a break to distract his attention." This communication method demonstrates understanding and care, helping to alleviate the child's negative emotions. P7 remarked, "When going out, I prefer to complete plans with my child and discuss our activities together rather than simply informing him." Through communication and interaction in jointly planning riding trips, parents can encourage children to explore and grow independently.

As another interviewee, P3, mentioned,"I believe that more encouragement and patient companionship can help him grow." This kind of encouragement and patient companionship helps children build confidence and a positive attitude. In summary, parents' emphasis on emotional guidance, trust building, and other aspects during their children's riding demonstrates spiritual and emotional support, particularly evident in encouraging comfort, positive guidance, and jointly setting goals. The emotional support contributes to children's healthy growth and development.

4.3 Instructional Support

Instructional Support refers to providing support and resources that aid individual learning and growth. In this regard, families play a crucial role as they are the earliest educators for children [18]. Apart from offering emotional support, families also provide children with a learning environment and emotional motivation, encouraging them to be brave in learning and exploring.

P8 mentioned, "Every time my child and I go riding, we set a goal, establish clear time limits or locations. This helps him quickly set goals and execute them." This goal-oriented education emphasizes the systematic nature of learning, enabling children to establish clear directions in the learning process.

P4 stated, "I cultivate riding as my child's interest. When participating in competitions, I care more about his safety than his ranking. I often emphasize phrases like 'safety first' to him." Several interviewees mentioned safety education, demonstrating parents' emphasis on their children's safety.

P10 said, "I regularly communicate with the coach and, based on my child's feedback, develop his learning plan. This helps clarify my child's needs and abilities, providing targeted assistance to improve his riding skills." In the educational process, timely and effective feedback enables coaches to implement personalized teaching better, inspiring children's interest and motivation to learn, thus promoting each child's maximum development [3].

Parents' guide their children's riding activities through various instructional methods, creating a more flexible, interactive, and personalized learning environment for them. This contributes to promoting children's comprehensive development and cultivating their lifelong learning abilities.

4.4 Material Support

Material support refers to the act of providing material resources or financial assistance to meet specific needs or promote particular activities. In parent-child riding interactions, material support is quite common.

P9 mentioned, "I bought my child his first bike as a birthday present and also purchased some protective gear. Safety is paramount." This behavior of purchasing riding equipment and protective gear to ensure the child's safety is also common among parents. Additionally, some respondents emphasized the importance of professional training and learning environments. P3 said, "I believe enrolling my child in professional riding courses was one of the best decisions I made. He can receive professional guidance and instruction at specialized facilities, while also meeting like-minded partners. The coach and I can collaborate to decide on equipment, courses, growth objectives, and so on. This environment is highly beneficial for my child's development." P2 stated, "Children often get engrossed in riding and easily overlook their physical condition. I need to remind him frequently to wear protective gear, stay hydrated, etc." As parents, they often worry about their child's health and always strive to provide timely support to ensure their well-being. P8 remarked, "My child and I often indulge in some activities after riding, like having an ice cream cone or buying a toy. This method makes him look forward to riding every time." Establishing this reward mechanism can enhance the child's interest in riding and maintain a positive attitude towards learning and activities. The material support provided by parents not only satisfies the child's basic needs such as food, medical health, etc., but also offers excellent educational resources to promote the child's learning and growth.

4.5 Non-positive Supports

During riding, the interaction between parents and children is not always positive and willingly accepted by both parties. Sometimes, non-positive interactions may occur, mainly reflected in excessive intervention and Lack of Affection. Parents may excessively intervene and protect their children during riding due to excessive worry, anxiety, or desire for control [16]. However, such intervention may not truly meet the child's needs and may not be reasonable. Additionally, some parents may set excessively strict goals or growth paths for their children, leading to non-positive reactions when deviations from these goals or paths occur. This kind of intervention may have a negative impact on the child's growth and autonomy.

Regarding Lack of Affection, parents should first examine whether they exhibit behaviors such as impatience or lack of support. Additionally, some parents may lack awareness of their children's emotional needs, making it difficult for them to meet their children's genuine needs [19]. For example, the attention parents provides may not match what the child expects, or parents may lack sensitivity to their child's emotional changes.

In conclusion, these typical non-positive interactions can have a negative impact on the child's riding activities. Therefore, it is necessary for us to examine these non-positive interactions and strive to improve the way we interact with our children to ensure the smooth progress of their riding activities [20].

5 Concluding Remarks

Based on in-depth interviews, this study identified parent-child interaction patterns in child riding setting. These patterns include: Participatory Support, Emotional Support, Instructional Support, and Material Support. Building upon these patterns, the paper proposes a series of design opportunities for digital interaction in children's riding and offers a set of intervention strategies to enhance parent-child interaction within this context.

5.1 Design Opportunities and Strategies

Firstly, compared to adults, children's emotional expressions are often more straightforward, with their facial expressions typically reflecting their feelings and states accurately. In current riding scenarios, parents may not always be able to promptly capture their child's emotional changes due to physical constraints such as distance and speed. Moreover, due to limited understanding of child psychology and education among parents, they may not always interpret their child's emotions well or respond appropriately. By integrating digital interactive technology, utilizing methods like cameras and emotion recognition algorithms [8], real-time recording and recognition of a child's emotional state can be achieved, providing timely feedback to parents, which greatly benefits parent-child interaction.

Secondly, children's movements and the posture of the ride are closely related to the child's riding status, reflecting their level of physical activity and directly impacting riding safety. Through digital interactive technology, capturing a child's movements, monitoring ride posture, and conducting data collection and analysis can provide insights into the child's riding status. Utilizing these scientific means not only enhances the safety of children's riding but also offers opportunities for improving their riding skills. Digital interactive tools make education and parent-child interaction more tangible, effectively optimizing the parent-child interaction process in children's riding scenarios.

5.2 Contribution to HCI Research

This paper contributes to the understanding of digital interaction methods in child riding settings. While there are numerous studies on digital applications for children, such as reading books and playing games [21], the discussion on digital interactive applications in children's riding scenarios has been largely overlooked. Our research focuses on this gap and makes contributions to this area. Based on the discovered parent-child interaction patterns in child riding settings, this study provides two digital interaction design strategies in children's riding environments, effectively enhancing parent-child interaction during the process. It enriches the potential applications of digital interaction technology in children's riding scenarios and fills the gap in human-computer interaction in this direction.

5.3 Limitations and Implications for Future Research

While the study has provided an abundance of detailed and lively contextual information crucial for responding to our research questions, it is important to acknowledge that there are also several limitations to the research that was undertaken.

First, this study solely relied on interview data collection methods. The researchers did not incorporate observational methods, and they did not directly participate in riding activities, thus lacking triangulation of data. This may result in a lack of support for the validity of the conclusions. To enhance the generalizability and credibility of the research findings, subsequent studies should include a wider range of data types and conduct cross-validation.

Second, as an exploratory study, we did not establish specific hypotheses. We encourage future researchers to propose more design strategies and develop prototypes related to digital interactive technology interventions based on the findings of this study, and then validate and test them in future research.

References

Jung, H., Stolterman, E.: Digital form and materiality: propositions for a new approach to interaction design research. In: Proceedings of the 7th Nordic Conference on Human-Computer Interaction: Making Sense Through Design (NordiCHI '12). Association for Computing Machinery, New York, NY, USA, pp. 645–654 (2012). https://doi.org/10.1145/2399016.2399115

Lindberg, S., Wärnestål, P., Nygren, J., Svedberg, P.: Designing digital peer support for children: design patterns for social interaction. In: Proceedings of the 2014 Conference on Interaction Design and Children (IDC '14). Association for Computing Machinery, New York, NY, USA, pp. 47–56 (2014). https://doi.org/10.1145/2593968.2593972

Sadka, O., Erel, H., Grishko, A., Zuckerman, O.: Tangible interaction in parent-child collaboration: encouraging awareness and reflection. In Proceedings of the 17th ACM Conference on Interaction Design and Children (IDC '18). Association for Computing Machinery, New York, NY, USA, pp. 157–169 (2018). https://doi.org/10.1145/3202185.3202746

Sadka, O., Zuckerman, O.: From parents to mentors: parent-child interaction in co-making activities. In: Proceedings of the 2017 Conference on Interaction Design and Children (IDC '17). Association for Computing Machinery, New York, NY, USA, pp. 609–615 (2017). https://doi.org/10.1145/3078072.3084332

Jones, C., McIver, L., Gibson, L., Gregor, P.: Experiences obtained from designing with children. In: Proceedings of the 2003 Conference on Interaction Design and Children (IDC '03). Association for Computing Machinery, New York, NY, USA, pp. 69–74 (2003). https://doi.org/10.1145/953536.953547

Toombs, A.L., Morrissey, K., Simpson, E., Gray, C.M., Vines, J., Balaam, M.: Supporting the complex social lives of new parents. In: Proceedings of the 2018 CHI Conference on Human Factors in Computing Systems (CHI '18). Association for Computing Machinery, New York, NY, USA, Paper 420, pp. 1–13 (2018). https://doi.org/10.1145/3173574.3173994

Garg, R.: Its Changes so Often: parental non-/use of mobile devices while caring for infants and toddlers at home. Proc. ACM Hum.-Comput. Interact. 5, 1–26 (2021). https://doi.org/10.1145/3479513

Balbino, F.C., Anacleto, J.C.: Improving users communication to promote the organicity of online social networks. In: Proceedings of the 28th ACM International Conference on Design of Communication (SIGDOC '10). Association for Computing Machinery, New York, NY, USA, p. 261 (2010). https://doi.org/10.1145/1878450.1878499

Mejtoft, T., Lindahl, H., Norberg, O., Andersson, M., Söderström, U.: Enhancing digital social interaction using augmented reality in mobile fitness applications. In: Proceedings of the 2023 5th International Conference on Image, Video and Signal Processing (IVSP '23). Association for Computing Machinery, New York, NY, USA, pp. 95–100 (2023). https://doi.org/10.1145/3591156.3591170

Jo, E., Bang, H., Ryu, M., Sung, E.J., Leem, S., Hong, H.: MAMAS: supporting parent--child mealtime interactions using automated tracking and speech Recognition. Proc. ACM Hum.-Comput. Interact. 4, 1–32 (2020). https://doi.org/10.1145/3392876

Hoffman, G., Gal-Oz, A., David, S., Zuckerman, O.: In-car game design for children: child vs. parent perspective. In: Proceedings of the 12th International Conference on Interaction Design and Children (IDC '13). Association for Computing Machinery, New York, NY, USA, pp. 112–119 (2013). https://doi.org/10.1145/2485760.2485768

Sandelowski, M.: Using qualitative research. Qual. Health Res. 14(10), 1366–1386 (2016). https://doi.org/10.1177/1049732304269672

Vinayagamoorthy, V., Brogni, A., Steed, A., Slater, M.: The role of posture in the communication of affect in an immersive virtual environment. In: Proceedings of the 2006 ACM International Conference on Virtual Reality Continuum and Its Applications (VRCIA '06). Association for Computing Machinery, New York, NY, USA, pp. 229–236 (2006). https://doi.org/10.1145/1128923.1128961

Hsieh, H.-F., Shannon, S.E.: Three approaches to qualitative content analysis. Qual. Health Res. 15(9), 12771288 (2005). https://doi.org/10.1177/1049732305276687

Kang, S., Kim, K., Chi, S., Kim, J.: Interaction control for postural correction on a riding simulation system. In: Proceedings of the 2014 ACM/IEEE International Conference on Human-Robot Interaction (HRI '14). Association for Computing Machinery, New York, NY, USA, pp. 194–195 (2014). https://doi.org/10.1145/2559636.2563705

Desmet, P.: Designing emotions. Doctoral dissertation, Delft University of Technology, Delft, The Netherlands (2002)

Shin, J.Y., Rheu, M., Huh-Yoo, J., Peng, W.: Designing technologies to support parent-child relationships: a review of current findings and suggestions for future directions. Proc. ACM Hum. -Comput. Interact. 5, 1–31 (2021). https://doi.org/10.1145/3479585

Patil, S.G., et al.: GesturePod: enabling on-device gesture-based interaction for white cane users. In: Proceedings of the 32nd Annual ACM Symposium on User Interface Software and Technology (UIST '19). Association for Computing Machinery, New York, NY, USA, pp. 403–415 (2019). https://doi.org/10.1145/3332165.3347881

Li, C., Androulakaki, T., Gao, Y.A., Yang, F., Saikia, H., Peters, C., Skantze, G.: Effects of posture and embodiment on social distance in human-agent interaction in mixed reality. In: Proceedings of the 18th International Conference on Intelligent Virtual Agents (IVA '18). Association for Computing Machinery, New York, NY, USA, pp. 191–196 (2018). https://doi.org/10.1145/3267851.3267870

Ghekiere, A, Cauwenberg, V.J., Carver, A., et al.: Pyschosocial factors associated with children's riding for transport: a cross-sectional moderation study. Prev. Med. 86, 141–146 (2016)

Shahid, S., Krahmer, E., Swerts, M.: Child-robot interaction: playing alone or together? In: CHI'11 Extended Abstracts on Human Factors in Computing Systems (CHI EA '11). Association for Computing Machinery, New York, NY, USA, pp. 1399–1404 (2011). https://doi.org/10.1145/1979742.1979781

Research and Application of Grid System Design for Version Aesthetics in Book Design

Jun Zhang[✉]

Beijing Technology Institute, Zhuhai 519088, China
81901765@qq.com

Abstract. To explore the grid - lines in traditional Chinese book layout. To sort out the rules and version specifications of Chinese character arrangement in classical books. Study its version aesthetics. Establish a grid system in line with modern Chinese book design. Methods: Based on typology. Through the research of modern layout design grid system. Compare the differences between Chinese and western layout lines and grids. This paper analyzes the design standards of Chinese traditional book layout and line. Clarify the use of lines in a layout. Results: Taking the development of Chinese traditional books as the context. Study the generation of grid idea in various forms. Finding the beauty of a version has a lot to do with the grid system. Grid systems have always existed in ancient Chinese writing systems and version designs. The beauty of the grid is both ancient and modern.

Keywords: Grid System · Chinese Traditional Book · Layout Design · Book Design

1 The Emergence of Grid Systems

At present, the grid system is widely used in the visual communication professional design discipline. This system is one of the most important bases of layout design. It plays a vital role in the mastery of design. The first prototype of the grid design system was in 1692. France set up a royal commission responsible for the management of printing and improving the level of domestic printing. Under the leadership of mathematician Nicholas Gazon, a scientific numerical and example analysis of various original typography was carried out. The relationship between decorative details and communication function is also studied. This is the world's first scientific practice of typeface and layout. Ultimately based on the Roman style. On the printed surface of 2304 small squares. Carry out font design and layout. The idea of using squares for design is the beginning of the Western grid system. In 1928, he taught graphic design at the Bauhaus Academy in Germany. A set of rational design system and method, which uses grid to redesign on neat square grid, is applied to the design field. It is argued that design should be developed from simple geometric figures. Segment, cross and repeat simple geometric shapes such as circles and squares. The square grid is used as the design basis. All design elements are proportionally arranged in a grid with a highly unified form. This is

© The Author(s), under exclusive license to Springer Nature Switzerland AG 2024

C. Stephanidis et al. (Eds.): HCII 2024, CCIS 2114, pp. 112–122, 2024.
https://doi.org/10.1007/978-3-031-61932-8_14

a typical feature of modern grid layout design. The grid design system was continuously practiced and improved in West Germany and Switzerland in the 1940s and 1950s. And through the Swiss graphic design magazine to the world. Become the mainstream layout design pattern. It has a wide influence on modern graphic design of Western language.

In 2005, China translated the Western grid system book "Grid Composition of Layout design". It was edited by Hans Rudolf Borthard of Switzerland and published by Niggli. The book uses a lot of text and design examples. The theory and application of grid structure design are systematically and deeply explained. It introduces the concepts of order and constructivism into design. It makes it possible to harmonize all design elements - pictures, words, and points, lines, and surfaces. Grid system has become an excellent layout design form law. It emphasizes the sense of proportion, order, integration, times and rigor. Create a simple, simple layout art expression style [1].

Similarly, grid systems play an important role in book design. Use grid to form design rules. Combine design practice. Integrate feeling, cultivation and skill. Create both practical value and artistic book design.

2 Grids in Traditional Chinese Books

Traces of grid use can be seen everywhere in the life of ancient Chinese people in the past. For example, the pre-Qin writing culture used the grid system. Qin, Han and Tang Dynasties have preserved a large number of commemorative inscriptions. You can experience a uniform grid system.

What is the relationship between grid system and traditional Chinese books? What is the relationship between the aesthetic qualities in ancient Chinese books and the grid system? This is another starting point for discussing grid systems. From the oracle bone inscriptions in Yin Ruins to the end of the 19th century by the influence of western printing, the design of ancient books in China has experienced more than 3000 years. In this long historical period, books are influenced by economy, culture, philosophy, aesthetics, politics, science and technology, materials, etc., and their forms are constantly developing and changing. There are carved oracle-bone inscriptions, jade plates of writing prototypes, bamboo slips and wooden slips, inscriptions of casting technology, stone inscriptions and so on; There are rolling books that appear in paper and write with a brush dipped in ink, dragon scale (cyclone), folded; And after the invention of printing, the butterfly, the bag, the thread-bound book and other forms. The most culturally representative is the various book forms that appeared under the block printing technique of the Song and Ming dynasties. The layout of books in this period appeared lines and graphic elements such as sky head, ground foot, boundary, column (Wenwu column), fishtail, elephant trunk. These elements are often used in combination with standardized grid systems in book layout design and mass printing [2].

2.1 The Plain Grid System Predates the Use of Paper

Before paper was invented, the carrier for recording knowledge was chosen by the wise ancients to keep the material longer. Such as: pottery, oracle bones, jade plates, bronze vessels, stone tablets, bamboo slips and wooden slips. This process went on for a long time. Writing text on these hard objects is difficult. The writing surface that these materials provide - that is, the size of a folio page today. It is limited, uneven, irregular. Carrier sources are precious and difficult to obtain. Therefore, before writing and writing, we must think carefully and consider the layout of elements such as text and decoration. This process is the core idea of modern layout design. Through the study of a large number of materials left by the ancients. The text pays great attention to layout aesthetics. And has its own set of writing standards (see Fig. 1).

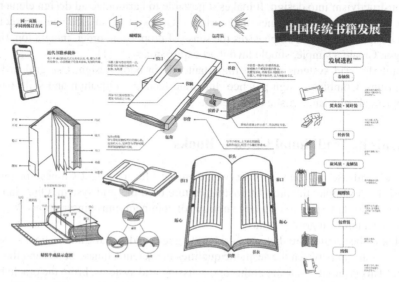

Fig. 1. Chinese traditional book development infographic designed by Li Yongyi

A large number of oracle bones have been unearthed from current excavations. It can be clearly seen that the written text is top-down, the literal size is basically the same, and the number of words in each vertical column is basically the same. Horizontally, the text is basically aligned at the bottom, without too strong jumps, forming a relatively balanced horizontal line. This shows that there is an invisible grid supporting the writing. The original simple grid system is reflected in a large number of subsequent works. The size of bone area provided varies according to different bone shapes. When writing characters, pay attention to the balanced position of the characters on the bone surface. Combine the shape of bone surface to make clever text position arrangement. The layout of the letters varies with the shape of the bones. This may be the earliest appearance of Layout design thinking - Layout (the English name of layout design, is the layout). At the same time, the text and pattern are mostly located in the middle of the bone surface for writing safety considerations. There is a margin around it. It is also the embodiment of the layout heart in modern layout design [3].

Through research found. The various forms of books before paper embodied the concept of a simple grid system. This intellectually rigorous grid system was used to write monumental, formal, and official classics. The existence of the grid gives them a solemn and sublime form. So that the spiritual core of national culture can be passed on. This tradition continued in the later era of printing (see Fig. 2).

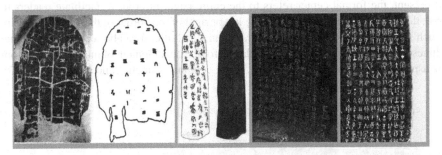

Fig. 2. Layout design thinking of oracle bone inscriptions, jade plates, inscriptions,

2.2 The Development of Grid Systems in the Printing Age: Row Grids

The invention of block printing in the late Sui and early Tang dynasties. It is an epoch-making event in the history of human culture communication. It opened a new era in the history of Chinese books. There appeared to be engraving printing based on the iris, packaging, thread bound books and other forms. These forms pay attention to "the collection is in order, the style is elegant". Both spiritual products and material products. It has rich cultural connotation. The format, arrangement structure and binding method are all influenced by the idea of "harmony between nature and man" in Chinese traditional culture. Many valuable design ideas and forms. It still influences the current design activities. Most importantly, at this time, the Song engravings of books formed a well-structured grid system: line and horizontal. A large number of books and excellent works have appeared [4].

After the Northern Song Dynasty, block printing flourished unprecedentedly. Its printing efficiency increased, and the output of books soared. The book is beautiful in shape. You have the book structure of front cover, back cover, illustrations, page numbers, chapters, table of contents, and so on. The idea of making books coincides in some ways with current book design. The morphological difference is not significant. In other words, many of the current book design ideas come from the traditional Song engravings. According to the process flow of Song engraving, it can be understood that the line grid system has been very perfect. And there are systematic writings.

Carved books have maintained the vertical and straight lines of writing that began with oracle bone inscriptions. The tradition of writing from right to left. The page is enclosed by four sidebar lines (a plate frame). The real space occupied by the printed plate is called the layout. It is the basic area for the arrangement of elements such as text and image. There is a virtual space left in the page that is not printed, which is called the top of the sky, the bottom of the foot, the sides of the side, and the right side is used for binding into the spine. The multiple vertical single lines in the plate frame are called boundaries. The space used for writing between the two boundaries is the boundary grid, the boundary line, also known as the line grid. The line with the fishtail and elephant trunk symbols in the middle is called the center and is used for folding and binding. There is a difference between the format of engraved books and that of modern books. At present, the format center refers to the entire page. In order to facilitate readers to read, there is a book ear structure on the left or right of the border of the butterfly layout, which is used to mark the page number, volume, and title. It can be seen that traditional Chinese books have laid a certain foundation for the development of modern books from the aspects of function, craft, structure, form, content, aesthetics and so on (see Fig. 3).

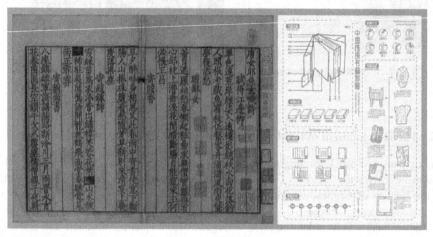

Fig. 3. Engraving book layout. Important form of traditional books. Designed by Huang Baozhen

3   Traditional Book Layout and Grid: Row Grids

There are many different copies of traditional ancient books in circulation. Although the content and volume are the same, there are many different layout specifications and lines. In the layout design, the center of the plate, the axis of the left and right pages are relative. The text layout is strictly limited. Kerning and line spacing have a uniform size standard. There are strict corresponding standards for the depth of text ink and the black and white relationship between the images embedded in the plate center. Column division is the basic design method of traditional layout design.

3.1   Number of Lines and Word Count

The number of words in the lines of ancient books is the main basis for the versionists to distinguish the versions. The number of lines and words in a book, usually measured on half a page. This is similar to the total number of words on the copyright page of modern books (words per line × number of lines per side × total number of faces). The purpose is to facilitate the reasonable arrangement of the number of words in the layout, easy to read. We often hear the idiom "ten lines at a glance", which ostensibly describes reading a book very fast. In fact, it refers to the ancient book half page 10 lines, each line fixed number of words, generally 20 words. In addition, in the past, the ancient imperial examinations were said to be able to recite about 500,000 words of various classics in order to succeed in the examination. To keep these contents in mind, in addition to reading hard, but also rely on the line. Because what the rows provide is a way of memorizing positions. That is, each word in the specific position and chapter of the book [1].

3.2 Layout and Folio

The size of traditional books is not much different from the size of books today. This is also an ergonomic option. The layout has become very unified with the help of various guidelines. And it hasn't changed much over the centuries. It's a respect for tradition. The blank space outside the page border is relatively large. The main function is to protect the text. The top of the sky can be used to write the eyebrow. The base section can also be used to write footnotes. In addition, large white space can clearly separate the content of the book from the outside world. When reading, the eyes and attention are more focused within the border. Like the mounting of modern paintings, the more white space, the more sense of work. The layout is divided into two sections. The upper part is generally smaller for annotations, and the lower part is larger for text. Three-section edition, both above and below can be used to annotate the content, the middle is the body. In terms of the size of the folium, the Ming Dynasty's "Yongle Grand Ceremony" has a plate heart of 216×315 mm, and the ratio of width and height is 1:0.626, which is only 0.08 different from the golden section. In the book, a series of elements such as heaven and earth, gray scale group, space dimension and so on, all show the relaxation degree of rhythmic beauty.

3.3 The Change of the Row

Flexible lines refer to the flexibility of layout and the use of movable type. Why are there different rows? The first factor is the alphanumeric version change caused by layout design. Different aesthetics in different periods lead to changes in the number of words in the layout and bring different experiences. Finding changes under normalization is the core idea of grid system. The grid system is not meant to make the design mechanized or template-based. It's a variable in a quantity. The design idea of flexible grid is an excellent use of grid system.

The ancient book version carries the ancient information and wisdom, is a kind of aesthetic expression, and becomes a cultural symbol. Chinese admire Song Dynasty books. Not only because of its rarity, but also because of its quaint beauty. Elegance presents the beauty of order bearing the words, and it is also the beauty of design. The establishment and search for order took thousands of years. And it is closely connected with various forms of traditional books. Form a grid system of reading and communication. The grid determines the format framework and visual structure of ancient book editions [6].

4 Grid System in Modern Chinese Books

Book design in the face of complex text style. When designing ideas, there should be an overall sense of framework and systematization. This system is called the grid system. Like Joseph Miller. In his book Grid Systems in Graphic Design, Brockman said: "In typesetting, the resources in the layout are used as much as possible to achieve the maximum possible order and economy". Resources are both a provision and a limitation. Design is a method of solving problems under various constraints. An open-ended design is a castle in the air. Order: Use resources, limits, and grids to integrate complex text with effective communication to establish visual logic.

4.1 Modern Grid System and Book Design

To understand the relationship between the grid system and book design, it is necessary to understand the size and proportion of paper. Only the space range of the design is determined, that is, the size of the folio. Before you can start designing. To build a grid system. The size and proportions of paper do not create beauty in themselves. Only through the combination of all visual elements can beautiful objects be produced. Likewise, the grid itself has no character. Need to combine font, graphic elements, ink, paper color, structure and other elements, and finally form a useful grid relationship. "The grid system is an aid, not a guarantee, it allows for many possible uses, and each designer can look for solutions that suit his personal style". But you have to learn how to use the grid. It's an art that takes practice" [7].

There are infinite variations in the proportions and sizes of paper. In the early days, people used various scientific experiments to find the answer to the most beautiful ratio. The golden ratio is considered one of the most beautiful. Surprisingly, however, this ratio rule is rarely applied to typography. Because the size of the paper first meets the technical setting of the printing field. While maintaining an economic edge. German Industrial Standard (DIN) size ratio 1:1.414, A0 = 841 mm*1189 mm. Repeatedly folding the long side in half does not change the original proportional relationship. Under this standard, different sizes of folios were produced. The grid system is actually based on the size of the folio. The width of the layout is the standard. Design according to the size and change of the layout column (see Fig. 4).

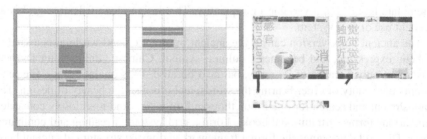

Fig. 4. Center, grid, Folio. Designed by Liu Yilin

4.2   The Rational Beauty of Book Design Under Grid System

The guarantee of the orderly combination of design elements is the grid. Use a flexible combination of grids. Break through the grid regularly and divide the grid reasonably. The purpose is to make the layout flexible and beautiful. The combination of grid system and layout design is not a simple grid and module. De-populate elements unconsciously. Instead, we use well-set, rational columns and frameworks to do rational thinking. Provide a reasonable position for each element, presenting an orderly mathematical beauty. Reasonable grid system design can rationally control the layout design of books. Enhance visual beauty. It provides a design approach for the innovation of book layout design [8].

Composition of book layout under grid system: In book layout design, Le Corbusier was the first to use the golden ratio method and designed 44 grid design templates for the book "Modulus". Provides a selection of templates for book layout design. At present, there are columnar grid, modular grid, 20-type, 32-type grid, compound grid and other forms in use. The grid system is used to rationally place elements such as title, text, picture and illustration. Create a satisfying visual relationship. Through the layout of the visual elements of the primary and secondary positioning. Establish visual hierarchy to form a sense of order. Make the various messages to be conveyed at a glance. There is a very close relationship between the form of the grid and the theme and content of the book. Different theme content will design different grid systems to present the layout style. For example, the composite grid system, its form is active and clever, and the corresponding content is often a more entertaining theme. On the contrary, in the more serious content of the topic, it is necessary to use a more rational, such as symmetric grid system form.

5   Principles of Using Grid System in Book Design

The grid system follows the principle of proportion and moderation. Excellent layout design with good proportions. Various proportions formed by mathematical aesthetics, such as arithmetic series, arithmetic series, gold ratio, etc., are widely used in layout design. The grid system is a scale of the elements. The visual form of book design is controlled by the text content. Here the grid system provides the principle of moderation. In particular, the agreement between the design form and the design content. The harmonious relationship between whole and part. Book layout should be adapted to the visual psychology of readers. Convey layout beauty and design aesthetics. Take the audience's perception and acceptance as the appropriate standard. The principle of alignment is another basic principle of grid design system, which can reflect the designer's overall sense and overall view. Arrange design elements such as text and pictures in an orderly manner according to certain reference lines. Avoid cluttered layouts. It is one of the most common basic methods for dealing with book design layout. Use the horizontal and vertical coordinate lines of the grid to align left, middle, right, top, bottom, etc. The layout has coherence and time and space [9].

5.1 Grid System Establishes Information Architecture for Book Design

A large number of graphic and visual information materials in book design constitute a huge database or information base. How to choose data and information for different audiences. How to spread to achieve the best results. The most effective way is to visualize it, that is, to use visual information design. Visualization expands the scope and degree of information dissemination and builds communication space. The construction of this communication space must be based on the visualization, accuracy, authenticity and compound of information. Grid architecture is helpful to the establishment of information architecture. 1) The information system established under the grid system has authenticity and accuracy, and the grid system helps to make the information clear, concise, specific and clear. 2) In the construction of information system, the grid system makes complex information simpler and easier to understand by layering, zoning, integrating and designing all kinds of information. Third, the grid system strengthens the identifiability of information symbols and the orientation of communication. Fourth, the grid system emphasizes the guiding function of the infographic through the design, combines all kinds of information, attracts the audience's attention, strengthens the memory, and expands the influence of the information.

5.2 Grid Design of Chinese Characters

Font size and layout: The grid system of Latin characters is different from that of Chinese characters. This is determined by two completely different writing systems. Chinese characters are square characters. Although the words have size, length, simple and complex strokes, it is only for the literal. Each Chinese character is framed on a fixed square. It is located in a 1:1 square and occupies the corresponding position. If the unit is mm. You will encounter a situation where the text cannot be arranged within the line. For example, set a 90 mm column width, which can hold how many Chinese characters? Using 10pt Chinese characters, it is found that 25.52 characters will appear (90 mm/0.3527 mm/10pt = 25.52 characters, 1pt = 0.3527 mm). Chinese characters do not have a hyphen "-"and cannot place half of the text in a line. 0.52 words are eventually assigned to 24 kernels. We all know the importance of kerning and line spacing in layout design. For the beauty of the layout. Constantly trying to fine tune the kerning, line spacing. This passive distribution is not what we want. The most effective method is to use pt to set the field width and center size. Even the folio. 25 10pt words are 250pt, and the field width is 250pt. In InDesign software, there is already an artboard in the layout grid mode, which is completely developed to adapt to the layout of Chinese characters [10].

Line spacing and font size: Which line spacing is used. Depends on how the design wants the reader to feel visually. Also taking 10pt words as an example, the line spacing can be set to 10pt and the word spacing can be set to 5pt to achieve a ratio of 1:1:0.5. This ratio can be adjusted as needed. Of course, the best integer setting, easy to calculate. Put 25 10pt text in a row, spacing is 5pt, the width of the column is 370pt = (25*10pt) + (24*5pt). The column width can also be converted to millimeters. 370pt*0.3527 = 130.499 mm, as long as the line width is set to 131 mm, you can get a whole word and neat effect (see Fig. 5).

Fig. 5. Chinese layout, grid system. Designed by Cheng Biying

Modular unit: The modular unit layout in the grid system refers to a square as a unit. Design the square with 0.3527 mm. That is, the height, the width can fit the whole Chinese character. Because other levels of text use the magnification relationship. Using the smallest square, arrange the square repeatedly within the plate center. Get a rigorous scientific layout, also known as the square layout. This modular unit layout sorts out a lot of information and arranges each element reasonably to form an effective information layout and guidance (see Fig. 6).

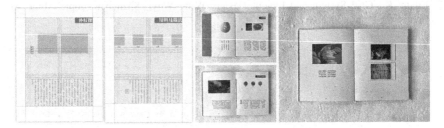

Fig. 6. Grid system and modular units. Designed by Luo Siyin

Negative space in the grid system: from the perspective of reading experience, the text and graphic information on the page is too crowded, which will hinder the comfortable reading experience. The more negative space in the layout, the easier the text is to read and understand. Negative space is not simply a blank space. The area it refers to is not necessarily white. It is the space embodied in many different forms, and it is the blank space surrounding each element in the layout. Including charts, gaps, pictures, margins, column spacing, etc., also includes text line spacing space. Although there are no design elements inside the negative space. However, it is the main element that creates the beauty and expression of the layout. The good control of negative space by designers is the embodiment of their design literacy and ability.

6 Conclusion

At present, the grid system established in combination with the history and characteristics of Chinese characters has a profound guiding significance for book design. The grid system applies science and scientific methods to book design to show the inherent structure and profound meaning of the text.

References

1. Brockman, J.M.: Grid Systems in Graphic Design. Xu Chenxi, Translated by ZHANG Pengyu. Shanghai People's Fine Arts Publishing House, Shanghai, p. 163 (2006)
2. Tsien, J.: History of Chinese Paper and Printing Culture, p. 33. Guangxi Normal University Press, Guilin (2004)
3. Hongyi, C.: Collection and Appreciation of Ancient Books. Shaanxi People's Publishing House, Xi'an, p. 92 (2008)
4. Kimberly Elam translated by Li Leshan. Design Geometry: A Study on Proportion and Composition. Water Resources and Hydropower Press, Beijing, p. 120 (2008)
5. Wenyin, C.: General Knowledge of Ancient Books. Zhonghua Book Company, Beijing, p. 133 (2009)
6. Needham, J.: History of Science and Technology in China, p. 149. Science Press, Beijing (2018)
7. Lijuan, Z., Youqing, C.: Song Edition, p. 25. Jiangsu Ancient Books Publishing House, Nanjing (2002)
8. Shaoming, Z.: The Social History of Books, p. 14. Peking University Press, Beijing (2009)
9. Jingren, L.: Book Art Asked: Lu Jingren Book Design, pp. 157–169. Shanghai People's Fine Arts Publishing House, Shanghai (2017)
10. Eilam, K.: Grid System and Layout Design. Wang Wuyi. Shanghai People's Fine Arts Publishing House, Shanghai, p. 77 (2013)

User Experience Evaluation Methods and Case Studies

Exploration of Alert Response Strategy Modeling Method Based on MBSE

Lin Du[1(✉)], Meihui Su[1], Xiaoli Wang[2], and Wei Guo[2]

[1] Shanghai Aircraft Design and Research Institute, No. 5188 JinKe Road, PuDong New District, Shanghai 201210, China
dulin@comac.cc

[2] COMAC Beijing Aircraft Technology Research Institute, Yingcai North 1st Street, Changping District, Beijing 102211, China

Abstract. A key component of flight safety in commercial aviation is the cockpit crew alert system. However, due to the increasing integration and complexity of modern civil aircraft systems, a single failure can quickly propagate to other systems, while each affected system also generates different types of alert information. Faced with multiple alerts generated by this cascading effect of failures, it's difficult for pilots to accurately and quickly identify the source of the failure and select effective means of addressing it, which can lead to delays in addressing failures and affect flight safety. Therefore, it is becoming more and more urgent to accurately identify the direct effects of the alerts. Traditional methods are often limited to reviewing specific areas or documents, making it difficult to view the system as a whole. Model-Based Systems Engineering (MBSE) provides a comprehensive framework for modeling, analyzing, and managing systems throughout their lifecycle.

This research examines the modeling of alerts in the context of Model-Based Systems Engineering (MBSE) using suitable modeling languages. The focus on the individual components of the alert system, but also the in-depth consideration of the relationships between these components within the overall system and their dynamic behavior in different system states, is the unique strength of this method. Important modeling details, such as alert triggering conditions, the association between system states and alerts, system architecture, and failure mode analysis, are emphasized by embedding alerts in the overall system engineering model. This research effectively demonstrates the practicality and effectiveness of the modeling approach in real-world applications through a detailed analysis of practical model cases. The study provides robust theoretical and empirical support for enhancing system security.

By integrating the alert system into the overall engineering model, this approach promotes a comprehensive and integrated approach to systems engineering. It contributes to a better understanding and planning of the system's response to alert conditions. Alert triggers are typically associated with predefined conditions or events, such as system failures, abnormal states, or important safety and reliability events. The purpose of this study is to provide theoretical and empirical evidence for the improvement of system safety. Through the modeling of alert-triggering strategies with the help of MBSE, new perspectives and methods are provided for research and practice in the field of human-computer interfaces.

© The Author(s), under exclusive license to Springer Nature Switzerland AG 2024
C. Stephanidis et al. (Eds.): HCII 2024, CCIS 2114, pp. 125–131, 2024.
https://doi.org/10.1007/978-3-031-61932-8_15

Although some progress has been made, challenges such as the choice of modeling language and the management of model complexity are still in need of further attention. Future research will be focused on the proposal of more efficient and intelligent methods for the modeling of alert triggering policies.

Keywords: MBSE Framework · Failure Modeling · Alert System Modeling

1 Introduction

Flight safety in civil aviation is of paramount importance. It affects the lives and property of millions of passengers. The cockpit crew alert system is a crucial component of flight safety. Researchers have conducted extensive research to improve the level of understanding, analysis, and integration of alert systems within a broader systems engineering framework. For instance, Yuqiao et al. proposed a safety analysis method based on the state of the operational process. The method establishes a hierarchical system functional framework oriented to the operational process through state machines for dynamic assessment of fault states. In contrast, Zhengjie et al. proposed a methodology for modeling and evaluating cockpit-integrated alert messages in civil aircraft. However, the design and management of alert systems face many challenges due to the continuous integration and complexity of modern civil aircraft systems. To address this problem, a more integrated and systematic modeling approach is needed, as traditional approaches often fail to fully consider the system as a whole.

The Model-Based Systems Engineering (MBSE) approach offers a new methodology to comprehensively analyze the behavior of an alert system within a systems engineering framework. This paper clarifies the functions and interrelationships between subsystems and devices through system-subsystem-device modeling. Based on this, we performed system failure mode modeling to identify possible failure modes of the system and devices. Furthermore, we associated the system/device state with the alert state to better reflect the system state.

Additionally, we propose a logical operation modeling method for alert signals. This method specifies the alert triggering conditions by formally defining the characteristics and attributes of the alerts. It establishes a logical flow of information.

2 Alert Triggering Strategy Modeling Method

In the Model-Based Systems Engineering (MBSE) approach, the system is modeled from the top-down, starting with the system and then moving to the subsystems and equipment. The following outlines the steps involved in establishing an alert model.

2.1 System-Subsystem-Equipment Modeling

First, the entire system is modeled using the MBSE system modeling method. Then, the system is subdivided into different subsystems. An appropriate modeling language, such as SysML, should be used to create system-level and subsystem-level models that clarify the functions of each subsystem and their upstream and downstream relationships. The subsystems should then be further refined to the equipment level to clarify the functions and characteristics of each equipment. Each subsystem should be modeled in detail, identifying and describing each equipment, including its inputs, outputs, interfaces, and relationships with other equipment (refer to Fig. 1).

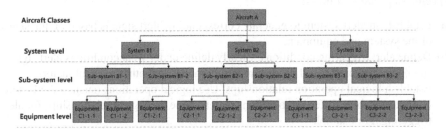

Fig. 1. The system architecture analysis diagram

2.2 System Failure Mode Modeling

Identify the potential failure modes of the system and equipment using methods such as Failure Modes and Effects Analysis (FMEA). This section aims to identify the potential failure modes of the system and equipment. We will use methods such as Failure Modes and Effects Analysis (FMEA) to analyze the failures of the system and equipment, and identify potential failure modes (see Fig. 2). The states of the system/equipment should be associated with the alert states. System/equipment failures that are detectable should be characterized with signals. Signals should be generated and transmitted through changes in the system/equipment states.

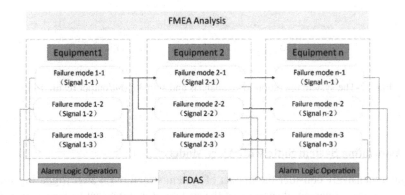

Fig. 2. The FMEA safety analysis of equipment

2.3 Alert Signal Logic Operation Modeling

Formalize the concept of alerts using the selected MBSE modeling language, clarify the characteristics and attributes of alerts, define the conditions for triggering alerts in the system, and represent the relationships and constraints of alert triggering conditions using MBSE tools to ensure the accuracy and reliability of the model (see Fig. 3). The specific steps are as follows:

a) Establish an alert system to generate corresponding alert signals based on the states of the system and equipment.
b) Define alert triggering conditions: Clearly define under what conditions alert signals should be triggered based on system failure modes and other relevant factors.
c) Establish logical operation relationships: Use logical operations (such as AND, OR, NOT) to combine different conditions to determine the logical relationships for alert triggering. For example:

AND logic: A specific alert triggering condition can be set so that an alert is generated only when two or more specific conditions are triggered simultaneously.

OR logic: A specific alert triggering condition can be set so that an alert is generated as long as any one of the conditions is triggered.

NOT logic: The opposite condition of a specific alert triggering condition can be set to generate an alert when that condition is not triggered.

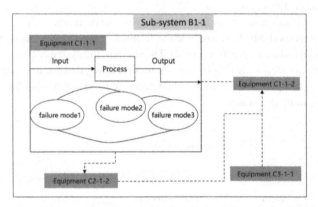

Fig. 3. The system operation logic analysis and signal input/output relationship

2.4 Associating System State with Alert Models

To comprehensively consider the impact of system structure on alert triggering strategies and improve the overall security of the system, it is important to associate system architecture with failure modes. It is necessary to clearly define the path for alert signals to be transmitted from the system level to the subsystem and equipment levels, ensuring that alert information accurately reflects the system's state. The system's state should be

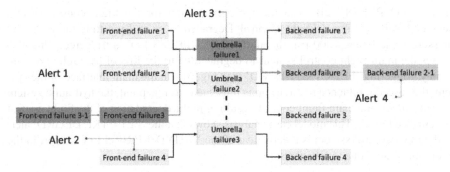

Fig. 4. The system failure and alert signal logic trigger analysis

associated with the alert state. To describe how changes in the system's state trigger the generation and transmission of alerts, use MBSE modeling language (refer to Fig. 4).

Through the above steps, a comprehensive model from the system to the equipment level has been established, which includes the logic operations of failure modes and alert signals. Additionally, it facilitates the identification and resolution of potential issues during both the design and operation phases.

3   Alert Trigger Strategy Modeling Demo

The modeling environment MagicDraw supports the SysML language to create BDD diagrams that describe the functional definition and decomposition, logical component definition and decomposition, and physical component definition and decomposition of an aircraft system. Using the umbrella alert '--HYD 1 PRESS LO--' as an example, an IBD diagram was created to describe the functional, logical, and physical architectures of the avionics (FDAS) system, the hydraulics system, and the main flight control system (see Fig. 5).

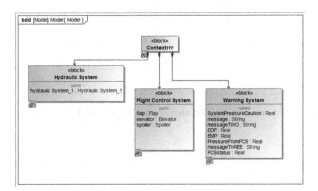

Fig. 5. The system architecture model

Construct the alert triggering logic model, where the logic expression for the hydraulic system low pressure alert #1 is Out = (HYD_1_LO_PRESS_T1A ∥

HYD_1_LO_PRESS_T2B), and the logic expression for the flight control system degraded alert is Out = (Flight_Control_Degraded = = 1). By setting the hydraulic pressure value below 1800 psi, the alert 'HYD 1 PRESS LO' is triggered. This also causes the main flight control system to degrade due to the loss of hydraulic pressure supply, triggering 'FLT CTRL DEGRD' (see Fig. 6). On the main interface of the system, the cascade influence relationship is presented. At this point, the hydraulic system cascade affects the main flight control, resulting in the degradation of the flight control system (see Fig. 7). This model case analysis shows that the 'FLT CTRL DEGRD' alert in the flight control system is a derivative of the '---HYD 1 PRESS LO---' alert in the hydraulic system due to low pressure.

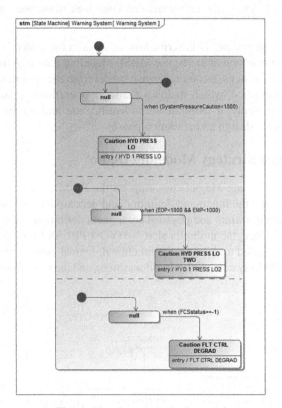

Fig. 6. The alert trigger logic model

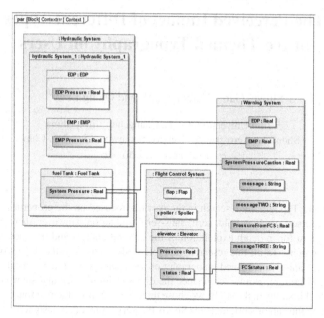

Fig. 7. The main interface for cascading impact analysis

4   Conclusion

According to studies, incorporating alerting systems into the overall engineering model helps promote a comprehensive and integrated approach to systems engineering. The Model-Based Systems Engineering (MBSE) approach provides new perspectives and methods for studying and practicing human-machine interfaces, enhancing the safety and reliability of systems. However, challenges such as managing model complexity and selecting modeling languages still require further attention. In conclusion, this study highlights the significance of utilizing MBSE to model cockpit crew alert systems for enhancing the safety of commercial aviation flights. Future research will concentrate on proposing more effective and intelligent alert triggering strategy modeling methods to address the challenges identified in this study.

References

1. Yuqiao, W., Gang, X., Miao, W.: Cascading failure analysis method of avionics based on operational process state. IEEE Access, 148425–148444 (2020). https://doi.org/10.1109/ACC ESS.2020.3016026
2. Zhengjie, C., Gang, X., Yuqiao, W.: A method of civil aircraft cockpit integrated alert information modeling and evaluation based on MBSE. In: 2019 IEEE/AIAA 38th Digital Avionics Systems Conference (DASC), pp 1–8 (2019). https://doi.org/10.1109/DASC43569.2019.908 1699

The Perceived Impact of Different Types of Ice-Themed Typography on Users

Shiwei Gao[1], Yufeng Guo[1], and Qiang Li[2(✉)]

[1] Jilin University of Arts, Changchun, Jilin, China
[2] Shenyang Aerospace University, Shenyang, Liaoning, China
qiangli@sau.edu.cn

Abstract. Typography research in the past has focused on the properties of the typeface itself, such as bold, serif, sans-serif, and so on. However, there is still much room for in-depth exploration of the cultural context and user perception of typography. To fill this research gap, this study focuses on the impact of different ice and snow-themed typography on user perception in the context of ice and snow culture, aiming to enhance the dissemination of ice and snow culture through this study. In the study, we chose three ice and snow-themed font designs, including the author's original "Ice Sports Imagery" font, other designers' ice and snow-themed font, and regular bold font, and presented them on the same web banner. The three font types were evaluated by using 15 pairs of adjectives, and participants' perceptions of the different font types and designers were collected through a questionnaire. The results of the study showed that there were significant differences in participants' perceptions of different ice-themed fonts. When web banners were presented using fonts that were considered inappropriate, participants perceived the fonts as unserious and unprofessional in personality. On the contrary, the author's "Ice Sports Imagery" typeface received positive feedback in the banner presentation. From the semiotics point of view, "Ice Sports Imagery "font successfully extracts the trajectory of ice and snow sports, which is full of dynamics and can fully express the imagery of ice and snow sports, and successfully integrates the imagery of "ice and snow" with the glyphs, which improves the function of ideograms. And from an imagery point of view, the typeface evokes the association of sliding snow and ice for an immersive experience. This strong image experience comes from the clever shape of the strokes and the organic rhythm between the strokes, which can form emotional resonance.

Keywords: Ice Culture · Perception · Emotion · Semiotics · Typography

1 Introduction

Typography is not just a tool for text presentation, it plays an important role in visual communication and directly affects the way information is interpreted and received. Especially in the application of ice and snow theme, the font design is no longer limited to the basic function of words, but forms an expression of emotional perception. For example [1]. The study investigated the effects of choosing different fonts on email

© The Author(s), under exclusive license to Springer Nature Switzerland AG 2024
C. Stephanidis et al. (Eds.): HCII 2024, CCIS 2114, pp. 132–143, 2024.
https://doi.org/10.1007/978-3-031-61932-8_16

perceived personality, gender and temperament of email writers. The study found that when emails were presented using fonts that were considered inappropriate, the user's perceived personality of the email appeared less professional and less serious. Additionally, inappropriate font choices negatively impacted users' perceptions of the gender and temperament of email authors. This illustrates the significant impact of font choice on the way emotional perceptions are expressed, emphasizing the importance of employing appropriate fonts in scenarios such as email to convey more appropriate emotions and professionalismm [2]. The study examined the impact of font "personality" on readers' emotional information processing. In Study 1, personality trait words were presented in a brief manner, and their personalities were displayed through specific fonts, and perceptual differences were observed when the font personalities were consistent or inconsistent with the meaning of the words. The results show that readers who use consistent font personalities perceive faster in an affective lexical decision task. In Study 2, by presenting pages with different fonts, the researcher found that readers' quick judgments of the emotional tone of the page were significantly influenced by font personality. It is concluded that readers are able to immediately perceive and process font personality, which in turn influences their perceptual process of emotional processing on screen. This emphasizes the fact that font personality plays an important role in the perceptual process when it comes to expressing an emotional way of perception. In addition [3]. The results of the study showed that personality traits were associated with the design family of fonts (serif, sans-serif, modern, monospaced, script/funny) and correlated with appropriate use. The results of these studies further discuss the perceptual impact on online material and website design, emphasizing the critical role of typeface choice in conveying emotionally charged perceptual expressions.

In addition, scholars have delved into the impact of different fonts on user legibility. According to [4] the results of the study showed that the legibility of fonts had different effects on the subjective perception of easy-to-read and difficult-to-read poems, and the effect was most significant especially in the case of easy-to-read poems. Through three experiments, the authors examined the effects of poem difficulty and font readability on the subjective perception of poetry. Participants read poems that may have varying degrees of conceptual or structural difficulty, and these poems were presented in easy or difficult to read fonts. Participants then rated their subjective perceptions of the poems they read, as measured by four dependent variables, including overall preference, perceived poetic fluency, perceived thematic clarity, and structure. In a study assessing perceptions of font legibility [5], it was found that size 10 Tahoma was perceived as clearer compared to size 12 textbooks. In addition, the Verdana and Courier fonts at size 12 were perceived as sharper than the Comic, Schoolbook, and Verdana fonts at size 10. Interestingly, Georgia at size 10 is significantly more legible than Tahoma and Schoolbook at size 12. Arial at size 14 is perceived as clearer than Comic at size 14, and Arial at size 10 is also perceived as more legible than Tahoma at size 12. At size 14, only Arial is sharper than the other fonts (size 10 Schoolbook and Comic). [6] revealed that by improving font legibility, the similarity between the evaluations of the elements demonstrated a significant positive impact on consumers' evaluation of the aesthetic impression of packaging. This highlights the importance of the similarity between elemental evaluation and typeface legibility in the perceptual process when evaluating the aesthetic impression of a package. In addition, the findings of [7] showed that font type had a significant impact on readability for both subjects with and without dyslexia. Sans Serif, Equal Width, and Roman font styles significantly improved reading performance in the test compared to Serif, Proportional, and Italic fonts. Based on this finding, the study recommended a set of more perceptible fonts designed to enhance the reading experience of people with and without dyslexia, which is essential for improving the perception and understanding of text. In addition, the study by [8] assessed the perceived legibility of individual letters, numbers, and symbols in each font by asking participants to look at the characters in each font for a short period of time and to verbally identify them. By calculating the percentage of correctly recognized characters for each character and applying a graphical sunflower chart to highlight misrecognized characters, the results of the study clearly show that the ClearType fonts Consolas and Cambria, and the non-ClearType font Verdana, are more legible in terms of numbers and symbols compared to Times New Roman. This study provides substantial insights into the impact of perceiving different fonts on the screen reading experience, further emphasizing the importance of choosing more readable fonts.

Many scholars have also delved into the impact of different fonts on users' emotional responses. In a study by [9] researchers investigated which fonts were effective in conveying emotions and introduced these fonts into a mobile chat application. A survey was conducted to demonstrate how changes in message fonts can affect the meaning of the message conveyed. The results show that the use of a variety of fonts influences and reinforces the value perceived by the user, and that this variety elicits a positive response among users, leading to a more active emotional experience when sending text messages. This study emphasizes the potential importance of fonts in perceiving emotional responses. Researchers at [10] selected 20 simplified and 20 traditional characters and conducted a perceptual evaluation experiment, and simultaneously collected data on emotional evaluation of Japanese characters in order to study the differences between Chinese and Japanese in terms of emotion. The study found that participants from mainland China and Taiwan showed diametrically opposed classical and contemporary perceptions of the three widely used fonts: bold, loose, and open. And the perception of Taiwanese and Japanese showed a more consistent trend. This study deeply reveals the complexity of different fonts for users' emotional perception in different geographical and cultural backgrounds. In a study by [11], 102 participants shared their immediate emotional responses to 36 different font designs. The results of the study support the correlation between specific font characteristics (variety, contrast, pattern) and specific emotional parameters (amusement, excitement, concentration) and suggests various classroom approaches for purposeful font selection. This study emphasizes the importance of typography for users' emotional perceptions and provides practical guidance for real-world applications. [12] showed that satirical texts read in the new Roman font triggered more interest and anger compared to satirical texts read in Arial font, and that this strong association of emotional perception is consistent with the definition of satire. This apparent interplay between typeface type and the emotional quality of the text not only has an impact on marketing and advertising, but also plays out in persuasive literature. This study highlights the potential power of font choice in shaping users' emotional perceptions, with important implications for creators of various text forms and marketing practitioners. [13] study worked on constructing font recommendation guides in three languages, English, Burmese and Japanese, through a subjective evaluation approach. The results showed that the study succeeded in finding suitable fonts for each of the 36 perceptual adjectives and identified five clusters of adjectives and types. It is worth noting that, consistent with previous studies of English and Japanese scripts, there is a lack of similar studies in the field of Burmese. In addition, the study emphasizes the need to consider the initially specified font thickness when choosing fonts, and explores how the use of "exciting" perceptual fonts affects readability. This research provides useful emotional and perceptual guidance for font selection in different contexts.

In addition, a study by [14] proposed an affective font selection method for different national cultural contexts, highlighting the importance of affective font perception. First, the emotional data of the selected fonts were perceived through a series of evaluation experiments. Second, these fonts were organically categorized into several clusters with similar emotional tendencies through hierarchical cluster analysis. Third, by quantifying the relationship between perceptual clusters of types and impressions in depth through Quantitative Theory Type I, it is suggested that Latin and Japanese fonts be selected and combined in the clusters that are most closely related to the specified impression. The validation results show that the combination of Latin and Japanese font clusters works better than using the original Latin alphabet design with similar shape characteristics in the Japanese font pack. This not only emphasizes the critical role of perception in emotional font selection, but also provides deeper insights into typography. [15] delved deeper into the effects of font type and size on emotion, and through data collected with subjects found that Arial was more strongly associated with positive emotions, compared to Times New Roman, which showed a different tendency towards emotion. It is worth noting that the 8pt font size causes an unpleasant experience and is accompanied by a higher number of errors. In contrast, medium (12pt and 16pt) and large fonts are primarily associated with a pleasurable and comfortable experience. Such research helps to perceive the role of font choice in design more fully, providing more in-depth guidance for optimizing the user experience. In response to the current state of research, most studies revolve solely around the type, size, weight, height, color, and other factors of the font itself. There are also literacy studies on fonts, which test the clarity perceived by users of different font sizes and further measure the legibility of different fonts by evaluating the percentage of users who can read different fonts correctly within a specified period of time. Research on fonts and emotions has focused on font characteristics such as shape, traditional and simplified fonts, and other font attributes. However, there is a lack of research on the application of typography to regional cultural contexts. Therefore, this paper focuses on the impact of different fonts on users' emotional responses under the dimension of ice culture, and also includes an evaluation of the perceived personality of different fonts.

What is emotion, perception, and typography? There is no agreed upon definition of emotion, [16] defines emotion as a brief but violent mental fluctuation triggered by an intense experience, including fear, surprise, and joy, that causes sudden irritability within the individual. Overall, emotion is a positive or negative mental state that directly affects an individual's cognition and behavior. [17] This definition cannot be ignored because emotion has been viewed as a mere physiological response. [18] study by assessing students' and teachers' perceptions of legibility and emotion conveyed by 10 fonts showed that the majority of participants embraced the legibility of the fonts. In terms of affective assessment, four of the fonts proved to be consistent with the emotions conveyed and the remaining six fonts were inconsistent with the emotions conveyed. [19] showed that affective feelings towards fonts can be described by the appearance and evaluation dimensions of fonts. Specifically, the presence or absence of serifs and the style of appearance of the printed or handwritten typeface are the judgment criteria for distinguishing different fonts. The results showed that compared to color, font change had a greater effect on affective judgments such as "complex-simple", "beautiful-ugly", "luxurious-plain", "active-passive", "cause-effect-rule", and "like-dislike". "complex-simple", "beautiful-ugly", "luxurious-plain", "active-passive", "cause-effect-rule", and "like-dislike" affective judgments. Colors had a greater influence than fonts in judging the feelings "friendly-serious" and "soft-hard". [20] states that perception is a subjective experience that is associated and labeled with an individual's past experiences. Perception is personalized and autobiographical in nature due to the unique life experiences of each individual. [21] study presents the results of a subjective evaluation study of four variants of the Helvetica Neue font (Ultra Light, Light, Normal and Bold). These variants contain high vs. low contrast and positive vs. negative polarity. The results suggest that ultralight fonts are rated lower in legibility among users of different ages, but younger users may find them more aesthetically appealing than older users. Based on the results of the study, we provide recommendations on the use of lightweight fonts in user interface design. Considering the use of different combinations of font thickness, contrast, and polarity in a design can better satisfy users' aesthetic and reading needs. We recommend that designers not only consider legibility when choosing fonts, but also focus on the attractiveness of fonts to ensure a more interesting and engaging user experience. This may have a positive aesthetic effect on users of different ages, making them more willing to interact with the user interface [22] study confirms that people will match basic taste words (sweet, sour, salty, bitter) with different fonts that are rounded and angular on a perceptual level. The study concluded that there is a strong relationship between the degree of roundness/angularity of the typeface, the ease of handling and personal preference, which in turn influences the establishment of a correspondence between the typeface and the sense of taste at the perceptual level. [23] is based on relevant literature on the use of different languages on package labels and aims to investigate whether the use of exotic Chinese language in package design affects consumer preferences and perceptual evaluations of packages in different countries. The results of the analysis found that consumer preference for exotic Chinese package labels was associated with individual Chinese character recognition ability. In this study, packaging with exotic Chinese characters demonstrated attractiveness and aesthetics, with Chinese and Japanese subjects who could recognize Chinese characters scoring higher on the dimensions of attractiveness, aesthetics, innovation, sophistication, and engineering, while Thai subjects who did not know Chinese had the lowest scores on all dimensions. In terms of theories related to typography, [24] in the Handbook of Typography defines typography as the selection of appropriate fonts for specific needs, rationalization of space on the page, and consideration of the reader's reading comfort as much as possible. In the typographic process, the choice of fonts is consistent with the temperament of the typographic content, which allows the reader to effectively grasp the reading information. Exploring the theories of typography from the perspective of different cultural contexts, [25] proposed the concept of "exogenous", which is defined as "a design in which the typeface is a Latin character, and the design is clearly influenced by the characteristics of typefaces in different countries". The design of a typeface with Latin characters is clearly influenced by the characteristics of typefaces in different countries. The typeface design process may incorporate typeface features from the designer's home country, or it may draw on inspiration presented from different countries."

Therefore, in response to the previous discussion, the author proposes two hypotheses:

1. H1. The "Ice and Snow" font designed by the author for the theme of ice and snow culture will have an impact on the participants' emotional response.
2. H2. Different participants perceive different font personalities for the "Ice and Snow" font.

- **Study of independent variables, dependent variables:**
- Independent variables: Different types of ice and snow themed font designs, including the author's original ice and snow font designs and other designers' ice and snow themed fonts, as well as a regular bold font.

Cultural Context: Considering that culture may be an important factor influencing perception, cultural background was used as the independent variable. Different cultural groups were further covered to test the potential influence of culture on perception.

– Dependent Variable:

Subjective perception: This includes the user's subjective evaluation of font aesthetics and visual appeal. Users' subjective perception is quantified through questionnaires or subjective ratings.

Readability and comprehensibility: How well the user reads and understands the text. Assessed through screen viewing tests, comprehension questions or relevant questionnaires.

User preferences: user preferences for different types of ice-themed fonts. User preference information is obtained through questionnaires or rating systems.

Cognitive consistency: the consistency of users' perceptions of the ice-themed font design with their personal or cultural perceptions. Interviews or questionnaires were used to find out whether users' perceptions of the design were consistent with their expectations of the ice theme.

2   Research Methodology

This study used a variety of methods to delve into the possible effects of different cultural contexts on the perception of ice and snow themed fonts. These included questionnaire analysis, semi-structured interview analysis, and experimental tasks. First, by designing a structured questionnaire, we collected information on subjects' subjective feelings, preferences, and perceived effects of different types of ice and snow-themed fonts.

This approach allowed us to systematically understand subjects' perceptions in terms of ice-themed typography and to capture their perceptual tendencies. Second, using semi-structured interview analysis, we conducted face-to-face or remote interviews to communicate in depth with the participants in order to gain a more comprehensive understanding of their experiences, perceptions, and suggestions on ice and snow-themed typography. This type of in-depth communication helped to tap into the deeper perception and cognition of the subjects. In the experimental task, subjects engaged in interactions with different types of ice-themed fonts, including reading, recognition, or evaluation tasks. This step allowed us to observe how subjects reacted to the fonts in the actual task, and thus to assess more objectively the actual effects of the typography. Finally, through a cross-cultural comparative analysis, we considered cross-cultural factors when recruiting subjects to ensure that the findings were broadly applicable. This helps to identify potential differences in the perception of snow and ice-themed fonts across cultures, providing a more comprehensive understanding for further research.

2.1 Font Selection and Experimental Procedures

Three fonts are displayed in the cell phone banner page. The first one is the author's original font design "Ice Sports Imagery", which is inspired by the ice sports in the regional ice and snow culture. The author extracts the imagery of the characteristics of ice and snow sports, mainly from the words of "coherence", "power" and "agility" and other characteristics. In terms of font structure, the design is based on the running script of Chinese calligraphy. The overall effect seeks to create the shape of a "snowball" in terms of the characteristics of the strokes, adopting the rounded head of the strokes, and at the same time borrowing from the calligraphic style of the line to strengthen the dynamic connection between the strokes. In addition, the structure of the font adopts the right corner of the upward momentum, while increasing the contrast of the space within the word, making it more dynamic. The second font is a snow and ice theme font "Jiang Shuang Song" created by other font designers, while the third font is a regular bold font design. To ensure the credibility of the experiment, the designer of each font was not informed prior to the start of the experiment, and none of the subjects had seen the three fonts to be presented in advance. The experiment was divided into two parts. The first part divided all the participants into three groups of 50 each. In addition, participants in each group were fixed to look at one of the three fonts. In the second part, participants were asked to make a perceptual assessment of the viewed fonts, using a 7-point scale of 15 pairs of adjectives. Finally, participants were asked questions through a questionnaire, including "Do you know what type of font this font belongs to?", "How often on average do you pay attention to the knowledge about font design?" and "Do you consider yourself a typeface design enthusiast?" The questions included "Do you know what typeface this font belongs to? (Fig. 1).

(a) the author's original "Ice Sports Imagery " font
(b) other designers' ice and snow-themed font
(c) regular bold font

Fig. 1. Demonstration of three fonts

2.2 Participants

A total of 150 participants completed the experiment from a variety of majors in art and design, majoring in art and design, as well as majors related to typography, to ensure that they had an understanding of design elements and aesthetics. In addition, we recruited participants from different grade levels to ensure a diverse sample.

3 Results and Analysis

3.1 Semiotic Theory Analysis

Since its inception, semiotic theory has played an important role in the interpretation of visual works in terms of their symbolic meaning and impact [26]. Among them, the analytical method of the semiotician Saussure emphasizes the relationship between the "energy" and "reference" of symbols, as well as the connection between different symbols. "Energetic reference" refers to the sounds and images of symbols, which are manifested mainly through the physical dimension, including "the form of things presented by sensory stimuli, including text, sound, images, etc.". The "referent" is the extended meaning attached to the "capable". At the same time, the relationship between "energy" and "reference" is not static. [27] In addition, the semiotician Roland Barthes, relying on Saussure, proposed that "sign" is an element that develops at the level of culture and society, and argued that the sign can be embodied in two dimensions, namely, "inner meaning" and "outer meaning" and "extensible meaning". There is general agreement that "connotative meaning" includes implicit, associative and flexible meanings, while "denotative meaning" refers to direct linguistic meaning. The analytical approach of Saussure and Roland Barthes focuses on historical context and cultural context. The research theme in this paper combines the excavation and promotion of ice and snow culture with typography. Based on the analysis of semiotics, the font design of ice and snow theme is the result of the connection of multiple energetic and referential meanings. Relying on the context of semiotic theory, the author further refines the semiotic analysis method of typography by combining the studies of [28] and [29]: 1. Analyze the connotations of typography in depth, and identify their unique visual characteristics, in order to more profoundly identify the "visual assignments" embedded in typography. 2. Apply semiotic theory to standardize the translation of the corresponding visual meanings, so as to decode the relevant meanings for the typography. 3. Utilize the results of the perceptual assessment in the Semantic Difference Method to further validate the distilled visual meanings through the results of the Semantic Difference Method. The results of the perceptual evaluation in the semantic differential method will be used to further verify the refined visual meanings.

3.2 Discussion of Findings

The results of this study indicate that the ice and snow themed font design is related to the emotional response of the participants, and the participants perceive different font personalities for different font types. The survey results show that the "Ice Sports Imagery" designed by the author makes the participants feel more "elegant", "flexible", "exciting", "unruly", "expensive", "normative", "professional" and other themes. According to the structure of the calligraphy, smooth and powerful strokes reflect a certain writing speed, and a certain sense of continuous rhythm between strokes makes the font structure look more flexible and vivid. At the same time, the " Ice Sports Imagery" pays attention to the horizontal and vertical structure, and the stable and balanced shape is formed between the fonts and strokes, which may bring people a standardized and stable feeling. In addition, the font adopts special strokes, such as vertical strokes of the font, irregular vertical line shape, and the change in thickness reminds people of the rhythm of skiing tracks, which may make people feel that it is not in line with the regular personality. In addition, the "Jiang Shuang Song" typeface designed by other designers makes participants feel "rigid", "amiable", "masculine", "conformist", "old", "practical" and other themes, "Jiang Shuang Song" typeface is based on the Chinese Qing Dynasty calligrapher Jin Nong's lacquer book "Tong Meng Ba Zhang Juan". The letters in the lacquer book "Tong Meng Ba Zhang Juan" are like writing with a special horizontal brush, showing a thick sense of sweeping the brush, which may make participants feel rigid and masculine. In addition, the "Jiang Shuang Song" font in the horizontal and vertical strokes to a large extent reflects the Chinese calligraphy of "Dao Xie", " Dao Xie " brushwork makes the strokes appear first wide and then sharp, and at the same time, the longitudinal trend of the font is appropriately increased, so that the overall temperament of the font is like the pine and cypress standing tall in the snow, and the overall characteristics of the font have very obvious calligraphy characteristics in the lacquer book " Tong Meng Ba Zhang Juan ". This may make people perceive the characteristics of conformity and old age. The last font is a regular boldface font, and the results show that it makes people perceive more features such as "standard", "cheap" and "boring". Since boldface font is not specially designed for the theme of snow and ice, it may lead to a low professional score in the evaluation. However, because boldface font is more efficient in People's Daily life, this may lead to people feeling more normative, ordinary, cheap and other characteristics. The "Ice Sports Imagery" designed by the author makes most participants perceive the "professional" impression. According to Saussure's semiotic theory, the relationship between signifier and signified is established in culture. In terms of design concept, the " Ice Sports Imagery " chooses the shape of "snow ball" to spread out in the pen and the track of skiing. At the level of font expression, the calligraphy style of Chinese calligraphy is chosen to be displayed, and the stroke speed is accelerated and the stroke fluidity is strong. There is a clear correlation between the "able reference" of the characteristic image of running script and the cultural meaning of the ice and snow theme expressed in this image, i.e. the "reference", which makes the participants clearly feel the cultural concept of the ice and snow theme.

4   Conclusion

Our study further confirms that the category of fonts evokes different emotional perceptions in participants, and the results further apply semiotic theories to explain the perceptual impact of different font designs in terms of "referent" and "denotation" on participants. In addition, our study provides guidance on the development of font libraries and the affective demand aspects of typeface design, and in particular provides insights into the perceptual assessment of typeface design in the context of a geographic culture with a snow and ice theme. This study addresses the differences in assessed perceptions and perceived impact of three different fonts in the context of snow and ice culture. The results show that different fonts produce different feeling impressions. The "Ice Sports Imagery" gave participants a greater sense of the characteristics associated with ice and snow culture, with participants favoring adjectives such as "professional" and "elegant". The second typeface, "Jiang Shuang Song", is significantly less relevant to the perception of the snow and ice theme than Ice and Snow, evoking more "amateurish" participants, "rigid" and "customary" adjectives. The third regular bold font made participants feel more adjectives such as "uninteresting" and "cheap". In the process of font development, perceptual evaluation of fonts is more conducive for designers to grasp the significance that needs to be brought by the structure and stroke shapes of fonts. This will lead to more effective design strategies for fonts with different themes and needs to meet the needs of different users. Font design also follows the human-centered design concept, to let our font design to convey additional meaning, the need for designers to understand the font at the beginning of the "can mean" and "refer to" in the user's mind to present the perceived personality.

References

1. Shaikh, A.D., Fox, D., Chaparro, B.S.: The Effect of Typeface on the Perception of Email (2007)
2. Hazlett, R.L., Larson, K., Shaikh, A.D., Chaparo, B.S.: Two studies on how a typeface congruent with content can enhance onscreen communication. Inf. Des. J. **20**(3), 207–219 (2013). https://doi.org/10.1075/idj.20.3.02haz
3. Shaikh, A.D., Chaparro, B.S., Fox, D.: Perception of fonts: perceived personality traits and uses (2006)
4. Gao, X., Dera, J., Nijhof, A.D., Willems, R.M.: Is less readable liked better? The case of font readability in poetry appreciation. PLoS ONE **14**(12), e0225757 (2019). https://doi.org/10.1371/journal.pone.0225757
5. Usability News 41 - Bernard1 (2002)
6. Mukai, S., Miyazaki, G.: Effects of both similarity of the evaluation of impressions, between elements, and font legibility, on aesthetic impression of packaging. Int. J. Affect. Eng. **15**(3), 289–293 (2016). https://doi.org/10.5057/ijae.IJAE-D-16-00012
7. Rello, L., Baeza-Yates, R.: The effect of font type on screen readability by people with dyslexia. ACM Trans. Access. Comput. **8**(4), 1–33 (2016). https://doi.org/10.1145/2897736
8. Chaparro, B.S., Shaikh, A.D., Chaparro, A., Merkle, E.C.: Comparing the legibility of six ClearType typefaces to Verdana and Times New Roman. Inf. Des. J. **18**(1), 36–49 (2010). https://doi.org/10.1075/idj.18.1.04cha

9. Choi, S., Aizawa, K.: Emotype: expressing emotions by changing typeface in mobile messenger texting. Multimed. Tools Appl. **78**(11), 14155–14172 (2019). https://doi.org/10.1007/s11042-018-6753-3

10. Qiu, Q., Watanabe, S., Omura, K.: Emotional responses to Chinese characters: exploration for simplified, traditional Chinese and Japanese typefaces. Int. J. Affect. Eng. **20**(2), 79–85 (2021). https://doi.org/10.5057/ijae.IJAE-D-20-00018

11. Amare, N., Manning, A.: Seeing typeface personality: emotional responses to form as tone. In: 2012 IEEE International Professional Communication Conference, Orlando, FL, USA, pp. 1–9. IEEE (2012). https://doi.org/10.1109/IPCC.2012.6408605

12. Juni, S., Gross, J.S.: Emotional and persuasive perception of fonts. Percept. Mot. Skills **106**(1), 35–42 (2008). https://doi.org/10.2466/pms.106.1.35-42

13. Gabriel, N.V., Ryoke, M.: Communication through typefaces: affective selection of English, Myanmar and Japanese Typefaces. In: International Symposium on Affective Science and Engineering, vol. ISASE2020, pp. 1–4 (2020). https://doi.org/10.5057/isase.2020-C000039

14. Qiu, Q., Watanabe, S., Omura, K.: Affective font selection: the hybrid of Japanese and Latin typefaces. Int. J. Affect. Eng. **17**(2), 89–98 (2018). https://doi.org/10.5057/ijae.IJAE-D-17-00008

15. Bianchi, R.G., Da Hora Rodrigues, K.R., De Almeida Neris, V.P.: Emotional responses to font types and sizes in web pages. In: Proceedings of the XX Brazilian Symposium on Human Factors in Computing Systems, Virtual Event Brazil: ACM, pp. 1–11 (2021). https://doi.org/10.1145/3472301.3484325

16. Cabanac, M.: What is emotion? Behav. Process. **60**(2), 69–83 (2002). https://doi.org/10.1016/S0376-6357(02)00078-5

17. Cannon, W.B.: The James-Lange theory of emotions: a critical examination and an alternative theory (2024)

18. Gump, J.E.: The readability of typefaces and the subsequent mood or emotion created in the reader. J. Educ. Bus. **76**(5), 270–273 (2001). https://doi.org/10.1080/08832320109599647

19. Lee, W., Pai, S.: The affective feelings of colored typefaces. Color. Res. Appl. **37**(5), 367–374 (2012). https://doi.org/10.1002/col.20698

20. Shouse, E.: Feeling, Emotion, Affect. MC J. **8**(6) (2005). https://doi.org/10.5204/mcj.2443

21. Zlokazova, T., Burmistrov, I.: Perceived legibility and aesthetic pleasingness of light and ultralight fonts. In: Proceedings of the European Conference on Cognitive Ergonomics 2017, Umeå Sweden, pp. 191–194. ACM (2017). https://doi.org/10.1145/3121283.3121296

22. Velasco, C., Woods, A.T., Hyndman, S., Spence, C.: The taste of typeface. Percept. **6**(4), 204166951559304 (2015). https://doi.org/10.1177/2041669515593040

23. Yun, W., Kamchompoo, S., Takamitsu, T.: Study of consumer response on exotic Chinese font design styles in packaging design: focus on Korean-style Chinese fonts and Thai-style Chinese fonts as examples. 芸術工学会誌 **80**, 32–39 (2020). https://doi.org/10.15113/0002000163

24. Damayanti, L.: Color and font meaning in beauty clinics logo: a semiotic study (2013)

25. Celhay, F., Boysselle, J., Cohen, J.: Food packages and communication through typeface design: the exoticism of exotypes. Food Qual. Prefer. **39**, 167–175 (2015). https://doi.org/10.1016/j.foodqual.2014.07.009

26. Aiello, G.: Theoretical advances in critical visual analysis: perception, ideology, mythologies, and social semiotics. J. Vis. Lit. **26**(2), 89–102 (2006). https://doi.org/10.1080/23796529.2006.11674635

27. Suhaimi, S.N., Fauzi, T.A.: Visual semiotics: identity reflection in personal symbol creation. **9**(1) (2021)

28. Vallverdu-Gordi, M., Marine-Roig, E.: The role of graphic design semiotics in environmental awareness campaigns. Int. J. Environ. Res. Public Health **20**(5), 4299 (2023). https://doi.org/10.3390/ijerph20054299
29. Song, C.-M., Jeon, H.-Y.: A semiotic study of regional branding reflected in the slogans of Korean regions. Soc. Semiot.Semiot. **28**(2), 230–256 (2018). https://doi.org/10.1080/10350330.2017.1292628

Cognitive Biases in the Estimation of the Interface Updates: Facebook Users' Case

Nadezhda R. Glebko[✉]

National Research University "Higher School of Economics", Moscow, Russian Federation
nglebko@hse.ru

Abstract. The term "baby duck syndrome" is used to refer to the phenomenon when the user compares each new computer system with the one, he or she originally studied. It is assumed that the user, according to the results of this comparison, prefers exactly the type of interface with which they interacted for the first time. This hypothesis was tested on the case of a major Facebook update in 2020, when the design of the social network was significantly changed. The study involves 201 participants from 18 to 59 years old. First, the subjects described frequency and duration of using Facebook. Then they subsequently evaluate interface versions (108 people first evaluated the old version, others - the new). At the end, the participants answer the question which version they prefer and why. The data obtained reveal significant differences for the estimates of the old version depending on the frequency of use (but not to the new). Regarding the duration of use, no significant differences are found. In addition, the estimates of the new interface, depending on the type of presentation of the survey, differ significantly. Based on the results, it can be assumed that the frequency of use predominantly affects the evaluation of interface updates.

Keywords: The Baby Duck Syndrome · Cognitive Biases · Interface Updates · Human-Computer Interaction

1 Introduction

It is already difficult to imagine a world without computing devices and mobile phones with which we interact every day to perform a wide variety of tasks. The interface in this vein sets a new interaction context - it is a digital environment [1]. The digital environment is an interesting object of study because the interface can be called a kind of prism for the transformation of cognitive processes [2]. The familiarization of such a new multifunctional cultural tool can have an impact not only on the direct activity of the subject, but also on the mechanisms of the mental functions in general. For example, it can lead to the emergence of new cognitive biases - systematic patterns of deviation from norm or rationality in judgment [3]. They affect decision making regarding various objects and phenomena of the surrounding world [4]. Thus, the study of user interaction with the interface and related phenomena is extremely relevant and important for the development of modern psychology.

© The Author(s), under exclusive license to Springer Nature Switzerland AG 2024
C. Stephanidis et al. (Eds.): HCII 2024, CCIS 2114, pp. 144–147, 2024.
https://doi.org/10.1007/978-3-031-61932-8_17

In this paper, such a phenomenon as the "baby duck syndrome" is considered. In usability, this term is used to refer to the phenomenon when a user compares each new computer system with the one, he or she originally learned [5]. It is assumed that the user, based on the results of this comparison, will prefer exactly the type of interface with which he or she interacted for the first time. And its subsequent variations will be rated much lower, at least initially. The first impression is decisive for further interaction with any object, including the interface. For example, it was found [6] that high visual complexity has a negative effect on intent to use websites, but this is entirely mediated by first impression attitudes towards the website. It can be assumed that the lower score for interface updates and the preference for the old version are similar cognitive biases, since updates usually suggest improvements based on user opinion.

Since the "baby duck syndrome" is closely related to the practical use of the interface, laboratory conditions are only partially suitable for studying this phenomenon. However, some case studies provided the empirical evidence. Such a case is a major update of the Facebook interface in 2020. This is the biggest social network design update since the founding of Facebook. The updated design has become more modern, there are light and dark versions and much more. In connection with this event, it was decided to conduct a survey of Facebook users a week after the release of the new version of the interface [7]. The purpose of this work is to study a practical case where it is possible to detect cognitive biases in user assessment. According to the "baby duck syndrome" hypothesis, users will prefer the old version of Facebook and rate lower the new one. However, these estimates may differ depending on how long the user have been familiar with the interface and the frequency of interaction.

2 Methods

The study involved 201 subjects (82 are males) from 18 to 59 years old (M = 31.67, SD = 10.32). The data was collected through the Toloka platform using the survey method. The survey consists of three parts. The first part concerned: socio-demographic characteristics (gender, age, education); duration of using (the last couple of months/ more than six months/ more than a year/ more than three years and beyond); frequency of using (every day/ 2–3 time a week/ a couple of times per month/ once a month and less) of using Facebook.

The second and third parts dealt with the assessment of the old and new interface versions using the System Usability Scale questionnaire [8]. In order to exclude the influence of the sequence of presentation, two Types of the survey were made. In Type 1, subjects evaluate the old version first, then the new one (108 participants); in Type 2 - on the contrary (93 participants). At the very end, the question was asked which version the user likes best and why. Further, all questionnaires were processed, and all survey data was collected into a common dataset.

3 Results

The R-studio environment was used for the analysis. First, descriptive statistics were calculated. Table 1 presents the average scores of the old and new versions of Facebook - both in general (Average) and depending on the Type of survey.

Table 1. Mean SUS scores for types of survey.

Condition	Mean SUS scores with SD	
	Old version	New version
Type 1	57.01 (20.37)	64.12 (18.02)
Type 2	55.1 (20.64)	56.42 (19.07)
Average	56.13 (20.47)	60.56 (18.89)

The results show that, on average, the new version of the interface is rated higher than the old one, while the distribution of ratings remains almost the same. In particular, there is significant difference in the assessment of the new interface depending on the Type of survey ($p = 0.022$).

If we talk about the influence of any factors on the assessment of the interface, then neither gender, nor age, nor the duration of use have a significant impact on the assessment of either the old or the new versions of Facebook ($p > 0.05$). However, significant differences were found in the evaluation of the old version depending on the experience of using ($p = 0.0002$); no differences were found for the new version ($p = 0.054$). SUS scores depending on the frequency of use are presented in Table 2 (the number of people is indicated as "n"). It represents that the more often the user interacts with the interface of the version, the higher he or she rates it.

Table 2. Mean SUS scores for frequency of use.

Version	Mean SUS scores with SD			
	Every day (n = 63)	2–3 time a week (n = 36)	A couple of times per month (n = 44)	Once a month and less (n = 58)
Old	64.52 (18.94)	55.76 (22.05)	56.25 (18.76)	47.16 (18.98)
New	66.45 (18.97)	60.97 (19.19)	58.86 (16.24)	55.27 (19.05)

As for the final question of the preferred version, 72 people chose the old version, and the remaining majority - the new one. As arguments for the old version, the usual design was mainly used, and for the new one - attractiveness and novelty.

4 Discussion

The results obtained did not support the main hypothesis. First, the new version of Facebook was indeed rated higher than the old one. It is possible that the new design is more attractive than the old one. However, it is important to note the effect of survey Type on the scores of the new version. This is probably the effect of framing, since in the Type 2 the scores of the new version is slightly lower than the old version in Type 1. The scores of the old version do not differ so much, which may be a consequence of users' attachment to the interface.

It is also important to note that it is the frequency of use, not the duration of use, that is critical when evaluating an interface. This statement confirms the result that significant differences were found when evaluating the old version. It is important to note that "everyday" users rated the old and new versions almost equally. This is a partial confirmation of the duckling syndrome hypothesis. The less often a person uses the interface, the higher he evaluates the new version. This is probably because the new design is closer to modern interface usability. Regular users, on the other hand, adapt to the existing design and are less critical of it.

To sum it up, the Facebook interface update case study is great for learning about the "baby duck syndrome". The results obtained can serve as a partial confirmation of the existence of this phenomenon and can also expand knowledge in the field of cognitive psychology and usability. In addition, the study of interaction with the digital environment is extremely important for understanding the cognitive processes of a modern person.

Acknowledgments. The study was carried out as part of the HSE Program for Fundamental Research in 2020.

Disclosure of Interests.   The author has no competing interests to declare that are relevant to the content of this article.

References

1. Kallinikos, J., Aaltonen, A., Marton, A.: The ambivalent ontology of digital artifacts. Mis Q., 357–370 (2013)
2. Barr, N., Pennycook, G., Stolz, J.A., Fugelsang, J.A.: The brain in your pocket: evidence that Smartphones are used to supplant thinking. Comput. Hum. Behav. **48**, 473–480 (2015)
3. Haselton, M.G., Nettle, D., Andrews, P.W.: The Evolution of Cognitive Bias. In: Buss, D.M. (ed.) Hoboken, pp. 724–746. John Wiley & Sons Inc., NJ, US (2005)
4. Wilmer, H.H., Sherman, L.E., Chein, J.M.: Smartphones and cognition: a review of research exploring the links between mobile technology habits and cognitive functioning. Front. Psychol. **8**, 605 (2017)
5. Novin, A., Meyers, E.M.: Four biases in interface design interactions. In: Marcus, A., Wang, W. (eds.) DUXU 2017. LNCS, vol. 10288, pp. 163–173. Springer, Cham (2017). https://doi.org/10.1007/978-3-319-58634-2_13
6. Crutzen, R., de Kruif, L., de Vries, N.K.: You never get a second chance to make a first impression: the effect of visual complexity on intention to use websites. Interact. Stud. **13**(5), 469–477 (2012)
7. The Daily Star, https://www.thedailystar.net/shout/news/unsettling-2020-1966305. Accessed 10 Sept 2020
8. Lewis, J.R.: The system usability scale: past, present, and future. Int. J. Hum.-. Interact. **34**(7), 577–590 (2018)

Force-Based Modeling of a Resilient Helping Role in Coordinated Behavior of a Triad

Jun Ichikawa[1]([⊠]) ⓘ and Keisuke Fujii[2,3,4] ⓘ

[1] Shizuoka University, 3-5-1 Johoku, Chuo-ku, Hamamatsu, Shizuoka, Japan
`j-ichikawa@inf.shizuoka.ac.jp`
[2] Nagoya University, Furo-cho, Chikusa-ku, Nagoya, Aichi, Japan
`fujii@g.sp.m.is.nagoya-u.ac.jp`
[3] RIKEN Center for Advanced Intelligence Project, 744 Motooka, Nishi-ku, Fukuoka, Fukuoka, Japan
[4] PRESTO, Japan Science and Technology Agency, 4-1-8 Honcho, Kawaguchi, Saitama, Japan

Abstract. The aim of this study was to understand complex and dynamic coordination, which refers to the nonverbal interaction of more than three members. This would be applied to smooth and effective role-sharing, as in multiplayer games with AI characters. Our previous study indicated the importance of resilient help using a coordinated drawing task involving a triad. In the experiment, each participant operated a reel to change the thread tension and moved a pen connected to the three threads to draw an equilateral triangle. Three heterogeneous roles were shared: the pulling and relaxing roles moving the pen as if pulling it closer to the hand and supporting its smooth movement, respectively. However, these roles alone cannot draw a triangle's side because of the task specifications. The adjusting role must moderately intervene in the two roles to correct the pen trajectory, which can deviate. The multiple regression model using pen position and tension data revealed that the third role was related to the high task performance of the pen's quick movement while minimizing deviation. To constructively understand this resilient helping role, this study conducted multi-agent simulation using equations of motion. Here, the tension in the adjusting role was changed as optimally as possible so that the resultant force of the three roles would coincide on a side. The results showed that the proposed model partially replicates the pen trajectory. Overall, this role might anticipate the forces of the other roles based on the performance information, that can be perceived.

Keywords: Coordinated group behavior · Role sharing · Computer simulation

1 Introduction

Group coordination achieves works that cannot be done alone or higher task performance [1]. Scientific research has been conducted in various fields to inves-

ⓒ The Author(s), under exclusive license to Springer Nature Switzerland AG 2024
C. Stephanidis et al. (Eds.): HCII 2024, CCIS 2114, pp. 148–155, 2024.
https://doi.org/10.1007/978-3-031-61932-8_18

tigate this mechanisms. The findings would contribute to smooth and effective role-sharing with computers, including AI. Meanwhile, the nonverbal adjustment processes of more than three humans is not fully understood because of complex and dynamic interactions [2,3], as in team sports and haul seines. We focused on the resilient helping role, which is crucial for complex and dynamic coordination, and aimed to constructively understand this role using a multi-agent simulation approach.

Next, we explain a series of our previous studies considering the above problems. Related work has identified an important role in coordinated group behavior based on the sharing of heterogeneous roles was identified [4]. Here, a coordinated drawing task involving a triad [5] was introduced (Fig. 1a). In the experiment, each participant operated a reel to change the thread tension and moved a pen connected to the three threads to draw an equilateral triangle (length: 30 cm, width: 2 cm; Fig. 1b). Three heterogeneous roles were shared (Fig. 1b). The pulling and relaxing roles moved the pen as if each operator pulled it closer to the hand and supported its smooth movement, respectively. However, these roles alone cannot draw a triangle's side because of the task specifications, as indicated by the dashed blue arrow in Fig. 1a. The adjusting role must moderately intervene in the two roles to correct the pen trajectory, as indicated by the dashed black arrow in Fig. 1a. The six triads repeatedly engaged in the task, and the multiple regression model using pen position and tension data revealed that the third role was related to the high task performance of the pen's quick movement while minimizing deviation. It suggests that this role resiliently helps others to maintain an overall balance. However, this experiment alone cannot explain how to adjust. Thus, to constructively understand the adjusting role, we modeled the above three roles using equations of motion [6]. The results of computer simulation showed that the proposed model partially replicates the pen trajectory. This suggests that in the adjustment process, the resilient helping role may use the performance information reflected in others' motions. In the coordinated drawing task, the degree of pen deviation is related to operating procedures and forces. However, the previous model could not replicate on all the sides.

Therefore, we modeled the adjusting role of the coordinated drawing task using a different rule in the previous study [6]. The task performance in this simulation was compared with that in the behavioral experiment [4]. The purpose of this study was to constructively investigate the resilient adjustment process. The main contribution of our study is the understanding of primitive social interactions, which is expected to be applicable to role-sharing in field sports and multiplayer games with computer characters.

2   Method

In the coordinated drawing task, each operator turns a reel to change the tension and the triad moves the pen. Thus, we can simply explain each role using equations of motion according to human operations. The force vectors of the three heterogeneous roles at the current time frame f are expressed using Eq. (1):

$$F_f = F_f^p + F_f^r + F_f^a,$$ (1)

where F_f^p, F_f^r, and F_f^a represent the tensions (N) in the pulling, relaxing, and adjusting roles, respectively. These vectors comprise two dimensions: the x- and y-components. In the following sections, we briefly describe the rule-based model for each role.

2.1 Pulling and Relaxing Roles

These rules follow those in our previous study [6]. $|F_f^p|$ is expressed as in Eq. (2):

$$|F_f^p| = \begin{cases} \overline{F^p} + r_f^p & if\ f \leq f_{tau}, \\ \beta_0^p + \beta_1^p Dev_{f-f_{tau}} & otherwise, \end{cases}$$ (2)

where the sensorimotor delay f_{tau} is 0.25 s [7]. $\overline{F^p}$ is the average tension peak value (0.57 N) through the triads based on the analysis of the behavioral experiment [4]. r_f^p is random noise, which is the product of a random number with a standard normal distribution, the SD of the tension peaks (0.12 N), and the tuned amount of noise (0.1). An operator pulls the pen at a certain tension until the current time frame reaches the delay as exception handling. After f_{tau}, $|F_f^p|$ is linearly regressed on the degree of pen deviation at the time frame before f_{tau}, $Dev_{f-f_{tau}}$ (cm). This is the distance between the pen position and the median width line on each triangle's side, as indicated by the dotted black line in Fig. 1a. Depending on whether the pen is positioned inside or outside the side, the value is negative or positive, respectively. The intercept and slope of the regression are also analyzed using the experimental pen position and tension data, respectively ($\beta_0^p = 0.67$, $\beta_1^p = 0.14$). Here, the operator changes the tension based on the performance information reflected in the operations of the other roles.

Next, $|F_f^r|$ is represented by Eq. (3):

$$|F_f^r| = \begin{cases} 0 & if\ f \leq f_{tau}, \\ 0 & else\ if\ (f > f_{tau})\ and\ (|Dev_{f-f_{tau}}| \leq D_s/2), \\ r_f^r & otherwise, \end{cases}$$ (3)

This role does not need to pull the thread; $|F_f^r|$ is 0 in principle. Meanwhile, if $|Dev_{f-f_{tau}}|$ is larger than a threshold, an operator would try something to handle as noise r_f^r, which is the product of a random number, the SD of the minimum tension peaks through the triads (0.03 N), and the tuned amount of noise. D_s is the threshold for operation switching (1 cm), which is half the width of a side.

Both $|F_f^p|$ and $|F_f^r|$ are decomposed into two dimensions based on θ_f^p and θ_f^r in Fig. 1a.

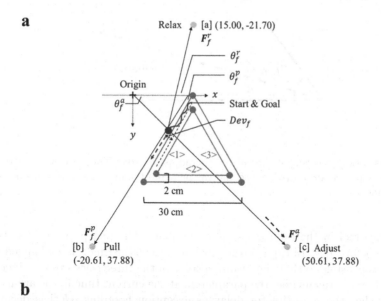

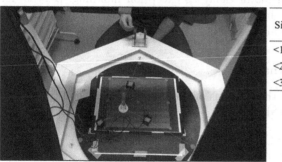

Side	Operator agent's role		
	[a]	[b]	[c]
<1>	relax	pull	adjust
<2>	adjust	relax	pull
<3>	pull	adjust	relax

Fig. 1. Coordinated drawing task. (a) Pattern diagram and used symbols when drawing side <1> in this simulation. Brackets represent the x- and y-positions. (b) Behavioral experiment from our previous study [4] and the table with three heterogeneous roles on each side. The image of our previous study itself is licensed under CC BY.

2.2 Adjusting Role

In this study, $|F_f^a|$ is determined using the following rule in Eq. (4):

$$|F_f^a| = \frac{\tan\theta^{o'}_{f-ftau}|F^p_{f-ftau} + F^r_{f-ftau}|}{\sin\theta^o_{f-ftau} - \cos\theta^o_{f-ftau}\tan\theta^{o'}_{f-ftau}}, \tag{4}$$

where θ^o_{f-ftau} represents the angle between the median width line on each triangle's side and the position vector of the reel in the adjusting role and the pen. $\theta^{o'}_{f-ftau}$ indicates the angle between the median width line and the position

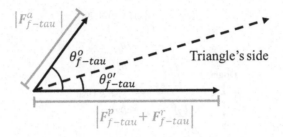

Fig. 2. Illustration diagram of the rule in the adjusting role. The position vectors of the reel in the pulling or adjusting role and the pen, and the median width line on each triangle's side.

vector of the reel in the pulling role and the pen[1]. The pen position is at the time frame before f_{tau}. In Eq. (4), the tension in the adjusting role is changed as optimally as possible so that the resultant force of the three roles would coincide on a side (Fig. 2). Meanwhile, the parameters at the current time frame are used until it reaches the sensorimotor delay as exception handling. $|F_f^a|$ is decomposed into two dimensions based on θ_f^a in Fig. 1a. That is to say, such ideal role is implemented hypothetically.

2.3   Simulation and Analysis

Once F_f is determined by the tensions of the three heterogeneous roles, the pen acceleration a_f is calculated using Eq. (5):

$$a_f = F_f/m. \tag{5}$$

where m is the pen mass (0.085 kg), and the pen position in the next time frame is calculated by the second-order integration of a_f. The time frame interval is 0.05 s.

If the distance between the pen and the triangle vertex is within the threshold, it reaches the goal and the roles are switched counterclockwise to draw the next side. The threshold is 1 cm when drawing sides <1> and <2>, and 2 cm when drawing side <3>. This study ran the multi-agent simulation six times, that is, the number of participant triads [4] was the same as in the previous simulation [6]. These were conducted using the MATLAB R2016b software.

3   Results and Discussion

The operator agents were able to draw all the triangles' sides. In task performance, Fig. 3 shows the average pen deviations (cm) on each side. The Mann-Whitney U test was conducted to compare the pen deviation in the simulation

---

[1] The position vector of the reel in the relaxing role is not considered because the force in this role is extremely small (see the Pulling and Relaxing roles section).

with the behavioral experiment [4] on each side. The p-values were corrected using the Bonferroni method to avoid the multiplicity problem. Notably, no significant difference was confirmed on side <3> at the 5% level. However, significant differences between the simulation and behavioral experiment were confirmed on the other sides ($ps < .01$).

The results showed that the proposed model partially replicated the experimental pen trajectory, which was similar to those of our previous study [6]. The participant triads could watch the pen deviation during the task [4]. In the previous simulation, the adjusting role mainly determined the tension based on the degree of pen deviation, and this role could not use the forces of the other roles, as in this study. Therefore, considering the findings in the current study, the resilient helping role might anticipate the forces of the other roles based on the performance information. It is a crucial discussion to complement the previous findings and to constructively understand the adjustment process for group coordination. Meanwhile, this study did not also replicate the pen trajectory on all the sides. In addition, the side on which no significant difference was confirmed differed from that of the previous simulation. The previous study replicated the trajectory on side <2> and this study did on side <3>. These might have emerged because of the exception handling and environmental settings. Additional features are required to develop a real human model. Group coordination in sports is achieved through both top-down and bottom-up processing [8]. The former includes a group goal and instructions, and information of other

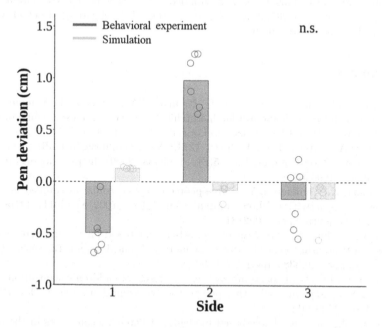

Fig. 3. Task performance. Average pen deviations on each triangle's side in the simulation and behavioral experiment [4].

members based on task knowledge. The rule-based model involves top-down processing. The latter indicates data-driven handling through sensory information, for example reinforcement learning of the adjustment from the tensions and pen deviation. The integration of both types of processing is required.

The series of our studies contribute to the understanding of complex and dynamic coordination, which is nonverbal interaction of three members. This study is expected to be applicable to role-sharing in field sports and multiplayer games with AI characters.

4 Conclusion

This study modeled the three heterogeneous roles in the coordinated drawing task, using equations of motion. We focused on the adjusting role, which is crucial for coordination. This role resiliently helps the other roles to maintain an overall balance. The results of computer simulation showed that our rule-based model of top-down processing partially replicates the task performance of the behavioral experiment. Considering the findings of the previous and current simulation studies, a resilient helping role might anticipate the behaviors of other roles based on performance information. Future work can improve the proposed model by tuning the exception handling and integrating top-down and bottom-up processing such in reinforcement learning.

Acknowledgments. This work was supported by JSPS KAKENHI Grant Numbers 21K18033 and 24K20562, and AY 2023 (Special Application) Research Grants of Amano Institute of Technology.

References

1. Fujii, K., Yokoyama, K., Koyama, T., Rikukawa, A., Yamada, H., Yamamoto, Y.: Resilient help to switch and overlap hierarchical subsystems in a small human group. Sci. Rep. **6**, 23911 (2016). https://doi.org/10.1038/srep23911
2. Braun, D.A., Ortega, P.A., Wolpert, D.M.: Nash equilibria in multi-agent motor interactions. PLoS Comput. Biol. **5**(8), e1000468 (2009). https://doi.org/10.1371/journal.pcbi.1000468
3. Yokoyama, K., Yamamoto, Y.: Three people can synchronize as coupled oscillators during sports activities. PLoS Comput. Biol. **7**(10), e1002181 (2011). https://doi.org/10.1371/journal.pcbi.1002181
4. Ichikawa, J., Fujii, K.: Analysis of group behavior based on sharing heterogeneous roles in a triad using a coordinated drawing task. Front. Psychol. **13**, 890205 (2022). https://doi.org/10.3389/fpsyg.2022.890205
5. Maruno, S.: Effects of social interaction on preschool children's acquisition of procedural knowledge and "self-other perspectives coordination". Jpn. J. Dev. Psychol. **1**(2), 116–127 (1991)
6. Ichikawa, J., Fujii, K.: Force-based modeling of heterogeneous roles in the coordinated behavior of a triad (2023, Manuscript submitted for publication)

7. Tsutsui, K., Fujii, K., Kudo, K., Takeda, K.: Flexible prediction of opponent motion with internal representation in interception behavior. Biol. Cybern. **115**, 473–485 (2021)
8. Steiner, S., Macquet, A.C., Seiler, R.: An integrative perspective on interpersonal coordination in interactive team sports. Front. Psychol. **8**, 1440 (2017). https://doi.org/10.3389/fpsyg.2017.01440

Automating User Task Performance: Introducing Task Experience Score (TES) for Complex Cloud Platforms

Xiang Li[✉] and Yuwei Yang

Alibaba Cloud Design, Alibaba Group, Beijing, People's Republic of China
{lx140892,yuwei.yang}@alibaba-inc.com

Abstract. For IT companies with complex back-end systems, it is crucial to enhance the usability and user experience by facilitating users to operate tasks smoothly and efficiently. Continuously measuring task performance is an essential aspect of experience design and management. Traditional usability metrics in industry and academia often depend on task testing and user feedback, demanding considerable time and resources. There is a scarcity of methods for rapidly, cost-effectively benchmarking and tracking the task performance of multiple products. This paper introduces an automated task performance scoring method and process entirely based on user behavior data for the Alibaba Cloud Console, which encompasses hundreds of cloud products. Utilizing objective raw data captured from web analytics tools, we formulated specific metrics that contribute to the Task Experience Score (TES). This scoring enables various stakeholders, particularly data-sensitive developers, to quickly grasp the experience levels of different products and tasks. TES can also complement other subjective experience measurement indicators, providing more comprehensive guidance for resource allocation and experience optimization in the design of complex back-end products. A preliminary study applied TES on 53 task flows across 10 products within the Alibaba Cloud Console. The results showed that TES closely corresponded with the results obtained through user surveys. Furthermore, we tracked the changes in TES for 8 task flows after optimizing the user interface. The results indicated that TES could evaluate the effectiveness of our design improvements to a certain extent. This simple and efficient method, initially designed for our online cloud platform, is likely adaptable to various types of user interfaces.

Keywords: Task Performance · Usability Evaluation · User Behavior Data · Cloud Computing Products

1 Introduction

In the process of user interaction with software products, the analysis of user task performance is an important aspect of measuring product usability and user experience [1]. Within enterprise settings, appropriate evaluations can ensure that the experience improvement process is always in the right direction.

© The Author(s), under exclusive license to Springer Nature Switzerland AG 2024
C. Stephanidis et al. (Eds.): HCII 2024, CCIS 2114, pp. 156–163, 2024.
https://doi.org/10.1007/978-3-031-61932-8_19

The Alibaba Cloud Console is a complex web application that provides a graphical interface for millions of users to conveniently manage and utilize hundreds of cloud products and their functionalities. Due to variations in development teams and resource investments, there is a noticeable disparity in the user experience across different products. Our design team has relied on usability research methods such as task testing and questionnaire surveys to evaluate the usability levels of various products. With rapid product iterations, these traditional research methods have proven complex in implementation, consuming substantial human and temporal resources without focusing on the finer domain of task performance. Moreover, in IT companies where user behavior and web analytics tools are increasingly prevalent, an over-reliance on subjective feedback metrics makes it challenging for non-design background personnel to quickly understand and reach a consensus.

How can we let different stakeholders understand the task performance levels and differences of each product at a glance? And how can we continuously and cost-effectively track and validate the task performance improvements? In response, we aim to design an automated, objective behavior data-based method of measuring task performance to serve the experience design of hundreds of cloud products.

2 Related Work

For the majority of complex back-end web products, the experience of task completion is a key concern for users and is intimately linked to the overall perception of the product's use. Task performance metrics effectively reflect the aspects of effectiveness and efficiency within product usability [2]. Academic research on usability measurement often favors comprehensive evaluation frameworks that combine task performance with self-reported results [3]. However, practical methods for measuring task performance have been seldom discussed [4, 5].

From an industry application perspective, traditional manual usability assessment methods based on standardized questionnaires and task tests have drawbacks such as high time and labor costs, and susceptibility to subjective factors [6]. Automated evaluation based on data analysis is a more economical and practical alternative, which has led to the continual proposal of tools for automated usability metrics of web and mobile applications [7, 8]. Post-launch, automated data-driven methods play a vital role, especially in large-scale evaluations [9, 10]. Yet, current research tools for automated usability assessments are often designed for specific requirements and are not well-suited to more complex software scenarios [11], and they typically require the deep involvement of usability experts [12]. To measure task performance for the Alibaba Cloud Console on a large scale and at a low cost, we have developed an automated evaluation method and process based entirely on objective web behavior data metrics.

3 The Metric

Task performance metrics are typically categorized into five aspects: task success, time-on-task, errors, efficiency, and learnability [2]. Using basic user log analysis tools, we can easily gather various user behavior data that reflect these five dimensions. For complex cloud computing platforms, failure to complete designated operational goals can lead to serious issues such as business disruptions, which might result in negative public sentiment and increased post-sales service costs. The speed at which users achieve operational goals directly mirrors the design and development quality of various products. Consequently, we aim to devise a composite, singular score based on objective data indicators of task success and efficiency—two aspects most critical to our business—to evaluate the task performance of different product consoles. Indicators reflecting errors and learnability, such as interface error rates or ticket support request rates, are more suitable for analyzing and pinpointing specific issues and have not been included in our scoring metric design.

3.1 Relative Completion Rate (RC)

Initially, the common automated metric of task Completion Rate (C) measures whether users can successfully achieve operational goals. Within a set timeframe, we denote the number of users who successfully complete a task as "s" and the total number of users who attempted the task as "S". The formula for calculating C is as follows, with values ranging from 0 to 1.

$$C = s/S \tag{1}$$

However, the value of C can be heavily influenced by the complexity of the task, making cross-comparison between different tasks seem inequitable. Hence, we have devised the "Relative Completion Rate (RC)" metric. We begin by categorizing tasks into different complexity levels based on the median number of user actions required for each task, such as "simple," "medium," and "complex." Simple tasks require fewer average user actions, while complex tasks demand more. During this categorization, we ensure that tasks within each category have a similar and relatively low variance in their completion rates. Subsequently, based on further measurement practices, we calculate the average completion rate for tasks of different complexity levels, which allows us to define a constant expected completion rate "p" for each category. This value is then automatically used to calculate the RC. In other words, for a task with a completion rate of "C", we first determine its complexity category based on the median number of actions collected, and select the corresponding expected completion rate "p". The final formula for RC is as follows, with values ranging from 0 to 1.

$$RC = \begin{cases} \frac{1}{2} * \frac{1+C-2p}{1-p}, & C \geq p \\ \frac{C}{2p}, & C < p \end{cases} \tag{2}$$

3.2 Relative Efficiency (RE)

In terms of efficiency, it is necessary to facilitate horizontal comparability amongst tasks of varying complexity and to ensure that metrics can be collected automatically, circumventing manual measurement methods, such as expert testing. Therefore, we have introduced a metric called task completion Relative Efficiency (RE). RE measures the gap between the expected completion time and the average time it takes for users to complete the task, thus reflecting the level of efficiency. The expected time to complete a task can be represented by the average completion time of the faster segment of the user sample, with the percentile chosen to reflect the proportion of skilled or professional users within the overall product user base. For instance, we may take the median completion time of the fastest 5% of task completions as the expected completion time for a given task. The median duration of all successful completion samples is taken as the average time for users to complete that task. If we order all completion time samples in ascending order as $t\_1, t\_2, \ldots, t\_n$, then the formula for calculating RE is as follows, with values ranging from 0 to 1.

$$RE = median(t\_1, t\_2, \ldots, t\_\{0.05n\})/median(t\_1, t\_2, \ldots, t\_n) \tag{3}$$

3.3 Task Experience Score (TES)

Building on the RC and RE metrics, we propose a method for calculating the TES for the Alibaba Cloud Console. When combining RC and RE, we introduce the task Completion Rate (C) as a weighting variable. Given that RE is calculated based on the sample data of tasks successfully completed, when C is very low, such as when C equals 0, we consider the statistical significance of RE to be lost, and in this case, the task is assigned the minimum score of 0. When C is at the ideal value of 1, the score is the arithmetic mean of RC and RE, meaning the weight given to RE is at its maximum value of 0.5. To facilitate communication and comparison in business contexts, we convert the final calculation result into a 10-point scoring system. The formula is as follows:

$$TES = \frac{RC + RE*C}{1 + C}*10 \tag{4}$$

3.4 Product-Level Task Experience Score (PTES)

To evaluate the differences in task experience across various products, we calculate the arithmetic mean of the scores for each task that is monitored within a product to represent its overall task performance. The higher the score, the better the overall task performance of the product. The formula is as follows:

$$PTES = \frac{1}{n} \sum_{i=1}^{n} TES_i \tag{5}$$

4 Evaluation Process

The automated task performance measurement process is divided into four main steps. First, integrating a unified user behavior data collection and analysis tool is essential to commence the measurement activities. The second step involves each product identifying the core user operation flows to be measured. In selecting tasks, product management teams or product owners might refer to objective data such as API call frequency or button click rankings to make considered decisions that encompass the majority of user scenarios. The third step is to configure the start and end points of each task flow in the data analysis tool, initiating the automatic collection of user data. The starting point corresponds to the commencement of user action, such as opening an operation dialog, while the end point signifies the successful completion of the action, for example, the successful submission of a task-related API call. Additionally, to ensure the credibility of metrics such as RC and RE, we should verify based on the Cochran Formula [13] that the number of completed samples for each task flow exceeds 385 at the end of sampling. The final step is to calculate the task experience score for each task and product automatically, using the collected user data and the aforementioned formulas at specific intervals. As shown in Fig. 1, these scores are often presented in a data dashboard format, providing a visual comparison of task performance over time within products and between different product consoles.

For product teams, TES can be used to establish a benchmark for their product's task performance. Faced with tasks that score poorly, designers can analyze the points at which users drop off or encounter errors during their operations. This analysis can be combined with subjective feedback from users to propose appropriate experience optimization measures. Typically, simply by changing the frequency of metric collection, TES can be used to continuously track the effectiveness of improvements made to product task flows.

Fig. 1. A screen capture of our cloud platform TES data board

5   Discussion and Future Works

To preliminarily validate the reasonableness and feasibility of this measurement method and scoring system, we conducted a pilot study on the Alibaba Cloud Console, encompassing 10 major cloud products including cloud servers and load balancers. After discussions and consultations with the respective product designers and developers, we selected 53 core user task flows, which included tasks such as creating resources, deleting resources, and modifying configurations. Through the automated calculation of user raw data, we obtained the TES for each task flow, which allowed us to calculate the PTES for the 10 different products.

Table 1. Introduction of our ease-of-use questionnaire survey

Question description	Scale
Is the product generally easy to use?	1–10

We compared the PTES with the subjective ease-of-use rating based on a sample of 663 valid questionnaire responses (see Table 1) [14], and the results are depicted in Fig. 2. A Pearson's correlation test between PTES and ease-of-use rating demonstrated that the scores based on objective behavioral data analysis are very consistent with users' subjective assessments of product ease of use, with a correlation coefficient $r = 0.728$ ($p < 0.05$). In terms of the time cost invested in obtaining the measurement results, the PTES method showed significant time savings for each product compared to conducting Ease-of-Use questionnaire surveys. Additionally, 8 task flows from 4 products have already been optimized in design, in collaboration with designers and developers, and the second round of TES has been calculated post-improvement. We found that the

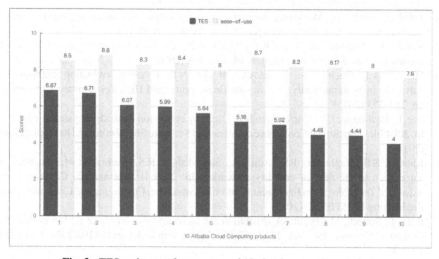

Fig. 2. TES and ease-of-use scores of 10 cloud computing products

increase in TES and the extent of the improvement matched the subjective expectations of the stakeholders for each product, indicating that TES can be used to some degree to evaluate the effectiveness of design optimizations.

However, during the pilot study, we also identified some limitations of this scoring method. On one hand, for products with a smaller user base, a longer data sampling period may be required to ensure an adequate sample size, which is not conducive to rapid comparative validation before and after the implementation of improvement measures. On the other hand, the calculation method for RC requires continuous iteration of the complexity grouping and the expected completion rate constant based on test data. When the average number of steps to complete a task is at the boundary of the complexity grouping, there can be discrepancies between the final score and expectations.

Overall, we believe that TES proposed in this paper is an effective and extremely low-cost task performance measurement method, particularly suitable for complex web applications like cloud computing platforms. The metrics are based entirely on objective and real user behavior data, allowing for continuous, automated tracking of user experiences across a multitude of products and tasks, and facilitating communication with development staff and others. In the future, we plan to extend TES to more interface types. Based on more extensive measurement results and score distributions, we will define a reasonable measurement scale and further refine the automation design of the measurement process or related tools to further reduce costs in terms of manpower and time. We hope that our practice in measuring task experience based on the Alibaba Cloud Console can inspire practitioners in the field of user experience and attract attention and discussion from the community.

References

1. Vermeeren, A.P., Law, E.L.-C., Roto, V., Obrist, M., Hoonhout, J., Väänänen-Vainio-Mattila, K.: User experience evaluation methods. In: Proceedings of the 6th Nordic Conference on Human-Computer Interaction: Extending Boundaries (2010)
2. Tullis, T., Albert, B.: Measuring the user experience: Collecting, analyzing, and presenting usability metrics. Elsevier/Morgan Kaufmann, Amsterdam (2013)
3. Seffah, A., Donyaee, M., Kline, R.B., Padda, H.K.: Usability measurement and metrics: a consolidated model. Software Qual. J. **14**, 159–178 (2006)
4. Martins, A.I., Queirós, A., Silva, A.G., Rocha, N.P.: Usability evaluation methods. In: Advances in Systems Analysis, Software Engineering, and High Performance Computing, pp. 250–273 (2015)
5. Paz, F., Pow-Sang, J.A.: Current trends in Usability evaluation methods: a systematic review. In: 2014 7th International Conference on Advanced Software Engineering and Its Applications (2014)
6. Khasnis, S.S., Raghuram, P.S., Aditi, A., Samrakshini, R.S., Namratha, M.: Analysis of automation in the field of usability evaluation. In: 2019 1st International Conference on Advanced Technologies in Intelligent Control, Environment, Computing and Communication Engineering (ICATIECE) (2019)
7. Ruiz, J., Snoeck, M.: Feedback generation for automatic user interface design evaluation. Commun. Comput. Inf. Sci. **1622**, 67–93 (2022). https://doi.org/10.1007/978-3-031-115 13-4_4

8. Weichbroth, P.: Usability of mobile applications: a systematic literature study. IEEE Access. **8**, 55563–55577 (2020)

9. Maia, C.L., Furtado, E.S.: A systematic review about user experience evaluation. Design, User Experience Usability: Design Thinking Methods **9746**, 445–455 (2016). https://doi.org/10.1007/978-3-319-40409-7_42

10. Castro, J.W., Garnica, I., Rojas, L.A.: Automated tools for usability evaluation: a systematic mapping study. Social Computing and Social Media: Design, User Experience and Impact. **13315**, 28–46 (2022). https://doi.org/10.1007/978-3-031-05061-9_3

11. Khasnis, S.S., Raghuram, P.S., Aditi, A., Samrakshini, R.S., Namratha, M.: Analysis of automation in the field of usability evaluation. In: 2019 1st International Conference on Advanced Technologies in Intelligent Control, Environment, Computing & Communication Engineering (ICATIECE) (2019)

12. Bakaev, M., Mamysheva, T., Gaedke, M.: Current trends in automating usability evaluation of websites: can you manage what you can't measure? In: 2016 11th International Forum on Strategic Technology (IFOST) (2016)

13. Cochran, W.G.: Sampling techniques. New York: Wiley (1977)

14. Gao, X., Zhi, S., Wang, X.: Investigating the relationship among ease-of-use, NPS, and customers' sequent spending of Cloud Computing Products. HCI International 2021 – Posters, 417–422 (2021)

Examining the Influence of Front-Facing Camera Layout on the Aesthetic Experience of Smartphone User Interfaces

Qiang Li[✉], Zhen Chen, and Tianqi Wu

Shenyang Aerospace University, Shenyang, China
qiangli@sau.edu.cn

Abstract. The primary research objective of this paper is to explore the direct impact of the front-facing camera layout on users' aesthetic experiences, specifically investigating how different layouts of the front-facing camera influence the aesthetic experience of the user interface (UI) on smartphones. The ultimate goal is to provide practical design recommendations for future smartphones and potential support for mobile application developers. To achieve this objective, we recruited 120 volunteers from a university and evaluated interfaces with different layouts of the front-facing camera across four experimental groups (1. Left-aligned pill-shaped screen, 2. Centered notch screen, 3. Centered pinhole screen, 4. Centered triple-hole screen), conducting a comprehensive assessment for each experimental group. After the experiments, the results were analyzed using a mixed-factor analysis of variance (ANOVA), and the total scores of various indicators were comprehensively calculated. Each indicator underwent meticulous categorization for detailed comparative analysis. The evaluation covered ten dimensions, including creativity, attractiveness, aesthetics, complexity, symmetry, and others, to assess the impact of different front-facing camera layouts on user aesthetics. The research findings indicate that different front-facing camera layouts significantly influence users' aesthetic experiences. Specifically, a centrally positioned layout on the smartphone interface is most preferred by users, and the size of the layout also significantly affects user evaluations. The practical significance of this study is twofold. Firstly, it provides valuable guidance for the design of future smartphones. Designers can take note of these research findings and apply them to their creative endeavors. Secondly, the study can assist mobile application developers in creating interfaces that are both user-friendly and aesthetically pleasing, thereby improving user satisfaction by understanding how different layouts impact user experience. In summary, this study contributes to an enhanced understanding of user experience with mobile devices, offering valuable insights to enhance the design of smartphones and mobile applications.

Keywords: Positioning of the front-facing camera · Aesthetic · User experience

© The Author(s), under exclusive license to Springer Nature Switzerland AG 2024
C. Stephanidis et al. (Eds.): HCII 2024, CCIS 2114, pp. 164–170, 2024.
https://doi.org/10.1007/978-3-031-61932-8_20

1   Introduction

In today's society, amidst the rapid evolution of the information age, mobile phones have become an indispensable element in our daily lives, intricately intertwined with various aspects of contemporary society [1]. Furthermore, mobile devices have evolved into portable information hubs in our daily lives, akin to computers in functionality [2, 3]. Santayana posits that our society is increasingly emphasizing visual aesthetics, extending this focus to the aesthetic design of smartphone interfaces [4]. According to the research conducted by Lavie and Tractinsky, interface visual aesthetics play a pivotal and determining role in user satisfaction and pleasure. Additionally, Lavie suggests that aesthetics hold a certain level of significance across most domains of life, with a particular difficulty to be replaced in the importance of human-computer interaction [5]. Experimental findings from Tractinsky regarding the perception of aesthetic appeal and usability in computer systems suggest a strong correlation between the perceived aesthetics and perceived usability of a system [6]. Phillips and Chapparro study revealed that users' perceptions of web interfaces are primarily influenced by the visual attractiveness of the web. Users tend to give higher ratings to webpages with high visual appeal but lower usability, whereas they give lower ratings to webpages with high usability but lower visual attractiveness [7].

In the interface of mobile devices, the layout stands as a pivotal design characteristic. The arrangement of interface elements directly influences its aesthetic appeal, while the coherent placement of visual interface elements ensures smooth communication between humans and machines [8]. Sonderegger research indicates that visual appearance positively impacts performance, potentially reducing task completion time and minimizing user error opportunities to enhance overall user experience [9]. In mobile interfaces, different layouts of interface elements influence users' experiences. Altaboli's experiments break down interface layout into balance, unity, and sequence, considering these three metrics as crucial factors in evaluating interface aesthetics [10]. Generally, two methods exist for assessing interface aesthetics: the first employs an objective approach by analyzing the correlation between screen design layout elements and users' perception of visual aesthetics. This method, rooted in empirical research, seeks to establish a scientific, objective evaluation standard. For instance, Bauerly's experiment utilized 30 black-and-white geometric images to validate computational aesthetic quantification algorithms against participant ratings, alongside realistic webpages as stimuli [11]. The second method is subjective, primarily employing questionnaire tools to measure users' perception and evaluation of visual aesthetics, aiming to understand users' actual experiences and satisfaction regarding interface aesthetics [5].

In the interface of mobile devices, the front-facing camera has become a standard feature in nearly all smartphones in recent years, playing a pivotal role across various phone models in the market. Given the diverse strategies adopted by different manufacturers concerning the position of the front-facing camera in current market smartphones, this paper rigorously delves into the substantial impact of the front-facing camera on users' aesthetic perceptions and interactive experiences across different screen layout positions. This study holds significant theoretical and practical value, providing robust support for furthering the humanization and user-friendliness of mobile design.

Therefore, this study investigated the impact of front-facing camera placement in user interface layout on aesthetic perception and interactive experience through simulated experiments. The experiment aimed to explore the potential influence of front-facing camera UI layout on user aesthetics. This experiment contributes to unveiling the inherent connection between UI layout in smartphone interfaces and user aesthetic perception, providing a scientific basis for optimizing smartphone design and front-facing camera placement.

2   Materials and Methods

2.1   Participants

In order to conduct this study, all participants in the experiment were informed about the informed consent form prior to the commencement of the study. Personal information of the participants will be strictly confidential and used solely for the purpose of this research, without any other application. The subjects of the study were students at a certain university, mainly undergraduate or graduate students with experience in using smartphones. The average age of participants was 21.1 years (SD $\pm$ 1.9), and all participants volunteered without compensation. The descriptive statistics of participants are shown in Table 1.

Table 1. Descriptive statistics of participants.

Characteristics	Items	Number of people	Percentage
Sex	Male	46	38.33%
	Female	74	61.67%
Mobile phone System	Android	51	42.50%
	IOS	69	57.50%
impact of front-facing smartphone camera position on the user interface	Yes	67	55.83%
	No	53	44.17%

2.2   Apparatus and Prototypes

In this study, to authentically explore the impact of front-facing smartphone camera position on the user interface, we employed the Realme X model as our experimental device. The front-facing camera of this phone is not visibly embedded on the screen, as presented in Fig. 1. (Interface A). The entire experiment involved the creation of a simulated online application, utilizing an Android device with a 6.53-inch screen, 1080 $\times$ 2340 pixels, and 394 ppi. Each participant accessed the experiment through an application icon on their mobile phone. Four distinct UI interface layouts were developed for the experiment.

In the first experimental group, the front-facing camera is situated on the left side of the phone in a configuration resembling a rounded rectangle. The simulated phone interface mirrors that of an Android device, and model is 'HUAWEI meat 40 pro', as presented in Fig. 1 (Interface B).

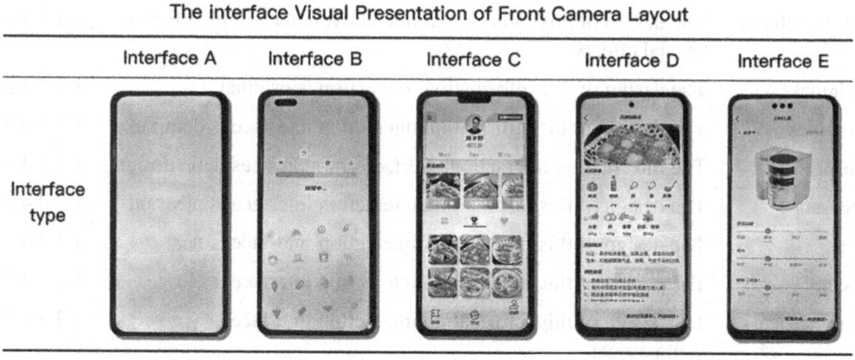

The interface Visual Presentation of Front Camera Layout

Fig. 1. The experimental equipment and user interface utilized in the experiment.

The front-facing camera layout in the second experimental group is positioned in the middle of the phone. The simulated phone interface replicates an iOS device, and model is 'iPhone 14', as presented in Fig. 1 (Interface C).

In the third experimental group, the front-facing camera layout is situated at the center of the phone and is circular in shape. The simulated phone interface replicates an Android device, and model is 'HUAWEI P30 Pro', as presented in Fig. 1 (Interface D).

In the final experimental group, the front-facing camera layout is centered on the phone, featuring a configuration of three circular cutouts. The simulated phone interface replicates an Android device, and model is 'HUAWEI Mate 60 Pro', as presented in Fig. 1 (Interface E).

2.3 Experiment Design

Before the experiment commenced, researchers used interview methods to gather basic user information and assess their smartphone usage experiences. This included inquiries into participants' preferences regarding smartphone operating systems and their opinions on whether the positioning of the front-facing camera on a smartphone might affect the interface. Additionally, instructions and tasks for the experiment were explained. At the start of the experiment, the devices were handed to participants for their experience, each user interface remained identical, with variations only in the layout of the front-facing camera across different user groups. To ensure procedural clarity, participants were instructed to fill out a rating sheet immediately after viewing their assigned user interface, allowing for prompt assessment of their experiences.

This paper employed Lavie's aesthetic perception tool to assess these four simulated interfaces. Lavie believes that this tool contributes to a better understanding of human-computer interaction phenomena, such as the relationship between aesthetics

Table 2. Survey questions [5].

Indicator	Question	Score
Created	This information interface is creative	1 2 3 4 5
Attractive	The design of this information interface is appealing	1 2 3 4 5
Special effects	The design of this information interactive interface incorporates special effects	1 2 3 4 5
Original	The design of this information interaction is original	1 2 3 4 5
Complex	The design of this information interaction interface is complex	1 2 3 4 5
Beauty	The information interaction interface embodies aesthetic design	1 2 3 4 5
Pleasant	The design of this information interaction interface is pleasant	1 2 3 4 5
Neat	The design of this information interaction interface is neat	1 2 3 4 5
Clear	The design of this information interaction interface is clear	1 2 3 4 5
Symmetrical	The design of this information interaction interface is symmetrical	1 2 3 4 5

and usability [5]. Nasar believes that factors like attractiveness, pleasantness, cleanliness, clarity, and symmetry are design attributes of a human-computer interface applied to the dimension of 'visual clarity' [12], Additionally, Johnson suggests that these factors embody the qualities encompassed in the classic concepts of aesthetic design [13]. Thus, five-point Likert scales whose values ranged from 1 to 5 were used for questionnaire surveys. The survey questions are shown in Table 2.

3   Result and Discussion

Based on the experimental findings, variance analysis was conducted on ten dimensions individually, as presented in Table 3. Post-hoc analysis revealed that the arrangement of the front camera at varying positions significantly influenced users' aesthetic perceptions, the impact was ranked as follows: Interface C > Interface E > Interface D > Interface B.

For further analysis, the total scores of the ten dimensions were aggregated and statistically analyzed, and a bar chart was generated as illustrated in Fig. 2. It was

Table 3. The descriptive statistics of indicators.

Experimental group		Interface B	Interface C	Interface D	Interface E
Indicator	Created	0.79	0.51	0.62	0.71
	Attractive	1.04	0.70	0.67	0.81
	Special effects	0.92	0.81	0.65	0.90
	Original	0.72	0.51	0.74	1.17

(*continued*)

Table 3. (*continued*)

Experimental group		Interface B	Interface C	Interface D	Interface E
	Complex	1.08	0.67	0.92	0.86
	Beauty	0.81	0.64	0.76	1.13
	Pleasant	1.08	0.67	1.14	1.01
	Neat	1.36	0.53	0.33	1.36
	Clear	0.70	0.60	0.52	0.82
	Symmetrical	0.72	0.63	0.39	1.50

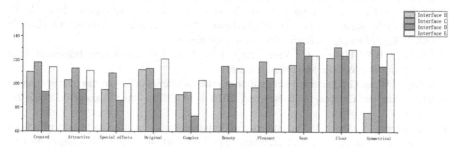

Fig. 2. Score line statistics chart.

observed that the Interface C group outperformed other experimental control groups in the evaluation of eight dimensions: creativity, attraction, special effects, aesthetic design, pleasantness, neatness, clarity, and symmetry. Moreover, a comprehensive mixed-factor analysis of variance (ANOVA) indicated that the evaluation of the experimental group Interface C was superior to that of the other groups.

4 Conclusions

The front-facing camera, an integral component of mobile devices, is a pivotal focus in this study. The primary aim was to explore the impact of diverse front-facing camera layouts in smartphones on the aesthetic user experience within the UI. The intention is to offer practical reference recommendations for future smartphone designers and potential assistance for mobile application developers. A total of 120 volunteers participated in this research, engaging in a series of experiments and rating each experimental group. Findings indicate that varying front-facing camera layouts indeed significantly influence users' aesthetic experiences.

Throughout users' interactions with mobile devices, the positioning of the front-facing camera may evoke distinct experiential perceptions during similar interactions. This study solely addresses the influence of front-facing camera layouts on users' aesthetic experiences, with potential future research intending to delve further into these issues and refine experimental designs.

References

1. Laghari, A.A., Wu, K., Laghari, R.A., Ali, M., Khan, A.A.: A review and state of art of Internet of Things (IoT). Arch. Comput. Methods Eng. **29**, 1395–1413 (2022). https://doi.org/10.1007/s11831-021-09622-6
2. Walker, G.H., Stanton, N.A., Jenkins, D., Salmon, P.M.: From telephones to iPhones: applying systems thinking to networked, interoperable products. Appl. Ergon. **40**, 206–215 (2009)
3. Laghari, A.A., He, H., Shafiq, M., Khan, A.: Impact of storage of mobile on quality of experience (QoE) at user level accessing cloud. In: 2017 IEEE 9th International Conference on Communication Software and Networks (ICCSN), May 2017. https://doi.org/10.1109/iccsn.2017.8230340
4. Santayana, G.: The Sense of Beauty; Being the Outline of Aesthetic Theory, June 1996
5. Lavie, T., Tractinsky, N.: Assessing dimensions of perceived visual aesthetics of web sites. Int. J. Hum. Comput. Stud. **60**, 269–298 (2004). https://doi.org/10.1016/j.ijhcs.2003.09.002
6. Tractinsky, N., Katz, A.S., Ikar, D.: What is beautiful is usable. Interact. Comput. **13**, 127–145 (2000). https://doi.org/10.1016/s0953-5438(00)00031-x
7. Chaparro, B.S., Phillips, C.: Visual Appeal vs. Usability: Which One Influences User Perceptions of a Website More? January 2009
8. Deng, L., Wang, G.: Quantitative evaluation of visual aesthetics of human-machine interaction interface layout. Comput. Intell. Neurosci. **2020**, 1–14 (2020). https://doi.org/10.1155/2020/9815937
9. Sonderegger, A., Sauer, J.: The influence of design aesthetics in usability testing: effects on user performance and perceived usability. Appl. Ergon. **41**, 403–410 (2010). https://doi.org/10.1016/j.apergo.2009.09.002
10. Altaboli, A., Lin, Y.: Investigating effects of screen layout elements on interface and screen design aesthetics. Adv. Hum. Comput. Interact. **2011**, 1–10 (2011). https://doi.org/10.1155/2011/659758
11. Bauerly, M., Liu, Y.: Computational modeling and experimental investigation of effects of compositional elements on interface and design aesthetics. Int. J. Hum. Comput. Stud. **64**, 670–682 (2006). https://doi.org/10.1016/j.ijhcs.2006.01.002
12. Nasar, N.: Perception and evaluation of residential street scenes. In: Directions in Person-Environment Research and Practice (Routledge Revivals), pp. 259–278 (2016). https://doi.org/10.4324/9781315542553-21
13. Johnson, P.-A.: The Theory of Architecture: Concepts, Themes & Practices, January 1993

A Comparative Study of Icon Style Based on Cognitive Behavior

Miao Liu[ID] and Linyi Zheng[✉][ID]

East China University of Science and Technology, Shanghai 200237, People's Republic of China
linyi_zheng0410@163.com

Abstract. With the rapid development of mobile applications and the popularity of intelligent living environments, people's demand for the experience of using mobile devices is constantly increasing. As an important element in the interaction between users and mobile devices, the design form of interactive interface icons is also evolving. This study starts with the development trend of icon style in the interactive interface, adopts the research method of cognitive behavior, designs behavior experiments with the help of E-prime, a computerized behavior research platform, and compares the influence of flat icons and neumorphic icons on users' search performance and use experience in combination with subjective evaluation, to provide a quantitative decision-making basis for icon design decisions. According to the statistical results of experimental test data, the flat icon is slightly better than the neumorphic icon in icon search performance, the neumorphic icon has advantages in user preference and eye comfort, and the flat icon has certain advantages in clarity. The evaluation data of the flat icon and neumorphic icon are weighted by the weight of the evaluation index, and finally, it is concluded that the comprehensive performance of the flat icon is better than that of the neumorphic icon, which provides a reference for the design of interactive interface icon.

Keywords: Cognitive behavior · Icon style · Search performance

1 Introduction

With the rapid development of service design and experience economy, users' awareness of Internet products is getting deeper and deeper. Instead of simply measuring products through visual presentation, users pay more and more attention to the ease of use and experience of products. In order to obtain a high-quality user experience, the digital interface is constantly developing and innovating with the changes of the living environment, technological development and product innovation, and its visual performance is also changing with the changes of environment, users' psychology, usage habits, etc. Every media change will lead to a new direction of interface icon design, and in order to adapt to the update iteration of media, the style of icon design is also accelerating transformation.

In this paper, from the perspective of cognitive behavior, based on the development trend of icons, we conduct a comparative study on the current main-stream flat icons and

© The Author(s), under exclusive license to Springer Nature Switzerland AG 2024
C. Stephanidis et al. (Eds.): HCII 2024, CCIS 2114, pp. 171–179, 2024.
https://doi.org/10.1007/978-3-031-61932-8_21

neumorphic icons to provide reference for the selection of icon styles for user interaction interface, so as to make the interaction of human-computer interface more friendly and efficient.

2 Related Work

From the creation of icons to today's perfect development, icons have only gone through several decades of history. Along with the iteration of computer display technology, the interactive interface has gone through the process of formation, development and maturity from command-line language interface to natural interactive interface.

Iconography became known to the public due to the launch of Apple's ios1 system in 2007. The anthropomorphic style of icons at this time pursued realism and complexity. The purpose was to eliminate the barrier between the user and the product and machine, and to reduce the cognitive cost and memory load of the user in use [1].

With the continuous development of mobile technology, in order to make the interface icon become efficient and concise, and improve the loading speed of the interface, the flat icon form came into being. Apple ios7 system is an example (Fig. 1), at this time the icon abandoned excessive decoration and three-dimensional effect, so that the design tends to simplify, the sense of real objects greatly reduced [2], visually more concise and clear, reduce the user's visual burden.

Fig. 1. Apple ios7 interface

The flat icon style continued until 2019. At this time Ukrainian designer Alexander Plyuto published a series of system interfaces one after another on the design website Dribbble, and a visual style called neumorphic emerged (Fig. 2). The neumorphic style combines anthropomorphic icons with the respective characteristics of flat icons. The sense of things in the icons retains some of the physical characteristics of the original objects, and slightly adds layers of shadows based on flat simplicity, which is a great improvement in terms of expressiveness and visual effect.

In response to the debate on the advantages and disadvantages of icon styles, most scholars believe that flat icons are better in terms of recognition efficiency, while some scholars believe that even though flat design is as strong as ever, anthropomorphic design still has its necessity and space to exist. Some scholars believe that the future trend will be the result of the fusion of flat and anthropomorphic design. For example, by comparing the ease of use and learning cost of flat icons and anthropomorphic icons,

Fig. 2. Alexander Plyuto Design Interface

Xia Tao et al. believe that the subsequent icon development trend is to find the balance point between flat icons and anthropomorphic icons [3]. The current research on icons is mainly carried out through qualitative methods such as questionnaires, or eye movement research methods, Ren Hong et al. used ERP technology to study the impact of flat and anthropomorphic icons on users' cognitive efficiency [4]. This paper, on the other hand, compares the flat and neumorphic icons based on cognitive behavioral science, combined with subjective evaluation.

3 Methods

3.1 Cognitive Behavioral

Cognitive behavioral science is a discipline based on the study of people's behavior and then infer people's psychology, which is complex and multi-faceted [5]. In recent years, it has been widely applied in the field of interactive interfaces, such as interface layout and color matching, but in the area of icon evaluation, it is still little involved. The reaction time and correctness rate required for a person to obtain information, process information, and give feedback with behaviors such as body or language can effectively measure cognitive performance. From a cognitive-behavioral perspective, higher correctness and lower reaction time reflect higher cognitive performance. The two can be considered comprehensively through the ratio, with E representing the recognition efficiency, A representing the recognition accuracy, and T representing the recognition time, the recognition efficiency is the ratio of the recognition accuracy to the recognition time, and the formula is as follows: $E = A/T$. A higher recognition efficiency indicates a higher degree of information recognisability and better cognitive performance [6]; conversely, a lower recognition efficiency indicates a lower degree of information recognisability and worse cognitive performance.

3.2 Development of Evaluation Indicators

Based on the current research status of cognitive behavioral science, this paper comprehensively applies the behavioral test method, subjective evaluation method and entropy value method to construct an evaluation system, and conducts a comparative study on the icon schemes of the 2 manifestations of flat icons and neumorphic icons.

Computerized cognitive behavioral research refers to the objective data processing of users' cognitive behaviors through the interactive interface of computer or APP with concise and clear steps and highly structured multi-media interaction. The computerized behavioral research platform E-prime 3.0 is an effective tool for collecting cognitive behavioral information, covering trial generation, millisecond precision data collection and preliminary data analysis of the psychological trial operating system [7]. During the trial process, according to the preset procedures, the correctness of the subject's judgment and the reaction time can be accurately recorded when the subject makes a judgment, to obtain the subject's cognitive situation.

Subjective evaluation mainly focuses on the user's overall feeling during the interaction with the icon, including physiological feeling evaluation and emotional feeling evaluation. Comfortable physiological feelings and positive emotions can improve cognitive performance, while uncomfortable physiological feelings and negative emotions will reduce cognitive performance [8].

Considering cognitive behavior and subjective feelings, four evaluation indexes are drawn up, namely: one evaluation index of cognitive performance, that is, identification efficiency; There are three subjective evaluation indicators, namely, preference, clarity and eye comfort [9]. Among them, user preference belongs to emotional feelings, reflecting the aesthetic characteristics of icons; Clarity is an experiential index, which refers to the experience of icon clarity, recognition and readability; Eye comfort belongs to the physiological level.

4   Experiment

4.1   Experimental Design

The experiment used nine flat icons with nine neumorphic icons of the same grey scale as stimuli. To avoid the icons being affected by familiarity, this study selected nine icon semantics common in life to design two styles of icons respectively. The icon schemes are shown in Fig. 3, Scheme A is a flat icon, all elements are 2D graphics, without adding any highlights, shadows, gradients, bevels and other three-dimensional effects; Scheme B is a neumorphic icon, with the addition of projections and highlights, forming a three-dimensional "relief" effect.

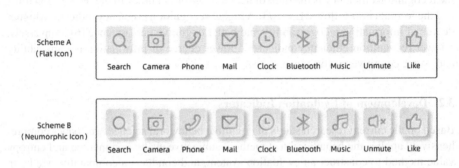

Fig. 3. Icon scheme

The experimental program was prepared using E-Prime 2.0 and the experiments were conducted on a Lenovo Y7000 computer with a screen size of 15.6 in., a resolution of 1920 × 1080 pixels, and a refresh rate of 60 Hz. The experiments were conducted in a brightly lit, quiet room, with the subjects 60 cm away from the monitor, with their eyes at approximately the same height as the center of the monitor screen. Subjects responded to keystrokes via a keyboard, and the response time and correctness of the subjects were recorded.

The experimental flow is shown in Fig. 4. Firstly, the screen displays the test instruction, and after the subjects fully read it, they press the space bar to continue; then the center of the screen presents a red cross focus as the focus of attention to ensure visual concentration, which lasts for 500 ms; then the semantics of the icons that need to be identified is presented, which lasts for 1,500 ms; then a set of icons is presented on the screen, with no time limitation, and the subjects need to identify the icon that matches the icon semantics and press the corresponding numeric keys on the keyboard to give feedback; then the experiment moves to the next trial, during which the target icon location is randomized. A total of 2 groups of tests were conducted, namely, the flat icon recognition test and the neumorphic icon recognition experiment. Subjective evaluation was conducted at the end of the behavioral experiments, and the subjective evaluation scale was a Likert 5-level scale, see Table 1. After performing the test procedure, the subjects scored the 2 icon schemes according to their personal feelings on 3 indexes, including clarity, user preference, and eye comfort, respectively.

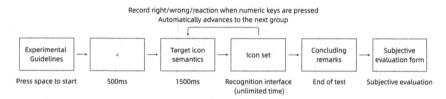

Fig. 4. Experimental process

Table 1. Subjective evaluation form

Evaluation indicators		Very bad	Bad	Fair	Good	Very good
Scheme A	Clarity	1	2	3	4	5
	Preference	1	2	3	4	5
	Eye Comfort	1	2	3	4	5
Scheme B	Clarity	1	2	3	4	5
	Preference	1	2	3	4	5
	Eye Comfort	1	2	3	4	5

Twenty-seven college students were randomly selected as subjects with an overall age distribution between 20 and 28 years old. The subjects had normal visual acuity or corrected visual acuity and no color blindness or color weakness. Preparations were made before the test to ensure that the subjects were familiar with the test methods and procedures.

4.2 Data Analysis

Behavioral and subjective data collected from 27 subjects in the test trials were analyzed and calculated to obtain the mean value of each evaluation indicator. The experimental test data are shown in Table 2.

Table 2. Experimental test data statistics

Icon type	Clarity	Preference	Eye comfort	Recognition efficiency
Flat Icon	4.11	4.07	4.00	4.18
Neumorphic icon	3.78	4.22	4.04	4.07

Experiments are conducted for m icon style schemes, and n experimental data indicators are used as icon style evaluation indicators, where the raw data for the jth evaluation indicator of the ith icon scheme is x_{ij}, a judgement matrix $X = (x_{ij})_{m \times n}$ is built from the experimental data:

$$X = \begin{bmatrix} 3 & 4 & 4 & 3.98 \\ 4 & 3 & 4 & 4.27 \\ \vdots & \vdots & \vdots & \vdots \\ 3 & 4 & 4 & 3.80 \end{bmatrix}$$

Since the four icon evaluation indicators are all positive indicators, the original matrix is normalised according to the formula $y_{ij} = \frac{x_{ij} - \min x_{ij}}{\max x_{ij} - \min x_{ij}}$ to obtain the normalised matrix $Y = (y_{ij})_{m \times n}$:

$$Y = \begin{bmatrix} 0.33 & 0.67 & 0.67 & 0.32 \\ 0.67 & 0.33 & 0.67 & 0.37 \\ \vdots & \vdots & \vdots & \vdots \\ 0.33 & 0.67 & 0.67 & 0.29 \end{bmatrix}$$

Through the formula $p_{ij} = \frac{y_{ij}}{\sum_{i=1}^{n} y_{ij}}$, the weights of the indicators of the different icon programmes under the four indicators, p_{ij}, can be derived, yielding the weight matrix $P = (p_{ij})_{m \times n}$:

$$P = \begin{bmatrix} 0.0095 & 0.0172 & 0.0183 & 0.0172 \\ 0.0190 & 0.0086 & 0.0183 & 0.0199 \\ \vdots & \vdots & \vdots & \vdots \\ 0.0095 & 0.0172 & 0.0183 & 0.0155 \end{bmatrix}$$

The entropy value E of each evaluation index is calculated according to $e_j = -\frac{1}{\ln n}\sum_{i=1}^{n} p_{ij}\ln(p_{ij})$:

$$E = \begin{bmatrix} 0.9726 & 0.9803 & 0.9707 & 0.9661 \end{bmatrix}$$

The indicator weight $W = w_j$ is obtained by $w_j = \frac{1-e_j}{\sum_{j=1}^{m}(1-e_j)}$ and thus the indicator weight of the item indicator:

$$W = \begin{bmatrix} 0.2489 & 0.1784 & 0.2656 & 0.3071 \end{bmatrix}$$

Finally, according to $z_i = \sum_{j=1}^{n} y_{ij}w_j$, the evaluation data of each program is weighted and calculated by the weights of evaluation indexes, and finally the reasonableness of its design is judged on the basis of the weighted scores, and the scores of the 2 icon styles under the four evaluation dimensions are obtained as Z, with Z_A as flat icon, Z_B as neumorphic icon, $Z_A = 0.5842$, $Z_B = 0.5625$, Z_A (flat) $> Z_B$ (neumorphic).

4.3 Result

The evaluation data are shown in Fig. 5. From the individual scores of each index, it can be concluded that the 2 icon forms have their own advantages and disadvantages. According to the statistical results of the experimental test data, it can be seen that the flat icon has advantages in terms of clarity and recognition efficiency, and the neumorphic icon has certain advantages in terms of user preference and eye comfort.

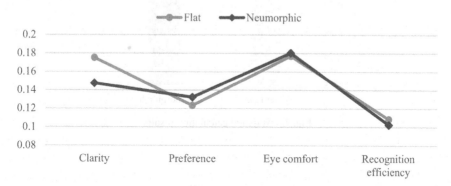

Fig. 5. Index data for flat icons and neumorphic icons

The evaluation index weights are shown in Fig. 6. From the weights W of the icon scheme, it can be found that the weight value of recognition efficiency is the largest, followed by eye comfort, so when carrying out the evaluation of the icon scheme and scheme optimisation, the user's recognition efficiency and eye comfort should be considered.

The weighted calculation results are shown in Fig. 7. From the final judgment result of weighted score Z, it can be judged that the overall performance of flat icons is better than neumorphic icons, with better cognitive performance and user experience. Therefore,

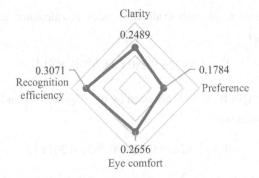

Fig. 6. Weight of evaluation indicators

flat icons can be used preferentially in UI interface design to ensure the readability and clarity of the icons and enhance the efficiency of human-computer interaction. Since there is little difference between flat icons and neumorphic icons in terms of recognition efficiency, neumorphic icons with high user preference and eye comfort can also be used in some interfaces with low demand for icon recognition, such as games and entertainment interfaces.

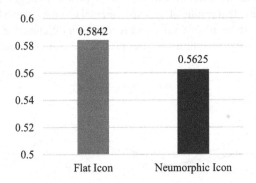

Fig. 7. Weighted calculation results

5 Conclusion

This paper explores the advantages and disadvantages of comparing flat icons with neumorphic icons from a cognitive behavioral perspective. The computerized cognitive-behavioral system E-prime is applied as a new tool for icon style evaluation, which accurately and intuitively presents the quantitative relationship between icon style and response time and correct response rate. Meanwhile, combined with subjective evaluation, the aesthetic function, experiential and physiological comfort of icons were included in the evaluation scope. Through entropy calculation, the icon scheme is evaluated, which is more scientific and rigorous than the traditional method. The evaluation method provides a new idea for icon style design and evaluation, which is of great inspiration and reference significance.

References

1. Zhu, Y.: Research on UI interface visual style based on color and texture. Fashion Color (10), 31–33 (2022)
2. Bi, X., Zhou, R.: Object sense design of mobile terminal interface graph. Ind. Eng. Des. **4**(04), 78–84 (2022)
3. Xia, T.: Analysis on the trend of skeuomorphism and flat design of smart phone app icons. Design (01), 122–123 (2017)
4. Ren, H., Zou, Y., Wang, D., et al.: Cognitive efficiency of flat and skeuomorphic icons based on ERP. Packag. Eng. **39**(18), 186–190 (2018)
5. Zhang, H., Jia, J., Wang, G.: Color evaluation analysis of silk fabric on cognitive behavior. Mod. Silk Sci. Technol. **33**(05), 13–16 (2018)
6. Feng, S., Wang, J., Zhi, J., et al.: Evaluation index system of visual ergonomics for human-computer interface in the situation of quickly capturing the target. Packag. Eng. **41**(06), 176–180 (2020)
7. Chen, Y., Zou, C.: Research on the standardization of icon symbols. Stan. Sci. **01**, 15–18 (2017)
8. Zhang, Q., Lu, Y., Zhang, P.: Research on evaluation method of construction machinery icon design based on cognitive behavior. Constr. Mach. Equip. **53**(05), 73–79+11 (2022)
9. Zhang, Q., Li, L., Ma, R.: Research on computer icon based on cognitive psychology. Microelectron. Comput. **10**, 126–130 (2004)

Analysis of Participants' Synchronization Behaviors and Big Five Personalities in Dyadic Conversation

Koutaro Okada[1] and Yuya Okadome[2]([✉]) [iD]

[1] Tokyo University of Science, Tokyo, Japan
[2] RIKEN Information R&D and Strategy Headquarters, Kyoto, Japan
okadome@rs.tus.ac.jp

Abstract. Gestures during conversation and personality are not independent. However, there are few studies on the relationship between smile synchronization and personality. In this study, we analyze the relationship between synchronization and personality traits during dyadic conversation using dialogue data. The targets of the analysis are the relationship between the Big Five personalities and smile synchronization and wrist movements. From the results, we obtain the following findings. A strong negative correlation coefficient was obtained between the probability of synchronized smiles and intelligence scores. There are weak negative correlation coefficients between the delay of synchronized smiles and Extraversion, Conscientiousness, Emotional Stability, and Intelligence scores. These insights suggest that personality traits affect the synchronization strategy of conversation.

Keywords: Dyadic conversation · Big Five · Behavior Synchronization

1 Introduction

Thanks to recent advances in artificial intelligence technology, many communication robots have been developed [3,5], and the opportunity to communicate with these robots has been increasing. The robot communicating with humans is required to be operated in the actual environment such as people living. Most of these robots consider the dyadic conversation situation.

Gestures expressed in human-human conversation are different for each people [13]. For instance, there are individual differences in the frequency of nodding [14]. In human-robot communication, the "natural" communication is expected to be achieved by changing the robot's reaction depending on the other person.

The synchronization [8,9] and personality traits [7] affect the reaction expressions during conversation. Nodding [8] and smiling [9] seems to be synchronized in human–human communication. The relationship between personality traits and non-verbal body gestures are investigated [7]. The behavior rules of a communication robot is designed by analyze synchronization and personality traits during conversation.

© The Author(s), under exclusive license to Springer Nature Switzerland AG 2024
C. Stephanidis et al. (Eds.): HCII 2024, CCIS 2114, pp. 180–186, 2024.
https://doi.org/10.1007/978-3-031-61932-8_22

Fig. 1. The example scene of recorded video. Two participants sit in person.

In this study, the relationship between smile synchronization, hand movements, and personality traits in small talk are analyzed. Our target is a dyadic conversation, and the video and audio data and personality traits data of two participants are collected. Big Five [6] is used as the personality traits, and the Big Five express the personality traits by five factors: extravarsion, agreeable, conscientiousness, emotional stability, and Intelligence. Smile labels are given to collected data, and the annotated data is analyzed in terms of smile synchronization. The velocity of wrists and length of utterance are also analyzed.

A strong negative correlation is obtained between the intelligence score of the Big Five personality and the probability of smile synchronization. There is a medium negative correlation between the intelligence score and the delay of smile expression in the synchronization. A weak positive correlation is obtained between the velocity of wrists and extravarsion, conscientiousness, emotional stability, and intelligence scores. These results suggest that personality traits affect behaviors and synchronizations during conversation.

2   Collection of Dyadic Conversation Data

In this study, the conversation of six pairs (ten male and two female university students, aged 18–21) are collected. Ten minutes of conversation for each pair is recorded by video cameras with 4k resolution. Figure 1 shows the example scene of the video. The behavior information during conversation is extracted from gathered videos. After recording the video, participants answer the questionnaire for measuring the Big Five.

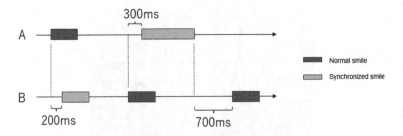

Fig. 2. The scheme of detecting smile synchronization. Blue and yellow boxes are unsynchronized and synchronized smiles, respectively. A and B are the dummy IDs of the participants. (Color figure online)

In this study, because all participants are Japanese university students, we use the Japanese questionnaire of the Big Five. To reduce the workload of participants, the questionnaire designed by Murakami et al. [11] which has 70 questionnaire items with a binary scale is adopted.

2.1 Calculation of Smile Synchronization

Facial Action Units (FAUs) are extracted from collected videos using OpenFace [2]. The smile label of each participant is defined as simultaneously activating FAU6 and FAU12 which are Cheek Raiser and Lip Corner Puller.

The smile synchronization is calculated from the labeled smile interval. The smile interval of each participant for each conversation pair is compared, and the interval in which the participant smiles within 500 ms after the conversation partner smiles is defined as the synchronized smile. Figure 2 shows the scheme of calculation of smile synchronization. The smile synchronization probability is obtained on the number of smile intervals and smile synchronization, and the mean delay of synchronization is calculated. Note that the two participants' data is not considered due to the error of FAU detection of OpenFace.

2.2 Wrist Velocity and Voice Activities

The author annotates "speech interval" and "behavior interval" (e.g., gestures) for gathered data. For the speech interval, the cumulative speech time length is used as the feature for analysis.

Positions of right and left wrists are extracted by MediaPipe [10]. The maximum velocity of the wrist for each behavior interval is calculated, and then the mean of maximum velocity for each interval is obtained.

The velocity of the wrist is calculated as

$$v = \sqrt{(x_{k+1} - x_k)^2 + (y_{k+1} - y_k)^2} * \frac{1}{\Delta t}, \tag{1}$$

where (x_k, y_k) and Δt wrists' (x, y) position from MediaPipe and time interval of the video (i.e., the reciprocal number of frame rate), respectively. The velocities

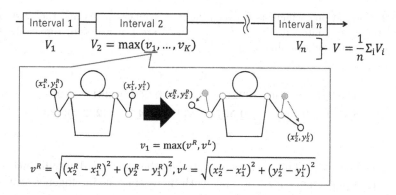

$$V_1 \quad V_2 = \max(v_1, \ldots, v_K) \qquad V_n \quad \bigg\} \quad V = \frac{1}{n}\Sigma_i V_i$$

$$v_1 = \max(v^R, v^L)$$

$$v^R = \sqrt{\left(x_2^R - x_1^R\right)^2 + \left(y_2^R - y_1^R\right)^2}, v^L = \sqrt{\left(x_2^L - x_1^L\right)^2 + \left(y_2^L - y_1^L\right)^2}$$

Fig. 3. The procedure of calculating the wrist velocity. K is the number of frames in the interval. V_i and V and the wrist velocity of i-th behavior interval and the output wrist velocity of a certain participant.

Table 1. Correlation coefficients between the Big Five personality and the smile synchronization and the delay of synchronization. Ex, A, C, Em, and I are Extraversion, Agreeable, Consciousness, Emotional Stability, and Intelligence, respectively.

	Ex	A	C	Em	I
Probability of smile sync	0.102	**0.287**	0.0184	0.144	**−0.766**
The delay of smile sync	**−0.343**	0.056	**−0.231**	**−0.379**	**−0.473**

of right and left wrists are obtained by Eq. 1, and a larger maximum velocity is used as the "wrist velocity". Figure 3 shows the calculation procedure of output wrist velocity.

3   Results of Analysis

The result of analysis about the smile synchronization is described in the Sect. 3.1, and the wrist velocity and speech interval are in Sect. 3.2.

3.1   Results of Smile Synchronization

Correlations between Big Five personality traits and the probability of smile synchronization and mean delay of the smile synchronization are investigated. Table 1 shows correlation coefficients. The bold and underline in the table mean the absolute values of the coefficient are larger than 0.2 and 0.4.

The coefficient of smile synchronization and intelligence score is −0.766 which the value is a strong negative correlation, and the value of the synchronization and agreeable score is 0.287 which is a weak positive correlation. There are no correlations between other scores and smile synchronization.

Correlation coefficients between the delay of synchronization and extraversion, consciousness, and emotional stability scores are −0.343, −0.230, and

Table 2. Correlation coefficients between the Big Five personality and the wrist velocity and the speech interval. Ex, A, C, Em, and I are Extraversion, Agreeable, Consciousness, Emotional Stability, and Intelligence, respectively

	Ex	A	C	Em	I
The wrist velocity	**0.222**	−0.104	**0.234**	**0.381**	**0.201**
Speech interval	**<u>−0.567</u>**	−0.148	**<u>0.547</u>**	**−0.222**	**<u>0.483</u>**

−0.377, respectively. The coefficient between the delay and intelligence score is −0.474. In particular, in accordance with increasing the intelligence score, the rate of synchronization and the delay of smile expression tend to decrease.

3.2   Results of Wrist Velocity and Speech Interval

Correlations between Big Five personality traits and the wrist velocity and the speech interval are investigated. Table 2 shows correlation coefficients. The bold and underline in the table mean the absolute values of the coefficient are larger than 0.2 and 0.4.

From the table, there are weak positive correlations between the wrist velocity and extraversion, consciousness, emotional stability, and intelligence scores. The medium correlation are in speech interval and extraversion, consciousness, and intelligence score, and these values are −0.567, 0.547, and 0.483, respectively.

4   Discussion

In the analysis of the wrist velocity, weak positive correlations with personality traits are obtained, and the results are consistent with previous studies [12], in Japanese). From this, insights of our analysis are not specific results derived from image features.

Intelligence score is related to knowledge, analytical ability, and thinking ability [1,4]. If the intelligence score is high, the probability of synchronization becomes small because the person considers whether to express a smile or not against the conversation partner's smile. Because the person with a high intelligence score rapidly judges whether to synchronize, the delay of synchronization is small.

Extraversion score is the personality trait that prefers engaging in cheerful conversations with a wide range of people, utilizing fluent eloquence and adept wit. A negative correlation is obtained between the extraversion score and the delay of synchronization because the person with higher extraversion has a rich conversation experience and rapidly responds to the conversation partner. The reason for the negative correlation between extraversion score and speech interval is that the participants let the conversation partner speak and continued the conversation as listeners, thus shortening their utterances. Upon reviewing

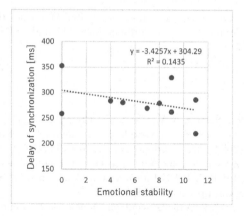

Fig. 4. The scatter plot of emotional stability and the delay of smile synchronization. The vertical and horizontal axes are the delay and the score, respectively. Blue points and line are data of each participant and regression line. (Color figure online)

the videos, the author observed that participants with high extraversion scores tended to facilitate conversation by asking questions of their partners.

The low emotional stability score relates to better sensitivity and insight ability. Because the person with low emotional stability is skilled at reading conversation partners' inner workings and rapidly expresses a smile, we assume a positive correlation between the emotional stability score and the delay of synchronization is obtained. However, the correlation between the score and the delay is a negative value. Figure 4 is the scatter plot of the emotional stability score and the delay of smile synchronization. The outlier which is the person with a low emotional stability score and large delay of synchronization seems to affect the result.

5 Conclusion

In this paper, we analyze the relationship between personality traits and behavior during small talk sessions. The strong negative correlation between the intelligence score and the probability of smile synchronization is obtained. For the delay of smile synchronization, negative correlations are observed in extraversion, consciousness, emotional stability, and intelligence scores. Designing the communication robot using the above insight and testing the developed behaviors are our future directions.

In addition to this, we analyze communication data with other related information. The analysis based on the combination of personality traits between both participants is an important issue for unveiling the property of human-human communication. The relationship between both participants affects the behavior during the conversation. Adding this information for analysis is also one of our future tasks.

Acknowledgment. This work was supported by JST Moonshot R&D Grant Number JPMJMS2011 (Development of Semi-autonomous CA) and JSPS KAKENHI Grant Number JP23K16977.

References

1. Furnham, A., Viren Swami, A.A., Chamorro-Premuzic, T.: Cognitive ability, learning approaches and personality correlates of general knowledge. Educ. Psychol. **28**(4), 427–437 (2008). https://doi.org/10.1080/01443410701727376
2. Baltrusaitis, T., Zadeh, A., Lim, Y.C., Morency, L.P.: Openface 2.0: facial behavior analysis toolkit. In: 13th IEEE International Conference on Automatic Face and Gesture Recognition, pp. 59–66. IEEE (2018)
3. Bartneck, C., Forlizzi, J.: A design-centred framework for social human-robot interaction. In: 13th IEEE International Workshop on Robot and Human Interactive Communication, pp. 591–594 (2004)
4. Chamorro-Premuzic, T., Furnham, A., Ackerman, P.L.: Ability and personality correlates of general knowledge. Personal. Individ. Differ. **41**(3), 419–429 (2006). https://doi.org/10.1016/j.paid.2005.11.036, https://www.sciencedirect.com/science/article/pii/S0191886906000870
5. Forlizzi, J.: How robotic products become social products: an ethnographic study of cleaning in the home. In: Proceedings of the ACM/IEEE International Conference on Human-Robot Interaction. HRI 07, pp. 129–136. Association for Computing Machinery, New York, NY, USA (2007). https://doi.org/10.1145/1228716.1228734
6. Goldberg, L.R.: The structure of phenotypic personality traits. Am. Psychol. **48**(1), 26 (1993)
7. Ishii, R., Ahuja, C., Nakano, Y.I., Morency, L.P.: Impact of personality on nonverbal behavior generation. In: Proceedings of the 20th ACM International Conference on Intelligent Virtual Agents, pp. 1–8 (2020)
8. Kwon, J., Ogawa, K.I., Ono, E., Miyake, Y.: Detection of nonverbal synchronization through phase difference in human communication. PLOS ONE **10**(7), 1–15 (2015). https://doi.org/10.1371/journal.pone.0133881
9. Li, R., Curhan, J., Hoque, M.E.: Predicting video-conferencing conversation outcomes based on modeling facial expression synchronization. In: 11th IEEE International Conference and Workshops on Automatic Face and Gesture Recognition, vol. 1, pp. 1–6. IEEE (2015)
10. Lugaresi, C., et al.: Mediapipe: a framework for building perception pipelines. arXiv preprint arXiv:1906.08172 (2019)
11. Murakami, Y., Murakami, C.: Construction of scales for the big five personality inventory. J. Personal. Psychol. Res. **6**(1), 29–39 (1997). https://doi.org/10.2132/jjpjspp.6.1_29. (in Japanese)
12. Nakano, Y., Oyama, M., Nihei, F., Higashinaka, R., Ishii, R.: The generation of agent gestures expressing personality traits. Hum. Interface Soc. **23**(2), 153–164 (2021). https://doi.org/10.11184/his.23.2_153. (in Japanese)
13. Nowicki, S., Duke, M.P.: Individual differences in the nonverbal communication of affect: the diagnostic analysis of nonverbal accuracy scale. J. Nonverbal Behav. **18**, 9–35 (1994)
14. Osugi, T., Kawahara, J.I.: Effects of head nodding and shaking motions on perceptions of likeability and approachability. Perception **47**(1), 16–29 (2018)

Optimization and Evaluation of Tablet Keyboard Layout in the Unsupported Case

Yuhang Qiu, Ruishan Zheng, Bojun Wei, and Yun Chen[✉]

Beijing Institute of Technology, Beijing, China
yun.chen@bit.edu.cn

Abstract. Tablet PCs are mobile devices that possess a mid-range size and processing speed, situated between that of cell phones and computers. They are highly favored for their easy-to-use and portable features and thus are popularly employed in light office settings due to their availability to a wide user base.

Nevertheless, the virtual keyboards on tablets currently available possess layouts and designs that are derived from the physical keyboards of computers or the full 26-key keyboards of smartphones. These keyboards, merely stretched and scaled to fit the tablet screen, lack ergonomic design considerations for specific tablet usage scenarios. As a result, users engaged in text-based office work may experience inconvenience.

Therefore, we created a customized, ergonomic, and optimized virtual keyboard for touchscreen tablets by combining different existing keyboard layouts. Our goal was to address the common issues faced by users who hold the tablet with both hands and type with their thumbs. We based the keyboard design on the comfortable typing area of the fingers on a tablet device and developed a test prototype. To minimize interference of existing layout proficiency, we replaced familiar letters of the alphabet with special symbols. An equal number of male and female participants underwent testing comparing the traditional keyboard layout to the new one. Researchers measured the length of the participants' thumbs, administered subjective scale questionnaires, and separately recorded the time and accuracy of each participant's use of both keyboards.

A regression analysis was conducted to examine the relationship between finger length and typing efficiency among subjects, concerning existing studies. The subjects were divided into three groups based on their finger length - short, medium, and long. Notably, the short-finger group comprised mostly female participants. Results demonstrate that the curved arrangement of the split keyboard significantly improved typing efficiency for users in the short-finger group, while showing no significant change for the other groups. However, there were some negative effects on the correctness rate. It was found that finger length was negatively correlated with the enhancement effect.

Keywords: Typing input · keyboard layout · Tablet

© The Author(s), under exclusive license to Springer Nature Switzerland AG 2024
C. Stephanidis et al. (Eds.): HCII 2024, CCIS 2114, pp. 187–194, 2024.
https://doi.org/10.1007/978-3-031-61932-8_23

1   Introduction

1.1   Background

Since the first-generation iPad's release in 2010, tablet PCs have emerged as a favored type of mobile office equipment, and their popularity continues to grow rapidly [8] .Tablets are easier to carry and can be operated conveniently and flexibly by way of touchscreen technology, in comparison to desktop computers. Additionally, tablets offer larger displays than cell phones, providing a superior experience for paperless learning and office work.

In recent years, there has been a significant increase in the global tablet market, particularly in China. The COVID-19 pandemic has acted as a catalyst for this trend, with remote learning and teaching driving the demand further. Tablets are also valuable tools for grading, creating lecture materials, and recording meeting notes [7]. As a result, an increasing number of businesses and households now possess tablet devices. According to IDC data, the tablet market in China shipped 28.46 million units in 2021, marking a year-on-year increase of 21.8%, the largest increase in shipments seen in the last seven years. Furthermore, shipments are expected to grow by 5.2% in 2022 [3,6]. Despite this high demand, improvements to the ergonomic design of tablet devices are still necessary.

1.2   Related Work

Typing input on tablet devices has been partly examined, with some studies focused on the tilt angle of the keyboard or the user's typing posture [1,9]. S. Lee and colleagues found that 67.9% of tablet users experience musculoskeletal symptoms, with females being 2.059 times more likely than males to experience symptoms [5]. Gender was identified as a correlate of symptomatology. During mobile device usage, research suggests that typing on a physical keyboard results in increased activity of thumb, finger flexors, and wrist extensors compared to typing on a similarly sized touchscreen device [4]. Therefore, further investigation into the ergonomic benefits of tablet device usage is warranted, including an examination of any potential gender differences.

Of course, there have been designs and studies conducted on virtual keyboard layouts. For instance, a prior study revealed that an optimized split keyboard with a Qwerty layout for tablet devices heightened user comfort during two-handed typing scenarios [10]. Current research mainly focuses on one-handed virtual keyboards for large-screen smartphones in the context of thumb typing. For instance, Yincheng Wang et al. (2018) proposed a correlation between the size of the arc-shaped curved keyboard and user input reaction time, which necessitates a more precise redefinition of the functional areas of keyboard input [11]. Thomas and colleagues conducted experiments on tablet devices with 20 participants to compare single and dual finger input. The results showed that the split keyboard introduced by the iOS system does not outperform traditional keyboards in terms of input performance and accuracy [2]. While some studies have suggested that a more rational keyboard layout can reduce finger movement distance [13], this research did not investigate tablet devices in landscape mode.

2   Method

2.1   Experimental Design

Thumb length and keyboard types were the independent variables, while the dependent variables were the input time required per 500 characters and the correct rate. The keyboard factor was categorized into two types- the normal soft keyboard and the arc-type developed in this study.

2.2   Participants

Twenty participants were recruited for the study, all of whom were university students. There were an equal number of male and female participants (10 each), whose ages ranged from 19 to 22 years old. All participants had been using the iPad for study or office purposes for an extended period of time. Nineteen participants were proficient in using the 26-key input method (95%).

2.3   Task

This experiment involved copying characters or patterns as a task. To mitigate the potential impact of participants' familiarity with the traditional 26-key keyboard layout on the results, the participants were asked to copy 500 randomly-displayed characters or patterns using a predetermined keyboard. The 26 characters all come from the familiar and commonly used section of the Unicode standard character library, with the selected characters ensuring that participants will not be affected by orientation during recognition. Before and after the test, participants need to complete a questionnaire on their personal keyboard usage and a five-point Likert scale survey regarding their feelings about using the two types of keyboards, respectively.

2.4   Equipment

The type of study's equipment is the iPad Pro with an 11-inch display (horizontal state). The virtual keyboard consisted of 26 characters excluding the function keys, derived from the Unicode character library. Notably, that the 26 letters were not utilized during the experiment, and the backspace function was disabled throughout. The text was coded in the Swift Playgrounds application, and the 500 characters to be copied were randomly generated and displayed in groups of 100 above the participant's input box.

2.5 Prototype Design

Based on the results of the pre-test questionnaire, approximately one-third of users frequently employ a two-handed posture while typing with their thumbs on tablet devices; about two-thirds reported difficulty accessing the center portion of the virtual keyboard while typing in this manner. Consequently, we aimed to develop a virtual keyboard which could enhance text input efficiency in such circumstances.

Prior to conducting the formal experiment, we conducted an investigation to determine the optimum range for comfortable typing on a tablet device while holding it with both hands. An iPad Pro (11-inch) was utilized as the operating device, and 30 volunteers were recruited for the study. The experimenter was instructed to hold the tablet with both hands, keep the device away from any support or desk, and use both thumbs to click the screen in a relaxed state. The volunteer's clicks were recorded for 30 s, and the resulting traces were combined to generate a single image. This image displayed the most comfortable range of thumb movement during tablet device use for the volunteer. To create a heat map, 30 images were superimposed.

Based on the test results, the most comfortable areas for clicking thumbs were found to be the left and right sectors beneath the tablet device, for both hands. Therefore, we have redesigned the QWERTY keyboard by framing it with the left and right sectors, preserving the traditional key arrangement, and maintaining individual key size and spacing (Fig. 1). Our goal is to enhance typing efficiency and optimize the user's typing experience when using both thumbs.

2.6 Procedure

To maintain standardized environmental conditions, all 20 participants underwent individual testing in an unoccupied classroom. Before conducting the experiment, each participant provided responses to a questionnaire that queried aspects such as their tablet device usage, typing posture, and issues related to usage. The measurements were based on the method previously defined by J. Xiong and S. Muraki in their study, where thumb length was the distance between the top of the thumb tip and the proximal protuberance of the metacarpal bone [12]. Before the experiment, the thumb length of each participant (Fig. 2) was measured and recorded with a 150 mm long slide caliper that had an accuracy of 0.2 mm.

Participants completed the character copying task using a standard keyboard and a split arc-type (Fig. 2). The timer for the task will start as soon as the first character is typed into the text box and will end when 500 characters have been copied. The program randomly generated a sequence of 500 characters or patterns, which was then divided into 5 groups and presented in a 20 * 5 format. Upon completion, an automatic window displayed the participant's total typing time (in seconds) and correct rate. Participants were instructed to hold the tablet with both hands and enter text using their thumbs in a two-handed state. After finishing the text-entry task, participants completed a questionnaire regarding

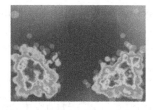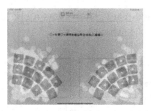

Fig. 1. The figure illustrates the process from test experiments to the determination of the keyboard layout, moving from left to right.

Fig. 2. (A) Thumb length measurement. The distance between A and B represents the thumb length. (B) The left shows the program interface of a standard keyboard while the picture on the right shows the interface of a split arch-type keyboard. (The standard keyboard layout is identical to the system's default keyboard layout, except that it has been omitted the function keys such as backspace.)

their perceptions of using the two keyboards. The questionnaire included measures of comfort, acceptability, adaptability, fluency, and satisfaction.

2.7 Analyse

The efficiency and accuracy of typing input are automatically calculated by the program script. Input time is determined based on the duration it takes for participants to complete a replication task of 500 patterns (unit: seconds). Accuracy is computed as the error rate generated through the calculation of the Levenshtein distance between the input text and the source text (Fig. 3). Participants were divided into three groups based on thumb length: short thumb group, medium thumb group, and long thumb group. (The dividing lines are half a standard deviation above and below the mean.)

3 Result

3.1 Performance

Observing the experimental results reveals that the effects produced by the new layout have a certain correlation with finger length. According to the previous grouping, the short group showed a noticeable improvement in time consumption, while the medium and long groups did not exhibit significant differences.

In terms of accuracy, there was a slight decline across all groups, but the difference was not significant.

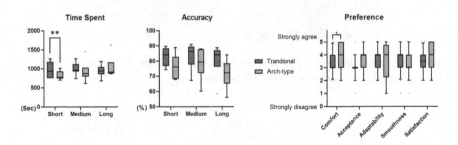

Fig. 3. Graph A respectively depicts the differences in typing task completion time and Graph B depicts accuracy between male and female participants. Graph C illustrates the differences in participants' subjective perceptions when using the two keyboards.

To further explore the specific connection between layout effects and finger length, we conducted a detailed analysis through linear regression. Using thumb length as the independent variable (unit: cm) and Time Decrease Rate as the dependent variable (Time Decrease Rate calculation method: (1-Time of arc-type/Time of traditional)×100%), the trend of the dependent variable with respect to the independent variable can be deduced from the graph: the longer the thumb, the lower the ratio of additional time spent using the standard keyboard compared to the arc-shaped keyboard. Graph A is based on linear regression analysis. We speculate that such differences in results may be related to the difference in thumb lengths between males and females. By analyzing the connection between finger length and gender through a scatter plot (Fig. 4.A), it is not difficult to find that females have a larger proportion in the short group, and overall, the range for females tends to be shorter than that for males.

3.2   User Preference

Subjective evaluations of five aspects of use for each of the two keyboards are presented as box plots (Fig. 4). The new keyboard layout offers a significant improvement in comfort compared to traditional keyboards.

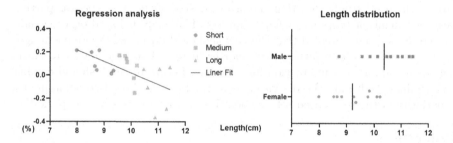

Fig. 4. Graph A uses linear regression to analyze the correlation between Time Decrease Rate and thumb length; Graph B shows the distribution of finger length in male and female subjects.

4 Discussion and Conclusion

Building on other researchers' studies on arc-type and segmented keyboards, we redesigned the experiment and applied it to tablet devices. In terms of input time, the feedback from the short thumb group met expectations, with the new layout design enhancing text input efficiency compared to the conventional layout. This enhancement is likely due to participants spending less time touching the central area of the screen with their fingers. For subjects with medium to long fingers, the input efficiency was not significantly affected by the keyboard type, which we speculate is due to them needing more time for eye movements to recognize keys spread across the screen sides. However, in terms of preference, there were positive results; participants unanimously found the design of the segmented, two-handed arc-shaped keyboard more comfortable. This preference is based on the results of the initial survey conducted before the experiment, positioning the keyboard layout in what users generally consider the most comfortable typing area. Notably, participants did not subjectively feel that typing on the segmented keyboard was smoother than on traditional keyboards, possibly because this was their first encounter with a divided keyboard layout, requiring more time to adapt, or because it took them more time to identify patterns and characters on both sides. Moreover, with more resources in the future, we can learn from the detailed research directions in traditional layouts, further adjusting and optimizing details such as key spacing to provide a better user experience.

The study's findings are derived from a single data collection with a limited sample size. The majority of participants utilized the split arch-type for the first time during the experiment. The unfamiliarity with the pattern had an impact on participant reaction time during the experiment. To gauge any changes in the effectiveness of both keyboards over an extended period of time, ongoing follow-up experiments could be conducted to observe participant adaptation and learning. In a comparative experiment conducted on tablet devices in landscape mode between the segmented arc-type keyboard layout and the traditional layout, the results indicated that the layout design of the Arc-type was particularly beneficial for users with shorter fingers. The analysis based on the gender ratio of each group revealed that the new keyboard layout was more meaningful for female users, who typically have shorter fingers. This contributes to ensuring equal comfort and interaction for everyone. Future research should conduct longitudinal studies on the design of segmented soft keyboards to examine the superiority of the segmented soft keyboard over a longer observation period.

References

1. Albin, T.J., McLoone, H.E.: The effect of tablet tilt angle on users' preferences, postures, and performance. Work **47**(2), 207–211 (2014)
2. Aschim, T.B., Gjerstad, J.L., Lien, L.V., Tahsin, R., Sandnes, F.E.: Are split tablet keyboards better? A study of soft keyboard layout and hand posture. In: Lamas, D., Loizides, F., Nacke, L., Petrie, H., Winckler, M., Zaphiris, P. (eds.) INTERACT 2019. LNCS, vol. 11748, pp. 647–655. Springer, Cham (2019). https://doi.org/10.1007/978-3-030-29387-1_37
3. Bi, X., Smith, B.A., Zhai, S.: Quasi-qwerty soft keyboard optimization. In: Proceedings of the SIGCHI Conference on Human Factors in Computing Systems, pp. 283–286 (2010)
4. Kietrys, D.M., Gerg, M.J., Dropkin, J., Gold, J.E.: Mobile input device type, texting style and screen size influence upper extremity and trapezius muscle activity, and cervical posture while texting. Appl. Ergon. **50**, 98–104 (2015)
5. Lee, S.P., Hsu, Y.T., Bair, B., Toberman, M., Chien, L.C.: Gender and posture are significant risk factors to musculoskeletal symptoms during touchscreen tablet computer use. J. Phys. Ther. Sci. **30**(6), 855–861 (2018)
6. Li, F.C.Y., Guy, R.T., Yatani, K., Truong, K.N.: The 1 line keyboard: a qwerty layout in a single line. In: Proceedings of the 24th Annual ACM Symposium on User Interface Software and Technology, pp. 461–470 (2011)
7. Mock, K.: Teaching with tablet PC's. J. Comput. Sci. Coll. **20**(2), 17–27 (2004)
8. Müller, H., Gove, J., Webb, J.: Understanding tablet use: a multi-method exploration. In: Proceedings of the 14th International Conference on Human-Computer Interaction with Mobile Devices and Services, pp. 1–10 (2012)
9. Straker, L.M., Coleman, J., Skoss, R., Maslen, B.A., Burgess-Limerick, R., Pollock, C.M.: A comparison of posture and muscle activity during tablet computer, desktop computer and paper use by young children. Ergonomics **51**(4), 540–555 (2008)
10. Trudeau, M.B., Catalano, P.J., Jindrich, D.L., Dennerlein, J.T.: Tablet keyboard configuration affects performance, discomfort and task difficulty for thumb typing in a two-handed grip. PLoS ONE **8**(6), e67525 (2013)
11. Wang, Y., Ai, H., Liang, Q., Chang, W., He, J.: How to optimize the input efficiency of keyboard buttons in large smartphone? A comparison of curved keyboard and keyboard area size. In: Stephanidis, C., Antona, M. (eds.) HCII 2019. CCIS, vol. 1088, pp. 85–92. Springer, Cham (2019). https://doi.org/10.1007/978-3-030-30712-7_11
12. Xiong, J., Muraki, S.: Effects of age, thumb length and screen size on thumb movement coverage on smartphone touchscreens. Int. J. Ind. Ergon. **53**, 140–148 (2016)
13. Yang, N., Mali, A.D.: Modifying keyboard layout to reduce finger-travel distance. In: 2016 IEEE 28th International Conference on Tools with Artificial Intelligence (ICTAI), pp. 165–168. IEEE (2016)

Assessing the Usability of Statistical Software Using a Discrete Choice Experiment

Jacob Rhyne[✉], Mark Bailey, Joseph Morgan, and Ryan Lekivetz

JMP Statistical Discovery LLC, Cary, NC 27513, USA
{Jacob.Rhyne,Mark.Bailey,Joseph.Morgan,Ryan.Lekivetz}@jmp.com

Abstract. The usability [2,3] of modern statistical software is increasingly important as users with limited statistical training become more reliant on such tools to help them address complex real-world problems [1,13]. This paper presents a case study that illustrates how a discrete choice experiment [16] may be used to assess the usability of the complex controls that are becoming more prevalent in such software. The case study focuses on an interactive plot intended for novice users of a commercially available statistical application, who need to interpret a linear model used to analyze the results of an experiment. Effective selection of model terms is critical for identifying important experimental factors and the accuracy of model predictions. The ability to easily determine whether terms should be entered into a model, or the reason for their inclusion, is essential for interpretability [4,15] and to ensure user satisfaction of the application.

Keywords: Design of experiments · Usability · Statistical software

1 Introduction

As the analytic capabilities of modern statistical software become more complex, users of these tools find that the graphical user interface (GUI) controls that they need to use are also becoming more complex. This is particularly problematic for users with limited statistical training who may find it difficult to distinguish between the complexity of the controls and the complexity of the underlying methods. One way that software developers can ameliorate the cognitive burden that such users face is to both minimize the amount of information that users must digest while making the controls that users interact with more intuitive. This is partly a usability challenge and one that has recently garnered some attention in the literature [1,13].

In this paper, we address the usability of a complex control for an application in a commercially available statistical software package by using a discrete choice experiment to evaluate the perceived preferences of users of the application. The application for which we conduct the usability study allows users to fit a model to data collected for a designed experiment. The result of the model fit (see Fig. 1) is an interactive visualization of the model that requires users to interpret the

© The Author(s), under exclusive license to Springer Nature Switzerland AG 2024
C. Stephanidis et al. (Eds.): HCII 2024, CCIS 2114, pp. 195–205, 2024.
https://doi.org/10.1007/978-3-031-61932-8_24

results of the fit and to use the visualization as a control to interact with the model. To do this effectively, users must either have some understanding of the rules for how effects are added to or removed from a model, or the control must be sufficiently intuitive that users can quickly discover the necessary rules. This interactive visualization control had undergone previous usability studies prior to the current study and so the development team hypothesized that any additional changes needed to enhance usability would not be design changes but, instead, would be changes to various attributes of the control. Such attributes include those related to the appearance of the control (i.e., visual attributes) as well as those that provide information about the visualization, such as dynamic hover help, icons, etc. (i.e., textual attributes).

A discrete choice experiment seemed appropriate for this type of usability evaluation. Since the intent was to investigate how changing various attributes of the control would be perceived by different user groups, this experimental setup allowed us to vary multiple hypothesized changes simultaneously. The burden to a subject is minimal, as they simply needed to indicate their favorite each time among sets of configurations presented. Conceptually, from the perspective of the subjects, the experience is like that of a usability study based on a conjoint analysis [8, 12], but the underlying analysis is different. We refer readers to Louviere et al. (2010) [10] for an in-depth discussion of discrete choice experiments versus conjoint analysis.

2   Methodology

We first introduce necessary notation used in our discrete choice experiment. An *attribute* is a feature that we intend to vary in the experiment, with corresponding *levels* that represent the values the attribute can take on in the experiment. In traditional designed experiments, an attribute is also referred to as a factor. A *profile* reflects a combination of different attributes, while a *choice set* represents a collection of profiles. In subsequent sections we will use the term *configuration* instead of profile to distinguish this usage from the statistical usage for univariate plots. For each choice set, a respondent will choose one of the profiles as their "choice".

Underlying the choice experiment is a random utility model. The random utility model assumes some latent utility with the explainable components that we can use to model the probability that a respondent chooses a particular option among a set of competing options. Formally, we represent the utility that a respondent attaches to profile j in choice set s, U_{js}, as

$$U_{js} = \mathbf{x_{js}^\intercal}\beta + \epsilon_{js}, \tag{1}$$

where k represents the number of parameters to be estimated, $\mathbf{x_{js}}$ is a $k \times 1$ vector containing the attribute levels of alternative j with β the corresponding $k \times 1$ vector of parameters. The ϵ_{js}'s are independently identically distributed random variables following a Gumbel distribution (Extreme Value Type I) and reflect random components for unexplained differences, whether from individuals or attributes that are unaccounted for [11]. Following model (1) for utility, we can consider the probability of a particular profile j (out of J profiles) being chosen as preferred among a specified choice set s, p_{js}, using a conditional logit model as follows:

$$p_{js} = e^{\mathbf{x}_{js}^{\mathsf{T}}\beta} / \sum_{t=1}^{J} e^{\mathbf{x}_{ts}^{\mathsf{T}}\beta}. \tag{2}$$

In using a discrete choice design, there are two important aspects of interest in our experiments. First, do any of the attributes contribute to the utility in a significant way? This allows us to study which attributes have the biggest impact (in terms of utility) on the control, while also providing potential insight into attributes for subsequent studies. Such a model also allows the ability to test if interactions between various attributes significantly affects the utility. Secondly, beyond investigating which attributes are important, we can use the model to compare profiles. This is especially useful to compare "promising" profiles (according to the utility) to the current control as well as estimating the probability of a new profile being preferred to the current control.

When appropriate, one can use a prior probability distribution for the parameters in model (2) [5]. We had no evidence to suggest higher utility for particular levels of attributes, so we used a utility-neutral design where all choices within a choice set are equally probable [6].

3   Usability Case Study

3.1   Background

Figure 1 is a screenshot of the interactive visualization control that was evaluated for this case study. The control consists of an interactive plot and tabular data which both represent the output of a model fitting method for data collected from a designed experiment. The plot shows 95% confidence interval estimates for each term in the model. The intervals are presented relative to a reference line at zero, which can be interpreted as the null hypothesis that the estimate of the term is zero and should not be included in the model. Line color is used to denote whether terms are included in the model or not and line style is used to denote whether terms are statistically significant. Removing a term sets its estimate to zero and computes prospective confidence intervals, showing what the confidence interval would be if the term were included, given the current model.

Clicking a line segment will either remove the associated term from the model or enter it into the model, with green and red used to indicate if the term is included or excluded. The legend above the plot explains the meaning of the line color and style. Also, a hint is provided to aid in discovering this interactivity, by instructing the user that line segments are interactive controls and can be clicked. The presentation avoids information that does not directly assist in choosing terms.

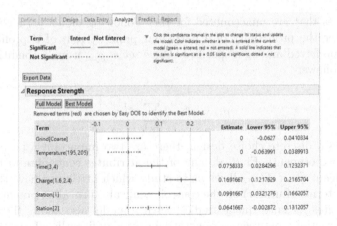

Fig. 1. Term estimates and effect tests for the analysis of a coffee tasting experiment.

3.2   Motivation for a Usability Study Powered by a Designed Experiment

Motivated by the shortcomings of the initial design of this control, it was enhanced to make it easier to interpret the fitted model. One of the main issues addressed was providing support for heredity. Regression models for experimental data generally benefit from maintaining effect heredity. This means that if a higher-order term is included in the model, then lower-order terms with the same factors should also be included, even if they are not statistically significant. Empirical evidence suggests that the assumption of heredity is a reasonable one, and many users familiar with designed experiments expect heredity to be enforced by fitting methods [9]. However, the development team recognized that not all users understand the rationale for model heredity, so simply adding this capability would likely confuse or even surprise those users. So, the team recognized that a mechanism was needed to aid interpretability when heredity was being enforced.

Also, a usability study found that not all users read, or even noticed, the legend above the plot and not all users discovered that tooltips/hints were available. Furthermore, some users had difficulty interpreting the legend. The study also showed that users who discovered tooltips were more successful in interpreting the output. The development team believed the content of tooltips could be further improved. Motivated by this, a dynamically generated, context appropriate, tooltip (i.e., hover hint) mechanism was added to the control to help users interpret each confidence interval.

Additionally, since tooltips were not easily discovered, as they require a user to hover over individual line segments, the development team added a new column to the tabular content of the control, using icons to also indicate tooltip information. We refer to this new column as a "Preview Column" in subsequent sections. However, optimal locations for the "Preview Column" or its associated legend were not clear.

In total, there were 51 possible variations of this enhanced output, including different color schemes, location of the Preview Column, and tooltip messages, that were considered. With this many potential configurations to consider, the development team decided to employ a discrete choice experiment for usability evaluation that would limit the number of distinct configurations that subjects would consider, by changing several attributes at once, and would therefore allow subjects to quickly choose between alternative configurations.

3.3 Designed Experiment for the Usability Study

To create our usability study, we used the "Choice Design" tool in JMP [7]. Our study comprised two discrete choice experiments. The first experiment focused on the color scheme used in the interactive plot and the location of the "Preview Column", while the second experiment focused on the wording and location of the dynamic, contextual, tooltips. We decided on two separate experiments because, although we wanted to explore potential interactions, we did not expect interactions between the tooltip wording and the color scheme or "Preview Column" location. However, the study presented both experiments seamlessly, in succession, and participants were not aware that two experiments were being conducted.

Table 1. Factors for discrete choice experiment #1

Name	Levels
Color Scheme	Green or Red, Blue or Orange, Blue or Red
Preview Column Location	End of Table, Appended to Term, Next to Term
Preview Legend Location	Above, Below, None

The factors in Table 1 specify which factors are presented together in a choice set during the initial eight exercises of the usability study. As participants did the usability study, they were presented with three different color schemes, three different locations for the Preview Column, and three different locations for the legend. Each experimental run of the design corresponds to a different choice set.

Table 2 outlines the three parts of the tooltip considered. That is, the Entered, Significance, and Heredity Messages. The Entered Message indicates whether the term is entered in the model, the Significance Message indicates whether the term is statistically significant and, finally, the Heredity Message indicates if the term is included in the model to maintain heredity. Note that the Heredity Message is only included if heredity applies to the term. In each case, the levels represent either an existing message or one or two alternate messages. The fourth factor indicates the location of the tooltip, that is appearing either over the confidence interval or the Preview Column.

Table 2. Factors for discrete choice experiment # 2

Name	Levels
Entered Message	Status Quo, Alternate
Significance Message	Status Quo, Alternate
Heredity Message	Status Quo, Alternate 1, Alternate 2
Tooltip Location	Confidence Interval, Preview Column

The statistical model for the discrete choice experiments allowed us to determine the utility of each factor, given the observed data. Our model is set to estimate all first-order effects (i.e., main effects) and as many two-factor interactions as possible, given run size constraints. We decided to use three surveys with eight choice sets per survey in each experiment. Therefore, our usability study had 3 different versions, with 16 total exercises in each version.

Each choice set was presented as two images created to match the combinations of factor settings. For example, the first row in Fig. 2 (left) determines the appearance of the first image in the first exercise (i.e., choice set) and the second row in Fig. 2 (left) determines the appearance of the second image in the first exercise.

We recruited colleagues from staff at JMP to complete the usability study and we aimed for a balanced representation of expert users of DOE and JMP, as well as newer users of both JMP and DOE.

Choice Set	Color Scheme	Preview Col Loc	Preview Legend Loc		Choice Set	Entered Message	Significance Message	Heredity Message	Hover Help Loc
1	Green and Red	Next to Term	Below		9	Alt 1	Alt 1	Status Quo	Preview Column
1	Green and Red	End of Table	None		9	Status Quo	Status Quo	Alt 1	Preview Column
2	Green and Red	Next to Term	None		10	Alt 1	Alt 1	Alt 1	Preview Column
2	Blue and Red	End of Table	None		10	Status Quo	Status Quo	Alt 1	Confidence Interval
3	Green and Red	Append Term	Below		11	Alt 1	Status Quo	Alt 1	Preview Column
3	Blue and Orange	End of Table	Below		11	Status Quo	Status Quo	Status Quo	Confidence Interval

Fig. 2. Design for participant 1 with choice sets for experiment #1 (left) and experiment #2 (right).

3.4 Usability Study

Our goal in delivering this usability study was to have participants complete the study independently, in an unmoderated setting. To do this, we created an application to deploy the study. With this application, we controlled test presentation to participants and managed result collection and analysis return [13]. The application provides explanations and instructions, and automatically assembles the images corresponding to choice sets from the experimental runs of the discrete choice designs.

To illustrate, consider the first exercise completed by the first participant in the study. In this case, the choice sets presented to the first participant were automatically generated from the specifications outlined in Table 3. Note that the user is shown two options, which are the color scheme and Preview Column configurations determined by the choice design.

Table 3. Specifications for Exercise 1 for Participant 1

Choice Set	Position	Color Scheme	Preview Col Loc	Preview Legend Loc
1	Left	Green and Red	Next to Term	Below
1	Right	Green and Red	End of Table	None

For each exercise (i.e. choice set), the subject was required to choose their favorite from the two options and, as they proceeded, their choices were saved (Fig. 3). They were then presented with a new set of images corresponding to the next run of the choice design. Note that the application included an integrated questionnaire, where subjects were given the option of answering a set of questions as well as providing additional feedback.

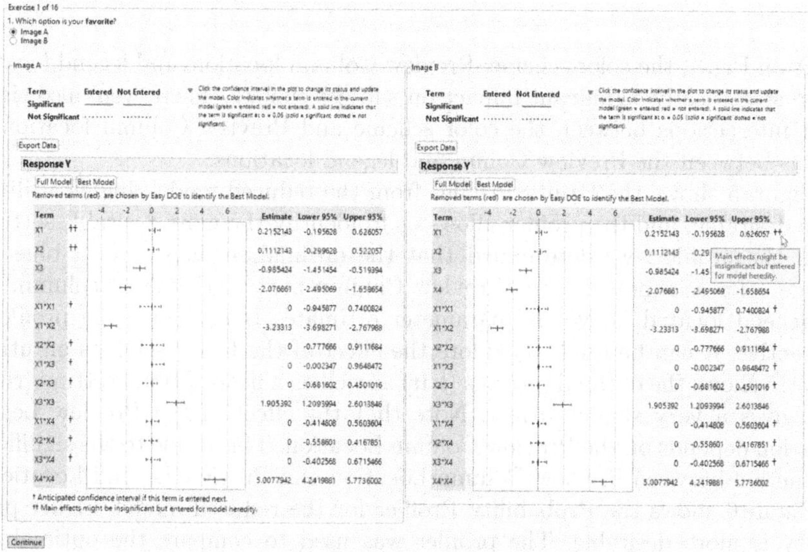

Fig. 3. Exercise 1 completed by Participant 1

4 Findings

The Choice modeling tool in JMP was used to analyze the results of the study. As two designs were used for the study, the results for each design were analyzed separately.

4.1 Choice Modeling for Design 1

The first design considered different color schemes, as well as the location of the Preview Column and legend. We first fit the full model, then removed the interaction effect for Color Scheme and Preview Legend Location as it was not significant. The results of the full and reduced models are presented in Fig. 4.

Source	L-R ChiSquare	DF	Prob>ChiSq	Source	L-R ChiSquare	DF	Prob>ChiSq
Color Scheme	9.898	2	0.0071*	Color Scheme	14.850	2	0.0006*
Preview Col Loc	2.575	2	0.2760	Preview Col Loc	15.571	2	0.0004*
Preview Legend Loc	14.790	2	0.0006*	Preview Legend Loc	19.988	2	<.0001*
Color Scheme*Preview Col Loc	11.387	4	0.0225*	Color Scheme*Preview Col Loc	13.481	4	0.0091*
Color Scheme*Preview Legend Loc	4.129	4	0.3888	Preview Col Loc*Preview Legend Loc	13.918	4	0.0076*
Preview Col Loc*Preview Legend Loc	9.892	4	0.0423*				

Fig. 4. Likelihood ratio tests for choice experiment #1 Full (left) and Reduced Models (right).

From Fig. 4, the color scheme, Preview Column location, and legend location had a statistically significant impact on subject choices. There were also significant interactions between the color scheme and Preview Column location, as well as between the Preview Colmn and legend locations.

Figure 5 shows the Utility Profiler from the reduced model, higher utility is more desirable, and the profiler allows us to identify the most desirable settings. From the profiler, we determined that the optimal settings were a blue and orange color scheme, with the Preview Column next to the Term column, and the legend located above the parameter estimates table. Since the profiler is interactive, it can be used to explore the effect of the factor settings on utility. Figure 5 shows the optimal settings (left) as well as a near-optimal setting (right) that gives a very similar utility. Note that the effect of the Preview Legend Location depends on the Preview Column Location. This is due to the significant interaction between Preview Column Location and Preview Legend Location.

Figure 6 shows the Probability Profiler for the reduced model, higher probability is more desirable. The profiler was used to compare the optimal and near-optimal settings to the current color scheme (green and red). As seen in Fig. 6, using the alternative color schemes instead of green and red coincides with a probability of preference of 0.99.

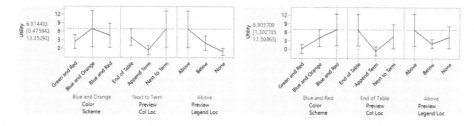

Fig. 5. Utility Profiler at optimal settings (left) and near-optimal settings (right).

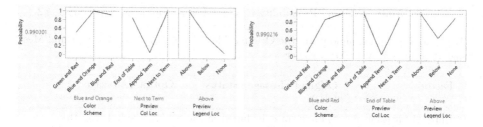

Fig. 6. Probability Profiler at optimal (left) and near-optimal settings (right).

4.2   Choice Modeling for Design 2

The second design considered the wording of the tooltip provided to assist in interpreting the confidence intervals, as well as the location of this tooltip. We fit the full model, then discovered that several effects were not significant, so we applied backward elimination to reduce the model [14]. The full and reduced models are presented in Fig. 7.

Figure 8 (left) shows the Utility Profiler from the reduced model. Using the profiler to determine the most desirable settings, the optimal configuration uses the alternative Entered Message and the second alternative Heredity Message. A summary of these messages is presented in Table 4.

Source	L-R ChiSquare	DF	Prob>ChiSq	Source	L-R ChiSquare	DF	Prob>ChiSq
Entered Message	6.249	1	0.0124*	Entered Message	5.307	1	0.0212*
Significance Message	0.000	1	1.0000	Heredity Message	6.436	2	0.0400*
Heredity Message	6.566	2	0.0375*				
Hover Help Loc	0.015	1	0.9018				
Entered Message*Significance Message	4.666	1	0.0308*				
Entered Message*Heredity Message	2.443	2	0.2948				
Significance Message*Heredity Message	5.332	2	0.0695				
Entered Message*Hover Help Loc	0.000	1	1.0000				
Significance Message*Hover Help Loc	1.211	1	0.2712				
Heredity Message*Hover Help Loc	4.035	2	0.1330				

Fig. 7. Likelihood ratio tests for choice experiment #2 Full (left) and Reduced Models (right).

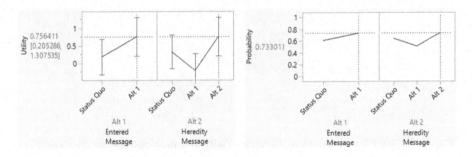

Fig. 8. Utility (left) and Probability Profilers (right) for choice experiment #2

Table 4. Tooltip example using the Original Message (status quo) and Optimal Message determined by Utility Profiler

Factor	Original Message (Status Quo)	Optimal Message
Entered Message	"This term is included in the model."	"X1 is included in the model."
Significance Message	"It is not significant at $\alpha = 0.05$."	"It is not significant at $\alpha = 0.05$."
Heredity Message	"Main effects might be insignificant but they are entered for model heredity."	"X1 is entered to maintain model heredity as X1*X2 is entered."

The Entered and Heredity Messages were found to have a different Optimal Message than the original, while the Significance Message remained unchanged. Note the status quo Significance Message is included in Table 4 for clarity, but it was not found to have a significant effect. The Original Message would read, "This term is included in the model. It is not significant at $\alpha = 0.05$. Main effects might be insignificant but they are entered for model heredity."

Our analysis indicated that the Optimal Message would instead read, "X1 is included in the model. It is not significant at $\alpha = 0.05$. X1 is entered to maintain model heredity as X1 * X2 is entered." The model indicates participants preferred seeing term specific help, particularly for the Entered and Heredity Messages.

Figure 8 (right) shows the Probability Profiler for the reduced model. The profiler presented compares using the alternative Entered and Heredity Messages to the Original Messages. As seen in Fig. 8, using these alternative messages coincides with a probability of preference of 0.733.

5   Conclusion

We found that a discrete choice experiment allowed us to efficiently investigate how changing various attributes of a complex control would be perceived by users. We were able to identify attributes that had a significant impact on preference, while also discovering interactions between various attributes. Secondly, beyond identifying important attributes and preferred configurations, we were able to provide empirical evidence to guide the development team as they refined the appearance of the control as well as the contextual help provided to aid users in interpreting the information provided by the control.

References

1. Abbasnasab Sardareh, S., Brown, G.T., Denny, P.: Comparing four contemporary statistical software tools for introductory data science and statistics in the social sciences. Teach. Stat. **43**, S157–S172 (2021)
2. Bevan, N., Carter, J., Harker, S.: ISO 9241-11 revised: what have we learnt about usability since 1998? In: Kurosu, M. (ed.) HCI 2015. LNCS, vol. 9169, pp. 143–151. Springer, Cham (2015). https://doi.org/10.1007/978-3-319-20901-2_13
3. Frøkjær, E., Hertzum, M., Hornbæk, K.: Measuring usability: are effectiveness, efficiency, and satisfaction really correlated? In: Proceedings of the SIGCHI Conference on Human Factors in Computing Systems, pp. 345–352 (2000)
4. Guidotti, R., Monreale, A., Ruggieri, S., Turini, F., Giannotti, F., Pedreschi, D.: A survey of methods for explaining black box models. ACM Comput. Surv. (CSUR) **51**(5), 1–42 (2018)
5. Kessels, R., Jones, B., Goos, P.: Bayesian optimal designs for discrete choice experiments with partial profiles. J. Choice Model. **4**, 52–74 (2011)
6. Huber, J., Zwerina, K.: The importance of utility balance in efficient choice designs. J. Mark. Res. **33**, 307–317 (1996)
7. JMP Statistical Discovery LLC 2022–2023. JMP® 17 Design of Experiments Guide. Cary, NC: JMP Statistical Discovery LLC
8. Kim, S.-H., et al.: Ergonomic design of target symbols for fighter aircraft cockpit displays based on usability evaluation. In: Stephanidis, C. (ed.) HCI 2018. CCIS, vol. 850, pp. 176–182. Springer, Cham (2018). https://doi.org/10.1007/978-3-319-92270-6_24
9. Li, X., Sudarsanam, N., Frey, D.D.: Regularities in data from factorial experiments. Complexity **11**(5), 32–45 (2006)
10. Louviere, J.J., Flynn, T.N., Carson, R.T.: Discrete choice experiments are not conjoint analysis. J. Choice Model. **3**(3), 57–72 (2010)
11. McFadden, D.: The choice theory approach to market research. Mark. Sci. **5**(4), 275–297 (1986). JSTOR
12. Michalski, R.: Examining users' preferences towards vertical graphical toolbars in simple search and point tasks. Comput. Hum. Behav. **27**(6), 2308–2321 (2011)
13. Rhyne, J., Bailey, M., Morgan, J., Lekivetz, R.: Assessing the usability of statistical software using designed experiments. In: Stephanidis, C., Antona, M., Ntoa, S., Salvendy, G. (eds.) HCII 2023. CCIS, vol. 1832, pp. 681–688. Springer, Cham (2023). https://doi.org/10.1007/978-3-031-35989-7_87
14. SAS Institute Inc.: SAS/STAT® User's Guide. The QUANTSELECT Procedure: Effect Selection Methods. SAS Institute Inc., Cary, NC (2024)
15. Silva, A., Schrum, M., Hedlund-Botti, E., Gopalan, N., Gombolay, M.: Explainable artificial intelligence: evaluating the objective and subjective impacts of XAI on human-agent interaction. Int. J. Hum.-Comput. Interact. **39**(7), 1390–1404 (2023)
16. Street, D.J., Burgess, L.: The Construction of Optimal Stated Choice Experiments: Theory and Methods. Wiley, New York (2007)

Preliminary Exploration of Technology Acceptance for Applying Virtual Assistants in Clinic Self-service Machine

Chien Tang and Chun-Ching Chen[✉]

Department of Interaction Design, National Taipei University of Technology, Taipei, Taiwan
t111ac8009@ntut.org.tw, cceugene@mail.ntut.edu.tw

Abstract. This study aims to investigate the impact of anthropomorphism level and dimensionality on clinic users' perceived enjoyment and social presence toward virtual assistants. We employ a mixed-design analysis of variance and utilize a questionnaire proposed. Findings revealed a significant interaction effect between anthropomorphism level and dimensionality on perceived enjoyment, with higher anthropomorphism levels associated with greater social presence. However, dimensionality showed no significant influence on social presence. Our study suggests that when designing virtual assistants, careful consideration of anthropomorphism level and dimensionality is crucial. Enhancing anthropomorphism can improve users' perceived enjoyment and social presence but may also heighten perceived fear.

Keywords: Virtual assistant · Self-service machine · Clinic · Anthropomorphism · Dimensionality

1 Introduction

In previous research on designing effective human-computer interaction, "human-computer trust" has always played an important role as an influencing factor (Hancock et al., 2011). According to Sheridan and Ferrell (1974), "trust is considered a fundamental determinant of users' choice to rely on complex automated systems rather than traditional service personnel for task execution." Many studies have shown that human-computer interaction with facial features enhances the impact on social, authenticity, and immersiveness aspects. Therefore, we planned to test the degree of facial anthropomorphism (X-axis) and the virtual-to-real ratio (Y-axis) as independent variables to understand the existence of an interaction effect between different levels of anthropomorphism and realism. The results of our pilot study have shown that users with a higher need for interaction with service personnel tend to exhibit lower willingness to use self-service machines. Therefore, in the experiment conducted in this study, we focused on measuring interaction and sociability as the dependent variables.

© The Author(s), under exclusive license to Springer Nature Switzerland AG 2024
C. Stephanidis et al. (Eds.): HCII 2024, CCIS 2114, pp. 206–214, 2024.
https://doi.org/10.1007/978-3-031-61932-8_25

2   Method

2.1   Research Framework

We will utilize the questionnaire proposed by Heerink (2010), selecting two dimensions, namely, perceived enjoyment and perceived sociability, along with questions related to the perception of fear toward virtual assistants. This will help us to study user behavior and perception when interacting with different styles of virtual assistants as well as their willingness to use these assistants. Through this approach, our goal is to understand the style of virtual assistant that is most effective in establishing user trust and influencing their usage decisions in clinical settings.

The variable descriptions for the research framework are as follows:

1. Control variables: The control variables referred to in this study are the operational task and voice of the virtual assistants. Each control variable is described as follows:
   (a) Operational task: The operational context of this study primarily focuses on the clinic check-in process.
   (b) Voice: To eliminate the influence of voice, this study will employ a single voice across nine different appearances of virtual assistants.
2. Independent variables: The independent variables in this study are degree of anthropomorphism (Dependent Sample Variable B) and perception of dimensionality (Independent Sample Variable A).
3. Dependent variables: The dependent variables in this study are perceived enjoyment and social presence.

2.2   Experimental Design

This study will be divided into two phases: Phase 1 (Preparation Phase), and Phase 2 (Experiment Phase).

Phase 1: Preparation Phase

1. Generate 24 different samples of virtual assistant images with varying dimensions and degrees of anthropomorphism using MidJourney.
2. Create an online survey using Google Forms to evaluate the dimensions and degrees of anthropomorphism of these virtual assistant images.
3. Select the top-scoring, lowest-scoring, and median images from each group, representing images with different degrees of anthropomorphism and dimensions (see Fig. 1).
4. Combine the selected images with voice using the D-ID AI video generator to create high-fidelity prototypes.

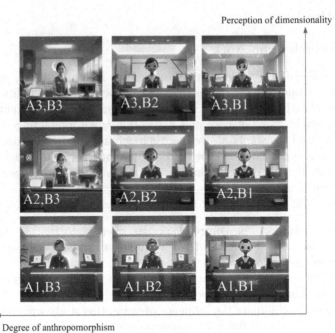

Perception of dimensionality

Degree of anthropomorphism

Fig. 1. Different levels of anthropomorphism and dimensions of virtual assistants.

Phase 2: Experiment Phase

1. Divide the nine sorted images from Phase 1 horizontally into three groups, each comprising virtual assistants with three different degrees of anthropomorphism (B) but equal dimensions (A).
2. Each group will consist of 20 participants, who will be asked to operate the machine in a clinic "check-in" scenario.
3. Initially, participants will be briefed on the task using images; then, they will be instructed to start the experiment.
4. Participants will be randomly assigned different virtual assistants with varying facial features that will help users complete their tasks.
5. The virtual assistants will instruct participants on how to fill out the questionnaire and provide them with the survey.
6. Statistical analysis will be conducted to examine whether the independent variables significantly impact the dependent variables, assessing participants' perceptions and willingness to use virtual assistants with different degrees of anthropomorphism and dimensions.

2.3   The Unified Theory of Acceptance and Use of Technology Questionnaire

This study employs the Unified Theory of Acceptance and Use of Technology (UTAUT) questionnaire proposed by Heerink (2010). The original scale comprises 12 constructs; however, for the purpose of this study, only two constructs were selected. The perceived enjoyment construct consists of three items, while the social presence construct comprises four items. A Likert five-point scale is utilized for scoring, where 1 indicates "strongly disagree" and 5 indicates "strongly agree" (Table 1).

Table 1. Variable Definitions

Variable	Definition
Perceived Enjoyment (PENJ)	Feelings of joy/pleasure associated with the use of the system.
Social Presence (SP)	The experience of sensing a social entity when interacting with the system

– **Items for Perceived Enjoyment**

- PENJ1: I enjoy doing things with this virtual assistant.
- PENJ2: I feel that this virtual assistant is friendly.
- PENJ3: I find this virtual assistant fascinating.

– **Items for Social Presence**

- SP1: When interacting with this virtual assistant I felt like I'm talking to a real person.
- SP2: It sometimes felt as if this virtual assistant was really looking at me.
- SP3: I can imagine this virtual assistant to be a living creature.
- SP4: I often think this virtual assistant is not a real person.

2.4 Participant Demographics

There were 60 participants in the main study. In terms of the gender distribution of participants, male and female participants accounted for 53.3% and 46.7% of the total, respectively. Moreover, the participants' ages varied widely. Overall, participants over the age of 45 and under 45 accounted for 51% and 49% of the total, respectively.

2.5 Data Processing and Analysis

This study employed a two-way analysis of variance (ANOVA) (mixed design) using SPSS 29.0.1.0 statistical software to analyze the data collected from the perceived enjoyment (PENJ) and social presence (SP) questionnaires.

2.6   Research Results

Results for Perceived Enjoyment

– **Summary table of two-factor mixed design ANOVA**
   Table 2 reveals that the F-value for the interaction effect is 3.931, with a p-value of 0.007, which is less than 0.05, indicating significance. Therefore, this suggests that under different degrees of anthropomorphism and their interaction, users exhibit significant differences in perceived enjoyment of the virtual assistant, necessitating further analysis of the main effects (Table 3).

Table 2. Summary table of two-factor mixed design analysis of variance.

Source of Variation	SS	df	MS	F	p-value
Dimensionality (Independent Variable)	1.97	2	0.985	0.977	0.383
Anthropomorphism (Dependent Variable)	20.56	2	11.70	16.07	<.001
Dimensionality x Anthropomorphism	10.06	2	2.86	3.93	0.007
Within	130.41	2			
Group (Between Subjects)	57.47	57	1.01		
Residual	72.94	100.14	0.73		
Total	162.99	13.82			

Table 3. Simple Main Effects Analysis Summary Table

Source of Variation	SS	df	MS	F	p-value	Post-hoc comparisons
Anthropomorphism						
Low Dim	8.21	2	4.11	5.70	0.0045	B3 > B1 > B2
Medium Dim	11.0	2	5.50	7.64	0.0008	B3 > 1; B3 > B2
High Dim.	10.9	1.43	7.61	10.57	0.00006	B2 > B1; B3 > B1
Residual	72.92	101.20	0.72			
Dimensionality						
Low Anthro	4.98	2	2.49	3.26	0.04	A1 > A3
Medium Anthro	4.46	2	2.23	2.92	0.056	
High Anthro.	2.59	2	1.30	1.70	0.185	
Residual	130.41	171	0.762			

– The Simple Main Effect Test of Dimensionality

- H_{a1}: When the level of anthropomorphism of the virtual assistant is set to low anthropomorphism, there is no significant difference in the perceived enjoyment mean values among different dimensionality levels.
- H_{a2}: When the level of anthropomorphism of the virtual assistant is set to medium anthropomorphism, there is no significant difference in the perceived enjoyment mean values among different dimensionality levels.
- H_{a3}: When the level of anthropomorphism of the virtual assistant is set to high anthropomorphism, there is no significant difference in the perceived enjoyment mean values among different dimensionality levels.

On the basis of the independent factor "dimensionality" in the simple main effect test, the significance levels of the hypotheses H_{a1}, H_{a2}, and H_{a3} are 0.04, 0.056, and 0.185, respectively. At a significance level of 0.05, only the significance of Ha1 is less than 0.05, reaching significance, while H_{a2} and H_{a3} are not significant. This indicates that when the anthropomorphism level of the virtual assistant is low anthropomorphism, there is a significant difference in the average perceived enjoyment of users among different dimensionalities, with L Dim. > H Dim.

– The Simple Main Effect Test of Anthropomorphism

- H_{b1}: When the dimensionality of the virtual assistant is set to low dimensionality, there is no significant difference in the perceived enjoyment mean values among different anthropomorphism levels.
- H_{b2}: When the dimensionality of the virtual assistant is set to medium dimensionality, there is no significant difference in the perceived enjoyment mean values among different anthropomorphism levels.
- H_{b3}: When the dimensionality of the virtual assistant is set to high dimensionality, there is no significant difference in the perceived enjoyment mean values among different anthropomorphism levels.

The simple main effect test of the dependent factor "anthropomorphism" reveals that the significance levels of hypotheses H_{b1}, H_{b2}, and H_{b3} are 0.0045, 0.0008, and 0.00006, respectively. The significance levels of H_{b1}, H_{b2}, and H_{b3} are all less than 0.05, indicating significance. This suggests that when the realism level of the virtual assistant is L Dim., there is a significant difference in the average perceived enjoyment of users among different anthropomorphisms, with H Anthro. > L Anthro. > M Anthro. When the virtual assistant's dimensionality is medium dimensionality, H Anthro. > L Anthro.; H Anthro. > M Anthro. When the virtual assistant's dimensionality is H Dim., M Anthro. > L Anthro.; H Anthro. > L Anthro.

Social Presence

– Summary table of two-factor mixed design ANOVA
According to Table 4, the F-value for the interaction effect is 2.373, with

a p-value of 0.056, which is greater than 0.05, indicating nonsignificance. Therefore, this suggests that under different perceptions of dimensionality and degrees of anthropomorphism, users do not perceive significant differences in social presence among virtual assistants.

However, from the F-value of the dependent factor "anthropomorphism," which is 22.279, with a p-value of less than .001, we conclude that we should reject the null hypothesis H6. This means that users perceive significant differences in social presence among virtual assistants with different degrees of anthropomorphism, and according to the means, H Anthro. (3.31) > M Anthro. (2.56) > L Anthro. (2.32).

Table 4. Summary table of two-factor mixed design analysis of variance.

Source of Variation	SS	df	MS	F	p-value
Dimensionality (Independent Variable)	0.90	2	0.45	0.32	0.728
Anthropomorphism (Dependent Variable)	31.84	2	15.92	22.28	<.001
Dimensionality x Anthropomorphism	6.78	4	1.70	2.37	0.056
Within	162.14	171			
Group (Between Subjects)	80.68	57	1.42		
Residual	81.46	114	0.72		
Total	201.66	179			

3   Conclusion

This study aims to investigate the impact of different levels of anthropomorphism and dimensionality of virtual assistants on users' perceived enjoyment and social presence. The research findings are as follows:

– **Perceived Enjoyment**

- The interaction between the level of anthropomorphism and dimensionality of virtual assistants significantly affects users' perceived enjoyment.
- When the level of anthropomorphism is low, dimensionality significantly affects users' perceived enjoyment, with users perceiving higher enjoyment with low-dimensionality virtual assistants compared to high-dimensionality ones.
- When the level of anthropomorphism is high, dimensionality does not significantly affect users' perceived enjoyment.

– **Social Presence**

- The level of anthropomorphism of virtual assistants significantly influences users' social presence perception, with higher levels of anthropomorphism leading to stronger perceived social presence.
- Dimensionality does not significantly influence users' social presence perception.

4 Discussion

Due to the typically referenced discomfort stemming from the similarity between the appearance and behavior of virtual characters and humans in the Uncanny Valley Theory, there is an interplay between this theory and the present study, which focuses on the social perception of virtual assistant appearance. Therefore, this study aims to specifically compare the similarities and differences between the Uncanny Valley Theory and the results of this study, which employs AI to generate the appearance of virtual assistants, potentially challenging the Uncanny Valley Theory. Since the appearance of AI-generated virtual assistants may possess more human-like features compared to previous cold and rigid robot appearances, while simultaneously possibly increasing anthropomorphism, this may conflict with the discomfort described as the "valley" in the Uncanny Valley Theory.

– **Perceived Enjoyment and the Uncanny Valley Theory:**

According to the research findings, when the anthropomorphism of virtual assistants is low, the perceived enjoyment of low-dimension virtual assistants is higher than that of high-dimension virtual assistants. This new aspect has not been explored in the Uncanny Valley Theory. According to the Uncanny Valley Theory, when the anthropomorphism of virtual characters reaches a certain level, human users may feel discomfort and aversion, leading to a decrease in perceived enjoyment. However, it does not explore whether other aspects under the same level of anthropomorphism will have a negative impact on users. According to post-experimental interviews, it has indeed been confirmed that users feel more fear when the robot's eyes have a stronger sense of hollowness, especially in low anthropomorphism (leaning towards robot appearance) situations.

– **Social Presence and the Uncanny Valley Theory:**

The research results show that the level of anthropomorphism significantly affects users' social presence, with higher anthropomorphism leading to a stronger perception of social presence. This is not entirely consistent with the "Uncanny Valley" phenomenon described in the Uncanny Valley Theory. According to the Uncanny Valley Theory, after a certain level of anthropomorphism, human users may feel discomfort, leading to a decrease in social presence. In this study, AI-generated virtual assistants may have succeeded in increasing social presence, which may indicate that an increase in anthropomorphism does not necessarily lead to the occurrence of the Uncanny Valley phenomenon under certain circumstances.

In conclusion, this data provides some insights into the effects of virtual assistant anthropomorphism and appearance features on user perception. The use of AI to generate the appearance of virtual assistants may challenge past understandings based on the Uncanny Valley Theory. If future research finds that AI-generated virtual assistant appearances can strike a balance between anthropomorphism and dimensionality, enhancing perceived enjoyment while reducing fear, this may challenge some assumptions of the Uncanny Valley Theory. Therefore, further research may be needed to explore these phenomena and ascertain the consistency and reliability of these results.

References

1. Hancock, P.A., et al.: Hum. Factors: J. Hum. Factors Ergon. Soc. **53**, 517 (2011)
2. Heerink, M.: Assessing acceptance of assistive social robots by aging adults. Doctoral dissertation, Universiteit van Amsterdam [Host] (2010)
3. Sheridan, T.B., Ferrell, W.R.: Man-Machine Systems: Information, Control and Decision Models of Human Performance. MIT Press (1974)
4. Mori, M.: The uncanny valley. Energy **7**(4), 33–35 (1970)

Positive-Right and Negative-Left: Affective Spatialization by Digital "Grab" Interactions

Sergio C. Torres[1]([⊠]) [iD], Susana Ruiz Fernández[2] [iD], and Peter Gerjets[1] [iD]

[1] Multimodal Interaction Lab, Leibniz Institut für Wissensmedien, Tübingen, Germany
s.cervera-torres@iwm-tuebingen.de

[2] Brandenburg University of Technology Cottbus – Senftenberg, Senftenberg, Germany

Abstract. Recent research exploring embodied interactions with digital interfaces indicate cognitive and affective implications regarding the processing of visual stimuli when the hands are near to them (hand-proximity effect). In this regard, the present study delves into the affective implications of digital "grabbing", particularly within the context of affective spatialization by hand dominance. Concretely, the Body Specificity Hypothesis (BSH) suggests that right-handers associate the right space with positivity and the left space with negativity. To test this assumption within an interactive environment, sixty right-handed participants performed lateralized grab interactions with forty pictures (20 positive and 20 negative) displayed at the right or left space of a touchscreen monitor. The results support an interactive positivity bias effect whereby grabbing positive (vs. negative) pictures at the right (vs. left) space was significantly faster. This finding is discussed against the background of the Spatial Affective Interaction (SAI) framework, integrating hand-proximity, affective spatialization, and approach-avoidance mechanisms to understand embodied digital interactions. Limitations include the need for further research on left-handed interactions and decontextualized stimuli. The findings highlight the relevance of considering ergonomics and emotional context in interface design.

Keywords: Affective Spatialization · Valence processing · Embodied Interaction · Spatial Affective Interaction (SAI) · Grab Interaction · Hand-proximity · Approach-Avoidance

1 Introduction

Touch-based interfaces like smartphones, tablets, or touch-monitors, popular for their intuitive use, support interactive manual gestures similar to the way we manipulate physical objects [1]. For example, interaction gestures such as reach-to-touch digital content, entail a sequence of actions (e.g., raising the hand or finger and moving them to finally touch the content) that might trigger mental representations of approach actions performed to grab tangible objects [2]. Notably, recent research indicates that interacting with digital content directly by hand facilitates the processing of said content (e.g., art pictures; [3]). This is in line with cognitive frameworks indicating that the

© The Author(s), under exclusive license to Springer Nature Switzerland AG 2024
C. Stephanidis et al. (Eds.): HCII 2024, CCIS 2114, pp. 215–223, 2024.
https://doi.org/10.1007/978-3-031-61932-8_26

attention to visual stimuli is intensified when placing the hands close to these stimuli i.e., hand-proximity effect [4, 5]. Recent research exploring embodied interactions with digital interfaces showed affective implications of such hand-proximity effect, indicating, in addition, that this effect is context-sensitive. For example, research reveals that interacting with affective digital pictures directly by hand may highlight motivational action-goals associated with pleasant outcomes (i.e., approaching positive and avoiding negative stimuli [6]). Interestingly, it has been proposed that people may also mentally represent affective outcomes in space based on hand dominance [7]. As elaborated below, the present study investigates how this postulate applies to digital "grabbing".

According to the Body Specificity Hypothesis (BSH [7]) right-handers form space-valence associations in terms of right-positive and left-negative. In contrast, left-handers tend to form the inverse associations. The proposed mechanism behind these associations refers to motor fluency. Specifically, actions within the dominant hand side might be perceived as more pleasant because they are typically more fluent than actions within the non-dominant hand side, which are less fluent. Experimental research based on stimuli-response paradigms have reported effects in line with that reasoning. For example, in studies requiring bimanual responses, affective stimuli were displayed in the middle of a screen (e.g., positive and negative words [8] or happy and sad face images [9]). Participants had to discriminate between positive or negative stimuli by pressing one of two response-buttons on a keyboard, one response-button assigned to each hand. The findings reveal that responses to positive stimuli are generally faster using the dominant right hand whereas responses to negative stimuli are faster using the non-dominant left hand. In a sense, this finding extends the space-valence associations proposed by the BSH to hand-valence associations (right hand-positive and left hand-negative). In addition, similar research has focused on dynamic unimanual responses as for example raising the hand from a centrally located response-button on a keyboard and pressing another response-button located either at the right or left side on the keyboard [10]. Here, reacting to positive stimuli was shown faster when the response required moving the dominant right hand toward the right space as compared to when moving it toward the left space. Interestingly, responses to negative stimuli were almost identical instead of being faster when moving the right hand to the left side as could have been reasonable to expect in the light of the BSH. This reinforces the idea that the dominant right hand is particularly linked to the processing of positive stimuli but also that the performed action (moving the hand to the right or to the left) modulates this link.

However, although experimentally relevant, it is very unclear whether and how these findings generalize to a more ecologically valid environment as it is the case when interacting with affective stimuli directly by hand. Accordingly, this study investigates whether the findings reported in the standard stimuli-response settings introduced above, may generalize to a more interactive environment, i.e., interacting with affective pictures through lateralized grab interactions by the dominant right hand. In line with the postulates of the BSH, symmetrical results could be expected whereby interacting with positive pictures at the right side and with negative pictures at the left side (congruent grab interactions) are performed faster than interacting with positive pictures at the left side and with negative pictures at the right side (incongruent grab interactions) i.e., an *interactive space-valence hypothesis*. Alternatively, asymmetries could also arise so that effects are only observed for grab interactions with positive pictures and not for negative ones. Concretely, rightward grab interactions could be particularly faster than leftward interactions i.e., an *interactive positivity bias hypothesis*.

2 Methods

2.1 Participants

Sixty participants from 18 to 49 years old ($M = 24.3$, $SD = 5.5$, $Mdn = 23$; 50% women) took part in this 40-min experiment. They were recruited through the SONA online system (https://www.sona-systems.com) in exchange for monetary reward. The following inclusion criteria were required: $18 \geq$ years, good or corrected-to-normal vision, right-handed, and German language skills.

2.2 Apparatus and Stimuli

Apparatus. A large touchscreen monitor (TM; Dell™-Monitor S2340T) connected to a laptop (Fujitsu lifebookE10, Intel Core i7 6500U, 2.50 GHz) was used to run the study. The TM featured 20.99″ (Horizontal) and 12.28″ (Vertical) Active-Matrix TFT-LCD and displayed a resolution of 1600 × 900 pixels.

Stimuli. Forty affective pictures (20 positive and 20 negative pictures with moderate arousal) were retrieved from the Nencki Affective Picture System (NAPS [11]) and the International Affective Picture System (IAPS [12]). The content included scenes of animals, landscapes, objects, and people. The pictures were displayed with a resolution of 397 × 340 pixels (10.5 cm × 9 cm). Pictures differed significantly in valence, $F(1,36) = 308.02$; $p < .001$, but not in arousal, $F(1,36) = 2.07$; $p = .15$, or luminance, $F(1,36) = .158$; $p = .69$ (see Table 1).

Table 1. Valence, arousal, and luminance of the positive and negative pictures.

Valence Category	Valence M(SD)	Arousal M(SD)	Luminance M(SD)
Positive	7.14 (.67)	4.92 (.59)	104.61 (31.67)
Negative	3.81 (.52)	5.19 (.62)	108.31 (25.8)

2.3 Experimental Procedure

Once at the lab, participants took a seat in front of the touchscreen monitor at approximately 60 cm. Before the experiment, participants were asked to wear a glove on their non-dominant left hand and leave this hand over their laps to prevent using it during the testing. The experiment consisted of two consecutive blocks, each of them introduced by specific instructions. One block required observing the affective pictures without any interaction involved. The other block required participants to interact with the pictures using the dominant right hand. The order of the blocks was counterbalanced across participants. After six training trials using gray squares instead of pictures, the 40 affective pictures were randomly displayed. Importantly, half of the positive pictures were shown on the right and the other half on the left. The same applied to the negative pictures. Participants had to react by performing grab interactions i.e., raise the hand from a centered initiation mark on the screen, approach the hand to the displayed picture and touch it. For a detailed description of a trial see Fig. 1.

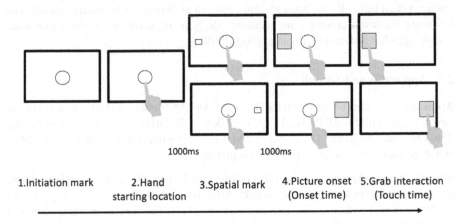

1.Initiation mark   2.Hand   3.Spatial mark   4.Picture onset   5.Grab interaction
                    starting location   (Onset time)   (Touch time)

Fig. 1. Illustration of leftward and rightward grab interactions in training trials. An initiation mark (white circle) was displayed first to control the starting location of the hand on the screen. After positioning the hand on this mark, a spatial mark (white square) indicates the location where the picture will appear. As soon as the picture appears, participants have to "grab" the picture.

3   Results

The analyses were carried out using Jamovi v2.3.21.0 [13]. After a descriptive analysis, Grab Times (ms) = Touch time - Pictures' Onset Time, were analyzed using a Generalized Linear Mixed Model (GLMM) approach via the GAMLj package [14].

3.1   Descriptive Analyses

Grab Times departed from a Gaussian distribution as indicated by the Shapiro-Wilkinson (S-W) test and standardized skewness and kurtosis (Table 2). An exclusion criterion of ±1.5 SD was established to reduce potential biases due to extreme observations (resulting in 8% exclusion of trials). The proportion of incongruent trials = 1077 (positive pictures-left side = 541 and negative pictures-right side = 536) and congruent trials = 1058 (positive pictures-right side = 533 and negative pictures-left side = 525) did not significantly differ after the trial exclusion, $X^2 = .169, p = .681$.

Table 2. Descriptive statistics of Grab Times

N	2315 (96.4%)
Missing	85 (3.5%)
M (SD)	.912 (1.30)
Mdn	.442
Skewness (SE)	3.83 (.0509)
$Z_{skewness}$	75.2
Kurtosis (SE)	21.4 (.102)
$Z_{kurtosis}$	209.8
S-W	.586**

** $p < .001$

3.2 Comparative Analyses

The analyses used a Gamma data distribution together with a log-link. Age and gender were included as covariates in the modeling.

A two-step data modeling included, first, the examination of general Congruency effects. The analysis addressed the fixed factor Congruency, which compared congruent trials (grabbing positive pictures-right side and grabbing negative pictures-left side) and incongruent trials (grabbing positive pictures-left side and grabbing negative pictures-right side). Subjects and pictures were included as random factors with random intercepts (1|id_subject; 1|id_picture) together with random slopes (Congruency|id_subject). The results indicated a main effect of Congruency. On average, grab interactions in the congruent trials were 14.1% faster than grab interactions in the incongruent trials. Age, and gender were not statistically significant (Table 3).

Second, a closer inspection of the interaction between the factors Grab Direction (right vs. left) and pictures' Valence Category (positive vs. negative) was carried out (i.e., 2 × 2 within-participants design). Subjects and pictures were also included as random intercepts. In this case, random slopes addressed the two factors (Valence|id_subject; Direction|id_subject; Direction|id_picture). The results showed a main effect of the Valence Category indicating that interacting with positive pictures was 13% faster than interacting with negative pictures, on average. This main effect was qualified by a highly significant interaction between the Grab Direction and the Valence Category. Concretely, interacting with positive pictures at the right side was faster than (a) interacting with positive pictures at the opposite left side and (b) interacting with negative pictures at both sides. Descriptively speaking, negative pictures showed lower Grab Times when interacting with them at the left side than at the right side. However, in this case, Grab Times did not reach statistical significance (Fig. 2). As in Step 1, age and gender were not statistically significant (Table 3).

Table 3. Fixed Effects Parameter Estimates and Estimated Marginal Means

95% CI						
Step 1	**b**	**SE**	**Lower**	**Upper**	**exp(b)**	**p**
Age	.009	.011	−.013	.031	–	.408
Gender	.171	.134	−.088	.439	–	.192
Congruency	−.152	.048	−.246	−.058	.859 (14.1%)	.002
	M	**SE**	**Lower**	**Upper**		
Congruent	.527	.057	.457	.609		
Incongruent	.614	.039	.512	.736		
Step 2	**b**	**SE**	**Lower**	**Upper**	**exp(b)**	**p**
Age	.021	.012	−.002	.044	–	.079
Gender	.169	.143	−.111	.450	–	.237
Direction	−.057	.045	−.146	.031	–	.205
Valence Cat	−.138	.064	−.265	−.012	0.870 (13.0%)	.032
Dir.*Valence Cat	−.205	.057	−.318	−.915	0.815 (18.5%)	<.001
	M	**SE**	**Lower**	**Upper**		
Positive	.525	.042	.448	.615		
Right	.484	.044	.404	.580		
Left	.568	.044	.488	.663		
Negative	.603	.054	.504	.721		
Right	.617	.063	.505	.754		
Left	.589	.051	.497	.699		

Note: Valence Cat. = Valence Category; Dir. = Direction; CI = Confidence Intervals

4   Discussion

The results supported an interactive space-valence hypothesis whereby congruent inter-actions (positive-right and negative-left) were faster than incongruent ones (positive-left and negative-right). However, a more detailed inspection revealed asymmetrical effects mainly driven by faster interactions with positive pictures, particularly when displayed at the right space i.e., an *interactive positivity bias hypothesis*. This result-pattern is in line with experimental findings observed in space-valence research based on valence discrim-ination tasks using unimanual lateralized button-presses on keyboards [10]. Nonetheless, a critical difference with this research is that grab interactions require to approach the stimuli directly with the hand. Therefore, it seems reasonable that assumptions based on space-valence associations should be considered together with other mechanisms that might take place when interacting manually with digital objects. In this regard, the Spa-tial Affective Interaction (SAI) framework [15] could be useful to interpret our findings.

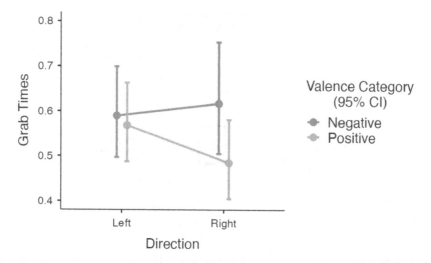

Fig. 2. Results of the Grab Times. Vertical bars represent 95% Confidence Intervals around the mean (colored dot).

The SAI framework proposes a more comprehensive understanding of embodied "affective" interactions with digital content by integrating the affective spatialization and hand-proximity mechanisms and, in addition, approach-avoidance dynamics within one framework (Fig. 3).

In line with this reasoning, "positive" interactions (with positive pictures) were faster than "negative" interactions (with negative pictures), on average. This is in line not only with space-valence research [8–10] but also with emotion [16, 17] and hand-proximity research [18], which indicates that negative stimuli lead to slower responses, probably due to preparatory mechanisms (e.g., focusing attention to detect danger) leading to avoidance behaviors.

In addition, as mentioned above, interactions with positive pictures were faster when pictures were displayed at the right space. This effect cannot be simply explained by an ergonomic motor advantage of ipsilateral (congruent hand-side) vs. contralateral actions (incongruent hand-side) since we would have expected an overall main effect of Direction i.e., rightward interactions being faster than leftward interactions, in general. It is plausible then, that as suggested by previous studies, interacting manually with the stimuli highlights motivational driven actions associated with more pleasant outcomes [6, 19]. In this study, this could refer to the pleasant outcome of "grabbing" with the dominant right hand a pleasant object at the "positive" right space (see BSH [7]).

As a limitation, this study does not allow to draw conclusions regarding affective implications associated with interactions using the non-dominant left hand because participants only used their dominant right hand. In addition, it would also be necessary to investigate interactive contexts where the pictures are not displayed at lateral locations, in order to disentangle the valence of the space from the valence of the pictures.

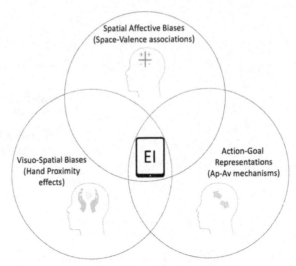

Fig. 3. Schematic representation of the SAI framework. The upper circle represents affective spatialization. The right circle represents action-goal representations in terms of approach (Ap) and avoidance (Av) mechanisms. The left circle represents visuospatial biases defined by the proximity of the hands to the visual stimuli. Note: EI = Embodied Interaction.

The results of this study might be useful for the design of interactive environments and particularly to provide insights on how manual interactions are associated with affective outcomes.

Acknowledgments. We thank Ulli Hagenlocher, Lisa Fritsch, Kathy El-Majzoub, Duygu Tuncay, and Lorea Versa for their invaluable help. The study was funded by the German Research Foundation (DFG) grant num. CE 426/1-1, awarded to Dr. Torres.

Disclosure of Interests. The authors have no competing interests to declare that are relevant to the content of this article.

References

1. Wigdor, D., Wixon, D.: Brave NUI World: Designing Natural User Interfaces for Touch and Gesture. Elsevier & Morgan Kaufman, Burlington (2011)
2. Fabbri, S., Selen, L.P., Van Beers, R.J., Medendorp, W.P.: Flexible visuomotor associations in touchscreen control. Front. Hum. Neurosci. **11**, 558 (2017)
3. Brucker, B., Brömme, R., Ehrmann, A., Edelmann, J., Gerjets, P.: Touching digital objects directly on multi-touch devices fosters learning about visual contents. Comput. Hum. Behav. **119**, 106708 (2021)
4. Qi, Y., Wang, X., He, X., Du, F.: Prolonged subjective duration near the hands: effects of hand proximity on temporal reproduction. Psychon. Bull. Rev. **26**, 1303–1309 (2019)
5. Thomas, L.E.: Action experience drives visual-processing biases near the hands. Psychol. Sci. **28**(1), 124–131 (2017)

6. Cervera-Torres, S., Ruiz Fernández, S., Lachmair, M., Riekert, M., Gerjets, P.: Altering emotions near the hand: approach–avoidance swipe interactions modulate the perceived valence of emotional pictures. Emotion **21**(1), 220–225 (2021)

7. Casasanto, D.: Embodiment of abstract concepts: good and bad in right-and left-handers. J. Exp. Psychol. Gen. **138**(3), 351–367 (2009)

8. de la Vega, I., Dudschig, C., De Filippis, M., Lachmair, M., Kaup, B.: Keep your hands crossed: the valence-by left/right interaction is related to hand, not side, in an incongruent hand response key assignment. Acta Physiol. (Oxf) **142**(2), 273–277 (2013)

9. Kong, F.: Space–valence associations depend on handedness: evidence from a bimanual output task. Psychol. Res. **77**(6), 773–779 (2013)

10. Milhau, A., Brouillet, T., Brouillet, D.: Valence–space compatibility effects depend on situated motor fluency in both right-and left-handers. Q. J. Exp. Psychol. **68**(5), 887–899 (2015)

11. Marchewka, A., Żurawski, Ł, Jednoróg, K., Grabowska, A.: The Nencki Affective Picture System (NAPS): introduction to a novel, standardized, wide-range, high-quality, realistic picture database. Behav. Res. Methods **46**(2), 596–610 (2014)

12. Lang, P., Bradley, M.M.: The International Affective Picture System (IAPS) in the study of emotion and attention. Handb. Emotion Elicitation Assess. **29**, 70–73 (2007)

13. The jamovi project. Jamovi (Version 2.3) (Computer Software) (2022). https://www.jamovi.org

14. Gallucci, M: GAMLj: General analyses for linear models. (jamovi module) (2019). https://gamlj.github.io/

15. Torres, S.C., Ruiz Fernández, S., Gerjets, P.: Spatial Affective Interaction (SAI): A Framework for Research on Affective Processing by Manual Interactions with Digital Objects (Manuscript submitted for publication) (2024)

16. Kauschke, C., Bahn, D., Vesker, M., Schwarzer, G.: The role of emotional valence for the processing of facial and verbal stimuli—positivity or negativity bias? Front. Psychol. **10**, 1654 (2019)

17. Torres, S.C., Gracia Laso, D.I., Minissi, M.E., Maddalon, L., Chicchi Giglioli, I.A., Alcañiz, M.: Social signal processing in affective virtual reality: human-shaped agents increase electrodermal activity in an elicited negative environment. Cyberpsychol. Behav. Soc. Netw. **27**(4), 268–274 (2024)

18. Du, F., Wang, X., Abrams, R.A., Zhang, K.: Emotional processing is enhanced in peri-hand space. Cognition **165**, 39–44 (2017)

19. Cervera Torres, S., Ruiz Fernández, S., Lachmair, M., Gerjets, P.: Coding valence in touchscreen interactions: hand dominance and lateral movement influence valence appraisals of emotional pictures. Psychol. Res. **84**, 23–31 (2020)

Design and Usability Evaluation of a Web-Based Pitch Control Training App for Transgender Women

Xiangyi Wang[1], Sam Weese[1], Tara McAllister[2], Victoria McKenna[1], and Vesna Novak[1(✉)]

[1] University of Cincinnati, Cincinnati, OH 45221, USA
novakdn@ucmail.uc.edu
[2] New York University, New York, NY 10012, USA

Abstract. Transgender people often experience dysphoria because the way their voice is perceived does not match their gender identity. Such dysphoria negatively affects mental health and quality of life, and is particularly an issue in trans women. Dysphoria can be reduced via gender-affirming voice and communication training provided by human experts, but the accessibility of such training is often limited. As a supplement or alternative to human-guided training, our team has thus developed an early prototype of voice training software for transfeminine users (i.e., trans women and nonbinary users who were assigned male at birth). The software is accessible via a web browser and provides three vocal pitch exercises together with real-time feedback about the user's pitch relative to a desired target pitch curve. This paper presents the main technical features and results of a single-session usability evaluation with 5 transfeminine participants. We further present future plans for expansion to other exercises and voice aspects (particularly resonance) as well as plans for clinical trials.

Keywords: Transgender Health · Computer-Aided Voice Therapy · Serious Games

1 Introduction

Transgender people often experience dysphoria because the way their voice is perceived does not match their gender identity – for example, trans women with low pitch [1]. Though this voice-gender mismatch should not be viewed as failure on part of the speaker [2], it negatively affects mental health and quality of life in trans men and women [1, 3]. This is particularly an issue in trans women, as hormone replacement therapy does not affect transfeminine voice due to irreversible effects of testosterone during puberty [4]. Voice can be modified using surgery, which can improve pitch and perceived femininity, but surgery is expensive, patient satisfaction is inconsistent, and there can be negative side-effects on other acoustic measures such as frequency range and loudness [5, 6]. As a result, transgender people tend to prefer noninvasive methods for voice modification.

© The Author(s), under exclusive license to Springer Nature Switzerland AG 2024
C. Stephanidis et al. (Eds.): HCII 2024, CCIS 2114, pp. 224–234, 2024.
https://doi.org/10.1007/978-3-031-61932-8_27

Gender-affirming voice and communication training (GAVT) has emerged as a common noninvasive way to modify transgender voice. It consists of structured exercises that target different voice aspects and must be performed repeatedly in order to learn how to speak differently. Such GAVT has been shown to improve self-perception of voice as well as objective acoustic measures such as pitch, resonance and intonation [7, 8]. However, the accessibility of GAVT is limited, as in-person GAVT is unavailable in many areas due to factors such as lack of trained providers [9]. Even when training is available, it is often expensive, requires many sessions (usually 15–25 [10]), is often not covered by health insurance [11], and has additional barriers such as anxiety [12]. As a result, some trans people do not attempt to modify their voice (and continue experiencing voice-related dysphoria) while others resort to self-guided GAVT based on online resources (e.g., Reddit forums, Discord servers) and peer advice [13]. However, self-guided voice regimens generally suffer from poor adherence [14] and consequently suboptimal outcomes.

The accessibility of GAVT could be improved through computer- or smartphone-based software that delivers information about voice, suggests exercises, and provides feedback on exercise performance. Such software is already used in other voice training protocols besides gender affirmation [15] and has been recommended for GAVT by the World Professional Association for Transgender Health [16]. It would be preferably used in conjunction with professionally guided GAVT (e.g., as "homework" between sessions provided by human experts [17]), but could also be used on their own by trans people who cannot access professionally guided GAVT. Indeed, a recent study found that a generic voice analysis app (not meant for GAVT) can provide some benefits when combined with professional GAVT guidance [17], emphasizing the potential of GAVT software.

The desired features of GAVT software have been identified through multiple studies involving interviews of potential end-users [13, 18]. They include features such as providing structured exercises, providing real-time feedback about the user's voice, and allowing longer-term performance tracking. Conceptually, such desired features are similar to those used for motor learning in diverse biomedical fields such as motor rehabilitation [19]. However, most existing GAVT software lacks such features. Basic GAVT apps (e.g., EvaF.app and Christella VoiceUp) have existed for years, but are limited in functionality and have not been broadly adopted [13, 18]; furthermore, EvaF.app was recently discontinued. One app, Project Spectra, attempted to develop features such as real-time feedback, but only produced a limited prototype before development stalled indefinitely [20]. Project Spectra is not available from an app store and must be installed on a smartphone via a relatively complex manual process. A second app, Attuned, was presented recently, but consists primarily of text descriptions and video of anatomy and exercises with no current plans for implementation of features like real-time feedback [21]. Furthermore, Attuned is available only on iOS, limiting accessibility.

This paper presents the first prototype of our GAVT software package that aims to be broadly accessible via a web browser (and thus not limited to specific operating systems) as well as provide real-time visual feedback about the user's voice during structured exercises. The software is currently focused on transfeminine people (i.e., trans women and nonbinary people who were assigned male at birth but now identify with aspects of femininity), who represent the largest and most enthusiastic subpopulation for GAVT [13]. Here, we present the current technical features and a brief usability evaluation; in the future, we will implement additional features and then evaluate the software's ability to guide voice modification.

2 Software Prototype

Our GAVT software prototype is, at the time of this writing, accessible at https://ceas5. uc.edu/transvoice. It consists of five top-level tabs that users can freely switch between: Introduction, Pitch, Volume, About, and User Account.

2.1 Introduction

The Introduction is the initial landing page and briefly welcomes users to the page and offers a "Begin Tour" button to move directly to the Pitch page. Alternatively, users can read a description of the Pitch module, which includes a description of the relationship between vocal pitch and gender, a description of the three pitch exercises that can be performed, and suggestions for which exercises the user should perform based on their experience with pitch modulation.

2.2 User Account

The User Account functionality is limited at this time, but the longer-term goal is to allow users to store their various exercise settings between sessions, obtain a log of their time spent exercising in the past, and gauge their progress with regard to various voice characteristics. Long-term performance tracking has been emphasized as potentially motivating by trans people [13]. As we eventually wish to perform clinical trials of the software, this functionality would also allow us to track the progress of clinical trial participants. However, user accounts will never be mandatory since trans people have also emphasized that they want the software to allow them to maintain their privacy (e.g., not provide an email address) and to be accessible with minimal effort [13].

2.3 Pitch

The pitch training page is the main component of the current version of the software, and allows users to practice modulating the pitch (fundamental frequency) of their voice. Studies show that vocal pitch is one of the main contributors to voice gender perception [22, 23], and it is relatively easy to understand compared to other contributors such as resonance [13]. Thus, although transfeminine people often validly emphasize that excessive focus is placed on pitch in GAVT [13, 18, 20], it was nonetheless selected as the first GAVT module to be implemented.

The main part of the pitch page is a real-time display of pitch as a function of time. As the user talks into their microphone, their current pitch is displayed as a black dot on the graph that leaves a red "trail" of dots to indicate their recent pitch history. Depending on the specific exercise, the black dot may either remain in the middle of the graph (with the red trail moving toward the left off the graph over time), or may move from the left to the right end of the graph over time (leaving the red trail on the graph as it moves). Separately from the user's pitch, a "target" pitch curve is also displayed in blue and should be matched by the user; this target curve takes different shapes depending on the specific exercise. Finally, depending on the exercise, reference text for the user to speak may be displayed both below the graph and next to the target curve.

So far, three exercises have been implemented: Constant Target, Stair Target, and Human Curve Matching. Screenshots of the real-time pitch display for the Stair Target and Human Curve Matching exercises are shown in Fig. 1.

The exercises are as follows:

- **Constant Target**: The user's pitch is displayed as a black dot in the center of the graph, and the red pitch history trail moves toward the left off the screen. A constant pitch target can be selected using a slider on the right, allowing the user to try to match it while vocalizing. The user is not required to say anything specific to match the target; they can, for example, choose to make vowel sounds at a specific pitch or try to sustain conversation at that pitch. If desired, an "Upload Text" button below the graph allows the user to upload a standard.txt file whose contents are then shown under the graph. The user can then read this text while trying to match the pitch curve, with additional Forward/Backward buttons allowing the user to move to the next/previous line in the .txt file.
- **Stair Target**: The user's pitch is again displayed as a black dot, which starts on the left side of the screen and moves across the screen, leaving a red pitch history trail behind it. The target pitch curve is a sequence of five different pitches whose heights can be adjusted using a slider on the right. The user can try to match these five pitches with any desired vocalization (e.g., a sustained vowel sound varying in pitch, or a five-syllable phrase with each syllable at a different pitch). If desired, a "Show/Hide Text" button below the graph enables the display of a five-syllable phrase (shown in green below the screen) for the user to speak while matching the five pitch targets. In this case, each individual syllable is shown atop one of the pitch targets, and additional Forward/Backward buttons allow the user to move to the next/previous five-syllable phrase. The phrase selection interface is further shown in Fig. 2.
- **Human Curve Matching**: The user's pitch starts on the left and moves across the screen, leaving a red trail as in the Stair Target exercise. In this exercise, the target pitch curve is extracted from a recording of a cis woman speaking a multisyllable phrase. Thus, while the Stair Target exercise allows the user to practice matching a sequence of artificially selected pitches, the Human Curve Matching exercise allows the user to practice matching the pitch curve of an actual human. Additional Forward/Backward buttons allow the user to move to the next/previous phrase. Finally, a Listen button next to the Forward/Backward buttons allows the user to play the recording from which the pitch curve was extracted. While the recording is played, a pitch indicator moves along the target curve, indicating how the pitch curve relates to the spoken sounds in the model.

Other than these three exercises, the pitch training page also has an Options submenu accessed via an Options button. These options are specific to pitch training and include the following:

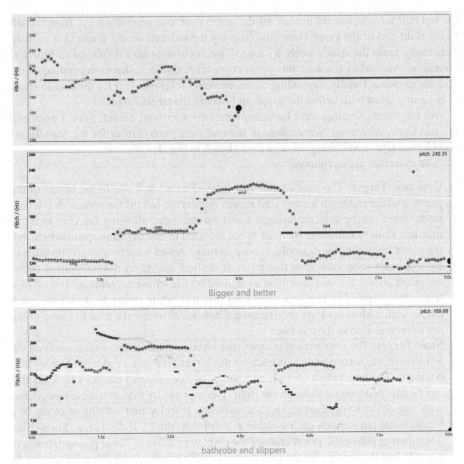

Fig. 1. Real-time pitch displays in the Constant Target (top), Stair Target (middle), and Human Curve Matching (bottom) exercises. The user's current pitch is shown as a black dot, with a red trail to indicate pitch history. A target pitch curve is shown in blue for the user to match, and turns yellow if the user's pitch is sufficiently close to it. In the Constant Target exercise, the target pitch curve is a constant. In the Stair Target exercise, the target pitch curve is a sequence of five different pitches. If desired, the user can select a target five-syllable phrase to match, which is displayed both under the graph and superimposed over the target pitch curve, with one syllable per pitch target. In the Human Curve Matching exercise, the target pitch curve is extracted from a recording of a human speaking a target phrase, which is also shown below the graph in green. (Color figure online)

- **Pitch scale type:** Allows the user to change the pitch scale between hertz (e.g., 123 Hz) and scientific pitch notation (musical note and octave, e.g., B2).
- **Pitch range:** Allows the user to change the minimum and maximum values of the pitch graph's scale. By default, this is set to 100–300 Hz since stereotypically "male" voices have a mean pitch around 110 Hz while stereotypically "female" voices have

a mean pitch around 200 Hz. However, the minimum and maximum can be adjusted independently in 10 Hz steps with the broadest possible scale being 50–600 Hz.

- **Auto-start when voice detected**: By default, the user must press a Play button underneath the pitch display to start recording their voice and displaying pitch (Fig. 2). However, this can be a problem in the Stair Target and Human Curve Matching exercises – after the user presses the Play button, their pitch indicator may already travel partway across the screen before the user starts talking, resulting in the user's pitch being delayed relative to the target pitch curve. Thus, this auto-start option, when enabled, starts displaying pitch as soon as it detects that the volume of incoming sound has exceeded a threshold, allowing the user to better match the target curve in Stair Target and Human Curve Matching exercises. When the option is enabled, the user can additionally set the threshold volume between 50 dB and 90 dB SPL.
- **Pitch indicator speed**: Allows the user to change the speed with which the black and red user pitch indicators move across the screen. This only has an effect in the Constant Target and Stair Target exercises, as the indicators are synchronized with the previously recorded target curve in the Human Curve Matching exercise.
- **Avatar selection**: Allows the user to select an avatar: a specific speaker associated with a set of prerecorded phrases used in the Human Curve Matching exercise. Once the user has selected their avatar, all target pitch curves used in the Human Curve Matching exercise come from that avatar's recordings. At this time, the selection of avatars consists of seven cis women who were native speakers of American English and enrolled as students in the University of Cincinnati's Department of Communication Disorders. The speakers vary with regard to baseline pitch, race, and regional dialect, allowing users to choose one they might identify most with. This option has no effect in the other two exercises.

If the user has made an account, all settings are saved to the user's account between sessions.

Fig. 2. Interface below the pitch graph in the Stair Target exercise. Show/Hide buttons allow optional target phrases to be displayed both below the graph and atop the pitch targets on the graph. The current target phrase is shown in green text while the next two target phrases are shown below it in grey text. Buttons below include a Play button (third from left), which starts and stops voice recording, Backward/Forward buttons (second/fourth), which change the phrase, and a Retry button (leftmost), which resets the pitch graph for the current phrase. (Color figure online)

2.4 Volume

The Volume page also currently has limited functionality and simply displays the user's vocal pitch in Hz and volume (i.e., loudness) in dB SPL simultaneously on a bar graph. While volume on its own is not an indicator of gender, our previous interview work has indicated that transfeminine and transmasculine people who manage to achieve a desirable pitch often find themselves speaking more quietly than they would prefer [13]. Thus, the long-term goal of this page is to allow users to simultaneously visualize and train two aspects of voice: pitch and volume. From a motor learning perspective, this is likely to represent a design challenge since two different aspects will have to be simultaneously visualized to the user in a way that is beneficial for learning [19].

3 First Evaluation

As an initial evaluation, the prototype was presented to 5 transfeminine participants who were all native English speakers, 26–55 years old. Four had socially transitioned and reported at least some past engagement with GAVT – either self-guided or received from a human expert. A link to the webpage was provided electronically, and participants were asked to interact with the software for 15–20 min on their own computer. After that, participants engaged in a brief interview with co-author Novak, who previously also conducted interviews in our initial qualitative research [13].

All participants agreed that voice is important to them, though they had mixed views regarding motivation for GAVT – three reported dysphoria regarding their voice and wanted to change it in order to reduce dysphoria, but two participants emphasized that they did not personally mind their voice and simply wanted to change it to avoid negative reactions from other people. None of the participants were interested in voice surgery, with one mentioning that she could not afford it, one mentioning that she had heard of too many negative side effects, and one mentioning that she was unlikely to pursue it since her job required her to regularly give presentations and lectures (preventing long voice surgery recovery). Two participants had previously tried another GAVT app (EvaF.app) and found it inadequate, so they were initially skeptical of whether software could be useful in GAVT. Three participants had previously tried a generic pitch tracker app not meant for transgender voice and felt that it provided insights but did not provide guidance, limiting usefulness.

With regard to the software, participants gave numerous suggestions for improving usability (e.g., renaming certain terms that were not understandable to casual users, changing the layout of different buttons) that will be addressed in future versions. They overall found the Introduction to be sufficient for someone with basic GAVT knowledge and felt that the exercises were presented in a sensible manner. Notably, one participant noted that the software needs to be straightforward and allow users to begin exercising quickly, as voice training "is overwhelming and it's easy to get discouraged if you don't know where to start, so you don't want to spend two hours installing an app and then getting 500 options that you don't know what to do with." We also noted that at least one user did not notice an option that already existed (ability to change the five target pitches in the Stair Target exercise), emphasizing that different options need to be presented in a clear and accessible manner.

Despite its simplicity, the Constant Target exercise was relatively well received, with one participant saying "I can do a lot with just seeing my pitch. I can just read something and see if I can keep my pitch going for a few minutes". In this regard, the option to upload text was also perceived positively, though participants did not like that only .txt format was supported – they requested the ability to copy-paste text into a text box or upload .doc/PDF files. The Stair Target exercise was also well received and perceived as sufficiently different from the Constant Target exercise. For example, one participant noted "just because you can hold one pitch doesn't mean you can change your pitch when you need to, so you know, I think it's helpful to be able to practice changing pitch." The Human Curve Matching exercise received mixed reactions. For example, one participant said "I don't know why I'd want to sound like someone else. I want to sound like me." Another participant said "Seems too complicated. I can see how she moves her pitch up and down on different words but I don't know if it'd help me to learn it that closely. I can just do the Constant exercise and say the same phrases at a good pitch. That seems good enough." However, one participant did note that the Human Curve Matching exercise "might be great for beginners who don't even know how pitch changes as they talk. They can hear someone else actually speak and see what's happening on the curve."

More broadly, participants generally appreciated the software but were divided about the usefulness of pitch training alone. Participants who had used EvaF.app or a generic pitch tracker felt that our current prototype had more potential since it combines feedback with specific exercises and does aim to go beyond just pitch training in the future. One participant noted that the app could potentially be very useful for users just getting started with GAVT, as "you don't really have to put a lot of effort in it. You can just go on this website and start trying it. You don't have to talk to a therapist or post on Reddit and make posts, you can just poke at a webpage and no-one will know." Another participant noted that the app "is what I was looking for when I first started." However, another participant noted that "pitch just isn't hard for me. I can put my pitch wherever I want. Other things about voice are way more important, like resonance." Two participants also felt that, while pitch training is useful, resonance training would be more important, with one saying that "everyone knows what pitch is. What even is resonance though? I've heard of exercises for it but I never know if I'm doing them right and I just feel silly." On the other hand, one participant said that "a lot of people say that pitch is easy and not that important, but it was still work for me. I spent hours figuring out how to get my pitch up consistently at the start, because I didn't have any singing experience or anything."

Finally, participants shared differing views of their own GAVT journeys and how this may affect GAVT software. Only one participant was satisfied with her voice, and described "not getting misgendered on the phone" as her indicator of success. Other participants expressed dissatisfaction with their own voice, but two specifically emphasized limited motivation to work on their voice. One participant described it like "learning a new language" and said that she was "already super busy with life so it's hard to do this [voice] thing regularly." Another participant who was currently engaged in GAVT with a speech-language pathologist noted that "the software is nice but I need to be on a schedule or I'll never do my practice. If I go to my therapist and haven't practiced, I'll feel bad, so I sometimes do it just for that reason."

4 Future Plans

At this time, we are working to expand the software with additional pitch exercises to help people both understand pitch as well as better control it. For example, we are implementing a "Heteronyms" exercise where the user practices saying two words that are spelled the same but sound differently and have different meanings – e.g., "address" can be a noun (a place where someone lives) or a verb (to direct a statement to). As both have different pitch patterns, this may help users understand how varying pitch over time may affect meaning.

At the same time, we are working to implement exercises for other aspects of voice. While the simultaneous pitch-volume module was already mentioned, we also plan to implement a resonance module, which was emphasized as important both in the current pilot evaluation and in our previous interviews with transfeminine participants [13]. Co-author McAllister previously implemented a lab-based intervention for short-term vocal resonance modification using real-time visual feedback [24], and we are working on ways to expand this to independent use with a variety of exercises.

Furthermore, as noted both in the current evaluation and in our previous interviews [13], users may have limited motivation to regularly engage in GAVT, particularly if they do not have a human expert to remind them and gauge their process. We have thus begun working on an Assessment module where users could perform predefined vocalizations (e.g., read a specific sentence) and have their voice analyzed. The assessment history could be stored in the user's account and periodically presented to users to show how their voice has changed over time. We will also implement features such as optional reminders if a user with an account does not engage with the software for some amount of time. To provide additional structure to users, we may also implement an automatic exercise recommender feature that would suggest specific exercises based on results of the Assessment module as well as the user's self-reported goals regarding voice. The prototype software currently already gives some broad suggestions on the Introduction page (e.g., "If you have limited ability to control your pitch, we recommend starting with the Constant exercise."), but this is likely insufficient.

Finally, once we have developed a suite of pitch, volume and resonance exercises, we plan to eventually test the software in a clinical trial where it would be used in combination with expert-delivered GAVT – similarly to a previous study that combined generic voice monitoring software with expert-delivered GAVT [17]. As a first trial, we would likely not examine voice improvements, but would simply test whether the software results in more time spent performing GAVT than a generic voice monitoring app. Since GAVT outcomes are correlated with the amount of exercise [7, 8, 10], positive results would suggest that our software has the potential to contribute to improved voice outcomes and thus reduce gender dysphoria for trans people.

Acknowledgments. This study was funded by National Institute of Deafness and Other Communication Disorders (grant number R21DC021537) and by a Collaborative Pilot Grant from the University of Cincinnati Office of Research.

Disclosure of Interests. The authors have no competing interests to declare that are relevant to the content of this article.

References

1. Hancock, A.B., Krissinger, J., Owen, K.: Voice perceptions and quality of life of transgender people. J. Voice **25**, 553–558 (2011)
2. Azul, D., Hancock, A.B.: Who or what has the capacity to influence voice production? Development of a transdisciplinary theoretical approach to clinical practice addressing voice and the communication of speaker socio-cultural positioning. Int. J. Speech Lang. Pathol. **22**, 559–570 (2020)
3. Watt, S.O., Tskhay, K.O., Rule, N.O.: Masculine voices predict well-being in female-to-male transgender individuals. Arch. Sex. Behav. **47**, 963–972 (2018)
4. Bultynck, C., Pas, C., Defreyne, J., Cosyns, M., den Heijer, M., T'Sjoen, G.: Self-perception of voice in transgender persons during cross-sex hormone therapy. Laryngoscope **127**, 2796–2804 (2017)
5. Song, T.E., Jiang, N.: Transgender phonosurgery: a systematic review and meta-analysis. Otolaryngol. - Head Neck Surg. (United States) **156**, 803–808 (2017)
6. Nolan, I.T., et al.: The role of voice therapy and phonosurgery in transgender vocal feminization. J. Craniofac. Surg. **30**, 1368–1375 (2019)
7. Chadwick, K.A., Coleman, R., Andreadis, K., Pitti, M., Rameau, A.: Outcomes of gender-affirming voice and communication modification for transgender individuals. Laryngoscope **132**, 1615–1621 (2022)
8. Kim, H.T.: Vocal feminization for transgender women: current strategies and patient perspectives. Int. J. Gen. Med. **13**, 43–52 (2020)
9. Matthews, J.J., Olszewski, A., Petereit, J.: Knowledge, training, and attitudes of students and speech-language pathologists about providing communication services to individuals who are transgender. Am. J. Speech-Language Pathol. **29**, 597–610 (2020)
10. Hancock, A.B., Garabedian, L.M.: Transgender voice and communication treatment: a retrospective chart review of 25 cases. Int. J. Lang. Commun. Disord. **48**, 54–65 (2013)
11. DeVore, E.K., et al.: Coverage for gender-affirming voice surgery and therapy for transgender individuals. Laryngoscope **131**, E896–E902 (2020)
12. Antoni, C.: Service delivery and the challenges of providing service to people who are transgender. Perspect. Voice Voice Disord. **25**, 59–65 (2015)
13. Bush, E.J., Krueger, B.I., Cody, M., Clapp, J.D., Novak, V.D.: Considerations for voice and communication training software for transgender and nonbinary people. J. Voice (2022, in press)
14. Bartlett, R.S., Carpenter, A.M., Chapman, L.K.: A systematic review of adherence strategies for adult populations in speech-language pathology treatment. Am. J. Speech-Language Pathol. **31**, 1501–1516 (2022)
15. van Leer, E., Lewis, B., Porcaro, N.: Effect of an iOS app on voice therapy adherence and motivation. Am. J. Speech-Language Pathol. **30**, 210–227 (2021)
16. Davies, S., Papp, V.G., Antoni, C.: Voice and communication change for gender nonconforming individuals: giving voice to the person inside. Int. J. Transgenderism. **16**, 117–159 (2015)
17. Hawley, J.L., Hancock, A.B.: Incorporating mobile app technology in voice modification protocol for transgender women. J. Voice **38**(2), 337–345 (2024)
18. Ahmed, A.A.: Trans competent interaction design: a qualitative study on voice, identity, and technology. Interact. Comput. **30**, 53–71 (2018)
19. Sigrist, R., Rauter, G., Riener, R., Wolf, P.: Augmented visual, auditory, haptic, and multimodal feedback in motor learning: a review. Psychon. Bull. Rev. **20**, 21–53 (2013)
20. Ahmed, A.A., Kok, B., Howard, C., Still, K.: Online community-based design of free and open source software for transgender voice training. Proc. ACM Human-Computer Interact. **4**, 258 (2021)

21. Pitti, M., Coleman, R., Chadwick, K., Andreadis, K., Rameau, A.: Interprofessional creation of a gender affirming voice modification mobile application: innovative solutions in service delivery. In: Proceedings of the 2021 ASHA Convention (2021)
22. Holmberg, E.B., Oates, J., Dacakis, G., Grant, C.: Phonetograms, aerodynamic measurements, self-evaluations, and auditory perceptual ratings of male-to-female transsexual voice. J. Voice 24(5), 511–522 (2010)
23. Leung, Y., Oates, J., Chan, S.P.: Voice, articulation, and prosody contribute to listener perceptions of speaker gender: a systematic review and meta-analysis. J. Speech, Lang. Hear. Res. 61, 266–297 (2018)
24. Kawitzky, D., McAllister, T.: The effect of formant biofeedback on the feminization of voice in transgender women. J. Voice 34, 53–67 (2020)

User Preferences for Icon Design Styles and Their Associations with Personality and Demographic

Xinyan Zhang and Haohan Wang[✉]

Hunan University, Changsha 410082, Hunan, People's Republic of China
haohanwang0026@163.com

Abstract. To gain a more comprehensive understanding of user preferences for icon design styles in different HCI interfaces, we investigated the associations between user preferences for icon design styles and the Big Five personality factors was investigated. 220 participants (100 males and 110 females) completed a questionnaire on icon design style preferences, personality traits, and background variables. The results showed that skeuomorphic and semi- skeuomorphic icons were more endorsed by those of higher age, and flat and semi-skeuomorphic icons were more endorsed by men than women. The remaining four personality factors (extraversion, agreeableness, conscientiousness, openness) and preferences for the three icon design styles were significantly correlated with each other, except for neuroticism. However, the correlations were low, indicating that user preferences for icon design styles are related to the user's personality traits or dimensions, and the correlation is low because there may be other factors that affect user preferences for icon design styles. It also indicates that these four personalities do not have aversive feelings toward icon styles. Overall, the results of the study confirm that icon design features are associated with user personality traits or dimensions and can help design appropriate icons and human-computer interaction interfaces to improve user satisfaction.

Keywords: Adaptive and Personalized interfaces · Icon design · Personality factors

1 Introduction

Human-computer interaction (HCI) is a knowledge and a multidisciplinary area that aggregates a vast and multifaceted community.

A current topic in the field of human-computer interaction (HCI) focuses on understanding and evaluating user-centered design, taking into account certain psychological factors related to the user's thought processes, feelings, and behaviors [1, 2].

Currently, most smart devices still use Graphical User Interface (GUI) as the main interaction interface mode. As one of the important components of the GUI interface, icons are widely used in action guidance, content differentiation, and status indication. They bear the important role of the carrier between the user and smart device interaction

© The Author(s), under exclusive license to Springer Nature Switzerland AG 2024
C. Stephanidis et al. (Eds.): HCII 2024, CCIS 2114, pp. 235–245, 2024.
https://doi.org/10.1007/978-3-031-61932-8_28

interface. Some characteristics of icons are capable of exerting different effects on user performance [3, 4], appropriate icon design can add visual aesthetics to the project and enhance the brand image, and meet the personalized needs of the user experience.

Most current research on icon design styles has focused on two styles: skeuomorphic and flat. Skeuomorphic icons feature such as textures, shadows, and highlights to imitate real-world objects, aiding users in understanding the interface. In contrast flat icons can reflect better humanization. Confusion arises when their usage on mobile devices conflicts with the actual usage habits implied by the visual metaphor of the icon [5]. Thus, flat design highlights the content subject by removing gratuitous shadows, gradients, and textures, aligning with minimalism's primary goal. However, it may also encounter readability issues and consequently be misused by users [6]. With the prevalence and improvement of icon design, the boundary between skeuomorphic and flat design has gradually blurred. In recent practice, a combination of skeuomorphic and flat designs has been used. The study by Kairu Zhao et al. [7] refers to this style as the semi-skeuomorphic style. A typical example is Google's material design language "flat 2.0". In contrast to the heavy texture of the skeuomorphic design, it is a lighter texture, with appropriate embellishments without disturbing the content. Compared to flat design, skeuomorphic design features a soft texture and innovative appearance, rendering such icons look more realistic, modern, futuristic, and attractive. However, it also has the disadvantages of poor visibility, low recognition, and reliance on the background color.

As an important element in the human-computer interaction interface, icons have been widely studied by scholars focusing on aesthetics and user experience. For instance, Luo, S.J et al. [8] analyzed the influence of icon background shapes and figure/ background area ratios on visual search performance and user preference. Xiaoming Zhang et al. [9] studied the influence of application icons on user experience and summarized the key factors affecting user experience in four dimensions including identification accuracy, cognitive validity, and degree of emotional arousal as well as emotional validity of icons. Ruoyu Chen et al. [10] explored the extent to which users can perceive the difference between icons designed in skeuomorphic and flat icons, and investigated how the design style affects visual search performance across different age groups.

Due to individuals' diverse cultural, psychological, and physiological backgrounds during interface interaction [11], designers are encouraged to develop intuitive availability, aligning with users' expectations when engaging with artifacts. The design interventions tested by Oded nov et al.'s [12] have been demonstrated to exert varying effects on individuals with different levels of personality traits, thereby elucidating the potential value of personality-oriented design. However, the integration of individual personality traits, which vary among users, has yet to be fully implemented in UI design. Linking UI design features to users' personality traits or dimensions can enhance users' ability to process and comprehend visual information effectively, thereby facilitating their interaction with the interface [13]. Samer Muthana Sarsam et al.'s [13] study indicates that certain personality dimensions can be used to increase user satisfaction with interface design, and users' attention may be influenced by the type of design elements placed in the UI based on their personality profile, potentially impacting the efficiency of their information processing This may potentially affect the efficiency of their information processing. When UI design is shaped according to the user's personality profile, it may affect the overall interaction experience generated through the close integration of visual information with other cognitive modalities to stimulate the visual system. Fuchs-Frohnhofen et al. [14] suggested that "an important aspect of human-centered system design is cognitive compatibility, which means that the structure of the human-machine interface of the computer should match the cognitive styles of the users." Given the aforementioned research perspective, this study was motivated by preferences for icon design styles and their associations with personality. Considering that various individual differences, including age, gender, job roles, language, culture, and fundamental idiosyncratic attributes, may influence technology [15], we incorporated demographics as variables.

Basic demographics are considered to be influential factors in user preference for icon style, with younger people preferring flat icons aesthetically. In contrast, older people aesthetically appreciate skeuomorphic icons more [10]. Younger people are more likely to understand most icons compared to older people [11]. Therefore, older people are less confident in interpreting icons. The skeuomorphic icon usually highly mimics the real world and it is less difficult to interpret Skeuomorphic icons than flat icons that are abstract, minimalistic, and symbolic for users, so this may be the reason why older people prefer skeuomorphic icons.

Personality is considered to be an individual's unique variation in the general evolutionary design of human nature. It is expressed as a developmental pattern of dispositional traits, characteristic adaptations, and self-defined life narratives. These elements are complexly and differentially situated in culture and social context [17]. Over the past century, as a result of continuous research on personality, many taxonomies of personality traits have been proposed. Eysenck, H. J. [18] proposed a "three-factor model" that divides personality traits into three factors: extraversion, neuroticism, and psychoticism. Alpert proposed the Theory of Personality Traits, which divided personality traits into common traits and individual traits, and differentiated them into three overlapping levels according to their different influences and effects on personality: primary traits, important traits, and secondary traits. Cattell et al. [19] used factor analysis to propose 16 mutually independent root traits and compiled the Cattell 16 Personality Factor Test (16PF). Analytical studies of these numerous personality models have revealed that the number of factors they include and the nature of the factors varies widely with little consistency. Currently, the personality trait classification that has received the most attention and support from personality researchers is the five-factor model [20]. It has been confirmed by research in several fields that the Big Five factors are relevant and valid dimensions of personality that reliably predict differences between individuals and are considered by many psychologists to be the best paradigm for personality structure. The model provides a comprehensive overview of five dimensions of personality, each containing specific traits; neuroticism, the presence of traits that make it difficult to balance emotions such as anxiety, hostility, repression, self-consciousness, impulsivity, and vulnerability, i.e., the inability to maintain emotional stability; conscientiousness, the presence of traits that show competence, fairness, organization, dutifulness, achievement, self-discipline prudence, and restraint; agreeableness, with traits such as trust, altruism, straightforwardness, compliance, humility, and empathy; openness, with traits such as imagination, aesthetics, emotional richness, dissimulation, creativity, and intelligence; and extraversion, showing traits such as enthusiasm, socialization, decisiveness, activity, risk-taking, and optimism [21].

There is no sufficient research to explain the relationship between user personality and preferences for icon design styles included in interfaces, so in this study, we will investigate whether different personality traits affect user preference for icon design styles.

The results of the study will help create guidelines for personalized interface design that depends on user psychological variables. This guide serves a dual purpose: firstly, aiding designers in identifying the types of users likely to be attracted to their icon designs; secondly, assisting designers in evaluating whether their icons are tailored to the intended target audience or need refinement to align with user personality traits, thereby enhancing user experience and reinforcing brand image.

2   Method

2.1   Participants

The study sample consisted of 210 smartphone users (100 men and 110 women) from different geographical regions of China, ranging in age from 18 to 60 years (M = 31, SD = 12), of which, 40% were married and 60% were unmarried. All the participants were volunteered and gave their informed consent to take part in the study.

2.2   Procedure and Instruments

Subjects were asked to complete a packet of three questionnaires in the following order: preference evaluation, the 40-item brief version of the Chinese Big Five Personality Inventory (CBF-PI-B), and the Background Data Inventory. It took approximately 8 min to complete all questionnaires. A total of 233 questionnaires were returned, and after eliminating invalid responses, a total sample size of 210 valid questionnaires was obtained.

The design of the preference evaluation test is as follows. First, we collected 16 commonly used functions from smartphone and web interfaces: camera, photo album, calendar, clock, calculator, browser, settings, music, calculator, flashlight, mailbox, address book, memo, map, wallet, and stock market corresponding to three styles (flat design, skeuomorphic design, and skeuomorphic design) of icons (48 in total). Participants were presented with a randomly disorganized list of 48 icons with functional descriptions on the right side of each icon, and participants were asked to rate their preference for liking each icon design on a scale of 1–5, with 1 indicating extreme dislike and 5 indicating extreme like (see Fig. 1). The results of participants' ratings were collected, and the 16 scores of participants for each of the three design style icons were summed to obtain the preference scores for each of the three styles, and statistical analysis was performed in SPSS.

The Chinese Big Five Personality Questionnaire Brief Version (CBF-PI-B) [22–24] consists of 40 entries to assess five personality constructs. The questionnaire is a personality questionnaire developed to fit Chinese people's verbal expression habits using

Fig. 1. A figure caption is always placed below the illustration. Short captions are centered, while long ones are justified. The macro button chooses the correct format automatically.

the Big Five model as a theoretical framework and assesses five dimensions of personality traits: Neuroticism, Conscientiousness, Agreeableness, Openness, and Extraversion. Zhang X et al. [24] study provided initial support for the utility of the CBF-PI-B by showing good factor structure, acceptable internal consistency reliability, and, as expected, convergent, discriminant, and criterion-related validity. The components of the questionnaire were as follows: Neuroticism (8 items; e.g., "I am often afraid"); Conscientiousness (8 items; e.g., "Once I set a goal, I stick to it and work hard to achieve it"); and Agreeableness (8 items; e.g. "I think most people are basically well-intentioned"); Openness (8 items; e.g. "My mind is often full of vivid images"); Extroversion (8 items; e.g., "At lively gatherings, I often take the initiative and have fun at lively parties"). In the current study, Cronbach's alpha coefficient was 0.81 for Neuroticism, 0.81 for rigor, 0.76 for Agreeableness, 0.78 for Openness, and 0.80 for Extraversion. The participants were asked to make a choice based on the degree to which each sentence matched their personality, with seven reverse scored entries, specifically: 5, 8, 13, 15, 18, 32, and 36. The reverse questions were the first reverse scored, and then each dimensional question was summed to obtain the five-dimensional scores.

The demographics were collected through a questionnaire that asked participants to indicate their gender, age, geographic location, marital status, and education level.

3   Results

3.1   User Preferences for Icon Design Styles and Sociodemographic Factors

A one-way ANOVA was conducted to examine the differences in preference for icon design styles between men and women. ANOVAs conducted for each icon design style indicated significant gender differences in all four styles: ANOVAs were conducted for the scores related to user preferences for icon design styles, and the results showed significant gender differences in the flat and skeuomorphic design: flat icons, $F(1, 208) = 6.898$, $p < 0.01$, ETA2 $= 0.032$; skeuomorphic icons, $F(1, 208) = 5.298$, $p < 0.05$, ETA2 $= 0.025$. Scores presenting female preference for flat icons (M $= 52.45$, SD $=$

9.741) and preference for semi- skeuomorphic icons (M = 53.54 SD = 9.89) were lower than men (M = 52.58, SD = 9.70; M = 53.67, SD = 9.85 for flat and semi- skeuomorphic icons, respectively).

We next tested the association between the preferences for three icon design styles and age using Pearson correlations. User preferences for flat icons R(209) = −0.242, p = 0.000, user preferences for semi- skeuomorphic icons R(209) = 0.275, p = 0.000, user preferences for skeuomorphic icons R(209) = 0.402, p = 0.000. This indicates that higher age is positively correlated with higher preference for the semi- skeuomorphic and skeuomorphic icons and negatively correlated with higher preference for the flat icons.

3.2 User Preferences for Icon Design Styles and Personality

Pearson correlations between user preferences for icon design styles and personality were calculated and the results are shown in Table 1, which shows that all factors except Neuroticism were significantly and positively correlated with higher preference for flat and skeuomorphic icons, but the correlation with skeuomorphic icons was stronger. The three factors extroversion, Agreeableness, and Openness were significantly and positively correlated with higher preference for semi- skeuomorphic and skeuomorphic icons, but the correlation was weaker. Conscientiousness was significantly and positively correlated with higher preference for semi- skeuomorphic icons with a moderate correlation.

Table 1. Pearson correlations between preference for icon design styles and the Big Five personality dimensions.

	Preference for icon design styles		
	Flat	Semi- skeuomorphic	Skeuomorphic
Extraversion	0.185**	0.214**	0.317**
Agreeableness	0.185**	0.259**	0.339**
Conscientiousness	0.341**	0.439**	0.456**
Neuroticism	−0.086	−0.083	−0.068
Opennes	0.283**	0.259**	0.300**

Note. ** p < 0.01

3.3 The Contribution of Demographic and Personality Factors to User Preferences for Icon Design Styles

A series of two hierarchical regressions were conducted to examine the unique and combined contribution of each study variable to the explained variance of the three icon design styles, with variables entered in a forced order in the regression analysis; socio-demographic variables (gender, age, education) in step 1; personality factors were added in step 2, and interactions between variables were added in step 3, using a stepwise approach so that only interactions showing significant interactions that showed significant contributions were entered into the equation. The results are shown in Table 2.

Table 2. Hierarchical regression coefficients (beta weights) for the prediction of user preferences for icon design.

	Preference for icon design		
	Flat	Semi- skeuomorphic	Skeuomorphic
Step 1			
Gender	17.906	29.160[*]	18.073
Age	-1.903[***]	-0.962	-0.246
Education	-4.752	5.298	-6.770
ΔR^2	0.068[**]	0.076[***]	0.162[***]
Step 2			
Openness	0.10	0.484	-1.497
Neuroticism	0.126	1.069[*]	0.933
Conscientiousness	0.278	0.854	1.383
Agreeableness	-0.003	0.146	0.230
Extraversion	-1.707[*]	-1.884[*]	-0.345
ΔR^2	0.095[***]	0.141[***]	0.138[***]
Step 3			
Openness x Gender	0.031	-0.269	0.111
Openness x Age	0.008	0.001	0.030
Openness x Education	-0.089	-0.171	0.259
Neuroticism x Gender	-0.364	-0.585	-0.179
Neuroticism x Age	0.015	0.007	0.005
Neuroticism x Education	-0.232	-0.490[*]	-0.400
Conscientiousness xGender	-0.202	-0.040	-0.096
Conscientiousness x Age	0.011	0.003	-0.009
Conscientiousness x Education	-0.059	-0.181	-0.275
Agreeableness x Gender	-0.355	-0.359	-0.607[*]
Agreeableness x Age	0.004	-0.004	-0.012
Agreeableness x Education	0.067	0.119	0.319

(continued)

Table 2. (*continued*)

	Preference for icon design		
	Flat	Semi- skeuomorphic	Skeuomorphic
Extraversion x Gender	0.328	0.348	0.267
Extraversion x Age	0.024	0.027^{*}	0.002
Extraversion x Education	0.369	0.450	0.173
ΔR^2	0.144^{**}	0.139^{***}	0.078
R^2	0.307^{***}	0.378^{***}	0.356^{***}

Note. * p < 0.05; ** p < 0.01; *** p < 0.001

As shown in Table 2, the independent variables explained a total of 9.5% of the variance in preferences for flat icons, a total of 14.0% of the variance in preferences for semi- skeuomorphic icons, and a total of 13.8% of the variance in preferences for semi-skeuomorphic icons.

In the analysis of preferences for flat icons, a significant contribution of age was found in step 1, indicating that younger people prefer flat icons over older people, and a significant contribution of extraversion was found in step 2, where people with high extraversion have a lower preference for flat icons.

In the analysis of preferences for semi- skeuomorphic icons, gender played a significant role in Step 1, indicating that women preferred the semi- skeuomorphic icons over men, and significant contributions of neuroticism and extraversion were found in Step 2, indicating that higher neuroticism and lower extraversion had higher preferences for the semi- skeuomorphic icons, and two significant interactions emerged in Step 3: neuroticism and education, extraversion and age.

Simple slope analyses were conducted to examine the source of these interactions, and the results are shown in Fig. 2. The analysis showed that higher neuroticism was significantly correlated with decreased preference for semi-skeuomorphic icons among the users with higher levels of education, b = −0.458, p = 0.001; but not among their less educated counters, b = 0.243, p = 0.085. Thus, users with higher levels of education and less Neuroticism may prefer semi-skeuomorphic icons. Users with higher Extraversion are significantly associated with increased preferences for semi-skeuomorphic icons among older users, B = 0.475, p = 0.000, but not among younger users, B = −0.035, p = 0.789. In other words, users who are older and more characterized by Extraversion may prefer semi-skeuomorphic icons.

No significant contribution was found in step 1, step 2, and step 3.

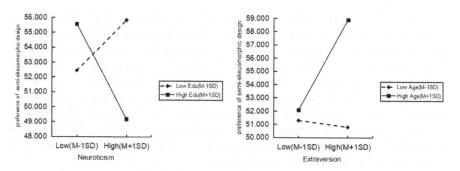

Fig. 2. Neuroticism x Education preference of semi-skeuomorphic design and Extraversion x Age preference of semi-skeuomorphic design.

4 Discussion

The present study aims to enhance understanding of factors associated with user preferences for three iconographic design styles: flat design, semi-skeuomorphic design, and skeuomorphic design. In order to provide as comprehensive a description as possible, personality, as well as basic demographics, were examined. This finding is consistent with previous research indicating that preferences for icon design styles differed between higher and lower ages, with higher preferences for skeuomorphic and semi-skeuomorphic icons at higher ages [8]. It was also found that gender could also be a basic predictor, with men exhibiting higher preferences for flat and semi-skeuomorphic icons compared to women.

In our study of personality factors, we found that, except for Neuroticism, the remaining four personality factors (Extraversion, Agreeableness, Conscientiousness, and Openness) were significantly correlated with user preferences for the three icon design styles ($p < 0.01$). However, the correlation was low, indicating that the user preferences for the icon styles were correlated with the user's personality traits or dimensions. Owing to the possibility of other factors affecting user preferences for icon design styles, the correlation values remain consistently low. Additionally, the correlation values of these four personality factors with user preferences for the three design styles were all positive. This suggests that individuals with these personality traits do not exhibit aversive emotions towards the three types of icons.

If we consider all the factors that uniquely contribute to user preferences for icon design styles, we find that flat icons are supported by the younger and people with less Extraversion. Semi-skeuomorphic icons are endorsed to a higher degree by men and middle-aged and older people. In the judgment regarding preferences for semi-skeuomorphic icons, for users with higher levels of education, it can be predicted by lower Neuroticism. On the other hand, for users of older age, it can be predicted by higher Extroversion.

The current study is the first attempt to integrate demographic and personality factors in order to gain a more comprehensive understanding of the factors influencing preference for the three icon design styles.

However, it is crucial to acknowledge several limitations of the study. Despite efforts to diversify the sample by including individuals from various age groups and geographic regions, a significant proportion of participants possessed high levels of education. While education was not found to be directly related to the three icon design styles, the findings do suggest potential differences between individuals with varying levels of education due to interaction effects. Therefore, employing a representative sample would be advantageous for outcome measures in future studies. Second, the non-significant results due to multiple tests suggest that many of the relationships are unexplained. Therefore, other independent variables not currently considered may help to better explain the reasons for preferences for different icon design styles.

Despite the limitations of the study, the current findings suggest that a multidimensional and holistic approach is necessary when related to drivers. Design approaches that consider the diverse personality traits and background variables of smart device users are more effective than unidimensional strategies.

A quantitative analysis of icon design styles can effectively address interface usability issues and provide valuable insights for designers in developing icons for smart device human-computer interaction interfaces, including those of computers, cell phones, and navigation systems. By considering various interface design elements such as color, layout, typography, and font size, alongside icon design style, future research can comprehensively explore their potential intrinsic connections with users' personality traits. This exploration aims to identify interface design elements that significantly influence user preferences and to develop design guidelines conducive to interface optimization. Through iterative refinement of these design elements, interfaces can be tailored to be more personalized, user-centric, reasonable, and conducive to enhancing the overall user experience and brand perception.

References

1. Deaudelin, C., Dussault, M., Brodeur, M.: Human-computer interaction: a review of the research on its affective and social aspects. Can. J. Learn. Technol. **29**, 89–110 (2003)
2. Farzan, R., Dabbish, L.A., Kraut, R.E., Postmes, T.: Increasing commitment to online communities by disigning for social presence. In: Proceedings of the ACM 2011 Conference on Computer Supported Cooperative Work, New York, pp. 321–330. ACM Press Digital Library (2011)
3. McDougall, S.J., de Bruijn, O., Curry, M.B.: Exploring the effects of icon characteristics on user performance: the role of icon concreteness, complexity, and distinctiveness. J. Exper. Psychol. Appl. **6**(4), 291–306 (2000)
4. Page, T.: Skeuomorphism or flat design: future directions in mobile device User Interface (UI) design education. Int. J. Mobile Learn. Organ. **8**(2), 130–142 (2014)
5. Moran, K.: The Characteristics of Minimalism in Web Design. https://www.nngroup.com/articles/characteristics-minimalism/. Accessed 12 July 2015
6. Zhao, K., Wang, X., Bai, L.: Interface adaption to elderly users: effects of icon styles and semantic distance. In: Gao, Q., Zhou, J. (eds.) HCII 2021, LNCS, vol. 12786, pp. 126–141. Springer, Cham (2021). https://doi.org/10.1007/978-3-030-78108-8_10
7. Luo, S., Zhou, Y.: Effects of smartphone icon background shapes and figure/background area ratios on visual search performance and user preferences. Front. Comp. Sci. **9**(5), 751–764 (2015)

8. Zhang, X., Wang, Q., Shi, Y.: Contrastive analysis on emotional cognition of skeuomorphic and flat icon. In: Zhao, P., Ouyang, Y. (eds.) PPMT2016, LNEE, vol. 417, pp. 225–232. Springer, Singapore (2017). https://doi.org/10.1007/978-981-10-3530-2_28

9. Chen, R., Huang, J., Zhou, J.: Skeuomorphic or flat icons for an efficient visual search by younger and older adults? Appl. Ergon. **85**, 103073 (2020)

10. Norman, D.: The Design of Everyday Things: Revised and Expanded. Basic Books, New York City (2013)

11. Nov, O., Arazy, O.: Personality-targeted design: theory, experimental procedure, and preliminary results. In: Proceedings of the 2013 Conference on Computer Supported Cooperative Work (CSCW 2013), pp. 977–984 (2013)

12. Sarsam, S.M., Al-Samarraie, H.: Towards incorporating personality into the design of an interface: a method for facilitating users' interaction with the display. User Model. User-Adapted Inter. **28**, 75–96 (2018)

13. Fuchs-Frothnhofen, P., Hartmann, E.A., Brandt, D., Weydandt, D.: Designing human-machine interfaces to match the user's mental models. Control. Eng. Pract. **4**, 13–18 (1996)

14. Alves, T., Natálio, J., Henriques-Calado, J., Gama, S.: Incorporating personality in user interface design: a review. Person. Individ. Diff. **155** (2020). Article109709

15. Ghayas, S., Al-Hajri, S.A., Sulaiman, S.: Experimental study: the effects of mobile phone icons characteristics on users' age groups. J. Comput. Sci. **14**(8), 1134–1143 (2018)

16. McAdams, D.P., Pals, J.L.: A new big five: fundamental principles for an integrative science of personality. Am. Psychol. **61**(3), 204–217 (2006)

17. Eysenck, H.J.: The biological basis of personality. Nature **199**, 1031–1034 (1963)

18. Cattell, R.B., Eber, H.W., Tatsuoka, M.M.: Handbook for the sixteen-personality factor questionnaire (16 PF): in clinical, educational, industrial, and research psychology, for use with all forms of the test. Champaign, Ill: Institute for Personality and Ability Testing (1970)

19. John, O.P., Srivastava, S.: The Big Five trait taxonomy: history, measurement and theoretical perspectives. In: Pervin, L., John, O.P. (eds.) Handbook of Personality: Theory and Research, 2nd ed., pp. 102–138. Guilford Press, New York (1999)

20. Peng, J.: General Psychology, 5th edn. Beijing Normal University Press, Beijing (2019)

21. Wang, M., Dai, X., Yao, S.: Development of Chinese Big Five Personality Inventory (CBF-PI)—theoretical framework and relability analysis. Chin. J. Clin. Psychol. **18**(5), 545–548 (2010)

22. Wang, M., Dai, X., Yao, S.: Development of the Chinese big five personality inventory (CBF-PI) II: validity analysis. Chin. J. Clin. Psychol. **18**(6), 687–690 (2010)

23. Wang, M., Dai, X., Yao, S.: Development of the Chinese big five personality inventory (CBF-PI) III: psychometric properties of CBF-pi brief version. Chin. J. Clin. Psychol. **19**(4), 454–457 (2011)

24. Zhang, X., Wang, M.C., He, L., Jie, L., Deng, J.: The development and psychometric evaluation of the Chinese big five personality inventory-15. PLoS ONE **14**(8), e0221621 (2019)

Emotions in HCI

Exploring the Emotional-Behavioral Relationship in Action Role-Playing Games: Diverse Player Responses to Varying Difficulty Challenges

Yucheng Cao[✉] [iD]

Beijing University of Posts and Telecommunications, Beijing 100083, China
caoyucyc@bupt.edu.cn

Abstract. One of the core objectives of video games is to elicit a range of emotional experiences in players, where the art and interactive levels in games induce a variety of positive and negative emotional responses. However, due to differing player types, the same game content can lead to diverse emotional experiences, which are reflected in the players' gaming behaviors. This study aims to explore the correlation between dynamic emotional changes and game difficulty during gameplay, and to investigate the potential impact of different personality types on gaming behavior. Utilizing action role-playing games as an experimental platform, we employed self-assessment and behavioral observation as methods to collect player experience data. We then analyzed the emotional variations and corresponding behavioral feedback of different types of players when faced with challenges of varying difficulties through statistical analysis. Our results indicate a significant increase in negative emotions and arousal levels when players face high-difficulty challenges. Additionally, we observed that players with high neuroticism displayed more aggressive behaviors, whereas those with low extraversion and low openness exhibited more exploratory behaviors. This study provides preliminary insights into the complex relationship between emotions and gaming behaviors among different types of players when faced with challenges of varying difficulties.

Keywords: Emotional-Behavioral Relationship · Personality Types · Emotional Experiences · Gaming Behaviors

1 Introduction

Past research has shown that emotions play a critical role in motivating and guiding players' behaviors, affecting their decision-making, exploration, and engagement within the game world [8,10,12,12]. However, there remains a knowledge gap regarding the dynamic nature of emotions throughout the gameplay process and the impact of different player personalities on their gaming behavior and overall emotional experience.

© The Author(s), under exclusive license to Springer Nature Switzerland AG 2024
C. Stephanidis et al. (Eds.): HCII 2024, CCIS 2114, pp. 249–259, 2024.
https://doi.org/10.1007/978-3-031-61932-8_29

Therefore, this study aims to investigate the following questions: 1. How do players' emotional states change with the varying levels of challenge difficulty during gameplay? 2. How are these emotional states reflected in players' gaming behaviors? 3. How does the emotional-behavioral relationship differ among different types of players?

By utilizing action role-playing games as an experimental setting, we designed an experiment to explore the relationships between player personality types, emotional states, and in-game behaviors. Our goal is to capture and analyze the dynamic changes in players' emotional responses throughout the gaming process and the behavior choices and strategies influenced by personality tendencies. This allows for effective management of in-game levels and AI content composition, providing players with appropriate levels of challenge difficulty.

2   Related Work

Research into players' emotions has demonstrated that various level elements within games and individual player factors can trigger dynamic changes in players' emotional experiences. Bopp et al. [2] investigated the causes and effects of players' emotional fluctuations through self-reports by players. Interestingly, they noted that players appreciate the negative valence emotions experienced during gameplay. In another study, Cole et al. [3] explored the motivations behind players seeking mixed emotional experiences and the significance of such emotional challenges to players through interviews. Compared to hedonistic gameplay experiences and designs, they found that players were more interested in a mix of positive and negative emotions. They suggested that game designs that pursue hedonism, seeking only fun or positive effects, need to be revised to focus instead on stimulating a mix of emotions and self-reflection in different players.

Bopp et al. [6] conducted a study focusing on players with psychopathic traits and their interactions with non-player characters (NPCs) that exhibit different emotional patterns. They observed that players' personalities influence their reactions and behaviors in a virtual environment. This research highlighted the role of personality traits in shaping social behaviors and emotional perceptions within players' gameplay.

3   Method

We designed an experiment to explore the relationship between player personality types, emotional states, and behaviors within the game. The experiment comprises five stages: two game stages, each lasting 20 min, and three survey stages. The content of the first game stage consists of a tutorial level, which is relatively easy, while the second game stage involves open-world exploration that includes an elite enemy, presenting a certain level of challenge. The choice of a 20-min gameplay duration was made to allow players ample time to try various game contents and achieve substantial progress.

The three survey stages are strategically placed: one before the first game stage, one between the two game stages, and one after the second game stage. During the game stages, players' gameplay will be recorded through screen recording.

3.1   Game Environment

We selected the video game "The Elden Ring" as the experimental environment to observe and collect data on players' emotions and behaviors (see Fig. 1). "The Elden Ring" is an open-world action role-playing game developed by FromSoftware. The design of the game integrates a rich combat system, vast exploration spaces, and complex narrative storytelling to create a multi-layered interactive experience. Set in a fictional world known as "The Lands Between," the game offers an environment filled with mystery and historical depth for players to explore. A core aspect of the game's mechanics is its sophisticated combat system, which demands high levels of strategic thinking and reactivity from players. This system challenges players' presuppositions and problem-solving abilities through diverse enemy and boss designs. Additionally, character development within the game is driven by players' choices and actions, allowing for customization according to individual gameplay styles.

Fig. 1. Game "The Elden Ring" Environment.

The world design of "The Elden Ring" is another distinctive feature. The game presents an expansive open world, including a variety of geographical terrains and intricately structured dungeons. This design not only encourages autonomous exploration but also uses environmental storytelling to convey elements of the game's lore and world background.

The narrative and quest design within the game is also meaningful. Beyond the main storyline, the game includes a multitude of side quests that complement the main narrative, offering players a deeper understanding of and engagement with the world. The game's non-directive design means players must learn its mechanics through exploration and experimentation, a factor that becomes especially apparent in high-difficulty combat situations.

Overall, as an experimental environment, "The Elden Ring" provides a complex system of interactions and a rich narrative context, making it an ideal choice for our study on the relationship between player types, player emotions, and player behaviors.

3.2 Participants and Experimental Procedure

A total of 43 individuals participated in the experiment, with ages ranging from 19 to over 53 years (M = 28, SD = 11). None of the participants had played "The Elden Ring" before. Participants first provided informed consent and were then introduced to the experimental procedure.

The experiment began with Survey Phase One, where participants were asked to complete a set of pre-survey questionnaires. This included a basic personal information questionnaire, the Big Five Inventory (BFI) for personality assessment, and the Positive and Negative Affect Schedule (PANAS) for measuring positive and negative affect.

After completing the questionnaires, participants commenced the first gaming stage, which involved completing the tutorial level before entering "The Lands Between," lasting between 15–20 min. To minimize the additional impact of equipment issues on the experiment, standardized computers and controllers were used. Moreover, to assist participants in acclimatizing to the game environment, beyond the game's own hints and tutorial mechanisms, participants could ask any gameplay-related questions.

Before the first gaming stage, we informed players that they would need to complete an "Affective Slider" (AS) digital self-assessment scale during each game stage. If a player forgot to complete the AS due to being in a state of flow, it was to be completed immediately after each gaming stage. During the first gaming stage, we recorded each player's in-game behavior data. After the first gaming stage ended, participants were required to complete the PANAS scale again to measure their subjective emotional experiences.

After completing the scale, participants began the second gaming stage, which involved unrestricted gameplay in "The Lands Between" for a fixed duration of 20 min, with in-game behavior data being recorded for each player. After the second gaming stage ended, participants were once again required to complete the PANAS scale to assess changes in their subjective emotional states.

3.3   Measures

The experimental methods include personality type assessment questionnaires, emotional assessment questionnaires, and game behavior observations.

Big Five Inventory (BFI). In the field of psychology, the Big Five Personality Traits model is a widely recognized framework for describing and measuring individual personality traits [9]. This model revolves around five key dimensions: Openness, Conscientiousness, Extraversion, Agreeableness, and Neuroticism, which together constitute the core aspects of personality. To effectively measure these dimensions, the Big Five Inventory (BFI) was developed as a concise and efficient psychological assessment tool. The BFI includes 44 items, each designed to assess one of the above five personality traits. Participants are required to rate themselves on a five-point scale (ranging from 1 "Strongly Disagree" to 5 "Strongly Agree") based on their self-perceived behaviors and attitudes. This self-assessment scale's design takes into account both comprehensiveness and ease of operation, making it widely applicable in psychological research, career guidance, educational assessment, and personal development planning.

Positive and Negative Affect Schedule (PANAS). The Positive and Negative Affect Schedule (PANAS) is a widely used tool in psychology to measure emotional states, designed to rapidly assess an individual's levels of Positive Affect (PA) and Negative Affect (NA) [4]. Developed by Watson, Clark, and Tellegen (1988), the PANAS includes two relatively independent dimensions measuring positive and negative emotional states. The scale consists of 20 items, with 10 assessing positive emotions, such as excitement, strong interest, or enthusiasm, and 10 assessing negative emotions, such as distress, hostility, or anxiety. Participants rate their recent (e.g., past week) or current emotional states on a five-point scale (from 1 "Very little or not at all" to 5 "Extremely"). The PANAS is extensively used due to its brevity, high reliability and validity, and cross-cultural applicability in mental health, emotion research, workplace emotional assessment, and clinical practice.

The Affective Slider(AS). The Affective Slider is a streamlined tool for the precise and real-time assessment of users' emotional states, designed for quick collection of emotional data in various research and application scenarios [1]. Based on Russell's Circumplex Model of Emotions, it offers a method to quantify emotional dimensions, specifically pleasure and arousal. With these dimensions, The Affective Slider captures a range from positive to negative emotions and from calm to excited arousal levels. It consists of two parallel sliders that users move to express their levels of pleasure and arousal. This intuitive design adapts to users of different ages and backgrounds, making it an ideal tool for interdisciplinary research on emotional states. Additionally, the digital design of The Affective Slider is especially suited for online surveys, remote user studies, and real-time emotion monitoring, providing researchers with a flexible and efficient method for data collection.

Game Behavior Observation. During the experiment, players' gameplay footage will be recorded to facilitate the observation and analysis of their behavior within the game. We categorized player behavior into four types: combat behavior, exploration behavior, decision-making behavior, and passive behavior. Combat behavior is further divided into offensive actions and defensive actions.

Labeling Process. Two observers annotate the video recordings of players' gameplay screens following a video tagging protocol [11]. The video annotation process involves two coders who watch the recorded videos independently and document the observed player behaviors in detail. The results obtained by the two coders are then compared and cross-checked to identify any discrepancies in their observations.

4   Results

After completing the behavior tagging and cross-checking of the participants' gameplay video footage, we categorized the game behavior data into fight behavior, exploration behavior, decision-making behavior and passive behavior (see Fig. 2). Descriptive statistics were then conducted on the data for these behaviors (see Table 1). First, we analyzed the differences in players' emotional experiences when facing game content of varying difficulties (see Table 2). Furthermore, we explored the correlation between players' personality traits and their behavior patterns (see Table 3). These results provided us with an initial understanding of the relationship between players' emotional changes, behavior patterns, and personality types during the gaming process.

Table 1. Summary of Player in-game Behavior Data.

Category	Min	Max	Mean	SD
Attack	13	47	31	17
Defence	8	17	11	5
Exploration	15	52	37	19
Decision-making	4	7	5	2
Negative	0	5	2	1

4.1   Analysis of Emotional Experience Data Facing of Different Game Difficulties

To investigate the potential impact of different levels of game difficulty (easy versus hard) on players' emotional experiences, independent samples T-tests

Category		Behavior	Behavior description
Fight	Attack	Melee attack	Light attack, heavy attack, close combat skills
		Remote attack	Bows and arrows, magic, long-distance combat skills
	Defense	Attack from behind	
		Jump attack	
		Proximity movement	Approaching the enemy, dangerous offensive moves Use to restore health and provide buffs and other props to stay
		Block	
		Roll	
		Use consumables	Use to restore health and provide buffs and other props to stay
		Retreat movement	Away from enemies and dangerous defensive moves.
Explore		Squat	
		Exploratory movement	Movement in non-combat exploration scenes, including
		Get props	Movement in non-combat exploration scenes.
		Watch plot dialogue and cg	Destroying wooden boxes, opening treasure chests, etc.
		Watch text tutorial	
		Observe the messages left by other players.	
		Use body movements.	
		Combat behavior in non-combat state.	
Decision		Open backpack	Organize props, change equipment, view instructions, change settings, etc.
		Interact with rest points	Recover health points, upgrade attribute
		Observe the scene and enemies	Allocation, non-moving or slow moving state, observe level scene behavior, etc.
		Open map	Teleport, mark map and other behaviors
Negative		Die of player	
		Wander	Passing through a certain location repeatedly in a short period of time

Fig. 2. Labeling behavior clustering in Action games.

Table 2. Results of Independent Samples T-Test of Players' Emotional Data facing Different Difficulty Content.

	Group 1 (Easy)	Group 2 (Hard)	t-value	p-value	Effect Size
Positive Emotion	29.75 (SD = 2.86)	28.34 (SD = 3.79)	1.19	0.24	0.42
Negative Emotion	15.75 (SD = 3.57)	20.17 (SD = 6.12)	−2.5	0.018	−0.88
Valence	2.13 (SD = 0.82)	2.94 (SD = 0.81)	−2.81	0.09	−0.99
Arousal	3.01 (SD = 1.03)	4.19 (SD = 1.10)	−3.13	0.0039	−1.11

were performed on the Positive and Negative Affect Schedule (PANAS) and Affective Slider (AS) scale data from participants in both stages (see Table 2).

PANAS scale data indicated that there was no statistically significant difference in positive affect between facing easy and hard game content (t = 1.19, p =

Table 3. Correlations between Personality and Player Exploring Behaviour (*p < 0.05).

Behaviour\Personality	Extraversion		Agreeableness		Conscientiousness		Neuroticism		Openness	
	R	p	R	p	R	p	R	p	R	p
Attack	0.578	0.059	−0.192	0.187	−0.467	0.231	0.465	0.044	0.548	0.073
Defence	−0.615	0.174	0.107	0.067	0.216	0.139	−0.478	0.102	−0.019	0.171
Exploration	−0.631	0.015	−0.401	0.121	−0.574	0.127	0.271	0.257	−0.578	0.02
Decision−making	−0.487	0.31	−0.359	0.785	0.678	0.412	−0.685	0.144	−0.326	0.189
Negative	−0.475	0.231	−0.752	0.154	−0.043	0.236	0.420	0.136	−0.544	0.29

0.24, effect size $= 0.42$). However, participants reported significantly lower levels of negative affect following the easy game stage compared to the hard stage (t $= -2.50$, p $= 0.018$, effect size $= -0.88$).

For the AS scale data, there were no statistically significant differences in valence (from displeasure to pleasure) or control (from controlled to uncontrollable) when facing easy versus hard game content. Nevertheless, there was a significant difference in arousal levels (from calm to excited), with participants showing significantly lower arousal following the easy game stage compared to the hard game stage (t $= -3.13$, p $= 0.0039$, effect size $= -1.11$).

4.2 Analysis of Player Personality Types and In-Game Behaviors

Based on the summary of in-game behavior data (see Table 1), players engaged in attacking behaviors (M $= 31$, SD $= 17$) and exploration behaviors (M $= 37$, SD $= 19$) with higher frequency, and there was considerable variability in the engagement of these two types of behaviors.

Further two-tailed Pearson correlation analyses were conducted on the player behavior data to examine the relationship between player personality types and in-game behaviors. As indicated by the data analysis in Table 3 on player personality and in-game behaviors, significant correlations were found between attacking behavior and the neuroticism trait, as well as exploration behavior and traits of extraversion and openness (p < 0.05, rejecting the null hypothesis).

5 Discussion

5.1 Differences in Players' Emotional Experiences When Facing Game Content of Different Difficulties

Analysis of emotional experience data when facing game content of varying difficulties indicates that although difficulty levels did not significantly impact positive emotions, there was a significant effect on negative emotions. This suggests that players' negative emotional experiences are more sensitive to changes in game content difficulty, and increased combat difficulty in games tends to correlate with higher levels of negative emotions in participants. This finding aligns with the general notion that heightened challenges can evoke a range of negative emotions, such as anxiety, fear, and frustration. Additionally, increased combat difficulty and reduced error tolerance may force players to adjust their cognitive strategies, making decisions within limited timeframes and constrained game mechanics to overcome formidable opponents, which could help activate complex emotional states in players.

We also observed that, compared to easier game segments, players reported higher arousal levels after challenging segments, reflecting a more agitated emotional state. The increase in arousal levels could be attributed to several factors related to game difficulty. Firstly, encounters with more challenging enemies in the game environment can increase uncertainty, which aligns with existing cognitive stress psychology research. It is known that uncertainty can trigger higher arousal responses in individuals. Facing unpredictable situations often leads to heightened vigilance and physiological arousal as they try to understand and adapt to unfamiliar environments. Players may feel a greater sense of anticipation and engagement as they formulate strategies and adjust gameplay to overcome difficulties. Secondly, a significant challenge faced by players is the final boss encounter, representing a critical moment of success or failure. The anticipation and emotional investment associated with such high-risk situations can trigger higher levels of excitement in players, including the satisfaction and sense of achievement from overcoming tough challenges, as well as feelings of defeat and reluctance when challenges are not met.

5.2 Relationship Between Player Personality and In-Game Behaviors

According to the data analysis in Sect. 5.2, we observed that players displayed a tendency to engage in more aggressive behaviors and exploration within the gaming environment, in line with game mechanics that require players to adopt more offensive rather than defensive strategies to progress in the game. Additionally, significant variability was observed among participants in aggressive and explorative behaviors, suggesting individual differences in players' tendencies towards aggression during gameplay. These differences may be influenced by a variety of factors such as personality traits, unique play styles, and emotional states, highlighting the need for further research to clarify the underlying factors driving these behavioral patterns.

Correlation analysis results showed that players with higher neuroticism exhibited more frequent aggressive behaviors in the game, while players with lower extraversion and openness displayed more frequent explorative behaviors. Individuals with high neuroticism tend to experience more negative emotions, such as anxiety, anger, and sadness. In the gaming environment, this higher emotional reactivity may lead players to prefer aggressive behaviors when facing challenges or competitors, as a way to cope with stress and negative emotions. Aggressive behaviors in games may also reflect a strong desire to win, especially in highly competitive settings. Players with high neuroticism, who are more focused on outcomes and sensitive to failure, may be more inclined to adopt proactive strategies to ensure victory, even if those strategies involve aggressive actions.

Furthermore, individuals with lower extraversion and openness, typically more introverted and less open to new experiences, tend to engage more in explorative activities in gaming environments. The higher frequency of explorative behaviors among these personality trait players may be attributed to their preference for internal stimuli and cautious attitude towards new situations. This phenomenon also demonstrates a stronger desire for knowledge and information-seeking within the game among such players.

5.3   Limitations and Future Work

This study still has several limitations, which we aim to address in our future work. First, our research has a relatively small sample size, which may affect the generalizability and reliability of our findings. In the future, we will increase the sample size to enhance the universality and dependability of our results. Second, our study did not perform statistical evaluations of inter-rater reliability. To what extent the coding results accurately reflect the anticipated behaviors of players in the game remains unclear. Our future research will incorporate tests of inter-rater reliability to bolster the credibility of the behavior data. Third, this research primarily relies on self-report measures and subjective assessments of player experiences and emotions, which may be biased. To address this issue, our future studies will include objective measurements, such as eye-tracking or other physiological measures, to provide a more comprehensive understanding of player emotions. Fourth, understanding the participants' exposure to video games and the types of games they are familiar with would be useful. To address this, we will conduct a pre-survey detailing the participants' previous exposure to video games and their familiarity with different types of games. This information will provide valuable context for understanding the gaming background of the participants, helping to explain their emotional responses and gaming experiences.

6   Conclusions

This study explored the dynamic emotional changes players experience during gameplay and the correlation with game difficulty, as well as investigating the potential impact of different personality traits on gaming behaviors. Our findings indicate that the level of difficulty has a significant impact on players' negative emotional experiences, with more challenging gameplay leading to an increase in negative emotions. Moreover, compared to easier gameplay, players exhibited higher arousal levels during more difficult gameplay, indicating a more excited emotional state. Additionally, we found substantial differences in gaming behaviors among players with different personality traits, highlighting the importance of individual differences in shaping gaming behavior and emotional experiences. Future research with larger sample sizes will strengthen our understanding of the complex interactions between player differences, emotions, and behaviors.

By acquiring this knowledge, game designers and researchers can create more immersive and engaging video game experiences that cater to the diverse emotional needs and preferences of players.

References

1. Betella, A., Verschure, P.F.: The affective slider: a digital self-assessment scale for the measurement of human emotions. PLoS ONE **11**(2), e0148037 (2016)
2. Bopp, J.A., Mekler, E.D., Opwis, K.: Negative emotion, positive experience? Emotionally moving moments in digital games. In: Proceedings of the 2016 CHI Conference on Human Factors in Computing Systems, pp. 2996–3006 (2016)
3. Cole, T., Gillies, M.: Emotional exploration and the eudaimonic gameplay experience: a grounded theory. In: Proceedings of the 2022 CHI Conference on Human Factors in Computing Systems, pp. 1–16 (2022)
4. Crawford, J.R., Henry, J.D.: The positive and negative affect schedule (PANAS): construct validity, measurement properties and normative data in a large nonclinical sample. Br. J. Clin. Psychol. **43**(3), 245–265 (2004)
5. Croissant, M., Schofield, G., McCall, C.: Theories, methodologies, and effects of affect-adaptive games: a systematic review. Entertain. Comput. 100591 (2023)
6. Dechant, M.J., Welsch, R., Frommel, J., Mandryk, R.L.: (Don't) stand by me: how trait psychopathy and NPC emotion influence player perceptions, verbal responses, and movement behaviours in a gaming task. In: Proceedings of the 2022 CHI Conference on Human Factors in Computing Systems, pp. 1–17 (2022)
7. Frommel, J., Fischbach, F., Rogers, K., Weber, M.: Emotion-based dynamic difficulty adjustment using parameterized difficulty and self-reports of emotion. In: Proceedings of the 2018 Annual Symposium on Computer-Human Interaction in Play, pp. 163–171 (2018)
8. Hudlicka, E.: Affective game engines: motivation and requirements. In: Proceedings of the 4th International Conference on Foundations of Digital Games, pp. 299–306 (2009)
9. John, O.P., Srivastava, S., et al.: The Big-Five Trait Taxonomy: History, Measurement, and Theoretical Perspectives (1999)
10. Kienzle, J., Vangheluwe, H., Verbrugge, C.: The 4th International North American Conference on Intelligent Games and Simulation (Gameon-NA), Eurosiseti, August 2008, Montréal, Canada (2008)
11. Oczak, M., et al.: Analysis of aggressive behaviours of pigs by automatic video recordings. Comput. Electron. Agric. **99**, 209–217 (2013)
12. Wang, Y., et al.: A systematic review on affective computing: emotion models, databases, and recent advances. Inf. Fusion **83**, 19–52 (2022)

Analysis Method for Audience's Emotional Changes During Watching Movies

Tatsuya Fujiwara[✉] and Midori Sugaya

Shibaura Institute of Technology, 3-7-5 Toyosu, Koto City 135-8548, Tokyo, Japan
{al20099,doly}@shibaura-it.ac.jp

Abstract. The realization of effective information transfer through stories (success of stories) will greatly contribute to the development of human society. Previous studies that have analyzed the success of movies, which are one type of stories, have shown that the emotional experience given to the audience by movies may be related to the success of the movies. In this previous study, emotional arcs were used as a method to analyze the emotional experiences of movie audience. However, the emotional arcs in the previous study can only analyze the emotional arousal intended by the movie creator and does not take into account the actual emotional experiences of the audience. To solve this problem, it is necessary to devise an appropriate method of analyzing the emotional experience of the audience for application to existing methods of analyzing the success of movies. Therefore, in this study, we extracted and analyzed the emotional changes of movie audiences during watching movies using heart rate variability as an analysis of the emotional experiences of the movie audience. As a result, the emotional changes of the movie audience analyzed by the method in this study could be effectively incorporated into existing methods for analyzing the success of movies, for example, by contrasting them with the emotional arousal intended by the creators.

Keywords: Emotion Analysis · Movie · Heart Rate Variability

1 Introduction

Stories have traditionally been used to pass on information and ideas [1]. For example, various social problems (drunk driving, obesity, smoking cessation, etc.) have been communicated in the form of stories to raise public awareness of social issues and change behavior [2, 3]. In the field of science, stories are used as a means of communicating scientific events that are difficult for non-scientists to understand in an easy-to-understand format [4]. These stories are widely communicated to people in society through video advertisements, novels, movies, academic papers, etc. [4–6]. Thus, stories play an important role in human society as a means of passing on various information and ideas [5]. The realization of effective information transfer through stories (success of stories) will greatly contribute to the development of various fields in human society.

One such study analyzing the success of stories is that of Vecchio et al. Vecchio et al. believed that the emotional experience that movies gives to the audience is largely

© The Author(s), under exclusive license to Springer Nature Switzerland AG 2024
C. Stephanidis et al. (Eds.): HCII 2024, CCIS 2114, pp. 260–267, 2024.
https://doi.org/10.1007/978-3-031-61932-8_30

related to the success of movies and analyzed the relationship between the emotional experience given to the audience by movies and the success of movies [7]. In their analysis, Vecchio et al. defined the emotional experience given to the audience by movies as an emotional arc. The emotional arc is the trajectory of emotional change contained in the emotional contents of a story [6, 7]. Vecchio et al. considered emotional arcs of movies as the audience's "emotional journeys," i.e., emotional experiences, and used the emotional arc as a method to analyze the audience's emotional experiences. Vecchio et al. extracted emotional arcs from subtitle scripts (mainly dialogues) of 6,174 movies [7]. The clustering of emotional arcs extracted from movie subtitle scripts revealed that they can be classified into six types, as shown in Fig. 1. The gray lines in Fig. 1 indicate the members (trajectories of emotional arcs) belonging to each cluster, and the red lines indicate members representing each cluster [7]. Vecchio et al. classified movies based on the results of this clustering and analyzed which movies with different emotional arcs were more successful or less successful. As a result, Vecchio et al. found that when box-office revenue is used as a measure of a movie's success, movies with emotional arcs belonging to the cluster in Fig. 2 tend to be more successful than movies with other emotional arcs. They also found that this may be due to the fact that emotional arcs belonging to the cluster in Fig. 2 achieve higher earnings by producing the most "talked about" movies [7]. Thus, the analysis of the emotional experience that movies gives to the audience from the perspective of the emotional arc indicates that the audience's emotional experience may be related to the success of the movies.

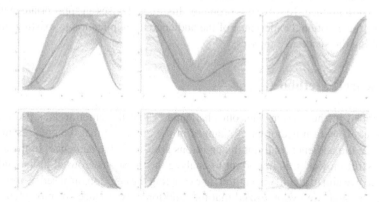

Fig. 1. Clustering results on emotional arcs extracted from movie subtitle scripts by Vecchio et al. [7].

As shown thus far, Vecchio et al. showed that the success of movies may be related to the audience's emotional experience during watching movies. On the other hand, there is an essential question regarding the method used by Vecchio et al. to extract the emotional arc as a representation of the audience's emotional experience during watching movies. Specifically, Vecchio et al. used movie subtitle scripts, i.e., dialogues describing characters or scenes in a movie, for the extraction of emotional arcs. However, dialogue is a technique for expressing the intention of the movie creators to arouse emotions in the

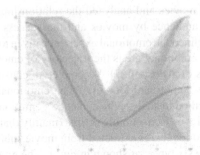

Fig. 2. The cluster representing the types of emotional arcs that tend to provoke discussion in the audience among the six types of emotional arcs in the study of Vecchio et al. [7].

movie by describing characters and scenes, not the emotions aroused in the audience. In other words, the emotional arc of Vecchio et al. does not express the emotional experience of the audience, but rather the change in emotion that the creator intends to evoke in the audience. Therefore, the analysis of the emotional arc conducted by Vecchio et al. is not so much an analysis of the actual emotions experienced by the audience, but rather an analysis of the creator's intention, i.e., the change in emotion that he wants to evoke in the audience.

The analysis of successful movies conducted by Vecchio et al. is based on the emotional arousal intended by the creators and is not based on the actual emotional experience of the movie audience. To solve this problem, this study devises an appropriate method of analyzing the emotional experience of the audience for application to existing methods of analyzing the success of movies.

2   Research Method

As described in the section one, our challenge is that the emotion arcs proposed by Vecchio et al. were trajectories of changes in the emotions that the creators intended to evoke in the audience, and not the emotions aroused in the audience. In the analysis of successful movies, it is important to analyze the emotions aroused in the audience. Therefore, we aim to identify a method for extracting the emotions aroused by movies. To achieve our goal, we hypothesized that the emotional experiences of movie audiences could be represented in a form that corresponds to the emotional arc. Based on this hypothesis, we extracted and analyzed the audience's emotional experiences collecting data of physiological reactions using biometric sensors of the audience, especially we use heart rate variability. Next, we explain the hypothesis and the analysis method.

Vecchio et al.'s emotional arc, which is considered to be the emotional experiences intended by the creator, is defined as a two-dimensional graph with the vertical axis representing "positive-negative" emotions and the horizontal axis representing the degree of progress of a movie [7]. Following this definition, this study assumes that the emotional experience of an audience is a time-series change in the "positive-negative" of the audience's emotional changes during watching movies. Possible methods for extracting people's "positive-negative" emotions include questionnaires of movie audience. However, in order to take a questionnaire at a timing that can capture emotional changes, it is necessary to have the audience answer the questionnaire in a short period of time during watching the movie, which may interfere with their emotional experiences during watching the movie. As a method to objectively measure emotions during watching the movie without disturbing them, we can consider extracting emotions by measuring physiological reactions using biometric sensors. Among these, heart rate variability (HRV), which can be acquired using a pulse wave sensor, is an accurate and non-invasive physiological method for measuring human autonomic nervous system activity [8]. Autonomic nervous activity is believed to cause physiological reactions that is associated with human emotions, and measuring minute changes in autonomic nervous activity is useful in understanding human emotional changes [8]. In particular, the autonomic nervous system can measure two human emotional states: "relaxed-tense". Therefore, we thought that we could extract the "positive-negative" emotional change expected in the emotional arc by continuously acquiring HRV, which can evaluate autonomic activity, from the audience during watching movies.

In the analysis of HRV, HRV indexes that quantify HRV in the time domain, frequency domain, and nonlinear domain are calculated and used. In this study, we calculated Root Mean Square of Successive Difference (RMSSD) [8], an index that quantifies HRV in the time domain. RMSSD can quantify HRV over a very short term [9]. Therefore, by dividing the HRV of the audience recorded during watching movies into short terms and looking at the variation of RMSSD calculated from the divided terms, it is thought that it is possible to capture the time-series changes in the emotions of the audience during watching movies.

The RMSSD is used for detecting the parasympathetic activity [10]. Therefore, a higher value of RMSSD corresponds to an emotional state of "relaxed" and a lower value to "tense". Thus, since the RMSSD can express positive/negative human emotions as relaxed/tense emotional states, the RMSSD can be mapped to "positive-negative" emotions, which is the definition of the vertical axis of the emotional arc.

Based on the above, this study uses RMSSD, one of the HRV indexes, to analyze time-series changes in the "positive-negative" emotions (hereafter referred to as "emotional change") of the audience during watching movies.

3   Experiment and Result

3.1   Experiment Method

In this study, an experiment was conducted to capture the HRV of the audience during watching a movie. In the experiment, HRV was calculated from the pulse wave of a participant during watching a short movie, which was measured using a pulse wave sensor. We use a pulse sensor (Switch Science, World Famous Electronics llc.) to measure the pulse wave. RMSSD was calculated from the HRV obtained from the sensor.

A short movie [11] with a running time of 2 min and 48 s was used as the movie presented to the participants. The purpose of this was to suppress the effect of fatigue on pulse waves by shortening the duration of the movie.

The experimental procedure consisted of the following four steps: 1) The participant sat in front of the display; 2) A pulse wave sensor was attached to the participant and pulse wave measurement began; 3) The participant is instructed to rest for 2 min to stabilize the pulse wave; 4) The participant watches the short movie.

Thirteen healthy male and female (8 males and 5 females) in their 20 s participated in the experiment. All data obtained from the participants were used in the analysis described below.

3.2   Experiment Result

Using the HRV of the experiment participants obtained in Sect. 3.1, we analyzed the emotional change of each participant during watching the short movie.

First of all, the emotional change of each participant during watching the short movie was structured as a time-series graph of RMSSD calculated from the HRV. Then, patterns of emotional change were extracted by clustering the structured emotional changes of each participant.

Structuring Emotional Changes of Participants During Watching the Short Movie with RMSSD.   To obtain the emotional changes of each participant during watching the short movie, RMSSD was calculated from the pulse wave of each participant, and time-series data of RMSSD during watching the short movie were generated. Figure 3 shows a graph of the RMSSD time-series data obtained from each of the three participants. For each graph, the vertical axis represents the RMSSD value, and the horizontal axis represents the run time of the short movie.

The top, middle, and bottom graphs in Fig. 3 show the time-series changes in RMSSD for each of the three participants during watching the short movie. There are individual differences in the variation of RMSSD between the graphs (Fig. 3). On the other hand, the first and second subjects from the top show similar variations of RMSSD in the interval after 60s. This partial similarity in the variation of RMSSD was also observed among the other participants. This suggests that there are some common patterns in the RMSSD variations of the participants during watching the short movie.

Clustering of Emotional Changes During Watching the Short Movie.   Based on the above hypothesis that "there are some common patterns in RMSSD variations among participants during watching the short movie," we conducted clustering on the RMSSD time-series data of all participants to extract patterns of emotional change among participants during watching the short movie.

The k-means method was selected as the clustering method because it is a clustering method that provides important intuition about the data structure [7]. Dynamic Time Warping was selected as the method for calculating the distance between the RMSSD time-series data during clustering, because it allows for nonlinear expansion and contraction in the time direction. Figure 4 shows the clustering results. The gray lines in Fig. 4 show the members belonging to each cluster, and the red lines show the added means in each cluster.

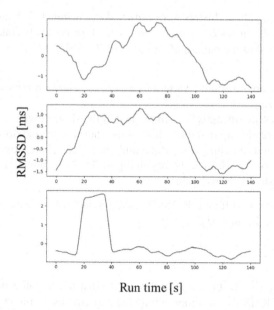

Fig. 3. Graphical results of RMSSD time-series data obtained from three participants.

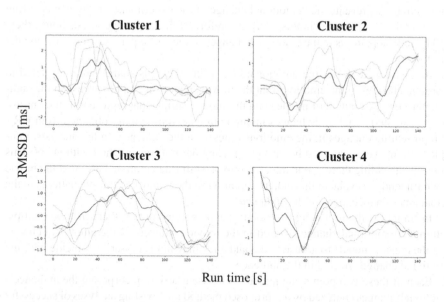

Fig. 4. Results of clustering on RMSSD time-series data obtained from all participants.

As shown in Fig. 4, four clusters were extracted as a result. 4, 3, 4, and 2 participants belonged to cluster 1, cluster 2, cluster 3, and cluster 4, respectively. Taking the additive mean shown in Fig. 4 as the pattern of variation of RMSSD, the pattern in each cluster is as follows.

- Cluster 1) There are no notable variations except for a large variation in the first half of the short movie.
- Cluster 2) It rises significantly toward the end of the short movie.
- Cluster 3) The trend is up in the first half of the short movie and down in the second half, with the trend switching around the midpoint of the short movie.
- Cluster 4) After a large drop at the beginning of the short movie, it rises for a short while and then slowly drops again.

Thus, four distinctly different RMSSD variation patterns were extracted as a result of the clustering for the analysis.

4 Discussion

Based on the clustering results, it is highly likely that the hypothesis that "there are several patterns of RMSSD variations among the participants during watching the short movie," which was set when clustering the time-series RMSSD data obtained from all the participants, is valid. This "variation in RMSSD of the participants during watching the short movie" represents the "emotional change of the experimental participants during watching the short movie" in this study. Therefore, if the above hypothesis holds, there will be several patterns in the emotional changes of the participants during watching the short movie.

As mentioned above, the emotional arcs in the previous studies are considered to represent changes in the emotions that the movie creators attempt to arouse in the audience through the content of movies and the subtitle scripts that represent it. In contrast, the present study analyzed changes in autonomic nervous activity obtained from HRV as representing changes in the emotions aroused in the audience. In the analysis, multiple patterns were extracted by clustering using the k-means method with DTW. This suggests that while there is one main emotional shift (the emotional arc) that the movie creator intends to evoke in the audience in movies, there may be multiple patterns in the actual emotional changes of the audience.

In summary, the following two points can be pointed out: 1) there may be multiple patterns of emotional change aroused in the movie audience; 2) the emotional change that the creator intends to arouse in the audience may not necessarily coincide with the emotional change aroused in the audience.

Each of these two points can lead us to devise a way to incorporate the audience's emotional changes analyzed by our proposed method into existing analyses of successful movies. The first is to use the pattern of audience emotion change itself as a new indicator. Specifically, in addition to classifying movies according to the emotional arc, which is done in existing analyses of successful movies, we can also classify audiences according to their emotional change patterns.

The second is to use the relationship between the emotional change intended to be aroused by the creator and the emotional change of the audience as a new indicator.

This relationship can be quantified by the degree of compatibility between the emotional change that the creator intended to evoke and the emotional change of the audience. Such a quantification index can be used as a new index for classifying movies and audiences.

Thus, we believe that the changes in audience's emotions analyzed by our proposed method are useful for considering methods to incorporate movie audience's emotions into existing methods for analyzing successful movies. They are also, to the best of our knowledge, the first and novel attempts.

5 Conclusion

In this study, we proposed a method for analyzing changes in audience emotion during watching movies using heart rate variability. The results indicate that there are multiple patterns in the changes in the emotions aroused in the audience, and that these patterns may not necessarily coincide with the changes in the emotions that the creator intends to evoke in the audience. Our results also suggest that the emotional changes of the audience analyzed by our proposed method can be incorporated into existing analyses of successful movies in various ways. To realize one of these methods, i.e., quantification of the degree of compatibility between the emotional change that the creator intended to evoke and the audience's emotional change, we extracted emotional arcs from movies and then conducted a contrast analysis between emotional arcs and the audience's emotional change analyzed with the method proposed in this study.

References

1. McIntyre, A.: After virtue Notre Dame, p. 266. University of Notre Dame Press (1984)
2. Hall, C.M.: Tourism and Social Marketing. Routledge (2014)
3. Kotler, P., Lee, N.: Social Marketing: Influencing Behaviors for Good, SAGE Publications (2011)
4. Wilson, E.O.: The Power of Story. American Educator (2002)
5. Finkler, W., Leon, B.: The power of storytelling and video: a visual rhetoric for science communication. J. Sci. Commun. **18**(05), A02 (2019)
6. Reagan, A.J., et al.: The emotional arcs of stories are dominated by six basic shapes. EPJ. Data Sci. **5**(1), 31–43 (2016)
7. Vecchio, M.D., et al.: Improving productivity in Hollywood with data science: Using emotional arcs of movies to drive product and service innovation in entertainment industries. J. Oper. Res. Soc. **72**(5), 1110–1137 (2021)
8. Hasnul, M.A., et al.: Electrocardiogram-based emotion recognition systems and their applications in healthcare—a review. Sensors **21**(15), 5051 (2021)
9. Salahuddin, L., Cho, J., Jeong, M.G., Kim, D.: Ultra short term analysis of heart rate variability for monitoring mental stress in mobile settings. In: 2007 29th Annual International Conference of the IEEE Engineering in Medicine and Biology Society, pp. 4656–4659, Lyon, France (2007)
10. Bertsch, K., et al.: Stability of heart rate variability indices reflecting parasympathetic activity. Psychophysiology **49**(5), 672–682 (2012)
11. The Black Hole | Future Shorts. https://www.youtube.com/watch?v=P5_Msrdg3Hk. Accessed 11 Mar 2024

Preliminary Evaluation of Manga's Emotional Impact Using Physiological Indexes

Tatsuhiro Hiraide[✉], Chen Feng, and Midori Sugaya

Shibaura Institute of Technology, 3-7-5 Toyosu, Koto-Ku 135-8548, Tokyo, Japan
al20018@shibaura-it.ac.jp

Abstract. The manga market has experienced significant expansion in recent years, necessitating the production of higher-quality content. Previous studies have highlighted that high-quality manga can effectively evoke emotions in readers. Consequently, gaining an in-depth understanding of the emotional impact manga has on its reader is crucial for enhancing manga quality. This study specifically aimed to quantify the emotional effects of manga on readers. Given manga's unique format of being consumed page by page, we utilized EEG and HRV sensors to capture emotion-induced physiological responses on a double-page spread basis. Findings from the EEG data indicated an increase in readers' concentration levels at plot twists. However, HRV did not show significant differences from one page to another. This suggests that changes in EEG indexes on specific pages might allow for emotion estimation from page to page, despite the lack of significant HRV findings.

Keywords: Manga · Page · EEG · HRV · Emotion · Concentration

1 Introduction

1.1 Background

Manga, which originated in Japan, has become a popular form of entertainment worldwide, and leads a strong cultural and economic impact. In recent years, the size of the Japanese market for manga has been expanding [1]. According to Okada's research, one of the factors responsible for the expansion of manga on the market is the competition among manga artists. This competition stems from popularity contests held in manga magazines. It encourages competition among artists by selecting and weeding works based on their reputation in the manga market, such as popularity contests. As a result of these contests, artists produce high-quality works over the long term [2]. It has been suggested that popular manga, i.e., manga that the majority of readers find interesting, have content that evokes emotions in readers [3]. Therefore, we assume that if we can understand the details of readers' emotional changes while reading manga, we are able to support the authors to create more high-quality works.

© The Author(s), under exclusive license to Springer Nature Switzerland AG 2024
C. Stephanidis et al. (Eds.): HCII 2024, CCIS 2114, pp. 268–277, 2024.
https://doi.org/10.1007/978-3-031-61932-8_31

1.2 Research Task

When manga artists create manga, they consider the reaction of the readers who read the manga. A common method for quantitatively evaluating reader response is to conduct reader surveys of manga works. Almost all manga magazines conduct reader surveys [2], and most of them ask readers to describe in order of interest the manga that they have read in the magazine. Manga artists can create and improve their manga based on the readers' evaluations of their own manga through this reader survey. However, manga evaluation methods such as reader questionnaires are not sufficient to evaluate what emotions are aroused in readers during their reading. Furthermore, based on our field research with manga publishers, it is mentioned that manga artists consider the effective use of the page in the production of their manga in terms of story direction. For example, they draw large spreads for scenes that they want to emphasize in their stories, and they intentionally draw scenes they want to show on the next page to give them more impact. The evaluation method based on the reader questionnaire is not sufficient to evaluate such detailed evocation of emotion on each page. In light of the above, there is a need for a method to objectively evaluate the emotions aroused by each page in the creation of manga.

1.3 Previous Research

Few previous studies have assessed emotions during manga reading [4], and there is room for debate regarding their understanding and assessment methods. As a method for assessing emotions, previous research has proposed a physiological signal-based emotion estimate method which combine the electroencephalogram (EEG) and heart rate variability (HRV). This method can objectively estimate human's emotional state in real-time by observing the changes of central and autonomic nervous system related to the changes on the emotional state [5]. We consider that this method could be used to assess emotions while reading.

1.4 Purpose/Proposal

The aim of this study is to elucidate the emotional state of each page while reading manga using EEG and HRV. In order to achieve the objective, we analyzed the EEG and HRV during reading by separating the manga into double page spread, calculated representative values for each page from two types of physiological indexes, and compared readers' emotional change of each page with the resting state by statistical analysis.

2 Experiment

2.1 Experimental Overview

The aim of this experiment was to obtain two types of biological information, EEG and HRV, while reading manga. A total of 10 participants, five males and five females in their 20s (Mean = 21.5, Mid = 21), collaborated in the experiment.

Sensing Method. In this experiment, we collected physiological signals with EEG sensor and PPG sensor. The EEG sensor is a NeuroSky MindWaveMobile2 (MWM2) [6], which consists of a single EEG electrode and an ear clip. The EEG electrode is placed in the left frontal region (FP1) according to the international 10–20 method. The single electrode is easy to wear and portable. The sampling frequency is 512 Hz.

The PPG sensor we applied is the Spark Fun Electronics' Pulse Sensor [7]. This sensor utilizes optical methods to monitor blood flow within blood vessels. It detects variations in light absorption by the skin, which occur due to changes in blood volume. These changes enable the measurement of physiological indexes, such as heart rate variability (HRV) and blood oxygen levels.

Experiment Material. The manga used in the experiment are described. The manga used in the experiment were selected to consider differences in the tastes of male and female, and to ensure that the ratio of male and female among purchasers was approximately the same. In addition, one episode of one volume was used in the experiment, considering the fatigue of the experimenters during the experiment. The manga used in the experiment is shown in Table 1, Fig. 1.

Table 1. Manga used in the Experiment [8]

Manga Name	Author	Number of Pages (double page spread)
The Witch of Thistle Castle	John Tarachine	24

Fig. 1. Manga used in the Experiment [8].

2.2 Experimental Procedure

The experimental procedure is shown in Fig. 2.

Fig. 2. Experimental Procedure

1. Sit in front of the display and put on the pulse wave meter and electroencephalograph.
2. Rest in a comfortable position for 1 min.
3. Read the manga shown on the display.
4. Answer a questionnaire about the manga you read.

In step (2), the participants were instructed to view a manga (black cross on a grey background) on the display. In step (3), one double-page spread of manga was shown on the display. The participants were asked to read the presented manga page by their own reading pace, and able to turn the next page on by clicking the mouse. And the participants were not allowed to go back to the previous page. The manga viewer created for this experiment saves a timestamp of when a page is turned in a csv file. This makes it possible to measure the timing of page transitions by participants. In step (4), the participants received an A4 sheet with the manga printed on it. On an A4 sheet of paper, eight images of double-page spread of manga are displayed per sheet. They were instructed to identify and mark three pages that made a significant impression on them.

3 Analysis Method

3.1 Physiological Indexes for Analysis

This section details the physiological indexes selected for the analysis, specifically focusing on EEG and HRV measures. These measures are chosen based on the emotion estimation method [4] outlined in Sect. 1.3, "Previous Research."

The EEG analysis utilized eight specific indexes—δ (delta), θ (theta), Lowα (low alpha), Highα (high alpha), Lowβ (low beta), Highβ (high beta), Lowγ (low gamma), and Midγ (mid gamma)—as defined by the MWM2 device. Additionally, the study incorporated the Lowβ/Lowα ratio, which is calculated by dividing the values of Lowα by Lowβ, following the methodology described in Shiraiwa et al. [9]. This ratio, Lowβ/Lowα, has been recognized as an effective index of cognitive processes related to thinking and concentration. Table 2 presents the association between these EEG frequency bands and their corresponding psychological states, as informed by literature [10].

Table 2. Frequency bands and psychological state [10]

Type(wave)	frequency band (Hz)	psychological state
δ	0.5–2.75	Deep sleep without dreaming, non-REM sleep, unconsciousness
θ	3.5–6.75	Intuitive, creative, recall, fantasy, illusion, dream
Lowα	7.5–9.25	Relaxed, but not languid, peaceful, conscious
Highα	10–11.75	Old SMR (sensory-motor rhythm), relaxed but concentrated, integrated
Lowβ	13–16.75	Thinking, Self and Environment Awareness
Highβ	18–29.75	Vigilance, motions
Lowγ	31–39.75	Memory. High level of mental activity
Midγ	41–49.75	visual information processing

HRV indexes can reflect the overall activity of autonomic nervous system activity [11]. Specifically, this study utilized the root Mean Square of Successive Differences (rMSSD), a time-domain HRV index, for analysis. The rMSSD is calculated by taking the root-mean-square of the successive differences between adjacent R-R intervals (see Eq. 1), and it is acknowledged as a measure reflecting parasympathetic nervous system activity [11]. A higher rMSSD value indicates a state of relaxation, and a lower value suggests less relaxation.

$$rMSSD = \sqrt{\frac{1}{N-1} \sum_{i=1}^{N-1} (x_i - x_{i+1})^2} \quad \begin{matrix} x_i : & RRI \\ N : & number\ of\ data \end{matrix} \quad (1)$$

3.2 Typical Value Calculation of Physiological Index for Each Page

This section describes the method used to calculate representative values for the EEG and HRV indexes on each page. The EEG and HRV indexes were analyzed for the data of 10 experiment participants.

For the EEG index, representative values were calculated using the mean value for the resting condition and the median value for each page of the manga reading condition for all participants in the experiment. This operation was performed for several EEG indexes (δ, θ, Lowα, Highα, Lowβ, Highβ, Lowγ, Midγ, Lowβ/Lowα).

For the HRV index, rMSSD is calculated for each page of data from all participants. rMSSD is calculated by setting the amount of data to the number of seconds in which a participant reads a single page spread.

3.3 Multiple Comparison Procedure

After calculating the representative values of each page for the EEG and HRV indexes while reading manga, we compared the resting state and each page by multiple comparisons. The Nemenyi test (correspondence, nonparametric) was used for multiple comparisons due to the small number of participants in this experiment. Friedman() function from scikit_posthocs (version 0.7.0), an external Python library.

3.4 Subjective Evaluation of Impressive Page

For the subjective evaluation, the participants were given A4 sheets of paper on which manga had been printed out, and asked to respond to three pages that left an impression on them. Each sheet of paper displays eight pages of one-page spreads, and the participants are asked to mark the pages that impressed them with a ballpoint pen provided. Subjective evaluation allows participants to identify for themselves which pages were most impressive to them. We consider that this will allow us to link EEG and heart rate measurement data with subjective impressions, and to understand what factors influence the emotional impact of the manga.

4 Results

4.1 Multiple Comparison Analysis Result of EEG Indexes

Of the results of the Nemenyi test for each EEG index, only the EEG indexes that showed significant differences between the resting state and the page are shown in Fig. 3, 4. The vertical axis indicates band power of EEG, and the horizontal axis indicates the page number. The red bars indicate the resting state.

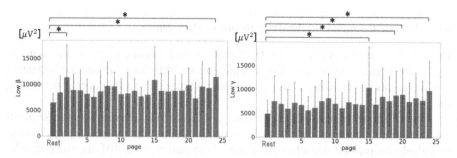

Fig. 3. Lowβ Nemenyi test (* < 0.05) (Left); Lowγ Nemenyi test (* < 0.05) (Right)

Figure 3. (Left) shows the results of the Nemenyi test for Lowβ. The results of the Nemenyi test showed that Lowβ significantly differed from the resting state between pages 2, 20, and 24. Page 2 was the description of the setting, page 20 was the spread where the rapid development of the story takes place, and page 24 was the description of the ending. Lowβ is believed to be involved in the degree of concentration [10], and

274   T. Hiraide et al.

the improvement of concentration was observed on pages 2, 20, and 24 compared to the resting state.

Figure 3 (Right) shows the results of the Nemenyi test for Lowγ. The results of the Nemenyi test showed that Lowγ was significantly different from the resting state on pages 15, 19, 20, and 24. Lowγ is considered to be involved in higher mental activity [10], and significant differences tended to be found in the latter pages of the story compared to the resting state.

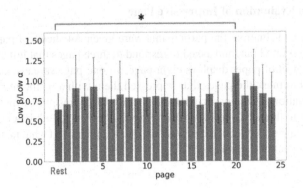

Fig. 4. Lowβ/ Lowα Nemenyi test (* < 0.05)

Figure 4 shows the results of the Nemenyi test for Lowβ/ Lowα. Lowβ/Lowα showed a significant difference from the resting state in the 20-page spread, which is the rapid development scene of the story. 20 is considered an index of arousal level [10], and Lowβ/Lowα showed an increase in arousal level in the rapid development scene of the story.

4.2 Multiple Comparison Analysis Result of HRV Index

The results of the Nemenyi test for HRV index at rest and at each page are shown in Fig. 5. The vertical axis of each figure represents the rMSSD value and the horizontal axis represents the number of pages. Red bars indicate mean value during the resting state.

Figure 5 Shows the results of the Nemenyi test for rMSSD. The results of the Nemenyi test showed no significant difference between the resting state and each page. Due to the calculation method of each page, if there is an outlier in the IBI, the value may be extremely high. In addition, since the minimum period for calculation of rMSSD is 30 s [12], the results of this HRV index are unreliable and unlikely to reflect the HRV index of each page during manga reading. Therefore, further research on the calculation method of the HRV index for each page is needed.

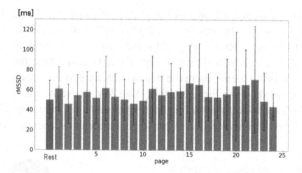

Fig. 5. rMSSD Nemenyi test (* < 0.05).

4.3 Subjective Evaluation of Impressive Page

Figure 6 presents the aggregate results of participants' selections of the three most impressed pages. The vertical axis represents the total number of responses, while the horizontal axis denotes the page numbers.

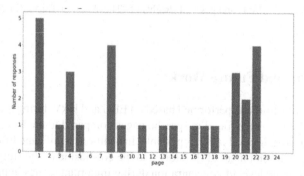

Fig. 6. Subjective evaluation of pages which impressed participants

In the subjective evaluation, pages 1, 8, and 22 garnered a higher number of responses compared to other pages. These pages were compared with those that exhibited significant differences in EEG and HRV indexes. However, no correlation with subjective evaluations was observed. This suggests that pages inducing physiological index changes during reading did not necessarily leave an impressive impact on the participants.

5 Discussion

Of the nine EEG indexes analyzed, significant differences were found between rest and page 20 for Lowβ (4.1 Fig. 3. Left), Lowγ (4.1 Fig. 3. Right), and Lowβ/Lowα (4.1 Fig. 4), while no significant differences were found for the other EEG indexes. These three indexes were interpreted as EEG indexes of high concentration. Pages 20 were significantly different for Lowβ (4.1 Fig. 3. Left), Lowγ (4.1 Fig. 3. Right), and Lowβ/Lowα (4.1 Fig. 4). And pages 24 were significantly different for Lowβ (4.1 Fig. 3. Left) and Lowγ (4.1 Fig. 3. Right). Page 20 is the scene where the main character gets into trouble, as shown in which shown in Fig. 7 (Left), and where the story takes an abrupt turn. Page 20 is the scene where the main character gets into trouble and the story takes a sudden turn, as shown in Fig. 7 (Right), Page 24 is the scene where the story ends, and significant differences were found for important scenes in the manga. These results suggest that the level of concentration improves in important scenes in the manga.

Fig. 7. Pages 20 (Left) and page 24 (Right) of "The Witch of Thistle Castle" [8]

6   Conclusion and Future Work

Page-by-page evaluation was performed based on EEG and HRV during manga reading. Significant differences were found in specific pages compared to the resting state, suggesting that page-by-page evaluation is possible. In addition, significant differences were found in the rapid development of the story and the conclusion of the story, suggesting an improvement in the level of concentration during important scenes in the story.

In the analysis of this experiment, the number of seconds used to calculate the HRV index for each page was set to the number of seconds in which the experimental participants read a double page spread. However, the rMSSD has a minimum period for calculation to ensure the reliability of the calculation results [12]. Therefore, the analytical method used in the experiment would have compromised the reliability of the calculation results. In light of the above, it is necessary to consider a calculation method that ensures the reliability of the calculation results of the HRV index on each page.

Acknowledgments. The authors would like to thank Mr. Takeshi Hanada, Mr. Taiyo Nakashima, Mr. Kumpei Takasaki, and Mr. Yu Matsumoto of Coamix Inc. For their assistance in this research.

References

1. National Association of Publishers and Institute of Publication Science. "Publishing Monthly Report February 2023. (in Japan). https://shuppankagaku.com/news/. Accessed 14 Jun 2023
2. Okada, M.: Development of Japanese manga business: explanation from the viewpoint of comics business system. Econ. Stud. **63**(1), 45–64 (2013). (in Japan)
3. Tamada, K.: Exploring study for the content analysis of manga. In: The Annual Convention of the Japanese Psychological Association. The 74th Annual Convention of the Japanese Psychological Association. The Japanese Psychological Association, 2010. (in Japan)
4. Augereau, O., et al.: A survey of comics research in computer science. J. Imaging. **4**(7), 87 (2018)
5. Ikeda, Y., Sugaya, M.: Estimate emotion method to use biological, symbolic information preliminary experiment. In: Schmorrow, D.D.D., Fidopiastis, C.M.M. (eds.) AC 2016. LNCS (LNAI), vol. 9743, pp. 332–340. Springer, Cham (2016). https://doi.org/10.1007/978-3-319-39955-3_31
6. Narosky, Mind Wave Mobile2. http://store.neurosky.com/. Accessed 31 Jan 2023
7. SparkFunElecronics, Pulse Sensor. https://pulsesensor.com/. Accessed 31 Jan 2023
8. John, T.: Witch of Thistle Castle, vol. 1. 2019. (in Japan)
9. Shiraiwa, G., Sugaya, M.: Verification of improvement in motivation to learn by robot's voice. IEICE Technical Report, BioX2019-62, CNR2019-45(2020-03) (2020). (in Japan)
10. Hirai, F., Yoshida, K., Miyaji, I.: Comparison analysis of the thought and the memory at the learning time by the simple electroencephalograph. In: Multimedia, Distributed, Cooperative and Mobile Symposium 2013, pp. 1441–1446 (2013)
11. Takase, B.: What can heart rate variability tell us? J. Jpn. Soc. Intensive Care Med. **12**(2), 89–92 (2005). (in Japan)
12. Baek, H.J., et al.: Reliability of ultra-short-term analysis as a surrogate of standard 5-min analysis of heart rate variability. Telemed. e-Health **21**(5), 404–414 (2015)

Estimation of Riemannian Metric in a High-Dimensional Facial Expression Space from Low-Dimensional Subspaces

Keisuke Hosaka, Daigo Mihira, Haruto Horie, and Jinhui Chao[✉]

Department of Information and System Engineering, Chuo University, Tokyo, Japan
jchao@ise.chuo-u.ac.jp

Abstract. To determine the Riemannian metric tensor in the psychophysical space of facial expression images demands a large amount of psychophysical experiments and coping with observation noise. We propose a new algorithm to estimate high dimensional Riemannian metric tensor of facial expression spaces using ellipse/ellipsoid fitting in low dimensional subspaces. The proposal based on conformality between different cross-sections of a hyperellipsoid with low dimensional affine subspaces and a method to find the conformality factor. We evaluate the proposed algorithms using artificial discrimination data containing noise, comparing the least square and maximal likelihood fitting, and show that they are noise robust and data efficient. The method is then applied to construct 10D facial expression spaces.

Keywords: Facial expression · Psychophysical space · Discrimination threshold ellipsoids · Riemannian metric

1 Introduction

In recent years, there have been interests in building psychophysical spaces of facial expressions instead of psychological spaces of expressions used in the dimensionality theory [1]. In 2017, Sumiya et al. proposed a psychophysical space of facial expressions by measuring expression discrimination thresholds in expression image spaces to show that it is a Riemannian space [2]. This space has been investigated further and found various applications since then [3–6].

A major obstacle in building a psychophysical expression space is to derive the Riemannian metric tensor defined by the expression discrimination thresholds. According to [7], the dimension of a facial expression image space could be as high as 50. To estimate the Riemannian metric tensor by e.g. the least square fitting demands 1275 discrimination measurements for each point, which is difficult in practice. Another problem is that psychophysical measurements often contain observation noise in discrimination data.

To overcome the first difficulty, [5] proposed to estimate the Riemannian metric of a high dimensional space from low dimensional subspaces by using

© The Author(s), under exclusive license to Springer Nature Switzerland AG 2024
C. Stephanidis et al. (Eds.): HCII 2024, CCIS 2114, pp. 278–286, 2024.
https://doi.org/10.1007/978-3-031-61932-8_32

e.g. ellipse and ellipsoid fitting in 2D and 3D subspaces. This method, however, works only for data points close to these 2D or 3D subspaces.

In this paper, we proposes a general method for estimating Riemannian metric of high-dimensional psychophysical spaces such as facial expression spaces from low-dimensional subspaces to reduce the amount of psychophysical measurements. We also evaluate its performance for noisy data and shown that it is noise robust and data efficient comparing with direct estimation in high dimensional spaces. We then applied it to construct 10D facial expression spaces.

2   Psychophysical Facial Expression Space and Riemannian Metric Tensor

A n-D psychophysical space is a space of physical stimuli in which subjective discrimination threshold at every point is available, which defines a Riemannian metric tensor or a $n \times n$ symmetric non-negative definite matrix $G = (g_{ij})$ such that

$$x^T G x = \sum_{i,j} g_{ij} x_i x_j = 1, \quad x = (x_1, ..., x_n)^T \in \mathbb{R}^n, \quad G = (g_{ij})_{1 \leq i,j \leq n}, \quad (1)$$

[5] used the fact that cross-section of the hyperellipsoid (1) by a 2D subspace $[X_i, X_j]$ is an ellipse defined by a 2D submetric or the 2×2 submatrix G_{ij} of G:

$$x_{ij}^T G_{ij} x_{ij} = g_{ii} x_i^2 + g_{jj} x_j^2 + 2g_{ij} x_i x_j = 1, \quad (2)$$

$$x_{ij} := (0, ..., x_i, ..., x_j, ..., 0)^T, \quad G_{ij} = \begin{pmatrix} g_{ii} & g_{ij} \\ g_{ji} & g_{jj} \end{pmatrix}. \quad (3)$$

Thus, if one projects data points close to $[X_i, X_j]$ to find G_{ij} using ellipses fitting in different 2D subspaces, G can be eventually obtained.

The same strategy applies to intersection of the hyperellipsoid with a 3D subspace $[X_i, X_j, X_k]$, an ellipsoid defined by a 3D submetric or the 3×3 submatrix G_{ijk} of G, which can be found by ellipsoid fitting using data points in $[X_i, X_j, X_k]$.

$$x_{ijk}^T G_{ijk} x_{ijk} = g_{ii} x_i^2 + g_{jj} x_j^2 + g_{kk} x_k^2 + 2g_{ij} x_i x_j + 2g_{ik} x_i x_k + 2g_{jk} x_k x_k = 1$$

$$x_{ijk} := (0, ..., x_i, ..., x_j, ..., x_k, ..., 0)^T, \quad G_{ijk} = \begin{pmatrix} g_{ii} & g_{ij} & g_{ik} \\ g_{ji} & g_{jj} & g_{jk} \\ g_{ki} & g_{kj} & g_{kk} \end{pmatrix},$$

These methods work well for data points close to the subspaces. But when data points are not close to the subspaces, one obtains a smaller ellipse or ellipsoids.

3   A New Algorithm to Estimate High Dimensional Metric from Low Dimensional Subspaces

We show an algorithm to estimate high dimensional metric by estimating submetrics in low dimensional subspaces using arbitrary data points. Here we explain the case using ellipse fitting in 2D plane $[X_i, X_j]$ to estimate G_{ij}.

3.1   Conformality in Cross-Section Ellipses

First we show a fact that every point P on the hyperellipsoid (1) lie on an ellipse which is conformal to the ellipse cross-section (2) on $[X_i, X_j]$. For such a $P = (c_1, ..., c_n)^T$, substitute coordinates $x_k = c_k, k \neq i, j$ into (1), one gets the 2D section of the hyperellipsoid with the plane through P parallel to $[X_i, X_j]$ as an ellipse with x_i, x_j as free variables

$$g_{ii}x_i^2 + g_{jj}x_j^2 + 2g_{ij}x_ix_j + Ax_i + Bx_j + C = 1 \tag{4}$$

$$A := 2(\sum_{k \neq i,j} g_{ik}c_k), B := 2(\sum_{k \neq i,j} g_{jk}c_k), C := \sum_{k,l \neq i,j} g_{kl}c_kc_l \tag{5}$$

or $(\boldsymbol{x}_{ij} - \boldsymbol{c})^T G_{ij}(\boldsymbol{x}_{ij} - \boldsymbol{c}) = r^2$. Its center $\boldsymbol{c}$ and radius r are different from (2) on $[X_i, X_j]$ but with the same G_{ij}. Meanwhile A, B, C depend on P and G_{ij}.

Now we transform (4) such that RHS is 1, a form obtainable from estimation

$$g'_{ii}x_i^2 + g'_{jj}x_j^2 + 2g'_{ij}x_ix_j + A'x_i + B'x_j = 1 \tag{6}$$

$$G'_{ij} = \gamma G_{ij}, \ A' = \gamma A, \ B' = \gamma B, \ C' = \gamma C, \ \exists \gamma > 0 \tag{7}$$

Metric matrices such as G_{ij}, G'_{ij} different by a factor γ are called conformal to each other with γ as the conformal factor. Two Riemannian manifolds with conformal metric tensors at every point are called conformal. So all cross-section ellipse (6) are conformal to (2). In experiments with ellipse fitting using all data points, all cross-sections with different 2D subspaces have the same comformal factor.

3.2   Ellipse-Fitting of Arbitrary Data Points to Estimate 2D Submetric

We use two ways to estimate the submetric G_{ij} or G_{ijk} by either Least Square (LS) or Maximal Likelihood (ML) fitting. Below we show the 2D LS fitting.

For arbitrary data point $P_d = (c_1^{(d)}, ..., c_n^{(d)})^T, d = 1, ..., D$, based on (6) we define

$$X_{ij} := \begin{pmatrix} (c_i^{(1)})^2 & c_i^{(1)}c_j^{(1)} & (c_j^{(1)})^2 & c_i^{(1)} & c_j^{(1)} \\ \vdots & \because & \because & \because & \vdots \\ (c_i^{(D)})^2 & c_i^{(D)}c_j^{(D)} & (c_j^{(D)})^2 & c_i^{(D)} & c_j^{(D)} \end{pmatrix} \tag{8}$$

$$\boldsymbol{\alpha} := (a, b, c, e, d)^T \quad \boldsymbol{1} := (1, ..., 1)^T \tag{9}$$

$$X_{ij}\boldsymbol{\alpha} = 1, \qquad \boldsymbol{\alpha} = (X_{ij}^T X_{ij})^+ X_{ij}^T \boldsymbol{1} \tag{10}$$

Estimate of $\boldsymbol{\alpha}$ then gives the submetric

$$G'_{ij} = \begin{pmatrix} g'_{ii} & g'_{ij} \\ g'_{ij} & g'_{jj} \end{pmatrix} = \begin{pmatrix} a & c/2 \\ c/2 & b \end{pmatrix}. \tag{11}$$

The Maximal Likelihood or RBF fitting also provides an estimate of G_{ij}.

3.3   To Find the Conformal Factor γ

If one used arbitrary data points in the fitting, the estimated ellipse will be in the form of (6) with a unknown coformal factor γ. Now we show how to find γ. First, we calculate A', B', C' directly from (5) for every P_d

$$A'_d = 2\sum_{k\neq i} g'_{ik}c_k^{(d)}, B'_d = 2\sum_{k\neq j} g'_{jk}c_k^{(d)}, C'_d = \sum_{k,l\neq i,j} g'_{kl}c_k^{(d)}c_l^{(d)} \quad (12)$$

so the estimate of the cross-section ellipse (4) through P_d is

$$g'_{ii}x_i^2 + g'_{jj}x_j^2 + 2g'_{ij}x_ix_j + A'_dx_i + B'_dx_j + C'_d = 1. \quad (13)$$

Now if i, j-th coordinates $c_i^{(d)}, c_j^{(d)}$ of P_d are substituted into LHS of (13), the RHS will be $\delta_d \neq 1$.

$$g'_{ii}(c_i^{(d)})^2 + g'_{jj}(c_j^{(d)})^2 + 2g'_{ij}c_i^{(d)}c_j^{(d)} + A'_dc_i^{(d)} + B'_dc_j^{(d)} = \delta_d \quad (14)$$

Compare the target ellipse (4) with the above equation, we find γ and G_{ij} as

$$\frac{\delta_d}{\gamma_d} = 1 - C = 1 - \frac{C'_d}{\gamma_d}, \quad \gamma_d = \delta_d + C'_d, \quad \gamma = \frac{1}{D}\sum_{d=1}^{D}\gamma_d \quad G_{ij} = \frac{1}{\gamma}G'_{ij}.$$

This method can be extended to other low dimensional subspaces.

4   Evaluation Experiments

We evaluated the proposed algorithm to estimate 4D and 8D metrics from 2D and 3D subspaces. Since it is impossible to obtain the true discrimination data, we use instead artificial discrimination data generated from matrix $G = V\Lambda V^T$ with random eigenvalues $\Lambda := \text{diag}\{\lambda_1, ..., \lambda_n\}$, the orthogonal matrix V as Walsh-Hadamard matrix W_{2^n}.

$$W_2 = \frac{1}{\sqrt{2}}\begin{pmatrix} 1 & 1 \\ 1 & -1 \end{pmatrix}, \quad W_{2^n} = W_2 \otimes W_{2^{n-1}} = \frac{1}{\sqrt{2^n}}\begin{pmatrix} W_{2^{n-1}} & W_{2^{n-1}} \\ W_{2^{n-1}} & -W_{2^{n-1}} \end{pmatrix}$$

e.g. $W_4 = W_2 \otimes W_2 = \frac{1}{2}\begin{pmatrix} W_2 & W_2 \\ W_2 & -W_2 \end{pmatrix}, \quad W_8 = W_2 \otimes W_4 = \frac{1}{2\sqrt{2}}\begin{pmatrix} W_4 & W_4 \\ W_4 & -W_4 \end{pmatrix}$

To generate artificial discrimination data x such that $x^TGx = 1$, one first generates $y := (y_1, ..., y_n)^T$ with random $y_i, i = 1, ..., n$, then substitute it into the ellipsoid equation $y^TGy = a \neq 1$. A random discrimination point x is obtained as $x := \frac{1}{\sqrt{a}}y$. The Normalized Mean Square Error (NMSE) $= \frac{\sum_{i,j}(g_{ij} - \hat{g}_{ij})^2}{\sum_{i,j}g_{ij}^2} \times 100$ is used to evaluate accuracy averaged over 100 experiments.

Metric estimations are also conducted when the data is polluted by Gaussian noises of standard deviation $\sigma = 0.3, 0.5, 1.0, 2.0$, compared with noise-free data. It seemed the proposed methods are noise robust, especially ML fitting.

The first row of Fig. 1 shown NMSE for $\sigma = 0.3$. The data points need to achieve 20% NMSE are 52 and 100 if one directly estimates the 8D metric in 8D space with LS and ML. The same accuracy can be achieved with 55 and 97 points for estimation from 2D subspace, 43 and 88 from 3D subspaces, with LS and ML respectively. The second row of Fig. 1 shown NMSE for $\sigma = 0.5$. The data points need to achieve 30% NMSE are 59 and 54 for direct estimate in 8D space with LS and ML. but reduced to 37 and 40 for estimation from 2D subspace, 31 and 42 from 3D subspaces. The third row in Fig. 1 shown NMSE for $\sigma = 1$. The data points required to reach 30% in NMSE is 100 and 55 with LS and ML for direct estimate in 8D space, 62 and 45 from 2D subspaces, 52 and 50 from 3D subspaces, with LS and ML respectively.

Therefore, estimations from low dimensional subspaces are data efficient than the direct estimation.

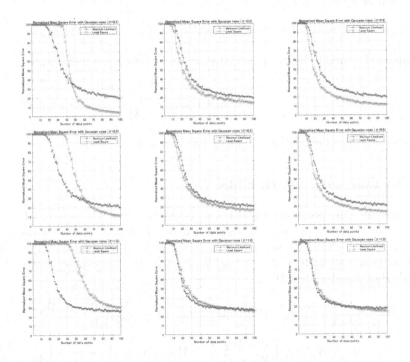

Fig. 1. NMSE by direct estimate (Left), from 2D subspaces (Middle) and from 3D subspaces (Right), The 1st, 2nd and 3rd rows are of $\sigma = 0.3, 0.5, 1$ respectively.

4.1   Matching of 2D and 3D Cross-Section Ellipse/ellipsoids

Since it is hard to imagine how well the estimated metric agree with the true one in high dimensional space with a certain NMSE, we visually compare 2D and 3D cross-sections of 8D true and estimated hyperellipsoids for noisy data.

It turned out the 2D and 3D estimated cross-sections agree with the true cross-sections well in low dimensional subspaces and only slightly disagree in the high dimensional subspace, i.e. the plane of the 7–8th dimensions or the 3D subspace of 6–7–8 th dimensions. So we only shown for the 7–8 th plane and 6–7–8th subspace with the greatest deviations from the ellipse/ellipsoid cross-sections of the true hyperellipsoid in Fig. 2, 3 for $\sigma = 0.3, 0.5, 1$ and Fig. 4 for

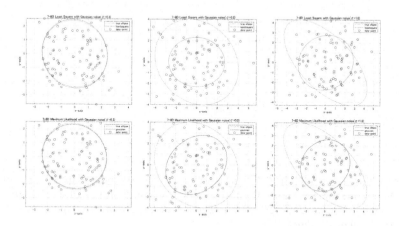

Fig. 2. Ellipse sections in 7–8th subspace of 8D hyperellipsoid (green) and hyperellipsoid estimated from 2D subspaces by LS in the 1st row (red, NMSE = 14%, 17%, 26%) and by ML in the 2nd row (blue, NMSE = 20%, 22%, 27%), the columns are of $\sigma = 0.3, 0.5, 1$ (Color figure online)

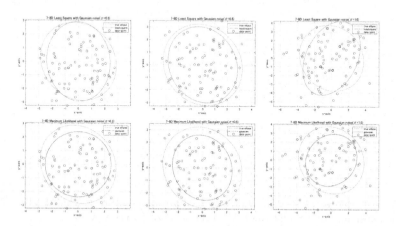

Fig. 3. Ellipse sections in 7–8th subspace of 8D hyperellipsoid (green) and hyperellipsoid estimated from 3D subspaces by LS in the 1st row (red, NMSE = 12%, 14%, 25%) and by ML in the 2nd row (blue, NMSE = 20%, 20%, 28%). The columns are of $\sigma = 0.3, 0.5, 1$. (Color figure online)

$\sigma = 0.5, 1, 2$. It seemed that the shape of ellipse/ellipsoids is not very sensitive to the estimation error or NMSE.

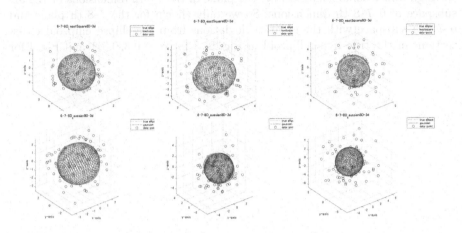

Fig. 4. Ellipsoid sections in 6–7–8th subspace of the 8D hyperellipsoid (green) and hyperellipsoid estimated from 3D subspaces by LS (red, NMSE = 14%, 25%,50%) and by ML (blue, NMSE = 20%, 28%,50%). The 3 columns are of $\sigma = 0.5, 1, 2$ from left to right. (Color figure online)

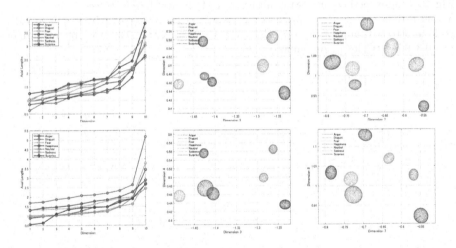

Fig. 5. Principle axial lengths (Left) and ellipse sections in 3–4th (Middle), 7–8th (Right) subspaces by LS (1st row), ML (2nd row) of observer A

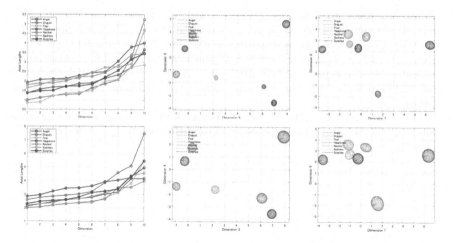

Fig. 6. Principle axial lengths (Left) and ellipse sections in 3–4th (Middle), 7–8th (Right) subspaces by LS (1st row), ML (2nd row) of observer B

5   Construction of 10D Facial Expression Spaces

The algorithm using 3D subspaces is applied to discrimination data of two observers A and B (A in [2]) which are redused to 10D by nonmetric MDS and 10D metrics are estimated. Lengths of principle axes of the 10D threshold hyperellipsoids at basic expressions, as reciprocals of the square-root of eigenvalues of the metrics by LS and ML, are shown in the Left of Figs. 5 and 6, which can be used to determine effective dimensions of facial expression spaces according to the definition in [4]. The ellipse cross-sections in 3–4th and 7–8th 2D subspaces by LS and ML are also shown for observers A and B respectively.

References

1. Russell, J.A., Bullock, M.: Multidimensional scaling of emotional facial expressions: similarity from preschoolers to adults. J. Pers. Soc. Psychol. **48**(5), 1290 (1985)
2. Sumiya, R., Lenz, R., Chao, J.: Measurement of JND thresholds and riemannian geometry in facial expression space. In: Kurosu, M. (ed.) HCI 2018. LNCS, vol. 10901, pp. 453–464. Springer, Cham (2018). https://doi.org/10.1007/978-3-319-91238-7_37
3. Sumiya, R., Chao, J.: Transform facial expression space to Euclidean space using Riemann normal coordinates and its applications. In: Kurosu, M. (ed.) HCII 2019. LNCS, vol. 11567, pp. 168–178. Springer, Cham (2019). https://doi.org/10.1007/978-3-030-22643-5_13
4. Shinto, M., Chao, J.: How to compare and exchange facial expression perceptions between different individuals with Riemann geometry. In: Kurosu, M. (ed.) HCII 2019. LNCS, vol. 11567, pp. 155–167. Springer, Cham (2019). https://doi.org/10.1007/978-3-030-22643-5_12

5. Shinto, M., Lenz, R., Chao, J.: Definition and estimation of dimension in facial expression space. In: Kurosu, M. (ed.) HCII 2021. LNCS, vol. 12762, pp. 604–621. Springer, Cham (2021). https://doi.org/10.1007/978-3-030-78462-1_47
6. Shinto, M., Chao, J.: A new algorithm to find isometric maps for comparison and exchange of facial expression perceptions. In: Kurosu, M. (ed.) HCII 2021. LNCS, vol. 12762, pp. 592–603. Springer, Cham (2021). https://doi.org/10.1007/978-3-030-78462-1_46
7. Calder, A.J., Burton, A.M., Miller, P., Young A.W., Akamatsu, S.: A principal component analysis of facial expressions. Vision Res. **41**(9), pp. 1179–1208 (2001). Elsevier

Designing Korean Emotion Analysis System Combining KoBERT Model and Ensemble Machine Learning Model Considering Emotion Words

Hyeonji Kim[1] and Yoosoo Oh[2(✉)]

[1] Department of Information and Communication Engineering, Daegu University, Gyeongsan-Si, Republic of Korea
hyunji-k@daegu.ac.kr
[2] School of AI, Daegu University, Gyeongsan-Si, Republic of Korea
yoosoo.oh@daegu.ac.kr

Abstract. Emotions can be expressed through language, facial expressions, voice, and other means. However, facial expressions and voice can be hidden or distorted by an individual's will. However, language has less distortion of emotions due to the situation and linguistic meaning. Therefore, in this paper, we propose a Korean emotion analysis system using only linguistic expressions. The proposed system considers the emotional elements of words. The emotion word dictionary considered the characteristics of the Korean language by using FastText, which learns subwords using n-grams. The proposed system proposes a deep learning module learned through KoBERT Fine-tuning and a sentiment analysis module through machine learning ensemble machine learning for sentiment analysis. This paper improves the accuracy of the Korean emotion analysis system by combining deep learning modules and machine learning modules.

Keywords: Sentiment Analysis · Deep Learning · Machine Learning · FastText · KoBERT

1 Introduction

Human emotions can be expressed through language, voice, and facial expressions. Language contains emotional elements because it is expressed by composing words with meaning depending on the situation. However, an individual can hide or control the way emotions are expressed through voice and facial expressions [1]. However, language can infer emotions even if we take actions that hide emotion due to the context and meaning of the words. Therefore, this paper designs an emotion analysis system using only linguistic expressions. This paper proposes an emotion analysis system that reflects the characteristics of the Korean language. Unlike English, Korean has compound words and homonyms whose meanings change depending on the situation. For example, onomatopoeia such as "Ha…" expresses the word sigh, joy in positive situations, and sadness

© The Author(s), under exclusive license to Springer Nature Switzerland AG 2024
C. Stephanidis et al. (Eds.): HCII 2024, CCIS 2114, pp. 287–295, 2024.
https://doi.org/10.1007/978-3-031-61932-8_33

or frustration in negative situations. In this way, the meaning of homonyms can be understood by understanding the context of the sentence. Among deep learning models, the BERT model is a natural language processing algorithm that can understand context. The BERT model learns by randomly masking words in sentences and then predicts the masked words through two-way learning. [2] The BERT model can understand the relationships between words within context but fails to consider the emotional elements contained in words. In this paper, we propose the design of a sentiment analysis system that includes emotional elements of words based on KoBERT, which was learned with a large Korean corpus, and the RandomForest algorithm among ensemble machine learning. The proposed system analyzes six emotions (joy, sadness, anger, shame, wound, and worry). The proposed system consists of an emotion word dictionary, an emotion analysis deep learning module, an emotion analysis machine learning module, and a final emotion calculation module. The proposed system builds an emotional word dictionary according to emotion to identify emotional elements of words. The proposed emotional word dictionary tokenizes emotional sentences and performs preprocessing. FastText is applied to preprocessed words to generate word vectors containing emotions. FastText is a neural network model that performs word embedding for n-grams, each character unit of a word. [3] FastText shows high performance in OOV (Out-Of-Vocabulary). [3] The proposed system builds an emotional analysis deep learning module (DL_Emotioner) by fine-tuning the KoBERT model learned with Korean data. The emotion analysis machine learning module (ML_Emotioner) learns emotion word dictionary data constructed using an ensemble machine learning algorithm. Ensemble machine learning combines multiple classifiers to achieve higher accuracy than using a single classification model. [4] The emotion analysis machine learning module (ML_Emotioner) analyzes the emotion of each word that makes up a sentence. The proposed emotion analysis machine learning module (ML_Emotioner) analyzes the emotion for each word and integrates the analysis results to derive results. The proposed system analyzes the final emotion by multiplying the probability value for each emotion of the emotion deep learning module (DL_Emotioner) and the emotion machine learning module (ML_Emotioner) derived through the final emotion calculation module by weight. In this paper, we verify the performance of the proposed emotion analysis system through accuracy, recall, precision, and F1-Score. [5] The proposed system analyzes emotions for single words by learning about emotion words.

2   Related Research

The BERT Model can understand context by learning using Next-Sentence-Prediction (NSP) [2]. Baek et al. proposed a method for analyzing public opinion through Korean news articles and comments [6]. Beak et al. used Word2vec to improve performance by focusing on the frequency of terms [6]. Additionally, comments were analyzed using KoBERT. Beak et al. confirmed an emotion classification accuracy of over 90% through the fusion of word2vec and KoBERT emotion analysis models [6].

Fasttext is a word embedding algorithm that complements the limitations of Word2vec word embedding. Fasttext uses the Subword model for n-grams to reflect the intrinsic information of words [7]. Therefore, Fasttext can calculate similarity even for words that have not been learned. Fasttext shows high performance in solving the Out of Vocabulary problem [7]. S. Thavareesan et al. propose an emotion vocabulary expansion method using Word2vec and Fasttext word embedding [8]. Thavareesan et al. improved sentiment analysis performance by constructing a lexicon through Word2vec and then expanding the vocabulary through Fasttext [8].

Ensemble machine learning is a method of combining multiple classification models to create a model with improved performance [9]. Among ensemble machine learning, RandomForest is an algorithm that combines multiple Decision Trees. Ensemble machine learning reduces the overfitting of a single model [10]. X. Dong et al. proposed the Adaboost-RandomForest hybrid model method to predict readmission of diabetic patients. As a result of model performance verification, it was confirmed that the proposed hybrid model showed superior performance in precision, recall, and AUC than the single classification model [10].

Previous research in Emotion analysis analyzed contextual emotions without considering the emotional elements of words. Therefore, this paper creates an emotional lexicon through Fasttext word embedding and identifies emotional elements of words through ensemble machine learning. In addition, emotions according to context are analyzed through fine-tuning of the KoBERT model, a BERT model learned with the Korean corpus [11]. Additionally, the final emotion is analyzed by combining the learned deep learning model and the machine learning model.

3   Proposed System

This paper proposes the design of a Korean emotion analysis system that combines the KoBERT model and ensemble machine learning model considering emotional words. Figure 1 is an operation diagram of the proposed system. The proposed system consists of an emotion word dictionary, an emotion deep learning module (DL_Emotioner), an emotion machine learning module (ML_Emotioner), and a final emotion calculation module. The emotion word dictionary identifies the emotional elements of words by constructing an emotion word vector dictionary according to emotion. The emotion deep learning module (DL_Emotioner) identifies and learns sentence data from past and current sentences. The emotion analysis machine learning module (ML_Emotioner) analyzes the emotion of each word that makes up a sentence. The proposed emotion analysis machine learning module (ML_Emotioner) analyzes the emotion for each word and integrates the analysis results to derive results. The proposed system analyzes the final emotion by multiplying the probability value for each emotion of the emotion deep learning module (DL_Emotioner) and the emotion machine learning module (ML_Emotioner) derived through the final emotion calculation module by weight.

3.1   Emotion Dictionary

In this paper, to build an emotion dictionary, we used human sentence 1 and emotion main classification column data from the emotional conversation dataset provided by AI_Hub [12]. Table 1 is part of the human sentence 1 and emotion major classification data set used for training. The proposed emotion dictionary uses Konlpy Okt morpheme

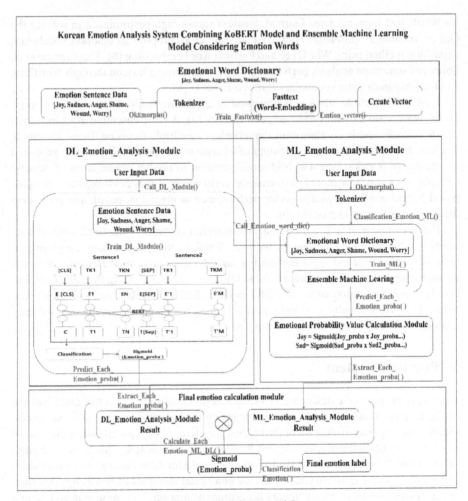

Fig. 1. Diagram of proposed System

analyzer to analyze morphemes on a noun-by-noun basis. Konlpy Okt morph is an open-source Korean morpheme analysis developed by Twitter that was developed for social networks and reflects informal words well [13]. The emotion word dictionary learns morphologically analyzed data using the Fasttext algorithm and then vectorizes the emotion words. Additionally, in the case of overlapping words, the frequency of emotion label categories for each word was confirmed, and emotion dictionary data was constructed using only the most frequent emotion label.

In this paper, for learning Fasttext, hyperparameters were set to vector_size = 2 and min_count = 1. In this paper, the vector size was set to 2 to reduce the amount of calculation, and min_count, the number of occurrences, was set to 1 to filter out duplicate words. The Fasttext learning results are shown in Table 2.

Table 1. Part of the human sentence 1 data used for training.

	Emotion Label	Human sentence1
1	joy	I feel so good right now
2	worry	I'm anxious that my next contract with my client will fall through
3	wound	I had a health checkup yesterday and my condition was very bad
4	shame	I failed the interview again
5	angry	I received a call from the place where I interviewed that I was rejected

Table 2. Vectors generated through Fasttext training

Emotion Word	Vectors generated through Fasttext training
ha	array([1.1001561, 1.1285814], dtype = float32)
laugh	array([0.26387474, 0.22757697], dtype = float32)
quarantine	array([0.24860919, 0.08018682], dtype = float32)
social phobia	array([-0.12159092, 0.00394389], dtype = float32)

3.2 Emotion Machine Learning Module (ML_Emotioner)

The emotion analysis machine learning module analyzes emotions through machine learning using vector data from the constructed emotion word dictionary. This paper learns through the ensemble machine learning algorithm among machine learning algorithms. An ensemble machine learning algorithm is an algorithm that combines multiple single machine learning models to achieve better performance. This paper uses the RandomForest algorithm, which combines several decision tree classification machine learning models among ensemble machine learning algorithms [10]. When the proposed ML_Emotioner receives a user sentence, it tokenizes the user sentence and then analyzes the emotions of each word used in the sentence. To normalize the probability value of the emotion of each derived word, the final emotion is analyzed through the ML_Emotioner module through the Sigmoid function, which derives a value between 0 and 1. The Sigmoid function used is as shown in Eq. 1 [14].

$$ML\_Result\_Sigmoid(x) = \frac{1}{1 + e^{-x}}$$

Equation 1. Sigmoid function equation used (x: sentiment analysis probability value).

3.3 Emotion Deep Learning Module (DL_Emotioner)

We propose a deep learning module (DL_Emotioner) using the BERT model to analyze emotions in sentences and context. The BERT model is capable of two-way learning and can understand contextual meaning through MLM (Masked Language Model) and NSP

(Next-Sentence-Prediction) learning. This paper analyzes sentiment through fine tuning the KoBERT model learned with a large Korean corpus [11]. This paper was trained using 30,000 human sentences and 6 major emotion categories (Sad, Angry, Happy, Wound, Embarrassed, Unrest) data from AI_Hub [12]. The composition of the data used is the same as the data in Table 2 used in the emotional word dictionary. In this paper, for KoBERT Finetuning, we found the optimal value through repeated experiments and learned with hidden_size = 728, max_len = 32, learning rate = 1e-5, log_interval = 200, and epoch = 500. The proposed DL_Emotioner finally derives probability values for six emotions.

3.4 Deep Learning Machine Learning Convergence Model

This paper proposes a fusion module to analyze the final emotion based on the constructed deep learning emotion module and machine learning emotion module. The proposed fusion model analyzes the final emotion through the Sigmoid function, which multiplies the emotion probability values obtained through deep learning and machine learning emotion analysis modules and derives a value between 0 and 1. The Sigmoid function is as shown in Eq. 1. Table 3 shows the results of emotion analysis through the proposed module.

Table 3. Results of the emotional analysis through the proposed model

	User Input	Emotion Label
1	Ha…it's so hard today	sadness
2	Ha…I'm so angry today	angry
3	I was playing with my friend, and he got hurt	sadness
4	I didn't finish my homework. I'm scared to go to school	wound
5	I was told never to buy stocks, but I did it secretly and ended up ruined	shame

4 Experiments

In this paper, the number of data for each emotion was set to approximately 200 to build an unbiased dictionary of emotion words. This paper identified the optimal ensemble machine learning algorithm among ensemble machine learning. For the experiment, the accuracy was derived and compared through a voting algorithm that can learn by combining several classification algorithms. Figure 2 is a graph showing the accuracy according to the combination of single classification machine learning algorithms.

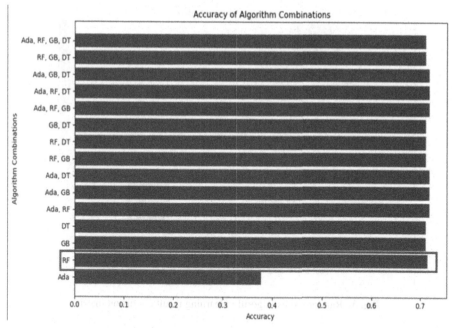

Fig. 2. Accuracy graph for each combination of classification machine learning algorithms (Ada: Adaboost, RF: RandomForest, GB: GradientBoosting, DT: Decision Tree)

As a result of the experiment, it was confirmed that RandomForest achieved the highest performance compared to other algorithm combinations at 0.718. Therefore, in this paper, a model was built using Random-Forest. After learning through the Random Forest algorithm, learning Accuracy = 0.718, Precision = 0.714, Recall = 0.714, F1-score = 0.708 were derived. Figure 3 is the confusion matrix generated after RandomForest learning.

This paper confirmed the deep learning emotion analysis module (DL_Emotioner) Train_Accuracy = 0.98, Test_Accuracy = 0.78 and Loss = 0.0024. Figure 4 is a graphical representation of Train/Test Accuracy and Loss values for each 100 epoch.

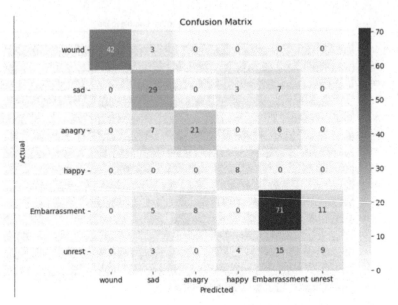

Fig. 3. RandomForest algorithm learning result confusion matrix

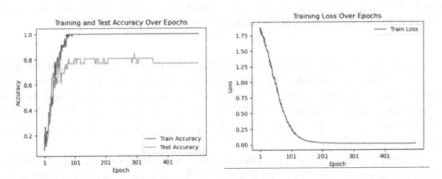

Fig. 4. Sentiment analysis Deep learning module Train/Test Accuracy, Loss graph

5   Conclusion

This paper proposes an emotion analysis system that combines emotional word dictionary deep learning and machine learning for Korean emotion analysis. This paper aimed at detailed emotional analysis by proposing a system that considers the emotional elements of words. The accuracy of the machine learning module according to the current emotional word dictionary results in a low score of 0.71. Due to the nature of the Korean language, there are many homonyms, so emotion labels for each emotion word (e.g. word: laughter - emotion label: joy, word: laughter - emotion label: sadness, etc.) are confusing in this model. Therefore, we plan to measure the accuracy of the fused model by collecting more data and preprocessing homonyms in the future. The proposed system is an emotion analysis system, and it is expected that the model can be used when customized services (chatbots, recommendation systems, etc.) are needed. Therefore, in future research, we plan to build an AI service model using the proposed emotion analysis system.

Acknowledgments. This work was supported by the Ministry of Education of the Republic of Korea and the National Research Foundation of Korea (NRF-2022S1A5C2A07091326).

References

1. Dawel, A., et al.: Perceived emotion genuineness: normative ratings for popular facial expression stimuli and the development of perceived-as-genuine and perceived-as-fake sets. Beh. Res. Meth. **49**, 1539–1562 (2017)
2. Devlin, J., et al.: Bert: pre-training of deep bidirectional transformers for language understanding. arXiv preprint arXiv:1810.04805 (2018)
3. Santos, I., Nedjah, N., de Macedo Mourelle, L.: Sentiment analysis using convolutional neural network with fastText embeddings. In: 2017 IEEE Latin American Conference on Computational Intelligence (LA-CCI). IEEE (2017)
4. Gao, X., et al.: An adaptive ensemble machine learning model for intrusion detection. IEEE Access **7**, 82512–82521 (2019)
5. Wang, R., Li, J.: Bayes test of precision, recall, and F1 measure for comparison of two natural language processing models. In: Proceedings of the 57th Annual Meeting of the Association for Computational Linguistics (2019)
6. Baek, C., Kang, J., Choi, S.: Online unstructured data analysis models with KoBERT and Word2vec: a study on sentiment analysis of public opinion in Korean. Int. J. Fuzzy Logic Intell. Syst. **23**(3), 244–258 (2023)
7. Bojanowski, P., et al.: Enriching word vectors with subword information. Trans. Assoc. Comput. Linguist. **5**, 135–146 (2017)
8. Thavareesan, S., Mahesan, S.: Sentiment lexicon expansion using Word2vec and fastText for sentiment prediction in Tamil texts. In: 2020 Moratuwa Engineering Research Conference (MERCon), Moratuwa, Sri Lanka, 2020, pp. 272–276 (2020). https://doi.org/10.1109/MERCon50084.2020.9185369
9. Han, J., Micheline, K.: Data Mining Concepts and Techniques. Morgan KaufmMLP (2001)
10. Dong, X., Yu, K., Cui, Z.: Readmission prediction of diabetic patients based on AdaBoost-RandomForest mixed model. In: 2022 3rd International Conference on Big Data, Artificial Intelligence and Internet of Things Engineering (ICBAIE), Xi'an, China, 2022, pp. 130–134 (2022). https://doi.org/10.1109/ICBAIE56435.2022.9985819
11. Lee, S., et al.: Kr-Bert: a small-scale Korean-specific language model. arXiv preprint arXiv: 2008.03979 (2020)
12. This research (paper) used datasets from 'The Open AI Dataset Project (AI-Hub, S. Korea)'. All data information can be accessed through 'AI-Hub (www.aihub.or.kr) Min, Moohong, Jemin J. Lee, and Kyungho Lee. "Detecting illegal online gambling (IOG) services in the mobile environment." Security and Communication Networks 2022 (2022)
13. Datta, L.: A survey on activation functions and their relation with xavier and he normal initialization. arXiv preprint arXiv:2004.06632 (2020)
14. Cho, J., Jung, H., Park, C., Kim, Y.: An autonomous assessment of a short essay answer by using the BLEU. In: Korean HCI Conference 2009, vol. 2, pp. 606–610 (2009)

Conversion from Dimensional Emotions to Discrete Emotions

Ray F. Lin[✉] [iD], Ching-Wen Hsiao, and Tzu-Hsuan Liu

Department of Industrial Engineering and Management, Yuan Ze University,
135 Yuan-Tung Road, Chung-Li, Taiwan
juifeng@saturn.yzu.edu.tw

Abstract. Recognizing user emotions while interacting with computers and consumer products is challenging due to similar physiological or behavioral responses for certain discrete emotions. Because the dimensional emotion model with three emotional indexes measured in a continuum correlated to physiological responses, measuring and differentiating dimensional emotions might be more effective and could provide more knowledge of biological reactions. Could dimensional emotions, however, be transformed into discrete emotions for practical application? Twenty-four adults watched IAPS graphical stimuli as part of this study to get the answer to the question. Subjective feelings were gathered for discrete and dimensional emotions after viewing images. The potential conversion from dimensional emotions to discrete emotions was demonstrated by the discriminant analyses of discrete emotions and the visualization of conversion between two types of emotions. However, positive emotions are confused with positive emotions (e.g., joy and interest), whereas negative emotions are primarily confused with negative emotions (e.g., angry and fear). Although the found discriminability from dimensional emotions to discrete emotions is reasonable, it shows the conversion limitation from dimensional emotions to discrete emotions.

Keywords: Discrete Emotion · Dimensional Emotion · Emotion Recognition · Emotion Discrimination

1 Introduction

1.1 Emotion Recognition in Human-Computer Interaction

With the advancement of computer computing power, cloud storage services, and artificial intelligence technology, smart, smart healthcare, and smart schools are no longer distant goals. These advancements hold immense potential to personalize and improve our interactions with technology. Imagine a smart home system that adjusts lighting and temperature based on your emotional state, or an educational platform that tailors lessons to your level of engagement. To achieve such advances, researchers have tried to develop artificial intelligence (AI) models that can recognize human emotions using multiple types of human information.

© The Author(s), under exclusive license to Springer Nature Switzerland AG 2024
C. Stephanidis et al. (Eds.): HCII 2024, CCIS 2114, pp. 296–303, 2024.
https://doi.org/10.1007/978-3-031-61932-8_34

1.2 Discrete Emotion vs. Dimensional Emotion

There are multiple perspectives on the definition of emotions, but the two most widely accepted taxonomies are "discrete emotions" and "dimensional emotions" [1]. Discrete emotions categorize emotions into several commonly recognized emotional states, such as happiness and anger. The content and number of discrete emotions have varied greatly with research developments. Early studies by Mowrer [2] proposed two emotions: happiness and sadness. Later studies proposed 6–7 emotions [3–5], ten emotions [6], 11 emotions [7, 8], 15 emotions [8], 18 emotions [9], and even 22 emotions proposed by Bradley, Codispoti [10].

Ekman and Friesen (1971) proposed that all emotional expressions can be composed of six primary discrete emotions: anger, disgust, fear, happiness, sadness, surprise, and neutral. In later studies, he added other secondary emotions, such as interest, contempt, contentment, embarrassment, excitement, pride, relief, satisfaction, pleasure, and shame. However, the increasing number of discrete emotions in different studies makes it difficult to reach a consensus. Additionally, the excessive number of emotion categories and their similar physiological responses hinder the development of emotion recognition models [11].

In addition to discrete emotions, another research approach commonly used by some psychologists is dimensional emotions. Building on the dimensional model, Russell and his research team [12–16] proposed to differentiate emotions using three main emotional dimensions: valence, arousal, and dominance. Valence refers to the variation of emotions from unpleasant to pleasant. Arousal represents the change of emotions from an unaroused state to a high-aroused state. In most studies, emotions are categorized using the above two dimensions. However, some studies also include dominance as a third emotional dimension. This dimension refers to the difference in people's ability to control or influence the emotions they feel, from submissive to dominant [16].

1.3 Research Objective

As discussed in the literature review, emotions are mainly categorized into "discrete emotions" and "dimensional emotions" for analysis. However, using only one type of emotion label data for modeling will have limitations in application. For example, using only discrete emotion data will limit the development of emotion models, while using only dimensional emotion data cannot directly predict people's discrete emotions.

Most current studies focus on modeling discrete emotions that are commonly recognized by people. However, from a psychological perspective, the selected discrete emotions may not have different physiological responses [11], which also affects the development of emotion recognition models. In addition, although there are a few studies that have developed models for dimensional emotions, there is no further research on how to convert predicted dimensional emotions to discrete emotions.

While limited research has explored the conversion of continuous dimensional emotions into discrete emotional categories, this study aimed to investigate the relationship between dimensional emotions and discrete emotions. Specifically, we examined (1) the mapping of discrete emotions onto a three-dimensional emotional space defined by valence, arousal, and dominance and (2) the performance of discriminating discrete emotions based on dimensional emotion features.

2   Method

2.1   Participant

The study recruited twenty-four Yuan Ze University students (11 males, 13 females) above the age of 20. The Institutional Review Board approved the experimental protocol.

2.2   Experimental Settings and Apparatus

The experiment was carried out in a quiet room with a temperature of $23 \pm 1°$ and a moisture content of 40% to 50%. A personal computer with a monitor on a table displayed graphical stimuli and questionnaires to the participants.

Affective stimuli were obtained from the International Picture System [IAPS, 17]. Ninety images from a collection of 1,182 pictures were selected to depict the nine combinations of high, medium, and low valence and arousal (i.e., ten images in each combination).

2.3   Experimental Procedures

After the informed consent procedure, the participant sat in front of the computer desk to watch affective stimuli and report discrete and dimensional emotions using DES [Discrete Emotions Questionnaire, 18] and SAM [Self-Assessment Manikin, 19–21], respectively.

The experiment consisted of two sessions separated by a 15-min break. During each session, participants viewed 45 images presented on a computer monitor, each displayed for six seconds. Following each image, participants verbally reported their emotional responses of angry, disgust, sadness, fear, calm, interest, and joy using the DES [18], and emotional responses of valence, arousal, and dominance using SAM [19–21]. After completing their ratings for one image, a 10-s rest period was given before the next image appeared.

2.4   Data Analyses

The degree to which dimensional emotions could be transformed into discrete emotions was demonstrated using a two-step analysis. The participant's responses to discrete emotions for affective stimuli were first plotted in a three-dimensional space based on valence, arousal, and dominance. The graphic mapping allowed us to see how discrete emotions differ from one another in a three-dimensional emotional space. In the second step, the ability to classify discrete emotions using three-dimensional emotions was tested using linear and quadratic discriminant analysis techniques.

3   Results

3.1   Collected Discrete and Dimensional Emotions

The distributions of participants' discrete and dimensional emotions responses to 90 affective stimuli were shown in Fig. 1. As shown in the figure, participants' reported emotions on the 90 images were quite different. Regarding discrete emotions (Fig. 1a), some participants (e.g., participants 5, 10, 14, and 23) were not sensitive to these affective stimuli and had many calm responses. In contrast, some participants were more sensitive to the images and reported relatively evenly to the seven discrete emotions (e.g., participants 2, 3, 6, 20, and 24). The distributions of demonsional emotions are reflected in the distributions of reported discrete emotions. For example, individuals who exhibited a high number of calm responses also exhibited a high number of medium valance (Fig. 1b), low arousal (Fig. 1c), and great dominance (Fig. 1c) responses. When we visualize these relationships in the following section, they become more evident.

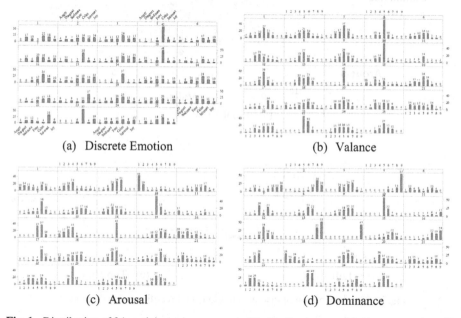

(a) Discrete Emotion   (b) Valance

(c) Arousal   (d) Dominance

Fig. 1. Distribution of 24 participants' responses to 90 affective images. (a) discrete emotion, (b) dimensional emotion of valance, (c) dimensional emotion of arousal, (d) dimensional emotion of dominance.

3.2   Visualization of Conversion from Dimensional Emotions to Discrete Emotions

This study created a three-dimensional scatter plot of the discrete emotions that participants reported feeling at a scale level greater than or equal to 4. As shown in Fig. 2, the positive emotions of discrete emotions (i.e., joy and interest) are distributed in places with higher scores in valence, while the negative emotions (i.e., anger, disgust, and sadness) are distributed in places with lower scores in valence. Calm is located in the areas with a score of 5 in valence. Hence, the relationship between valence and arousal levels presents an inverted U-shaped distribution (see Fig. 2c). In terms of dominance, a low level of arousal directly corresponded to a high degree of dominance (see Fig. 2b). Specifically, when they were calm, they exhibited a high degree of dominance and a low level of arousal. However, when they were experiencing negative emotions, such as fear and anger, their arousal level was high and their dominance level was low. Positive emotions experience a similar trend—Dominance was low at high arousal levels.

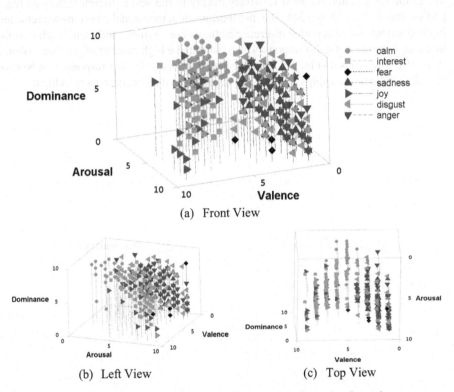

Fig. 2. The distribution of discrete emotions in three-dimensional emotions.

3.3 Discriminability of Discrete Emotions from Dimensional Emotions

Tables 1 and 2 display the discriminability of linear and quadratic discriminant analyses, respectively. While the quadratic model performed marginally better than the other, both models performed comparably in terms of discrimination. The accuracy of the quadratic model was 0.521, while the accuracy of the linear model was 0.477. The models did not appear to have a high degree of discriminate accuracy. The two models did, however, perform reasonably well. Positive emotions are often confused with positive emotions, but not with negative ones. Negative emotions are primarily confused with negative emotions. On the other hand, interest was easily confused with joy, but anger was easily confused with fear.

Table 1. Discriminability of discrete emotions using linear discriminant analysis. Note: darker red indicates higher frequency, whereas darker blue indicates lower frequency.

Predicted Emotion	Reported Emotion						
	Angry	Disgust	Sadness	Fear	Calm	Interest	Joy
Angry	31	68	61	54	7	6	0
Disgust	9	39	34	44	6	0	0
Sadness	6	17	15	28	19	1	0
Fear	14	50	35	80	44	9	2
Calm	4	32	29	46	512	76	34
Interest	1	6	7	21	85	136	88
Joy	0	1	4	5	33	102	168
Total N	65	213	185	278	706	330	292
N correct	31	39	15	80	512	136	168
Proportion	0.477	0.183	0.081	0.288	0.725	0.412	0.575

Accuracy: 0.477

Table 2. Discriminability of discrete emotions using quadratic discriminant analysis. Note: darker red indicates higher frequency, whereas darker blue indicates lower frequency.

Predicted Emotion	Reported Emotion						
	Angry	Disgust	Sadness	Fear	Calm	Interest	Joy
Angry	23	31	40	20	7	7	0
Disgust	13	51	33	45	9	0	0
Sadness	2	9	11	10	10	3	0
Fear	23	85	63	146	34	8	0
Calm	4	30	26	37	531	74	30
Interest	0	6	7	11	49	89	35
Joy	0	1	5	9	66	149	227
Total N	65	213	185	278	706	330	292
N correct	23	51	11	146	531	89	227
Proportion	0.354	0.239	0.059	0.525	0.752	0.27	0.777

Accuracy: 0.521

4 Discussion and Conclusion

To test the conversion from dimensional emotion to discrete emotion, this study simultaneously collected two types of emotion responses from 24 participants after they viewed graphic affective images.

Visualization of discrete and three-dimensional emotions in a three-dimensional space shows reasonable relationships between two types of emotions. As shown in Fig. 1, the three-dimensional scatter plot shows beautiful relationships between discrete and three-dimensional emotions. However, it is worth noting that this study only included data with a discrete emotion level greater than or equal to 4 for presentation and did not use data with more minor levels.

The two discriminate models also show reasonable discriminability of discrete emotions from three-dimensional emotions. Unlike drawing the three-dimensional visualization, we used all the data (i.e., all discrete emotion levels) in discriminate analyses. Hence, we found confused discrimination among some positive discrete emotions, especially joy and interest, and negative emotions, especially angry and fear. The main reason was that participants had a varied degree of discrete emotions. Hence, two positive discrete emotions (or two negative discrete emotions) with low degrees are difficult to discriminate from each other.

In conclusion, this study demonstrates the potential of predicting discrete emotions based on three-dimensional emotions. While many studies focus on predicting discrete emotions by building artificial intelligence models, another alternative is to build models to predict dimensional emotions. Given the relationship between dimensional emotions and physiological responses, constructing dimensional-emotion models could yield more effective results. This study has demonstrated the potential of converting dimensional emotions to discrete emotions to obtain discrete emotions.

Acknowledgments. We thank the National Science and Technology Council (NSTC111-2628-E-155-002-MY2) for their grant support.

Disclosure of Interests. The authors declare no conflict of interest. The funders had no role in the design of the study; in the collection, analyses, or interpretation of data; in the writing of the manuscript, or in the decision to publish the results.

References

1. Brave, S., Nass, C.: Emotion in human-computer interaction. Hum.-Comput. Interact. Fundam. **20094635**, 53–68 (2009)
2. Mowrer, O.: Learning Theory and the Symbolic Processes (1960)
3. Ekman, P., Friesen, W.V., Ellsworth, P.: Emotion in the Human Face: Guidelines for Research and an Integration of Findings, vol. 11. Elsevier (2013)
4. Ekman, P.: An argument for basic emotions. Cogn. Emot. **6**(3–4), 169–200 (1992)
5. Ekman, P., Friesen, W.V.: Constants across cultures in the face and emotion. J. Pers. Soc. Psychol. **17**(2), 124 (1971)

6. Izard, C.E., Weiss, M.: Maximally Discriminative Facial Movement Coding System. University of Delaware, Instructional Resources Center (1979)
7. Eckman, P.: Universal and cultural differences in facial expression of emotion. In: Nebraska Symposium on Motivation (1972)
8. Ekman, P.: Basic emotions. In: Handbook of Cognition and Emotion, vol. 98, no. 45–60, p. 16 (1999)
9. Frijda, N.H.: The Emotions. Cambridge University Press (1986)
10. Bradley, M.M., et al.: Emotion and motivation II: sex differences in picture processing. Emotion 1(3), 300 (2001)
11. Dzedzickis, A., Kaklauskas, A., Bucinskas, V.: Human emotion recognition: review of sensors and methods. Sensors 20(3), 592 (2020)
12. Russell, J.A.: Core affect and the psychological construction of emotion. Psychol. Rev. 110(1), 145 (2003)
13. Russell, J.A., Barrett, L.F.: Core affect, prototypical emotional episodes, and other things called emotion: dissecting the elephant. J. Pers. Soc. Psychol. 76(5), 805 (1999)
14. Russell, J.A.: A circumplex model of affect. J. Pers. Soc. Psychol. 39(6), 1161 (1980)
15. Mehrabian, A., Russell, J.A.: An Approach to Environmental Psychology. MIT Press (1974)
16. Russell, J.A., Mehrabian, A.: Evidence for a three-factor theory of emotions. J. Res. Pers. 11(3), 273–294 (1977)
17. Lang, P., Bradley, M., Cuthbert, B.: International Affective Picture System (IAPS): Affective Ratings of Pictures and Instruction Manual. University of Florida, Gainesville (2008). Tech Rep A-8
18. Harmon-Jones, C., Bastian, B., Harmon-Jones, E.: The discrete emotions questionnaire: a new tool for measuring state self-reported emotions. PLoS ONE 11(8), e0159915 (2016)
19. Lang, P.J.: The emotion probe: studies of motivation and attention. Am. Psychol. 50(5), 372 (1995)
20. Lang, P.J., Bradley, M.M., Cuthbert, B.N.: Emotion, attention, and the startle reflex. Psychol. Rev. 97(3), 377 (1990)
21. Lang, P.J., Bradley, M.M., Cuthbert, B.N.: International affective picture system (IAPS): Instruction manual and affective ratings. In: The Center for Research in Psychophysiology. University of Florida (1999)

Investigation of a Method for Evaluating the Effect of Interior Colors on Emotions

Shukuka Ninomiya[✉], Narumon Jadram, and Midori Sugaya

College of Engineering, Shibaura Institute of Technology, 3-7-5, Toyosu, Koto-ku 135-8548, Tokyo, Japan

{a120113,nb23107,doly}@shibaura-it.ac.jp

Abstract. When designing an interior space, it is expected to consider not only the functions required for the space but also the emotions desired by the users in the space. Color plays an important role in evoking specific emotions. There are many studies that have investigated the effect of color on emotion and the effect of color in interior spaces on emotion. However, the difference between the effect of color on emotion and the effect of space color on emotion has not been sufficiently investigated and is not clear. In this study, to clarify the effect of color on emotion in interior spaces, we evaluated the difference in the effect of the same color on emotion with and without furniture using physiological indexes and a questionnaire. As a result, the physiological indexes showed that viewing spatial design images was more comfortable than viewing plain color images, and the arousal level was higher when viewing interior spatial design images. In addition, a comparison between hues showed the same tendency for plain color and spatial design images. The questionnaire evaluation showed that spatial design images and plain color images of the same color gave similar impressions. Thus, spatial design images and plain color images tended to be similar in hue comparison. Therefore, it is possible that the effect of color on emotion has the same effect on spatial design.

Keywords: emotion · colors · interior spaces design

1 Introduction

When designing an interior space, it is expected to consider not only the functions required for the space but also the emotions desired by the users in the space [1]. For example, in the design of a bedroom, if a user wishes to feel relaxed, it is expected that the space should be designed using colors and materials that can evoke such feelings [2].

Interior spaces contain various elements such as colors, materials, and shapes. Colors play an important role in evoking certain emotions [1, 3]. For example, red and orange evoke feelings of "excitement," while blue and green evoke feelings of "calmness" and "tranquility" [3]. By understanding how the colors of a space affect emotions, we can design interior spaces with colors that better correspond to the target emotions.

© The Author(s), under exclusive license to Springer Nature Switzerland AG 2024
C. Stephanidis et al. (Eds.): HCII 2024, CCIS 2114, pp. 304–312, 2024.
https://doi.org/10.1007/978-3-031-61932-8_35

Various studies have investigated the effects of color on emotion [3, 4]. Valdez et al. evaluated emotional responses to 10 color samples with the same brightness and saturation but varied hues [4]. The results showed that blue and green were more comfortable, while the yellow was less comfortable. Several studies also investigated the effects of colors in interior space on emotions [5, 6]. Yildirim et al. used the Semantic Differential (SD) method [7] to evaluate the effects of warm, cold, and achromatic colors in three living room images on mood and preferences [5]. The results showed that warm colors tended to evoke emotions such as "high arousal," "exciting," and "stimulating." Cool colors tended evoke emotions such as "not very arousing," "spacious" and "restful." The results also showed that the achromatic color interiors were evaluated more negatively for all the bipolar items except those related to feelings of calm and peacefulness. Kondo et al. examined the effect of the accent wall and wooden floor on the impression and apparent size of living room [6]. The SD method and the Magnitude Estimation method, which evaluates the apparent size of the stimulus model (ME method) [8], were used for the evaluation. In the experiment, the colors similar to the architectural materials (yellow and gray) and the primary color hues (red, green, and blue) were selected. As a result, warm colors (red, yellow) had high average values in the evaluation of "warm", "soft", and "bright" impressions, while cool colors (blue, achromatic gray) resulted in low averages. These studies examined the effect of color on emotions and the effect of interior space color on emotions. However, the difference between the effect of color and the effect of color in space on emotions has not been sufficiently investigated and is not clear.

This study aims to clarify the effect of the colors in interior space design on emotions. To achieve this goal, we conducted an experiment to compare the differences in the effect of color between two types of images: plain color images and spatial design images. The spatial design is an image of a living room with wall colors identical to those in the plain color images. We evaluated the differences in the effects on emotion using physiological indexes and SD method. The purpose of physiological index evaluation is to objectively compare subtle differences in unconscious emotions [9].

2 Comparison of Emotions with and Without Interior Space

2.1 Experimental Setup

The objective of this experiment was to compare the emotional responses evoked by plain color images and spatial design images with physiological indexes and SD method. In the experiment, four plain color images and four spatial design images were presented to the participant on a display monitor. To evaluate emotional response, physiological data, which include Electroencephalogram (EEG) and Heart Rate Variability (HRV), were obtained using an electroencephalograph (EEG sensor) and a pulse wave sensor during the experiment. Moreover, after each image was presented, participants were asked to answer a questionnaire using the SD method. Seven university students in their 20s (4 males and 3 females) participated in the experiment.

2.2 Image Stimuli

The colors are specified by three dimensions: hue (red, green, etc.), saturation (difference from achromatic stimuli), and brightness (perceived light intensity) [10]. Among these, hue has a greater effect on mood and impression than saturation and brightness [11]. In this experiment, we used red, yellow, green, and blue (the four primary psychological colors [12]).

Eight images including four plain color images and four spatial design images were used in the experiment. The spatial design images were created on the website Voice of color [13], which allows the users to edit the colors of walls and ceilings in spatial design images. The four plain color images and four spatial design images used in the experiment are shown in Fig. 1. The hue, saturation, and brightness of each image is shown in Table 1.

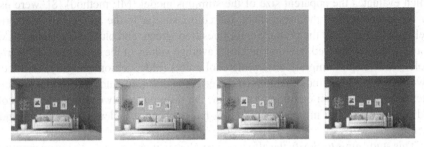

Fig. 1. The four color of image stimuli used in the experiment plain color image (top), spatial design image (under).

Table 1. Hue, saturation, and brightness of each image.

color	Hue (°)	saturation (%)	brightness (%)
Red	359	54	49
Yellow	59	55	49
Green	100	40	52
Blue	228	37	41

2.3 Emotional Evaluation Method

In this study, we conducted a quantitative emotion evaluation using physiological indexes. The reason for quantitative emotion evaluation using physiological indexes is that, as described in Sect. 1, it is thought to be possible to objectively compare subtle differences in unconscious emotions [9]. Furthermore, among physiological indexes, EEG is important for understanding cognitive and attentional states [14]. In addition, HRV are important for understanding the states of relaxation and tension [9]. Recently, an emotion visualization method called "emotion map" has been proposed to combine these two indexes [15]. Emotion maps have the advantage that physiological indexes such as EEG and HRV indexes can be evaluated more intuitively and differences between individuals can be easily compared. This method is a two-dimensional coordinate visualization of an emotion estimation model [9] that maps physiological indexes to Russell's circular model [16], which expresses the relationship between valence, arousal, and emotion used in psychology (Fig. 2). The X-axis represents valence, and the Y-axis represents arousal. The HRV index was used for evaluating the valence level. The EEG is used for evaluating the arousal level. The emotions of each stimulus were evaluated by mapping the average values of HRV and EEG indexes measured during a stimulus condition. The baseline for the emotion map is determined by the average resting state, which is assigned as the values at an origin point (x = 0, y = 0) on the emotion map. The distance and direction from the origin in both axes on the emotion map visualize the emotion evoked by stimuli. In this study, we used the emotion map to classify emotions into four categories: high valence/high arousal, low valence/high arousal, high valence/low arousal, and low valence/low arousal, as shown in Fig. 2.

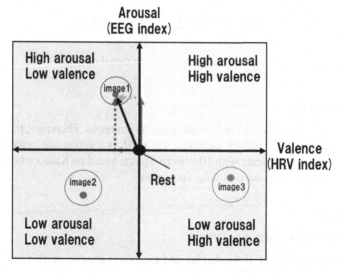

Fig. 2. The emotion map in two dimensions: valence (X-axis) and arousal (Y-axis) classified four categories of emotions. The origin point of emotion map is determined based on the resting state. The red point represents the classified emotion as high valence high arousal.

2.4 Physiological Indexes

EEG and HRV are highly reliable as they measure human emotions from the central and autonomic nervous systems (ANS) [17, 18]. In this study, we use the Lowβ/Lowα ratio as the EEG index to evaluate the arousal level [19]. This ratio represents the power spectrum of Lowβ to Lowα obtained from the brainwave sensor (Neurosky's MindWave

Mobile2 [20]). The summary of the frequency bands and their interpretations of the EEG are shown in Table 2. In this study, a higher ratio indicates a higher level of arousal.

Table 2. EEG frequency bands and related mental states [21].

EEG Index	Frequency Band (Hz)	Related mental states
Lowα	8–9	Relaxed, peaceful, conscious
Lowβ	13–17	Thinking, aware of self & surroundings

HRV is measured using Pulse sensor [22] from Switch Science. The HRV index is used as an index to measure the state of the autonomic nervous system [9]. In this study, we used pNN50 to evaluate the degree of valence. pNN50 is the percentage of heartbeats in which the difference between consecutive adjacent heartbeats exceeds 50 ms, and the calculation method is shown in Eq. (1). In this study, a high value of pNN50 is interpreted as comfort, and a low value is interpreted as tension.

$$pNNx = \frac{\Sigma_{i=1}^{30}(if(|m_i - m_{i-1}| > x); 1)}{30} \tag{1}$$

$$m_i = heart\ rate\ interval,\ x = threshold(ms)$$

2.5 Questionnaire

To evaluate the effect of colors in interior space on emotions. Therefore, the SD method, one of the questionnaire survey methods, was used as a subjective evaluation. In this study, we used a 7-point scale with 10 adjective pairs, based on Kato's study [2]. Table 3 shows the adjective pairs used in this experiment.

2.6 Procedure

The experiment procedure is as follows:

1. Participants sit in front of the display and wears a brainwave sensor and a pulse rate sensor as shown in Fig. 3. During the experiment, to collect the best quality of EEG, participants were asked to not to move his/her body as much as possible.
2. Participants rest with eyes open for 1 min to stabilize the physiological data measurement. During the resting state, the gray color image with a black cross in the center were presented on the display monitor.
3. Participants rest with eyes open for 1 min.
4. Participants view the display monitor presented image stimuli for 1 min.
5. Participants answer the SD-scale questionnaire.
6. Repeat steps 3–5 for eight times to look at four colors for two types of image stimuli. The image stimuli were presented randomly to prevent order effects.
7. After the experiment, the participants were asked to rank their favorite images presented during the experiment.

Table 3. Adjective pairs used in the experiment.

No.	SD adjective pairs	
1	Like	Dislike
2	Bright	Dark
3	Wide	Narrow
4	Light	Heavy
5	Comfortable	Uncomfortable
6	Warm	Cold
7	Relax	Oppressed
8	Stimulating	Sedate
9	Soft	Hard
10	Calm	Restless

Pulse Sensor   MindWave Mobile2
(pulse rate sensor)   (brainwave sensor)

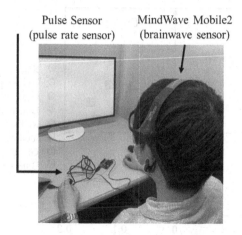

実験中の様子

Fig. 3. Experimental scene.

3　Results and Discussion

3.1　Physiological Indexes Results

To evaluate emotional response of each image, we analysis data as follows. Firstly, we calculated the average of pNN50 and Lowβ/Lowα indexes during the initial rest and for each stimulus for each participant. In this study, the initial rest was used as the neutral state because the initial rest was not affected by any stimulus. Secondly, to compare the change of emotion response between viewing each stimulus and the neutral state, we calculated the difference of the average of the physiological indexes (pNN50 and Lowβ/Lowα) during the stimulus and first rest. Finally, the emotion map was plotted by fitting the obtained pNN50 values to the X-axis of the emotion map and the Lowβ/Lowα values to the Y-axis.

The average of the emotion maps of all participants is shown in Fig. 4. Figure 4 shows that each spatial image has a larger pNN50 value than the plain color image of the same color, resulting in a more relaxed result. This may be due to the use of a living room image in the spatial design images, which may facilitate a relaxed state of mind. In addition, each spatial design image had a higher Lowβ/Lowα value than the same color plain color image, resulting in a higher arousal level. This may be because the spatial design images have more elements than the plain color images, and the participants spent more time concentrating on the images.

A comparison between each hue showed that yellow was more arousing and less comfortable than red, green, and blue. This trend was observed in both plain color and spatially designed images.

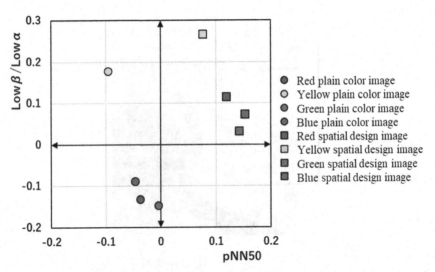

Fig. 4. Average of the emotion maps of all participants in the experiment. Plain color images are represented by circles (●) and spatial design images by squares (■). Red, yellow, green, and blue images are each shown in the same color.

3.2 Subjective Evaluation Results

We evaluated participants' impressions and emotional responses to each image using data obtained from the SD method. Figure 5 shows the average scores for each adjective pair from all participants. The solid line shows the plain color image, and the dotted line shows the spatial design image. Looking at the like-dislike adjective pairs in the first column, the difference between the spatial image and the plain color image is 0.14 for red, 1.57 for yellow, 0 for green, and 0.28 for blue. Thus, when comparing the spatial and plain color images of the same color, the differences for the same adjective pairs were all less than 2, indicating a trend toward giving similar impressions.

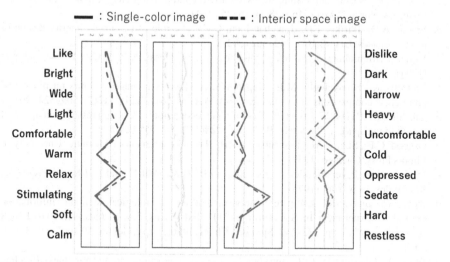

Fig. 5. Average scores for each adjective pair from all participants. Plain color images are represented by straight lines (–) and spatial design images represented by dotted lines (- - -). Red, yellow, green, and blue images are shown using the same colors.

4   Conclusion

To clarify the effect of the color of the interior space design on emotion, we conducted an experiment in which a plain color image with only one color and an image with the same color but with a spatial design were presented and evaluated the difference in the effect on emotion. As a result, the physiological indexes showed that the participants were more comfortable and had a higher arousal level when viewing the spatial design images than when viewing the plain color images. Comparison between hues showed the same trend between plain color and spatial design images. The questionnaire evaluation showed that spatial design images and plain color images of the same color gave similar impressions. Thus, spatial design images and plain color images tended to be similar in hue comparison. Therefore, it is possible that the effect of color on emotion has the same effect on spatial design.

In this experiment, we used a spatial design image that does not actually exist because we changed the wall color of the living room image as a spatial design image. In future experiments, we will use images of actual indoor spaces to evaluate the effect of color on emotion. Since multiple colors are used in actual space design, it is necessary to evaluate the effect of a space composed of multiple colors on emotion.

References

1. Ćurčić, A., Kekovic, A., Ranđelović, D., Momcilovic-Petronijevic, A.: Effects of color in interior design. Zbornik radova Građevinskog fakulteta **35**, 867–877 (2019)
2. Yukie, K.R., Hashimoto, Isamu, A.: Psychological and physiological responses to color of a room. J. Color Sci. Assoc. Jpn. **28**(1), 16–25 (2004)
3. Enwin, A.D., Ikiriko, T.D., Jonathan-Ihua, G.O.: The role of colours in interior design of liveable spaces. EJTAS **1**(4), 242–262 (2023)
4. Valdez, P., Mehrabian, A.: Effects of color on emotions. J. Exp. Psychol. Gen. **123**(4), 394–409 (1994)
5. Yildirim, K., Hidayetoglu, M.L., Capanoglu, A.: Effects of interior colors on mood and preference: comparisons of two living rooms. Percept. Mot. Skills. **112**(2), 509–524 (2011)
6. Takehiro, K., Ryota, Y.: Effect of all color and wooden floor on the impression and apparent size in living space. J. Architect. Build. Scie. **24**(57), 747–750 (2018)
7. Osgood, C.E., Suci, G.H., Tannenbaum, P.H.: The Measurement of Meaning. University of Illinois Press, Chicago (1957)
8. Stevens, S.S.: Psychophysics: Introduction to Its Perceptual Neural and Social Prospects. John Wiley, New York (1975)
9. Ikeda, Y., Sugaya, M.: Estimate emotion method to use biological, symbolic information preliminary experiment. In: Schmorrow, D.D.D., Fidopiastis, C.M.M. (eds.) AC 2016. LNCS (LNAI), vol. 9743, pp. 332–340. Springer, Cham (2016). https://doi.org/10.1007/978-3-319-39955-3_31
10. Wilms, L., Oberfeld, D.: Color and emotion: effects of hue, saturation, and brightness. Psychol. Res. **82**(8), 96–914 (2018)
11. Katayama, l., Zhang, X., Aoki, T.: Application of coior appearance model to coior Image evaluation. Trans. Jpn. Soc. Interior Stud. **12**, 3 (2002)
12. Kazumichi, H., Aya, T.: Playing with colors using watercolors by four psychological primary colors -for understanding color of donor. Res Bullet. Kindai Univ. Kyushu Jr. **48**, 136–143 (2018)
13. Voice of Colour. https://www.visualizecolor.com/. Accessed 23 May 2023
14. Khosla, et al.: A comparative analysis of signal processing and classification methods for different applications based on EEG signals. Biocybernet. Biomed. Eng. **40**(2), 649–690 (2020)
15. Ueno, S., Zhang, R., Laohakangvalvit, T., Sugaya, M.: Evaluating comfort in fully autonomous vehicle using biological emotion map. In: Stanton, N. (ed.) AHFE 2021. LNNS, vol. 270, pp. 323–330. Springer, Cham (2021). https://doi.org/10.1007/978-3-030-80012-3_38
16. James, A., Russell, A.: Circumplex model of affect. J. Pers. Soc. Psychol. **39**(6), 1161–1178 (1980)
17. Suzuki, K., Laohakangvalvit, T., Matsubara, R., Sugaya, M.: Constructing an emotion estimation model based on EEG/HRV indexes using feature extraction and feature selection algorithms. Sensors **21**(9), 2910 (2021)
18. Dzedzickis, A., Kaklauskas, A., Bucinskas, V.: Human emotion recognition: review of sensors and methods. Sensors (Basel) **20**, 592 (2020)
19. Eoh, H.J., Chung, M.K., Kim, S.-H.: Electroencephalographic study of drowsiness in simulated driving with sleep deprivation. Int. J. Ind. Ergon. **35**, 307–320 (2005)
20. NeuroSky, MindWave Mobile. http://store.neurosky.com/. Accessed 20 June 2023
21. Nafea, M., Hisham, A.B., Abdul-Kadir, N.A., Harun, F.K.C.: Brainwave-controlled system for smart home applications. In: 2018 2nd International Conference on BioSignal Analysis, Processing and Systems (ICBAPS), pp. 75–80. IEEE (2018)
22. PulseSensor. https://pulsesensor.com/. Accessed 20 June 2023

Analysis of Relation Between Facial Emotions and Comprehension Level in Listening

Yoko Nishihara[✉], Seina Hiramichi, and Junjie Shan

Ritsumeikan University, Shiga, Japan
{nisihara,shan}@fc.ritsumei.ac.jp

Abstract. Speaking in a way others can comprehend is essential when communicating with others. If people realize that the other does not understand what they say by observing their expressions, they can use easier words and give examples, which achieves good communication. The authors argue that people can tell whether they are being comprehended by looking at the other's face. Therefore, this study focuses on facial emotions and explores whether there is a relation between facial emotions and comprehension level while listening to other. In this study, the authors implemented a user interface that estimates human emotions from facial images using FER (Facial Emotion Recognition). The implemented user interface detects facial area of a frame and outputted the distribution of likelihoods of seven emotions. The authors examined the above assumption, conducted experiments with participants and analyzed the experimental data. The experiment measured participants' facial emotions while taking English listening tests of two difficulty levels (easy and hard). The distributions of seven emotion likelihoods were analyzed. Experimental results showed that when they had the easy listening test, they expressed neutral emotion if they comprehended it. However, they expressed other emotion (sad) if they could not comprehend it. In contrast, when they had the difficult listening test, they expressed the emotion sad if they did not comprehended it. However, they expressed neutral emotion if they gave up comprehension.

Keywords: Listening comprehension · Facial emotion recognition · Distribution of emotions

1 Introduction

When communicating with others, people should speak in a way that the others can comprehend. If people have a message that they want to deliver to others, they should choose words and phrases by considering the others' backgrounds (their ages, their knowledge levels, etc.) to make their words easier at understanding and get a better communication.

If people realize that the audiences might not comprehend what they just said, they can adjust their speeches by adding explanations or changing their

© The Author(s), under exclusive license to Springer Nature Switzerland AG 2024
C. Stephanidis et al. (Eds.): HCII 2024, CCIS 2114, pp. 313–318, 2024.
https://doi.org/10.1007/978-3-031-61932-8_36

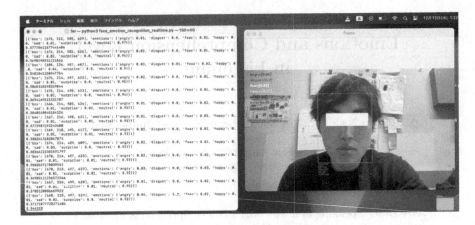

Fig. 1. Example of the implemented user interface's screen.

expressions. People make this judgment primarily by observing their audiences' facial emotions. The authors guess that people can judge whether they are being comprehended by looking at their facial emotions. Therefore, in this study, the authors conduct facial emotion recognition and analyze the relation between facial emotions and comprehension level when in listening.

In the study, the authors implemented a user interface that estimates human emotions from facial images. Then, evaluation experiments were conducted to measure participants' facial emotions while listening to speech content of two difficulty levels. The emotion distributions were analyzed to find the relation between facial emotions and comprehension level.

Previous research on support for audiences' comprehension have been conducted. Features of voice and videos related to comprehension level are studied in order to evaluate the comprehension level in presentations [1]. The authors would support the audiences in real-time communication instead of prepared communication, so this study analyzes the relation between human emotion and comprehension level in listening. For real-time communication, the quality of communication has been analyzed in previous research. Some methods used dialogue acts for the analysis [3]. This study uses the human emotions for the analysis instead of the dialogue acts.

2 Implemented User Interface

This section explains how to implement a user interface that estimates human emotions from facial images. The authors implemented an interface that estimates seven emotions for each face frame using Face Emotion Recognition [2]. The interface can estimate seven emotions: angry, disgust, fear, happy, neutral, sad, and surprise.

Figure 1 shows an example of implemented user interface's screen. The implemented interface first detects a facial area in a captured frame. Then, the facial

Table 1. Averaged likelihoods of seven emotions.

	Easy:correct	Easy:incorrect	Hard:correct	Hard:incorrect
Angry	0.061	0.088	0.162	0.081
Disgust	0.002	0.001	0.023	0.007
Fear	0.085	0.059	0.07	0.068
Happy	0.015	0.012	0.003	0.005
Sad	**0.189**	**0.272**	**0.24**	**0.222**
Surprise	0.01	0.001	0.006	0.005
Neutral	**0.609**	**0.521**	**0.492**	**0.605**

area is used for facial emotion estimation. Finally, the likelihood distribution of seven emotions is outputted for each frame. The user interface can capture and conduct emotion recognition three times in a second.

3   Experiments

This section describes the experiments to evaluate the relation between facial emotions and comprehension level through listening tests of different difficulties.

3.1   Experimental Procedures

The experimental procedures were as follows.

1. The experimenter assigns a listening test to a participant.
2. The experimenter measures participants' facial expressions during their listening tests using the implemented interface.
3. The experimenter scores quizzes in the listening test and analyzes the relation between facial emotions and comprehension level.

The experimenter was the 2nd author of this paper. The participants were 10 undergraduate/graduate students (8 male and 2 female). Their ages were 18–22 years old. All of them were Japanese and their native language was Japanese.

The experimenter used past listening tests of Eiken Test in Practical English Proficiency (like TOEIC and TOEFL) in the experiments. The listening test had 10 questions. The duration for answering was 10 min. The experimenter chose two listening tests of Level 1 and 4 as difficult and easy listening tests, respectively.

The experimenter asked the participants to have a seat in front of the implemented user interface while taking the listening tests. The distance between the participant and the screen was set to about 50 cm. The screen size was 13.6 in. (2560 * 1664 pixels). The experiment was conducted twice for each participant. The order of listening test assignment was different among the participants. The experiments were conducted from October to November, 2023.

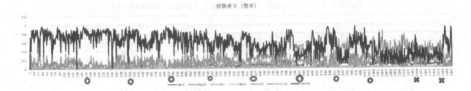

Fig. 2. Example of expressed emotions in easy listening test. The circle denotes a correct part while the cross denotes an incorrect part. The participant basically expressed the neutral emotion in answering easy listening test. However, other emotions would be expressed when they have trouble when answering easy listening test.

3.2   Evaluation Method

The experimenter cut the emotion recognition results for every quiz and classified the cut parts into two classes. One class is that the answer was correct, which meant the participants highly comprehended the speech part. The other class is that the answer was incorrect, which meant the participants did less comprehended the speech part. The authors had four groups of the results by the comprehension level and quiz's score. The distributions of emotion likelihood were averaged in each group.

- Easy:correct (correct part in the easy listening test)
- Easy:incorrect (incorrect part in the easy listening test)
- Hard:correct (correct part in the hard listening test)
- Hard:incorrect (incorrect part in the hard listening test)

3.3   Experimental Results and Discussion

Table 1 shows the averages of seven emotions for four groups (easy/hard × correct/incorrect). The emotion of neutral marked the highest likelihood in each group, followed by sad. The correct rate in easy listening test was 85% while that in the hard listening test was 15%.

Firstly, the authors discuss the estimated emotions in the easy listening test. The neutral emotion was more estimated than other emotions in Easy:correct group compared to the Easy:incorrect group. The participants could comprehend the easy listening test so they behaved calmly in answering quizzes. In contrast, the emotions sad were more estimated than the emotion neutral in Easy:incorrect group. Figure 2 shows the example of estimated emotions in the easy listening test. In the figure, the circle denotes a correct part while the cross denotes an incorrect part. The participants could not find the correct answer of a quiz that should be easy, so they might expressed other emotions. From the experimental results, the authors found that the emotion neutral was often expressed in easy listening test. However, if people could not find the correct answer in easy listening test, the other emotion sad would be expressed.

Next, the author discuss the estimated emotions in the hard listening test. The emotion neutral was more estimated than other emotions in Hard:correct

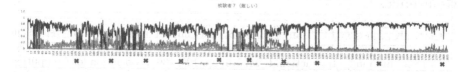

Fig. 3. Example of expressed emotions in the hard listening test. The circle denotes a correct part while the cross denotes an incorrect part. If the participant gave up comprehension, the emotion neutral was recognized more.

group. However, the averaged likelihood of neutral was smaller than that in Easy:correct group. Compared to the easy listening test, participants expressed more often other emotions during the hard listening test. This is because they could not comprehend the hard listening test. On the other hand, the participants expressed the emotion neutral more in Hard:incorrect group. Figure 3 shows the example of estimated emotions in the hard listening test. Since the participants could not comprehend the hard listening test, then they stopped expressing their emotions. Therefore, the emotion neutral was recognized. From the experimental results, the authors found that the emotion neutral was less expressed in the hard listening test than in the easy listening test. However, if people gave up comprehension, the emotion neutral would be expressed more.

4   Conclusion

In this paper, the authors analyzed the relation between the facial emotions and comprehension levels in listening test. The authors implemented a user interface to estimate facial emotions in real-time. In the evaluation experiments, the authors prepared the easy/hard listening tests. Participants' facial emotions were recognized and recorded while they were taking the listening test. Experimental results showed that the emotion neutral was more expressed in answering quizzes in the easy listening test. However, if they failed to answer the quizzes in the easy listening test, they showed the emotion sad instead of the emotion neutral. The results also showed that the participants expressed less emotion of neutral when answering the quizzes in the hard listening test than in the easy listening test. However, if they gave up comprehension in the hard listening, the emotion neutral was recognized more.

References

1. Curtis, K., Jones, G.J.F., Campbell, N.: Speaker impact on audience comprehension for academic presentations. In: Proceedings of the 18th ACM International Conference on Multimodal Interaction. ICMI '16, pp. 129–136. Association for Computing Machinery, New York, NY, USA (2016). https://doi.org/10.1145/2993148.2993194
2. Goodfellow, I.J., et al.: Challenges in representation learning: a report on three machine learning contests. In: Lee, M., Hirose, A., Hou, Z.-G., Kil, R.M. (eds.) ICONIP 2013. LNCS, vol. 8228, pp. 117–124. Springer, Heidelberg (2013). https://doi.org/10.1007/978-3-642-42051-1_16
3. Nishihara, Y., Tsuji, S., Sunayama, W., Yamanishi, R., Imashiro, S.: A generation method for the discussion process model during research progress using transitions of dialog acts. Int. J. Adv. Syst. Meas. 14(1&2), 17–26 (2021)

The Role of Exposure Time and Emotional Scene on the Perception of the Six Basic Facial Expressions

Junchen Shang[1(✉)], Xuejiao Hou[2], Jiafan Qin[3], and Yuqing Tian[4,5]

[1] Department of Medical Humanities, School of Humanities, Southeast University, Nanjing 211189, China
shangjc@seu.edu.cn
[2] College of Education, Suihua University, Suihua 152061, China
[3] Second-High Middle School of Yingkou City, Yingkou 115000, China
[4] Shaoyang Polytechnic, Shaoyang 422004, China
[5] College of Psychology, Liaoning Normal University, Dalian 116029, China

Abstract. Numerous studies have demonstrated the impact of emotional scenes on the interpretation of facial expressions. Nevertheless, limited research has explored the extent to which the exposure time of facial expressions influences the effect of emotional scenes on the categorization of facial expressions that convey congruent or incongruent emotional valence with the scene. To address this gap, the current study employed the Micro Expression Training Tool (METT) to examine the influence of emotional scenes on the perception of facial expressions presented for varying durations, including 120 ms or 200 ms (i.e., microexpressions) and 600 ms or 1000 ms (i.e., macroexpressions). Forty-seven participants were asked to categorize facial expressions displayed on the scene. The results showed that recognition of fear was more accurate in negative scenes than in positive scenes, while recognition of surprise was more accurate in positive scenes than in negative scenes. Nevertheless, the exposure time of facial expression did not impact the effect of emotional scenes. Therefore, this study indicates that the perception of both microexpressions and macroexpressions of fear and surprise are influenced by emotional scenes, and the minimal condition under which the effect of emotional scenes manifests is 120 ms of exposure.

Keywords: Emotional Scene · Facial Expression · Microexpressions · Exposure Time

1 Introduction

People can judge others' emotions by their facial expressions. In real life, expressions are not presented in isolation and are always in a particular context. Context information, such as natural scenes [1, 2], emotional body postures [3, 4], emotional sentences [5, 6], and other facial expressions [7, 8], could affect human recognition of target expressions [9, 10]. The majority of studies used natural scenes as context and suggested that the

© The Author(s), under exclusive license to Springer Nature Switzerland AG 2024
C. Stephanidis et al. (Eds.): HCII 2024, CCIS 2114, pp. 319–330, 2024.
https://doi.org/10.1007/978-3-031-61932-8_37

emotions of surrounding scenes influence the discrimination of expressions, that is, the emotional consistency effect, although the findings were not consistent. For example, Righart and de Gelder [11] asked participants to identify facial expressions that were positioned centrally on emotional scenes simultaneously for 200 ms. They found that happy faces were recognized faster in happy and neutral scenes than in fearful scenes. However, there was no significant difference in the reaction time of fearful expression in different scenes. Righart and de Gelder [2] used the same task and found that the recognition accuracy of disgust expressions was greater in disgusting and happy scenes than in fearful scenes. The recognition accuracy of fearful expressions was greater in fearful and happy scenes than in disgusting scenes, while the recognition accuracy of happy faces was greater in happy scenes than in fearful scenes. When the task load was increased, the recognition accuracy of facial expressions of disgust was greater in disgusting scenes than in fearful and happy scenes; however, the recognition accuracy of happiness and fear was not impacted by scenes. Milanak and Berenbaum [12] varied the intensity level of four types of facial expressions and included four categories of emotional scenes (happy, sad, fear, and disgust). All facial expressions except happy were more accurately recognized when the emotions of the face and context were congruent and less accurately recognized when they were incongruent. Xu et al. [13] presented emotional scenes and facial expressions for 300 ms and found that happy faces were recognized faster in positive scenes than in negative scenes, while fearful expressions were recognized faster in fearful scenes than in positive scenes. However, the emotional scenes did not impact the recognition accuracy of expressions.

Some studies have also adopted event-related potentials (ERPs) to investigate the neural mechanisms for the influence of emotional scenes on face processing. Fearful and neutral faces induced larger N170 amplitudes in fearful scenes than in neutral scenes [14]. Moreover, fearful and happy faces induced larger N170 amplitudes in fearful than in happy and neutral scenes [11]. A recent study [15] revealed that for both high-intensity fear expressions and low-intensity fear expressions, the N170 amplitudes were greater when faces appeared in neutral scenes compared with happy and fearful scenes, suggesting that facial expressions and emotional contexts are integrated during the early processing stage. In contrast, Xu et al. [13] did not observe an influence of scenes on N170 amplitudes but found that happy faces induced larger LPP amplitudes in positive than negative scenes, and fearful faces induced larger LPP amplitudes in negative than positive scenes.

The controversies in behavioral results and ERP results in the above studies may be because of the difference in exposure time and categories of facial expressions. Previous research only tested the influence of emotional scenes on facial expressions that were presented for greater than 200 ms. However, the effect of emotional scenes on the perception of facial expressions that were presented for less than 200 ms is not clear. Shen et al. [16] classified facial expressions presented for longer than 200 ms as macroexpressions, whereas facial expressions that are displayed for shorter than 200 ms should be classified as microexpressions [17]. Microexpressions are more difficult to recognize than macroexpressions [16]. Other researchers have suggested that microexpressions are facial expressions that usually last from 1/25 s to 1/5 s, revealing the real emotions that individuals are trying to conceal [18, 19]. The primary aim of the current study is to investigate whether the effect of emotional scenes on the perception of marcoexpressions is different from that on the perception of microexpressions.

Moreover, Righart and de Gelder [2] found that the effect of emotional scenes on the classification of facial expressions was related to the diversity of facial expressions. Most studies included two, three or four categories of facial expressions [2, 11–13] except for surprise faces. Surprise is emotionally ambiguous and can be easily mistaken as fear [20–23]. To the best of our knowledge, it remains unclear how emotional scenes influence the recognition of facial expressions if the diversity of facial expressions is increased and ambiguous facial expressions are included. The present study used six basic expressions (happy, disgust, anger, fear, surprise, sad) to avoid potential ceiling effects from easy face affect recognition (as suggested by Milanak and Berenbaum [12]). Positive and negative emotional scenes were used to explore whether the valence of context impacted the categorization of facial expressions presented for different levels of exposure time.

In sum, the objective of the present study is to investigate the role of exposure time and the effect of emotional scenes on the perception of facial expressions. We adopted the Micro Expression Training Tool (METT) paradigm [17, 24], in which facial expressions were presented for 4 durations, including 120 ms or 200 ms (i.e., microexpressions) and 600 ms or 1000 ms (i.e., macroexpressions) with the accompanying emotional scenes, while they were forward and backward masked with the neural face of the same model. The first hypothesis is that the effect of emotional scenes on microexpressions would be weaker than that for macroexpressions since microexpressions were presented more briefly and were more difficult to recognize than macroexpressions [16]. To test this hypothesis, we predicted a three-way interaction between the valence of the scene, exposure time, and facial expressions. Moreover, according to the emotional consistency effect [2, 11], the classification of facial expressions would be more accurate when the emotional valence of the face was congruent with the valence of the scene, as opposed to when it was incongruent. The ambiguous facial expression (surprise) would also be influenced by the emotional scene.

2 Materials and Methods

2.1 Participants

MorePower software was used to estimate the sample size for the $2 \times 4 \times 6$ within-subjects design. To induce a moderate effect with $\eta_p^2 = 0.06$, a sample size of at least 42 participants was required at $\alpha = 0.05$ with 0.80 statistical power [25]. To prevent possible loss of participants, 47 undergraduate students were recruited. The data of one participant was excluded because of a technical error. The main analysis consisted of 46 participants (30 females, $M_{age} = 21.5$, $SD_{age} = 5.60$). All participants reported physical and mental health, with normal or corrected-to-normal vision and no color weakness or color blindness. They all signed informed consent before the experiment. The experiment was approved by the ethics committee of Liaoning Normal University.

2.2 Materials

Fifty-six facial expressions were selected from the NimStim face set [26] for the formal experiment, including 7 categories of facial expressions (happy, disgust, anger, fear, surprise, sad, neutral) photographed by 8 models. We used the 31 scenes (consisting of 10 negative pictures, 10 neutral pictures and 11 positive pictures) in Cui et al. [27]. These scenes were originally selected from the International Affective Picture System (IAPS) [28]. Twenty-one participants (18 females, $M_{age} = 20.14$, $SD_{age} = 1.27$) who did not participate in the formal experiment were recruited to rate the emotional valence and arousal of scenes with the SAM scale (Self-Assessment Manikin) [29]. They were asked to click the corresponding number with the mouse button based on their gut feelings about the scene on a 9-point Likert scale (valence: 1 = most unpleasant, 5 = neutral, 9 = most pleasant; arousal: 1 = the least awake or the least excited, 5 = neutral, 9 = the most awake or the most excited. From 1 to 9, the degree of valence and arousal increases gradually).

The mean valence rating and arousal rating of each scene were calculated according to the average scores of the participants. We selected 8 scenes with the highest valence ratings and 8 scenes with the lowest valence ratings for the formal experiment. Two separate one-way ANOVAs were performed on the valence ratings and arousal ratings. The valence of the positive scenes ($M = 7.08$, $SD = 0.46$) was greater than that of the negative scenes ($M = 2.38$, $SD = 0.30$), $F(1, 14) = 587.51$, $p < 0.01$, $\eta_p^2 = 0.98$. The arousal of the negative scenes ($M = 6.91$, $SD = 0.24$) was greater than that of positive scenes ($M = 5.86$, $SD = 0.35$), $F(1, 14) = 48.60$, $p < 0.001$, $\eta_p^2 = 0.776$.

We used Photoshop 8.0 to position the facial expressions in the center of the scenes. The faces did not cover critical parts of the scenes. Each facial expression was combined with both a positive scene and a negative scene. A total of 112 compound pictures were generated. The facial expressions were presented at a visual angle of $5.3° \times 6.3°$, and the scenes were presented at a visual angle of $29.1° \times 21.7°$.

2.3 Design

A 2 (scene: positive, negative) × 4 (exposure time: 120 ms, 200 ms, 600 ms, 1000 ms) × 6 (facial expressions: happy, disgust, anger, fear, surprise, sad) within-subjects design was employed. The dependent variable was the recognition accuracy of facial expressions.

2.4 Procedure

The experimental paradigm was programmed using E-Prime 2.0 (Psychology Software Tools, Inc., 2007) and operated using an HP280 Pro G2 MT computer. The stimuli were presented on a Lenovo 17-in. monitor (the resolution was 1440 × 900, with a refresh rate of 60 Hz). The participants were comfortably seated in a chair, with a viewing distance of approximately 57 cm from the screen.

We adopted the same METT paradigm from Zhao et al. [17]. There were 12 practice trials before the formal experiment for the participants to become familiar with the task. The facial expressions and scenes in the practice trials were not shown in the formal experiment. The participants started a trial by pressing the space bar. In the beginning, a neutral expression was presented in the center of a scene for 2,000 ms. Afterward, the neutral expression was replaced by one of the six basic expressions for 120 ms, 200 ms, 600 ms or 1,000 ms. Then, the neutral facial expression was presented again for 2,000 ms. Immediately afterward, the participants were asked to identify which expression was transiently displayed on the scene by selecting among the six emotional labels (happy, disgust, anger, fear, surprise, sad) with the mouse with no time constraints. There were 48 images of target facial expressions. Each facial expression was presented twice for each level of exposure time, once on a positive scene and once on a negative scene. The formal experiment consisted of 384 trials that were presented in randomized order. The participants rested for 30 s after finishing every 48 trials. The experimental procedure is shown in Fig. 1.

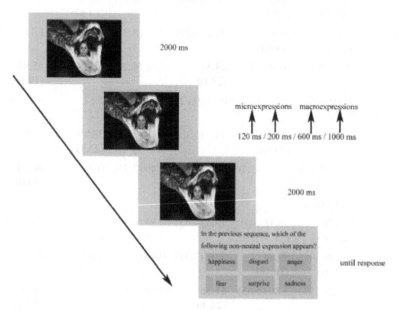

Fig. 1. Schematic of a single trial in the facial expression categorization task.

3 Results

A 2 (scene: positive and negative) × 4 (exposure time: 120 ms, 200 ms, 600 ms and 1,000 ms) × 6 (facial expressions: happy, disgust, anger, fear, surprise, sad) repeated-measures ANOVA was conducted on the recognition accuracy of facial expressions. All pairwise comparisons were Bonferroni corrected (p-values are reported). Greenhouse–Geisser corrections were applied to correct p-values and η_p^2 (uncorrected dfs were reported) for the violation of the sphericity assumption. The mean percentage of recognition of each facial expression is shown in Table 1.

Table 1. Percentages of correct and erroneous recognitions of six basic facial expressions (M ± SD) across four levels of exposure time. Bold numbers refer to correct identifications of facial expressions, and numbers in standard font are percentages of errors.

True Type	Categorized Type					
	Anger	Disgust	Fear	Happy	Sad	Surprise
	120 ms					
Anger	**35.60 (21.69)**	46.60 (22.70)	1.77 (3.88)	0.95 (2.27)	11.14 (10.37)	3.94 (7.02)
Disgust	20.25 (17.19)	**57.61 (19.94)**	8.02 (6.27)	0.14 (0.92)	7.88 (9.36)	6.11 (7.28)
Fear	1.63 (4.65)	6.39 (7.85)	**43.34 (23.10)**	2.58 (4.29)	0.68 (1.97)	45.38 (19.25)
Happy	0.68 (3.01)	1.77 (3.14)	0.14 (0.92)	**93.34 (15.67)**	2.17 (12.02)	1.90 (4.54)
Sad	5.03 (6.92)	45.38 (24.98)	4.48 (5.38)	0.95 (2.94)	**38.99 (23.91)**	5.16 (6.08)
Surprise	0.54 (2.22)	2.31 (4.24)	9.51 (12.06)	1.49 (2.70)	0 (0)	**86.14 (14.06)**
	200 ms					
Anger	**47.28 (22.69)**	38.18 (21.34)	1.63 (4.65)	0.14 (0.92)	9.78 (11.31)	2.99 (7.06)
Disgust	16.98 (13.09)	**59.24 (16.18)**	8.97 (7.41)	0.14 (0.92)	8.56 (10.97)	6.11 (7.28)
Fear	1.22 (3.87)	3.80 (6.65)	**51.36 (24.36)**	1.36 (2.92)	1.22 (3.64)	41.03 (20.40)
Happy	0.27 (1.29)	1.63 (4.46)	0 (0)	**95.38 (13.72)**	1.22 (6.54)	1.49 (4.41)
Sad	2.99 (4.88)	44.97 (22.73)	4.48 (6.80)	0.27 (1.84)	**43.07 (21.74)**	4.21 (6.19)
Surprise	0.41 (1.56)	1.63 (3.34)	11.14 (15.36)	1.09 (2.73)	0.68 (2.37)	**85.05 (16.27)**
	600 ms					
Anger	**58.29 (23.13)**	31.39 (21.43)	0.68 (1.97)	0.27 (1.29)	8.29 (11.34)	1.09 (2.73)
Disgust	14.67 (12.45)	**64.27 (17.76)**	9.78 (8.30)	0 (0)	8.56 (8.97)	2.72 (5.99)
Fear	0.54 (2.22)	3.67 (6.12)	**69.57 (19.44)**	0 (0)	1.22 (3.39)	25.0 (16.87)

(*continued*)

Table 1. (*continued*)

True Type	Categorized Type					
	Anger	Disgust	Fear	Happy	Sad	Surprise
Happy	0 (0)	0.41 (1.56)	0.27 (1.29)	**98.91 (2.73)**	0.41 (1.56)	0 (0)
Sad	2.85 (6.55)	37.23 (19.50)	5.43 (7.75)	0 (0)	**50.68 (17.79)**	3.80 (6.25)
Surprise	0 (0)	0.68 (2.37)	15.76 (18.34)	2.45 (4.46)	0.54 (2.89)	**80.57 (18.50)**
	1000 ms					
Anger	**59.78 (22.54)**	28.80 (18.93)	1.90 (4.73)	0.14 (0.92)	6.66 (7.62)	2.72 (5.21)
Disgust	13.45 (12.97)	**64.40 (19.36)**	8.97 (9.92)	0 (0)	10.05 (10.16)	3.13 (5.06)
Fear	0.27 (1.29)	2.72 (4.30)	**72.96 (19.59)**	0.27 (1.29)	0.95 (3.22)	22.83 (17.69)
Happy	0.14 (0.92)	0.41 (2.04)	0.27 (1.29)	**98.37 (4.46)**	0.27 (1.29)	0.54 (1.78)
Sad	0.95 (3.48)	33.97 (20.78)	7.07 (8.08)	0 (0)	**53.94 (20.97)**	4.08 (5.92)
Surprise	0.41 (1.56)	0.95 (2.62)	18.07 (19.60)	1.63 (3.34)	0 (0)	**78.94 (19.65)**

The main effect of scene was not significant, $F(1, 45) = 0.92, p = 0.34$. The interaction between exposure time and scene was not significant, $F(3, 135) = 1.46, p = 0.23$. The main effect of facial expressions was significant, $F(5, 225) = 76.38, p < 0.01, \eta_p^2 = 0.63$. The main effect of exposure time was significant, $F(3, 135) = 81.59, p < 0.01, \eta_p^2 = 0.65$. However, the three-way interaction between exposure time, scene, and facial expressions was not significant, $F(15, 675) = 1.04, p = 0.41$. The interaction between facial expressions and exposure time was significant, $F(15, 675) = 15.66, p < 0.01, \eta_p^2 = 0.26$. The interaction between facial expressions and scene was also significant, $F(5, 225) = 5.16, p < 0.01, \eta_p^2 = 0.10$.

3.1 Analysis of the Interaction Between Facial Expressions and Exposure Time

The simple main effect of exposure time on the recognition accuracy of anger was significant, $F(3, 135) = 57.547, p < 0.001, \eta_p^2 = 0.561$. Pairwise comparisons revealed that the recognition accuracy at the 120-ms exposure was lower than that at the 200-ms exposure, 95% CI [−0.174, −0.060], 600-ms exposure, 95% CI [−0.291, −0.162], and 1000-ms exposure, 95% CI [−0.308, −0.176], $ps < 0.001$. The recognition accuracy at the 200-ms exposure was lower than that at the 600-ms exposure, 95% CI [−0.168, −0.052], and 1000-ms exposure, 95% CI [−0.174, −0.076], $ps < 0.001$. The accuracies stabilized at the 600-ms exposure, and no significant changes were observed for the increase to 1000-ms exposure, $p = 1.000$.

The simple main effect of exposure time on the recognition accuracy of fear was significant, $F(3, 135) = 56.293, p < 0.001, \eta_p^2 = 0.556$. Pairwise comparisons revealed that recognition accuracy at the 120-ms exposure was lower than that at the 200-ms exposure, $p = 0.004$, 95% CI [−0.141, −0.020], 600-ms exposure, 95% CI [−0.352, −0.173], and 1000-ms exposure, 95% CI [−0.375, −0.218], $ps < 0.001$. The recognition accuracy at 200-ms exposure was lower than that at 600-ms exposure, 95% CI [−0.265, −0.099], and 1000-ms exposure, 95% CI [−0.293, −0.139], $ps < 0.001$. The accuracies stabilized at the 600-ms exposure, and no significant changes were observed for the increase to 1000-ms exposure, $p = 0.347$.

The simple main effect of exposure time on recognition accuracy of sad was significant, $F(3, 135) = 18.391, p < 0.001, \eta_p^2 = 0.29$. Pairwise comparisons revealed that the recognition accuracy at the 120-ms exposure was lower than that at the 600-ms exposure, 95% CI [−0.183, −0.051], and 1000-ms exposure, 95% CI [−0.225, −0.074], $ps < 0.001$. The recognition accuracy at the 200-ms exposure was lower than that at the 600-ms exposure, $p = 0.005$, 95% CI [−0.135, −0.017], and 1000-ms exposure, $p < 0.001$, 95% CI [−0.174, −0.043]. There was no significant difference between the recognition accuracies at 600-ms and 1000-ms exposures, $p = 0.469$, nor between the recognition accuracies at 120-ms and 200-ms exposures, $p = 0.274$.

The simple main effect of exposure time on the recognition accuracy of disgust was significant, $F(3, 135) = 4.215, p = 0.015, \eta_p^2 = 0.086$. However, pairwise comparisons showed that no significant changes were observed for the increase from 120-ms exposure to 1000-ms exposure, $ps > 0.13$.

The simple main effect of exposure time on the recognition accuracy of happy was significant, $F(3, 135) = 3.832, p = 0.041, \eta_p^2 = 0.078$. Nevertheless, pairwise comparisons showed that no significant changes were observed for the increase from 120-ms exposure to 1000-ms exposure, $ps > 0.12$.

The simple main effect of exposure time on recognition accuracy of surprise was significant, $F(3, 135) = 4.682, p = 0.008, \eta_p^2 = 0.094$. However, pairwise comparisons showed that no significant changes were observed for the increase from 120-ms exposure to 1000-ms exposure, $ps > 0.07$.

3.2 Analysis of the Interaction Between Emotional Scenes and Facial Expressions

Paired-sample t tests revealed that fear faces were more accurately recognized in negative scenes than in positive scenes, $t(45) = 3.79, p < 0.01$. In addition, the surprise faces were more accurately recognized in positive scenes than in negative scenes, $t(45) = 2.50, p = 0.02$. The recognition accuracies of angry, happy, sad, and disgust faces in scenes of congruent valence were not different from those in scenes of incongruent valence, $ts < 0.95, ps > 0.35$. The recognition accuracy of facial expressions in different emotional scenes is shown in Fig. 2.

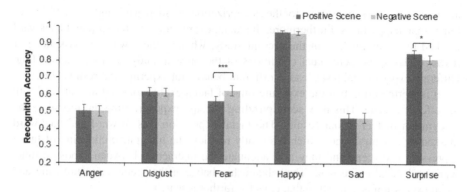

Fig. 2. The recognition accuracy was estimated as the proportion of correct classifications as a function of different emotional scenes for six basic facial expressions. Standard errors of the means are represented by error bars. * $p < 0.05$, *** $p < 0.001$.

4   Discussion

Previous studies have shown that the emotions of surrounding scenes influence the recognition of facial expressions at 200 ms of exposure or longer exposures [2, 11–13]. The present study manipulated the exposure time of target facial expressions to compare the effect of emotional scenes on the recognition of microexpressions and macroexpressions and investigate the minimal condition for the scene effect to occur. Our findings suggest that emotional scenes influence the categorization performance of fear and surprise even at the shortest exposure of 120 ms.

Consistent with previous research [2, 11, 12], the results showed that the recognition of fear faces was more accurate in negative scenes than in positive scenes. Moreover, the surprise faces were identified more accurately in positive scenes than in negative scenes. Surprise and fear expressions have some similar characteristics (wide-eyed), and it is not easy to distinguish these two expressions [20–23]. Therefore, surprise and fear are harder to identify than other expressions. People rely more on the information in the corresponding emotional scenes to categorize surprise and fear. Fear is a negative expression and is easier to identify in negative scenes, confirming an emotional consistency effect [2, 11]. In contrast, since surprise expresses neither explicitly positive nor negative emotion, the recognition of surprise is more likely to be influenced by emotional scenes [30]. Some studies have found that surprise conveys more positive valence than fear [23, 31]. This may help explain why the recognition accuracy of surprise was greater in positive scenes than in negative scenes.

However, there is no effect of emotional scenes on the recognition of happiness, anger, sadness and disgust. It is possible that the participants were asked to identify more categories of emotions in our study (6 basic expressions) than in previous studies (2, 3 or 4 basic expressions). Therefore, the task of this study was more difficult. Righart and de Gelder [2] also found that the emotional consistency effect became weaker when perceptual load increased; that is, the recognition performance of happy and fearful faces was not affected by emotional scenes. Moreover, Milanak and Berenbaum [12] observed an emotional consistency effect for the categorization of sad, fearful, and disgustful faces rather than happy faces. Furthermore, the facial expression was forward and backward masked by a neutral face in the present study, whereas there was no mask in prior research. Thus, the perceptual conditions of the present study are more demanding. Different experimental tasks lead to different behavioral experimental results [11].

It is worth noting that the exposure time of facial expressions did not interact with the effect of scene. This may seem puzzling because exposure time did modulate the recognition of fear in our results. The facial expression was forward and backward masked by a neutral face, which efficiently restricts the integrative encoding of facial expression and scene and may also attenuate the interaction between exposure time, scene and facial expression. The relationship between the scene, exposure time and facial expression is a question that calls for further research.

5 Conclusions

In sum, the current research demonstrates that as minimal an exposure time as 120 ms is sufficient for emotional scenes to influence perception of fear and surprise faces. Recognition of fear was more accurate in negative scenes than in positive scenes, whereas recognition of surprise was more accurate in positive scenes than in negative scenes irrespective of exposure time of the target emotion. Nonetheless, there is no scene effect on the perception of happy, angry, sad and disgustful faces.

Acknowledgments. This research was funded by Social Science Application Research Boutique Engineering Project of Jiangsu Province (23SYB-112), Humanities and Social Sciences Research Project of the Ministry of Education (23YJAZH119), the National Natural Science Foundation of China (31400869), Start-up Research Fund of Southeast University (RF1028623132), and the research funds for ideological and political education in postgraduate courses of Southeast University (yjgkcsz2229).

Disclosure of Interests. The authors have no competing interests to declare that are relevant to the content of this article.

References

1. Barrett, L.F., Kensinger, E.A.: Context is routinely encoded during emotion perception. Psychol. Sci. **21**(4), 595–599 (2010)
2. Righart, R., de Gelder, B.: Recognition of facial expressions is influenced by emotional scene gist. Cogn. Affect. Behav. Neurosci. **8**(3), 264–272 (2008)
3. Aviezer, H., Dudarev, V., Bentin, S., Hassin, R.R.: The automaticity of emotional face-context integration. Emotion **11**(6), 1406–1414 (2011)
4. Noh, S.R., Isaacowitz, D.M.: Emotional faces in context: age differences in recognition accuracy and scanning patterns. Emotion **13**(2), 238–249 (2013)
5. Aguado, L., Dieguez-Risco, T., Villalba-García, C., Hinojosa, J.A.: Double-checking emotions: valence and emotion category in contextual integration of facial expressions of emotion. Biol. Psychol. **146**, 107723 (2019)

6. Wieser, M.J., Gerdes, A.B., Büngel, I., Schwarz, K.A., Mühlberger, A., Pauli, P.: Not so harmless anymore: how context impacts the perception and electrocortical processing of neutral faces. Neuroimage **92**, 74–82 (2014)
7. Masuda, T., Ellsworth, P.C., Mesquita, B., Leu, J., Tanida, S., De Veerdonk, E.V.: Placing the face in context: cultural differences in the perception of facial emotion. J. Pers. Soc. Psychol. **94**(3), 365–381 (2008)
8. Mumenthaler, C., Sander, D.: Social appraisal influences recognition of emotions. J. Pers. Soc. Psychol. **102**(6), 1118–1135 (2012)
9. Barrett, L.F., Mesquita, B., Gendron, M.: Context in emotion perception. Curr. Dir. Psychol. Sci. **20**(5), 286–290 (2011)
10. Hassin, R.R., Aviezer, H., Bentin, S.: Inherently ambiguous: facial expressions of emotions, in context. Emot. Rev. **5**(1), 60–65 (2013)
11. Righart, R., de Gelder, B.: Rapid influence of emotional scenes on encoding of facial expressions: an ERP study. Soc. Cogn. Affect. Neurosci. **3**(3), 270–278 (2008)
12. Milanak, M.E., Berenbaum, H.: The effects of context on facial affect recognition. Motiv. Emot. **38**, 560–568 (2014)
13. Xu, Q., Yang, Y., Tan, Q., Zhang, L.: Facial expressions in context: electrophysiological correlates of the emotional congruency of facial expressions and background scenes. Front. Psychol. **8**, 2175 (2017)
14. Righart, R., de Gelder, B.: Context influences early perceptual analysis of faces-an electro-physiological study. Cereb. Cortex **16**, 1249–1257 (2006)
15. Song, S., Wu, M., Feng, C.: Early influence of emotional scenes on the encoding of fearful expressions with different intensities: an event-related potential study. Front. Hum. Neurosci. **16**, 866253 (2022)
16. Shen, X., Wu, Q., Fu, X.: Effects of the duration of expressions on the recognition of microexpressions. J. Zhejiang Univ. Sci. B (Biomed. Biotechnol.) **13**(3), 221–230 (2012)
17. Zhao, M., Zimmer, H.D., Shen, X., Chen, W., Fu, X.: Exploring the cognitive processes causing the age-related categorization deficit in the recognition of facial expressions. Exp. Aging Res. **42**, 348–364 (2016)
18. Ekman, P., Friesen, W.V.: Nonverbal leakage and clues to deception. Psychiatry **32**, 88–106 (1969)
19. Wu, Q., Xie, Y., Liu, X., Liu, Y.: Oxytocin impairs the recognition of micro-expressions of surprise and disgust. Front. Psychol. **8**, 2175 (2022)
20. Kim, H., Somerville, L.H., Johnstone, T., Alexander, A.L., Whalen, P.J.: Inverse amygdala and medial prefrontal cortex responses to surprised faces. NeuroReport **14**(18), 2317–2322 (2003)
21. Kim, H., et al.: Contextual modulation of amygdala responsivity to surprised faces. J. Cogn. Neurosci. **16**(10), 1730–1745 (2004)
22. Song, S., et al.: The effect of mouth-opening on recognition of facial expressions in the NimStim Set: an evaluation from Chinese college students. J. Nonverbal Behav. **47**, 5–18 (2023)
23. Zhao, K., Zhao, J., Zhang, M., Cui, Q., Fu, X.: Neural responses to rapid facial expressions of fear and surprise. Front. Psychol. **8**, 761 (2017)
24. Ekman, P.: MicroExpression Training Tool (METT). University of California, San Francisco (2002)
25. Campbell, J.I.D., Thompson, V.A.: MorePower 6.0 for ANOVA with relational confidence intervals and Bayesian analysis. Behav. Res. Methods **44**, 1255–1265 (2012)
26. Tottenham, N., et al.: The NimStim set of facial expressions: judgments from untrained research participants. Psychiatry Res. **168**(3), 242–249 (2009)
27. Cui, Q., Zhao, K., Chen, Y., Zheng, W., Fu, X.: Opposing subjective temporal experiences in response to unpredictable and predictable fear-relevant stimuli. Front. Psychol. **9**, 360 (2018)

28. Lang, P.J., Bradley, M.M., Cuthbert, B.: International affective picture system (IAPS): instruction manual and affective ratings. Technical report A-8. FL: University of Florida, Gainesville (2008)

29. Bradley, M.M., Lang, P.J.: Measuring emotion: the self-assessment manikin and the semantic differential. J. Behav. Ther. Exp. Psychiatry 25(1), 49–59 (1994)

30. Li, S., Zhu, X., Ding, R., Ren, J., Luo, W.: The effect of emotional and self-referential contexts on ERP responses towards surprised faces. Biol. Psychol. 146, 107728 (2019)

31. Vrticka, P., Lordier, L., Bediou, B., Sander, D.: Human amygdala response to dynamic facial expressions of positive and negative surprise. Emotion 14(1), 161–169 (2014)

Enhancing Emotional Induction in Virtual Reality: Innovative Fusion of Speech and Realistic Non-Verbal Emotional Expression

Wen Wei, Xinyu Zhang, and Shiguang Ni[✉]

International Graduate School at Shenzhen, Tsinghua University, Shenzhen, China
ni.shiguang@sz.tsinghua.edu.cn

Abstract. Virtual reality (VR) provides an unparalleled platform for exploring the intricate interplay between non-verbal and verbal cues in emotion induction. However, the efficient implementation of non-verbal expressions in VR has often been hindered by a lack of rapid and realistic execution. In this paper, we address this gap by introducing an innovative processing pipeline that seamlessly integrates non-verbal cues to enhance the emotional impact of VR experiences. A novel processing pipeline was employed for non-verbal expression, utilizing a text-dictionary matching approach for body movements and audio-driven lip synchronization for realistic lip movements. Additionally, facial expressions were analyzed at the sentence level using GPT-generated prompts for sentiment analysis. Our experiment comprised two distinct groups: the Speech Group and the Speech+Motion Group, where participants not only heard the negative emotional speech but also witnessed corresponding virtual characters displaying synchronized body movements and facial expressions. Both groups exhibited adverse effects on positive emotions. Negative emotion induction in the Speech+Motion Group surpassed that of the Speech Group, particularly in the dimension of anger, reaching a statistically significant difference. Our findings underscore the impact of multimodal stimuli on emotional experiences in VR and introduce a processing pipeline that enables rapid and realistic integration of non-verbal cues.

Keywords: Non-Verbal Emotional Expression · Virtual Reality · Novel Processing Pipeline

1 Introduction

When humans interact with others, they utilize a plethora of implicit mechanisms beyond language to convey information about their emotions and states. These mechanisms, collectively known as non-verbal communication [1], are manifested through various channels of the body. Emotions play a pivotal role in human communication, serving as the foundation of interpersonal relationships and offering insights into our internal states [2]. Many psychological disorders, such as depression, are characterized by frequent and intense negative emotions [3]. Consequently, emotional induction significantly correlates with the therapeutic process and outcome across various psychotherapy modalities [4].

© The Author(s), under exclusive license to Springer Nature Switzerland AG 2024
C. Stephanidis et al. (Eds.): HCII 2024, CCIS 2114, pp. 331–337, 2024.
https://doi.org/10.1007/978-3-031-61932-8_38

The field of virtual reality (VR) offers a convenient platform for exploring the impact of both verbal and non-verbal elements on emotion induction [5]. However, non-verbal expressions in VR often lack swift and realistic execution [6]. Thus, developing an efficient processing pipeline for non-verbal expressions is crucial for enhancing the emotional experience in VR environments.

This paper aims to introduce our innovative processing pipeline to address this gap and presents experiments to validate its effectiveness. Initially, we will discuss the construction of VR scenes and emotionally induced language scripts for the experiments. Subsequently, the paper will delve into how this processing pipeline manages non-verbal expressions, with a particular focus on lip animation, facial expressions, and body animation. Finally, the experimental results of this processing pipeline on subjects' emotional induction will be presented, followed by a discussion on the methodology employed.

2   Materials and Methods

2.1   Participants and Experimental Procedures

We recruited 20 subjects (6 females and 14 males) between the ages of 22 and 27 years (M = 24.4, SD = 1.43) to rate virtual reality emotion-evoking scenarios. Subjects were required to complete the following two questionnaires to obtain baseline emotion levels prior to the start of the experiment:

1. Self-Assessment Manikin (SAM) [7]: This scale uses an image-based cartoon manikin to represent basic emotional dimensions. Emotional valence ranges from 1 = "sad" to 9 = "happy," while emotional arousal ranges from 1 = "calm" to 9 = "excited.
2. Visual Analog Scale (VAS) [8]: it is a cross-sectional scale that ranges from 0 to 100 and has two verbal descriptors on each scale. The emotions to be rated by the subjects are: joy, anger, calmness, sadness, relaxation, disgust, happiness, fear, anxiety and dizziness.

Subjects were required to wear virtual reality devices in the experiment, and after completing each emotion inducing scenario, subjects rated their emotions using the SAM and the VAS, respectively. Finally, experimental data were collected and analyzed to compare differences in emotional responses between groups.

2.2   Construction of VR Scenes and Verbal Scripts

Construction of Emotionally Inducing VR Scenes. For the scene setting we chose the emotionally inducing scenario of parent-child conflict. Through qualitative interviews, it was learned that the scene of emotional conflict between parents and children was mainly the child's bedroom. Therefore, this study selected the adolescent's bedroom in virtual reality as the emotive scene.

The interaction employed in this project in the virtual reality scenario only requires the user to use handheld joystick buttons. In order to further reduce the fatigue and dizziness of the subjects in the virtual scene, the UI user interface in this project will be designed to always be at the front end of the user's entry into the emotionally evoking scene, reducing the frequency and magnitude of head movements.

Construction of Emotional Dialog Scripts. In conjunction with the pre-experimental interviews and the summarized causes of parent-child conflict, we designed two sets of dialogue scripts for the father and mother roles.

Since the audio generated by current text-to-speech technology for Chinese text with emotional tone is rather flat, it does not meet the expectation of actual emotional dialog tone. Therefore, instead of using text-to-speech (TTS) technology to convert the text into natural speech, we invited professional voice actors to record audio for the script. We edited the recordings into single-sentence clips of 3 to 10 s in length. These served as the basis for the subsequent animation of the avatars.

2.3 Non-Verbal Emotional Expression Processing Pipeline

In order to better control avatars for emotional expression, this study proposes a fusion pipeline to control the animation of avatars from three levels: lip animation, facial expression, and body animation to make it more realistic (Fig. 1).

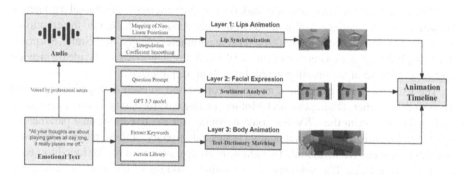

Fig. 1. Non-Verbal Emotional Expression Processing Pipeline

Lip Animation. Lip animation is driven by audio data to achieve highly realistic lip opening and closing. We pre-process the recorded audio data with noise reduction, filtering, and audio feature extraction. The audio signal is analyzed to extract relevant features, where SPL(t) represents the sound intensity at time t, P_ref is the reference sound pressure level, and the signal intensity is |x(t)|. A common mapping function that maps sound intensity to mouth opening is logarithmic mapping, where there is a logarithmic relationship between sound intensity and lip opening. This mapping can better model the nonlinear relationship between sound intensity-lip movement during human articulation. The mapping function can be expressed as:

$$M(t) = k * \log 1 + a * SPL(t) \tag{1}$$

In Eq. M(t) is the lip tension at time t, SPL(t) is the sound intensity at time t, and k and a are parameters that are adjusted according to the needs of the study. The generated mouth tensor M(t) is used in unity scenes to generate lip animation sequences, which is realized in this study using an interpolation method:

$$M(t) = a * M(t - 1) + (1 - a) * M(t) \tag{2}$$

The a in this equation is an interpolation factor used to smooth the lip animation. The lip animation sequence M(t) is synchronized with the avatar's mouth model to ensure that the avatar's mouth responds appropriately to the audio signal.

Facial Expression. In this paper, we aim to analyze the mapping scores of various sentiments through single-sentence level sentiment analysis. Previous studies have demonstrated the superior performance of GPT-related models in hybrid sentiment analysis tasks. Therefore, our approach combines the GPT3.5 model with Prompt-based Sentiment Prediction to evaluate the scores of each sentence on five sentiment dimensions: Angry, Sad, Smile, Surprise, and Thoughtful, with each score ranging from 0 to 100, indicating emotion intensity. To guide language models effectively, we employ cue engineering principles to refine input prompts. Our carefully crafted prompt is as follows:

"You are a social scientist and your task is to analyze a series of emotional parameters extracted from the text of a parent-child conflict conversation. Please rate the emotional intensity of each sentence from 0-100 on the five parameters Angry, Sad, Smile, Surprise, and Thoughtful. In cases where emotions are difficult to categorize clearly, please provide your best estimate of the emotion score. Let's think step by step".

The five emotional parameters analyzed correspond to each dialogue snippet and are stored as Father_Dialog.csv and Mother_Dialog.csv for Unity editor integration. Each audio snippet in the CSV file contains values for the five emotional parameters. Upon data loading, a script dynamically creates a dictionary of these parameters based on column names. We instantiate two emotion control scripts in the Unity editor, each assigned to a different PlayableDirector. Real-time updating of the avatar's blendshape occurs by retrieving the audio clip name currently playing in the timeline.

Body Animation. In this study, avatars perform animated actions such as Angry Point, Talking, Crazy Gesture, and Yelling, applicable to both female and male models. These actions are typically provided through skeletal animation or motion capture data, comprising keyframes and skeletal poses. We developed a text-action dictionary to correlate text fragments with corresponding actions or action sequences. This dictionary functions as an associative array, utilizing the text as a key and the corresponding action as its value. Upon receiving audio for specific text, we utilize the dictionary to trigger the appropriate action, employing conditional statements or lookup tables for implementation.

To ensure synchronization between actions and speech, we analyze keyframes and frame rates of the action data to determine the duration of each action in seconds. Timestamps are generated for each field in the audio based on corresponding fields in the text and audio. Finally, we apply the selected action sequences to the avatar model, including the manipulation of the avatar's bones and joints to reflect poses, gestures, and other body movements. This approach enhances the avatar's ability to express emotions and intentions vividly.

3   Results

A one-way analysis of variance (ANOVA) was conducted using group as the independent variable (with levels including baseline scores, speech group, and speech+motion group) on measures of emotional valence/arousal and visual analog scales. Homogeneity of variances was required for the ANOVA. The analysis revealed significant differences in emotional valence ($F(2, 57) = 14.98$, $p < 0.001$), emotional arousal ($F(2, 57) = 3.39$, $p < 0.05$), joy ($F(2, 57) = 8.08$, $p < 0.001$), anger ($F(2, 57) = 18.83$, $p < 0.001$), calmness ($F(2, 57) = 14.85$, $p < 0.001$), sadness ($F(2, 57) = 5.34$, $p < 0.01$), relaxation ($F(2, 57) = 16.48$, $p < 0.001$), happiness ($F(2, 57) = 8.63$, $p < 0.001$), and fear ($F(2, 57) = 6.81$, $p < 0.01$).

Then, we did the analysis of differences between groups by means of LSD test. In terms of emotional valence, both the speech group ($M = 3.35$, $SD = 1.60$) and the speech+motion group ($M = 3.75$, $SD = 1.65$) were significantly lower than the baseline group ($M = 5.80$, $SD = 1.28$). This indicates that the emotional induction of dialogue content in virtual reality scenes reduced participants' emotional valence, making them feel more saddened. Regarding emotional arousal, the speech+motion group ($M = 5.80$, $SD = 1.40$) was significantly higher than the baseline group ($M = 4.50$, $SD = 1.96$), while the speech group did not differ significantly from the other groups. This suggests that the speech+motion group significantly enhanced participants' arousal levels in virtual reality scenes.

In the joy, both the speech group ($M = 34.55$, $SD = 18.96$) and the speech+motion group ($M = 34.00$, $SD = 23.05$) were significantly lower than the baseline group ($M = 55.85$, $SD = 16.20$); in the calmness, both the speech group ($M = 35.85$, $SD = 18.58$) and the speech+motion group ($M = 32.45$, $SD = 15.96$) were both significantly lower than the baseline group ($M = 61.15$, $SD = 19.83$); in the relaxation, both the speech group ($M = 35.60$, $SD = 19.60$) and the speech+motion group ($M = 28.00$, $SD = 19.54$) were significantly lower than the baseline group ($M = 61.55$, $SD = 19.00$); and in the happiness, the speech group ($M = 33.70$, $SD = 21.43$) and speech+motion groups ($M = 34.30$, $SD = 22.27$) were both significantly lower than the baseline group ($M = 58.70$, $SD = 21.42$). The above results indicate that both the speech group and the speech+motion group were successful in reducing the subjects' positive emotions (Fig. 2).

In the anger, both the speech group ($M = 42.25$, $SD = 23.00$) and the speech+motion group ($M = 58.00$, $SD = 20.63$) were significantly higher than the baseline group ($M = 16.40$, $SD = 21.23$) and the speech+motion group was significantly higher than the speech group in the anger score; in the sadness, only the speech+motion group ($M = 52.95$, $SD = 29.85$) was significantly higher than the baseline group ($M = 26.25$, $SD = 23.08$); and in the fear, both the speech group ($M = 35.80$, $SD = 26.23$) and the speech+motion group ($M = 46.50$, $SD = 31.59$) were significantly higher than the baseline group ($M = 15.35$, $SD = 22.82$). The above results suggest that the speech+motion group was more effective than the speech-only group on negative emotion elicitation, especially in anger and sadness emotions (Fig. 3).

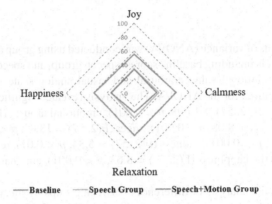

Fig. 2. Average Positive Emotion Scores Comparison Across Three Groups

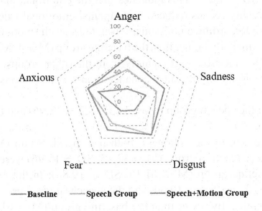

Fig. 3. Average Negative Emotion Scores Comparison Across Three Groups

4 Conclusions and Future Work

The findings corroborate the significance of integrating non-verbal cues into VR environments to evoke authentic emotional responses. By effectively simulating anger in the parent-child conflict scenario, our processing pipeline demonstrates its potential to create immersive and emotionally engaging VR simulations. This highlights the importance of considering the nuanced interplay between verbal and non-verbal elements in designing emotionally compelling VR experiences [9].

Moving forward, further exploration is warranted to refine and expand upon the capabilities of our processing pipeline. Furthermore, exploring real-time adaptation algorithms to dynamically adjust emotional cues based on user feedback and physiological signals holds promise for creating more personalized and immersive VR experiences [10]. Overall, continued advancements in understanding and harnessing the potential of multimodal stimuli in VR have the potential to revolutionize the landscape of immersive storytelling and therapeutic applications.

Funding Information. This study was funded by Shenzhen R & D sustainable development funding (KCXFZ20230731093600002), Guangdong Digital Mental Health and Intelligent Generation Laboratory (Grant No. 2023WSYS010), the Shenzhen Key Research Base of Humanities and Social Sciences (Grant No. 202003).

References

1. Brooks, A.G., Arkin, R.C.: Behavioral overlays for non-verbal communication expression on a humanoid robot. Auton. Robot. **22**(1), 55–74 (2007)
2. Zhang, Y., Chen, Z.J., Ni, S.: The security of being grateful: gratitude promotes risk aversion in decision-making. J. Posit. Psychol. **15**(3), 285–291 (2020)
3. Cassiello-Robbins, C., Barlow, D.H.: Anger: the unrecognized emotion in emotional disorders. Clin. Psychol. Sci. Pract. **23**(1), 66 (2016)
4. Terhürne, P., et al.: Validation and application of the non-verbal behavior analyzer: an automated tool to assess non-verbal emotional expressions in psychotherapy. Front. Psych. **13**, 1026015 (2022)
5. Bönsch, A., Radke, S., Ehret, J., Habel, U., Kuhlen, T.W.: The impact of a virtual agent's non-verbal emotional expression on a user's personal space preferences. In: Proceedings of the 20th ACM International Conference on Intelligent Virtual Agents, pp. 1–8. ACM, New York (2020)
6. Maloney, D., Freeman, G., Wohn, D.Y.: "Talking without a Voice" understanding non-verbal communication in social virtual reality. In: Proceedings of the ACM on Human-Computer Interaction, vol. 4(CSCW2), pp. 1–25 (2020)
7. Bradley, M.M., Lang, P.J.: Measuring emotion: the self-assessment manikin and the semantic differential. J. Behav. Ther. Exp. Psychiatry **25**(1), 49–59 (1994)
8. Tabbaa, L., et al.: Vreed: Virtual reality emotion recognition dataset using eye tracking & physiological measures. Proc. ACM Interact. Mobile, Wearable Ubiquitous Technol. **5**(4), 1–20 (2021)
9. Etienne, E., Leclercq, A.L., Remacle, A., Dessart, L., Schyns, M.: Perception of avatars nonverbal behaviors in virtual reality. Psychol. Mark. **40**(11), 2464–2481 (2023)
10. Elor, A., Kurniawan, S.: The ultimate display for physical rehabilitation: a bridging review on immersive virtual reality. Front. Virtual Reality **1**, 585993 (2020)

Human Robot Interaction

Using Virtual Reality Simulations in Safety-Critical Human Computer Interaction

Stefan Friesen[✉], Jan-Torsten Milde, Rainer Blum, Tabea Runzheimer,
Sven Milde, and Kerstin Geis

Department of Applied Computer Science, Fulda University of Applied Sciences,
Fulda, Germany
{stefan.friesen,torsten.milde,rainer.blum,tabea.runzheimer,
sven.milde,kerstin.geis}@cs.hs-fulda.de
https://www.hs-fulda.de/

Abstract. Virtual reality (VR) simulations have proven to be a crucial tool in offering a safe environment to test interactions between robots and human subjects in experiments. This paper describes the design and cration of such a VR simulation as part of the development of the CityBot, a self-driving modular vehicle with an interactive avatar that supports gesture and speech control. When such robotic systems are at an early stage of development they would pose a security risk if tested with human subjects in reality. To simulate gesture and speech control and gain an understanding of the users' hand movements and usage of speech in a safe manner, we decided to implement a VR simulation. A central technical requirement was to utilize standalone VR headsets based on the Android operating system that support hand tracking, microphone input, remote controllability and different options of movement compatible with these interactions. Implementing said interactions with the Wizard of Oz method enables early evaluation of human robot interaction without putting the testers in harm's way.

Keywords: VR · HCI · HRI · Wizard of Oz · ROS

1 Introduction

Studying Human-Computer-Interaction (HCI) in VR has proven to be a new way to base HCI development upon. This concept turned out in earlier studies of the authors [6] to be promising for an immersive experience, that enables usability testing without the need of physically present robot prototypes. The robot prototype described in this paper is the CityBot, a self-driving robotic vehicle with a modular design to adapt for different tasks like personal transport or maintenance of greenery. Development and testing of the ecosystem is part of the Campus FreeCity project [14], which consists of a consortium of scientific and commercial partners to implement a scalable vehicle fleet in larger

© The Author(s), under exclusive license to Springer Nature Switzerland AG 2024
C. Stephanidis et al. (Eds.): HCII 2024, CCIS 2114, pp. 341–348, 2024.
https://doi.org/10.1007/978-3-031-61932-8_39

city environments. This was the first step to a safer testing environment and was further explored in the work reported here, by increasing safety in a scenario that secures the user from other VR limitations. Implementing VR interactions with the Wizard of Oz method [1] during the first described study of the Campus FreeCity project was realized with the 3D game engine Unity, utilizing hand tracking capabilities integrated on Meta and PICO devices with third party extensions in the engine and the Open Sound Protocol (OSC) [2] for local network communication between control systems and VR headsets. This type of communication between networked applications allowed the use of headsets from different vendors to work interchangeably with the 3D scene.

Admittedly, specific endangerments for test subjects exist also in a VR environment: One of the main issues in studying vehicle interactions while crossing the street virtually was with users endangering themselves by trying to leave the designated VR space, even though a moderator introduced them beforehand to acclimate and to show its limitations. The used methodology to solve this problem is described in Subsect. 3.1 "Safety during VR immersion".

2   Related Work

Increased interest in virtual environments by the scientific community is shown in a bibliometric analysis by Lee et al. [18], showing more developments in the VR space especially laid out in autonomous vehicle testing as described by Tran et al. [19].

In a 2017 thesis by Anantha Pillai [7], pedestrian behavior towards autonomous vehicles was studied using a similar VR simulation. The aim of the tests was to understand how important an interaction with the driver of a vehicle is and how this translates to self-driving vehicles where no driver is present. As stated in the discussion, VR technology of the time was not able to provide the necessary freedom of movement during the experiment and therefore did not have the need to look for a more secure way of movement in VR since the user stood on a designated spot for the duration of the test.

Stadler et al. [4] and Deb et al. [5] also tested HMI concepts and pedestrian safety in VR with simulated traffic, proving that use cases of VR go beyond the gaming industry. The limitations in this form of simulation are described by Deb et al. [5] with heightened nausea, disorientation, eyestrain and oculomotor disturbance after prolonged exposure to virtual reality from 25 to 35 min. This is also taken into account in the studies of the Campus FreeCity project, limiting user studies to this timeframe. Nevertheless, the benefits of no physical risk of the user entering the path of virtual cars and precise tracking and monitoring in the simulation have shown to outweigh other technologies. The drawbacks described in the conclusion of Deb et al. [5] requiring more space for room-scale virtual environments will be mitigated by introducing an alternative way of movement in the form of VR treadmills (see Fig. 1, left), keeping the complete freedom of movement in the simulation.

The advantages of usability testing in VR for hazardous environments are also noted by Rebelo et al. [15], encouraging further implementations of VR in UX research. Concerns raised in performance of VR applications, like delay, latency and cybersickness by Chandra et al. [16] or perspective distortion and lack of visual clarity by Martens [17], are considered in development, taking advantage of technological advancements in standalone Android VR headsets and the optimizations of 3D environments in game engines for such devices.

3 Methods

3.1 Safety During VR Immersion

Fig. 1. Left: User interacting with modular self-driving "CityBot" in VR. Right: Moderator avatar in a Passthrough VR environment.

Initial own experiments were setup to support a walkaround of the vehicle in a lab environment constrained to an area of about 4 by 4 m, posing a risk of injury to the tester if they were to leave this space while being in a VR environment. Circumventing these limitations didn't prove to be easy, since most tracking systems in VR headsets have trouble with supporting larger interaction spaces. Since immersion in the scenario is also a big factor of correctly assessing gesture interactions with the tested vehicle models, the hands should be free to use and not be constrained by usage of dedicated VR controllers for movement, this being the standard form of movement in VR applications. Because of this, we opted for the implementation of a VR treadmill (see Fig. 1, left) that could be integrated in our system for the subjects to use their own feet to safely walk in the simulation and to allow for a smaller footprint of the testing system in real life. The treadmill system we implemented is connected to a computer via USB, tracks the positions of both users' feet, calculates the velocity of the user in a Unity 3D environment for matching coordinate systems and sends these coordinates via the established local ROS network to the headset. Tracking of feet positions is handled with specialized shoes that have an integrated laser sensor similar to a computer mouse, which allows for a more natural walking feeling compared to conventional VR movement techniques like teleportation or movement of the hands to simulate the whole body moving.

Gesture and speech recognition for vehicle interaction is handled by a separated system that uses additional skeletal data of a stereoscopic camera image of the user and additionally attached lavalier microphones. The integrated hand tracking of the VR devices for gesture recognition is not used for direct control of the vehicle in the application and serves mainly as a way to precisely log hand position and rotation in relation to the vehicle model. After our first run of studies, we reevaluated all systems to support larger interaction areas and dynamically changeable network addresses via the Robot Operating System (ROS). The larger interaction areas simulate the real-life areas as large as whole football stadium parks, in which the CityBot is used. Here, the limitations should only be in the size of the rendered scene in the 3D engine itself and not the space available in real life. Changing from OSC to ROS for network communication is important to allow for multiple control systems changing the VR application simultaneously without the need to reconfigure hardcoded addresses.

3.2 WebGL, WebRTC and VR Streaming

During the first and second study of the project [6], test observers had limited possibilities to track what happened in the VR environment since Android VR headsets are only able to cast to one computer. Inspired by the work of Lyu et al. on WebTransceiVR [3], we utilized a combination of WebGL rendered virtual cameras and a cloud-based virtual camera streaming service integrated in Unity to be able to control and monitor ROS message based environment changes and what exactly the user is able to see in VR from multiple desktop, web and mobile clients (see Fig. 3, right). With this setup, observers are able to track the point of view of the user in the top right using a cloud-based WebRTC stream, a simulated camera view from the vehicle cameras perspective int the bottom left and a mirror of the current state of the VR environment in the top left without the need to interact with a VR headset (see Fig. 2).

3.3 Realtime HCI Moderation with Avatars

Based on the 10 golden rules of usability testing by Dumas et al. [8], interacting with test participants in the form of a confident appearance of the moderator with smiling and making eye contact is a large factor in successful testing. To facilitate this in virtual reality, we opted for the design of a moderator avatar (see Fig. 1, right), following the user around during the entire test. Key to balancing a realistic appearance for an improved avatar-user relationship [9] and mobile performance on VR headsets was the utilisation of Ready Player Me avatars [10] and the full list of blendshapes by Apple's ARKit [11,12].

Fig. 2. Screenshot of a browser window containing all available environments for control of the VR application.

From the moderator side, the avatar is controlled by a web service that uses a webcam to capture and stream the face of the moderator. To take advantage of the already existing local ROS network for the VR application, the webcam image is translated to blendshape values with Google's MediaPipe face landmark detection [13] and their integrated Blendshape prediction model, resulting in streamable floating point number values representing different facial expressions and positions of eyes, nose and mouth. These are directly received and translated in Unity to the avatar model.

4   Results

The initial system developed by the authors for the purpose of two studies [6] was primarily designed to be a mobile VR solution, having the ability to setup the entire system with a standalone Android VR headset and a computer hosting the network and controlling the VR system with a web client. This approach proved to be very convenient in portability and ease of setup but was not secure enough for test participants unfamiliar with VR immersion, holding the risk of users injuring themselves. Compared to a tethered PC experience the VR immersion is still higher because of the restraints of a required USB and display cable connection, limiting freedom of movement by the user. Bringing together the described changes in a redesign of the Android VR environment provided additional securities for the user in the form of a VR movement system with a

VR treadmill and improved moderator communication with avatars, sacrificing some of its mobility for a safer user experience.

Fig. 3. Left: Using an external device to control the VR environment. Center: the VR environment itself, modeled after the Deutsche Bank Park. Right: Screenshot of testing application with WebRTC stream in a preview.

5   Further Work

Purpose of the VR system described here is the possibility to simulate any 3D environment, where robots and humans might interact in a safety-critical way and test interactions without endangering test subjects. Key part of these interactions is also the ability to control the simulation via local network (see Fig. 3, left) - a requirement of typical scenarios of Wizard of Oz tests. This concept can also be expanded upon with further testing of interaction modalities apart from the described speech and gesture control or different types of robot systems, requiring additional research and development of suitable VR solutions.

Acknowledgments. This work is part of the Campus FreeCity project, which is funded by the German Federal Ministry for Digital and Transport (BMDV).

References

1. Dahlbäck, N., Jönsson, A., Ahrenberg, L.: Wizard of Oz studies - why and how. Knowl.-Based Syst. **6**, 258–266 (1993). https://doi.org/10.1016/0950-7051(93)90017-N

2. Wright, M., Freed, A.: Open SoundControl: A New Protocol for Communicating with Sound Synthesizers (1997). https://opensoundcontrol.stanford.edu/files/1997-ICMC-OSC.pdf. Accessed 20 Feb 2024

3. Lyu, H., et al.: WebTransceiVR - asymmetrical communication between multiple VR and non-VR users online. In: CHI '22 Extended Abstracts (2022). https://doi.org/10.1145/3491101.3519816

4. Stadler, S., Cornet, H., Theoto, T.N., Frenkler, F.: A tool, not a toy: using virtual reality to evaluate the communication between autonomous vehicles and pedestrians. In: Augmented Reality and Virtual Reality, pp. 203–216 (2019). https://doi.org/10.1007/978-3-030-06246-0_15

5. Deb, S., Carruth, D.W., Sween, R., Strawderman, L., Garrison, T.M.: Efficacy of virtual reality in pedestrian safety research. Appl. Ergon. **65**, 449–460 (2017). https://doi.org/10.1016/j.apergo.2017.03.007

6. Milde, S., et al.: Studying multi-modal human robot interaction using a mobile VR simulation. In: Kurosu, M., Hashizume, A. (eds.) HCII 2023. LNCS, vol. 14013, pp. 140–155. Springer, Cham (2023). https://doi.org/10.1007/978-3-031-35602-5_11

7. Pillai, A.: Virtual Reality based Study to Analyse Pedestrian Attitude towards Autonomous Vehicles (2017). https://aaltodoc.aalto.fi/bitstream/handle/123456789/28563/master_Pillai_Anantha_2017.pdf. Accessed 20 Feb 2024

8. Dumas, J., Loring, B.: Moderating Usability Tests, Principles & Practices for Interacting (2008). https://uweb.engr.arizona.edu/~ece596c/lysecky/uploads/Main/Lec7.pdf. Accessed 05 Mar 2024

9. Kim, D.Y., Lee, H.K., Chung, K.: Avatar-mediated experience in the metaverse: the impact of avatar realism on user-avatar relationship. J. Retail. Consum. Serv. **73** (2023). https://doi.org/10.1016/j.jretconser.2023.103382

10. Ready Player Me (2024). https://readyplayer.me/. Accessed 05 Mar 2024

11. Kang, S., Song, H., Yoon, B., Kim, K., Woo, W.: Effects of different facial blendshape combinations on social presence for avatar-mediated mixed reality remote communication. In: IEEE International Symposium on Mixed and Augmented Reality Adjunct (ISMAR-Adjunct) (2023). https://doi.org/10.1109/ISMAR-Adjunct60411.2023.00094

12. Apple ARKit Blendshapes, (2024). https://developer.apple.com/documentation/arkit/arfaceanchor/2928251-blendshapes. Accessed 05 Mar 2024

13. Google MediaPipe face landmark detection (2024). https://developers.google.com/mediapipe/solutions/vision/face_landmarker. Accessed 05 Mar 2024

14. Campus FreeCity (2024). https://www.campusfreecity.de/. Accessed 14 Mar 2024

15. Rebelo, F., Noriega, P., Duarte, E., Soares, M.: Using virtual reality to assess user experience. Hum. Factors **54**, 964–982 (2012). https://doi.org/10.1177/0018720812465006

16. Chandra, A.N.R., El Jamiy, F., Reza, H.: A review on usability and performance evaluation in virtual reality systems. In: International Conference on Computational Science and Computational Intelligence (CSCI) (2019). https://ieeexplore.ieee.org/stamp/stamp.jsp?arnumber=9071019. Accessed 14 Mar 2024

17. Martens, D.: Virtually Usable: A Review of Virtual Reality Usability Evaluation Methods (2016). https://www.researchgate.net/publication/315032573_

Virtually_Usable_A_Review_of_Virtual_Reality_Usability_Evaluation_ Methods. Accessed 14 Mar 2024

18. Lee, S., Park, E.J.: Scientific landscape of embodied experience in the virtual environment: a bibliometric analysis. In: Buildings 2022, vol. 12, p. 844. (2022). https://doi.org/10.3390/buildings12060844

19. Tran, T.T.M., Parker, C., Tomitsch, M.: A review of virtual reality studies on autonomous vehicle-pedestrian interaction. IEEE Trans. Hum.-Mach. Syst. **51**(6) (2021). https://doi.org/10.1109/thms.2021.3107517

Use of Robot Operating System for Remote Manipulation of Robot Arm Based on Hand Gestures

Seiji Hayashi[1]([✉]) and Tomoki Kurasawa[2]

[1] Department of Electronics and Computer Systems, Faculty of Engineering,
Takushoku University, Tokyo, Japan
`shayashi@es.takushoku-u.ac.jp`
[2] Mechanical and Electronic Systems Course, Graduate School of Engineering,
Takushoku University, Tokyo, Japan

Abstract. We have been investigating various robot manipulation systems based on human hand gestures. In the present study, we constructed a prototype system incorporating a robot operating system (ROS) that uses an AI-based camera to recognize hand movements for intuitive operation of a robot arm. The major difference between this and our previous work is the use of ROS communication. We developed nodes and topic messages for the ROS package, including a topic message (handtracker_topic) for human hand camera coordinate system data acquired using a DepthAI-based camera, a node (handtracker_pub) to publish this topic message, and a node (handtracker_bridge) that obtains camera coordinate system data and performs transformation processes, including adjustment of the operating range of the robot arm coordinate system. We applied our prototype system to operate a real scalar robot via the scara_controller node based on hand gestures, and at the same time emulated a gazebo robot via the scara_controller_gazebo node. Although the performance test was successful, we believe that it is still necessary to improve the correspondence between hand gestures and the movements of the robot. This can be achieved by adding sensitivity adjustment and acceleration control functions to make the movements more natural.

Keywords: remote control · scara robot arm · ROS · hand gestures

1 Introduction

We have presented various manipulation systems based on human hand gestures at this series of conferences over the last few years [1,2]. Today, a variety of robotic arms are used in production and service. The robot arm control system that we developed is intuitive, and involves recognition of hand movements from images obtained using a camera, enabling work from a distance and work with hazardous materials. The robot development software ROS is a highly versatile

© The Author(s), under exclusive license to Springer Nature Switzerland AG 2024
C. Stephanidis et al. (Eds.): HCII 2024, CCIS 2114, pp. 349–356, 2024.
https://doi.org/10.1007/978-3-031-61932-8_40

system for robot applications because it allows multiple software components to communicate with each other [3], and is suitable for handling communications between a camera and a robotic arm. The purpose of this study is to build a prototype system with a robotic arm that can be controlled using ROS based on hand coordinate data acquired by a camera. Although the use of ROS is not new, as many other gesture recognition frameworks for robotics are based on it, and it has been used for many years in the field of robotics. However, the originality of this paper is that it presents an example of a bridge between a gesture application and a robotic arm.

2   Software and Robot Used in This Research

In this research, ROS was adopted as the robot development software. The Academic SCARA Robot by Vstone Corporation was used for the robot arm. We used the program `depthai_hand_tracker`(hereinafter referred to as DHT) to obtain hand coordinates [6].

2.1   ROS

ROS is an easy-to-use software system with many useful tools and libraries. There are multiple versions of ROS, and version-matching must be performed with the Ubuntu operating system. In this research, a combination of Ubuntu 20.04 and ROS Noetic, which is the latest version of ROS available at present, was used.

2.2   Academic SCARA Robot

The Academic SCARA Robot is a horizontally articulated robot arm with easy coordinate transformation, which enables robot control programming to be performed based on object transport movements (Fig. 1). The robot can be controlled and simulated using ROS, making it suitable for a wide variety of educational fields. The robot arm is a low-cost version of an industrial robot arm, and represents an effective learning platform for robot control [4].

2.3   Depthai-hand-tracker

DHT (Fig. 2) is a Python script that runs Google Mediapipe on a Luxonis DepthAI-based camera [5]; it consists of a two-stage pipeline, where the region of interest around the detected hand is calculated in the first stage and fed to the second stage. The second stage attempts to identify landmarks in the region of interest, and if the confidence level is sufficiently high, the next region of interest is directly determined without using the first stage (Fig. 3) [6].

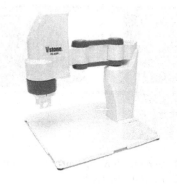

Fig. 1. Academic SCARA Robot

Fig. 2. Implementation of depthai-hand-tracker

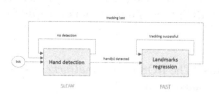

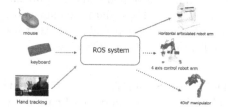

Fig. 3. DHT two-stage pipeline [6]

Fig. 4. Schematic diagram of ROS communication system

3 Robotic System Developed in This Study

ROS was installed on a prototype system consisting of different manipulation devices and the SCARA robotic arm (Fig. 4). Tracking of hand movements for controlling the robotic arm was implemented using DHT, and a node was created to publish the resulting hand coordinate data as ROS messages.

3.1 Checking Operation of SCARA Robot

The SCARA Robot can be controlled in ROS by downloading the ROS package, which is publicly available, and running the SCARA Robot model. We confirmed that the SCARA Robot operated normally by connecting the PC on which ROS was installed and the SCARA Robot via a USB and executing a program to control each joint (Fig. 5).

3.2 Development of ROS Communication System

Here, we describe the details of the ROS communication system developed to transmit hand coordinate data acquired by DHT to the SCARA Robot after some processing steps.

Fig. 5. Checking operation of SCARA Robot.eps

Fig. 6. Screen showing output of hand coordinate data to ROS

ROS Messaging for Hand Coordinate Data. DHT is used to track the operator's hand movements and to publish (xyz) coordinate data in the DHT program (Fig. 6). These data are managed by the ROS master. DHT is implemented as a ROS node *handtracker_pub* that uses a ROS topic **/handtracker_topic** for publication to other ROS nodes.

DHT and SCARA Robot Connections. The ROS node *handtracker_bridge* subscribes to the hand coordinate data obtained from DHT and publishes it to the program for communication with the SCARA Robot. Each node and topic is shown in Fig. 7.

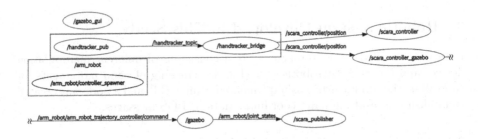

Fig. 7. Nodes and topics for ROS communication system

3.3 Processing Data Obtained from DHT

Maximum Range of Motion for DHT and SCARA Robot. DHT and the SCARA Robot both use the same (xyz) coordinate system, but have different maximum ranges, as shown in Table 1.

Table 1. Maximum range for DHT and SCARA Robot

Hand_X_d	$-250 \sim 250$	Scara_X_d	$-100 \sim 120$
Hand_Y_d	$-150 \sim 150$	Scara_Y_d	$-150 \sim 150$
Hand_Z_d	$400 \sim 900$	Scara_Z_d	$-1.00 \sim 1.00$

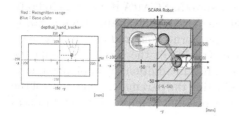

Fig. 8. Recognition range for x-y plane   **Fig. 9.** Schematic of coordinate transformation method

Determination of Recognition Range for DHT and SCARA Robot.
The camera coordinate system requires appropriate coordinate control at the edge of the screen. However, the SCARA Robot cannot move the tip of its arm outside its operating range or near its main support pillar. Therefore, the maximum operating range in DHT is reduced by 100mm in both the x-and y-directions to prevent the robotic arm from attempting to move outside its physical range, as shown in Fig. 8. In addition, it is not allowed to move into a 100 mm × 100 mm region in the x-y plane around the pillar.

DHT and SCARA Robot Coordinate Transformation.
Coordinate transformation between DHT and the SCARA Robot was performed so that the human hand and the arm of the robot were oriented in the same direction, as shown in Fig. 9. The transformations between the camera coordinate system and the robot coordinate system are shown in Table 2.

Table 2. Axis transformations for DHT and SCARA Robot

hand_x	$-200 \sim 200$	$\rightarrow$	scara_y	$100 \sim -100$
hand_Y	$-100 \sim 100$	$\rightarrow$	scara_z	$-1.00 \sim 1.00$
hand_Z	$450 \sim 850$	$\rightarrow$	scara_x	$-100 \sim 100$

4   Results and Discussion

4.1   Implementation of ROS Communication System

In this study, we managed DHT with a ROS master to build a ROS node *hand-tracker_pub* and ROS topic **/handtracker_topic** that publishes (xyz) coordinate data. In addition, we built a ROS node *handtracker_bridge* to publish the ROS topic **/scara_controller/positon** connected to the SCARA Robot's main body, after subscribing to hand coordinate data acquired from **/handtracker_topic** and processing the data using coordinate transformations and moving averages. By executing the constructed ROS nodes (package), the robot arm could be moved using the hand coordinate data (Fig. 10). In addition, by applying a moving average to the coordinate data and adjusting the parameters that control the movement interval of the robot body, it was possible to improve the naturalness of robot arm operation.

Fig. 10. ROS communication system in action

4.2   Figure 10 Execution Screen Details

The details of the sub-screens indicated by the numbers in Fig. 10 are given below.

① Screen captured from depth camera: Performs hand recognition and reads data in the camera coordinate system.

② SCARA Robot emulator screen: Emulates the behavior of the robot

by subscribing to robot coordinate system messages via the ROS topic
/**scara_controller/positon**.

③ Hand coordinate data obtained from DHT: As shown in Fig. 11, camera coordinate system messages are published from node *handtracker_pub* to node *handtracker_bridge* via topic /**handtracker_topic**.

④ Processed data to be sent to SCARA Robot: As shown in Fig. 11, messages in the robot coordinate system are subscribed to by the SCARA Robot node by way of topic /**scara_controller/positon** from node *handtracker_bridge*.

⑤ Node diagram showing the relationship between the ROS nodes managed by the ROS master at runtime.

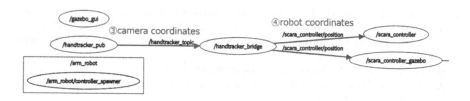

Fig. 11. Moving messages from DHT to SCARA Robot

4.3   Considerations

It should be noted that the current version of the prototype suffers from several problems. First, the robot arm cannot keep up with rapid movements of the operator's hand. However, this is a minor issue if the arm moves over the required range. In addition, the coordinates of the robot arm are slightly different from the expected coordinates, so that a calibration function is required. Finally, the arm tip does not move stably even when the hand is stopped when the arm tip is kept at a certain point. To address this issue, the arm should be improved so that it continues to stop by adjusting the sensitivity of the play when the hand is stopped by judging the state of the stopped hand.

5   Conclusion

In this study, a communication system was constructed to operate a robot arm based on hand coordinate data acquired by an AI-based camera using the robot development software ROS. Hand coordinates obtained by DHT were communicated to the SCARA Robot as ROS messages. This allowed the robot arm to be successfully operated using hand movements. However, there is still room for improvement with regard to positioning accuracy and the smoothness of movement of the robot arm. In future work, we plan to make further improvements to the developed system. Specifically, we will review the operating range of DHT and the SCARA Robot and control their mutual movement speeds. In addition, to improve the sensation of naturalness during operation, we will implement two-stage sensitivity adjustment and acceleration control.

References

1. Hayashi, S., Muxin, H.: Implementation of remote control of a robot arm by hand gestures. In: Stephanidis, C., Antona, M., Ntoa, S. (eds.) HCI International 2022 Posters. HCII 2022. Communications in Computer and Information Science, vol. 1581, pp. 18–27. Springer, Cham (2022). https://doi.org/10.1007/978-3-031-06388-6_3
2. Hayashi, S., Igarashi, H.: Touchless information provision and facial expression training using Kinect. In: Stephanidis, C., Antona, M., Ntoa, S. (eds.) HCII 2021. CCIS, vol. 1420, pp. 90–97. Springer, Cham (2021). https://doi.org/10.1007/978-3-030-78642-7_13
3. ROS.org. https://wiki.ros.org/. Accessed 20 Feb 2024
4. Academic SCARA Robot. https://www.vstone.co.jp/products/scara_robot/index.html. Accessed 20 Feb 2024
5. OAK-D Lite - Luxonis. https://shop.luxonis.com/collections/oak-cameras-1/products/oak-d-lite-1?variant=42583102456031. Accessed 20 Feb 2024
6. Hand tracking with DepthAI. https://github.com/geaxgx/depthai_hand_tracker. Accessed 20 Feb 2024
7. Kurasawa, T., Hayashi, S.: Research on manipulation of robotic arms by hand gestures using ROS. In: The 2023 IEICE Engineering Sciences Society/NOLTA Society Conference, A-14-1 (2023)

The Influence of Culture in Shaping Anthropomorphic Attitudes Towards Robots: A Literature Review

Geyi Kou[1](✉) and Shunan Zhang[2]

[1] University of Edinburgh, Edinburgh EH8 9NT, UK
S2489183@ed.ac.uk
[2] Sungkyunkwan University, 25-2 Seonggyungwan-ro, Jongno-gu 03063, South Korea
970205@g.skku.edu

Abstract. The ongoing evolution of robotic technology reveals a noticeable trend toward endowing robots with human-like traits, seen in their external design and language communication. However, there has been controversy about whether people accept and what factors influence their attitudes toward making robots more human-like. Despite studies emphasizing the impact of cultural backgrounds on attitudes towards robot anthropomorphism, existing research lacks sufficient classification and comparison of these cultural factors. This study, through an in-depth literature review, reveals that cultural factors, such as religious beliefs, popular culture, media exposure, social norms, values, and cognitive patterns, exert a substantial influence on user attitudes towards robot anthropomorphism. This influence varies across geographic regions and national contexts. Non-cultural factors such as technological acceptance, loneliness, and the uncanny valley effect also play a role. This review, crucial for human-robot interaction and cultural integration, proposes distinct cultural perspectives and classifications, offering valuable directions for future research.

Keywords: Robot · Human · Cultural Differences · Anthropomorphic · Cross-culture

1 Introduction

With the rapid development of technology, robotic technology is penetrating various aspects of our daily lives at an unprecedented pace. From industrial manufacturing to healthcare, and from education to entertainment, robots have become an indispensable component of daily life [5, 15, 27]. No longer confined to being mere tools, robots have evolved into societal entities, exerting a significant impact on social practices. One prominent feature of this trend is the anthropomorphism of robots, enabling them to play increasingly complex roles in practical applications such as medicine, therapy, and companionship [30]. The rapid advancement in this field not only brings convenience to production and daily life but also triggers profound reflections on the application of technology and cultural issues globally.

© The Author(s), under exclusive license to Springer Nature Switzerland AG 2024
C. Stephanidis et al. (Eds.): HCII 2024, CCIS 2114, pp. 357–371, 2024.
https://doi.org/10.1007/978-3-031-61932-8_41

Robotics, a cutting-edge field, is shaped by various pressures—demographic, economic, cultural, and institutional [31]. Culture, a crucial factor, deeply influences technology related to humans, offering new perspectives for robotics. Previous studies show individual cultural backgrounds significantly influence perceptions, feelings, and behaviors in human-robot interactions [20, 26]. In recent years, robot design has gradually tended to simulate human appearance, as seen in the trend of using legs instead of wheels [6]. This trend not only enhances the friendliness and usability of robots but also simulates emotional communication among humans to a certain extent. However, it is in this fusion process that cultural factors profoundly influence the anthropomorphism of robots. The anthropomorphism of robots exhibits markedly different features in diverse cultural environments, reflecting unique expectations and fears regarding human-machine interaction. While some studies explore the cultural impact on robots, existing research lacks a comprehensive examination of cultural factors influencing attitudes toward robot anthropomorphism.

2 Literature Review

2.1 Robot and Culture

Culture profoundly shapes human behaviour and societal structures. Human-robot interaction, mirroring interpersonal dynamics, is intricately linked to individual cultural backgrounds and personal experiences [34]. The theory of culturally adaptive machine agents, highlighting culture's multifaceted impact on human-agent interactions, designing robots should consider users' cultural backgrounds [25]. Recent research underscores that an individual's cultural context, including beliefs, values, and social norms, significantly shapes their perception and interaction with robots [19, 23].

While the origins, differences, and intricate classifications of culture extend beyond the scope of this discussion, understanding individuals' perceptions of East-West individualism and collectivism differences becomes crucial in the context of shaping robots. According to the cultural dimensions of Hofstede [14], individualism and collectivism are core dimensions summarizing fundamental differences in relationships between individuals and society. This cultural dimension is widely applied in interdisciplinary studies such as human-robot interaction and psychological sociology. Research suggests that individuals raised in a collectivist background tend to perceive robots as group members and are more inclined to maintain smaller social distances with robots [12, 19]. Religion further influences human-robot interaction; Christian expectations favor artificial intelligence over humanoid robots, while Shintoism in Japan makes participants more receptive to humanoid robots, perceiving them as unlikely threats to human uniqueness [4].

2.2 Anthropomorphism and Culture

Anthropomorphism, from the Greek "Anthropos" (human) and "morphe" (shape or form), involves attributing human characteristics to non-living artifacts [10]. Robots engaging in meaningful social interaction with humans inherently require anthropomorphism or human-like qualities in form, behavior, or both [9]. People prefer collaborating with robots having social capabilities, human-like appearance, and the ability for verbal and non-verbal behaviors [10]. Anthropomorphism goes beyond mere human resemblance, with the cognitive aspects of how humans perceive it in robots being crucial [16].

The anthropomorphic design features of robots and user cultural backgrounds may influence users' attitudes toward robot anthropomorphism, consequently impacting their interaction patterns. For instance, a study suggested that Japanese participants, influenced by Japanese popular culture, exhibited a more positive perception of anthropomorphism compared to Australian participants [3]. Moreover, due to differences in cultural backgrounds, individuals demonstrated distinct preferences for robot appearances [2].

Among 71 articles from 2008 to 2023 on robot culture and anthropomorphism, only a few provide comprehensive reviews. Papadopoulos and Koulouglioti [26] explored culture's impact on attitudes toward humanoid and animal-like robots. Lim et al. [20] focused on cultural factors shaping societal expectations and responses to robots, integrating empirical evidence from the past two decades of Human-Robot Interaction (HRI) research. Gasteiger et al. [11] aimed to synthesize literature on human factors for designing personalized or culturally adaptable robots. Out of the aforementioned 71 articles, only 22 dealt with specific empirical research and cultural comparisons. However, most literature only involves comparisons between two or three national cultures, and there is currently no literature systematically organizing these comparisons. In-depth investigation is needed to identify which cultural factors influence robot anthropomorphism and.

2.3 Research Questions

1. What cultural factors are key in shaping attitudes toward anthropomorphized robots, and are there notable variations in these attitudes among different cultures?
2. Apart from cultural factors, what other variables influence individuals' attitudes toward anthropomorphism in robots?

3 Methodology

This investigation followed the Preferred Reporting Items for Systematic Reviews and Meta-Analyses (PRISMA) standards [21], utilized electronic searches and snowballing to gather pertinent studies. The Web of Science database, renowned for its authority, was systematically searched on December 5, 2023. The search covered the years from 2000 to 2023, focusing on peer-reviewed empirical studies for article quality. Following full-text screening, a snowballing approach, unearthed additional relevant articles. Utilizing the characteristics of the Web of Science database, relevant keywords were applied in the search area.

3.1 The Screening Process

See Fig. 1 for flowchart showing the phases of the literature search and decisions for inclusion and exclusion.

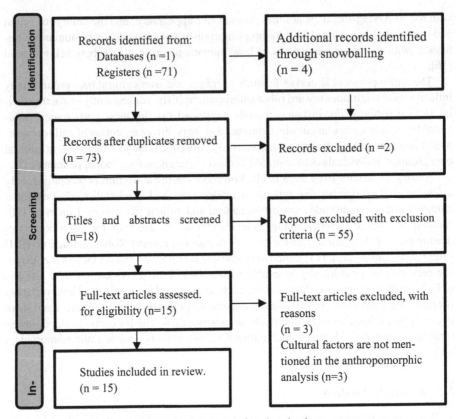

Fig. 1. PRISMA flow chart of study selection process

4   Result

The impact of individuals' cultural backgrounds on their attitudes toward the anthropomorphism of robots is currently influenced by four primary factors, alongside several non-cultural influences. Those factors are elaborated as follows.

4.1   Religious and Belief

As seen in Table 1, in Japan, Shintoism significantly influences robot culture, with research indicating that it leads to a stronger inclination toward anthropomorphism by attributing human characteristics and souls to non-human agents [3]. Eastern philosophies like Christianity, Buddhism, and Confucianism also play a pivotal role in shaping attitudes toward robot anthropomorphism. Western cultures, influenced by Christianity, approach humanoid robots cautiously, considering humans as uniquely endowed with spiritual privileges [7]. In contrast, East Asian cultures, influenced by Buddhism and Confucianism, are more accepting of humanoid robots, believing that souls can exist in non-human entities [7]. Japanese preferences for highly humanoid robots differ fundamentally from Americans, reflecting cultural and religious disparities [4]. In

Table 1. Summary of studies included the influence of religious and belief factors on robot anthropomorphic

Authors Year	Countries	Method	Findings	Cultural factor
Castelo and Sarvary (2022)	Japan; USA	Experiment	Japanese participants perceive robots to be more animate, having more of a mind, a soul, and consciousness, relative to American participants	Shintoism; Animism
Bernotat and Eyssel (2018)	Japan; Germany	Experiment	Japanese participants generally showed a stronger tendency to anthropomorphize nonhuman agents and attributed more mind than German participants	Shintoism
Lee and Sabanović (2014)	South Korea; Turkey; The United States	Survey	Korean participants were more likely to prefer robots with a human-like appearance and expressive faces, while US and Turkish participants preferred machine-like robots made of metal and without faces or facial expressions	Animism
Dang and Liu, (2021)	USA; China	Experiment	American participants perceived robots more ambivalently than Chinese participants, indicating cultural variations in the attitudes towards AI robots	Buddhism; Confucianism; Christianity

(*continued*)

Table 1. (*continued*)

Authors Year	Countries	Method	Findings	Cultural factor
Li et al. (2022)	China; America	Experiment	The Chinese participants had a higher score on anthropomorphism and perceived warmth than the American participants	Animism
Spatola, Marchesi and Wykowska (2022)	Korea; Japan, Germany; The United States	Experiment	Individuals from East Asian countries (e.g., Korea, Japan) may have a more positive and anthropomorphic view of robots compared to individuals from Western countries (e.g., Germany, United States)	Animism

Chinese culture, the belief in "everything has a spirit" contributes to a greater inclination to anthropomorphize robots [19]. Animism beliefs indirectly influence attributions of mental anthropomorphic characteristics to robots [32]. Lee et al. [18] reveal varied perspectives, with participants influenced by animism beliefs, but overall, a majority do not endorse the idea of robots possessing a soul. Additionally, the research shows that participants from Turkey, compared to those from South Korea, are more reluctant to accept the notion of robots having a soul, indicating a heightened aversion to overly anthropomorphic robots.

4.2 Popular Culture and Media Exposure

As shown in Table 2, exposure to robots in popular culture markedly shapes perceptions of their appearance, capabilities, and societal roles. In Japan, a hub of rich robot culture, media exposure strongly influences attitudes towards anthropomorphic robots [33]. For instance, the prevalence of robot images in works like "Astro Boy" fosters a preference for traditional robots among Japanese participants [2]. Television, film, and manga further amplify this impact, with media molding perceptions and attitudes toward robots, especially favoring those closely resembling humans [13]. However, Bernotat [3] reveals a contrasting trend, suggesting that highly anthropomorphic robots may not receive positive evaluations from Japanese participants, potentially leading to a focus on technological flaws. Some Japanese citizens express concerns about the negative societal impacts of robots, highlighting the influence of media and popular culture on their perceptions [17].

Table 2. Summaries of the influence of Popular culture and media exposure on robot anthropomorphic

Authors Year	Country	Method	Findings	Cultural factor
Bernotat and Eyssel (2018)	**Japan; Germany**	survey	Japanese participants generally showed a stronger tendency to anthropomorphize nonhuman agents and attributed more mind, particularly on the experience dimension, to both robot types than German participants	Animated film; Media exposure
Bartneck (2008)	**USA; Japan**	Experiment	Japanese participants favoured traditional robots, whereas American participants, on average, expressed greater liking for robots. However, with highly human-like androids, the preference reversed	Animated film; Science fiction
Haring et al. (2014)	**Japan; Europe**	Survey	Japanese participants favored robots with greater human resemblance when compared to their European counterparts	Media exposure; Movies; comics
Kamide and Arai (2017)	**USA; Japan**	Experiment	Japanese participants show a preference for traditional robots, while Americans favor robots with highly human-like features	Manga; animated movies

(continued)

Table 2. (*continued*)

Authors Year	Country	Method	Findings	Cultural factor
Trovato and Eyssel (2017)	**Japan; Italy**	Experiment	Japanese students attributed a higher level of mind to the outgroup robot, which had a Caucasian appearance, compared to the ingroup robot, which had a Japanese appearance	Media exposure

Table 3. Summaries of the influence of social norm on robot anthropomorphic

Authors Year	Country	Method	Findings	Cultural factor
Said et al. (2023)	Japan; USA	Survey	The Japanese users provided higher ratings for robots with human elements of anthropomorphism, intelligence, and safety compared to other users	Social norms
Nomura et al. (2008)	USA; Japan Korea	Questionnaire	Japanese students perceived humanoid robots relationships with humans as similar to human-to-human connections, while Korean and US students tended to view these relationships as akin to interactions between humans and tools	Respect the old and love the young; The use of honorifics

(*continued*)

Table 3. (*continued*)

Authors Year	Country	Method	Findings	Cultural factor
Lee and Sabanović (2014)	South Korea; Turkey; the United States	Survey	Korean participants showed a preference for robots resembling humans with expressive faces, whereas US participants favored machine-like robots made of metal without faces or facial expressions	Confucian social norms

4.3 Social Norms

As shown in Table 3, social norms significantly impact perspectives on robot anthropomorphism. For hotel guests, social norms profoundly influence the acceptance of humanoid service robots [29]. Cultural differences among South Korean, Japanese, and American students shape perceptions of humanoid and animal-like robots' emotional capabilities. Japanese students attribute higher emotional capabilities to humanoid robots, Korean students believe both types possess some emotional capabilities, while American students generally think these robots lack emotional capabilities [23]. In Korean culture, there is an expectation for robots to adhere to social norms, displaying social attributes and subordination through polite language [23]. Influenced by Confucian social norms, Korean participants advocate for enhancing robot anthropomorphism, including capabilities like bowing and using respectful titles when interacting with older individuals [18].

4.4 Values and Cognitive Models

As shown in Table 4, cultural differences significantly impact the values and cognitive models of individuals regarding robot attitudes. Westerners typically exhibit an analytical cognitive style and emphasize independent values, leading to a more negative attitude towards robots with human-like features. In contrast, east Asians display a holistic cognitive style and emphasize interdependent values, making them more accepting of humanoid robots [7]. According to Nomura [24], values such as trust, safety, and privacy affect people's perceptions and interactions with robots. Additionally, cognitive models, such as theories of mind, also influence people's perceptions and interactions with robots, especially in terms of anthropomorphism. Cultural dimensions of individualism and collectivism [14], affect social distance, thus influencing individual views and attitudes towards robots. Cultural differences between Chinese and American participants significantly influence their social distance from humanoid robots. Chinese participants, as collectivists, score lower on social distance, perceiving robots as group members, particularly service robots [19].

Table 4. Summaries of influence of Values and cognitive model on robot anthropomorphic

Authors Year	Country	Method	Findings	Cultural factor
Dang and Liu (2021)	USA China	Experiment	American participants perceived robots more ambivalently than Chinese participants	Values of independence and interdependence
Nomura, Syrdal and Dautenhahn (2015)	Japan UK	Survey	The UK people felt more negative toward humanoid robots than the Japanese people	Theory of mind
Li et al. (2022)	China America	Experiment	The Chinese participants had a higher score on anthropomorphism and perceived warmth than the American participants	Individualism and collectivism

4.5 Other Factors

As shown in Table 5, firstly, the acceptance of technology influences people's perspectives on the anthropomorphism of robots. For instance, in the hotel industry, Japanese has a higher acceptance of robots, and Japanese users have a higher perception of the practicality of humanoid robots and the ease of use, which may significantly affect the concept of anthropomorphism and the adoption of robots [29]. Perceived loneliness is a crucial factor affecting robot anthropomorphism. Although loneliness does not necessarily lead individuals to be more inclined towards anthropomorphizing robots or preferring anthropomorphic robots, studies indicate that anthropomorphized social robots can help alleviate feelings of loneliness [8]. Lastly, the Uncanny Valley effect is an important theory in human-computer interaction, demonstrating the relationship between individuals' perceptions and attitudes towards anthropomorphism. Research confirms Uncanny Valley theory [22], indicating that likability sharply decreases when the similarity between robots and humans reaches a certain threshold.

Table 5. Summaries of the influence of non-cultural factors on robot anthropomorphic

Factor	Authors Year	Country	Method	Findings
Technology Acceptance	Said et al. (2023)	Japan USA	Survey	The Japanese users provided higher ratings for robots with human elements of anthropomorphism, intelligence, and safety compared to users from other cultural backgrounds
loneliness	Dang and Liu, 2023)	China America	Mixed method: experimental designs and surveys	Lonely people in Chinese culture showed less preference for anthropomorphic robots compared to non-lonely individuals, while this effect was not observed in American culture. Consumers who purchased robots with higher levels of anthropomorphism as less lonely, and this effect was more pronounced in Chinese culture compared to American culture
Uncanny Valley Effect	Kamide and Arai (2017)	USA Japan	Experiment	Japanese participants show a preference for traditional robots, while Americans favour robots with highly human-like features

5   Discussion

The primary goal of this literature review is to comprehensively analyze the factors contributing to individual variations in the perception of humanoid robots across diverse cultural backgrounds. Synthesizing existing literature, we find that religious beliefs, popular culture, media exposure, social norms, values, cognitive patterns, and factors like technological acceptance and perceived loneliness collectively shape individuals' perspectives on humanoid robot personification.

We found that the Japanese exhibit a greater acceptance of humanoid robots compared to Western countries. The influence of film culture, portraying robots as benevolent, patient, or possessing a strong sense of justice, contributes to the more positive attitudes of the Japanese towards robots [20]. However, we have also identified that excessive media exposure exacerbates individuals' scrutiny of robot technology, thereby making people more prone to contemplate technological flaws. Furthermore, previous research exploring individuals' attitudes towards robots in diverse cultural backgrounds has underscored the significance of symbolic communication, such as the linguistic expression style of robots, in influencing people's perceptions of robot interactions [1, 28]. Nevertheless, within the realm of anthropomorphism research on robots, there is currently a lack of emphasis on how language and communication forms specifically impact individuals' attitudes towards the anthropomorphism of robots.

This study contributes theoretically by enriching the literature at the intersection of robotics and culture, being one of the first to integrate cultural elements into the research domain of humanoid robot personification. Through a literature review, we categorize the influencing factors of culture on robot anthropomorphism into dimensions such as religious beliefs, popular culture and media exposure, social norms, values, and cognitive patterns. This innovative classification establishes a foundation for future research.

From a practical perspective, our research provides crucial insights for culturally sensitive design. Understanding how different cultures perceive humanoid robot personification aids in designing technology aligned with regional and community needs. Considering cultural differences in individualism and collectivism during design allows customization for broader acceptance and an enhanced user experience. Our research also highlights the importance of studying acceptance of humanoid robot personification in different cultures for societal acceptance. Addressing alleviating concerns can better manage public apprehensions, fostering a favorable environment for robot technology's practical application and commercialization.

6 Limitations and Future Research

This study solely incorporated publications from the Web of Science database. Future studies can consider more database for example google scholar and Scopus, to provide in-depth cultural analysis. Secondly, this study is qualitative in nature and the research method is single. We highly recommend future investigations to employ quantitative research method (e.g., meta-analysis) or mixed research method. Lastly, although our study provides cultural analysis, the diverse methodologies and questionnaire designs employed across different articles hinder our ability to definitively determine which country or region holds the most negative or positive attitudes towards humanoid robot personification. In future studies, a concerted effort should be made to establish a common research framework and standardized measurement tools to facilitate cross-cultural comparisons.

7 Conclusion

This study adopts a cultural perspective to examine how individuals from diverse cultural backgrounds perceive and interpret the anthropomorphism of humanoid robots. We identify that cultural factor such as religion, popular culture, media exposure, values, and cognitive patterns, along with non-cultural factors like technological acceptance and the uncanny valley effect, significantly influence individuals' attitudes toward anthropomorphism. A comprehensive examination of the interplay between anthropomorphism and culture highlights the intricate relationship between these two factors. This research contributes to advancing a more profound cultural and ethical discourse on humanoid robot anthropomorphism, offering novel cultural classifications and perspectives.

References

1. Andrist, S., et al.: Effects of culture on the credibility of robot speech. In: Proceedings of the 20th Annual ACM/IEEE International Conference on Human-Robot Interaction, pp. 157–164. Association for Computing Machinery, New York (2015)
2. Bartneck, C.: Who like Androids more: Japanese or US Americans? In: Proceeding of the 17th IEEE International Symposium on Robot and Human Interactive Communication, Munich, Germany, pp. 553–557 (2008)
3. Bernotat, J., Eyssel, F.A.: "Can't wait to have a robot at home? - Japanese and German Users" attitudes toward service robots in smart homes. In: Proceedings of the 27th IEEE International Symposium on Robot and Human Interactive Communication. Nanjing, China, pp. 15–22 (2018). https://doi.org/10.1145/2696454.2696464
4. Castelo, N., Sarvary, M.: Cross-cultural differences in comfort with humanlike robots. Int. J. Soc. Robot. **14**, 1865–2187 (2022)
5. Chen, X., et al.: Application and theory gaps during the rise of artificial intelligence in education. Comput. Educ. Artif. Intell. **1**(1), 100002 (2020)
6. Chin, M.G., et al.: Measuring individual differences in anthropomorphism toward machines and animals. In: Proceedings of the Human Factors and Ergonomics Society Annual Meeting, vol. 48, pp. 1252–1255. SAGE Publications (2004). https://doi.org/10.1177/154193120 404801110
7. Dang, J., Liu, L.: Robots are friends as well as foes: ambivalent attitudes toward mindful and mindless AI robots in the United States and China. Comput. Hum. Behav. **115**, 106612 (2021). https://doi.org/10.1016/j.chb.2020.106612
8. Dang, J., Liu, L.: Do lonely people seek robot companionship? A comparative examination of the loneliness-robot anthropomorphism link in the United States and China. Comput. Hum. Behav. **141**, 107637 (2023)
9. Duffy, B.R.: Anthropomorphism and the social robot. Robot. Auton. Syst. **42**(3–4), 177–190 (2003)
10. Fink, J.: Anthropomorphism and human likeness in the design of robots and human-robot interaction. In: Social Robotics: 4th International Conference, Chengdu, China, pp. 199–208 (2012)
11. Gasteiger, N., Hellou, M., Ahn, H.S.: Factors for personalization and localization to optimize human-robot interaction: a literature review. Int. J. Soc. Robot. **15**(4), 689–701 (2021). https://doi.org/10.1007/s12369-021-00811-8
12. Eresha, G., Häring, M., et al.: Investigating the influence of culture on proxemic behaviors for humanoid robots. In: The 22nd IEEE International Symposium on Robot and Human Interactive Communication, Gyeongju, Korea, pp. 430–435 (2013)

13. Haring, K.S., Mougenot, C., Ono, F., Watanabe, K.: Cultural differences in perception and attitude towards robots. Int. J. Affect. Eng. **13**(3), 149–157 (2014). https://doi.org/10.5057/ijae.13.149

14. Hofstede, G.: Culture's Consequences: International Differences in Work-Related Values. Sage Publications, Beverly Hills (1984)

15. Johnson, D.O., et al.: Exploring the entertainment value of playing games with a humanoid robot. Int. J. Soc. Robot. **8**(2), 247–269 (2015)

16. Kahn, P.H., Ishiguro, H., Friedman, B., Kanda, T.: What is a human? - toward psychological benchmarks in the field of human-robot interaction. Robot Hum. Interact. Commun. **8**(3), 363–390 (2006)

17. Kamide, H., Arai, T.: Perceived comfortableness of anthropomorphized robots in US. and Japan. Int. J. Soc. Robot. **9**, 537–543 (2017)

18. Lee, H.R., Sabanović, S.: Culturally variable preferences for robot design and use in South Korea, Turkey, and the United States. In: Proceedings of the 2014 ACM/IEEE International Conference on Human-Robot Interaction, pp. 17–24. Association for Computing Machinery, New York (2014)

19. Li, L., Li, Y., Song, B., Shi, Z., Wang, C.: How human-like behavior of service robot affects social distance: a mediation model and cross-cultural comparison. Behav. Sci. **12**(7), 205 (2022). https://doi.org/10.3390/bs12070205

20. Lim, V., Rooksby, M., Cross, E.S.: Social robots on a global stage: establishing a role for culture during human-robot interaction. Int. J. Soc. Robot. **13**(6), 1307–1333 (2020). https://doi.org/10.1007/s12369-020-00710-4

21. Moher, D., Liberati, A., Tetzlaff, J., Altman, D.G.: Preferred reporting items for systematic reviews and meta-analyses: the PRISMA statement. Ann. Intern. Med. **151**(4), 264–269 (2009). https://doi.org/10.1016/j.ijsu.2010.02.007

22. Mori, M., MacDorman, K., Kageki, N.: The uncanny valley [from the field]. IEEE Robot. Autom. Mag. **19**(2), 98–100 (2009)

23. Nomura, T., Suzuki, T., et al.: What People Assume about Humanoid and animal-type robots: cross-culture Analysis between Japan, Korea, and the United States. Int. J. Humanoid Rob. **05**(01), 25–46 (2008)

24. Nomura, T., Syrdal, D.S., Dautenhahn, K.: Differences on social acceptance of humanoid robots between Japan and the UK. In: Proceedings of the 4th International Symposium on New Frontiers in Human-Robot Interaction, pp.115–120. The Society for the Study of Artificial Intelligence and the Simulation of Behavior (AISB), UK (2015)

25. O'Neill-Brown, P.: Setting the stage for the culturally adaptive agent, pp. 93–97. CA: AAAI Technical report, Washington (1997)

26. Papadopoulos, I., Koulouglioti, C.: The influence of culture on attitudes towards humanoid and animal-like robots: an integrative review. J. Nurs. Scholarsh. **50**(6), 653–665 (2018). https://doi.org/10.1111/jnu.12422

27. Preising, B., Hsia, T.C., Mittelstadt, B.: A literature review: robots in medicine. IEEE Eng. Med. Biol. Mag. **10**(2), 13–22 (1991)

28. Rau, P.L.P., et al.: Effects of communication style and culture on ability to accept recommendations from robots. Comput. Hum. Behav. **25**(2), 587–595 (2009)

29. Said, N., et al.: Customer acceptance of humanoid service robots in hotels: moderating effects of service voluntariness and culture. Int. J. Contemp. Hosp. Manag. **36**, 1844–1867 (2023)

30. Samani, H., Saadatian, E., et al.: Cultural robotics: the culture of robotics and robotics in culture. Int. J. Adv. Rob. Syst. **10**(12), 400 (2013)

31. Sherry, T.: A Nascent Robotics culture: New Complicities for Companionship, pp. 107–116 (2006)

32. Spatola, N., Marchesi, S., Wykowska, A.: Different models of anthropomorphism across cultures and ontological limits in current frameworks the integrative framework of anthropomorphism. Front. Robot. AI **9** (2022)
33. Trovato, G., Eyssel, F.A.: Mind attribution to androids: a comparative study with Italian and Japanese adolescents. In: 26th IEEE International Symposium on Robot and Human Interactive Communication, Lisbon, Portugal, pp. 561–566 (2017)
34. Zanatto, D., Patacchiola, M., Goslin, J., Cangelosi, A.: Investigating cooperation with robotic peers. PLoS ONE **14**(11), e0225028 (2019)

The Impact of Age on Children's Selective Trust in Misleading Social Robots

Jiaxin Li(✉) , Yi Pang , and Qianxi Jia

Central China Normal University, Wuhan 430070, Hubei, People's Republic of China
{jiaxinlee,pangyi,qianxijia}@mails.ccnu.edu.cn

Abstract. As technology advances, young children are interacting with social robots more frequently and seeing them as a source of information. However, social robots do not always provide correct information; do 3- and 4-year-old toddlers trust social robots unconditionally? The aim of this study was to investigate whether selective trust scores of 3- and 4-year-old toddlers differ when confronted with a social robot that provides incorrect information, and to analyze whether theory of mind and inhibitory control may have an impact on this. The results found that there was a significant difference between age and young children's selective trust scores, and that theory of mind and inhibitory control were positively correlated with selective trust scores.

Keywords: Social robot · Selective trust · Young children · Child-robot interaction

1 Introduction

With the development of AI technology, more and more AI products will come into our lives, and the development of AI is highly emphasized. The United Nations Children's Fund (UNICEF) released "Policy Guidance on AI for Children" in 2021, which states that AI systems are expected to improve educational opportunities. In China, the Ministry of Industry and Information Technology and seventeen other departments issued the "Robot +" Application Action Implementation Plan, which clearly states that by 2025, the density of manufacturing robots will double compared to 2020, and the depth and breadth of application of service robots and special robots will be significantly increased. Development of interactive, teaching, competition, and other educational robot products and programming systems, categorized construction of robotics service platform. Increase the guidance of robotics education, improve the robotics teaching content and practice environment at all levels of institutions, actively cultivate new modes and forms of robotics campus services, and deepen the application of robots in teaching and research, skills training, campus security, and other scenarios. The 2019 Global Educational Robotics Development White Paper estimates that the market size of educational robots will exceed US$330.8 billion by 2023, and the revenue of educational service robots will account for more than 77.5% of the entire market. The white paper's survey of 1,032 teachers, 1,345 parents, and 857 students of all school levels: teachers,

© The Author(s), under exclusive license to Springer Nature Switzerland AG 2024
C. Stephanidis et al. (Eds.): HCII 2024, CCIS 2114, pp. 372–380, 2024.
https://doi.org/10.1007/978-3-031-61932-8_42

parents, and students have a positive attitude toward the use of educational robots, with 85% of students and 90% of teachers expressing the desire to own an educational robot. It can be seen that robots supported by artificial intelligence technology will be widely used and developed in various fields of social life.

Social robots are one type of artificial intelligence products that are autonomous or semi-autonomous robots that interact and communicate with humans by displaying social behaviors and adhering to human social norms [1]. Social robots are making an unstoppable influx into homes, schools, and public spaces in a variety of roles, and the opportunities and frequency of children's passive or active exposure to this type of technology have increased [2, 3]. For example, social robots can act as guides in shopping malls or museums [4], and can also act as tutors, peers, and students to help children learn as they learn [5–8]. It has been demonstrated that social robots not only promote children's knowledge learning but also promote young children's social development [9–11]. Thus, it is clear that social robots will become a part of human social life that cannot be ignored.

According to social epistemology, most of an individual's knowledge comes from information (also known as testimony) in the external environment [12, 13]. The early childhood stage is an important stage for acquiring information from the outside world to understand the world, in which young children are full of curiosity and always take the initiative to ask "why" from the outside world in order to acquire knowledge [14]. Due to their limited cognitive development, young children find it difficult to acquire information through direct experience, so they mostly rely on indirect experience to acquire information. Parents, teachers, and artificial intelligence devices are the main sources of indirect information for young children. As Baier [15] pointed out, children are entirely dependent on other people, and so have little choice but to trust those around them. It has been demonstrated that young children unconditionally choose to trust information provided by adults. For example, Jaswal's [16] study found that when categorizing objects and making inferences about an object's attributes, young children were ready to abandon their initial categorization if they heard a different categorization proposed by an adult. Jaswal et al.'s study found that when adults verbally or gesturally went to a young child to tell them where an object was located (e.g., the location of a sticker), they would act on the information they received [17].

Learning from others can help young children acquire knowledge and accomplish learning efficiently, but learning from others comes with certain risks. This is because informants may provide incorrect information, either unintentionally or intentionally. The role of trust in interpersonal communication is self-evident, but not all the information we receive is correct, especially in the information explosion, and identifying the truth of information is important not only for adults but also for young children at the "blank slate" stage.

When choosing different informants for learning, young children take into account both epistemic cues and social cues of the informants [18]. Cognitive cues reflect the level of knowledge or competence (e.g., prior accuracy) of the informant, and young children can obtain more and more reliable information by choosing to trust informants with more extensive and accurate knowledge [19]. Sociability reflects the influence of social and interpersonal relationships, whereby young children can integrate into a specific group by trusting a particular information provider, which facilitates the transfer of socio-cultural information for learning, as well as the establishment and maintenance of good social relationships [20]. Intellectual and social also interact when independently influencing young children's choice judgments separately [21], but it is not clear whether young children prioritize cognitive or social cues when selectively trusting. Younger toddlers are more likely to be influenced by social cues [22], and as they age toddlers are influenced by cognitive cues [23], but toddlers are unable to make trust judgments about relevant cognitive issues when faced with multiple conflicting cues [24].

Although young children have some ability to recognize misinformation [25, 26], it is still difficult for them to resist misinformation provided by informants. 3-year-olds also unconditionally choose to believe adults when confronted with misinformation [27] and 4-year-olds, although they may show paranoia, may believe "liars" [28]. 3-year-olds may unconditionally choose to believe adults when they are misinformed [27], and 4-year-olds may show paranoia but may also believe "liars" [28]. Therefore, there is a need to understand the development of cognitive vigilance in young children, to increase cognitive vigilance, and to help young children identify and resist misinformation.

Artificial intelligence devices are more accessible, have a wider range of information sources, and have a lower threshold for information acquisition [29], making them an important source of information for children. Voice assistants and social robots are among the more common AI devices in young children's lives. It has been found that young children will use voice assistants more as a source of information than as an entertainment tool [30], and will be more likely to ask voice assistants questions in natural domains [31]. Social robots possess more social characteristics than devices without a form of mental agency (e.g., voice assistants) and are also viewed as information providers by young children. A meta-analysis showed that young children can interact with and learn from robots [32]. As "digital natives," young children have more access to AI and more opportunities to obtain information from AI. A study by Breazeal et al. [33] found that 3–5-year-olds could view robots as informants and that 5-year-olds were able to recognize human informants and non-human informants [34]. This shows that social robots are an important source of information for young children.

Social robots are a difficult ontological concept for young children and even adults to distinguish, and it is difficult to define whether they are animate or inanimate. On the one hand, robots can move and talk like humans and even have a high degree of physical resemblance to humans. On the other hand, robots are artifacts made of metal or plastic. It has been found that young children interact with and learn from robots as information providers [32, 33]. However, it is undeniable that robots have yet to upgrade their technological capabilities and are not able to communicate as flexibly as real people and even make mistakes in many cases. When social robots provide misinformation to 3- and 4-year-old toddlers, do the toddlers choose to trust the robots as much as they trust adults? This study hypothesizes that 3-year-olds are more likely to unconditionally trust a social robot that provides misinformation compared to 4-year-olds.

A number of researchers have found a link between selective trust and theory of mind and inhibitory control in young children [35, 36]. Both theory of mind and selective trust require young children to make guesses about the intentions of others' beliefs, and young children with a high level of theory of mind can realize that everyone's beliefs and knowledge are different and that not every provider of information is correct [37]. Selective trust requires young children to notice and remember relevant characteristics of information providers, to self-regulate to select appropriate information providers when faced with unknown domains, and to inhibit inappropriately dominant responses when confronted with inauthentic information, similar to inhibitory control, a major component of executive functioning. Therefore, the present study hypothesized that there is an association between the theory of mind and young children's selective trust in social robots; there is also an association between inhibitory control and young children's selective trust in social robots.

2   Method

2.1   Participants

Sixty-six children from a kindergarten class in Wuhan City, Hubei Province, were randomly selected to participate in the experiment; one invalid subject (who withdrew halfway due to emotional problems) was excluded, and Sixty-five children finally completed the experiment. According to the age of the subjects on the day they participated in the experiment, the subjects were divided into the 3-year-old group ($n = 35$, $M = 43.29$ months, $SD = 3.01$; 14 boys, 21 girls) and the 4-year-old group ($n = 30$, $M = 51.27$ months, $SD = 2.08$; 18 boys, 12 girls).

2.2   Materials

Theory of Mind. This study adopts Wellman et al.'s [37, 38] revised scale of psycho-theoretical development to test the level of psycho-theoretical development of young children. In this scale the level of psycho-theoretical development is divided into five tasks: different desires, different beliefs, knowing and not knowing, content false beliefs, and hidden emotions, each task is scored as 1 if it passes, and 0 if it doesn't pass, with a total score of 0–5, and the higher the score represents the better the level of psycho-theoretical development.

Inhibitory Control. The McClelland et al.'s [39] head and feet task was taken to test the level of inhibitory control development in young children. Inhibitory control is divided into 4 times rule practice stages and 6 times of formal test stages, the score of the rule practice stage is not counted in the total score, in the formal test stage each time to make the correct action is recorded as 1 point, do not do the action or make the wrong action is recorded as 0 points, the total score of 0–6 points, the higher the score represents the better the level of development of inhibitory control.

Selective Trust. A single source of information paradigm was chosen for this study, taking Heyman et al.'s [40] item location task to test selective trust in young children. Subject 2 will assist the robot in playing the hide the sticker game with the subject together. There were 2 paper cups on the table, red and green. The robot would tell the toddler which color paper cup he or she hid the sticker in, but the robot consistently provided the wrong answer. When the toddler chooses to believe the information provided by the robot, she will not get the sticker and will be scored 0. The robot will also tell the toddler that she did not get the sticker. When the toddler chooses to reject the information provided by the robot, she will get the sticker, scoring 1 point, and the robot will also tell the toddler that you got it and can put the sticker you got on the plate. At the end of the game, Master Test 2 will tell the children that it was just a game and that the robot did not mean to provide incorrect information. The game is played for 6 rounds, with a total score of 0–6, with higher scores representing better levels of selective trust development.

Information Provider. In this study, a humanoid robot named "Wukong" is chosen as the information provider. The Wukong robot is 245 mm high, 149 mm wide, 112 mm thick, and weighs about 700 g. It has strong interactive functions, can answer human questions, communicate and dialog with humans, and can sing, dance, tell stories, etc. Its eyes have LCD screens, and it can show expressions of joy, anger, sadness, and happiness. Its eyes have LCD screens, which can present expressions of joy, anger, sadness, and happiness. Its arms, knees, neck, and other joints can move and can make some movements. For example, the Wukong robot can walk, dance, play Tai Chi, and so on. Besides, it also has a programming function, and users can program it through an APP to realize the control of the Wukong robot. In this study, the researcher programmed the robot through the APP to ensure that the experimental conditions faced by each young child were the same.

Procedure. The experiment was conducted in two quiet rooms in the kindergarten, where the toddlers were brought to the room where the experiment was conducted by a lab assistant. Main test 1 was responsible for conducting the tests of the toddlers' level of development of the theory of mind and inhibitory control. Main test 2 was responsible for conducting the test of selective trust of the toddlers. At the end of the game the children were allowed to take away the stickers they had received during the experiment and Main Test 2 would reward the children who had not won a sticker with one.

3 Data Analysis

In this study, the data were organized and data were analyzed using SPSS and processed through Spearman's correlation analysis and Mann-Whitney U-test. It was found that there was a significant difference between age and toddlers' selective trust scores ($U = 668.5, n1 = 35, n2 = 30, p < 0.05$). Specifically, 4-year-olds had higher selective trust scores than 3-year-olds, suggesting that as they get older, toddlers show more caution and selectivity when confronted with social robots that may provide misinformation. In addition, theory of mind was positively correlated with selective trust scores ($r = 0.26, n = 65, p < 0.05$), as was inhibitory control ($r = 0.48, n = 65, p < 0.01$). This implies that young children with stronger theories of mind and higher inhibitory control are more likely to be reserved and cautious about robots that provide misinformation.

4 Discussion

This study examined whether there would be a difference in selective trust scores between 3- and 4-year-old toddlers when confronted with a social robot that provides misinformation, and analyzed whether theory of mind and inhibitory control might have an effect on this. The results of the study show a significant difference between age and the selective trust scores of toddlers, a result that is consistent with the finding that humans were used as information providers. As Harris and Corriveau [27] showed, 3-year-olds still tended to trust familiar caregivers when confronted with inaccurate information, whereas 4- and 5-year-olds were more likely to choose whom to trust based on the accuracy of the information, even if it meant rejecting a familiar caregiver's information. The results of the study showed that the selective trust scores of 4-year-olds were higher than the selective trust scores of 3-year-olds. This shows that as they get older, toddlers will pay more attention to the cognitive cues of the informant, i.e., prior accuracy when making selective trust decisions. This implies that toddlers' decision-making mechanisms for selective trust when interacting with social robots may be similar to those when interacting with humans. However, this study only explores the characteristics of selective trust in young children when they face a single information provider. In real life, toddlers face more complex situations and may face two or even more information providers. One researcher used the conflicting information source paradigm to investigate the effect of prior knowledge accuracy on selective trust in 3-year-old toddlers. Using two different colored Nao robots as information providers and manipulating the accuracy of the robots' prior information through an item naming task, the study found that 3-year-olds were more likely to learn from the robot that had previously provided accurate information than the robot that had previously provided inaccurate information [41]. This shows that 3-year-olds do not blindly trust the robot. Thus, future research could be about younger toddlers' selective trust in social robots.

This study also found that young children's theory of mind was positively correlated with young children's selective trust scores for social robots, which is consistent with findings with human-as-informant studies that link young children's selective trust with the theory of mind and inhibitory control [35, 36]. As shown by Ding et al., [42] increased levels of psycho-theoretical cognition facilitated children's understanding of the concept of lying and the ability to recognize lying as a behavior that intentionally creates false beliefs in the listener through factually incorrect statements. Young children's inhibitory control was positively correlated with young children's selective trust scores in social robots, which is consistent with the findings with human-as-informants that there is a link between young children's selective trust and inhibitory control [36]. Li et al.'s [43] study also found that young children with a high level of inhibitory control recognize misinformation provided by the other party and resist abduction behaviors. This suggests that young children with stronger theories of mind and higher inhibitory control are more likely to be reserved and cautious about social robots that provide misinformation.

However, there are some limitations to this study. First, the number of subjects in this study was small, and the number of subjects should be increased in the future. Second, only one kindergarten child was selected for this study, which was in an economically developed area, and future studies should also expand the scope of the subjects by selecting kindergartens in economically underdeveloped areas to improve the representativeness of the results. Further, only one type of social robot was selected for this study in the experiment, and future studies should increase the types of social robots for research to explore the effects of different appearances of social robots on selective trust in young children.

Acknowledgments. We sincerely thank the children, teachers, and parents who supported and participated in this experiment.

References

1. Bartneck, C., Forlizzi, J.: A design-centred framework for social human-robot interaction. In: RO-MAN 2004. 13th IEEE International Workshop on Robot and Human Interactive Communication (IEEE Catalog No. 04TH8759), pp. 591–594. IEEE (2004)
2. Benitti, F.B.V.: Exploring the educational potential of robotics in schools: a systematic review. Comput. Educ. **58**(3), 978–988 (2012)
3. Druga, S., Williams, R., Breazeal, C., Resnick, M.: "Hey Google is it ok if I eat you?" Initial explorations in child-agent interaction. In: Proceedings of the 2017 Conference on Interaction Design and Children, pp. 595–600 (2017)
4. Satake, S., Hayashi, K., Nakatani, K., Kanda, T.: Field trial of an information-providing robot in a shopping mall. In: 2015 IEEE/RSJ International Conference on Intelligent Robots and Systems (IROS), pp. 1832–1839. IEEE (2015)
5. Han, J.H., Jo, M.H., Jones, V., Jo, J.H.: Comparative study on the educational use of home robots for children. J. Inf. Process. Syst. **4**(4), 159–168 (2008)
6. Movellan, J., Eckhardt, M., Virnes, M., Rodriguez, A.: Sociable robot improves toddler vocabulary skills. In: Proceedings of the 4th ACM/IEEE International Conference on Human Robot Interaction, pp. 307–308 (2009)
7. Baxter, P., Ashurst, E., Read, R., Kennedy, J., Belpaeme, T.: Robot education peers in a situated primary school study: personalisation promotes child learning. PLoS ONE **12**(5), e0178126 (2017)
8. Tanaka, F., Matsuzoe, S.: Children teach a care-receiving robot to promote their learning: field experiments in a classroom for vocabulary learning. J. Hum.-Robot Interact. **1**(1), 78–95 (2012)
9. Belpaeme, T., Kennedy, J., Ramachandran, A., Scassellati, B., Tanaka, F.: Social robots for education: a review. Sci. Robot. **3**(21), eaat5954 (2018)
10. Peter, J., Kühne, R., Barco, A.: Can social robots affect children's prosocial behavior? An experimental study on prosocial robot models. Comput. Hum. Behav. **120**, 106712 (2021)
11. Jia, Q., Lee, J., Pang, Y.: Praise for the robot model affects children's sharing behavior. In: Zaphiris, P., Ioannou, A. (eds.) HCII 2023. LNCS, vol. 14041, pp. 327–335. Springer, Cham (2023). https://doi.org/10.1007/978-3-031-34550-0_23
12. Yuan, M., Deng, Z., Ji, P.: Children's social epistemology: children's selective trust in informants. Adv. Psychol.Sci. (03), 480–486 (2013). (in Chinese)
13. Wah, C.Y., Ki, C.L.: Epistemic trust: how preschoolers selectively learn from others. Adv. Psychol. Sci. (01), 86–96 (2014). (in Chinese)
14. Csibra, G., Gergely, G.: Natural pedagogy. Trends Cogn. Sci. **13**(4), 148–153 (2009)
15. Baier, A.: Trust and antitrust. In: Feminist Social Thought, pp. 604–629. Routledge (2014)
16. Jaswal, V.K.: Don't believe everything you hear: preschoolers' sensitivity to speaker intent in category induction. Child Dev. **75**(6), 1871–1885 (2004)
17. Jaswal, V.K., Croft, A.C., Setia, A.R., Cole, C.A.: Young children have a specific, highly robust bias to trust testimony. Psychol. Sci. **21**(10), 1541–1547 (2010)
18. Terrier, N., Bernard, S., Mercier, H., Clément, F.: Visual access trumps gender in 3- and 4-year-old children's endorsement of testimony. J. Exp. Child Psychol. **146**, 223–230 (2016)
19. Sobel, D.M., Finiasz, Z.: How children learn from others: an analysis of selective word learning. Child Dev. **91**(6) (2020)

20. Bernard, S., Proust, J., Clément, F.: Four-to six-year-old children's sensitivity to reliability versus consensus in the endorsement of object labels. Child Dev. **86**(4), 1112–1124 (2015)
21. Landrum, A.R., Pflaum, A.D., Mills, C.M.: Inducing knowledgeability from niceness: children use social features for making epistemic inferences. J. Cogn. Dev. **17**(5), 699–717 (2016)
22. Mascaro, O., Sperber, D.: The moral, epistemic, and mindreading components of children's vigilance towards deception. Cognition **112**(3), 367–380 (2009). https://doi.org/10.1016/j.cognition.2009.05.012
23. Einav, S.: Does the majority always know best? Young children's flexible trust in majority opinion. PLoS ONE **9**(8), e104585 (2014)
24. Brosseau-Liard, P.E., Birch, S.A.J.: Epistemic states and traits: preschoolers appreciate the differential informativeness of situation-specific and person-specific cues to knowledge. Child Dev. **82**(6), 1788–1796 (2011)
25. Marble, K.E., Boseovski, J.J.: Content counts: a trait and moral reasoning framework for children's selective social learning. Adv. Child Dev. Behav. **58**, 95–136 (2020)
26. Mills, C.M.: Knowing when to doubt: developing a critical stance when learning from others. Dev. Psychol. **49**(3), 404 (2013)
27. Harris, P.L., Corriveau, K.H.: Young children's selective trust in informants. Philos. Trans. Royal Soc. B Biol. Sci. **366**(1567), 1179–1187 (2011)
28. Vanderbilt, K.E., Liu, D., Heyman, G.D.: The development of distrust. Child Dev. **82**(5), 1372–1380 (2011)
29. Mao, Y., Tong, Y., Li, H., Wang, F.: Artificial intelligence and child development: research based on robots and voice assistants. Chin. J. Appl. Psychol. (05), 413–423 (2022). (in Chinese)
30. Oranç, C., Ruggeri, A.: "Alexa, let me ask you something different" Children's adaptive information search with voice assistants. Hum. Behav. Emerg. Technol. **3**(4), 595–605 (2021)
31. Li, Z., Liu, Z., Mao, K., Li, W., Li, T., Li, J.: The epistemic trust of 3- to 6-year-olds in digital voice assistants in various domains. Acta Psychologica Sinica (09), 1411–1423 (2023). (in Chinese)
32. Stower, R., Calvo-Barajas, N., Castellano, G., Kappas, A.: A meta-analysis on children's trust in social robots. Int. J. Soc. Robot. **13**(8), 1979–2001 (2021)
33. Breazeal, C., Harris, P.L., DeSteno, D., Kory Westlund, J.M., Dickens, L., Jeong, S.: Young Children treat robots as informants. Top. Cogn. Sci. **8**(2), 481–491 (2016)
34. Baumann, A.-E., Goldman, E.J., Meltzer, A., Poulin-Dubois, D.: People do not always know best: preschoolers' trust in social robots. J. Cogn. Dev. **24**, 1–28 (2023)
35. Brosseau-Liard, P., Penney, D., Poulin-Dubois, D.: Theory of mind selectively predicts preschoolers' knowledge-based selective word learning. Br. J. Dev. Psychol. **33**(4), 464–475 (2015)
36. Ding, X., Sang, B., Pan, T.: Relations between selective trust, theory of mind, and executive function in preschoolers: evidence from longitudinal study. J. Psychol. Sci. (05), 1129–1135 (2017). https://doi.org/10.16719/j.cnki.1671-6981.20170516. (in Chinese)
37. Wellman, H.M., Liu, D.: Scaling of theory-of-mind tasks. Child Dev. **75**(2), 523–541 (2004). https://doi.org/10.1111/j.1467-8624.2004.00691.x
38. Wellman, H.M., Fang, F., Liu, D., Zhu, L., Liu, G.: Scaling of theory-of-mind understandings in Chinese children. Psychol. Sci. **17**(12), 1075–1081 (2006). https://doi.org/10.1111/j.1467-9280.2006.01830.x
39. McClelland, M.M., Cameron, C.E., Connor, C.M., Farris, C.L., Jewkes, A.M., Morrison, F.J.: Links between behavioral regulation and preschoolers' literacy, vocabulary, and math skills. Dev. Psychol. **43**(4), 947–959 (2007). https://doi.org/10.1037/0012-1649.43.4.947
40. Heyman, G.D., Sritanyaratana, L., Vanderbilt, K.E.: Young children's trust in overtly misleading advice. Cogn. Sci. **37**(4), 646–667 (2013)

41. Brink, K.A., Wellman, H.M.: Robot teachers for children? Young children trust robots depending on their perceived accuracy and agency. Dev. Psychol. **56**(7), 1268 (2020)
42. Ding, X.P., Wellman, H.M., Wang, Y., Fu, G., Lee, K.: Theory-of-mind training causes honest young children to lie. Psychol. Sci. **26**(11), 1812–1821 (2015)
43. Li, Q., Wu, X., Zhai, Y., Zhang, Z., Zhang, N.: Development trend of 3-to 5-year-old children's resistance to abduction and the predictive effect of theory of mind on children's resistance to abduction. Chin. J. Appl. Psychol. (05), 433–440 (2022). (in Chinese)

Effects of the Exoskeleton on Human Physiological Stress

Yang Liu[1]([⊠]), Erkang Hui[1], Yanmin Xue[1], Xiaoling Li[2], Mengcheng Wang[1], Xin Zhou[1], Xiaowen Liu[1], and Dan Hui[1]

[1] School of Art and Design, Xi'an University of Technology, Xi'an 710049, China
105388@xaut.edu.cn
[2] Xi'an Jiaotong University, Xi'an, 710049, China

Abstract. Despite the advantages of powered exoskeletons for occupational safety, their design, including characteristics such as weight and volume, may induce localized physiological burdens on operators. The current understanding of how exoskeleton characteristics impact physiological stress is unclear. Therefore, this study designed an experimental exoskeleton with the capability for external feature expansion (EXOT). EXOT comprises four parts for the upper and lower limbs, each coupled to the human body through commonly used strapping methods in exoskeletons. The experiment utilized a polr heart rate monitor to collect heart rate variability (HRV), and Rating of Perceived Exertion (RPE) questionnaires were collected at the beginning and end of each task for physiological stress assessment. The results indicated a significant increase in the LF and HF ratio of HRV with an increase in load weight compared to the control group, with the highest activation observed in the upper limbs. The LF and HF ratio exhibited significant inter-group differences between M1 and M2 under varying walking speeds. Participants in the M1 and M2 configurations showed an increasing trend in RPE compared to the control group. This study suggests that higher exoskeleton mass exacerbates the physiological stress.

Keywords: Exoskeleton · Physiological Stress · HRV · Load Mass · Work Safety

1 Introduction

The intervention of exoskeletons maintains a continuous human-machine coupling during movement, allowing operators to select exoskeletons with different assistive features based on task conditions and specific operational characteristics. Although powered exoskeletons contribute to occupational safety, the design characteristics such as weight, stiffness, and volume may impose localized physiological burdens on operators and affect their mobility, potentially further intervening in metabolic processes [1, 2]. However, the current understanding of how exoskeleton characteristics affect movement is unclear, and it remains uncertain which characteristics of exoskeletons' influence can be reflected in the response of typical physiological parameters. Therefore, the accuracy of exoskeleton assessment will be affected by the impact of exoskeletons as external loads

© The Author(s), under exclusive license to Springer Nature Switzerland AG 2024
C. Stephanidis et al. (Eds.): HCII 2024, CCIS 2114, pp. 381–386, 2024.
https://doi.org/10.1007/978-3-031-61932-8_43

on energy consumption calculation. This study will conduct experimental research on the intervention of human movement by exoskeletons with different wear characteristics, analyze the response characteristics of physiological parameters, and explore factors influencing changes in physiological stress.

2 Method

2.1 Exoskeleton

In order to independently vary the impact of exoskeleton load attributes such as weight, volume, and stiffness as much as possible, an experimental exoskeleton with the capability for external feature expansion (EXOT) was designed. Figure 1 illustrates the EXOT, composed of four limb parts and a back part, connected to the human body through commonly used strapping methods in exoskeletons. The total weight of the 3D-printed EXOT was controlled to be 1.68 kg. Given the research goal of altering multiple attributes of the exoskeleton in different configurations within the human-machine coupling, materials representing detachable configurations were chosen. This approach aimed to minimize variations in the other two attributes. To achieve this, flat sets of weights were used for load variation, while simultaneously restricting increases in volume characteristics. The selected weights were adhesive and could be affixed to the load-bearing structure of the EXOT arms, legs, and back. Lightweight foam blocks with a volume of 20 L were used to augment the exoskeleton's volume configuration. Additionally, different torque coil springs and elastic rubber pads were added to the joint connection points in the EXOT to modify the stiffness of the exoskeleton at the elbow, knee, and spine sections. These additional components could be attached to all body regions and adapted to different load configurations.

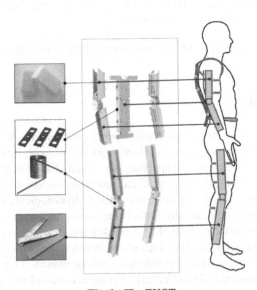

Fig. 1. The EXOT

2.2 Experimental Design

The test comprised one control group and six exoskeleton configurations: (a) control group (without exoskeleton); (b) unilateral upper and lower limb load masses (M1, M2) of 0.5 kg, 1 kg, and 1.5 kg, respectively; (c) back load masses (M3) of 1 kg, 1.5 kg, 2 kg, 2.5 kg, and 3 kg; (d) an increase of 20L in volume for each part (B20); (e) moderate stiffness (S1), high stiffness (S2). Load sizes were determined based on existing exoskeleton weights as a reference [3]. Following safety recommendations from NOISH, the selected total mass did not exceed 33% of the subject's body weight. The experiment took place in a thermally neutral environment at 23 °C.

2.3 Test Procedure

Ten male young adults (with a weight of 71.17 kg ± 4.23 kg, height of 174 cm ± 3.21 cm, and age of 26.77 ± 2.65) participated in the experiment. To investigate the effects of walking speed and load position on metabolic rate, participants had additional mass attached to their upper limbs, lower limbs, and back. Under various load positions and load weight conditions, participants were required to walk at speeds of 4 km·h-1, 5 km·h-1, and 6 km·h-1. Prior to each test, participants underwent a 10-min warm-up, followed by the commencement of the testing tasks in sequence. There was a minimum rest period of 1 h between each task. Due to the inclusion of subjective parameter collection, a Latin square design was used to control for the effects of experimental sequence. All experiments were conducted on a treadmill with zero gradient. Respiratory parameters were measured, and metabolic rate (MR) was calculated, with heart rate (HR) and mean skin temperature (MST) data collected for all participants simultaneously. Following the completion of each task, participants rated their perceived exertion using the Borg Rating of Perceived Exertion (RPE) questionnaire. Subsequent paragraphs, however, are indented.

2.4 Analysis

Statistical analysis was conducted using SPSS 22 (IBM). The Shapiro-Wilk test was utilized to assess the normality of the data. As all data, except for RPE, followed a normal distribution, parametric statistical tests were employed. A repeated measures ANOVA was performed to determine if there were differences in physiological parameters, followed by LSD post-hoc tests. A significance level of $p < 0.01$ was set to determine significant differences, while p-values between 0.01 and 0.05 were considered marginally significant. The Friedman two-way analysis of variance by ranks, a non-parametric test, was used to examine the differences in RPE scores across different exercise configurations ($p < 0.05$).

3 Results

3.1 HR, RPE and Metabolic Rate

Table 1 presents the physiological response results under exoskeleton loads. Observations from the results indicate that metabolic rate (MR) only exhibited significant differences compared to the control group in the M1, M2, and M3 modes ($p < 0.05$).

The average heart rate (HR) was slightly higher than that of the control group, but no significant difference was observed between them (p > 0.05). It can be observed that the average heart rate fluctuated within the range of 139 b·min-1 to 133 b·min-1 across all conditions. Mean skin temperature (MST) did not show significant differences among different configurations throughout the exercise range (p > 0.05). However, in the Rating of Perceived Exertion (RPE) results, participants reported greater perceived exertion under the M1, M2, and M3 configurations compared to the control group, with the perceived exertion level under M1 being similar to that under M3, indicating that energy expenditure is only influenced by exoskeleton mass. MR seems to respond to changes in subjective exertion level, leading to slight fluctuations in heart rate, but the specific underlying mechanisms require further analysis.

Table 1. The results of HR, RPE and Metabolic rate.

	Control Group	M1*	M2**	M3*	B20	S1	S2
HR/b·min-1	134.9 ± 10.5	137.7 ± 10.9	139.0 ± 6.4	133.4 ± 11.1	133.4 ± 8.7	132.5 ± 9.0	135.7 ± 12.3
MST/°C	33.4 ± 0.12	32.8 ± 0.30	34.7 ± 0.19	33.4 ± 0.58	34.3 ± 0.22	31.4 ± 0.55	34.1 ± 0.23
RPEScale	10 ± 3	13 ± 1	15 ± 2	13 ± 1	10 ± 2	10 ± 2	10 ± 1
MR/W·m-2	137.36 ± 12	149.59 ± 21	177.13 ± 17	146.61 ± 13	131.95 ± 11	138.44 ± 15	133.75 ± 19

3.2   HRV

Since the Polar heart rate monitor itself includes RR interval data, which represents heart rate variability (HRV), it can be directly extracted for sympathetic nervous system activity analysis. Figure 2 illustrates the RR intervals during upper limb exoskeleton loading exercise range.

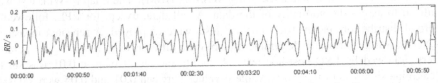

Fig. 2. Time-domain plot of RR intervals during upper limb exoskeleton loading exercise range.

The HRV spectrum consists of high frequency (HF) ranging from 0.15 to 0.4 Hz and low frequency (LF) ranging from 0.04 to 0.15 Hz [4]. An increase in LF power indicates dominance of sympathetic nervous system (SNS) activity, whereas an increase in power in the high frequency (HF) band suggests enhanced parasympathetic nervous system (PNS) activity. Spontaneous regulation behaviors related to muscle movement and environmental adaptation are manifested in SNS activity, with LF increasing as the level of physical activity rises. Therefore, the study extracted LF and HF and combined

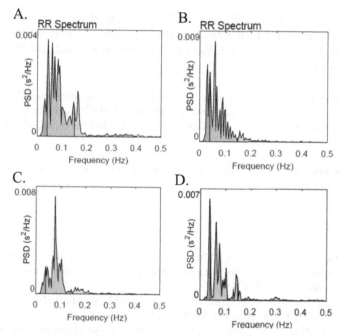

Fig. 3. The results of LF/HF ratio under exoskeleton weight configuration changes. (A: Control; B: M1; C: M2; D: M3.)

them into the LF/HF ratio as an index of sympathetic nervous system balance, analyzing the physiological mechanisms between exoskeleton mass variations and load changes.

Figure 3 presents the LF and HF activity results under varying load weights obtained using fast Fourier transform. Compared to the control group, the LF/HF ratio significantly increased with an increase in load weight ($p < 0.05$), with the highest activation observed in the upper limb; the LF/HF ratios for the control group, M1, M2, and M3 were 4.60, 8.56, 6.92, and 6.56, respectively.

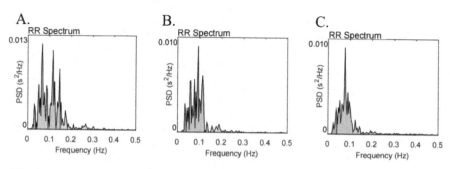

Fig. 4. The results of LF/HF ratio under changes in exercise speed. (A: M1; B: M2; C: M3.)

Figure 4 displays the LF/HF results under speed variations. There were significant intergroup differences in LF/HF ratios between M1 and M2, as well as between M1 and M3, with p-values less than 0.001. The LF/HF ratios for M1, M2, and M3 were 9.56, 7.92, and 7.36, respectively.

Acknowledgments. This research was funded by the Scientific· Research Program of Shaanxi· Provincial· Education· Department. (grant number 23JK0567), and by Shaanxi Province Natural Science Basic Research Program General Project (Youth) Project (2024JC-YBQN-0996).

Disclosure of Interests.   The authors have no competing interests to declare that are relevant to the content of this article.

References

1. Bach, A.J.E., Costello, J.T., Borg, D.N., et al.: The Pandolf load carriage equation is a poor predictor of metabolic rate while wearing explosive ordnance disposal protective clothing. Ergonomics **60**(3), 430–438 (2017)
2. Bastien, G.J., Willems, P.A., Schepens, B., et al.: Effect of load and speed on the energetic cost of human walking. Eur. J. Appl. Physiol. **94**(1–2), 76–83 (2005)
3. Liu, Y., Li, X., Zhu, A., et al.: Design and evaluation of a surface electromyography-controlled lightweight upper arm exoskeleton rehabilitation robot. Int. J. Adv. Robot. Syst. **18**(3) (2021)
4. Rombold-Bruehl, F., Otte, C., Renneberg, B., et al.: Lower heart rate variability at baseline is associated with more consecutive intrusive memories in an experimental distressing film paradigm. World J. Biol. Psychiatry **20**(8), 662–667 (2019)

Development of a Attentive Listening Robot Using the Motion Prediction Based on Surrogate Data

Shohei Noguchi[1]([⊠])(iD), Yutaka Nakamura[2](iD), and Yuya Okadome[1,2](iD)

[1] Tokyo University of Science, Faculty of Engineering, Department of Information and Computer Technology, Tokyo, Japan
noguchisho0201@gmail.com , okadome@rs.tus.ac.jp
[2] RIKEN Information R&D and Strategy Headquarters, Wako, Japan

Abstract. The development of nonverbal behavior functions such as nodding is also important for natural dialogue robots. However, since natural nonverbal dialogue functions is not developed, it is not possible to gather natural human-robot dialogue data. In this study, we developed the attentive listening robot system that uses human-human dialogue data as surrogate data. The nodding prediction model substitute human-human dialogue data for human-robot dialogue data to predict the behavior of the dialogue robot. The proposed system makes a judgment on whether to nod based on the output of the prediction model, audio and image information are input to the model. The results of the attentive listening experiment suggested that the proposed system that generates noddings that make it easier to speak was developed.

Keywords: Human robot interaction · Surrogate behavior · Dialogue robot · Nodding

1 Introduction

For a decade, the demand for communication robots has been growing because of the lobar shortage problem in the nursing care [1] and customer service fields. These robots communicate with humans through conversation and gestures. It is expected that they can interact with humans in a human-like manner, thanks to their physical presence.

There are two components to communication: verbal and non-verbal. Large language models, such as ChatGPT [2], dramatically enhance the performance of verbal aspects. In addition, improving non-verbal functions, such as facial expressions, gestures, and speaking tempo [3], is crucial for "natural" communication robots.

Researchers propose several studies on robots performing non-verbal actions. Joanna et al. [4] developed a robot system that performs three motions: nodding, gaze movement, and eye blinking, using voice volume as a criterion. Tojo et

© The Author(s), under exclusive license to Springer Nature Switzerland AG 2024
C. Stephanidis et al. (Eds.): HCII 2024, CCIS 2114, pp. 387–394, 2024.
https://doi.org/10.1007/978-3-031-61932-8_44

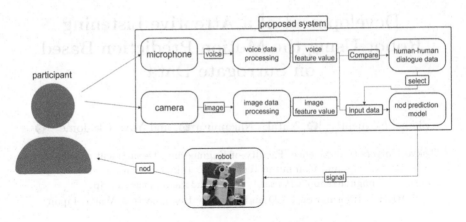

Fig. 1. Schematic diagram of this system

al. [5] developed a robot system that recognizes the direction of the speaker's face and speech content and performs actions such as nodding. Results show that people have a more favorable impression when the robot displays facial expressions and behaviors. Chaoran et al. [6] investigate the rule-based robot system that nods appropriately during speech. Chidchanok et al. [7] investigate the difference between several non-verbal functions that influence the human impression. However, designing actions that take into account all situations that occur in human-robot interaction is not easy.

We propose the attentive listening robotic system. The proposed system uses human-human dialogue data as surrogate action data [8] instead of human-robot dialogue data to predict the actions during attentive listening. The proposed system concatenates the observed speaker's voice, neck angle, gaze angles, and facial expressions with prepared surrogate data. The concatenated data is input into the nod prediction model, and then the decision whether nodding or not is output.

We conducted the attentive listening experiment using the proposed system. In this experiment, the participants speak to the attentive listening robot for 1 min, and during speaking, the robotic system performed a nodding motion. The experimental results indicate that the nodding of the system gives the impression that the speaker is more comfortable speaking.

2   Proposed Method

In this study, we propose the attentive listening robot that performs nodding as a non-verbal behavior. Figure 1 shows an overview of the proposed system. The first step is to preprocess the features extracted from the audio and image data observed. Then, features are input into the nodding prediction model.

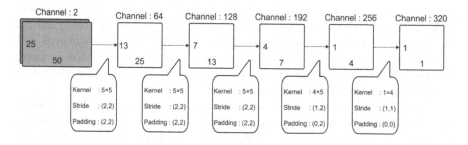

Fig. 2. Network structure of CNN

2.1 Pre-processing of Observed Data

Loudness normalization is used to preprocess the audio data. This process reduces the influence of voice volume fluctuations caused by changes in mouth position relative to the microphone.

Open Face [9] is used to extract facial features, such as the angles of the head and gaze, along with the Facial Action Units (FAUs), from the image data. Differential value angles of the head and eye and zero-order hold are used to preprocess the extracted features. Using differential value angles reduces the influence of the initial position of the participants. Zero-order hold is a method to compensate for missing head angle or gaze from the previous frame.

2.2 Nodding Prediction Model

A nodding prediction model determines whether a person will nod within 0.5 s. To reduce annotation costs, self-supervised learning with dyadic conversation is used to pre-train the model. Okadome et al.'s proposed data augmentation technique [8], called the lag operation, is used during self-supervised learning. The lag operation breaks the temporal structure embedded in the dialogue data by shifting the timestamps of one participant. The pre-training weight obtained by the process is used for training nodding prediction, such as a downstream task. Then, a small amount of annotated data with nodding labels is utilized for supervised learning to obtain the nodding prediction model. Furthermore, human-human dialogue data is utilized to train the nodding predictive model.

Output $\hat{l}$ is calculated as $\hat{l} = f(X_L(t), X_R(t); \omega)$, where f is the nodding prediction model. $X_L(t)$ and $X_R(t)$ represent the features of two persons for the past T steps from a time t. ω denotes the parameters of the prediction model. In this study, the structure of the nodding prediction model is a 5-layer CNN model shown in Fig. 2. Empirically, both image and audio data are downsampled to 10 fps.

2.3 Decision to Execute a Nodding

This section describes the method for selecting surrogate action data for input to the nodding prediction model. While the system is running, feature values of two persons are necessary, just as when training the nodding prediction model. However, during the conversation session, only one participant's feature value can be obtained. Therefore, another participant's feature value is substituted with a surrogate feature value. The input data is a concatenation of the speaker's feature value $X_R^T(t)$ and the surrogate feature value $\bar{X}_L^S$. Note that the role of participant L is the attentive listener.

Figure 3 shows an overview of the concatenation process. Since human movement is expected to be continuous at 0.1-second intervals, we assume that $\hat{l}(t)$ has a high probability of the same label as $\hat{l}(t - 0.1)$. Therefore, the two surrogate sets $\bar{X}_0^S, \bar{X}_1^S$ are selected based on the condition of the previous nodding prediction result. $\bar{X}_0^S, \bar{X}_1^S$ represent data with nodding and not nodding labels that are the subset of training data of the nodding prediction model.

The input data $X(t)$ is a concatenation of $X_R^T(t)$ obtained in real time and X_L^S. The index k of the selected surrogate data is calculated as follows:

$$c_i = \frac{\langle X_R^T(t), \bar{X}_{p,R_i}^S \rangle}{||X_R^T(t)|| \, ||\bar{X}_{p,R_i}^S||}, p = \hat{l}(t - 0.1), \tag{1}$$

$$k = \text{argmax}\{c|c = c_0, c_1, ...\}, \tag{2}$$

$\bar{X}_{p,i}^S = (\bar{X}_{p,L_i}^S, \bar{X}_{p,R_i}^S)$ represents the i-th surrogate data. c_i is the cosine similarity between $X_R^T(t)$ and the speaker's features $\bar{X}_{p,R_i}^S$ in the surrogate data. The input data can be expressed as $X(t) = [\bar{X}_{p,L_k}^S, X_R^T(t)]$ by using k derived from Eq. 2.

Based on the output probability from the nodding prediction model, the robot decides whether to nod or not. In this study, the robot nods only when the output probability exceeds the threshold (0.6) empirically.

3   Experimental Details

3.1   Experimental Procedure

The participants in the experiment are 12 male students (age 22.0 ± 1.0) from Tokyo University of Science. There are 10 valid responses, due to the error of sensors.

The participants sit facing the robot and speak to it. The following two systems are used in speech sessions. The participants evaluate their impressions of each robot system.

- Proposed:
  Predict nodding using surrogate data.
- Rule:
  When speech interval is for 0.2 s, the robot nods with 90% chance.

A Rule system is designed considering that the silent interval when occurring turn-taking is approximately 0.2 s [10].

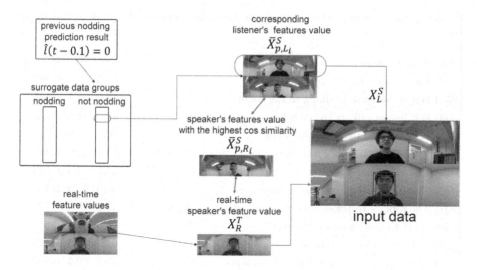

Fig. 3. Overview of data concatenation

3.2 Questionnaire

In this experiment, the 14-questions questionnaire with a 5-point Likert scale is utilized. The questionnaire content is based on the subjective evaluation questionnaire for attentive listening robots by Inoue et al. [11], and the number of questions is designed considering the workload of the participants. The Mann-Whitney U test is used to compare the differences between A and B for each question.

3.3 Experimental Results

Table 1 shows the questionnaire items and the test results. Note that the original questionnaire items in Japanese are listed in Appendix A. U1 represents the test statistic of Proposed, and U2 represents the test statistic of Rule. The items Q1, Q7, and Q10 are highlighted out of the 14 items in Table 1. These are "(Q1) It was easy to talk to the robot." with $p = 0.087$, "(Q7) The robot's response was human-like" with $p = 0.125$, and "(Q10) The robot was listening to me seriously" with $p = 0.173$. Since $p < 0.1$, there is a significant tendency in the (Q1) questionnaire item.

4 Discussion

In this section, we discuss the reasons for the significant tendency observed in the (Q1) questionnaire item, and the behavior of the proposed system. In the Proposed, there are cases where the robot nods even when the participant is still speaking. The participants may perceive such noddings during speech as

S. Noguchi et al.

Table 1. Test results. The original questionnaire items in Japanese are listed in Appendix

Questionnaire item	U1	U2	P Value
(Q1) Easy to talk to the robot	67.5	32.5	0.087^+
(Q2) Felt embarrassed talking to the robot	48.5	51.5	0.565
(Q3) Felt happy talking to the robot	52.0	48.0	0.448
(Q4) Feel uneasy talking to the robot	50.0	50.0	0.516
(Q5) The robot's behavior was natural	56.0	44.0	0.327
(Q6) The robot responded at the right timeing	46.5	53.5	0.623
(Q7) The robot's response was human-like	65.0	35.0	0.125
(Q8) The robot's response appropriately encouraged you to talk	43.0	57.0	0.725
(Q9) Want to talk to this robot again	45.5	54.5	0.657
(Q10) The robot was listening to you seriously	62.5	37.5	0.173
(Q11) The robot understood speech contents	39.5	60.5	0.814
(Q12) The robot showed interest in what you were saying	49.0	51.0	0.548
(Q13) The robot showed empathy towards you	47.0	53.0	0.610
(Q14) The robot was not listening to you very attentively	56.0	44.0	0.330

$+ : p < 0.1$

having the effect of encouraging them to continue speaking. However, there is no significant difference in the questionnaire item "The robot's response appropriately encouraged you to talk." (Q8), and some participants answered that they feel "hurried" in the free description. These results indicate that the amount and timing of the robot's nodding may not be appropriate. On the other hand, the results indicate that simple nodding motion can influence human speech, even if the surrogate data are used.

FAUs, representing the magnitude of the observed facial expression, strongly influence the nodding decision of the proposed attentive listening system. In particular, since the estimation results of FAUs in OpenFace are not stable for each participant, the robust FAUs estimator is necessary for developing a stable attentive listening system.

5 Summary

In this study, we developed the attentive listening robotic system using surrogate behavior. The system concatenates features obtained from a database as surrogate behavior with features obtained in real time. In addition, multimodal data, such as audio data, head and eye gaze angles, and facial expressions, is used. Experiments indicated that the system can generate nods that make it more comfortable for the speaker to speak.

The behavior of the nodding prediction model developed in this study is strongly affected by the FAUs. Therefore, improving the system to estimate facial expressions more accurately is a future issue. Another issue is the implementation of functions to respond by sounds such as "un" and "ah".

Acknowledgment. This work was supported by JSPS KAKENHI Grant Number JP23K16977.

Appendix A The Original Questionnaire Items in Japanese

Questionnaire item
(Q1) しゃべりやすかった
(Q2) ずかしさを感じた
(Q3) 嬉しい分になった
(Q4) 落ち着かない部分があった
(Q5) ロボットの振る舞いは自然だった
(Q6) ロボットはタイミングよく反していた
(Q7) ロボットの反は人らしかった
(Q8) ロボットの反はあなたのを切に促してた
(Q9) このロボットとまたしたい
(Q10) ロボットは真面目にをいていた
(Q11) ロボットはを理解していた
(Q12) ロボットはにする心を示していた
(Q13) ロボットはあなたにして共感を示していた
(Q14) ロボットはあまり集中してをいていなかった

$+ : p < 0.1$

References

1. Vercelli, A., Rainero, I., Ciferri, L., Boido, M., Pirri, F.: Robots in elderly care. ICT Neurodegener. Dis. [special issue] **2**(2), 37–50 (2018)
2. ChatGPT OpenAI. (https://openai.com/chatgpt). Reading Date 11 Feb 2024
3. Saunderson, S., Nejat, G.: How robots influence humans: a survey of nonverbal communication in social human-robot interaction. Int. J. Soc. Robot. **11**, 575–608 (2019)
4. Hall, J., Tritton, T., Rowe, A., Pipe, A., Melhuish, C., Leonards, U.: Perception of own and robot engagement in human-robot interactions and their dependence on robotics knowledge. Robot. Auton. Syst. **62**, 392–399 (2014)
5. Tojo, T., Matsusaka, Y., Ishii, T., Kobayashi, T.: A conversational robot utilizing facial and body expressions. In: SMC 2000 Conference Proceedings. 2000 IEEE International Conference on Systems, Man and Cybernetics. 'Cybernetics Evolving To Systems, Humans, Organizations, and their Complex Interactions' (cat. no.0), pp. 858–863, October 2000

6. Liu, C., Ishi, C.T., Ishiguro, H., Hagita, N.: Generation of nodding, head tilting and eye gazing for human-robot dialogue interaction. In: 2012 7th ACMIEEE International Conference on Human-Robot Interaction (HRI), pp. 285–292, March 2012

7. Thepsoonthorn, C., Ogawa, K., Miyake, Y.: The relationship between robot's non-verbal behaviour and human's likability based on human's personality. Sci. Rep. **8**, 8435 (2018)

8. Okadome, Y., Ata, K., Ishiguro, H., Nakamura, Y.: Self-supervised learning method for behavior prediction during dialogue based on temporal consistency. Trans. Jpn. Soc. Artif. Intell. **37**(6), 1–13 (2022). (in Japanese)

9. Baltrusaitis, T., Zadeh, A., Lim, Y.C., Morency, L.-P.: Openface 2.0: Facial behavior analysis toolkit, pp. 59–66, May 2018

10. Skantze, G.: Turn-taking in conversational systems and human-robot interaction: a review. Comput. Speech Lang. **67**, 101178 (2021)

11. Inoue, K., Lala, D., Yamamoto, K., Nakamura, S., Takanashi, K., Kawahara, T.: An attentive listening system for autonomous android Erica: comparative evaluation with human attentive listeners. Trans. Jpn. Soc. Artif. Intell. **36**(5), 1–12 (2021). (in Japanese)

Investigating Hospital Service Robots: A Observation Study About Relieving Information Needs at the Hospital Reception

Domenic Sommer[(✉)], Stefan Fischer, and Florian Wahl

Deggendorf Institute of Technology,
Dieter-Görlitz-Platz 1, 94469 Deggendorf, Germany
{Domenic.Sommer,Stefan.Fischer2,Florian.Wahl}@th-deg.de

Abstract. Hospital receptions (HRs) are a vital area to meet information needs. Deploying Service Robots (SRs) is increasingly important in HR due to staff shortages and increasing healthcare demands in Germany. To evaluate the effectiveness of SR in HR, we conducted a consecutive study during one week in September 2023 in a rural Bavarian hospital. The study involved 1,703 interactions, primarily handled by HR staff (89.9 %), with SRs addressing 10.1 %. HR was mainly requested from 10:00 to 15:00 and the SR between 13:00 to 19:00. Each interaction was mainly under one minute. The requests were predominantly regarding orientation by both the SR and the hospital staff. Our results indicate that SR can reduce workload, saving 2.15 working hours during the study. The findings suggest SRs' utility in information provision yet highlight the need for more comprehensive studies with advanced SRs in healthcare to optimize their role in information management.

Keywords: Service Robots · HCI · Information Needs · Hospital Reception

1 Introduction

Hospital stakeholders desire information, and Hospital Receptions (HRs) serve as the initial contact point for patients, visitors, and externals [1,4]. Because HRs can influence the overall hospital experience and satisfaction, studies emphasize the role of HR in being customer-centered [18]. HR plays a vital role in meeting the information and support needs, such as way-finding [11,12,15]. HR is important for hospitals' core processes, ensuring that the right patients get guided to their treatments timely [2]. HRs assist administrative, forward people and answer Frequently Asked Questions (FAQs) [11].

The related work regarding HRs is limited, even though meeting information needs in HR is a common challenge that binds capacities [16]. This is paralleled by the difficulties patients and families face in dealing with the complexities of

The research is funded by the *Federal Ministry of Transport* under grant 45FGU120.

© The Author(s), under exclusive license to Springer Nature Switzerland AG 2024
C. Stephanidis et al. (Eds.): HCII 2024, CCIS 2114, pp. 395–404, 2024.
https://doi.org/10.1007/978-3-031-61932-8_45

the hospital setting [4]. Predominantly, information needs in HR are handled by staff, including answering questions regarding COVID-19, managing appointments, and location guidance, often within a short interaction time frame [14].

In the face of growing healthcare demands and higher case numbers due to demographic shifts, an increase in HRs information needs is expected [10]. Managing information at the HR becomes critical, but Germany faces a healthcare staff shortage. A vital role in relieving the burden on staff and solutions to cope with the increasing demands can be the introduction of service robots [3]. Service Robots (SRs) are shown potential in meeting the information needs in hospitals and relief staff to focus on special requests and in-depth communication, such as direct patient support, advice, and emotional empowerment [5]. Jet service robot adoption in HR remains limited, but SRs will get more accessible [13].

We deploy SR within the HR to assess the effectiveness of the robot in meeting information needs previously identified in the HR. This paper compares information needs from different stakeholders, their answers by HR-staff and SRs, and examines information flow and staff relief. Therefore, we conducted a one-week observation and evaluation of the robot logs between November 13th and 19th, 2023 in a HR, answering the question: **How effective is the deployment of SR in HR regarding meeting information needs and relieving HR staff?** Our study includes the following sub-questions:

RQ1 Which inquiries are primarily handled by the robot vs. HR staff?
RQ2 How do patient, visitor, and employee information needs vary?
RQ3 In what manner and speed do the robot and HR staff respond to inquiries?
RQ4 To what extent is assistance required after interaction with the SR?
RQ5 What is the average waiting time for information seekers at the HR?

Our paper is structured as follows: After the related work, in Sect. 2, we outline the methodology (Sect. 3). In Sect. 4 we present our results. Closing this paper, in Sect. 5, we discuss our findings and conclude in Sect. 6.

2   Related Work

Examining information needs is vital for human-centered robot deployment [13].

Information Needs at the HR: HRs are the first step to meet extensive hospital information needs [4]. Meeting HR information needs influences workflows, satisfaction, and health outcomes [11,15]. Difficulties in meeting information needs can lower staff productivity, who are frequently asked for assistance [19].

The spectrum of HR information needs is diverse, ranging from information about treatments, orientation, registration, appointment management, forwarding to specific persons and FAQs, e.g., related to opening hours or policies [2,11,12]. Zenka et al. highlighted the role of navigational needs, which can be a stressor for patients and visitors [19]. In a prior study, influenced by the pandemics, we confirmed the diversity and prevalence of HR information needs. We underscored that in HR was an information demand in 1,499 cases in a rural hospital during one week [14]. People asked regarding COVID-19 testing (20.9 %), followed by requests about patients (14.5 %) and appointments (10.8 %) [14]. Navigation questions accounted for 6.7 %, while information about visiting rules accounted for 4.7 % of total inquiries. Visitors and patients have most information needs between 10:30 and 15:30, indicating peak periods for HR staff. In Summary, due to the lack of research and comparability to German healthcare, there needs to be more research HR information needs.

Usage of Service Robots (SR): SR, in the face of healthcare workforce limitations, are gaining prominence in healthcare settings, offering assistance in various tasks, including information provision in HRs [3,7,9,12]. Because the accessibility of robots improves and cost decreases, robots are expected to rise beyond surgical applications in the next decade [3]. SRs are a promising tool to smart hospitals [6]. Robots don't get tired from repetitive FAQs and aren't contagious.

The functionality of SR differs depending on the usage and the variety of robots used. In clinics the functionalities of (semi-) or fully autonomous navigation, are important [3,7]. SRs can perform from logistics, cleaning, and disinfection to direct patient interaction, including social assistance and COVID-19 testing [3,7]. There are many commercial SRs available in the robotics market. Still, only a few, like Pepper (Softbank Inc.) for social assistance and Temi (Temi Inc.) for monitoring, are focused on healthcare. In the HR domain, SRs needs to be social to streamline operations by addressing FAQs, allowing staff to focus on complex tasks. SRs can facilitate wayfinding to Point of Interests (POIs) [12].

First, research shows that SR are accepted, but the integration of SR in hospitals is nascent [8]. Germany is lacking in SR usage, while countries such as Japan with similar demographics are deploying SRs widespread [17]. Primary studies focus on technical issues and are influenced by disinfection use cases for pandemics [7,9]. As robotics are evolving, further research about SR application for meeting information needs in the HR is needed.

3 Methodology

To answer the Research Questions (RQs), a cross-sectional *participatory observation* with SRs in a HR was conducted from November 13th to 19th, 2023.

3.1 Intervention of Service Robots in the HR

During the observation, we deployed SRs centrally in the HR, consisting of the humanoid Pepper (Softbank Inc.) and non-humanoid Temi (Temi Inc.). Pepper uses gestures and engages individuals to use Pepper after recognition. The human-computer interaction is designed based on prior research by Sommer et al. [14]. The robots respond to FAQ regarding opening hours, building orientation, and room numbers. The SRs collaborate, including that Pepper can summon Temi with autonomous robot guidance to POI when needed.

For this study, Pepper's speech recognition was disabled, and Pepper was operated through touch interactions. For informed consent, we provided an informational poster about the SRs. Furthermore, our SRs doesn't request or provide personal data, including individual patient information and medical advice. Personal patient data requests are handled exclusively by staff.

3.2   Data Collection and Analysis

Our seven-day consecutive data collection in November 2023 at the HR of *Kliniken Am Goldenen Steig*, a rural Bavarian hospital with 1,000 employees and 365 planned beds, consisted of (i) a *participatory observation* and (ii) the *evaluation of robot logs*. Table 1 shows the recorded study data. The study period covered a regular week during the opening times of the HR, without any disrupting factors, such as construction work or holidays. The HR was opened on working days during *06:45 to 20:00* and on the weekend between *08:00 to 18:00* with hospital staff and service robots meeting the information needs.

Table 1. Overview of recorded interaction data in the HR.

Data	Description
Timestamp[i,ii]	Timestamps at the start and end of an interaction
Question[i,ii]	Notes on the main topic of an interaction*
Language[ii]	Language of the inquirer
Answer[i,ii]	Response and context information about the response*
Disturbances and Barriers[ii]	Barriers, incl. waiting times within the HR
Stakeholder Details[ii]	Classification (patient, staff, visitor)* and demographics*
Interaction Duration[ii]	Calculated duration from question to complete answer
Robot Use[ii]	Use of the robot before (further) inquiry to HR staff

[i] Documented by robot logs. [ii]Documented by observation. * Without personal data.

Participatory Observation and Robot-Logs: We used a standardized protocol with closed- and open-ended questions organized in a spreadsheet. The observers consisted of the authors, were trained prior, and performed a pre-test. The protocol included 12 criteria, summarized in Table 1. We noted the original inquiry from the information seeker, the answer, timestamps, and contextual information. We also noted robot usage and further help needed by the HR staff. Interaction data with the SR was captured through the tablet's user interface without recording personal data or media streams. The logs included timestamps, log levels, battery status, output language, software module, active User Interface (UI), and UI interactions such as button clicks.

Data Analysis: Open-ended questions were categorized on-site according to the qualitative content analysis of our prior study [14], showing the results in Table 2. All data, including the robot logs, were evaluated descriptively with IBM SPSS.

4   Results

The results are presented according to the HR staff and the SRs. *Interactions* refer to any communication between stakeholders, while *requests* are focused on questions topic. The same person can make multiple requests in one interaction.

4.1   Requests to the HR Staff

Varying Information Needs: 1,068 (N) interactions, leading to 1,531 requests, were handled by the HR staff. As Table 2 shows, most HR requests consist mostly of orientation with 45.2 % of all inquiries. This is followed by appointment registration (17.8 %) and specific information about the patient (9.3 %). Information needs about orientation (> 40 %) and appointment registration (> 15 %) are frequent in all stakeholders. Other requests, like small talk or depositing items, are more common in *patients* and *visitors*. Forwarding to doctors was needed if pain was expressed in the HR. *Employees and suppliers*, which were encountered as one category, had fewer information needs as shown in Table 2.

Table 2. Requests to HR per category by stakeholder type

Category	All		Patients		Visitors		Employees	
	n	%	n	%	n	%	n	%
Orientation & Way-finding	692	45.2	326	42.8	273	48.3	93	45.6
Appointment registration	273	17.8	128	16.8	108	19.1	37	18.1
Information about patient	142	9.3	92	12.1	34	6.0	16	7.8
Arriving person with pain	110	7.2	73	9.6	20	3.5	17	8.3
Deposit items[1]	67	4.4	32	4.2	29	5.1	6	2.9
Small Talk	65	4.2	31	4.1	28	5.0	6	2.9
General Administration	62	4.0	21	2.8	30	5.3	11	5.4
Patients de-registration	21	1.4	14	1.8	6	1.1	1	0.5
Payment / Billing	20	1.3	9	1.2	11	1.9	0	0.0
Information about doctors	18	1.2	11	1.4	2	0.4	5	2.5
Other[2]	61	4.0	25	3.3	24	4.2	12	5.9
Sum	**1,531**		**762**		**565**		**204**	

[1] belongings, documents, parcels [2] patient pick up, regulations, opening hours

Locations: Looking at the locations leads to 172 (23.8 %) requests for patient rooms and 170 (23.5 %) for emergency rooms (ERs). The nursing ward was requested by 132 (18.3 %), medical on-call service by 89 (12.3 %), radiology by 59 (8.2 %), anesthesia by 36 (5.0 %), and surgery by 31 (4.3 %). Other POIs sum up to 33, including navigation to toilets (1.8 %) or parking (1.0 %). Anesthesia, surgery, and radiology are requested in the median before 12:00. ERs was asked the whole day, with a median at 13:36 o'clock. POIs that includes asking for patient room numbers occur later, with a median of 14:23.

Timing of the HR Requests: Figure 1 shows the timing of all HR requests, indicating that requests concentrate between 10:00 and 15:00. Especially, appointment registration starts in the morning, requests peak around midday, and decline post-lunch. Orientation requests also start early and have a median around lunch. The majority of request does not drastically differ between weekdays and weekends. However, orientation, appointment registration, and patient information tend to commence later on weekends, suggesting a shift in HR demand pattern. The administration, e.g., mailing and handling orders is requested less on weekends, and persons with pain start earlier.

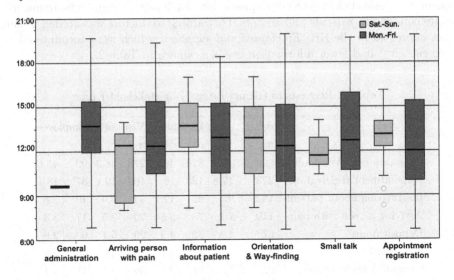

Fig. 1. Temporal distribution of most frequent request types.

Duration and Waiting for the Answer: It should be noted that all requests could be solved by the HR staff. Figure 2 shows that most information needs could be solved without long answers or high complexity. HR interactions last on average 52 s and have a median of 27 s. 90 % of the interactions (n = 1,073) were made within 122 s. At maximum, an interaction rarely takes 11:27 min. The duration significantly varies during weekdays and weekends, indicating a longer weekend duration. People under 30 and over 60 years, on average, interact longer. Analyzing deeper, the mean of administration queries (186 s), orientation questions (83 s), information about patients (82 s), and appointment registration (67 s) is higher, meaning they are, on average more time-consuming. In addition, waiting at the HR wasn't common, with 991 times (92.4 %) being served directly. If a waiting queue was formed, in 74 cases (7 %), one person was in front.

Demographics and Accessibility: Most interactions related to people between 30 to 60 years (61.2 %) and from people aged over 60 (30.0 %). Stakeholders under 30 years were less common (8.8 %). The language was in 99.4 % German, and handicaps, e.g., crutches or wheelchairs, occurred to 3.2 % in HR. During the observation, in six cases, a language barrier occurred, so gestures or written aids were necessary. In seven cases, a phone call was necessary to solve issues.

4.2   Requests to the Service Robots

In total 461 SR requests in 172 people-interactions were made. According to Table 3, our SR logs indicate that orientation (44.9 %), visiting times (26.3 %), and opening times (20.0 %) requests were most common. For the orientation POIs, patient rooms, toilets, medical on-call service, kiosk, and radiology were often inquired. At summarized opening and visiting times, a regular ward and the on-call service are asked the most. Furthermore, the robot guidance was requested in 8.9 % of all requests. The SRs guided people to nursing wards (14 times), to the kiosk (10), to on-call service (9), and to the toilets (8).

Table 3. Characteristics of the SR requests (N = 461)

Category	n = 461		Orientation[1] (n = 207)		Times[1] (n = 213)	
	Count	%	Location	%	Location	%
Orientation	207	44.9	Patient rooms	38.2	Regular ward[1]	53.1
Visiting times	121	26.2	Toilets	32.9	On-call service	26.8
Opening times	92	20.0	On-call service	14.0	Radiology	7.5
Robot guidance	41	8.9	Kiosk	7.7	Kiosk	6.6
			Radiology	5.8	Intensive ward[1]	3.8

[1]Top 5 answers, [2]Visiting Times, separated in the UI

4.3   Relief of HR Staff Through Service Robots

Share of Requests During the Day: Figure 2 shows the daily schedule and interaction duration. In total, 1,703 interactions were made, where the majority (89.9 %) were answered by HR staff, and a smaller portion (10.1 %) was handled by SR. The SR is primarily by 76.7 % used in the afternoon (13:00-19:00).

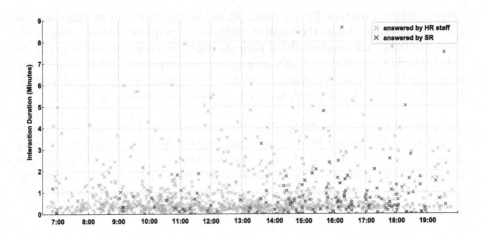

Fig. 2. Scatter about the duration of HR and SR interactions during the day.

Relief Through SR: The SR required staff assistance 0.6 % (six times) post-use. Interaction duration averaged 45 s, totaling 128.9 min or 2.15 h for the study week. This equates to approximately 8.6 h monthly and 103.1 h annually. Considering an hourly wage of € 20, the SR potentially saves about € 2,063 in annual labor costs.

5 Discussion

Contribution: This paper confirms that there is a variety of information needs at HR, changed post-COVID compared with our prior study [14] to above 40 % orientation requests. That orientation requests are common in hospitals, also stated by Zenka et al. [19]. Our study expands limited HR informational needs research with SR usage, which is in 172 interactions and indicates further potential to relieve hospital staff. The most common requests are related to orientation and details about visiting and opening hours. As the requests are within a minute, value is generated through SR as hospital staff is interrupted through requests, and most requests aren't complex, e.g., asking for toilets.

Limitations: The study focused on HR and excluded other locations, such as side entrances. We used a robust observation protocol, but the SR faces potential network issues due to outdated SR hardware. Logs may not capture all SR interactions fully. Privacy constraints mean the robot can't identify users, and interactions are tallied based on one-minute inactivity, possibly leading to undercounting. Curiosity-driven uses of the robot are not distinguished from necessary interactions. Furthermore, the robot's information is limited by its tablet interface and predefined selections. In summary, the potential of SR wasn't fully utilized, meaning that increased SR usage is expected in future iterations.

6   Conclusion

In HR, information needs focus on orientation and appointment registration, as seen in Table 2 and Table 3. Patients (49.8 %) made the most requests, followed by visitors (36.9 %) and employees (13.3 %) from 10:00 to 15:00. The SR was used already within its limited capabilities, in 10.1 % of all interactions, with orientation queries as the most common, reducing the hospital staff workload. Given the limited functionality of SRs, further research employing more advanced robots, diverse locations, and extended periods is essential.

Declarations. Informed Consent was provided. Our research is approved by the joint ethics committee of the universities of Bavaria under No. *GEHBa-202309-V-128.*

References

1. Carpman, J.R., Grant, M.A.: Design that Cares: Planning Health Facilities for Patients and Visitors. John Wiley & Sons, New York (2016)
2. Garg, A., Dewan, A.: Manual of Hospital Planning and Designing. For Medical Administrators, Architects and Planners, Springer, Singapore (2022). https://doi.org/10.1007/978-981-16-8456-2
3. Holland, J., et al.: Service robots in the healthcare sector. Robotics **10**(1), 47 (2021). https://doi.org/10.3390/robotics10010047
4. Kendall, L., Mishra, S.R., Pollack, A., Aaronson, B., Pratt, W.: Making background work visible: opportunities to address patient information needs in the hospital. AMIA Ann. Symp. Proc. **2015**, 1957–1966 (2015)
5. Kodur, K., Kyrarini, M.: Patient–robot co-navigation of crowded hospital environments. Appl. Sci. **13**(7), 4576 (2023). https://doi.org/10.3390/app13074576
6. Kwon, H., et al.: Review of smart hospital services in real healthcare environments. Healthcare Inform. Res. **28**(1), 3–15 (2022). https://doi.org/10.4258/hir.2022.28.1.3, https://synapse.koreamed.org/articles/1158770
7. Lee, I.: Service robots: a systematic literature review. Electronics **10**(21), 2658 (2021). https://doi.org/10.3390/electronics10212658
8. Lee, J.H., et al.: User perception of medical service robots in hospital wards: a cross-sectional study. J. Yeungnam Med. Sci. **39**(2), 116–123 (2022). https://doi.org/10.12701/yujm.2021.01319
9. Ozturkcan, S., Merdin-Uygur, E.: Humanoid service robots: the future of healthcare? J. Inf. Technol. Teach. Cases **12**(2), 163–169 (2022). https://doi.org/10.1177/20438869211003905
10. Parliament, E.: Demographic outlook for the EU 2022, May 2022. https://www.europarl.europa.eu/thinktank/en/document/EPRS_STU(2022)729461
11. Philipp, R., Hughes, A., Wood, N., Burns-Cox, C., Cook, N., Fletcher, G.: Information needs of patients and visitors in a district general hospital. J. R. Soc. Health **110**(1), 10–12 (1990)
12. Prochnow, A.G., dos Santos, J., Pradebon, V.M., Schimith, M.D.: Reception in the hospital environment: perspectives of companions of hospitalized patients. Revista Gaucha de Enfermagem **30**(1), 11–18 (2009)
13. Radic, M., Vosen, A., Graf, B.: Use of robotics in the German healthcare sector. In: Salichs, M.A., et al. (eds.) ICSR 2019. LNCS (LNAI), vol. 11876, pp. 434–442. Springer, Cham (2019). https://doi.org/10.1007/978-3-030-35888-4_40

14. Sommer, D., Greiler, T., Fischer, S., Wilhelm, S., Hanninger, L.M., Wahl, F.: Investigating user requirements: a participant observation study to define the information needs. Commun. Comput. Inf. Sci. 157–166 (2023). https://doi.org/10.1007/978-3-031-35992-7

15. Szpiro, K.A., Harrison, M.B., Van Den Kerkhof, E.G., Lougheed, M.D.: Patient education in the emergency department: a systematic review of interventions and outcomes. Adv. Emerg. Nurs. J. 30(1), 34–49 (2008)

16. Vermeir, P., et al.: Communication in healthcare: a narrative review of the literature and practical recommendations. Int. J. Clin. Pract. 69(11), 1257–1267 (2015)

17. Vogt, G., König, A.S.L.: Robotic devices and ICT in long-term care in Japan: their potential and limitations from a workplace perspective. Contemp. Japan 35(2), 270–290 (2021). https://doi.org/10.1080/18692729.2021.2015846

18. Wong, E.L.Y., Poon, C.M., Cheung, A.W.L., Chen, F.Y., Yeoh, E.K.: Relationship between patient experience and hospital readmission. BMC Med. Res. Methodol. 22(1), 1–10 (2022)

19. Ženka, J., Macháček, J., Michna, P., Kořízek, P.: Navigational needs and preferences of hospital patients and visitors. Int. J. Environ. Res. Public Health. 18(3), 974 (2021) https://doi.org/10.3390/ijerph18030974

Trust, (Dis)Comfort, and Voice Quality: Anthropomorphism in Verbal Interactions with NAO

Caja Thimm[1]([✉]), Phillip Engelhardt[1], Patrick Nehls[1], Jiliane Hens[1], Mira Biehler[1], Christopher Hermanns[1], Philipp Huzel[1], Maren Bennewitz[2], Jesper Mücke[2], and Nils Dengler[2]

[1] Media Department, University of Bonn, 53113 Bonn, Germany
thimm@uni-bonn.de
[2] Humanoid Robots Lab, University of Bonn, 53113 Bonn, Germany

Abstract. The endeavour to develop technologies which approach human faculties, whether in functionality or physical resemblance, has gained heightened momentum, leading to intensified attention to anthropomorphism in human-machine interaction. Anthropomorphism can be characterized as the process of attributing human properties, such as motivation, behaviours, and social roles to non-human entities. This inclination is notably pronounced in interactions with social robots, which can exhibit varying degrees of human-like attributes such as facial expressions and voices resembling those of human. Human-like voices. With machines becoming increasingly conversational and escalating expectations for more personalized interactions, voice-based interfaces have assumed more and more significance in human-machine relations.

In this study, two groups of participants (A, B) verbally interacted with a NAO robot about an emotionally charged topic ('depression'). In group (A) NAO's voice was synthetic. In group (B) NAO's voice replicated a female human voice, created from a pre-recorded voice sample. Visual analysis during interactions and post-experimental interviews showed that NAO's voice significantly contributed to emotional states like feelings of uneasiness or discomfort. A majority of participants described the relationship between the physical appearance of NAO and the human-like voice as incongruent. In the post-experimental interviews, participants indicated ambivalent attitudes, with references to the uncanny valley phenomenon. The following paper argues that voice-based anthropomorphization can be disrupted by artificial embodiment and inappropriate topics.

Keywords: Anthropomorphism · Robot Voice · Uncanny Valley

1 Anthropomorphization of Voice-Based Conversational AI-Interfaces

1.1 Anthropomorphization in Sociotechnical Communication

Machines have advanced notably over the last years. Whether in physical appearance, skills or functional applicability, their role in the life of many humans has changed. Large Language Models (ChatGPT, LaMDA), social robots (Paro, NAO) and voice-assistants

© The Author(s), under exclusive license to Springer Nature Switzerland AG 2024
C. Stephanidis et al. (Eds.): HCII 2024, CCIS 2114, pp. 405–412, 2024.
https://doi.org/10.1007/978-3-031-61932-8_46

(Alexa, Siri) operate in diverse social environments, generate natural speech, images and text, and some even provide company in domestic environments or take over care responsibilities for handicapped individuals (Thimm et al., i.pr). Machines are designed, utilized, and perceived as communication partners (Guzman and Lewis 2020), they are supposed to be friendly (Fröding and Peterson 2021), intelligent and trustworthy (Kok and Soh 2020).

Particularly the human-like design has elicited a tendency to anthropomorphize embodied systems (Thimm and Bächle 2019). Although the distinction between natural and artificial communicators is reliably detected and readily upheld, users perceive even complex information provided by AI as more and credible and trustworthy, and empathy with their technological counterparts is increasing (Malinowska 2021). Additionally, more and more machines are characterized as 'autonomous', thereby questioning fundamental differences between natural and artificial actors (Chiodo 2023). As a consequence, we regard anthropomorphism as a key element in human-machine relations, defined as the process of attributing human properties (motivation, behaviours, intentions or social roles) to non-human entities. This points at a transition in human-machine relations, in which the boundary between anthropological and technological conversationalists becomes more and more obscured, calling for legal and ethical measures of control (Thimm and Thimm-Braun, i.pr.). Some researchers even claim that the insistence on the very notion of their distinction should be rendered 'anachronistic'(Guzman (2020).

1.2　Robotic Voices and Anthropomorphism

The voices of robotic systems play a significant role in anthropomorphization. Based on the psycholinguistic relevance of voices in human relations, allowing for the attribution of several properties like gender, age, affect and intent, robot voices are considered "a particularly strong anthropomorphic cue" (Schreibelmayr and Mara 2022, 2). Contextual cues also proved to be relevant factors for voice-based attributions, as the combination of speech content (praise, empathy, humour) and paralinguistic cues (pitch, loudness, velocity) influence the user's perception of the machine's social competence to a large degree (Seaborn et al. 2021).

In alignment with these observations empirical research shows that anthropomorphization of robotic voices increases in direct proportion to the human-likeness of the voice in tone, vocal colour, pronunciation and timing (Marge et al. 2022). This observation leads to the description of anthropomorphization as a *linear process*: the more human-like a certain technological behaviour appears the more likely human users are to reproduce and apply social heuristics. Several studies (Kühne et al. 2020; Baird et al. 2018; Romportl 2014) describe anthropomorphization as linear, using a variety of cues and user data. Some users, for example, reproduced gender stereotypes or accommodated their linguistic behaviour to machines resembling human-to-human communication (Thimm et al. i.pr.). Similar effects were observed for anthropomorphic embodiment.

However, research suggests that the interaction between high levels of human-likeness and user attitudes has its limits. Robots with anthropomorphic embodiment or pronounced facial expressions are repeatedly rejected by study participants, citing feelings of eeriness and discomfort (Zhang et al. 2020; Mara et al. 2022). These reactions, described by Mori (2012) as the 'uncanny valley phenomenon', are characterized by a sharp decline of user acceptance in the last instance of approximation towards human-likeness. The prevailing explanation for this decline predominantly centers on cognitive conflicts. Participants unconsciously strive to classify robots within the established dichotomy of human versus technology. This cognitive dissonance arises from the awareness of the robot's intrinsic artificial nature juxtaposed with its visibly human-like physical attributes and its emulation of expressive and communicative behaviors.

Empirical findings associated with this phenomenon indicate a similar nonlinear relationship for voice-based conversational agents. But there are also important contextual conditions which additionally influence voice perception: "Irrespective of the voice type, participants were generally more skeptical of applying talking robots to social domains that, like caregiving, require typically human skills" (Schreibelmayr and Mara 2022, 13). It is noteworthy that elevated levels of human-likeness exhibit a positive correlation with anthropomorphization. However, such attributes demonstrate no discernible impact when these systems are intended to engage in social interactions. This suggests a conflicting dynamic between anthropomorphism and other humanoid characteristics.

2 Robotic Voices and Human-Machine Conversations

2.1 Hypotheses

Based on the existing literature as introduced we assume that embodied robotic voices have clear effects on user attitudes. As we are following the idea of human vs. non-human voices in a first step before embarking onto more detailed voice cues, we designed a study with two voice conditions:

1. Synthetic voice
2. Human voice

The following hypotheses were empirically examined:

- **H1**: In instances where the robotic voice is incongruent with the physical appearance of the robot, there is a decrease in performative anthropomorphization, coupled with an increase in negative participant responses.
- **H2**: Performative anthropomorphization of robotic voices is contingent upon the nature of the conversational topics.

2.2 The Study

To test our hypotheses, we conducted a lab experiment in our 'Humanoid Robots Lab' (University of Bonn, Germany). Two groups of student participants engaged in a 15-min conversation with the humanoid robot NAO about an emotionally charged topic (*depression*). The first group (A) of participants communicated with a NAO with a synthetic robot voice, the other group of participants (B) conversed with a NAO which was equipped with human female voice, which was created from prerecorded voice materials. The objective of the experiment was to foster intimate conversations and provide the human participants with the challenge to discuss personal matters of a psychological nature with a robot. The study involved eight participants, comprising five females and three males, aged between 18 and 34 years. Each experimental group consisted of four individuals.

2.3 Procedure

Prior to the experiment, the participants engaged in a pre-experiment interview. In this interview we collected data regarding participants' individual technological proficiency, attitudes towards robots, preferred domains of application, and personal experiences. Participants entered the robot lab without further instructions and sat down across a table from NAO. NAO's verbal responses, gesturing and body movements were pre-programmed according to the conversational script. Mimic expressions were implemented using NAO's colour coding. The NAO robot utilizes colours as a means of communicating emotions through a predefined color-coding system. By using these color-coded signals, the NAO robot can effectively convey a range of emotions and states to facilitate communication with users.

The synthetic voice for group (A) was pre-programmed, the natural female voice for group (B) was pre-recorded by a person outside of the experimental team. The interactions were filmed and audio recorded. After the experiment participants were asked to partake in a post-experiment interview with the aim of gathering data about how NAO was perceived. Open questions inquired about feelings of sympathy and trust and focused on the robotic voice. Answers were also audio recorded.

2.4 Results

Pre-experiment Interview. Five out of eight participants had previous experiences with robots or artificial intelligence, this particularly concerned interactions with Voice Assistants like Alexa. All participants had positive attitudes towards robots and agreed that robots were an important part of the future of modern societies. To fulfill these expectations effectively from their point of view, the robots should possess the capacity for verbal communication, physical movement, and the ability to store pertinent information. However, practices distinctive to human-to-human communication, such as facial expressions, gestures, and eye contact, were deemed to be of less importance. Regarding their preferred domains of use the participants pointed to work settings, but were hesitant on personal and private environments.

Post-experiment Interview. To be able to analyse the results of the post-experimental interview, nine coding categories were established inductively to classify specific parts of the interviews systematically in a content analysis.

- Trust
- Distrust
- Sympathy
- Description NAO
- Expectations NAO

- Voice
- Communication with NAO
- Depression as topic of conversation
- Conjoint physical exercise

With regards to voice-based anthropomorphization several semantic categories delivered relevant results. Both groups showed a diverse set of **expectations** towards the communication by NAO. Predominantly, these anticipations encompassed anthropomorphic attributions. Respondents cited expectations related to *linguistic comprehension, mimicry, facial expressions, pleasant vocal tones, organic movements, politeness,* and *humor*. Two participants stated explicitly that a likeable robot needs to be human-like in its behaviour. Additionally, **descriptions** of NAO entailed positive attributes like *agile, anthropomorph, fascinating* and *unpredictable* and negative attributions such as *inactive mimics, jerky movements, missing personality* and *machine-like*, suggesting that NAO partially matches the aforementioned **expectations**.

The category **voice** was differentiated between group A (synthetic voice) and B (natural voice). Results show that in group (A) three participants were content with NAO's voice. None could image NAO with a different voice. One participant described the synthetic voice as *likeable* and participant two describes the alternative natural voice as *creepy*:

I: *What did you think of his voice?*
P2: *Quite pleasant. Very neutral. Neither decidedly masculine nor decidedly feminine, just a classic robot voice. That's kind of what you'd expect. I think it would be weirder if NAO spoke with an actual recorded human voice. I think that's kind of weird.*
I: *Do you think if NAO had had a more human voice, without it being recorded, that you would trust robots more?*
P2: *I don't think so. I think it would go the other way. I'd find that creepy, so I'd be kind of uncomfortable.*

Results in group B were quite different. Participants couldn't image NAO without the natural voice, but one person reported that the natural voice *didn't fit* NAO's robotic appearance. Three participants described it as pleasant and friendly. The voice also had an impact on perceived **trust**. Two participants (B) reported an increase in trust due to the natural voice. Three participants mentioned that they wouldn't perceive a natural or synthetic voice from the other group as more trustworthy.

Distrust towards Group (A) primarily stemmed from issues pertaining to the embodiment of NAO. Participants cited jerky movements as a barrier to establishing trust, noting that moments of affinity were frequently disrupted. Conversely, for Group (B), a comparable evaluation emerged. One participant highlighted a mismatch between the natural voice and the artificial embodiment:

I: *What effect did that have on you? Hearing the human voice from this body?*
P5: *It's a bit strange because you imagine a real person and not a robot. So, I didn't think it was a typical robot voice, but more something where you immediately imagine a human face.*

I: *Would you trust a robot with a robot voice more or less?*
P5: *Less. Because I didn't have the feeling that people had bothered to program it or put less thought and effort into programming it so that it was tailored to me.*

Additionally, participants in group (B) indicated that a natural voice would be better suited to discuss emotionally charged topics.

I: *So, if the voice had been more mechanical, you would trust it less?*
P4: *Yes, I think so. The conversation would just be weirder. You don't have a conversation with Siri or anything like that. If it was a typical robot voice all the time, it would seem demanding to me and remind me of an instruction rather than a conversation.*
I: *That means you would classify a human voice as more for conversational interaction and a robot voice as more for instructions?*
P4: *Yes, exactly. That's what you've actually become more familiar with so far. I've never interacted with a human voice like that before. You could already tell that it wasn't a robot voice. And yes, I feel you're more likely to engage in a conversation.*

When coding for **sympathy,** the post-experimental interviews yielded very different results between groups for levels of anthropomorphization and likability. Overall, group B had more positive attitudes toward the NAO. One participant (group B) addressed NAO with the female pronoun in response to the natural female speaking voice:

I: *How did you find the communication between you and NAO?*
P4: *You immediately recognize that you are dealing with a robot and that she cannot respond to all of your cues. But with regards to the topic, I thought it was as personal as it could have been since she was talking about depression among other things.*

Gendered pronouns were not used by group (A).

2.5 Discussion

The aim of this study was to show whether and how participants anthropomorphize voice-based, embodied conversational agents. It has been hypothesized that anthropomorphization declines if the robotic voice is incongruent to the robot's physical appearance (H1) or the topic of the conversation (H2). The results show that the group interacting with a NAO equipped with a human-voice (group B) anthropomorphized NAO more than group (A). According to the content analysis of the interactions themselves and the statements in the post-experimental interviews, this effect must be ascribed to the difference between natural (B) and synthetics voices (A). Across both groups, initial **expectations** by the participants included human-like body movements as well as verbal behaviour from NAO. NAO's description entails both anthropomorphic and nonanthropomorphic attributions regardless of group affiliation. However, as soon as the different voice types are introduced the attitudes change. The synthetic voice was described as threatening, inappropriate for emotionally charged conversations and participants did not address NAO with a personal (gendered) pronoun. The natural voice was described as pleasant and friendly and more appropriate for personal encounters. Nevertheless, at the same time participants perceived the natural voice as incongruent to the robot's physical appearance. The anthropomorphic impression was disrupted in these cases and some participants reported a decrease in trust and likability. These results explicitly support H1. The relationship between voice based anthropomorphization and embodiment appears to be nonlinear and points to specific cognitive conflict if the two factors fail to equally elicit anthropomorphic attributions on the spectrum between natural and artificial. The same can be said with regards to H2: group (A) indicates that a natural voice would be a better fit for emotional topics of conversation.

2.6 Conclusion

This study has delivered specific empirical data to support the claim that voice-based anthropomorphization must always be regarded as contextualized and depends on factors like embodiment, conversation topics and application scenarios. If one of those factors disrupts the ascription of human-like qualities, the ensuing cognitive conflict triggers the uncanny valley phenomenon and attitudes such as trust, likeability and acceptance decrease. Further studies need to add to the spectrum of anthropomorphization and check for signs of uncanniness on an implicit and a performative level.

Funding. This work was partially funded by Federal Ministry of Education and Research within the project "BNTrAinee" (funding code 16DHBK1022).

Disclosure of Interests. The authors have no competing interests to declare that are relevant to the content of this article.

References

Baird, A., Parada-Cabaleiro, E., Hantke, S., Burkhardt, F., Cummins, N., Schuller, B.: The perception and analysis of the likeability and human likeness of synthesized speech. In: Proceedings of the Interspeech 2018, pp. 2863–2867 (2018). https://doi.org/10.21437/Interspeech.2018-1093

Chiodo, S.: Technology and the Overturning of Human Autonomy. Springer, Cham (2023). https://doi.org/10.1007/978-3-031-26159-6

Fröding, B., Peterson, M.: Friendly AI. Ethics Inf. Technol. **23**, 207–214 (2021). https://doi.org/10.1007/s10676-020-09556-

Guzman, A.L.: Ontological boundaries between humans and computers and the implications for human-machine communication. Hum.-Mach. Commun. **1**, 37–54 (2020). https://doi.org/10.30658/hmc.1.3

Guzman, A.L., Lewis, S.C.: Artificial intelligence and communication: a human– machine communication research agenda. New Media Soc. **22**(1), 70–86 (2020). https://doi.org/10.1177/1461444819858691

Kok, B.C., Soh, H.: Trust in robots: challenges and opportunities. Curr Robot Rep **1**, 297–309 (2020). https://doi.org/10.1007/s43154-020-00029-y

Kühne, K., Fischer, M.H., Zhou, Y.: The human takes it All: humanlike synthesized voices are perceived as less eerie and more likable. Evidence From a subjective ratings study. Front. Neurorobot. **14**, 105 (2020). https://doi.org/10.3389/fnbot.2020.593732

Malinowska, J.K.: What does it mean to empathise with a robot? Mind. Mach. **31**, 361–376 (2021). https://doi.org/10.1007/s11023-021-09558-7

Mara, M., Appel, M., Gnambs, T.: Human-like robots and the uncanny valley. A meta-analysis of user responses based on the godspeed scales. Zeitschrift für Psychologie **230**(1), 33–46 (2022). https://doi.org/10.1027/2151-2604/a000486

Marge, M., et al.: Spoken language interaction with robots: Recommendations for future research. Comput. Speech Lang. **71** (2022). https://doi.org/10.1016/j.csl.2021.101255

Mori, M., MacDorman, K.G.F., Kageki, N.: The uncanny valley [from the field]. IEEE Robot. Autom. Mag. **19**(2), 98–100 (2012). https://doi.org/10.1109/MRA.2012.2192811

Romportl, J.: Speech synthesis and uncanny valley. In: Sojka, P., Horák, A., Kopeček, I., Pala, K. (eds.) TSD 2014, pp. 595–602. Springer, Cham (2014). https://doi.org/10.1007/978-3-319-10816-2_72

Schreibelmayr, S., Mara, M.: Robot voices in daily life: vocal human-likeness and application context as determinants of user acceptance. Front. Psychol. **13**, 787499 (2022). https://doi.org/10.3389/fpsyg.2022.787499

Seaborn, K., Miyake, N., Pennefather, P., Otake-Matsuura, M.: Voice in human–agent interaction: a survey. ACM Comput. Surv. **54**(4) (2021). https://doi.org/10.1145/3386867

Thimm, C., Thimm-Braun, L.: Policies, regulation and legal perspectives on social robots. In: Edwards, A., Fortunati, L. (eds.) De Gruyter Handbook of Robots in Society and Culture. De Gruyter (2024/i.pr.)

Thimm, C., Engelhardt, P., Schmitz, J.: Machines as partners: anthropomorphism and communication accommodation to voice assistants in disability contexts. In: Habscheid, S., Hector, T., Hoffmann, D., Waldecker, D. (eds.) Voice Assistants in Private Homes. Media, Data and Language in Interaction and Discourse. Springer (2024/i.pr., to appear)

Thimm, C., Bächle, T.C. (eds.): Die Maschine: Freund oder Feind? Mensch und Technologie im digitalen Zeitalter. Springer, Wiesbaden (2019). https://doi.org/10.1007/978-3-658-22954-2

Zhang, J., Li, S., Zhang, J.-Y., Du, F., Qi, Y., Liu, X.: A literature review of the research on the uncanny valley. In: Rau, P.-L.P. (ed.) HCII 2020. LNCS, vol. 12192, pp. 255–268. Springer, Cham (2020). https://doi.org/10.1007/978-3-030-49788-0_19

Emotional Study on Octopus Arm Robots and Behavioral Parameterization

Meng-shiuan Tsai[(⊠)] [iD] and Yinghsiu Huang[iD]

Department of Industrial Design, National Kaohsiung Normal University, Kaohsiung, Taiwan
{611272004,yinghsiu}@mail.nknu.edu.tw

Abstract. As robotics tech progresses, robots' role as everyday aids grows, spanning from companions to service bots. Beyond functionality, they must enhance human interaction. This study seeks to quantify how humans perceive robot personalities and adjust robot behavior accordingly. Using an octopus arm as the robot arm, researchers employed regression analysis to model how personality traits affect its posture. They developed a formula linking "openness" and "neuroticism" to the arm's bending angle, aligning postures with perceived personality traits. This framework aims to guide future research on human-robot emotional interaction.

Keywords: HCI · Octopus · Service Robot · Motion

1 Introduction

With advancements like AI, 5G, and sensors, robots are increasingly present in logistics, subways, hospitals, restaurants, malls, hotels, and homes (Intel 2022). Termed service and medical robots (ISO 2021), they differ from industrial robots. According to Precedence Research, the global service robot market was valued at $41 billion in 2022 and is projected to surpass $169.5 billion by 2032, reflecting a 15.30% compound annual growth rate from 2023 to 2032 (Precedence Research 2023).

Creating humanoid robots may enhance user experience, but they might not always be the best choice for specific tasks. For instance, in robotic arms, traditional discrete models, resembling human arms, consist of several rigid links enabling precise and swift movements. Yet, their rigidity and weight hinder their use in confined and intricate settings like homes. Continuum robotic arms, akin to octopus arms, offer increased flexibility and fault tolerance in confined and intricate spaces, resembling octopus arms (Trivedi et al. 2008). With the rising importance of practicality and interactivity in robotics, they are deemed safer and more suitable for home robot deployment (Ansari et al. 2015; Guan et al. 2023).

Based on the above, researchers selected the octopus arm as a model for the robotic arm stimulus and utilized Grasshopper, a parametric tool within the Rhinoceros modeling software, to regulate it. Researcher investigated the translation of user sensations into robot motion parameters, enabling developers to modify corresponding parameters to evoke anticipated sensations in users, aligning with developers' expectations.

© The Author(s), under exclusive license to Springer Nature Switzerland AG 2024
C. Stephanidis et al. (Eds.): HCII 2024, CCIS 2114, pp. 413–420, 2024.
https://doi.org/10.1007/978-3-031-61932-8_47

Researchers selected the Big Five personality traits as the sensations for participants to evaluate. These traits include openness (curious/cautious), conscientiousness (efficient/careless), extraversion (outgoing/reserved), agreeableness (friendly/critical), and neuroticism (nervous/confident), which have become one of the most widely used personality structure model in the past 20 years, with minimal overlap between the five personality domains (Cooper et al. 2010).

The research objectives are outlined as follows:

1. Octopus arm motion simulation model: Generating different postures of the octopus arm through basic parameter control.
2. Relationship between motion parameters and sensations: Analyzing the relationship between sensations and corresponding actions through multiple regression analysis.
3. Controlling motion based on sensations: Converting sensations into parameters to control the octopus arm through equations.

2   Method

This study employed the Semantic Differential (SD) scale to have participants rate 27 octopus arm models on five bipolar adjectives, analyzing the relationship between adjectives and postures to derive parameter combinations corresponding to different perceptions.

2.1   Research Process

The study consisted of five stages (Fig. 1): 1. Setting two types of model motion parameters: bending angle and leaning degree, generating 27 different motion models, and rendering them into realistic images as stimuli. 2. Selecting 5 bipolar adjectives pairs as the content of the SD scale. 3. Distributing questionnaires through the internet, with 10–30 data points for each stimulus. 4. Analyzing the linear relationship between numbers and personality through multiple regression analysis. 5. Establishing a model of personality corresponding to motion parameters.

| Generating stimuli based on action parameters | Creating a SD scale with five bidirectional adjectives | Collecting survey data online | Conducting multiple regression analysis | Constructing a model for sensory-controlled actions |

Fig. 1. Research Process

2.2   Participants

The online questionnaire targeted participants aged 18 to 35 primarily from Taiwan. This age range was selected because perceptions may vary between older and younger individuals, with older respondents generally leaning towards positivity.

2.3 Materials

Using modeling software, a series of octopus arm models were constructed, excluding those that were too similar. After rendering, more realistic images were obtained, totaling 27 (Fig. 2). All octopus arms had one side with suction cups facing to the right.

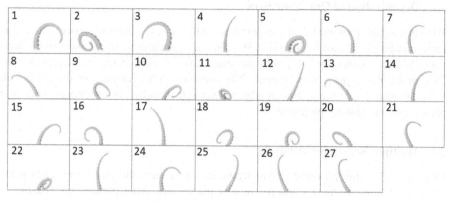

Fig. 2. Octopus arm stimulant

The octopus arm has 6 segments, with "bending angle" and "leaning degree" controlling its positions. The bending angle rotates each segment (-90 to $90°$); positive values bend right (towards suction cups), with the previous segment's endpoint as the rotation center. Leaning degree indicates lateral arm movement (-50 to 50 units), positive values move right (Fig. 3).

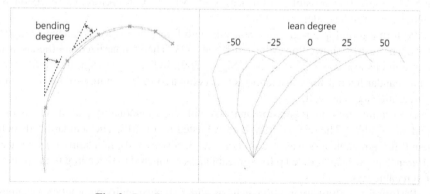

Fig. 3. Bending angle (left); leaning degree (right)

The adjectives of SD scale are the Big Five personality traits, including openness (curious/cautious), conscientiousness (efficient/careless), extraversion (outgoing/reserved), agreeableness (friendly/critical), and neuroticism (nervous/confident). Each image along with its corresponding five questions. The order of the images, questions, and bipolar adjectives is randomized. Additionally, the questionnaire includes an attention test, requiring the selection of specific options, and finally, participants are asked to assess their own understanding of the questionnaire.

3   Results

3.1   Organization of Questionnaires

109 participants took part in the experiment. After a dual screening process based on understanding level and attention test, 56 valid questionnaires were obtained. Individuals aged 19–25 accounted for 50%, while those aged 26–35 made up 32% of the participants. 73% of the participants were female. The average ratings for each of the 27 stimuli were calculated across five bipolar adjectives. Each stimulus corresponded to bending parameters and leaning parameters.

3.2   Multiple Regression Analysis

Using SPSS for multiple regression analysis, the aim is to establish the linear relationship between motion parameters and personality parameters. After preliminary analysis, it was found that the influence of bending parameters on the five personality traits exhibits a quadratic equation relationship, and the curves between 0 to 90 and 0 to $-90°$ are symmetrical. Therefore, researcher transformed the bending parameters into absolute values. On the other hand, impact of leaning parameters on personality traits is almost negligible and deemed to have no effect.

Using the five personality as independent variables and the "absolute value of bending angle" as the dependent variables, multiple regression analysis was conducted (Table 1). The results showed an Adjusted R^2 of .611. The VIF for extraversion was found to be 5.132, indicating possible collinearity since VIF > 5. Therefore, extraversion was removed as an independent variable.

Performing multiple regression analysis with four personality as independent variables. The results showed an Adjusted R^2 of .603. The standardized coefficient β for conscientiousness was .052 (t = .379, Sig = .709), indicating no significant difference in the standardized β for conscientiousness compared to 0. Leading to the removal of conscientiousness as well.

Performing multiple regression analysis with three personality parameters as independent variables. The results showed an Adjusted R^2 of .618. The standardized coefficient β for agreeableness was $-.144$ (t = $-.913$, Sig = .370), indicating no significant difference in the standardized β for agreeableness compared to 0, leading to the removal of agreeableness.

Performing multiple regression analysis with two personality parameters (openness, neuroticism) as independent variables. The results showed an Adjusted R^2 of .620. The unstandardized beta for openness was -17.302 (t = -2.855, Sig = .009), and for neuroticism was 15.478 (t = 2.372, Sig = .026), with the constant being 48.845. Therefore, the equation for the effect of openness and neuroticism on bending angle can be written as

"Absolute value of bending angle" = -17.302*openness + 15.478*neuroticism + 48.845
"Absolute value of bending angle" > 0

(1)

Please note that Eq. (1) calculates the bending angle considering only positive values. Therefore, Eq. (2) is required to consider negative values.

$$\text{"Negative value of bending angle"} = 17.302*openness - 15.478*neuroticism - 48.845$$
$$\text{"Negative value of bending angle"} < 0$$

$$(2)$$

Table 1. Regression analysis coefficients

Model		Unstandardized Coefficients		Standardized Coefficients	t	Sig.	Collinearity Statistics	
		B	Std. Error	Beta			Tolerance	VIF
1	(Constant)	87.615	72.781		1.204	.242		
	Openness	−6.358	9.453	−.176	−.673	.509	.219	4.560
	Conscientiousness	1.567	8.074	.027	.194	.848	.780	1.282
	Extraversion	−11.211	9.319	−.333	−1.203	.242	.195	5.132
	Agreeableness	−7.686	11.550	−.116	−.665	.513	.491	2.038
	Neuroticism	11.993	7.521	.308	1.595	.126	.402	2.490
2	(Constant)	64.173	70.833		.906	.375		
	Openness	−13.440	7.471	−.371	−1.799	.086	.358	2.792
	Conscientiousness	3.051	8.060	.052	.379	.709	.799	1.252
	Agreeableness	−11.009	11.328	−.166	−.972	.342	.520	1.922
	Neuroticism	15.493	7.006	.398	2.211	.038	.472	2.117
3	(Constant)	78.936	58.017		1.361	.187		
	Openness	−14.473	6.824	−.400	−2.121	.045	.413	2.419
	Agreeableness	−9.528	10.431	−.144	−.913	.370	.591	1.692
	Neuroticism	14.747	6.597	.379	2.236	.035	.513	1.950
4	(Constant)	48.845	47.593		1.026	.315		
	Openness	−17.302	6.060	−.478	−2.855	.009	.521	1.921
	Neuroticism	15.478	6.525	.397	2.372	.026	.521	1.921

Dependent Variable: Absolute bending angle

3.3 Modeling Sensory Control of Posture

In Grasshopper, set the parameters of openness and neuroticism from 1 to 7 (because the questionnaire is a seven-point scale) and incorporate them into formulas (1) and (2). Since the bending angle ranges from −90 to 90°, formulate (1) as follows: 0 < "Absolute value of bending angle" < 90, and (2) as: −90 < "Negative value of bending angle" < 0.

The formula results are inputted into the rotation angle parameters to generate octopus arm models (Fig. 4).

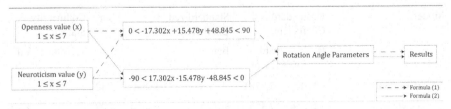

Fig. 4. Parametric Modeling Flow Chart

3.4 Checking the Compliance of the Results with the Data

Through simple regression analysis, it is evident that the standardized β for openness and neuroticism are −0.692 (t = −4.799, Sig < 0.001). Therefore, by computing the linear relationship between the standard scores of the two parameters, can assess the disparity between the expected standardized score of variable and the actual standard score of variable, and the suitability of the parameter combinations can be further calculated.

The calculation proceeds as follows: Converting openness parameter into standard score x_1. Then, x_1^* −0.692 to obtain the corresponding neuroticism parameter y_2. Similarly, acquire the standard score y_1 for the neuroticism parameter and its corresponding openness parameter x_2. Taking the average of $|x_1 - x_2|$ and $|y_1 - y_2|$ yields the average difference in standard scores ranging from 0 to 8, where higher values indicate greater disparity from the experimental data (Fig. 5), with scores being converted to colors: green represents 0 and red represents 8.

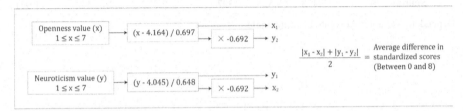

Fig. 5. Calculation of the compliance degree of the parameters with the data

3.5 Results

The results of controlling posture based on sensation are presented in Fig. 6. The color indicates the degree of compliance with experimental data. The left and right panels depict two different postures corresponding to the same set of parameters: bending to the right and bending to the left. The area in the bottom right corner of the images is empty but aligns with the experimental data. The area in the top left corner represents angles beyond the range of the original stimuli, as bending angles greater than 90° or less than −90° tend to cause irregular deformations.

The model of sensation-controlled postures aligns well with the experimental data. In regions where the compliance with the data is higher (light green area), when the bending angle approaches 0, the mean value of openness is close to 5, and the mean value of neuroticism is close to 3, which corresponds well with the average data.

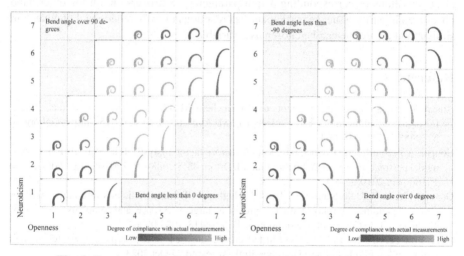

Fig. 6. Bend angle > 0 (left); Bend angle < 0 (right) (Color figure online)

4 Conclusion

The study attempts to construct a framework and process for mapping personality parameters to action parameters, providing developers with a reference when designing similar robotic arms to ensure that the sensations brought about by the robots meet expectations.

Researchers chose bending angle and leaning as parameters for controlling the octopus arm. However, experimental data indicate that people's perception of personality seems to be predominantly influenced by the bending angle. The larger the bending angle, the smaller the openness and the greater the neuroticism. Additionally, people's perception of whether the octopus arm bends to the right or left does not differ significantly. Both approximately opposite postures correspond to the same combination of openness and neuroticism parameters, indicating that the direction of the suction cups on the octopus arm does not seem to be a factor influencing perception.

Ultimately, the sensation control posture model constructed by researcher aligns with the experimental data. Furthermore, using standard scores calculated and presented in color to indicate the "degree of compliance with data" helps distinguish parameter combinations that are less consistent with average sensations. This study only addresses the situation where two independent variables control one dependent variable. If additional variables are to be added, more research effort would be required, and calculating the degree of compliance with experimental data when adding more variables might encounter difficulties.

The leaning used in the initial model construction did not have a significant impact on the experimental data, possibly because the variation in leaning is smaller compared to that of the bending angle, causing participants to focus on the degree of bending. Regarding other personality traits (conscientiousness, agreeableness), researchers believe that applying them to the octopus arm may be more abstract, leading participants to lack clear sensations or corresponding action parameters. Extroversion, on the other hand, poses a collinearity issue, as participants' perceptions of extroversion and openness are similar, and either one can be chosen as a variable.

References

Ansari, Y., Hassan, T., Manti, M., Falotico, E., Cianchetti, M., Laschi, C.: Soft robotic technologies for industrial applications. Eur. Projects Knowl. Appl. Intell. Syst. (2015). https://doi.org/10.5220/0007900900350064

Cooper, A.J., Smillie, L.D., Corr, P.J.: A confirmatory factor analysis of the Mini-IPIP five-factor model personality scale. Personality Individ. Differ. **48**(5), 688–691 (2010). https://doi.org/10.1016/j.paid.2010.01.004

Guan, Q., Stella, F., Della Santina, C., Leng, J., Hughes, J.: Trimmed helicoids: an architectured soft structure yielding soft robots with high precision, large workspace, and compliant interactions. Npj Robot. **1**(1) (2023). https://doi.org/10.1038/s44182-023-00004-7

Intel: How Service Robots Are Used in Different Industries (2022). https://www.intel.com/content/www/us/en/robotics/service-robot.html. Accessed 27 Oct 2023

International Organization for Standardization: ISO 8373:2021 Robotics — Vocabulary (2021). https://cdn.standards.iteh.ai/samples/75539/1bc8409322eb4922bf680e15901852d2/ISO-8373-2021.pdf. Accessed 27 Oct 2023

Precedence Research: Service Robotics Market Size, Share, Growth, Sales, Trade, Shipment, Export Value And Volume With Sales And Pricing Forecast By 2032 (2023). https://www.precedenceresearch.com/service-robotics-market. Accessed 27 Oct 2023

Trivedi, D., Rahn, C.D., Kier, W.M., Walker, I.D.: Soft robotics: biological inspiration, state of the art, and future research. Appl. Bionics Biomech. **5**(3), 99–117 (2008). https://doi.org/10.1155/2008/520417

Social Robots for Service Environments in Academia

Mireya Zapata[1] (ID) and Jorge Álvarez-Tello[2,3](✉) (ID)

[1] Centro de Investigación en Mecatrónica y Sistemas Interactivos – MIST, Universidad Indoamérica, Av. Machala y Sabanilla, Quito 170103, Ecuador
mireyazapata@uti.edu.ec
[2] Facultad de Ciencias Empresariales, Av. Quito km. 1 1/2 vía a Santo Domingo de los Tsáchilas, Quevedo, Ecuador
jorge.alvarez@cisde-ec.com
[3] Centro de Innovación Social y Desarrollo, Quito, Ecuador

Abstract. The increase of social robots in services has generated academic interest in their design and development to enhance human-robot interaction across various contexts, from home assistance to educational and medical environments. Design criteria increasingly explore the software development aspect, but interdisciplinary focus on sustainability also pursues hardware improvement for human-robot interaction in contexts ranging from home assistance to medical environments. With this background, the research question arises: What key features should be considered for the development of a social robot in academia? A systematic metadata review according to PRISMA of 698 studies from the SCOPUS database was conducted, selecting 10 relevant ones to explore functions and applications that allow characterizing hardware and software in the design of social robots for development in academia. Preliminary results indicate a focus on creating smarter, safer, and more adaptable robots, utilizing advances in hardware and software such as flexible electronics and artificial intelligence. It is concluded that the balance between hardware and software proposes the prototyping of a robotic platform with LiDAR/ROS technology, flexible electronics, and ultralightweight material structure, for sustainable, low-power consumption, and low-cost developments. Collaboration among researchers, educators, and developers is crucial to create educational social robots that are both useful and accepted.

Keywords: Social Robots · Service Environments · Academic Integration

1 Introduction

The integration of social robots in service environments has experienced exponential growth in the last decade, recognized for their potential to enhance the educational experience in academia [1]. These robots represent a convergence of robotics and technological innovation, applicable from home assistance to education and healthcare. Particularly, their potential to improve the educational experience in academia is an emerging field of study deserving specialized attention [2]. The integration of social

© The Author(s), under exclusive license to Springer Nature Switzerland AG 2024
C. Stephanidis et al. (Eds.): HCII 2024, CCIS 2114, pp. 421–426, 2024.
https://doi.org/10.1007/978-3-031-61932-8_48

robots in academic environments poses unique challenges and opportunities [3]. These environments are dynamic and heterogeneous, requiring robots to adapt and effectively collaborate with students and academic staff [4] Additionally, introducing social robots in academia raises important ethical, social, and pedagogical questions that must be comprehensively addressed [4, 5]. It is crucial to examine technological advancements in robotics and human-robot interaction (HRI) to understand the role of social robots in academic settings [6]. Literature emphasizes the importance of designing robots that understand and respond to the subtleties of human behavior [7]. Recent research has explored advanced perception, learning, and planning techniques that enable robots to adapt and seamlessly collaborate with humans [8]. Designing socially accepted robots in the educational community requires understanding cultural norms, social expectations, and ethical concerns related to automation and artificial intelligence [9, 10]. Furthermore, research must adopt an interdisciplinary approach to rethink how the future of education can be shaped in the evolution of humanity [11]. It is essential to highlight that effective design of social robots in academic environments depends not only on advanced technology but also on the appropriate selection of materials, operating systems, and materiality considerations, all while maintaining low costs for widespread and sustainable implementation [12–14]. Design criteria increasingly explore the software development aspect, but interdisciplinary focus on sustainability also pursues hardware improvement for human-robot interaction in contexts ranging from home assistance to medical environments. With this background, the research question arises: What key features should be considered for the development of a social robot in academia?

2   Method

In this section, the Method for the metadata review of literature from the SCOPUS database is presented, covering the period between 2019 and 2024, following the PRISMA 2020 procedure (see Fig. 1). The search queries included the following Boolean equations (see Table 1) for search with SCOPUS filtering adjustments. Through this, a deeper understanding of the main characteristics for the design of social robots can be gained.

Table 1. List of the keywords used in the systematic review.

N°	Boolean equation	Paper
1	social AND robotics AND in AND higher AND education AND institutions	290
2	social AND robots AND design AND low AND cost	209
3	social AND robots AND design AND academia	21
4	social AND robotics AND as AND a AND service AND in AND higher AND education AND institutions	178

The total number of articles after searching and filtering from the SCOPUS database is 698. The reasons for exclusion of relevant articles $(62 + 46 + 10 + 74 = 192)$ are as follows:

R1.- Having more than 10 citations: (including $50 + 30 + 7 + 64 = 151$)
R2.- Document related to the development of hardware & software in social robotics (per title or abstract): (including $12 + 16 + 3 + 11 = 42$)
R3.- Service related to academia: (including $6 + 11 + 0 + 5 = 22$)

3   Results

The characterization of the analyzed papers is divided into two main groups: hardware and software. This division allows us to identify the minimum components that a social robot must consider for its design and development (see Table 2).

Table 2. List of main characteristics for Social Robotics for these 10 relevant papers

N°	Author	Hardware	Software
1	[15]	An economical telepresence robot for elderly individuals	Evaluation of the navigation and manipulation system of the robot
2	[16]	RASA robotic platform for teaching sign language	Evaluation of performance in sign language recognition
3	[17]	Low-cost robotic arm for online teaching	Human-machine interface for remote control of the robotic arm
4	[18]	Hybrid social robot with digital facial expressions and 3D features	Contextual virtual assistant with cloud-based artificial intelligence
5	[19]	Flexible electronics using cellulose as substrate and dielectric material	Not applicable
6	[20]	Branch and Bound (B&B) algorithms and Genetic Algorithms (GA)	Formulation of task assignment problems
7	[21]	2D LiDAR SLAM accelerator on FPGAs	Integration with SLAM methods such as scan matching and ROS
8	[22]	CPHS system for Industry 5.0 with human proximity detection	Algorithms for human presence detection
9	[23]	Social robots as a low-cost alternative	Qualitative analysis of online review data
10	[24]	Exploration and goal-oriented orientation in robotics applications in higher education	Dominance of chatbots in artificial intelligence for personalized and scalable learning in higher education

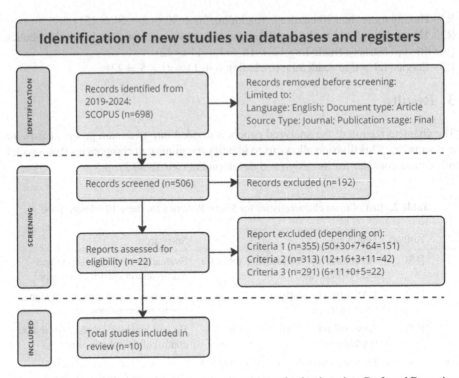

Fig. 1. A figure caption of the Flow chart for document selection based on Preferred Reporting Items for Systematic Review and Meta Analyses (PRISMA).

4 Conclusion

The development of social robots in academia requires a balance between hardware and software. In hardware, low power consumption, accessibility, and adaptability are key, while in software, natural and safe interaction with users is essential. Research should focus on optimizing the design and functionality of these robots, especially for vulnerable groups. Exploration of user interfaces, interaction methods, and impact assessments on learning is needed. Additionally, the role of artificial intelligence and other emerging technologies should be investigated. This careful approach has the potential to transform education in academic environments.

Finally, a proposed design for a social robot may be based on LiDAR technology, SLAM, ROS, FPGA/IoT, ultralightweight materials for the electromechanical platform, with flexible electronics and algorithms for recognition, evaluation, and assistance in human-robot interaction, for sustainable and low-cost developments. Subsequent research could explore the impact and effectiveness of social robots in educational environments and their influence on students.

References

1. Youssef, K., Said, S., Alkork, S., Beyrouthy, T.: Social robotics in education a survey on recent studies and applications. Int. J. Emerg. Technol. Learn. **18**(3), 67–82 (2023). https://doi.org/10.3991/IJET.V18I03.33529
2. Nocentini, O., Fiorini, L., Acerbi, G., Sorrentino, A., Mancioppi, G., Cavallo, F.: A survey of behavioral models for social robots. Robotics **8**(3) (2019). https://doi.org/10.3390/robotics8030054
3. Mayer, H.: RoboLabs: building surfaces of intelligibility. Front. Artif. Intell. Appl. **335**, 27–39 (2020). https://doi.org/10.3233/FAIA200898
4. Maples, B., Pea, R.D., Markowitz, D.: Learning from intelligent social agents as social and intellectual mirrors. In: AI in Learning: Designing the Future, pp. 73–89, January 2022. https://doi.org/10.1007/978-3-031-09687-7_5/COVER
5. Rossi, A., Dautenhahn, K., Koay, K.L., Walters, M.L.: 2020 29th IEEE International Conference on Robot and Human Interactive Communication (RO-MAN). IEEE (2020)
6. Mende, M., Scott, M.L., van Doorn, J., Grewal, D., Shanks, I.: Service robots rising: how humanoid robots influence service experiences and elicit compensatory consumer responses. J. Market. Res. **56**(4), 535–556 (2019). https://doi.org/10.1177/0022243718822827
7. Annamalai, N., Rashid, R.A., Munir Hashmi, U., Mohamed, M., Harb Alqaryouti, M., Eddin Sadeq, A.: Using chatbots for English language learning in higher education. Comput. Educ. Artif. Intell. **5**, 100153 (2023). https://doi.org/10.1016/J.CAEAI.2023.100153
8. Vaganova, O.I., Smirnova, Z.V., Kamenez, N.V., Bulaeva, M.N., Kutepov, M.M.: Organization of educational activities of volunteers as a social and educational project. Hum. Soc. Sci. Rev. **7**(3), 585–589 (2019). https://doi.org/10.18510/hssr.2019.7387
9. Ilori, M.O., Ajagunna, I.: Re-imagining the future of education in the era of the fourth industrial revolution. Worldwide Hosp. Tour. Themes **12**(1), 3–12 (2020). https://doi.org/10.1108/WHATT-10-2019-0066
10. Lopez-Caudana, E., Lopez-Orozco, C.F., Bárbara, C.M., Reyes, G.E.B., Ponce, P., Chong-Quero, J.E.: Physical therapy using robotics: a project-based learning experience for undergraduate students. Australas. J. Educ. Technol. **37**(5), 32–42 (2021). https://doi.org/10.14742/ajet.7139
11. Ponce, P., López-Orozco, C.F., Reyes, G.E.B., Lopez-Caudana, E., Parra, N.M., Molina, A.: Use of robotic platforms as a tool to support STEM and physical education in developed countries: a descriptive analysis. Sensors **22**(3) (2022). https://doi.org/10.3390/s22031037
12. Arora, A.S., Arora, A., Sivakumar, K., Taras, V.: The role of anthropomorphic, xˆenocentric, intentional, and social (AXˆIS) robotics in human-robot interaction. Comput. Hum. Behav. Artif. Hum. **2**(1), 100036 (2024). https://doi.org/10.1016/J.CHBAH.2023.100036
13. Brynjolfsson, E.: The turing trap: the promise & peril of human-like artificial intelligence. Daedalus **151**(2), 272–287 (2022). https://doi.org/10.1162/DAED_A_01915
14. Bartneck, C., Kulić, D., Croft, E., Zoghbi, S.: Measurement instruments for the anthropomorphism, animacy, likeability, perceived intelligence, and perceived safety of robots. Int. J. Soc. Robot. **1**(1), 71–81 (2009). https://doi.org/10.1007/S12369-008-0001-3
15. Koceska, N., Koceski, S., Zobel, P.B., Trajkovik, V., Garcia, N.: A telemedicine robot system for assisted and independent living. Sensors (Switzerland) **19**(4) (2019). https://doi.org/10.3390/s19040834
16. Meghdari, A., Alemi, M., Zakipour, M., Kashanian, S.A.: Design and realization of a sign language educational humanoid robot. J. Intell. Robot. Syst. Theory Appl. **95**(1), 3–17 (2019). https://doi.org/10.1007/s10846-018-0860-2
17. Benitez, V.H., Symonds, R., Elguezabal, D.E.: Design of an affordable IoT open-source robot arm for online teaching of robotics courses during the pandemic contingency. HardwareX **8** (2020). https://doi.org/10.1016/j.ohx.2020.e00158

18. Lima, M.R., Wairagkar, M., Natarajan, N., Vaitheswaran, S., Vaidyanathan, R.: Robotic telemedicine for mental health: a multimodal approach to improve human-robot engagement. Front Robot AI **8** (2021). https://doi.org/10.3389/frobt.2021.618866

19. Zhao, D., Zhu, Y., Cheng, W., Chen, W., Wu, Y., Yu, H.: Cellulose-based flexible functional materials for emerging intelligent electronics. Adv. Mater. **33**(28) (2021). https://doi.org/10.1002/adma.202000619

20. Martin, J.G., Frejo, J.R.D., García, R.A., Camacho, E.F.: Multi-robot task allocation problem with multiple nonlinear criteria using branch and bound and genetic algorithms. Intell. Serv. Robot. **14**(5), 707–727 (2021). https://doi.org/10.1007/s11370-021-00393-4

21. Sugiura, K., Matsutani, H.: A universal LiDAR SLAM accelerator system on low-cost FPGA. IEEE Access **10**, 26931–26947 (2022). https://doi.org/10.1109/ACCESS.2022.3157822

22. Fraga-Lamas, P., Barros, D., Lopes, S.I., Fernández-Caramés, T.M.: Mist and edge computing cyber-physical human-centered systems for Industry 5.0: a cost-effective IoT thermal imaging safety system. Sensors **22**(21) (2022). https://doi.org/10.3390/s22218500

23. Koh, W.Q., Whelan, S., Heins, P., Casey, D., Toomey, E., Droes, R.-M.: The usability and impact of a low-cost pet robot for older adults and people with dementia: qualitative content analysis of user experiences and perceptions on consumer websites. JMIR Aging **5**(1) (2022). https://doi.org/10.2196/29224

24. Chaka, C.: Fourth industrial revolution—a review of applications, prospects, and challenges for artificial intelligence, robotics and blockchain in higher education. Res. Pract. Technol. Enhanc. Learn. **18** (2023). https://doi.org/10.58459/rptel.2023.18002

Interactive Robotic Grinding: Interactive Building Metal Surface Design and Fabrication for Robotic Grinding

Weichen Zhang(✉) ⓘ

Politecnico di Milano, Piazza Leonardo da Vinci, 32, 20133 Milano, Italy
weichen.zhang@mail.polimi.it

Abstract. This paper presents an interactive robot grinding system that enables designers and workers to intuitively perform metal sheet grinding processes. This study involves three key elements: gesture-based interactive design, AR user interface, and robotic grinding. Different from regular patterns, the utilization of grinding to create irregular patterns on metal sheets hasn't been frequently practiced because of the unpredictability of the process and the inaccuracy of manual grinding. However, by proposing this augmented reality-based interactive system, users are allowed to interactively complete metal sheet grinding. Different from other augmented reality methods, it accomplishes this by visualizing control parameters as spatial operational interfaces through AR glasses and allowing for gesture-based control so users can edit the 3D custom geometry to change the control parameters. Finally, system test was conducted targeting designers, leading to the design and fabrication of a full-sized demonstrator consisting of 2 * 3 metal sheets using this system.

Keywords: Interactive fabrication · Augmented reality · Digital fabrication

1 Introduction

The AEC industry increasingly integrates robot fabrication as construction automation grows, focusing on customization, speed, and precision in component production amidst evolving design needs [1]. Robotic processes have optimized speed in many construction tasks, resulting in linear workflows with well-planned environments and materials.

Despite these advancements, automated tasks like facade grinding are less developed due to outcome unpredictability, needing human oversight for quality. The industry seeks varied patterns for building surfaces, employing methods like metal etching and stone carving. Metal grinding, in particular, offers novel pattern options, but consistency in fabrication and design remains a challenge. While robotic grinding allows controlled path creation, it falls short in supervision and predictability compared to manual grinding.

The IRGrinding system (see Fig. 1) combines a robot grinding device, gesture interaction, and augmented reality, using human gestures to program grinding paths. This approach overcomes manual grinding's time and control issues and improves the predictability and modifiability of robotic grinding.

© The Author(s), under exclusive license to Springer Nature Switzerland AG 2024
C. Stephanidis et al. (Eds.): HCII 2024, CCIS 2114, pp. 427–437, 2024.
https://doi.org/10.1007/978-3-031-61932-8_49

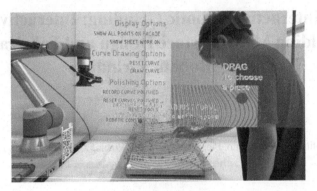

Fig. 1. IRGrinding system.

The paper first proposes pattern-oriented robot grinding and spatial augmented reality using HoloLens 2. It then outlines the structural framework of the system, explaining how it operates, the hardware and software components involved, and their interactions. Finally, the system's effectiveness is demonstrated using an example involving the processing of a 1 m x 3 m metal sheet surface composed of 2 × 3 panels.

2 Background

This section discusses further research on the application of pattern-driven robotic surface grinding, augmented reality through AR glasses, and human-machine collaboration in fabrication based on previous studies.

2.1 Human Machine Collaboration in Fabrication

Recent collaborative human-robot fabrication tasks have highlighted human creativity in digital fabrication. "RoMA" allows in-process design modifications [2], "CoilCAM" enables creative manual intervention in 3D printing [3], "The endless wall" lets users adjust robot-assembled brick walls [4], and "IRoP" translates human hand motions into robot trajectories for gypsum spraying [14, 15]. However, these studies mainly focus on additive fabrication or assembly, underscoring the benefits of human-robot collaboration.

2.2 Pattern Driven Robotic Surface Grinding

This study investigated pattern generation in robotic grinding, analyzing how speed, force, material, sandpaper roughness, and angle affect patterns (see Fig. 2). Key findings include the need for material and roughness compatibility, the significant impact of angle on the grinding area, and consistent patterns emerging from higher speed and greater force.

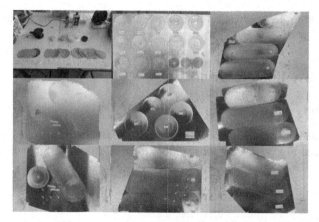

Fig. 2. Test to explore robot grinding factors.

Robot grinding enables controlled path and pattern generation, as summarized in "A Survey of Robotic Grinding" by Li et al. [18], with current practices focusing on smoothing complex geometries [16, 17]. In contrast, precision fabrication uses grinding for surface roughening without pattern addition [19]. Robotic grinding, more time-efficient and controlled than manual methods, is ideal for pattern creation despite its higher cost and equipment requirements (see Fig. 3). Collaborative robots enhance this process by ensuring tool adherence to metal surfaces, even on uneven sheets.

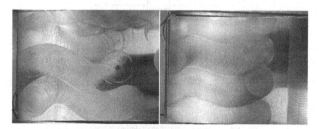

Fig. 3. Left: Manual grinding; Right: Robot grinding.

2.3 HoloLens (Head-Mounted Display) Based Spatial AR

Advances in AR technology provide real-time fabrication information, merging physical and digital worlds in construction [5]. Common AR methods include using tablet computers or smartphones [6, 7, 8], suitable for limited spaces but lacking immersive experiences. This system employs HoloLens 2 head-mounted displays, offering high accuracy and full-space scanning, with their compactness and ease of use making them popular in construction sites [9]. Projection-based AR, another method used in interactive fabrication [1], requires full surface and room projection in construction [10, 11, 12], but faces challenges like complex setup, portability issues, and precise operation needs, along with dependence on flat, clean surfaces and specific lighting conditions [13].

3 Interactive Robotic Grinding

3.1 Workflow

In the integrated design and fabrication process, IRGrinding is mainly assisted through four stages (see Fig. 4, Fig. 5): localization; filter selection; design, adjustment; robot machining.

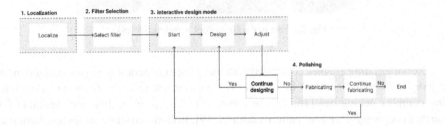

Fig. 4. The design and fabrication workflow.

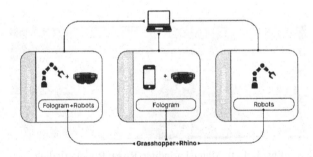

Fig. 5. Software and hardware System Overview.

In the localization stage, the workplane is set either through direct robot interaction or AR. Users then proceed through filter selection, design, adjustment, and machining, guided by a spatial UI of text and geometric blocks in HoloLens using Fologram. Interaction design involves sketching and editing 3D shapes (see Fig. 6). Completing curved grinding elements requires alternating between design and fabrication stages.

3.2 System Setting

As shown (see Fig. 7), the entire system mainly consists of two parts: gesture tracking and 3D AR interaction system, and robot grinding system.

Fig. 6. Left: AR system localization; Middle: Work plane localization; Right: Design and Adjust.

Fig. 7. Left: Gesture tracking and 3D AR interaction system; Right: Robot grinding system.

HoloLens-Based Gesture Tracking and 3D Interaction System. The system uses HoloLens 2 and a computer with Rhino, Grasshopper, and Fologram software, blending AR and computer processing for lightweight gesture tracking and 3D interaction. Rhino designs virtual spaces, Grasshopper transforms 3D models, and Fologram facilitates visualization and AR communication.

Robot Grinding System. The entire robot grinding system comprises a 6-degree-of-freedom collaborative robot (UR10e) and a pneumatic grinding head equipped with sandpaper ranging from P50 to P1500 for varying levels of surface roughness.

3.3 Computational Spatial Interaction

Gesture Tracking. The gesture tracking system in this project utilizes the gesture recognition feature of the Fologram plugin on the Grasshopper platform, using HoloLens 2 sensors for gesture detection and recording in a virtual 3D environment. Users activate tracking by pinching their fingers, recording gesture paths that can form curves.

The process varies with different filters; for instance, in robot motion path following, a 3D curve is generated in the z-axis direction from a drawn curve. The system then maps the distance between each point on this new curve and the original path to determine the robot's speed or force at that point (see Fig. 8).

In the sketching phase, the gesture-generated path curve (P) is projected onto the material surface plane, divided into points, and transformed into the robot's target plane (T). During speed/force adjustment, the distance (D) from each point on the speed/force curve to the path curve point is converted into the robot's motion speed/force (V). Consequently, a larger distance on the speed curve results in wider pattern spacing during grinding at that point.

Fig. 8. Left: Human input; Right: Robot output.

Robot Motion. Once the user has completed the design and adjustment steps, they start by turning on the compressed air switch for the grinding end effector. Then, by clicking the "construction" button, the generated code is imported into the robot controller, and the robot will move according to the specified path and speed.

Virtual Button (UI) Guiding System. IRGrinding's user interface features AR buttons for control in interactive design mode, encompassing steps like Localization, Design, Adjustment, and Recording. Users navigate steps and record/upload data via AR buttons, with each sub-step's UI displaying task-relevant 3D model information and controlling the gesture recognition switch.

The Interactive Steps: Localization; Design; Adjustment; Recording. It's worth mentioning that in these various process steps, an AR user interface containing several virtual buttons has been designed for controlling the gesture recognition feature, simplifying the number of 3D objects displayed in front of the user, indicating the current step the user is in, and facilitating movement between different steps (see Fig. 9).

Fig. 9. Left: Interactive step; Right: Virtual buttons.

4 User Experience

4.1 Filters Introduction

To achieve complex patterns and obtain precise human gesture design information and robot motion path planning, in a real project, several filters were designed initially for use by users who are not familiar with the system (see Fig. 10, Fig. 11).

Hand-Drawn Filter, Dot Matrix Filter, Straight Grid Filter and Curve Disturbance Filter are shown. For this case, the Curve Disturbance Filter was used (see Fig. 12).

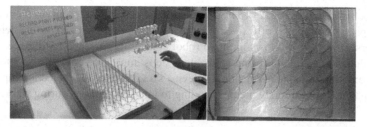

Fig. 10. Left: Dot Matrix Filter; Right: Outcome of Dot Matrix Filter.

Fig. 11. Left: Straight Grid Filter; Right: Outcome of Straight Grid Filter.

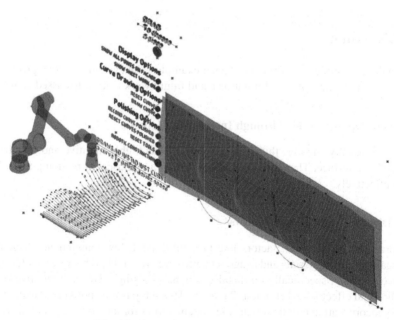

Fig. 12. Case of Curve Disturbance Filter.

4.2 Use Feedback

The system's true-scale design and fabrication allow immediate results, somewhat compensating for its inability to predict grinding outcomes, enhancing user engagement and design realization (see Fig. 13); The design method using abstract curves for controlling motion paths and speed is effective for knowledgeable users but may be challenging for beginners. However, it allows intuitive robot control through the AR device, with 3D images enhancing editability and adjustment steps improving control over robot speed and force; Limitations stem from the AR device's tracking and 3D projection capabilities, which may not be extremely precise, leading to minor deviations during work.

Fig. 13. Result sample.

5   Discussion

Through the completion of the mentioned examples, the system has been proven to be effective, and its advantages, limitations, and future work can be discussed as follows:

5.1   New Opportunities Through Interactive Methods

Users can readily embrace this system because of its highly intuitive and user-friendly interactive interface. The predefined filters further assist users in realizing their design ideas effectively.

5.2   Diverse Application Scenarios

For practical applications, factors like task fulfillment, low maintenance technology, and scalability in materials and usage scenarios are crucial [1]. This research focuses on surface grinding, specifically on metal components, using a UR collaborative robot, a grinding end effector, and Hololens 2 glasses. This setup is transportable and quick to set up. By incorporating mobile robots, the system allows for larger-scale robot movement, enabling direct surface processing and handling irregular areas like ceilings and corners.

5.3   Potential Responsibility Challenges

This system introduces a novel interaction between design and fabrication in the AEC industry, deviating from the traditional linear process with predefined drawings and plans. This approach can blur responsibility lines, generally fitting smaller projects under designer control. Project outcomes heavily depend on system design and filter choices, necessitating continuous filter updates and process optimizations tailored to specific tasks.

5.4 Low AR Accuracy

The AR glasses used in the system face accuracy challenges due to constant environment sensing and depth recognition, with direct eye projection causing misalignment. This affects robot path localization and AR object display. Future improvements could involve other AR tools and integrating computer vision to enhance object recognition and precision.

5.5 Possibility Towards Performing Arts

Grinding tasks are technically complex with variables impacting pattern outcomes, making prediction difficult and errors common. Errors require re-grinding the entire path due to the layering nature of grinding. Yet, the system's randomness and human-interactive creativity can steer it towards performance art. Humans guiding robots in pattern creation enable artistic expressions, with the overlaying of patterns offering rich visual and artistic effects.

5.6 Applicability to Different Materials

The system, initially for metal grinding, extends to other construction tasks like wall grinding post-painting. By incorporating a mobile robot base and lifting mechanism, it can traverse and grind entire wall surfaces, with potential for unique pattern creation on painted walls. Its versatility and suitability for tasks requiring human creativity make it broadly applicable in construction.

6 Conclusion

This project developed a system for robot grinding of metal sheets and assembling them into designed surfaces, combining interactive design, AR, and robot grinding. This integration reduces programming skill requirements and offers an intuitive integrated design-fabrication approach (see Fig. 14).

Grinding tasks, requiring skill for irregular patterns, are challenging to pre-design. This system, however, enables innovative metal grinding, adding patterns to surfaces like architectural facades and installations.

The project highlights interactive design interfaces in robot fabrication, enhancing human-machine collaboration and leveraging human intelligence and creativity. IRGrinding challenges traditional automation with gesture editing and AR's real-time feedback, allowing user-controlled processing.

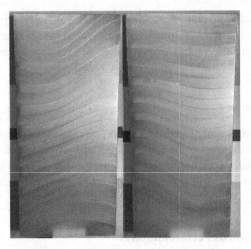

Fig. 14. Single chip experimental results.

References

1. Ahn, S., Han, S., Al-Hussein, M.: 2D drawing visualization framework for applying projection-based augmented reality in a panelized construction manufacturing facility: proof of concept. J. Comput. Civ. Eng. **33**(5), 04019032 (2019)
2. Atanasova, L., Mitterberger, D., Sandy, T., Gramazio, F., Kohler, M., Dörfler, K.: Prototype as artefact-design tool for open-ended collaborative assembly processes. In: Proceedings of the 40th Annual Conference of the Association for Computer Aided Design in Architecture: Distributed Proximities, ACADIA, vol. 1, pp. 350–359 (2020)
3. Azuma, R.T.: A survey of augmented reality. Presence Teleop. Virt. Environ. **6**(4), 355–385 (1997)
4. Benko, H., Wilson, A., Zannier, F.: Dyadic projected spatial augmented reality (2014)
5. Bourgault, S., Wiley, P., Farber, A., Jacobs, J.: CoilCAM: enabling parametric design for clay 3D printing through an action-oriented toolpath programming system (2023)
6. Chung, C.O., He, Y., Jung, H.K.: Augmented reality navigation system on android. Int. J. Electr. Comput. Eng. (IJECE) **6**(1), 406 (2016)
7. Dai, F., Olorunfemi, A., Peng, W., Cao, D., Luo, X.: Can mixed reality enhance safety communication on construction sites? An industry perspective. Saf. Sci. **133**, 105009 (2021)
8. Ferraguti, F., et al.: Augmented reality based approach for on-line quality assessment of polished surfaces. Robot. Comput.-Integr. Manuf. **59**, 158–167 (2019)
9. Hamdan, S., Öztop, E., Uğurlu, B.: Force reference extraction via human interaction for a robotic polishing task: force-induced motion (2019)
10. Helm, V., Ercan, S.A., Gramazio, F., Kohler, M.: Mobile robotic fabrication on construction sites: DimRob (2012)
11. Jones, B.D., et al.: 'RoomAlive', User Interface Software and Technology (2014)
12. Li, J., Zhang, T., Liu, X., Guan, Y., Wang, D.: A survey of robotic polishing (2018)
13. Milanfar, P.: A tour of modern image filtering: new insights and methods, both practical and theoretical. IEEE Signal Process. Mag. **30**(1), 106–128 (2013)
14. Mitterberger, D., Dörfler, K., Sandy, T., Salveridou, F., Hutter, M., Gramazio, F., Kohler, M.: Augmented bricklaying. Constr. Robot. **4**, 151–161 (2020)

15. Mitterberger, D., et al.: Interactive robotic plastering: augmented interactive design and fabrication for on-site robotic plastering. In: CHI Conference on Human Factors in Computing Systems (2022)
16. Ochoa, H., Cortesão, R.: Impedance control architecture for robotic-assisted mold polishing based on human demonstration. IEEE Trans. Ind. Electron. **69**(4), 3822–3830 (2022)
17. Peng, H., et al.: RoMA. In: Proceedings of the 2018 CHI Conference on Human Factors in Computing Systems (2018)
18. Wilson, A., Benko, H., Izadi, S., Hilliges, O.: Steerable augmented reality with the beamatron. CiteSeer X (The Pennsylvania State University), Pennsylvania State University (2012)
19. Zimmerman, J, Forlizzi, J., Evenson, S.: Research through design as a method for interaction design research in HCI. In: Proceedings of the SIGCHI Conference on Human Factors in Computing Systems - CHI 2007 (2007)

Author Index

© The Editor(s) (if applicable) and The Author(s), under exclusive license
to Springer Nature Switzerland AG 2024
C. Stephanidis et al. (Eds.): HCII 2024, CCIS 2114, pp. 439–440, 2024.
https://doi.org/10.1007/978-3-031-61932-8

Printed in the United States
by Baker & Taylor Publisher Services

Printed in the United States
by Baker & Taylor Publisher Services